THE MOTORBOAT ELECTRICAL AND ELECTRONICS MANUAL

By the same author

The Marine Electrical and Electronics Bible, Second Edition
The Great Cruising Cookbook: An International Galley Guide

THE MOTORBOAT ELECTRICAL AND ELECTRONICS MANUAL

JOHN C. PAYNE

SHERIDAN HOUSE

This edition first published 2002 by
Sheridan House Inc.
145 Palisade Street,
Dobbs Ferry, NY 10522

Library of Congress Cataloging-in-Publication Data

Payne, John C.
    The motorboat electrical and electronics manual / John C. Payne.
        p. cm.
    ISBN 1-57409-149-2 (Hardcover : alk. paper)
    1. Boats and boating—Electric equipment—Handbooks, manuals, etc. 2. Boats and
boating—Electronic equipment—Handbooks, manuals, etc. I. Title.

VM325 .P3923 2002
623.8'503—dc21   2002008304

Printed in the United States of America

ISBN 1-57409-149-2

CONTENTS

Sink Systems. Sewage Systems MSD's (Marine Sanitation Devices). Toilet Systems.

Uninterruptible Power Supplies. AC Circuit Protection Principles. Short Circuits, Causes and Calculations. Selecting Protection Equipment. AC Systems Installation. Ground Leakage Protection. Circuit Testing. Generators. Alternator Parameters and Rating Selection. Generator Rating Calculation. AC Equipment Ratings. Generator Systems, Protection, and Maintenance. Alternator Protection and Maintenance. Inverters.

SECTION TWO ELECTRONICS

INTRODUCTION

The world of the motorboat is as diverse as it is large. Boats range from luxury mega and super yachts, to sleek high-speed power vessels and trawler motor yachts. Anyone drawn to harbors and ports will see everywhere various fishing trawlers and shrimpers, crabbers, workboats and offshore supply boats. On the major river systems and canals the world over, there are tug boats, push and tow boats, pleasure and excursion boats, ferries and a variety of other motorized craft. Of course, ocean going ships ranging from 500,000-ton oil tankers to 28-knot container vessels are, on a very large scale, also motorboats.

Many of these boats are equipped with state of the art electronic systems, and many have electrical and electronic problems. While many systems work equally well for both sail and power, motorboats have specific systems and problems. This manual addresses the range of systems now installed on motorboats. It also answers the many questions I am asked by motorboat owners, from trawler men to commercial ship marine engineers. In this book I have tried to cover these topics that appear to cause the greatest problems.

This manual is very much a practical hands-on guide to systems and it distills many years of experience on motor vessels. Having spent my entire life afloat my main objective is to help fellow seafarers have safer passages in seaworthy boats. Remember there is no 24 hour breakdown and tow service out there.

ELECTRICAL SYSTEMS

Diesel Engines

1.1 **Basic Diesel Theory.** The diesel engine is the main propulsion source for most motorboats and power vessels. This opening chapter deals with the basics of diesel so that the important relationship between the engine and the electrical system of a vessel is fully understood. The diesel was invented in the late 19th century, and named after the pioneer engineer Rudolph Diesel. The diesel engine works on the principle of compression-ignition. Air is compressed to a point where fuel combustion will occur spontaneously. This manual deals with 4-stroke compression-ignition engines. The 4-stroke cycle comprises the air intake, compression, power and exhaust. Log on to www.penta.volvo.se; www.westerbeke.com; www.yanmar.com; www.manbwltd.com; www.cat.com; www.cummins.com; www.detroit-diesel.com; www.mtu-friedrichshafen.com; www.iveco.com; www.perkins-sabre.com; www.lister-petter.com; www.naval-technology.com (Scania); www.northern-lights.com (Lugger); www.wartsila.com; www.nannidiesel.com.

    a. **The Air Intake (Suction) Stroke.** At Top Dead Center (TDC), the inlet valves open. As the piston moves downwards, the air required for fuel combustion is drawn in via the turbocharger and air filter. At the bottom of the stroke, Bottom Dead Center (BDC), the inlet valves will close.

    b. **The Compression Stroke.** In the compression stroke, the piston moves upwards to compress the air. This raises the temperature within the engine cylinder, typically to around 1025°F (550°C). Fuel injection takes place before TDC and after an interval ceases.

    c. **The Power Stroke.** When the fuel is injected it will ignite spontaneously. Upon ignition, increased pressure is then generated in the cylinder, driving the piston down to BDC.

    d. **The Exhaust Stroke.** At BDC the exhaust valves open to expel the exhaust gases. At the end of the stroke the valves close at TDC.

1.2 **The Air System.** The air for fuel combustion is drawn in through an air filter and compressed. The amount of fuel that can be burned, and therefore the power of the engine, are limited by the air mass within the cylinder. The options are to pre-cool the air to increase the air density, or to use turbocharging. This raises the air density by increasing the pressure at which the cylinder is filled with air during the air intake stroke. This increases the engine power for the same cylinder size. The turbocharger is essentially a small air compressor driven by a turbine placed in the exhaust line. As the engine load increases, the exhaust gas output velocity also increases. This increases the turbine speed to drive the air compressor faster, which raises the air pressure into the cylinders. As the air is compressed into the engine cylinders, the air temperature also increases, reducing available oxygen. Some engines may have intercoolers installed. These cool the compressed air, which improves combustion.

1.3   Turbochargers Troubleshooting. Turbocharger faults cause reductions in power output, generate black exhaust smoke and increase oil consumption. The turbo shaft assembly should be inspected where possible to determine the fault. This requires the removal of the inlet and exhaust trunk. The turbine should be rotated by hand and the housing should be examined for signs of contact or rubbing. The oil drain should be checked and cleaned if fouled, and oil leaks should be investigated. Engines subject to low speeds or extended idle periods tend to leak and this usually disappears when the engine is loaded up. The most common cause of turbocharger failure is hot shutdown. When an engine is shutdown suddenly the turbo continues to rotate without oil. Turbo service life is reduced due to bearing wear from inadequate lubrication. Eventually bearing wear allows turbo casing to turbine contact and out of balance conditions. This can cause serious damage or destruction. When stopping an engine it is good practice to operate at slow speeds for a few minutes. This allows the turbocharger to spool down and for cooling to take place. The engine should never be revved prior to shutdown as the turbo will be rotating without lubrication, and this may damage the bearings. Turbochargers rotate at high speeds and generally use engine oil for lubrication, so maintaining clean oil is essential.

    a.   **Turbocharger Noise.** Turbochargers tend to make serious noises when something is wrong or degraded. The most common causes are:

        (1)   Restricted or clogged air inlet filters.

        (2)   Rotating turbine assembly binding or touching turbo housing.

        (3)   Flanges on the manifolds are loose, creating leaks.

        (4)   Object inside the compressor housing, inlet ducting or manifold.

    b.   **Turbine Assembly Binding**

        (1)   Ingress of material causing turbine or compressor damage.

        (2)   Turbine or compressor wheel is contacting the turbo housing due to bearing wear or failure.

        (3)   Accumulation of carbon deposits in turbine housing or on the turbine blades.

    c.   **Seal Leakage**

        (1)   Restricted or clogged air inlet filters.

        (2)   Oil drain lines are clogged.

        (3)   Crankcase breather is clogged.

        (4)   Bearings are worn or failing.

        (5)   Piston ring leakage or high crankcase pressures.

        (6)   Compressor wheel is damaged.

1.4   The Fuel System. Combustion is significantly influenced by the design of the fuel injection system. The fuel is drawn from the fuel tank, through pre-filters or separators, and then through the engine fuel filter to the fuel pumps. The pressurized fuel is then fed to the injectors. Although fuel is injected as a liquid, combustion efficiency requires proper vaporization. This requires thorough and rapid mixing of both the hot air and the fuel vapor. There are three mechanical fuel injection methods, which are the constant pressure system, the accumulator type and the jerk pump.

a.   **Constant Pressure System.** In the constant-pressure common rail system, the fuel is maintained at a constant pressure in the manifold. The manifold is connected to cam-actuated nozzles or distributor, and the timing valve and pressure activated injector nozzles. The pressure is maintained by compressing the diesel fuel using a pump and supplying fuel after each injection. Fuel is supplied from an accumulator and pressure regulating valve, which may be a governor or manually controlled. The quantity of fuel delivered at each injection is controlled by the injection pressure, the injector nozzle orifice area, and the time at which the nozzle valve lifts.

b.   **Accumulator System.** The accumulator system uses upper and lower plungers in a common bore. The lower plunger is driven by an eccentric cam and the upper plunger is spring loaded. As the bottom plunger is forced up the fuel between the plungers is pressurized by the spring force applied to the top spring. Fuel continues to pressurize until a delivery groove in the lower plunger indexes with the outlet passage. This pressurized fuel is then injected and continues until the upper spring forces the plunger downward, and closes the outlet passage.

c.   **Jerk Pump System.** The jerk pump system is the most common system in use for fuel pressurization, metering and timing. A camshaft activates the plungers and controls injection. The jerk pump system is the basis for distributor pumps and unit injectors. Engine makers such as Caterpillar use HEUI (Hydraulically actuated, Electronically controlled, Unit Injector) which have fuel injection pressures in the range 18–24,000 psi.

1.5   Injection Methods. There are two injection methods:

a.   **Direct Injection (DI).** The air is drawn in through special shaped inlet ports. This causes the air to swirl during compression, assisted by the piston crown. These engine types are more efficient, and deliver high power over small time periods. They have relatively small acceleration, as both the inlet and exhaust valves are restricted in diameter. This allows for a centrally located injector, and inhibits the aspiration process.

b.   **Indirect Injection (IDI).** These engine types have a greater fuel economy, and turbocharging can enhance this. An increased useful speed range is also obtained as larger valves are used, and noise is reduced. The air is made to swirl by forcing air through a special auxiliary chamber connected to the cylinder top housing the fuel injector. Fuel is injected close to completion of the compression stroke, as a stream of fine fuel droplets. When the fuel droplets mix with the heated air, combustion occurs. To increase the vaporization rate, the fuel must be injected into the cylinder as an atomized stream of fuel droplets. The pressure required to achieve this can exceed 7000psi. The fuel injector must meter the correct quantity of fuel to match the engine power requirements, and the injection period must be determined precisely. The droplet size of the fuel is critical to achieving good combustion. Large fuel droplets will require a longer period to vaporize, delaying combustion. Small fuel droplets move relatively slowly, reducing the oxygen mixing times. Both conditions will lead to incomplete combustion, with reduced efficiency, increased noise and exhaust emissions.

1.6 **Fuel Quality.** The quality of the diesel fuel is critical to good engine combustion and the US standard for diesel is the American Society of Testing and Materials ASTM D 975. The deterioration of fuel is almost inevitable, as contaminants are introduced into the fuel system through mixing, transferring and storage. During transportation and storage, fuel is in contact with air and water vapor. Diesel fuel can undergo changes as a result, sometimes forming sludge. This may block the fuel filters, or form gums that can damage the fuel injection equipment or leave deposits within the engine. Low quality fuels also cause injector fouling. When simple hole injectors in a DI engine become fouled, the spray patterns alter as the needles and seats become sticky. This causes leakage, poor combustion and excess exhaust smoke. The pintle injectors within an IDI engine can also become fouled. If the needles and injector bodies are dirty, the initial small fuel burst does not occur and all the fuel is delivered at once. No.2-D diesel fuel is unfortunately one of variable quality and purity, and ranges from very good to extremely poor. No.1-D is sometimes blended to improve cold temperature performance. The API specifications allow for acceptable levels of impurities such as sulfur, wax and other contaminants that include water, dirt and ash. Fuel contaminates are classified as either precipitates or particulates. The precipitates are commonly non-combustible materials that form when fuel oxidizes. As they are heavier than the fuel, they normally fall to the bottom of fuel tanks. Particulates are also known as asphaltines, which are black tar-like substances that plug fuel filters. Wax is added to fuels, however in colder conditions this may thicken if not suitable for the climate and can gel causing fuel blockages. The ignition delay period is crucial to engine starting. It can lead to white smoke after start up, diesel knock at idle speeds and lowering of overall engine performance. The normal method for describing ignition delay of a fuel is by the cetane number (CN). The longer the ignition delay, the lower the cetane number of fuel. Fuel supplies are generally within the 45–55 cetane number range. Assuming that the fuel is clean, the most important factor is the viscosity. Very high fuel viscosities impose severe strains on the fuel system. Low viscosities will cause leakage past the fuel pump. This can lead to unnecessary wear of vital components, as fuel also acts as a lubricant. This factor is also known as lubricity. Viscosity will impact on fuel combustion after injection, as this will affect the fuel droplet size and spray pattern. Water is the most common and damaging contaminant in fuel. It destroys the lubrication qualities of the fuel and damages the fuel pumps and injectors. The sulfur content is crucial in controlling exhaust emissions. In the combustion process, the sulfur compounds alter to form acidic byproducts. These are SO_2 and SO_3, which enter the exhaust gas causing air pollution. High sulfur levels will cause high engine wear rates and degrade the engine oil additives.

1.7　　**Water in Fuel.** Fuel tanks should be topped up to reduce condensation. Where possible, fuel tanks with a drain valve should have water drained off. After filling tanks, the prefilters should be monitored for excess water and drained. The most common method of water removal is stripping, which uses a silicon treated filter medium to inhibit water flow. The coalescing filter uses gravity to take water droplets out of the fuel. The absorption filter uses a filter medium to absorb water out of the fuel. The more commonly installed filter/separators use the stripping method. You invest in reliability when you install a filter/separator, either a Parker Racor unit or a Baldwin Dahl unit. I have used both and they have saved me from disaster more than once.

　　a.　　**Dahl Filter Operation.**

　　　　(1)　　Fuel from the tank enters the filter inlet port, and is directed down through the center tube. The depressurizer cone then spreads the fuel.

　　　　(2)　　As fuel is discharged from the depressurizer cone, 80% of the contaminants are separated from the fuel. The fuel rises upward and most of the solid contaminants and water settle into the bowl quiet zone. The system includes a reverse flow valve, to hold prime in the fuel system, and does not allow fuel flow back to the tank during shutdown. There is a removable primer plug at the top for use when complete priming is required.

　　　　(3)　　As the fuel rises upward, remaining small water droplets collect on the cone, baffle and bowl surfaces. The size and weight of the water droplets gradually increase causing downward flow into the sump.

　　　　(4)　　Fuel is then filtered completely by the 2-micron paper element. The clean fuel continues up through the outlet port to the pump and injection system. The transparent bowl holds up to 24 ounces of water capacity to reduce draining intervals, and this is done via the draincock.

　　b.　　**Racor Filter Operation.** The units also have optional heaters and electrical water continuity probe alarms. Some have a vacuum gauge to monitor pressure drop across the fuel filter elements.

　　　　(1)　　In the separation stage, a turbine separates large solids and free water using centrifugal force.

　　　　(2)　　In the coalescing stage, the smaller water droplets and solids coalesce on a conical baffle and drop into the collection bowl.

　　　　(3)　　The filtration stage uses a fine micron Aquabloc water repelling paper element.

1.8   Separators. Many larger motor vessels have centrifugal separators installed for the cleaning of both fuel and lube oils. The MOPX units from Alfa Laval and the Westfalia OTC2 mini-separators typify these. The basic process is that a positive displacement pump feeds oil from a day tank through a heater to raise it to separation temperature. The controller senses the temperature and flow rates, with the heated diesel and lube oil being then fed to the separator via a pneumatic changeover valve. The oil enters via a gravity disc that determines the oil and water interface position in the bowl, and a water seal is created within the separator bowl. The oil is fed to the center of the bowl, and this then rises through the disc stack. The water and solid particles are separated by centrifugal force and accumulate at the edge of the separator bowl. The clean oil is then discharged. The controller periodically activates a solenoid valve to discharge the sludge and water. The Alfa Laval EPC control systems used on the separators are quite sophisticated and very reliable. They have comprehensive alarm functions and self-diagnostic systems, with a range of fault codes.

1.9   Separator Electrical Systems. The 3-phase electric motor for the separator runs at 1500/1600 rpm depending on the nominal supply frequency. The bowl spindle rotates at around 7600 rpm. A disintegration risk exists if the bowl is unbalanced, and this is caused by caked-on sludge accumulating on the bowl if it is not cleaned. The drive motor power consumption is 4kW running, and any high currents are usually caused by the brake remaining engaged. The feed pump current draw is 1.6 amps. The most common electrical faults are caused by solenoid faults (there are at least 5); high and low pressure switches; Heatpac oil heater faults, with PT100 temperature sensor failures and temperature switches; the sticking of interlock switches on the cover and sludge valves and the tacho sensor. The EPC-41 controller controls the starting, separation, sludge discharge and stop sequences, and the heating

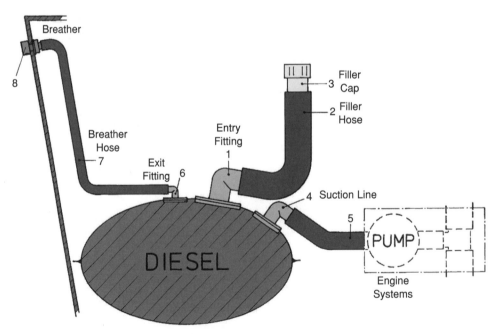

Figure 1-1 Fuel System Installation, *Courtesy of Vetus*

control via a PI controller. This is performed by a programmable microprocessor system, similar to a PLC. It inputs sensor data, processes the data and then outputs function commands and activates alarms. Sensor alarms are LED indicators, or numeric alarm codes. The system protection includes fuses on the PCB power inputs and main power supply. During installation, it is important to ensure that a minimum of 12" (0.3m) exists between the screened signal cables and power cables running parallel to avoid induced interference. The compressed air supply to the pneumatic solenoid block must be clean, dry and free from oil. Operation failures are usually due to loose connections, blown fuses, solenoid coil low voltages, coil burnouts or a valve fault. The changeover valve malfunctions are usually due to low air pressure and air leakages, or diaphragm problems. The worm-gear oil housing sight glass should be checked and be maintained between ¼ and ½ full. Oil changes should be carried out every 1000-1500 operating hours or yearly. Routine inspections should include leaks, abnormal noises and vibration. Perform a lamp test monthly to check that all alarms and indicators are functioning correctly.

1.10   Fuel Additives. The chemical makeup of fuel will determine the performance characteristics. There is no perfect fuel. Additives are added to diesel to improve the ignition delay periods. This gives improved combustion efficiency, less noise and exhaust smoke emissions. Detergents are added to keep the injectors clean and allow correct fuel metering. Anti-corrosive additives are used to protect the injection system, and anti-foam compounds are used to limit frothing. Uncontaminated fuel is essential to good combustion and efficient operation of the engine. There are many accounts of water-contaminated fuels being supplied to unsuspecting boats from bunker barges and fuel suppliers, and I have experienced this myself.

1.11   Microbe Growth. Moisture and water within the system can encourage microbiotic growth within the fuel. Algae, fungi and bacteria both aerobic and anaerobic will multiply rapidly and plug the filters. Once the system is infected, considerable flushing is required if it is to be eliminated. The solution is to add chemical biocides to kill or maintain quality. There are devices on the market called magnetic biocides, such as De-Bug (www.fuelmanagement.com). The theory is that single-celled organisms have electrical potential, usually positive on the cell wall and a negative interior. If this is disrupted the cell will die or rupture. This can be initiated by passing fuel over a strong permanent magnet or series of magnets. In the De-bug unit, the cells are exposed to 24 magnetic field changes within 20.2" of travel. The fluctuations destroy the cell by disruption of the cell ion and pH balances.

1.12   Fuel System Bleeding. If any part of the fuel system is disconnected or air has entered, all air must be bled from the system. Air in the fuel system causes many problems and can be difficult to expel. The injector pump and injector operate by having hydraulic pressure high enough to open needle valves, so that fuel can enter under sufficient pressure to atomize. Air absorbs the pump force and the injector will not open. Do not attempt to start the engine until the injection pump is filled and primed or damage can occur, as fuel is also a lubricant for the fuel pump. Paint the bleed screws with bright yellow paint to improve visibility in low light. Have the correct spanners always ready by the engine for use. Use caution with high-pressure fuel. Escaping pressure can penetrate the skin causing serious injury leading to gangrene. Tighten all connections before pressurizing the system, as any fluid injected into the skin must be surgically removed within hours. The fuel bleeding sequence is:

(1) Check that the fuel tank has sufficient fuel.

(2) Make sure all pipes and connections are tight. Check all hoses, fuel line fittings and steel lines where they may have chafed.

(3) Loosen the bleed screw on top of the engine fuel pre-filter or separator.

(4) Operate thumb/hand-priming lever on the lift pump, until a stream of bubble free fuel exits. Tighten the bleed screw.

(5) Loosen the bleed screw on top of engine fuel filter after the lift pump.

(6) Operate thumb/hand-priming lever on the lift pump, and operate until stream of bubble free fuel exits. Tighten the bleed screw.

(7) Repeat at the injection pump inlet connection.

(8) Loosen the bleed screws on the injection pump housing 2–3 turns and operate the lift pump until fuel is flowing bubble free.

(9) Tighten the furthermost injector from the inlet first, then the others in turn. Repeat with the other injectors, and crack the connection to allow any air to bleed out.

(10) Turn over the engine, and if the engine starts, the others will bleed automatically.

1.13 **Combustion.** Combustion efficiency is a measure of compression ratio, and is dependent on the control of ignition and fuel combustion. Factors controlling combustion are the air quantity, the fuel-air mixture, the compression temperature and pressure. The important factor is the delay period between the fuel injection, and the ignition. Both engine design and fuel quality are crucial to this. It affects engine performance, cold start characteristics, warm up times, engine power output, engine noise and the level of exhaust emissions. Short ignition delays do not generally cause problems. Long delays will allow fuel to accumulate in the cylinder prior to ignition. When this occurs the cylinder pressure will rise rapidly with incomplete and inefficient combustion. Ignition delay periods are mainly determined by fuel quality. Fuel injection starts just before Top Dead Center (TDC) and ends shortly afterwards. Injection delay is the time taken for the injection pump to build up pressure exceeding the opening pressure of the injector. Ignition delay is the time between fuel injection and ignition. This is dependent on fuel quality, compression temperature, compression pressure and fuel droplet sizes. The ignition delay must be short as possible. When ignition starts, combustion occurs quickly, and pressure increases rapidly. When delay is excessive, pressure rise is also fast, causing "knocking." During the final part of the combustion process the final fuel is burned. When the temperatures and pressure are high, the fuel droplets ignite immediately. Good combustion efficiency ceases at this point.

1.14   Engine Efficiency. Efficiency and losses in the process relate to fuel energy, incomplete combustion, and air/fuel mixing less than 100%, so that unburned fuel will exit in the exhaust gases. Losses are typically around 65% and are higher at low load than full load operation. Sources of losses include leakage through piston rings, friction, heat through combustion chamber walls, incomplete expansion, thermal loss via exhaust gasses and incomplete combustion. The air temperature, the air humidity and the air pressure affect the power ratings of an engine. In many engine spaces, engine power is reduced due to lack of air. The higher the engine space temperature rises, the greater the efficiency loss, and this is typically in the 10–15% range. The efficiency can be improved by the installation of an air inlet ducted to the engine air inlet, which provides cool external air. This is in addition to the normal machinery space ventilation air inlets and outlets or exhaust fans. Vetus makes kits that include air intake boxes and ducting.

1.15   Engine Exhaust. Stringent emissions legislation is now being introduced and becoming mandatory in many parts of the world. It is inevitable that some fuel will remain unburned after combustion, and come out in the exhaust. Maintenance is essential to reduce or maintain this to a minimum. The explosion of combustion is the source of an exhaust sound. The shock waves resonate through the cylinder liner and engine, and then reverberate through the exhaust outlet. Smoke color can be indicative of problems, normal exhaust has little to no color.

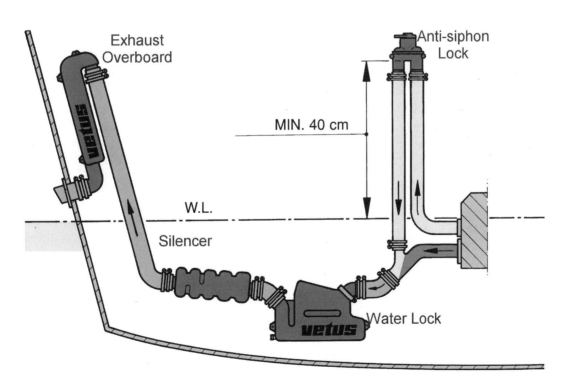

Figure 1-2 Exhaust System Installation, *Courtesy of Vetus*

9

a. **Blue-White Smoke.** This appears during cold starting. When the temperature is too low to burn the fuel, smoke is created by unburned fuel vapor. This indicates a lack of ignition and as the engine warms up the smoke will turn blue. Continuing blue smoke indicates worn or stuck piston rings, injector leaks, piston cracks, worn cylinder liners or valve guides. The unburned fuel particles are then exhausted and usually have a rich fuel smell. Another cause of white smoke at engine start up is faulty glowplugs or glowplug system. A low engine cranking speed can also create an excessive amount of white smoke. Once the engine is up to normal operating temperature, a faulty injector can be the cause. Other defects can include timing problems, low engine compression, injection pump, or air in the fuel system.

b. **Black or Gray Smoke.** This is caused by soot. It indicates improper air to fuel ratios and incomplete combustion; high exhaust back pressure; restricted air inlets; turbocharger malfunction; fuel injector problems; timing faults; engine overloads or low compression.

1.16   Engine Coolants. Most diesel engines have a heat exchanger with a closed circuit fresh water (FW) cooling system. The FW system has a pump that circulates the water from the expansion tank. It passes through the various engine water galleries to carry heat away, through the cooler and then back to the expansion tank. The exchanger provides the medium for transferring engine heat from FW to the primary sea water (SW) coolant. The SW is drawn through the SW inlet valve, the strainer, and to the suction side of the SW pump. The pressurized water is pumped to the cooler, where it passes through the cooler tubes and transfers heat from the FW. The SW then may be injected into the exhaust line and discharged overboard through the exhaust outlet. The coolant system controls the overall operating temperature of the engine, and proper heat transfer is essential. Sea water cooling circuits are dependent on maintenance, and coolers require regular inspection and cleaning. The fresh water cooling system must remain SW contamination free to prevent corrosion or formation of sludge and scale that may impede water flow or block coolers. This also reduces heat transfer rates by coating engine block water passages with insulating scale build-up. This will result in gradual overheating, with resultant damage. Inhibitors must be maintained at the correct concentrations if performance is to be optimized and damage avoided.

a. **Additives.** A number of additives are available to improve the performance of coolants. Coolant water may have sulfates, chlorides, dissolved solids and calcium. Coolant should also have an antifreeze additive to prevent freezing and engine damage in cold climates. Most ethylene glycol based antifreeze solutions contain the required inhibitors for normal operation.

b. **Corrosion Inhibitors.** These generally water-soluble chemical compounds protect the metallic surfaces within the system against corrosion. Compounds can include borates, chromates and nitrites. Soluble oil should not be used as a corrosion inhibitor.

1.17   Lubricating Oil System. Lubricating oil separates the various engine working surfaces to prevent metal-to-metal contact. The pistons must receive adequate oil supplies to prevent expansion and seizure that is caused by excess heat from increased friction on a dry cylinder wall. Lubrication has the dual function of lubricating the engine moving parts, and the removal of heat generated during the combustion process. Oil removes heat from the outside of cylinder liners, piston heat and inner liner walls and cools the main bearings.

a. **Circulation.** Oil is taken to the oil pump from a submerged suction in the oil sump or pan. Oil pumps are usually a 2-stage, positive displacement, gear type pump. They are driven off the timing gear train to maintain constant oil flow. A constant volume of oil is pumped, although flow will decrease slightly with increasing pressure. A non-adjustable pressure regulator valve is installed on the pump outlet side. A simple bypass valve is used to limit maximum oil pressure by diverting excess oil back to the sump. The pressurized oil is then passed through the oil filter and distributed around the various oil galleries and points within the engine. As oil reaches the crankcase bearings, flow is restricted, and the pump forces oil into the clearances between the main bearings and crankshaft. Oil is carried to the crank, connecting rod bearings, main and connecting rod journals. Oil may also be used in turbo bearings and sometimes under piston crowns. Liner, piston and rings are lubricated from oil thrown by the camshaft and crankshaft. The oil manifold supplies oil to the governor and rocker gear. Oil usually flows off the end of the rocker arms to lubricate valve springs and stems. Oil also lubricates the timing gear bearings. In many engines, the heat is dissipated through the oil cooler and through oil sump surfaces.

b. **Oil Filtration.** All oils contain contaminants and their levels must be minimized. These may be metals, fibers and microbial growth. Most damage is caused by hard particles that are slightly larger than the clearance of contact surfaces. Critical sizes are 0.5 to 45 microns and usually greater than 3–5 microns. Oil filters will remove these abrasive materials and contaminants. Oil also protects against corrosion, and assists piston rings to seal cylinders and reduce compression loss through the piston rings. Oil provides a strong film between all surfaces of working engine parts so that wear is reduced. Oil film may be typically around 0.08 mm thick between the shaft and bearings, and has to be strong enough to prevent surface contact.

c. **Oil Contamination.** In a 4-stroke diesel engine, oil reduces engine wear and absorbs contaminants that enter the engine. Most contaminants are expelled from the engine with exhaust gasses. Some remain in the cylinders and crankcase to corrode metal parts and form sludge and lacquer deposits. Most events that occur in the engine have an effect on the oil. When injection and combustion pressures are raised, the loads increase on pistons and bearings. Excess oil will bypass pistons and rings into the combustion chamber, where it burns to form carbon deposits. Oil is also affected by chemical composition, and the presence of nitrogen, phosphorus, potassium, sulfur. There are external growth factors such as temperature, pH values, water and oxygen. Oil neutralizes the acids that form and break up the deposits caused by combustion blow-by. Oil also cleans by dissolving sulfur that is converted to acid when the fuel is burned. High oil temperatures cause chemical breakdown of oil and maintaining engine temperatures is essential. The effect of acid formation can be reduced by operating the engine at the proper working temperatures. Humidity in combustion air also assists in acid formation.

d.   **Oil Standards.** It is essential that the correct grades of oil be used for the prevailing temperature conditions, and that the filter be changed regularly along with the oil. The nominal rating of oil viscosity must be maintained if correct lubrication is to be achieved. This is dependent on the engine remaining within the proper operating temperature ranges. Engine oil should comply with API CC/CD specifications, and may be synthetic, mineral, or blended. Mineral oils have various additives, and are suitable for infrequent use or under less hard service such as boats. Oils in generators changed at 500 hours and synthetic oils usually last longer by a factor of 10 times. This results in a cleaner engine, rings and liners and increases engine life by 40%, and decreases lube oil consumption by 75%. SAE standards match oil viscosity to operating temperatures. The W notation is the winter service rating defined at 0°F.

Table 1-1 Engine Oil Viscosity

Viscosity	Temperature
SAE 10W	-10°F to 70°F
SAE 30	+20°F to 100°F
SAE 40	+45°F to 120°F
SAE 10W-30	-10°F to +100°F
SAE 15W-40	+5°F to 120°F

e.   **Oil Additives.** Oil contains hundreds of chemical compounds and often additives to improve its lubrication characteristics. Oil additives allow continuous operation at high speed, or at raised engine temperatures. Oils have oxidation inhibitors and antioxidants to prevent oil thickening and formation of varnish and sludge that can seize fuel pump plungers. Anti-foaming agents are used to minimize foam formation, which can cause a loss of oil pressure and lubrication. Air bubbles in the oil retain heat and cooling ability is greatly reduced. Detergents are used to prevent combustion by-products adhering to metal surfaces, as deposits lead to excessive wear. Dispersal compounds such as calcium and barium prevent smaller particles within the oil agglomerating to form larger ones. This can cause damage, block oil galleries and passages. Dispersal compounds also keep particles suspended in the oil which can be filtered out. Zinc and phosphorus act as lubricants to resist pressure inside the cylinder. Magnesium inhibits excess wear and corrosion. Additives deplete in normal engine operation and require renewal. Remember that the longer an oil is used, the greater the oxidation, which alters the viscosity. Alkaline additives are also called buffers and prevent acid corrosion and wear on internal parts. The alkalinity of oil is referred to as Total Base Number (TBN) and the higher the TBN the greater the ability of the oil to neutralize acids.

f. **Oil Problems.** Problems that can occur are:

    (1) **Fuel in Oil.** Fuel in oil can create a crankcase explosion risk and is characterized by low lube oil viscosity.

    (2) **Water in Oil.** Water in the oil will cause emulsification and destroy the lubrication properties. The system must be completely flushed out after a leak repair and no moisture must remain. Stern tube and thruster oil seal leaks and failures can cause this condition.

    (3) **Microbe Growth.** Where water and oxygen are present, microbiotic growth within the oil and system can occur. Anaerobic microorganisms can live in oxygen free areas on partly mineralized hydrocarbons, and oil additives can stimulate growth of organisms. As the oil degrades the oil characteristics also change. It is caused by oil degradation and organisms that produce extracellular biopolymers (slime). These are usually bacteria and fungi, and also yeast contamination. Organisms start to produce surfactants and biopolymers when in contact with a hydrophobic culture medium, such as oil, which they can break down. This leads to increased exposure and oil breakdown, and the optimum temperature range is 3°–40°C. Once the system is infected, considerable flushing is required.

1.18 **Oil Testing.** With larger boats and engines, it makes sense to take oil samples at regular intervals for oil analysis. All leading oil companies offer this service. The analysis of the various trace metals found in the sample are good indicators of wear. Results can be obtained via the Internet with some companies. Different parts of an engine have different metals all washed by lube oil. Oils are analyzed using a spectrograph. As each element is burned in an electric arc the sample emits at a unique light frequency. The test results show amounts of each metal present in parts per million (ppm). The spectrochemical analysis is given in parts per million by weight. The analyst looks for wear metals, contaminants and oil additives. Oil analysis should be done at regular intervals, as trend analysis is more important than a single test. Wear metals have differing threshholds, usually indicating ranges of increased probability that problems are developing. Sharp increases in wear metals or a major shift in physical properties signal impending problems. The oil sample must be taken uniformly as wear metals are heavy, and sink to the bottom of the oil sump if oil is settled and not circulating. Take the oil sample within 20 minutes of engine shutdown, so that the oil material is equally dispersed in suspension. Do not sample from the sump bottom but from a point before the oil filter or suction, or out of the dipstick tube. Drop the suction hose to the sump bottom then raise an inch for sampling. New engines will show higher wear metal numbers than old engines. The baselines are best established after the engine is worn in. On the oil analysis reports, "normal" status indicates that the physical properties of the lubricant are within acceptable limits, and no signs of excessive contamination or wear are present. "Monitor" status indicates that specific test results are outside acceptable ranges, but not serious enough to confirm abnormal conditions. Initial abnormalities often indicate the same result patterns as temporary overloading or extended operations. "Abnormal" status indicates that lubricant physical properties, contaminations or component wear are unsatisfactory but not critical. "Critical" status is serious enough to warrant immediate diagnostic and corrective action to prevent major long-term performance loss or in-service component failure. There are typically 21 different elements present in lubricating oil. A simple test method is a viscosity test using a viscosity test stick. The new and used oil must be allowed to stand for an hour and stabilize at room temperature. The test stick is angled so that each oil sample runs down a channel. When the new oil reaches a mid-scale point on the graduated scale, the position of the used oil is read off. If the used oil has not reached the same point, it has a high viscosity, usually due to oxidation or high levels of insolubles. If the oil has run past the scale point the additives may be failing or there may be fuel oil contamination. These test kits should be part of any testing regime, as they are simple and easy to perform.

a. The **Soot Test** determines the amount of fuel soot. This is carbon suspended in the lubricant, and higher values indicate reduced combustion efficiency. This may be due to air intake or exhaust restrictions, injector malfunctions, or excess idling.

b. The **Oxidation Test** looks at chemical incorporation of oxygen into the oil. This causes a loss of lubrication performance due to aging, adverse or abnormal operating conditions or interval overheating.

c. The **Nitration Test** measures organic nitrates formed when combustion by-products enter the engine oil during normal service or as a result of blow-by past the compression rings.

1.19   Engine Operation. There are certain points to consider when operating diesel engines, and this applies to diesel generators.

a. **Warming.** Operate at 1200 rpm or less for 1–2 minutes, and extend this to 3–4 minutes in cold weather. Allow the engine sufficient time to reach normal operating temperature and for parts to expand.

b. **Oil Pressure.** Stop engine if oil pressure does not rise in 10 seconds.

c. **Idling.** Do not let the engine run on light or no-load for periods exceeding 10 minutes. This causes cylinder glazing and deposits within the engine, which increases maintenance costs. Prolonged idling also causes the coolant temperature to fall below normal range. Crankcase oil dilution can then occur due to incomplete fuel combustion. This permits formation of gummy deposits on valves, pistons and piston rings, and promotes rapid accumulation of engine sludge and unburned fuel in the exhaust system.

d. **Cooling Water.** Always visually check the sea water cooling overboard discharge after starting to ensure that coolant is passing through the engine. Do not wait for the high temperature alarm and possible engine damage. If the water is not coming out of the exhaust, or out of overboard discharge, stop the engine and investigate immediately. Do not allow the pump to run dry, or the engine to overheat.

e.   **Stopping.** Operate the engine for 5 minutes and allow temperatures to come down evenly. Avoid revving the engine prior to stopping as this effects the lubrication of moving parts, such as turbochargers.

Table 1-2 Engine Oil Analysis

Element	Indicators
Iron	High levels indicate wear from rings, shafts, gears, valve trains, cylinder walls, pistons or liners
Chromium	May indicate excessive wear from chromed parts such as rings, liners and some additives
Nickel	Secondary indicator of wear from some bearings, shafts, valves and valve guides
Aluminum	Wear from pistons, rod bearings, and certain shaft types
Lead	An overlay on main rods and bearings
Copper	Wear from bearings, rocker arm bushings, pin bushings, thrust washers, and other brass bronze parts
Tin	Wear from bearings and pistons in some engines
Silver	Wear from bearings. A secondary indicator of oil cooler problems, when coolant is detected
Titanium	Used as an alloy in steel for gears and bearings
Silicon	Airborne dust/dirt contamination indicates poor air cleaner servicing, and can accelerate wear
Boron	A coolant additive, and additive in some oils
Sodium	A coolant additive, and additive in some oils
Potassium	A coolant additive
Molybdenum	Wear from rings, and additive in some oils
Phosphorus	Anti-rust agents and combustion chamber deposit reducers
Zinc	An anti-oxidant, corrosion inhibitor, anti-wear additive, detergent and extreme pressure additive
Calcium	A detergent, dispersant and acid neutralizer
Barium	Corrosion inhibitor, detergent and rust inhibitor
Magnesium	Dispersant and detergent additive and alloying metal
Antimony	A bearing overlay alloy or oil additive
Vanadium	A heavy fuel contaminant

1.20   Engine Lay-up Maintenance Tasks

a.   Run engine until warm, then drain and replace the oil. Also change the oil filter. Drain and replace the transmission oil when warm. To avoid condensation, top up the oil.

b.   Top up the fuel tank, add biocide and stabilizer to the fuel. Circulate the treated fuel and check for leaks. Drain any water within the filter/separator bowl.

c.   Clean the sea water strainer. Rinse the sea water system with fresh water to dilute salt if this is possible.

d.   Treat the coolant with antifreeze, and run the engine to circulate properly.

e.   Lubricate the throttle and gear change linkages using a light machine oil.

f.   Tape over the exhaust outlet using duct tape.

1.21   Engine Spring Maintenance Tasks

a.   Change the oil before the start of the season or at the end of the lay-up period, including the oil filters. Run the engine, put in gear and add some load against the mooring lines. Run up to normal operating temperature.

b.   Operate the transmission and throttle cables over the full range several times and lubricate.

c.   Check and clean the sea water strainer.

d.   Check the engine mounts, clean and tighten.

e.   Check the electrical connections, clean and tighten.

1.22   Engine Maintenance. Maintenance should always be carried out in accordance with the engine manufacturer's recommendations. I have been extensively involved in preparing and implementing planned maintenance programs on commercial and offshore vessels. Good maintenance will significantly reduce machinery down time, and reduce overall operating costs. A quality and documented maintenance schedule may have significant benefits on boat resale values. The following maintenance tasks are guidelines only for both propulsion and generator diesel engines.

1.23   Engine Maintenance Tasks. The following essential maintenance tasks should be completed regularly, and will maintain optimum performance.

a.   **Water and Oil Coolers.** When temperatures cannot be maintained coolers need to be opened, inspected and cleaned. To do the task you require a soft wire brush and a soft metal rod (copper or brass).

(1)   Close any isolation valves.

(2)   Drain the cooler.

(3)   Remove the cooler end caps.

Table 1-3 Engine Maintenance

Task	Daily	150 h	300 h	1000 h
Check engine lube oil levels	X	X		
Change engine lube oil		X		
Replace engine lube oil filters		X		
Perform engine lube oil analysis			X	
Check for oil leaks	X			
Check pre-filter bowl for water	X			
Replace fuel pre-filters (Racor/Dahl)		X		
Drain water from fuel tank		X		
Replace engine fuel filters		X		
Check and clean crankcase breathers		X		
Replace air filter elements			X	
Check coolant water levels	X			
Replace coolant				X
Check water system anodes		X		
Check sea water pump impeller		X		
Check fresh water pump impeller		X		
Clean water and oil coolers			X	
Check and tighten fan belts		X		
Check alternator brackets for fatigue		X		
Check engine cable harness for chafe		X		
Check engine mounts are tight and clean		X		
Check flexible couplings are secure			X	
Tighten starter and alternator connections			X	
Tighten engine negative connections			X	
Check transmission oil levels	X	X		
Change transmission oil levels		X		
Check and tighten all hose clamps		X		
Check for oil and water leaks	X			
Stern drive anodes		X		
Adjust valve clearances				X
Test injectors				X

(4) Clean all accessible parts with a soft wire brush.

(5) Push the rod through each tube. The rod should be slightly smaller than the tubes. In severe cases of fouling, acid cleaning may be required.

(6) Flush the cooler and tubes well with fresh water.

(7) Inspect and renew the gaskets and seals if degraded or damaged.

(8) Re-assemble the cooler.

(9) Run the engine up to normal speed and observe oil and water temperatures. Inspect for leaks.

b. **Water Pump Impeller.** When temperatures are high, the impeller may be fatigued. Follow the simple change procedure.

(1) Remove the pump cover, making sure you do not damage the gasket.

(2) Carefully pry out the impeller with a screwdriver.

(3) Check the impeller for damage, cracks, and flexibility.

(4) Replace or renew and coat with grease or Vaseline.

(5) Refit gasket and pump cover, do not over-tighten the screws.

c. **Water Pump Impeller Troubleshooting.** If the impeller is damaged, the following are possible causes:

(1) Check if there are pieces missing out of the blade tips at the center of the impeller; pitting at the ends; or the edges have a hollowed out appearance. This is caused by cavitation, due to low pressures at the pump inlet. It can be rectified by reducing inlet pipe restrictions and lengths, and increasing inlet pipe diameters.

(2) Check if the impeller blade tips and end faces are worn, or the impeller drive is worn. This is caused by cavitation. This can also be caused by low pressures at the pump inlet, and the same corrective measures apply.

(3) Check if the end faces of the impeller have a hard and polished appearance, or if some or all blades are missing. This is caused by running the pump without water. The pump should not be run longer than 30 seconds without fluids, and be stopped as soon as the fluids are gone.

(4) Check if the impeller blades have excessive or permanent distortion or curving. This is caused by chemical action, excessive pump storage periods, or the end of the normal service life. Chemical actions are caused by pumping incorrect fluids. If an engine is stored for long periods or over winter, remove the impeller to avoid damage.

(5) Check if the impeller binds inside the pump housing, or the blades appear longer than the hub. Check if the impeller rubber is sticky and soft as this is caused by chemical actions, high fluid temperatures or long term immersion. Pumps should be flushed clean after use, and drained if being stored. High fluid temperatures should not be used.

(6) Check if the impeller blades are cracked by 50% or more, and if parts of the blade are missing. This is caused by the impeller reaching the end of normal operational life. It may also be caused by high output pressures. High or low temperature fluids and running the pump dry can cause similar damage. Check and reduce the pump pressures, outlet pipe restrictions such as long pipe runs or blockages.

1.24 Basic Diesel Troubleshooting. The most common faults in a diesel engine are a difficult start or a low power output.

a. **Electrical Causes.** Always check that the preheating system is operating, and the cranking speed is correct. Low battery voltages may not be turning the engine with sufficient speed. Check that the solenoids are operating in the injection pump. An audible click indicates that this is operating.

b. **Mechanical Causes.** An increase in smoke or rough running of the engine often indicates injector problems. This is possible with engines having high operating hours or extended service intervals. Injectors can have a reduction in opening pressure. Typically this can be 200 to 300 psi, and where this is exceeded the injectors may require resetting. Fuel injectors also may have poor atomization or be blocked. Air in the fuel system may be a problem, especially in engines that have not been started for long periods. Check that the fuel filters are not clogged or full of water. Where water may have passed through, the addition of a fuel lubricant additive to free up metering valves and plungers may resolve the problem. Engine timing and low compression problems are often found on engines with high operating hours. In some cases poor fuel quality may be the only cause.

Table 1-4 Engine Mechanical Troubleshooting

Symptom	Probable Fault
Engine will not start	Incorrect start procedure Fuel supply valve closed Fuel filter clogged Fuel lift pump fault
Low cranking speed	Air in fuel system Exhaust restriction Fuel pressure low, fuel pump fault Injector fault
Engine hard to start	Gearbox engaged Improper start procedure Air in fuel line, bleed the fuel line Cold weather, use starting aids Slow starter speed Oil too heavy, use correct oil viscosity Improper or low grade fuel type Water, dirt, air in fuel system. Clogged air filter, replace element Dirty or faulty injection nozzles.
Engine starts and then stops	Cold start, low engine temp Fuel filter clogged Air in fuel system Fuel incorrect Injector nozzles Engine timing
Lack of power	Intake air restriction, replace element Clogged fuel filter, replace elements Improper type of fuel Overheated engine Low temp, check thermostat Valve clearances out Dirty or faulty injection nozzles Injection pump out of time Turbo malfunction Leaking exhaust manifold gasket Restricted fuel line, replace hose

Table 1-5 Engine Mechanical Troubleshooting

Symptom	Probable Fault
High temperature	Water pump impeller fault Water pump V-belt loose Low coolant level, hose leaks Sea water strainer clogged Sea water pump fault Low oil level Air cleaner clogged Injector pump fault Thermostat fault Heat exchanger clogged Defective thermostat Water cap fault Engine overloaded
Low temperature	Thermostat fault
Low oil pressure	Oil filter clogged Oil cooler clogged Oil pump fault Bearing problem Wrong oil viscosity
High oil consumption	Oil leaks, lines and gaskets Crankcase vent clogged Wrong oil viscosity Air cleaner clogged
Exhaust smoke black/gray (incomplete combustion)	Low compression Injector pump fault Injector nozzles dirty/defective Restricted exhaust Head gasket leak Engine timing Turbocharger defect, seal leakage Low fuel quality
Exhaust smoke white (unburned fuel vapor)	Engine cold, low temperatures Valve stuck Low compression Head gasket leak Thermostat fault Injector nozzles Engine timing

Table 1-6 Engine Mechanical Troubleshooting

Symptom	Probable Fault
High fuel consumption	Clogged air filter
	Engine overload
	Valve clearances out
	Injection nozzles dirty
	Engine timing fault
	Defective turbocharger
	Low engine temperature
Engine misfiring/irregular	Low engine oil level
	One injector clogged or faulty
	Injection pump timing
	Low coolant temperature, thermostat
	Engine overheating
	Fuel problems
Engine knocks	Low coolant temperature, thermostat
	Clogged fuel filter, replace element
	Water, dirt, air in fuel system
	Dirty or faulty injection nozzles

Table 1-7 Engine Electrical Troubleshooting

Symptom	Probable Fault
Engine will not start	Flat battery Control power failure Stop solenoid jammed Loose corroded terminals Faulty start circuit relay Fuse blown control system
Starter will not crank (power on solenoid operates)	Starter brush jammed Starter bearings seized Starter mechanical failure Starter windings failed
Low cranking speed	Low battery voltage Battery terminal loose Starter motor fault
Generator will not hold load	Fuel filter clogged Air filter clogged Air in fuel system Governor fault Voltage regulator fault
High temperature (no mechanical fault observed)	Defective temp gauge or sensor
Low temperature (no mechanical fault observed)	Defective temp gauge or sensor
Undercharging	Excess loads on auxiliaries Engine low speed idles Connections loose Defect battery Alternator defect Drive belt loose
Battery water consumption increase	Overcharging High ambient temperatures High charge rate
Will not charge	Loose or corroded connections Sulfated batteries V- belt loose

1.25 **Sterndrive Gasoline Engines.** Many of the factors that apply for diesel engines also apply to gasoline units; the major difference is that equipment is ignition protected. Ignition protection is the mechanical design of equipment that prevents any ignition source within it causing flammable vapors such as gasoline to ignite. *All* equipment must be ignition protected by mandatory laws (i.e. USCG). A gasoline ignition engine requires electricity to operate. Starting systems are similar to diesels and the ignition system is the most common failure cause. Starting problems are usually due to low battery voltages. This is caused by loose main battery cable connections, engine negative connections or starter motor faults. Log on to www.mercurymarine.com.

a.   **Starting Control System.** When the key switch is turned on, a control voltage is applied from the battery to the starter motor solenoid and the ignition control system. A voltage is applied to the ignition coil, the distributor, then via the cables to the spark plugs. The solenoid closes, the starter motor turns, the engine rotates and the spark plugs ignite the fuel.

b.   **Starters.** These are of a special design. Explosions are caused by incorrectly designed and ignition protected starters. Another cause is improperly rebuilt, maintained or repaired starters. It is important not to replace starters with automotive types.

c.   **Ignition Control System.** Electronic control modules (ECM) use capacitive discharge ignition systems. They are considerably more complex than the simple add-on units I made at home in the early 1970s. The unit essentially comprises a capacitor, which charges up then discharges to the coil primary. The CDI unit performs the switching that times the high voltage correctly for ignition. Microprocessors perform the timing control and other functions. Ignition control modules must be properly installed or premature failure will occur. Make sure that the ground wires to the module chassis are attached and tight. Faults are typified by reduced engine speeds and a failure to start.

d.   **Ignition Coil.** The coil transforms the primary 12 volts to a secondary one up to 50,000 volts for ignition. The high voltage output is connected to the center of the distributor. Coils are very reliable, and terminals must be checked, tightened, and cleaned to prevent tracking and loss of voltage. They are a cause of erratic engine operation if excessive moisture is present causing surface tracking.

e.   **Distributor.** The distributor "distributes" the high voltage via a rotor to each cylinder ignition cable contact. The rotor is driven from the engine. The cylinder-firing order is determined by the sequence in which the cables are inserted in the distributor. Distributors should be clean and dry, and inspected for tracking. This should be both internal and external to each high voltage contact point. Check that all gaskets and seals are in good condition and replaced if degraded. The terminals often develop a "crust" that can be scraped off. Tracking, particularly in moist wet conditions, may cause misfiring and erratic engine operation. Typical are Mercruiser distributors, which are available in a range of types. These include conventional points units as well as

Thunderbolt and Delco Systems. Replacement of the distributor should be performed by approved technicians only, as timing if improperly carried out can lead to serious engine damage. Mercruiser assemblies are complete with internal ignition components, cap and rotor. When tuning the engine adjust the points before the timing. It is also good practice to smear on some dielectric grease to the distributor cam, as this prevents premature points failure.

f. **Ignition Cables.** The ignition cables carry the high voltage from the distributor to the spark plugs. Ignition cables will degrade, and should be kept clean and dry. The rubber protective boots over plug connections should be kept clean, and seal well. Vibration causes problems and the cables should be inspected for fatigue and cracking.

g. **Spark Plugs.** The spark plugs should be inspected regularly. They should be kept clean, the gaps measured and maintained according to the specific engine specifications. The external porcelain or ceramic insulation should also be clean and dry to prevent tracking and loss of ignition voltage. Renew the plugs each season. Misfiring and rough running are often caused by spark plug lead problems. A problem as simple as a failing plug or ignition cable can cause arcing on Mercruiser Thunderbolt coils, and many mistakenly replace the coils.

h. **Knock Modules.** The purpose of the Knock module is to monitor the Knock sensor AC voltage signal. A signal of 8–10 volts is supplied to the ICM when there is no knock. When a spark knock occurs the Knock control module stops sending the 8-10 volt signal to the ICM. This causes the ICM to switch off the MBT (Best-Mean-Timing) facility initiating a decrease in timing to a safe level. Mismatching of modules and sensors is a common cause of problems. When installing or replacing sensors the threads should not be coated with compounds as this will introduce resistance and cause sensor malfunction.

1.26   Outboard Engines. The outboard motor has become a sophisticated and complex machine. Typical units on larger boats have a range of systems. These include electronic fuel injection (EFI); modular CDI or digital inductive ignition systems; electronic multi-point variable-ratio oil injection lubrication systems; and high output alternators up to 60 amps rated output. Other systems include electrical power trim systems and comprehensive monitoring systems that detect overheat, low oil level and water in fuel. The majority of problems are related to corroded electrical connections, and water and moisture in the ignition systems. Starting problems are generally caused by bad connections, or batteries not fully charged or degraded due to inadequate charging.

Engine Electrical Systems

2.1   Engine Starting Systems. The systems that make up a typical electrical system include the battery; the engine control panel; the wiring loom; the preheating system; the starter motor and solenoid; shut-down solenoids; instrument sensors and transducers, and the alternator. There is a basic sequence of electrical functions that take place when starting the engine. When the key switch is turned to <ON>, this closes the circuit to supply voltage to the control circuit, and generally initiates alarms. When no audible or visual alarms occur, no power is on. When the key switch is turned to the <PREHEAT> position, this manually or automatically energizes the heating glowplugs or heating elements. When the key switch is turned to <START> or the engine <START> button is pressed, voltage is then applied to the starter motor solenoid coil. The solenoid pulls in to supply the main starting circuit current through a set of contacts. The contacts when closed supply current to the starter motor positive terminal. This turns over the starter motor to start the engine.

2.2   Electric Engine Starters. Essentially the electric starter consists of a DC motor, a solenoid, and a pinion engaging drive. The DC motor is typically series wound. This provides the high initial torque required to overcome engine friction and inertia, caused by factors such as high oil viscosity and cylinder compression. The starter motor then accelerates the engine to a point where self-ignition temperatures are reached and combustion starts. This is typically in the range 60–200 rpm depending on whether glowplugs are used. The pinion and ring gear transmit the starter motor torque to the flywheel. The drive gear pinion has a reduction gear of around 15:1.

    a.   Solenoids. The solenoid is essentially a large high current relay that consists of coil and armature, moving and fixed contacts. The solenoid is mounted directly to the starting motor housing, which reduces cables and interconnections to a minimum. When the solenoid coil is energized by the starting circuit, the solenoid plunger is drawn into the energized core. This then closes the main contacts to supply current to the starter motor. On some starters the solenoid also has a mechanical function. The solenoid activates a shift or engaging lever to slide the overrunning clutch along the shaft to mesh the pinion gear with the flywheel. When engaged, the starter motor then turns the engine, so meshing occurs before starting.

    b.   Starter Motors. The motor consists of four pole shoes or magnets. Some motors use permanent magnets. The poles are fitted with an excitation winding which creates the magnetic field when current is applied. The rotating part, called the armature, also incorporates the commutator. The four carbon brushes provide the positive and negative power supply. There are four basic DC motor types in use, and they are based on connection of the field windings. The field windings are connected either in series or in parallel with the armature windings.

(1) **Shunt (Parallel) Wound Motors.** The motor operates at a constant speed irrespective of loads applied to it. It is the most common motor used in industrial applications. It is suited to applications where starting torque conditions are not excessive.

(2) **Permanent Magnet Excited Motors.** The permanent magnet starter offers the advantages of reduced weight, physical size and generates less heat than normal field type motors. Current is supplied via the brushes and commutator directly to the armature. Another feature is that a reduction gear is used, which allows faster speeds and increased torque.

(3) **Series Wound Motors.** On this type of DC motor the speed varies according to the load applied; speed increases with a load decrease.

(4) **Compound Motors (Series/Shunt Wound).** This configuration is often used on large starter motors. It combines the advantages of both shunt and series motors, and is used where high starting torques and constant speeds are required.

c. **Pinion Engaging Drives.** The pinion engaging drive is located within the end shield assembly of the starter. It consists of the pinion engaging drive and pinion, the overrunning clutch, the engagement lever or linkage and the spring. When the motor operates, the drive gear meshes with the ring gear or flywheel teeth to turn the engine, and then disengages after starting. The overrunning clutch has two important functions, the first is to transmit the power from the motor to the pinion, and the second is to stop the starter motor armature from over-speeding and being damaged when the engine starts. Pre-engaged starters generally use a roller type clutch, while larger multi-plate types are used in sliding gear starters.

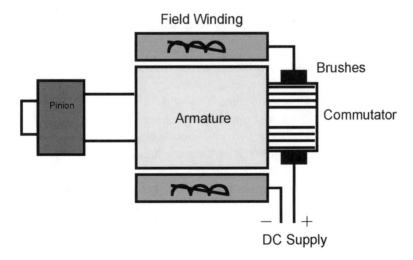

Figure 2-1 Starter Motor

2.3   Starter Types. There are several types of starters in use, the most common being the overrunning clutch starter and the inertia-engagement Bendix drive, which is now less common. There are four basic groups of starter motors:

a.   **Pre-engaged (Direct) Drive Starters.** The most common type of starter motor is the solenoid-operated direct drive unit and the operating principles are the same for all solenoid-shifted starter motors. When the ignition switch is placed in the Start position, the control circuit energizes the pull-in and hold-in windings of the solenoid. The solenoid plunger moves and pivots the shift lever, which in turn locates the drive pinion gear and connects it with the engine flywheel. When the solenoid plunger is moved all the way, the contact disc closes the circuit from the battery to the starter motor. Current now flows through the field coils and the armature. This creates the magnetic fields that cause the armature to rotate, which then turns the engine.

b.   **Gear Reduction Starters.** Some manufacturers use a gear reduction starter to provide increased torque. The gear reduction starter differs from most other designs in that the armature does not drive the pinion directly. In this design, the armature drives a small gear that is in constant mesh with a larger gear. Depending on the application, the ratio between these two gears is between 2:1 and 3.5:1. The additional reduction allows a small motor to turn at higher speeds and greater torque with less current draw. The solenoid operation is similar to that of the solenoid-shifted direct drive starter. The solenoid then moves the plunger, which engages the starter drive.

c.   **Sliding Gear Drive Starters.** These two-stage starters have either mechanical or electrical pinion rotation. The electrical units have a two-stage electrical pinion engaging drive. The first stage allows meshing of the starter pinion without cranking the engine over. The second stage starts when the pinion fully travels and meshes. This allows full excitation and current flow to the starter motor. The first stage of the mechanical units has a solenoid switch, which pushes forward the pinion engaging drive via a lever. When pinion meshing occurs, current is applied to the starter via the solenoid switch.

d.   **Bendix Drive Inertia Starter.** The Bendix friction-clutch mechanism drive was developed in the early 20th century. It uses a drive friction clutch, which has a drive pinion mounted on a spiral-threaded sleeve. The sleeve rotates within the pinion, and moves the pinion outwards to mesh with the flywheel ring gear. The impact of this meshing action is absorbed by the friction clutch. Once the engine is turning at a higher speed, it drives the Bendix gear at a higher speed than the starter motor. The pinion then rotates in the opposite direction to the spiral shaft and disengages. A common fault is where the drive pinion is thrown out of mesh and then stops. Always wait several seconds before attempting to restart as the drive mechanism may be damaged. Another fault is when the pinion does not engage after the starting motor is energized, and a high-pitched whine is emitted from the starter. Turn off the ignition immediately as the unloaded DC starter motor will overspeed and be seriously damaged. Problems can be minimized by ensuring that the sleeve and pinion threads are clean and lubricated, so that the pinion engages and disengages freely. The Bendix gear, shaft, bearings and end plates can be cleaned of dried grease with WD-40 and oiled with fine sewing machine oil.

2.4   Starter Installation, Maintenance and Troubleshooting. Starter installation is generally limited to two factors. The first is to make sure that it is mechanically secure. The second is that the attached cables are of the correct rating and the terminal nuts are properly tightened so that they do not work loose. In addition, the negative cable should be attached as close as possible to the starter. Starter motor design must generally be robust. Starter motors must withstand the shocks of meshing and engine vibration. They must also withstand salt and moisture laden air; water; oil; temperature extremes and high levels of overload. Preventive maintenance is essential to ensure reliability.

   a.   **Shaft Corrosion.** A common problem especially on idle vessels is the buildup of surface corrosion, or accumulated dirt on the shaft and pinion gear assembly. The lack of lubrication causes seizure or failure to engage. It is good practice to remove the starter every 12 months, clean and lightly oil the components according to the maker's recommendations.

   b.   **Starter Motor Maintenance.** Problems often occur with seized brushes, primarily because of lack of use. Always manually check that brushes are moving freely in the brush-holders, and that the commutator is clean. Remove all dust and particles using a vacuum cleaner. Wash out with a quality spray electrical cleaner if badly soiled. Follow the DC motor maintenance procedures described in Chapter 9. Never clean and polish the commutator with any abrasive materials.

   c.   **Starter Troubleshooting.** Many people are familiar with the loud click and then silence when the start solenoid operates but the starter fails to turn over. The main causes are a bad negative or positive connection, both caused by loose or dirty terminals. A solenoid plunger may also stick and not fully close, preventing the main contacts from closing.

2.5   Preheating Circuits. Some engines will not start without preheating. They often require extended starting turnover times which may overheat and damage the starter.

   a.   **Glowplugs.** Direct Injected (DI) engines commonly have glowplug heaters installed within each cylinder. They preheat the air in each cylinder to facilitate starting. In cold weather, this will dramatically decrease the electrical power requirements to start the engine.

      (1)   **Activation.** Prior to engine starting, the plugs are activated for an operator selected time period, or interlocked to a timer which is typically in the range 15 to 20 seconds.

      (2)   **Power Consumption.** The glowplugs can draw relatively large current levels for a short time. If your battery is low, allow a few seconds after preheating before starting, as this enables the battery voltage to recover from the heater load.

b.   **Air Intake Heaters.** These grid-resistor heaters are installed in the main air intake of IDI engines and there is normally only one heating element.

c.   **Pre-heater Control.** Many preheating circuits have relays, either timed or not timed. Timed relays are often a common failure cause. It is advisable to have a normal relay with a separate switch, and simply preheat manually for 15 seconds and then start the engine.

2.6   Pre-heater Maintenance. The following maintenance tasks should be carried out to ensure system reliability:

a.   **Electrical Connections.** Pre-heater glowplug connections must be regularly checked if they are to function properly. The connections must be cleaned, and tightened every six months.

b.   **Cleaning.** The insulation around the glowplug connections must also be cleaned. It is a common fault to have oil and sediment tracking across to the engine block with a serious loss of preheating power.

c.   **Glowplug Cleaning.** The plugs should be removed and cleaned yearly. Take care not to damage the heating element.

2.7   Pre-heater Troubleshooting. The following faults are the most common on pre-heating systems:

Table 2-1 Pre-heater Troubleshooting

Symptom	Probable Fault
No preheating	Loss of power (fuse failure) Connection fault on engine to first plug Relay failure Connection on ignition switch disconnected Terminal short circuiting to engine block
Partial preheating	One or more glowplugs failed Glowplug interconnection failure Dirt around glowplug causing tracking

2.8   Engine Starting System Diagrams. The following are simplified electrical systems for a variety of engines. Always check the electrical diagrams supplied in the operator's manual for your specific engine model. Make sure that you have the correct circuit diagram for the installed engine. It is a good idea to laminate a copy in plastic to have a working copy ready to use when troubleshooting. The following table gives equivalent color codes for various manufacturers.

Table 2-2 Engine Wiring Color Codes

Purpose	US Codes	Yanmar	Volvo	Perkins
Ignition start	yell/red	white	red/yell	white/red
Ignition stop	black/yell	red/black	purple	blk/blue
Preheat		blue	orange	brown/red
Negatives	blk or ylw	black	black	black
Alternator light	orange	red/black	brown	brown/yell
Tachometer	gray	orange	green	blk/brown
Oil pressure gauge	light blue	yellow/blk	light blue	green/yell
Oil warning light		yellow/wh	blue/wh	black/yell
Water temp gauge	tan	white/blk	light brn	green/blu
Water temp light		white/blue	brown/wh	blk/lt grn

Engine Starting Recommendations. Reference IRBES Section 1, Chapter 9 and 10. (See Chapter 7.2 Electrical Standards).

Rule 9.16. The power supply to the engine starting system should have an isolator installed as close as practicable to the battery in both the positive and negative conductor. The isolator should be accessible. Short circuit protection is not required. The isolator shall be rated for the maximum current of the starting circuit.

The starter cables should have an isolator as close as possible to the batteries, and accessible for isolation purposes. It should be rated for the maximum current starting circuit.

Rule 10.3. The main starting circuit positive and negative conductors shall be rated so as not to exceed 5% voltage drop at full rated current.

The main starter cables should have minimal voltage drop at full rated current. Cables should be kept as short and large as possible to minimize losses and maximize power availability.

a. **Caterpillar/Scania/MAN/Detroit/MTU Starting Systems.** The majority of engines have similar starting systems.

Table 2-3 Starting System Troubleshooting

Symptom	Probable Fault
Engine will not start	Shaft brake interlock switch
	Neutral position interlock switch
	Start button fault
	Key switch fault
	Starter solenoid connection off
	Start solenoid coil failed
	Main start connection loose
	Stop solenoid seized
	Stop button jammed in
	Negative connection fault
	Fuel rack jammed
	Starter seized
Engine will not stop	Stop solenoid seized
	Stop solenoid connection fault
No preheating	Air heater connection broken
	Key switch fault
	Negative connection fault
	Glowplug connection fault

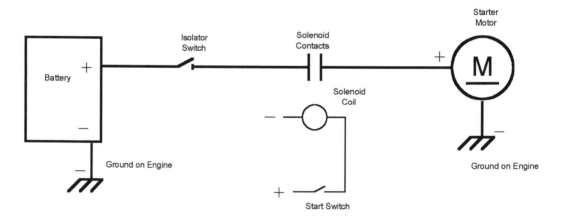

Figure 2-2 Basic Engine Starting Circuit

b. **Volvo Starting System.** The simplified circuit diagram of the starting system for typical Volvo engines is illustrated below.

Table 2-4 Volvo Troubleshooting

Symptom	Probable Fault
Engine will not start	Start button connection off Start button fault Control fuse failure Starter solenoid connection off Stop solenoid seized Stop button jammed in Negative connection fault Loom connector fault Stop solenoid connection fault
Engine will not stop	Stop solenoid seized Loom connector fault Fuse failure
No preheating	Key switch fault Negative connection fault Glowplug connection fault Fuse failure

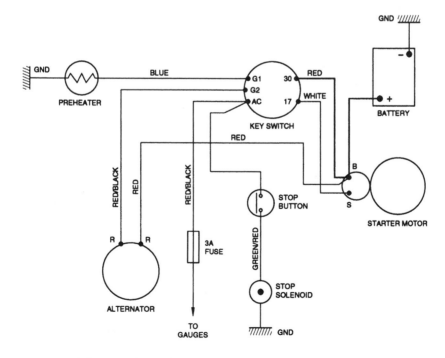

Figure 2-3 Typical Volvo Engine Starting System

c. **Yanmar Starting System.** The simplified circuit diagram of the starting system for typical Yanmar engines is illustrated below.

Table 2-5 Yanmar Troubleshooting

Symptom	Probable Fault
Engine will not start	Start button fault
	Key switch fault
	Starter solenoid connection off
	Stop solenoid seized
	Stop button jammed in
	Negative connection fault
Engine will not stop	Stop solenoid seized
	Stop solenoid connection fault
No preheating	Air heater connection broken
	Key switch fault
	Negative connection fault
	Glowplug connection fault

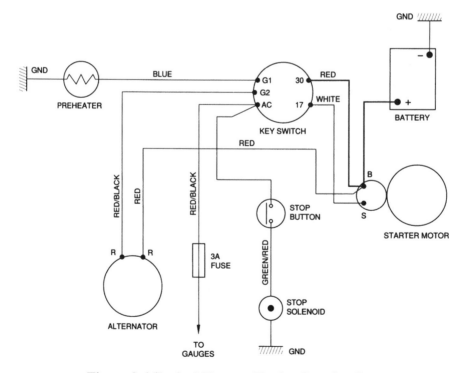

Figure 2-4 Typical Yanmar Engine Starting System

d. **Perkins Prima Starting System.** The simplified circuit diagram of the starting system for a typical Perkins Prima engine is illustrated below.

Table 2-6 Perkins Troubleshooting

Symptom	Probable Fault
Engine will not start	Start button connection off
	Start relay fault
	Starter solenoid connection off
	Stop solenoid seized
	Stop button jammed in
	Negative connection fault
	Stop solenoid connection fault
	Stop solenoid seized
	Stop solenoid connection off
	Loom connector fault
Engine will not stop	Diode failure
	Grounding relay fault
	Key switch fault
	Negative connection fault
	Glowplug connection fault
No preheating	Relay fault
	Grounding relay fault

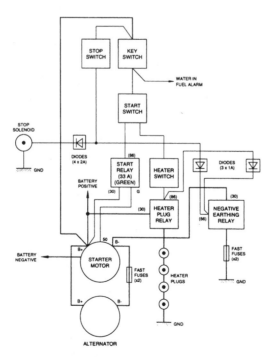

Figure 2-5 Typical Perkins Engine Starting System

2.9   Engine Starting System Configurations. There are several engine starting configurations and arrangements.

  a.   **Remote Battery Isolators.** Many boats have simple mechanical isolation switches to isolate the engine starter motor power supply. In many cases remote isolation circuits have relay type isolators. The control relay may be operated from a separate switch. It may also be interlocked to the main key switch, so that when the switch is turned the power is applied.

  b.   **Two Pole Engine Systems.** In many engines which have dual pole isolated systems, two battery isolation relays are installed, one on positive and one on negative. The relay coil is connected to the alternator D+ terminal and this energizes the coil when the alternator is operating. In remote isolation relay systems one relay can be used to energize both switches.

  c.   **Parallel Battery Starting Systems.** Some vessels have a 12-volt power system and a 24-volt engine system. The 12-volt batteries are connected to a relay. When the engine start switch is operated, the relay connects the 12-volt batteries in series to get 24 volts and supply the starter motor.

  d.   **Parallel Connected Starters.** Larger engines use two starter motors, which reduces the motor size. The system uses a large capacity double acting relay to supply current to both starter motors simultaneously.

2.10   Engine and Transmission Control Systems. While traditional engine controls have centered around push-pull Morse control cables, there is an ever-increasing use of fully electronic systems. Makers include ZF-Mathers, Teleflex Morse, Twin Disc and Kobelt. Systems may have an electronic throttle and shift arrangement or a mechanical shift with electronic throttle. Teleflex Morse have the Teleflex Intelligent System (TIS) MagicBus which uses the Control Area Network (CAN) protocol. In this system all engine control and monitoring signals, data, transducer inputs and outputs share the same network. The following is a basic description of the ZF-Mathers MicroCommander system. Other systems may vary but will have similar operating principles. Log on to www.ZFmarine.com.

  a.   **Control Head or Station.** This includes the throttle and gear change levers. The control head outputs a variable DC voltage to the actuators. Some systems may use a pulse width modulated (PWM) signal. The DC voltage value corresponds to the control lever position. The control heads also incorporate an LED visual and audible warning indication, and the control transfer button. The control head has three separate circuits and one common circuit. These are the potentiometer, transfer button, sound transducer and the LED indicator circuits.

  b.   **Actuators.** Actuators have an integral control circuit board, which accepts the variable DC command voltage, and converts the inputs into mechanical outputs. The outputs may be solenoid valves and linear actuators, with drive motors and coils. These operate the clutch or transmission ahead or astern, and control the fuel rack for speed control. The feedback loop to the control head or control module is via gear-operated potentiometers. The control systems are essentially closed loop controllers. A set point is used; for example, the throttle is moved to the required position, the control system increases engine speed to match via the actuators. The engine speed feedback signal is compared to the set point, and when there is no differential, no further speed signals are sent to the actuators. Synchronization for actuators and processors is required in twin-engine installations.

c.   **Push-Pull Cables.** The cables transfer the movement in the actuator to the clutch and engine throttle control.

d.   **Electrical Wiring.** Wiring interconnects the control heads, actuators and any electronic control module (ECM). These include the power supply cable, starter interlock cables, and multi-core cables (in the Mathers system this has 8 conductors). The starter interlock cables are connected to the starter solenoid and the actuator via a normally open relay. The multi-core cable connects the control head to the actuator.

e.   **Control Modules.** Some systems may have a separate control module. These modules include a power supply unit (PSU), and the microprocessor circuits (CPU) that input, process and output signals to the actuators. They perform the input signal conversion from the throttle and gear changes, and output signals to the actuators, via a distributed control network. Modules have displays to enable performance monitoring or troubleshooting using fault codes.

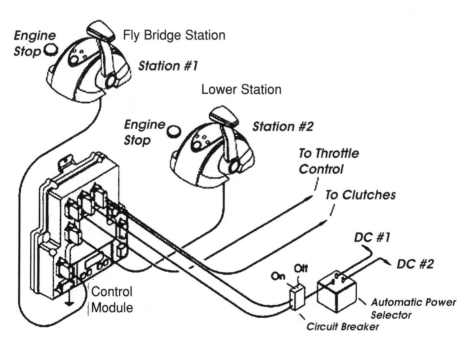

Figure 2-6 Mathers Control System, *Courtesy of ZFmarine*

f. **Safety and Control Systems.** Most mechanical and electrical controls incorporate several safety systems and operating features. Redundancy is important within any propulsion control system. Manufacturers of control systems and engine management systems incorporate backup sensors if the primary ones fail. This can include speed and injection timing; throttle position; boost pressure for fuel air ratio control; coolant temperatures and lubricating oil pressures. An auxiliary throttle is used in Mathers control systems for a backup speed signal. Systems may have combination visual LED and audible warning codes to indicate operation and fault status.

(1) **Neutral Interlock.** A micro-switch is used to activate a start-blocking relay. This prevents the starting of the engine when the transmission is selected ahead or astern until the clutch is disengaged. In addition the control system has to be switched on and command acceptance carried out. Switches and relays can cause problems, so always look at this first if you cannot get the engine started.

(2) **Shaft Brake Interlock and Control.** Shaft brakes incorporate a sensor that interlocks engine starting until the brake is off. Switches can cause problems and should be checked.

(3) **Reduction Gear Oil Pressure Interlock.** If gear oil pressure fails to build up or falls, the engine speed is reduced to idle. It is important to make sure the oil filters are clean and the oil levels are correct to avoid this occurring at speed.

(4) **Drive Train Reversal.** This is also called crash reversal. The control sequences the shift and speed functions. When an emergency reversal is requested, it provides the shortest possible reversal time without damage to the drive train or stalling the engine.

(5) **Warm-up Mode.** This enables engine speed adjustment with engine in the neutral (neutral fast idle mode) control position.

(6) **Engine Synchronization.** This is used to decrease vibration and noise, and reduce fuel consumption. It is an automatic function. In most cases, a leading engine is nominated and the following or slave engine speed is adjusted to match it. Some units use engine tachometers while others use a proximity sensor on the shafts that increases synchronization accuracy.

(7) **Trolling (Slow Speed Mode).** This is for speed control below normal idle speeds. A trolling valve comprises pressure reducing solenoid valves. The valves are operated by a servo, and associated control signal. When actuated a solenoid valve opens allowing fluid to go to the pressure reduction valve. The CAT trolling mode limits engine speed but allows full throttle engine speed for precise control.

g. **Installation.** Typical power consumption is 10 amps, and a stable power supply is required. This should not be taken from the engine starting batteries. It is also recommended that two power supplies be provided. This can be via a changeover switch so that control is available if the loss of one battery bank occurs. In noisy electrical environments a separate and isolated battery supply should be considered. Shielded, twisted pair data cables are used to prevent interference. The CPU should be isolated from any boat grounding system, in particular steel or alloy boats. Shielding at actuators and control stations should not be grounded to prevent circulating ground currents. Grounding of the cable shield is at the CPU only. Excess cable length should not be coiled up, but cut to fit.

Table 2-7 Engine Control System Troubleshooting

Symptom	Probable Fault
System dead	Power switched off
	Fuse failure or circuit breaker
	Flat battery
	Power cable fault
Engine not starting	Neutral interlock switch fault
	Shaft interlock switch fault
Actuator moving erratically	Feedback potentiometer faulty
	Wiring connection fault
All actuators erratic	Ground loop, isolate shields at actuator
Actuator jammed over	Feedback potentiometer fault
	Actuator failure
No synchronization	Wiring or connection fault
	Tachometer sensor faulty
	Wiring connection fault

2.11 **Engine Synchronizers.** While some complete engine control systems incorporate synchronization, systems for retrofitting are available. Typical of these is the AccuSync made by Sturdy Corporation (www.sturdycorp.com), and designed for installation to inboards, outboards and sterndrives. The actuator is placed in the helm throttle control to engine control cables. Speed signals are picked up from the nominated lead and following engines. When synchronization is required and activated, the system will match engine speeds whenever the throttles are within 15% of each other. Correct installation is essential and electrical connections must be tight. Power consumption is relatively low at just under 1 amp when in controlling mode.

2.12   Engine Management Systems. Control systems must interface correctly with different engine electronic fuel management systems. Some engine manufacturers have fully integrated systems. Caterpillar electronic engines have what is called open architecture allowing interfacing with various CAT monitoring systems or other engine monitoring and control systems. Features are extensive and include engine condition logging, data storage and trend analysis to detect abnormalities. MAN has the MMDS system, which also runs on a network with alarm and condition monitoring with automatic load limiting on certain critical conditions. MTU has the Blue Line system. The benefits of electronic management consist of improved fuel economy, which is achieved through fuel supply regulation, fuel injection pressure, timing and duration. Engine control systems such as the Caterpillar electronic unit injector (EUI) control the fuel delivery and injection timing though the injector process control. Smoke and emission reductions are to comply with new emission requirements, with smoother and more stable engine speed and acceleration. There is also a greater reserve power availability for changing sea states and conditions, loads such as fishing nets and hard turning. The Caterpillar electronic fuel and engine management system consists of the following elements:

a.   **Electronic Control Module (ECM).** This is a computer holding the operating software designed for a specific engine. It performs all the monitoring and control functions. The ECM supplies power to the electronics; processes sensor input information; outputs actuator signals; processes and outputs monitoring information; performs diagnostic routines and acts as a governor to control engine speed. When the ECM receives a requested throttle speed signal it controls the fuel injection. This maintains the engine speed by comparing required speed with actual speed fed back from the speed sensors. Speed is controlled through injection timing, and the quantity of fuel injected. CAT engines also have electric trim, which allows programming of increase or decrease of current duration to the solenoid to increase or decrease fuel delivery. This is based on the final injection test and compensates for the variability that exists between injectors and ensures smoother and more even running. Each injector has a specific correction code based on final delivery tests.

b.   **Sensors.** These consist of the pressure, temperature, speed and position transducers that input information to the ECM. The following characteristics, typical for Caterpillar, are similar for most sensors.

(1)   **Pressure.** The sensors are used for boost pressure, atmospheric pressure and oil pressure. These sensors have three wires and operate on + 5 VDC to provide a variable DC signal. The wires are voltage input; ground which is a zero reference, and the signal voltage. Typical operating range is 0.5 to 4.45 volts. The system monitors for short and open circuit; if signal voltage equals supply voltage it is open circuited, and if zero volts it is short circuited.

(2) **Temperature.** The sensors are used for coolant, fuel, air intake and oil temperature monitoring. These sensors have two wires, and they are resistance devices. They are also monitored and will indicate zero volts if short circuited and high resistance if open circuited.

(3) **Speed.** The speed-timing sensor consists of a permanent magnet and a coil. The teeth on the camshaft pass through the sensor magnetic field to generate a voltage. The time between voltage pulses is counted to calculate speed. Additional teeth are added to indicate Top Dead Center (TDC). These are a two-wire device that does not require a power supply. There are typically two sensors, one on the camshaft and one on the crankshaft. The camshaft unit is used for injector timing, and the crankshaft one is used for more accurate speed measurement. In two sensor systems one is used as a backup. In older engine models a single sensor system failure will cause engine to shutdown. The sensors are critical to the primary speed and timing function of the ECM that governs engine operation.

(4) **Position.** This is normally the throttle lever. It sends the requested speed signal to the ECM. It outputs a pulse width modulated (PWM) signal to the ECM. It has a 3-wire input, consisting of the supply voltage of 8 volts, the ground reference, and the output signal. The PWM output is a constant frequency square wave, either full voltage or zero, on or off signal. The duty cycle is the % of On time. In idle mode this is 10–22% and in high idle it is 75–90%. The ECM monitors the duty cycle, and if less than 5% or greater than 95% it indicates a fault.

c. **Injectors.** These inject the fuel into the engine cylinders. The injectors consist of several components that include the tappet; plunger; barrel; body; nozzle assembly (spring, check and tip) and cartridge valve (solenoid, armature, poppet valve, and poppet spring). In mechanical systems, push rods and cam lobes activate rocker arms and the injector plunger and barrel. In electronic systems the ECM energizes the solenoid. This magnetically attracts the armature and lifts the poppet valve to allow fuel pressure to build up. The check lifts and is then injected via the nozzle assembly into the cylinder. At the programmed end of injection the solenoid valve de-energizes and fuel flow ceases.

2.13 **Installation and Troubleshooting.** The reliability of systems depends on proper installation. Equipment must be located away from moisture and heat, and the power supply must be clean and stable. Units must withstand higher machinery space temperatures, vibration, electric currents, RFI and electrostatic discharges. Actuators are normally bonded to maintain equipotential levels. Many cables from control units and engine management systems use multi-core cables, most are also screened and the screens must be terminated correctly. It is important to identify locations where cables may chafe, have tight bends, or where mechanical damage is possible. Relay junction boxes must be mounted in locations that minimize mechanical damage, vibration and heat exposure. Troubleshooting is carried out by service technicians using computer based test programs. It is common to blame injectors for engine conditions such as misfiring, low power and rough or erratic operation. In many cases simple faults such as deteriorated solenoid connections, wiring faults or loose connectors are a cause of engine problems. When troubleshooting always clean and re-tighten connections first.

2.14   Steering Systems. Motorboat steering systems are either cable, or non-electric manual hydraulic systems using a pump unit and actuator cylinder. Larger systems have an electric powered hydraulic pump with a reversible DC motor. Typical power consumption for these pumps is in the 6–15 amp range. Pump units are usually plunger types and incorporate a relief valve. For autopilot operation or remote control devices, the motor direction is reversed to control pressurized oil to the actuator cylinder. Larger boats use electric systems that have a hydraulic power pack, with a continuously running gear oil pump and oil reservoir. Pressurized oil is directed to the actuators through electrically operated solenoid valves. System sizes are determined by the cylinder oil volumes and the required lock-to-lock times. Power consumption of the HPU ranges from 15 to 5 amps for 24-volt systems. More sophisticated steering systems are used on larger boats, such as the electronic full follow-up system from Kobelt. Steering systems may consist of single or multiple control stations, or dual independent systems. Log on to www.kobelt.com.

a.   **Hydraulics.** Hydraulic power is supplied via a HPU or engine mounted hydraulic pump.

b.   **Controller.** The controllers may consist of a wheel, lever, pilot or a joystick. A command is transmitted for the required rudder position. This opens the solenoid valves to direct pressurized oil to the actuator. This will then move the rudder in the required direction to the requested angle.

c.   **Amplifier.** The amplifier unit compares the command signal from the controller to the feedback signal from the follow-up unit. If any difference ex-

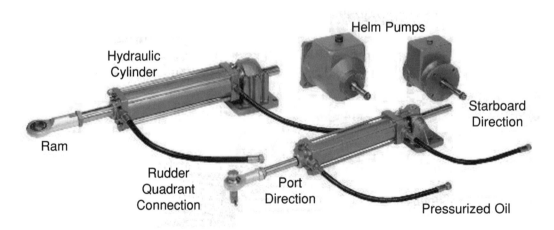

Figure 2-7 Hydraulic Steering System, *Courtesy of Vetus*

ists, a signal is transmitted to the solenoid valves to move the rudder in the required direction so that no difference exists.

d. **Solenoid Valves.** The pressurized oil is directed to the actuator via electrically activated solenoid valves, one for each direction. Dual rate systems may have both high and low speed solenoid blocks.

e. **Follow-up.** This consists of a hydraulic full follow-up telemotor. The rudder feedback unit has a signal proportional to the rudder angle, and is driven off the servo cylinder, not the rudder stock.

f. **Setup and Testing.** The rudder must be mechanically centered, and the rudder follow-up must also be aligned and mechanically centered. In initial commissioning directional control is tested. It is important to ensure that electronic limit settings stop travel before it reaches the mechanical limits or stops. Driving the rudder against the stops will cause considerable damage.

g. **Maintenance.** Hydraulic oil systems must be kept clean. All electrical connections should be tight and dry, and cables checked for chafe. The follow-up feedback sensor should be mechanically secured.

h. **Troubleshooting.** If a system does not start up, the power is either off or the supply circuit breaker is tripped, or a fuse has blown. This should be checked before going to sea. Erratic operation is often caused by faulty follow-up potentiometers, loose linkages, or sticking solenoid valves. Rudder hunting can be caused by amplifier problems and gain or deadband adjustments, which must be readjusted.

2.15 **Hydraulic Steering.** Hydraulic steering systems require the use of a reversible pump to be installed in the system for autopilot control. These systems consist of a steering wheel pump and steering cylinder. The wheel pump forces oil into the cylinder from either end depending on the direction required. The system should have a lock valve to prevent the rudder driving the wheel pump. Hydraulic systems are inherently more reliable than mechanical drives. Pump types are:

a. **Constant Running.** They are usually dual speed to save power in lighter conditions. Solenoid valves control oil pressure for directional activation of the hydraulic ram.

b. **Reversible Motor.** These pumps are the most typical and have low overall power consumption. The pump is controlled by autopilot command output signals. Typical power consumption is in the range 2–4 amps on units for vessels up to around 45' but have a maximum up to 20 amps. On larger vessels, this is typically 4–8 amps. The pump unit consists of an electric permanent magnet motor, valve block, and reversible gear pump. Gear pumps have positive displacement. They consist of two or more revolving gears that mesh and pick up fluid from the intake and force it out of the discharge under pressure. Non-return valves are installed on the directional outlets.

c. **Hydraulic Steering Types.** There are three basic types:

(1) **Two-Line System.** Pressurized fluid is pumped into the ram from either end depending on the direction required.

(2) **Two-Line Pressurized System.** This system has an external pressurized reservoir.

(3) **Three-Line System.** Pressurized fluid flows in one direction only. A uniflow valve is installed within the system to direct all fluid back to the reservoir.

d. **Installation.** There are a number of important considerations when installing pumps:

(1) Pumps must be mounted in a horizontal position. Units are often mounted vertically which is incorrect.

(2) The pump should be mounted adjacent to the steering cylinder.

(3) The pump must be securely mounted so that no vibration can arise.

(4) Non-return valves must be fitted to the helm pump to prevent the autopilot pump from driving it instead of the ram.

e. **Pump Maintenance and Testing.** Perform maintenance and testing as follows:

(1) **Test Rudder Operation.** Drive the rudder lock-to-lock using the pilot control unit. Make sure that the rudder moves to the same side as the required command signal. If reversed, the motor terminal connections require reversal at the autopilot control box. The oil expansion reservoir if fitted may require topping up. Make sure the rudder stops before the mechanical stops.

(2) **Maintenance.** Dismantle the pump after 1000 hours operation. Examine oil seals and replace them. It is recommended that this be done regardless of condition. Check the motor brushes, and replace if excessively worn. Clean the brush gear and ensure that brushes move freely in the brush-holders.

f. **Hydraulic System Troubleshooting.** The following faults and symptoms are applicable to most pump systems:

(1) **Spongy Steering.** This is common, and is caused by air trapped in the hydraulic system. The system must be bled according to the instruction manual. When bleeding ensure that the steering is operated stop-to-stop to expel air in the pump and pipe work.

(2) **System Cleanliness.** The system must be clean, and no particles of dirt introduced into the system. Clean hands, clean tools and clean oil are essential. Particles often lodge in check valves causing loss of pressure and back driving of the steering wheel.

Table 2-8 Hydraulic Steering Troubleshooting

Symptom	Probable Fault
Excessive pump noise	Air in hydraulic system
No piston movement on command	Oil valve closed Pump sucking in air Non return valve leaking
Rudder moves back to amidships	Non return valve leaking
Wheel moves with pump operation	Lock valve leaking
Piston moves erratically	Air in hydraulic system
Rudder movement stops with increase in rudder load	Pump under-rated Low pump motor voltage

2.16   Trim Tabs. The majority of planing hull and semi-displacement powerboats have trim tabs. These essentially consist of variable hydraulic rams or actuators that are electrically controlled. The electrical circuit is a simple switch supplying power to a solenoid valve, directing oil into either end of the actuator. Log on to www.bennetttrimtabs.com. Routine maintenance inspections are as follows:

> **a.**   Trim tab jamming due to marine growth or mechanical damage is common. Regular checking, cleaning and operation through the full operating range are required to maintain serviceability. In particular, check rams for pitting and ensure where possible that they are lightly coated with oil.

> **b.**   In some cases, corrosion of the tabs can be a problem. Anodes should be checked or installed as required. They should be installed on the upper surface only.

> **c.**   Electrical connections should also be inspected to ensure they are tight, and not degrading.

2.17   Stabilizers. Stabilizers are now found on boats in the 10 to 120 meter range. Systems such as those from Naiad, Trac and the SeaRocq from KoopNautic are hydraulic. They consist of a hydraulic pump; oil reservoir; oil filters and cooler; control valves; actuators; fins; roll sensors and the electronic control system. Stabilizer systems may be part of an integrated system. They can be powered from a central hydraulic power unit (HPU) that also may power a thruster, hydraulic powered generator and a windlass. Systems use variable delivery piston pumps with pressure compensation that are powered either from the main engine or other power take off (PTO). Hydraulic oil for the pump is supplied from an oil reservoir that usually has temperature and oil level sensors. The pressurized oil is supplied to the electro-hydraulic servo control valves located adjacent to the fin actuators. The actuators then direct oil to the two fin hydraulic actuator cylinders to vary the position. The roll stabilization process is very dynamic and the fin attack angles are altering continuously depending on sea states and the sensed roll. When the vessel moves through the water, the hydrodynamic flow of water over the foils creates lift. This generates a counteracting force to the rolling movement created by the wave action on the vessel. The foils are altered constantly to counteract the sensed roll.

a. **Control Systems.** A fin angle sensor is located on the main shaft to provide position feedback information to the control unit. In operation the control system computes the roll angle, velocity and acceleration based on sensor inputs that include a Gyrosens roll sensor. Older systems use mechanical gyros. Naiad has a patented hydraulic turbine-driven gyroscope that operates in the range of 10,000 to 20,000 rpm. This gives pressure control proportional to the vessel roll. Two signal lines are connected to a servo valve at each fin actuator. The feedback signals are amplified, processed and the output controls the direction, speed and degree of change of the fins directly proportional to the roll. TRAC systems use a solid-state inertial sensor to input roll and heel angle data to the control processor. Fin attack angle adjustment control signals output at a rate of 200 per second.

b. **Maintenance.** System performance relies on proper hydraulic system maintenance of oil and oil filters. Systems should be checked in operation for oil leaks. Feedback sensors must be checked and all connections and plugs kept tight and dry. Fin shaft seals should be checked for leakage. Where retractable fin systems are installed, the retract systems should also be visually checked.

2.18   Water Jet Propulsion. Rolls Royce Kamewa are the main makers of water jet systems. These systems are used as primary propulsion systems on some power vessels as small as 60–70 feet. In addition to the diesel engine speed controls, there are the water nozzle steering and control systems. These consist of actuators and feedback sensors. Steering and engine control are integrated as a propulsion unit. As there are considerable control electronics, cables and control equipment must be installed well clear of power cables and other sources of interference.

2.19   Electric Propulsion. I have been involved with large ship diesel electric propulsion systems for many years. These systems are now starting to appear on pleasure vessels. There are several variations available for electric propulsion in commercial applications. These systems operate using high voltage inputs and AC variable frequency drives (synchroconverters, cycloconverters) which are now common on deepwater drilling rigs and cruise liners. Older systems are DC powered with SCR drives for speed control and conversion. In motorboats, the technologies are similar with some variations and many exciting developments are now appearing.

a. **Fischer Panda.** (www.fischerpanda.de) Fischer Panda has a new system with a range of applications to suit sail and power. Like the big ship systems I am involved with, it has a podded, full azimuthing thruster type propulsion unit. The underwater podded unit contains the electric drive motor, which is powered via sliprings so that 360° azimuthing is possible.

b.   **Vetus.** The Dutch company Vetus has introduced a system that uses a brushless 2.2 kW 24 VDC electric motor. It operates at a speed up to a maximum of 1250 rpm allowing direct coupling to the shaft. The system also has a speed control module. The length of time the system can operate is dependent on the size of the battery bank.

c.   **The Electric Wheel.** This is an innovative development from Solomon Technologies (www.solomontechnologies.com). The system consists of just eight moving parts that include the electric wheel, which has two brushless, DC permanent magnet pancake type motors. They are connected to a special planetary gear transmission. The outer ring gear of the transmission is coupled to one motor and the inner sun gear is fastened to the hub of the other motor. A three-pinion planetary gear rides between the ring and sun gears, and this transmits torque to the drive shaft. This is unique as the electrical power and transmission are within one compact motor housing. For a 15-ton boat installation the system comprises a dual motor with a torque output of 58 lb-ft and 10 bhp (7.5 kW) at 900 rpm. The power supply is 144 volts DC and full load current of 64 amps. The controller uses a dual PWM technology system with a continuous rating of 40 amps and 20 amps.

Engine Instrumentation Systems

3.1 **Engine Alarms and Instrumentation.** Instrumentation is crucial to ensuring that engines operate correctly within the designed parameters. Instruments may consist of a bank of discrete analog meters, or an integrated system with digital and visual screen displays; most manufacturers have such systems. The latter is becoming more prevalent, and consists of trend analysis, alarm set-point management, alarm logging and other advanced features. A check of all sensor unit terminals and connections, along with a test of all alarm functions, preferably before you start a trip, is all that is required. Log onto FW Murphy www.fwmurphy.com, and www.vdokienzle.com.

   a.   **Oil Pressure Alarms.** A pressure alarm can be incorporated into a gauge sensor unit or it is a separate device. It consists of a pressure sensitive mechanism that activates a contact when the factory set pressure is reached. It is grounded to the engine block on one side. Activating it grounds the circuit, setting off the panel alarm. To test the alarm circuit, simply lift off the connection and touch it to the engine block.

   b.   **Water Temperature Alarms.** These stand-alone alarms have a bimetallic element that closes when the factory set temperature is reached. To test, simply remove the connection from the sensor terminal and touch it on the engine block to activate alarm. The sensor has two terminals: "G" is used for the meter, and "W" is used for the alarm contact. In many cases, damage occurs because the alarm did not function or was not noticed. The first reaction is often "What's wrong with the alarm?" instead of "What's wrong with the engine?" It is good practice to add a loud audible alarm, as some of the engine panel units are difficult to hear at times over ambient engine noise.

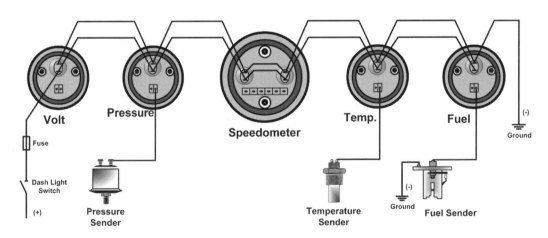

Figure 3-1 Engine Instrumentation Systems

3.2   **Pressure Monitoring.** The monitoring of pressures is fundamental to the proper operation of any engine. This includes lubricating oil and filter differential pressures, fuel and filter differential pressures, coolants (both seawater and freshwater), turbocharger charging air pressure and air inlet pressures, gearbox and transmission oil pressures and engine crankcase pressures.

Oil Pressure Monitoring. The oil pressure sensor unit is a variable resistance device that responds to pressure changes. It is very common to assume that the meter or alarm is wrong. Oil pressure sensor units should be removed every year and any oil sludge cleaned out of the fitting as this can clog up and cause inaccurate or no readings. Low oil pressure readings are caused by low lube oil level, or a clogged oil filter creating a lowering in oil pressure. A faulty oil pump also can cause a lowering in pressure; a rise in oil temperature due to an increase in engine temperature, or an oil cooler can also cause a problem. When sensor units are poorly grounded or Teflon tape is improperly applied to threads to make a high resistance contact, a problem can occur.

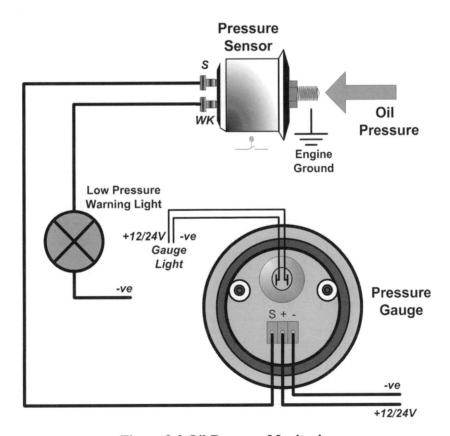

Figure 3-2 Oil Pressure Monitoring

3.3. **Temperature Monitoring.** The main temperature monitoring points utilizing the same sensor types include lubricating oil, transmission oil, coolants (seawater and fresh-water), fuel temperature, after-cooler and turbocharger inlet air.

Water and Oil Temperature Gauges. The monitoring of water temperature is essential to the safe operation of the engine. Temperature extremes can cause serious engine damage or failure. Sensor units are resistive; resistance within the sensor unit changes in a non-linear curve. If the gauge readings are not correct and a gauge test shows it to be good, check the sensor. Before you check the sensor unit, you must assume that the main causes of high temperatures are:

(1) Loss of freshwater-cooling can be caused by faulty water pump impeller, a loose rubber drive belt, low water levels, fouled coolers and increased combustion temperatures.

(2) Loss of salt water cooling can be caused by a blocked intake or strainer, a faulty water pump impeller, a clogged cooler or aeration caused by a leak in the suction side of the pump.

(3) Increased engine loadings caused by adverse tidal and current flows, or overloading. Sensor units are poorly grounded or Teflon tape is improperly applied to threads to make a high resistance contact.

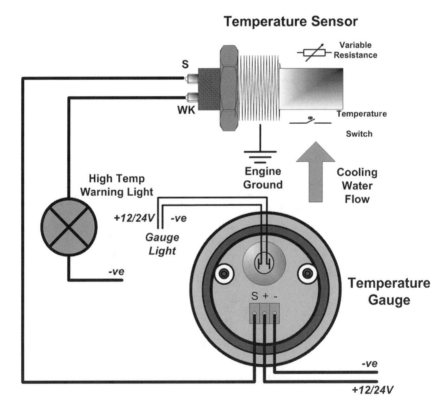

Figure 3-3 Water Temperature Monitoring

3.4 **Exhaust Gas Temperature Monitoring.** Exhaust gas temperature monitoring is used in commercial ships and is recommended on all motorboats. Engine problems are easier and faster to identify than water temperature and oil pressure monitoring. These can be problems within the cooling water system; increased engine loads caused by adverse tidal and current flows; air intake obstructions caused by clogged air filters, or where installed, blocked air coolers; combustion chamber problems caused by defective injectors, valves etc. Larger engine boats will also have cylinder monitoring, and this allows identification of problems specific to cylinders to be identified and monitored. Smaller engines will have a sensor installed on the main exhaust manifold. Pyrometer compensating leads and wiring should be routed clear of other cables to avoid induction and inaccurate readings.

> **Operating Principle.** Exhaust temperature sensors are called thermocouples, or pyrometers. These sensors consist of two dissimilar metals (iron/constantine; copper/nickel; platinum/rhodium; nicrosil/nisil, nickel/aluminum), which will generate a small voltage proportional to the heat applied to the sensor. The voltage is measured in millivolts (mV). The typical thermocouple consists of a sensing junction, and a reference junction. The open circuit voltage is measured with a high impedance voltmeter and is the temperature difference between the sensing junction and the reference junction. The thermocouple junction is also called the "hot junction." The compensating cables between the junction and the measurement meter are electrically matched to maintain accuracy. They are polarity sensitive, and must be connected positive to positive.

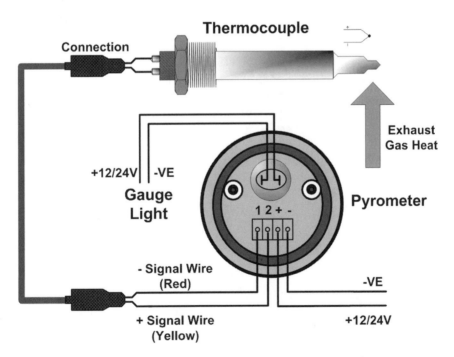

Figure 3-4 Exhaust Gas Temperature Monitoring

3.5 **Engine Tachometers.** The tachometer is used to monitor engine speed, differential or synchronization, shaft revolutions and turbocharger speed. This provides important information on fuel consumption and vessel performance. There are several tachometer types, based on the type of sensing system.

a. **Generator Tachometer.** This tachometer type receives a signal from a mechanically driven generator unit. The generator produces an AC voltage proportional in amplitude to the engine's speed. This is decoded by the tachometer. Variations in speed give proportional change in output voltage, which changes the meter reading. The most common fault on these units is drive shaft mechanism damage.

b. **Inductive Tachometer.** These tachometers have an inductive magnetic sensor. The sensor detects changes in magnetic flux as the teeth on a flywheel move past. This sends a series of on/off pulses that are decoded and displayed on the tachometer. Make sure that the sensor unit is properly fastened. A common cause of failure is that the flywheel damages the sensor head if it is adjusted too close.

c. **Alternator Tachometer.** This type of tachometer derives a pulse from the alternator AC winding, typically marked 'W'. The alternator output signal frequency is directly proportional to engine speed. The pick-up is taken from the star point or one of the unrectified phases. Typical connections for VDO tachometers are illustrated. If the alternator is faulty, there is no reading. There are a number of different alternator terminal designations used by various manufacturers; the main ones are W, STA, AC, STY, SINUS. If there is no output terminal, make the connection shown in the illustration when you install this tachometer.

d. **Synchronization Tachometers.** The synchronizer or differential tachometer is used to show the precise speed difference between each engine in a twin-engine installation. Use of the meter allows balancing to be carried out.

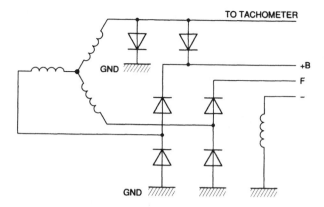

STAR WINDING, SINGLE PHASE

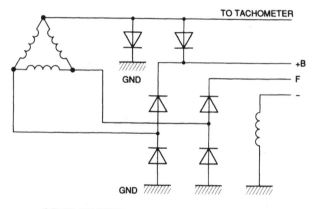

DELTA WINDING

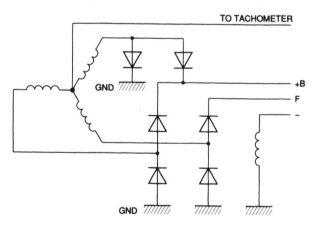

STAR WINDING, MULTI PHASE

Figure 3-5 Alternator Tachometer Circuits

3.6 **Bilge and Tank Level Monitoring** The monitoring of onboard fuel, water and bilge levels, is an essential task. A simple electrical gauge can be installed that provides the necessary information.

a. **Resistance Sensor.** The majority of tank sensors in use operate by varying a resistance proportional to tank level. The two basic sensor types are:

    (1) **Immersion Pipe Type.** This sensor consists of a damping tube, with an internal float that moves up and down along two wires. These units are only suitable for fuel tanks. The big advantage with these sensor types is that they are well damped, which eliminates fluctuating readings.

    (2) **Lever Type.** The lever type system consists of a sensor head located on the end of an adjustable leg. The sensor head comprises a variable resistance and float arm pivot. As the float and arm move relative to fluid levels, the resistance alters and the meter reading changes. Typical resistance readings are in the range 10–180 ohms. Lever type units should be installed longitudinally, as athwartships orientation can cause serious problems with the vessel rolling. In water sensor units, the variable resistance is located outside of the tank to avoid water problems, while the fuel unit has a resistance unit in the tank.

b. **Capacitive Sensors.** This type of transducer operates on the principle that the value of a capacitor depends on the dielectric between plates. The sensor unit measures the capacitance difference between air and the liquid.

    (1) **Output Values.** The sensing circuit outputs a voltage proportional to the level in the typical range of 0 to 5 volts.

    (2) **Faults.** The most common fault in these systems is water damage to the circuit board, usually because of tank condensation.

c. **Pressure Sensors.** These sensor are considerably more expensive, but very accurate and less prone to damage. The transducers are either placed at the bottom of the tank, or on a pipe to one side at the tank bottom. They are more common on computer based integrated monitoring systems.

    (1) **Output Values.** The sensors output either a 4-20 milliamps or 0.6 - 2.6 volts proportional to the pressure of the fluid in the tank. The pressure value is proportional to the tank volume.

    (2) **Faults.** If the sensor is located on a small pipe, it may become clogged.

d. **Air Sensors.** Air operated bilge switches such as the Jabsco Hydro Air use an air column to pressure activate a remote mounted switch. They can switch 20 amps, and are ignition protected. One advantage is they are less prone to jamming than float switches.

3.7 **Electrical System Monitoring.** There are a number of parameters for monitoring electrical systems and methods for installing instruments:

a. **Charging Voltmeters** Many instrument panels incorporate a voltmeter to indicate the state of the charging. Voltmeters are fairly coarse, and only partially useful in precisely assessing battery voltage, but they are a useful indicator on the charging system. Many voltmeters have a colored scale to enable rapid recognition of battery condition, red for under or overcharge and green for proper range.

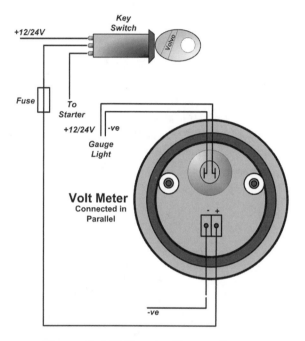

Figure 3-6 Voltmeter Connections

b. **Charging Ammeters** Charging ammeters are reasonably popular and are an easy guide to the level of charge current from the alternator. There are basically two types of ammeter:

(1) **In-line Ammeter.** This ammeter type has the main charge alternator output cable running through it. In many cases, the long run to a meter causes unacceptable voltage drops and undercharging. An additional problem with installing such ammeters on switch panels is that the charge cables are invariably run with other cables and cause radio interference. If you are going to install this type of ammeter, make sure that the meter is mounted as close as possible to the alternator. If these ammeters start fluctuating at maximum alternator and rated outputs, this is generally due to voltage drops within the meter and cable. The underrating of connectors is also a major cause of problems.

(2) **Shunt Ammeter.** The shunt ammeter overcomes the voltage drop problem. The shunt is essentially a resistance inserted in the charging line. Sense cables (16 AWG twisted pair) are connected across the output cable and can be run to any meter location without voltage drop problems as the output is in millivolts. The ammeter must always be rated for the maximum alternator output. Many installations do not do this; the shunt or meter is often damaged, and there are big voltage drops in the charging line.

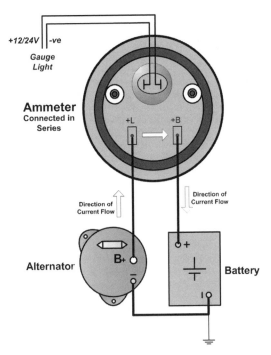

Figure 3-7 Ammeter Configurations

3.8 **Hour Counters and Clocks.** An hour counter is essential for keeping a record of maintenance intervals. Essentially it is a clock activated only when the engine is operating. There are a number of methods of activating hour counters:

a. **Ignition Switch.** This is the easiest and most practical method. The meter is simply connected across the ignition positive and a negative so that it operates when the engine is running.

b. **Oil Pressure Switch.** This is not a common method. Some installations activate through the switch, so that it operates only when engine is operating.

c. **Alternator.** In many installations the counter is activated from the alternator auxiliary terminal D+ or 61.

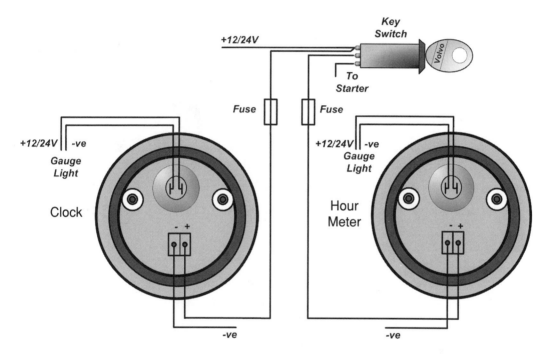

Figure 3-8 Hour Meter and Clock Connections

3.9 **Acoustic Alarm Systems** Acoustic alarms are generally connected to warning light circuits, and the buzzer is activated by a relay. Acoustic warnings are activated along with the lamp from sensor contact "W". The acoustic alarm should be activated through a relay, not through the sensor contact which is not rated for such loads.

a. **Buzzer Test.** Using a lead, connect a positive supply to the buzzer positive terminal, and check that a negative one is also connected. If buzzer operates, remove the bridges. A test function should be inserted into the circuit so that alarm function can be verified.

b. **Operating Test.** With alarm lights on, put a bridge from negative to the buzzer negative; sometimes a "lost" negative is the problem. Connect a positive supply to the relay positive, typically numbered 86. If the relay does not operate and the buzzer is working, then the relay is suspect. After removing it, verify using the same procedure. Note that sometimes a relay may sound like it is operating, but in fact the contacts may be damaged and open circuited. If a buzzer is not operating along with the lights, either a cable or connection is faulty, or the operating relay is defective.

c. **Mute Function.** On many home-built engine panels, it is essential to silence the alarm. This entails placing a switch in line with the buzzer. The lamp remains illuminated to indicate the alarm status.

d. **Time Delays.** During engine start up, a time delay is necessary to prevent the alarm from sounding before the oil pressure has reached normal operating level. Time delays are typically in the range of 15 to 30 seconds.

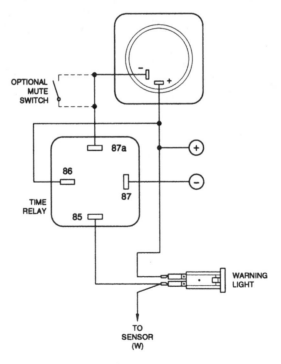

Figure 3-9 Acoustic Alarm System

e.   **Combination System.** The illustration below shows the use of both a switching relay and time delay relay. The system functions as follows:

(1)   **Switching Relay.** On ignition, the switching relay energizes. This illuminates the warning light and normally oil pressure will activate the alarm.

(2)   **Time Delay Relay.** The time delay relay is energized by the switching relay. The contacts that activate the audible alarm do not operate for 15 to 30 seconds. If oil pressure has risen to normal within that period, the alarm will not activate.

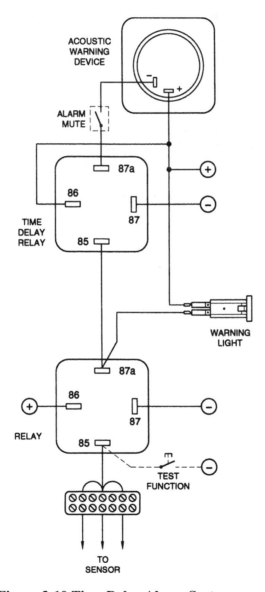

Figure 3-10 Time Delay Alarm System

3.10   Crankcase Oil Mist Detection. Large motorboats, offshore supply boats and super-yachts have larger output medium speed diesels, where crankcase explosions can cause fatalities and serious engine damage. Oil mist detectors such as the Schaller Visatron use an air supply at 0.5 bar to take atmosphere samples from each crankcase compartment, and measure the turbidity or opacity. The sample is passed between an infrared emitter and detector, where the oil mist absorbs some light reducing the light level at the detector. This opacity is measured as a percentage, with a typical operating range of 0%–7% with maximum alarm levels around 2.4%. The friction of non-lubricated metals causes very rapid overheating, and oil mist can rise to critical levels in 20-30 seconds. Oil mist is explosive at a quantity of 50mg of atomized oil per liter of air with ignition at 500°C. Systems must be calibrated correctly with all ventilation fans running. Detectors have LED fault and operating status indicators. The electronic PCBs are very static sensitive, and anti-static wrist straps should be used when handling.

3.11   Fuel Monitoring. Fuel computers such as those from FloScan (www.floscan.com) are typical of the systems in use. Many factors influence fuel consumption rates including bottom fouling, vessel trim, propeller and engine condition, as well as adverse tidal flows and currents. Burning excess fuel is very expensive. Optimizing consumption by varying speed to the most economical for prevailing conditions, or altering trim tab position, are possible based on accurate fuel consumption data. Performance drops show up in fuel consumption rates that can include propeller damage or bottom conditions. This can result in fuel consumption rate drops of up to 20% on a vessel with a clean bottom and matched propeller, and overall savings can exceed 30–35%. Flow monitors use a flow sensor, some use a paddle-wheel based system; FloScan use an opto-electronic turbine sensor with an infrared light source to count turbine rotations. A processor calculates fuel flow based on the speed of the fuel flow, and processing may use inputs from a log sensor or GPS to compute miles per gallon (mpg), liters per hour (lph) or gallons per hour (gph) rates. In systems with a return to the tank, a sensor is installed in forward and return lines, with return flow subtracted from forward flow rates. Engines such as Detroit and Caterpillar have fuel return flows at a much higher temperature than the forward flows, and compensation must be made for fuel expansion to eliminate errors. Each flow sensor must be calibrated and the calibration figures are used in systems commissioning and initialization.

3.12   Rudder Angle Indicators. The systems consist of a potentiometer connected to the rudder quadrant. Movement changes the resistance and the indication on the instrument in the console. Most problems arise from potentiometers, which have sustained accidental damage, or linkage damage, due to vibration.

3.13   **Gauge Testing.** If gauges are suspect, use the following testing procedures:

a.   **Open Sensor Test.** Remove the sensor lead marked "G" from the back of the gauge. Switch on meter supply voltage. The gauge needle should now be in the following positions:

(1)   Temperature Gauge: left-hand, hard-over position.

(2)   Pressure Gauge: right-hand, hard-over position.

(3)   Tank Gauge: right-hand, hard-over position.

b.   **Sensor Ground Test.** This test involves bridging the sensor input terminal "G" to negative. Remove the sensor lead and turn the meter supply on. The gauge needle should now be in the following position:

(1)   Temperature Gauge: right-hand, hard-over position.

(2)   Pressure Gauge: right-hand, hard-over position.

(3)   Tank Gauge: left-hand, hard-over position.

3.14   **Sensor Testing (VDO)** Disconnect the cables, and using a multimeter, digital or analog, set the resistance (ohms) range to approximately 200 ohms. Place the positive (red) meter probe on the terminal marked "G" on the sensor. If it has a dual alarm-and sensor-output, the alarm output is marked "W". Place the negative (black) meter probe on the sensor thread.

a.   **Temperature Sensors.** These approximate readings should be observed:

(1)   40°C = 200–300 ohms.

(2)   120°C = 20–40 ohms.

b.   **Pressure Sensors.** These approximate readings should be observed:

(1)   High Pressure (engine off) = 10 ohms.

(2)   Low Pressure (engine running) = 40psi: 105 ohms, 60psi:152 ohms.

c.   **Fuel Tank Sensors.** These approximate readings should be observed:

(1)   Tank Empty = 10 ohms. Tank Full = 180 ohms.

3.15   **Engine Alarm Set Points.** It is important to know when you are nearing the maximum values. Use the table to check your own and enter the specific values from your engine manual for reference. These figures cover normal ranges for alarms and automatic shutdowns for either main engines or generators. (1 bar = 14.4 psi; 1 psi = 0.07 bar).

Table 3-1 Engine Alarm Set points

Parameter	Typical Value	Your Boat Value
Lube oil temperature	90–95°C (194–203°F)	
Lube oil pressure	1–2 bar (14–28psi)	
LO filter differential	1–1.5 bar (14–20psi)	
Pre-lube pressure	1–2 bar (14–28psi)	
High crankcase pressure	0.01 bar (0.2psi)	
FW cooling out	100–105°C (212–220°F)	
FW cooling max	105–110°C (220–230°F)	
FW pressure	0.2–0.4 bar (3–6psi)	
Fuel pressure	2–3 bar (25–40psi)	
Fuel filter differential	0.5–0.8 bar (7–10psi)	
Fuel temperature max	65°C (149°F)	
Air inlet manifold temp	85–95°C (187–202°F)	
Air inlet manifold press	2.5–3.5 bar (35–50psi)	
Exhaust temp cylinder	500–550°C (933–1023°F)	
Exhaust temp manifold	600–650°C (1113–1203°F)	
Exhaust temp deviation	+/- 50°C (122°F)	
Exhaust temp to turbo	500–550°C (933–1023°F))	

3.16   PLC Control Systems. Large motor vessels and super-yachts have sophisticated programmable logic controller (PLC) automated control systems. PLCs are now found in engine control systems, desalinators, hydraulic control systems, vessel alarm systems, etc. A PLC is essentially a microprocessor-controlled system that replaces what were called relay logic control systems. The relay, timer and interlock functions are all programmed into the units and can have hundreds of operations. The program makes the electrical connections between inputs, outputs, internal relays, timers and counters. A PLC can contain all parts within an integral unit or, on larger systems, it will consist of three basic, usually modular parts. Lewmar have a winch hydraulic system. Manufacturers include Mitsubishi, Omron, GE-Fanuc, Allen Bradley and Modicon AEG. The main component parts are:

   a.   **The Power Supply Unit (PSU).** The voltage is stepped down to that required by the PLC circuits to operate. An isolation transformer should be used to power the PLC PSU to ensure a clean power supply. An LED is usually installed to show power status. Power supplies also have what is called a hold-up time, which is how long the system will operate during a brief power interruption. Typically this is in the range of 20–3000 milliseconds. The CPU, and I/O modules operate from a 5VDC source that is output from the PSU.

b. **The Central Processor Unit (CPU).** This unit stores the program in memory, and initiates program operations. Programming takes the form of ladder logic. Programs are usually entered using a handheld program unit or laptop computer via a serial cable. Memory in most marine applications is non-volatile: a small backup battery or capacitor is installed so that the program is not lost in case of a blackout. Memory depending on make is capacitor-backed RAM, EE-PROM, FLASH EEPROM and battery-backed RAM. Its life span is around 3–5 years. Capacitor backup lasts only 30 days maximum. In any cycle there is a scan of all inputs and reading of data; then a program scan to execute the instructions; this is followed by an output scan which outputs data. Some interconnected systems will then communicate via data links with others. The system also carries out internal housekeeping routines, memory management, etc. on each scan cycle. The PLC scans all the inputs and initiates any outputs as required. The scan time is around 30 milliseconds. Some PLC units have a key switch that may have various functions that include RUN in normal operation; REM for remote run or stop of a sequence; PROG for program mode; RESET to reset hardware or an operation error; LCL to clear latched devices. Indicators allow status monitoring and usually have the following function assignments:

(1) Forced I/O LED indicates an internal relay or an I/O logic state has been forced using the programmer.

(2) CPU LED indicates a CPU fault.

(3) ERROR LED indicates an error has been detected by self diagnostic routines during program sequence.

(4) RS232 LED may be fitted on networked systems and indicates function.

(5) BATTERY LED indicates the internal battery level is low and requires replacement.

(6) RUN LED indicates a program sequence is being executed. Flashing usually means an error has been detected by self diagnostic routines during program sequence.

(7) Power LED indicates 5 VDC is present.

3.17 **Input/Output (I/O) Modules.** The I/O modules typically have an ON status LED indicator, when the LED is on; the proper signal is present on either the input or output. I/O circuits are opto-isolated to ensure that no disruption or fault on an external system can affect the PLC circuits, and also to eliminate noise and interference on the circuits. I/O consists or various types depending on the applications.

a. **Digital Inputs.** There is digital I/O, which consists of switches that are on or off. These can be auxiliary contacts, micro-switches, proximity detectors, photoelectric switches, and push buttons.

b.   **Digital Outputs.** These can be relay and contactors, solenoids, indicator and alarm lamps and LED, electromagnetic clutches, etc. Manufacturers offer various output options that include AC/DC relay, AC triac and DC transistor. Solid-state relays (triacs) and transistor outputs are used where high switching rates are required. Triac outputs usually have an MOV inserted across the output for surge suppression, and where switching DC inductive loads, this is an IN4004 diode. These increase the relay contact life. Relay outputs have make and break ratings, typically 7–15A at 115/250VAC with continuous ratings of around 2 amps. DC ratings are much smaller at around 1.2 make and break and continuous rating of 2 amps.

c.   **Analog Inputs.** Analog input modules convert the signal to digital for use by the PLC. Analog I/O modules consist of RTD resistance inputs, thermocouple mV inputs. Typically these are 4-wire arrangements to suit 4– 20 mA, -10 to +10 VDC, and –20 to +20 mA. These have to convert the input signal and normally have a range of 0-100% of voltage or current. Circuits must also have filtering to eliminate noise on the inputs. RTD inputs can be configured for many of the 12 common types. Thermocouple inputs can be configured for many of the 8 common types, and provides automatic cold junction compensation and linearization. Thermocouple input cables should be the appropriate shielded extension cables, or if straight mV inputs, shielded twisted pair. Three wire Platinum PT100 sensors can be fed in directly.

d.   **Analog Outputs.** These output -10 to +10 VDC, and 4–20 mA to operate and control equipment and systems such as inverters, valves and other devices.

3.18   Programming. Most PLC units can be programmed using a handheld program unit or a laptop computer running the appropriate software. This allows on-line modification and testing, program editing, modification of the application program, monitoring in real-time, troubleshooting, observation of ladder logic and function descriptions. Programming is the writing and storing of the sequence of instructions within the memory. Ladder logic consists of rungs, which contain the instructions. Each instruction has a name (examine if open or closed, etc), a mnemonic (number or code), and an address. To execute the program all inputs are continually scanned and examined for status, either open or closed, and then output instructions are sent to the various output relays. The program is divided up into program files that store and control the main program and subroutines. The data files contain input and output status data, the processor timers and counters, etc. Each item of data has an associated address. Programs contain conditional input or output and instructions; comparison instructions; timer and counter instructions; communications instructions; I/O and interrupt instructions; math instructions (ADD, SUB, MUL, DIV, NEG); proportional integral derivative (PID) for controlling outputs of process loops such as temperature, pressure, flow and level; move and logical instructions; sequencer instructions and control instructions.

3.19   Installation. Heat dissipation must be considered when installing PLCs, and normally this is part of the equipment electrical control design. Ventilation must be adequate to maintain below maximum allowable operating temperatures. The PLCs must be protected from excess dust, moisture, gases, and high shock or vibration areas. While robust they are not indestructible, and they are rated up to around 50–55°C and 85% humidity without condensation. Use of desiccant crystals to reduce moisture is recommended.

    a.   All power input wiring must be wired clear of I/O wiring to reduce interference, and cross overs must be made at 90°C. Segregate the I/O signal types, such as RTD with RTD, and mV with mV etc. Run outputs with outputs and do not mix inputs with outputs if possible.

    b.   Emergency stop and safety isolation switches are always wired directly to starters and not through PLC I/O units.

    c.   Connections must be made with PLC power off. I/O cable sizes are typically 14 AWG or less. Color identification is preferred. Allen-Bradley suggests red for AC and blue for DC I/O cables. All wires must be identified and I/O labels marked.

    d.   Grounding within panels usually has the chassis bonded to an internal grounding bus that is connected to ground by an 8 AWG cable.

3.20   PLC Troubleshooting. PLCs are well developed, and are both reliable and robust. Problems are relatively rare and usually associated with the power supply unit. In many cases, system faults are wrongly attributed to the PLC CPU and not the peripherals. Resetting and rebooting often solve problems.

    a.   **LED Codes.** The specific PLC manual should be referenced to understand LED codes. Where a reset function is installed, perform a reset and then observe operation. If Power LED is on, CPU LED is on, then check I/O status LED's.

    b.   **Inputs and Outputs.** As the unit is a "logic" controller, the operating program for a PLC depends on the correct inputs to run. Where a system has stopped or frozen, and the PLC is clearly operational, troubleshooting should look initially at the various devices, such as switches and contacts that go to the input and output modules. This may be a pressure switch, an interlock or similar input device. If the inputs are correct, the I/O module channel may be at fault, but this is not common. Check that all connections are tight throughout the entire system.

3.21   Control Circuit Devices. Motor starters, hydraulic control systems, and many systems and equipment operate on sensor information.

    a.   **Pressure Switches.** The purposes include alarm activation, shutdown and interlock functions, control functions and inputs to PLCs. Pressure switches in general are the industrial brass and nitrile rubber diaphragm types on low pressure (20–200psi) with high accuracy; piston types when high pressure, high cycling use such as air compressors are required; and Bourdon Tube on high pressure and high accuracy applications. Switches are selected based on the pressure range, with the usually adjustable set point being at mid-range. Some switches require opening to adjust and on others the screw is top mounted. The set point is when the switch will activate. All switches have a dead-band, which is the pressure range between the set point and the point at which the switch resets on falling pressure. Switching mechanisms may be simple 3 terminal changeover, or sets of normally open or closed contacts.

b. **Temperature Sensors.** Temperature gauges or meters are generally of the bimetal or glass bulb type. PT100 Platinum Resistance sensors offer high accuracy and are used on many engine monitoring and automation systems. Thermistors have resistance changes with temperature changes. The negative temperature coefficient (NTC) units are used to drive alarms and temperature controllers. The positive temperature coefficient (PTC) units are used in over-temperature and over-current applications on motors and transformers, and in warning and trip circuits. The resistance temperature devices (RTD), like thermistors, have a changing resistance with temperature. Bimetal devices are frequently seen in snap action devices on refrigerator compressors or surface mounted on equipment. Infrared devices are typically on handheld units, which are very useful tools on motorboats. These can be used to monitor bearings, motors, or any object subject to heat. As they are non-contact, measurements are easy to take.

c. **Level Switches.** The traditional level switch is the float type, which is used in many applications. Other types in use are optical sensor switches, which use an infrared (IR) sensor as described in bilge system detectors. Some industrial switches that utilize probes for use in conductive liquids may cause corrosion problems on boats.

d. **Flow Switches.** Some systems use flow switches to monitor water flow. Flow switches generally have a normally open (NO) or normally closed (NC) reed switch. Reed switches can fail and the continuity of the switch must be checked. The reed switch is usually connected to a small control relay, which is then connected into the main control circuit. Flow switch paddles can jam or seize and may require checking.

e. **Limit Switches.** A variety of switches are in use; some use a plunger pin, roller plunger, roller lever and adjustable rod. They work by having the object travel until it strikes the actuator and this activates a set of either normally open or normally closed contacts. These contacts may be part of a control or indication circuit. It is important to check switches regularly, and hand actuate or exercise them when the system is off. In addition, application of lubrication to prevent corrosion of the mechanism is necessary. Problems stem from mechanical damage as the switches are designed to have an object strike the operating mechanism, and damage is often sustained.

f. **Proximity Switches.** Switches are either capacitive or inductive devices that detect objects at close ranges of around 15mm. Inductive sensors detect metal objects, and sensing distances vary for different metals. Capacitive sensors detect both metal and non-metal objects, including liquids. Sensors have either NPN or PNP solid-state outputs. NPN outputs are often referred to as sinking type devices as the load is wired between the output and the positive terminal. PNP outputs are often called sourcing types, as the load is wired between the output and the negative terminal. Sensors are very robust and the circuits are encased in epoxy. They are resilient to shock, vibration, heat and water. Clean and check the sensor faces for damage regularly.

g. **Photoelectric Sensors.** These sensors use light to detect the proximity of objects. They have a greater sensing range than inductive or capacitive sensor types. The two types are the light energized type, which have an output when light is detected, and the dark energized type with an output when no light is visible. The light sources are generally a red LED. The through beam device uses a light source and a detector, which are aligned opposite each other, and the sensor operates when the beam is interrupted. Retro-reflective detectors have a light source and detector integrated in one fitting. The source emits light and reflected light comes back to the detector from a reflector. Diffuse reflective sensors also have source and detector within one fitting and are able to distinguish different reflector target types and colors. Photo sensors are either NPN or PNP type semiconductor outputs rated at 100–200mA to switch relays or provide inputs to control systems. The typical response times for detection to output switching is around 0.5 to 2.5 milliseconds on DC detectors.

h. **Solenoid Valves.** Solenoid valves are part of many systems including hydraulics, refrigeration, air conditioning, air compressors, engine and water systems. Applying a voltage to a coil activates the solenoid. The most common in use on boat systems is the direct-acting type, which do not require differential pressure to operate. The energized solenoid coil directly activates the valve, as the coil magnetizes the plunger pulling it upwards along with the valve spindle. They are used on low to high-pressure systems. AC solenoids tend to be more powerful, and faster than DC and they have a higher inrush current. Solenoids generally have a duty cycle so repeated energization can overheat and burn the coils out. Continuous rating means it can stay on all the time, Duty Cycle + the On time divided by the On + Off Time. Many solenoids have plug on electrical connections, and these should have the retaining screw tightened. Regular inspection of connection pins is recommended for signs of corrosion and tracking between terminals. Solenoids that are not used regularly should be activated several times if possible to prevent seizure of the valve or solenoid mechanism. The solenoid has an audible metallic click when operating. Coils do burn out, and if you are testing, place a multimeter across the coil terminals or in the plug connector and check whether voltage is present. If full voltage is present, either the valve is jammed or the coil has failed.

i. **Remote Valves.** Larger vessels may have remote controlled gate and ball valves on seawater and freshwater systems. They should be routinely operated over the full range to exercise the mechanical systems, and to check operation of limit switches. Operation time is typically in the range 15–40 seconds. The control boxes should be inspected every year and cleaned, and all connections tightened. Lubrication should also be applied in accordance with the manufacturer's instructions.

j. **Relays and Contactors.** Most circuits have small relays in control applications, and contactors for supplying power to equipment. Both have a coil for operation and to close or open contacts. If a relay or contactor is suspected to be faulty, check the voltage at the coil, if voltage is applied and coil does not pull in then coil has failed. Generally the outer covering shows heat damage but not in all cases. In some cases the mechanical armature part is the problem and may be jammed. In contactors the current carrying contacts may have deteriorated and pitted so that poor or no contact is made when the coil pulls in, or the contacts weld together.

Table 3-2 Instrument Troubleshooting

Symptom	Probable Fault
Gauge does not operate	Power off Gauge supply cable off
Temperature gauge needle hard over	Sensor fault Cable fault
Pressure/tank gauge needle hard over	Sensor fault Cable fault Alternator fault
Alternator tachometer no reading	Lead off alternator terminal Alternator not "kicked" in Meter fault Broken drive mechanism
Generator tachometer no reading	Meter fault Generator fault Cable fault Sensor mechanically damaged
Inductive tachometer no reading	Sensor clearance excessive Sensor fault Meter fault Negative connections to engine
Low gauge readings	Block and sensors degraded Low oil pressure (oil pump fault)
Oil pressure alarm activated	Low oil level High oil temperature (cooling fault) Blocked sender unit Sender fault Cable fault High water temperature
Water temperature alarm	Low cooling water level Salt water cooling inlet blocked Cooling water pump fault Loose drive belt
No audible alarm	Sensor fault Relay fault Audible alarm fault Connection fault Lamp failure Lamp connection fault Alarm circuit board fault

Thruster and Propulsion Systems

4.1 **Thruster Operations.** Bow and stern thrusters are now common on many motorboats. They offer increased maneuverability in confined areas such as marinas and locks, and are invaluable on boats during high wind conditions. I work a lot with large offshore vessel thruster systems, both fixed and variable pitch, tunnel and azimuth. While these are somewhat more complex in terms of control systems, the average small boat unit is relatively simple. The major suppliers include MaxPower (www.maxpower.com), Lewmar (www.lewmar.com), Sleipner (www.side-power.com), Vetus (www.vetus.com), Wesmar (www.wesmar.com). There are many factors during both selection and installation that must be considered if thrusters are to be efficient. The basic operational factors to consider when using thrusters are:

(1)   Learn and understand the behavior of the vessel in wind conditions.

(2)   Avoid using the thruster unless moving very slowly or stopped.

(3)   Learn the maximum recommended run times and stay within the limits.

(4)   Do not use in short bursts, a single 5-second thruster period is more effective than 5 x 1 second bursts. This causes less strain and overheating on the motor, and uses less battery power.

(5)   Always switch off the control system when not in use to avoid accidental operation.

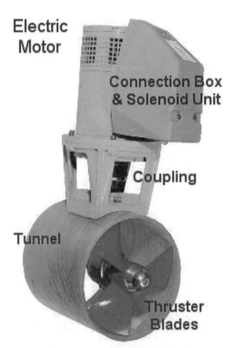

Figure 4-1 Electric Thruster —Vetus, *Courtesy of Vetus*

4.2 **Thruster Ratings.** Thrusters are specified in terms of the thrust output capability. It is the thrust and not the output of the electric motor in kW or HP that determines effectiveness. Thrust is a result of the power of the electric motor, the propeller shape and dimensions, the speed in rev/min, and of the tunnel efficiency losses. The thrust is typically in the range of 33–55 lbf (15–25 kgf) per hp (kW) of the electric motor. Thruster output forces are selected so that they equal or exceed the calculated or expected wind thrust forces, or to counter the sail plane effect. The draft also affects the drift rate, and shallow draft vessels tend to have a greater wind effect than deeper draft ones.

a. **Wind Pressure.** The wind pressure on a vessel has a quadratic increase with wind speed. The equation used by Vetus is pressure P (N/m^2) = $\frac{1}{2}$p x V^2 where p is the specific mass of air, and V is the velocity of air in m/s.

Table 4-1 Wind Force Table

Wind Force Beaufort	Description	Speed m/s	Pressure N/m^2 (kgf/m^2)
4	Moderate breeze	5.5 to 7.9	20–40 (2.0–4.1)
5	Fresh breeze	8.0 to 10.7	41–74 (4.2–7.5)
6	Strong breeze	10.8 to 13.8	75–123 (7.6–12.5)
7	Near gale	13.9 to 17.1	124–189 (12.6–19.2)
8	Gale	17.2 to 20.7	190–276 (19.3–28.2)

b. **Wind Draft.** The wind pressure must be multiplied by the wind draft area to calculate the actual wind force. This is determined by the boat surface area, wind speed and wind angle. The lateral surface areas and effects vary with the superstructure size and shape, the hull freeboard and therefore the hull surface area. The worst case is where the wind is on the beam or at 90°. A factor of 0.75 is used to account for streamlining and a less than flat and rectangular shape.

c. **Torque.** Torque is calculated by multiplying wind force by the distance between the center of effort of the wind and the center of rotation of the boat. The center of effort is dependent on the shape of the superstructure. The center of rotation tends to be more forward than center and is dependent on the underwater hull shape. The wind force torque is calculated by multiplying 50% of boat length by the wind force. Torque (T) = Wind Pressure (P) x Wind Draft (D) x 0.75 x Distance between the bow thruster center and the boat pivot point (½ vessel length). Nominally the pivot point is the stern. Thrusters should be installed as far forward as possible to maximize the leverage effect around the vessel's pivot point. They should be as deep as possible to prevent air being sucked in and maintain maximum water pressure.

4.3 **Thruster Types.** Thruster types depend on vessel types, sizes, and budgets. Propellers come in single, twin and counter rotation configurations. The latter arrangements are to increase efficiency and reduce cavitation. The range suits a variety of applications. Thrusters may be DC, single phase or three phase AC and hydraulic.

> a. **Swing Retractable.** The swing retractable thruster has the advantage of no drag, but the retract system is complicated. The Lewmar type uses a rotating lead screw to activate the arm, and MaxPower uses an innovative folding system. Interlock limit switches are installed in the control circuit for lead screw travel, and retracted position. These are prone to failure and must be maintained.

> b. **Vertical Retractable.** These also allow compact installations and reduced drag when retracted. Limit switches are also used to limit control of the up and down travel and must be maintained.

> c. **Transverse Tunnel.** The tunnel thruster is the simplest arrangement and is less complex in terms of mechanical components. Tunnels will cause some drag to the boat although not enough to bother most boat owners.

4.4 **Thruster Power Output Table.** The table shows figures quoted by Sleipner Side-power, and are a good general guide to all fixed pitch thrusters. Required thruster force (F) is calculated by dividing calculated torque (T) in Nm by distance between the bow thruster center and the boat pivot point in meters.

Table 4-2 Thruster Outputs

Thrust (kg/lbs)	Boat Size (ft)	Power (kW/hp)	Voltage (Volts)	Battery (Min CCA)
35/77	22–32'	2.2/3	12	300
55/121	28–40'	3.1/4	12/24	350/175
75/175	35–50'	4.4/6	12/24	50/250
95/209	42–58'	6/8	12/24	700/350
155/341	50–70'	8/10.7	24	600
220/484	60–84'	11.2/15	24	700
285/627	74–100'	15/20	48	2 x 450 (24V)

4.5 **Thruster Power Supply.** The efficiency of thruster motors is directly related to battery supply voltage levels, the available battery capacity, and the voltage drop in the supply cables during operation. Slow Blow fuses are used as the fluctuating loads must not cause fuse failure in normal service. The table is a general guide only; all circuits must be measured, and the appropriate cable size installed with the required protection.

a. **Batteries.** A common question is whether to use a separate battery located forward or not. This depends a great deal on the boat size and practical space considerations. In smaller boats, it is better to have the supply run off an increased engine start battery bank. If the engine battery is used, a large rated cable is required forward to supply the bow thruster. This make charging easier. The main propulsion engine is always operating when using the thruster. The alternator provides the additional power to the battery, with reduced battery drain. It is worth considering the installation of a high output alternator. In larger vessels, a separate battery bank is preferable, and additional battery charging must be considered. Larger vessels have a greater AC power supply and a large AC mains battery charger installed. In many cases the hydraulic thruster option or AC powered thruster is more practical. A major cause of reduced thrust is inadequate power availability from the batteries at full load, and maintaining them in optimum condition is essential. If the battery suffers a major voltage drop, the thruster will also suffer a reduction in thrust output. Where separate batteries are to be installed, my preference is for an AGM type battery bank, which can deliver the required current, requires no maintenance and has a high charge acceptance rate. A separate high output alternator on the engine is a good option and the 24-volt option should also be considered.

b. **Supply Cables.** The power supply cables must be rated for the maximum current requirements of the motor and allow for voltage drop, which ideally should not exceed 5% at full load. Voltage drop is a major cause of reduced thrust.

Table 4-3 Bow Thruster Electrical Installations

Thrust (kg/lbs)	Boat Size (ft)	Power (kW/hp)	Cable Size AWG/mm	Slow Blow Fuse Size
35/77	22– 32' (10)	12	2/35 mm²	125 A
55/121	28– 40' (11)	12/24	00/70 mm²	250 A
75/175	35– 50' (12–13)	12/24	0/120 mm²	355 A
95/209	42–58'(12–13)	12/24	0/120 mm²	355 A
155/341	50–70' (13–19)	24	100 mm²	355 A
220/484	60–84' (18–30)	24	0/120 mm²	425 A
285/627	74–100' (25– 35)	48	0/120 mm²	425 A

4.6   Thruster Control and Drive Motors. The thruster control systems are relatively simple. In general a joystick control lever, buttons, and in some cases a foot switch that activates a micro-switch are used. This supplies control power to a solenoid, which then closes current on to the motor. In variable pitch or azimuth systems, feedback sensors are used in the control system. These are a source of problems if mechanically damaged or loose. Electric motors generate heat, and thruster motors are limited by temperature rise. Generally, most thrusters are rated at between 3 to 5 minutes at full continuous output. Power supplies are critical as high currents cause large voltage drops. A 4 hp (3kW) motor will draw 250 amps or more at initial starting, and less power means loss of thrust. Larger vessels may have 3-phase AC motors with frequency drives for speed control. Motors generally have the following safety systems installed:

a. **Overheat Protection.** Once the temperature limit is reached, typically around 212°F (100°C), the motor windings are protected against damage by a winding embedded thermal cutout. Depending on the amount of heat within the winding, the time to reset the cutout varies from 1 to 5 minutes. To ensure availability the proper use is about 10-30 seconds per maneuver to prevent cutout operation.

b. **Drive Reversal Protection.** Some thrusters incorporate electronic time-lapse protection against sudden drive reversal.

c. **Protection.** Motors and cables are provided with Slow-Blow fuses for short circuit protection, as they must withstand the high instantaneous starting currents. Overload protection is provided by circuit breakers.

d. **Speed Control.** Vetus manufactures an adjustable speed control to ramp up the speed relatively slowly to suit certain 24-volt thruster models.

e. **Series/Parallel Switches.** In many cases, thrusters are only available in 24 or 48-volt versions. In 12-volt boats, two batteries will have to be connected in series to get 24 volts. The switches are usually modular and contain the switching relays.

f. **Motor Testing.** Under no circumstances operate the motor out of the water or with load off, coupling disconnected, or propeller off. The series wound DC electric motor will accelerate very fast to a point where it will be seriously damaged.

4.7 Thruster Maintenance and Servicing. Servicing and maintenance requirements are relatively simple. Some thrusters such as the composite leg types from MaxPower have sealed lubricated bearings and have no anodes or oil servicing.

a. **Anodes.** Anodes should be inspected regularly, at least every 6 months. New anodes where installed on the propeller shaft or the leg should be secured using Loctite. Gear cases are usually bronze, the anode protection is for the gear casing, propeller blades and shafting.

b. **Oil Tanks.** The gear case oil header tank should be checked and topped up prior to each trip. Side-power specify EP90 oil. Oil consumption usually indicates a leaking seal. If installation is properly done, there are no problems. If the oil header tank is installed at the wrong height there will not be enough oil overpressure, which leads to water ingress. I have seen this mistake even in commercial installations. A check should also be made on the oil tube to make sure there are no kinks or loops that can cause air locks or affect the oil flow and pressure. Oil should be changed at least every 2 years or in accordance with the manufacturer's instructions, usually timed when hauled out of the water. Make sure the oil drain screw is re-tightened securely and that oil is flowing through before doing so.

c. **Antifouling.** Coat the gear case and propellers only, and not the seals, anodes or propeller shafts. Where possible use antifouling designed specifically for propellers.

d. **Electric Motor.** Check and tighten the motor holding bolts every year. Vacuum out any carbon brush dust, and check the condition of the commutator and brush gear. Check and tighten all electrical connections on the electric motor, and the directional solenoids.

4.8 **Thruster Troubleshooting.** The following are the most common faults.

a. **Thruster Will Not Start**

(1) **Power Supply Loss.** Check the obvious causes such as: the isolator is open; the circuit breaker is off; or the Slow-Blow fuse is ruptured. Check that the voltage levels at the thruster are correct; at no load it should be a minimum of 12.7 or 25.4 volts. If lower, check the battery voltage first, and if acceptable check the connections. Check the voltage when trying to run the thruster. If the voltage has dropped lower than 8.5 volts, the battery condition is the probable cause and cannot deliver the required power.

(2) **Control Systems.** If the solenoids do not operate, a control signal is probably absent, as solenoids rarely fail. Check the voltage at the solenoid to confirm this. Check the power supply and protection fuse to the control panel. If this is good, check the control cable connections and control panel outputs. Retractable thrusters also may have interlocks on the retract systems. Check that the thruster is completely down and that the interlock limit switches are operating.

(3) **Electric Motor.** If the voltages are correct at the electric motor the thermal cut-out switch may be faulty, or the motor brushes are sticking. Turn off the power, open and manually check that the brushes are moving freely within the brush holders.

b. **Reduced Thrust.** The most common cause is reduced voltages, caused by battery failure or loose connections causing voltage drops. The brush gear can also cause reduced thrust problems, and the brushes and commutator should be checked. If electric circuit items are good, the thruster may be fouled with marine growth.

c. **Thrust Failure.** If the thruster stops during operation, check the protection equipment such as fuses, thermal cut-outs and circuit breakers first. If the motor is operating with no thrust output, check that the shearpins and flexible couplings have not separated due to the propeller jamming on debris. Large offshore vessels have even known whales and large tires to be sucked in!

4.9   Hydraulic Thrusters (Generators and Propulsion). The major advantage of hydraulic thrusters is that they have no restrictions on use, and are continuously rated. The hydraulic system is usually electrically powered, although some main engines have a belt driven electromagnetic hydraulic pump. Oil is suctioned from the reservoir by the hydraulic pump though the oil filter and an oil cooler where installed. The typical nominal oil temperature is 140°F (60°C). The cooler may be part of the existing seawater system on the engine or have a separate pump. The pressurized oil then passes through a directional control valve. This is activated from the thruster control station, either mechanically or electrically. The oil goes to the hydraulic motor, which is coupled to the thruster. The hydraulic motor speed control, where installed, is by means of a proportional control valve, although Wesmar use load sensing hydraulic pumps. The oil then returns to the oil reservoir. The system may have overload protection, which consists of a safety relief valve that vents back to the oil reservoir. In some installations, the system may power thrusters and a generator, and each function will have an electrically activated main solenoid valve. In variable pitch control systems, both on main propeller, tunnel or azimuth thrusters, hydraulic control is used. Hydraulic system reliability is dependent on good maintenance practices. Solenoid electrical connections should be dry, tight, and checked regularly.

   a.   **Oil System.** Oil must be kept clean, so oil filters must be changed and oil levels checked and topped up. Many gravity tanks are allowed to empty before refilling. Check the system regularly for oil leaks and repair them. Always bleed air from the system at the highest point.

   (1)   Oil is dark – indicates oil oxidation or overheating.

   (2)   Oil is milky or emulsified – indicates water in the oil.

   (3)   Bubbles – indicates air in the oil, low oil levels or a suction air leak.

   (4)   Contaminants – indicates wear, or dirt in the oil.

   (5)   Burned smell – indicates oil aging or overheating.

   b.   **Cooling System.** Ensure that oil coolers are maintained so that maximum heat transfer takes place. Anodes where installed must be checked and renewed. Where a separate seawater pump and inlet are used, check and clean the strainers regularly.

4.10   Hydraulic Power Units. Several hydraulic power pack units (HPU) are now available, and they are economical. These power packs can be diesel operated such as the unit from Vetus, or electrically powered such as the system from Lewmar. The HPU can power thrusters, windlass, winches, or generators. This is common on fishing trawlers where a dedicated diesel engine is used to drive the hydraulic pump to power drums, net trawl and line winches.

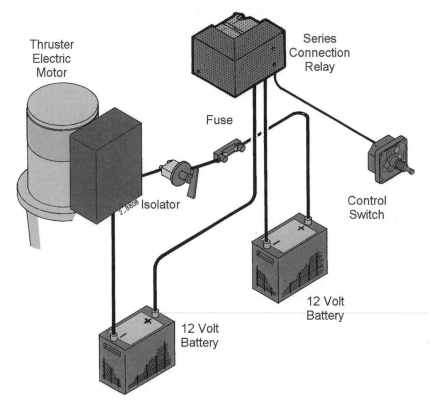

Figure 4-2 Electric Thruster Series Connection, *Courtesy of Vetus*

a. **HPU Pump Set.** This consists of the hydraulic reservoir; electric motors; motor control gear; oil cooler; pressure gauges; sight glasses and pressure relief valves. Motors are typically rated at 4 hp (3kW), up to 18 hp (14kW) and require considerable battery power. With maximum outputs of 2030 psi (140 bar) the 4 hp systems can draw 630 amps and specified battery capacity is 1200 Ah. A 24VDC system draws 400 amps. To prevent de-rating, the voltage drop must be minimal. For a 7m cable length, a 000 AWG (95mm^2) size cable is required, with 600 amp protection Slow-Blow fuse. Pump units can also be powered by single and three phase AC motors, with soft start options.

b. **Control System.** On some systems, this can be an integral electronic printed circuit board (PCB), which controls the directional solenoid valves. Systems that are more complex can be controlled by a PLC. The Lewmar system is illustrated. In addition, the motor contactor can be mounted locally or remotely. Control switch units are also installed to actuate functions.

c. **Valves (Directional Control, Check, Cushion).** The directional solenoid valves are mounted on manifold blocks, and feed each equipment circuit. Hydraulic control may include control valves, flow controls and pilot operated check valves. Check valves may also be used to prevent backpressure to the pump. Cushion valves reduce surges and overloads.

77

d.   **Oil Filtration System.** This consists of oil filters placed in the oil reservoir return line and they are typically 2–3 micron filter elements.

e.   **Maintenance.** Hydraulic oil levels must be checked and visual inspections of the system made for oil leaks. Oil filters should be cleaned or changed regularly. Oil coolers should be checked and cleaned. The oil condition should also be checked.

f.   **Troubleshooting.** The following are the most common faults.

   (1)   **Over Temperature.** Oil over-temperature alarms are generally due to plugged coolers, and blocked seawater cooling strainers. High oil temperatures will degrade the oil and cooling problems should be rectified.

   (2)   **Low Pressure.** Problems are normally due to plugged filters, low oil levels and high-pressure system leaks. With DC systems, pump motor problems can be caused by low voltages. Hydraulic pumps can also be a problem as well as high-pressure relief valves.

   (3)   **No Operation.** Failure to operate can be due to electrical control system faults, or pump motor failures.

   (4)   **Excessive Noise.** This results from cavitation in the pumps, and is caused by inlet restrictions due to high oil viscosity, clogged filters, collapsing hoses and debris. This causes a pressure drop across the restriction and can cause serious pump damage if allowed to continue. Another cause is aeration within the oil, which is often due to O-ring and seal failures. If a hydraulic pump is worn, noise will also be generated. Faulty relief valves may cause excess noise and require resetting.

4.11   PLC Hydraulic Control Systems. PLC systems will become standard on many systems, and hydraulic systems are an ideal application. The illustration below shows the Lewmar system configured for dual thrusters and dual windlasses. The description will assist in understanding operations:

a.   The main power input provides control power. This supplies PLC power via a control fuse, and the on/off switch S1. Another fuse supplies the pump clutch relay output. The switch S1 is closed, which inputs to the PLC. The output closes the relay, which activates the clutch control relay. The clutch is then energized to supply hydraulic oil to the system.

b.   The PLC has a speed sensor input to monitor under-speed and over-speed. If the PLC detects either condition, the clutch will disconnect. The PLC will then output and activate an alarm. If low oil level input is detected, an alarm is activated, and in very low oil levels, the clutch will be disconnected.

c. When the thruster joystick is moved, or the windlass switch is closed, this is input to the PLC. The PLC will output a signal to the directional control valves in the required direction.

4.12 Controllable Pitch Propellers (CPP). Many commercial ships, offshore oil industry vessels and many fishing trawlers have controllable or variable pitch propeller systems. They are also seen on a variety of pleasure vessels. They have many advantages over fixed pitch propellers. The main advantages are that CPP systems allow optimum engine performance over the entire boat speed range, where fixed pitch only allows maximum power at a single engine speed. CPP also allows good slow speed operation while still maintaining engine speeds. The propeller head is a relatively simple mechanical design. A servo valve activates a servo piston and a hollow propeller shaft carries the tie rod to the propeller cross head. This controls the propeller pitch position both ahead and astern. MerCruiser are currently developing a CPP system for sterndrives using hydraulic control and the ECU.

a. **Hydraulic Oil System.** Oil pumps may be directly driven off the engine or have a separate electrical motor. The pump supplies oil to the pitch servo system and in some cases hydraulic clutches.

b. **Solenoid Valves.** These are used to supply hydraulic oil to proportional control valves.

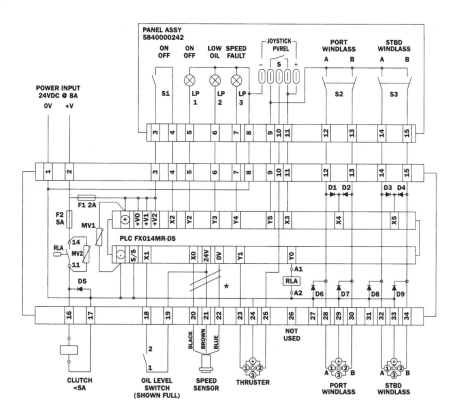

Figure 4-3 PLC Hydraulic Control System, *Courtesy of Lewmar*

c.   **Relief Valves.** These are used to vent any oil overpressure and maintain constant operating oil pressures.

d.   **Feedback Sensors.** These are used to indicate the actual blade position in closed loop control systems. When a pitch command is made, the feedback signal is compared and stops blade position control when the required angle is reached.

e.   **Maintenance.** The usual hydraulic system troubleshooting procedures are used to solve problems. Clean oil is essential so filters must be checked. Where oil coolers are used they must be kept clean to avoid high temperatures. Feedback sensors can be mechanically damaged and care should be taken when working near them. Oil leaks should be rectified as soon as possible as pressure losses can affect the operation. Oil lubricated stern tubes must have the oil gravity tank checked and topped up.

4.13   Hydraulic Generators. Hydraulic systems with larger outputs are a good proposition where vessels have long engine run times, such as canal boats and barges, workboats and trawler yachts. System outputs can be either single or 3 phase depending on the output required. These outputs range from 6.4 kW up to 120kW.

a.   **Pump Drive.** The system incorporates a directly coupled or belt driven hydraulic pump. In many cases these are powered off a hydraulic power unit (HPU).

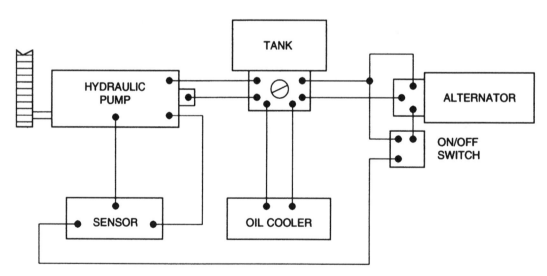

Figure 4-4 Hydraulic Powered Alternator System

b. **System Operation.** The electrical powered hydraulic pump suctions oil from the reservoir and delivers pressurized oil to the hydraulic motor via a manifold mounted valve system. An electrical operated solenoid valve directs oil to the generator hydraulic drive motor. The valve system maintains alternator at rated speed irrespective of engine speed or electrical loading. Generator frequency and voltage stability are normally maintained to within 2.5 Hz over the full engine speed range. Electronic feedback options can be incorporated to reduce this to 0.5 Hertz.

c. **Auxiliaries.** The system also incorporates an oil cooler and filter on the reservoir tank. Many systems offer an optional bow thruster off the same hydraulic system's HPU. The solenoids are electrically operated. The typical system is illustrated below.

d. **Maintenance.** Hydraulic oil levels must be checked and visual inspections of the system made for oil leaks. Oil filters should be cleaned regularly, and oil coolers checked and cleaned.

e. **Troubleshooting.** Oil over-temperature alarms are generally due to plugged coolers, and blocked seawater cooling strainers. Frequency instability is generally due to low oil levels, faulty regulator valves or pump problems. If a pump fails to operate, this can be caused by a faulty solenoid valve or regulator valve.

Batteries

5.1   Battery Selection. The battery has a primary role of a power storage device, and a secondary one as a buffer, absorbing power surges and disturbances that arise during charging and discharging. The foundation of a reliable and efficient power system is a correctly specified and rated battery. A battery is required to supply two different load types. References are from IRBES Section 1, Chapter 5 Power Supplies. (See Chapter 7.2 Electrical Standards.)

Rule 5.2. The service battery capacity shall be based on calculation of the boat power consumption for a 12-hour period. Sailing vessels should base calculations on a 24-hour period. The power calculations should include all equipment and systems that will run continuously or intermittently during the calculated period.

Service loads draw current over long periods. Equipment in this category include lights, instruments, radios, radar, autopilots, inverters and entertainment systems. The deep cycle battery is normally used for these applications. Calculations are based on the maximum power consumption over the longest period between battery recharging.

Rule 5.1. A separate battery shall be provided for starting each engine. The engine start battery capacity should be based on the provision of 10 consecutive start attempts of 5 seconds duration with a 30 second period between each attempt, at an ambient temperature of 5ºC. The engine manufacturer's recommendations should be the minimum battery specification.

Starting loads require large current levels for relatively short time periods. Loads in this category include engine starter motors, engine pre-heating, anchor windlass, electric winches, thrusters and electric toilets. The starting battery is normally used for these applications. The rating should allow for worst case starting scenarios. In cold temperatures battery efficiency is lowered and engine starting requires greater power due to increased oil viscosity.

Rule 5.3. Generator units should have a dedicated engine starting battery.

Generators should have an independent battery, which also increases starting power redundancy.

5.2   Battery Ratings. Manufacturers use a range of ratings figures to indicate battery performance levels. When selecting a battery it is essential to understand the ratings and how they apply to your requirements. The various ratings are defined as follows.

   a.   **Amp-hour Rating.** Amp-hour rating (Ah) refers to the available current over a nominal period until a specified final voltage is reached. Rates are normally specified at the 10- or 20-hour rate. This rating generally applies to deep cycle batteries. For example, a battery is rated at 84 Ah at 10 hour rate with a final voltage of 1.7 Volts per cell. This means the battery is capable of delivering 8.4 amps for 10 hours, when a cell voltage of 1.7 volts will be attained. (Battery Volts = 10.2 VDC). Where a battery is discharged faster than the nominal rating the available capacity also decreases. This is called the Peukert effect; the decline follows a logarithmic curve.

b. **Reserve Capacity Rating.** This rating specifies the number of minutes a battery can supply a nominal current at a nominal temperature without the voltage dropping below a certain level. This rating, normally applied to automotive applications, indicates the power available when an alternator fails and the power available to operate ignition and auxiliaries. Typically, the rating is specified for a 30-minute period at 25°C with a final voltage of 10.2 volts.

c. **Cold Cranking Amps (CCA).** This rating defines the current available at -18°C for a period of 30 seconds, while being able to maintain a cell voltage exceeding 1.2 volts per cell. This rating is only applicable for engine starting. The higher the rating, the more power available, especially in cold weather conditions.

d. **Marine Cranking Amps (MCA).** This newer rating defines the current available at 0°C for a period of 30 seconds, while being able to maintain a cell voltage exceeding 1.2 volts per cell. Again, this rating is only applicable for engine starting purposes. If you are in a cold climate area (UK/Europe and US) then CCA is more relevant.

e. **Plate Numbers.** Data sheets state the number of positive and negative within a cell. The more plates, the greater the plate material surface area. Greater plate surface area increases the current during high current rate discharges and subsequently improves cranking capacity and cold weather performance.

f. **Casing Type.** Battery casings are either a rubber compound or plastic. Where possible, always select the rubber types as they are more resilient to knocks and vibration.

g. **Marine Battery.** This often misused sales term applies to certain constructional features. Plates may be thicker than normal or there may be more of them. Internal plate supports are also used for vibration absorption. Cases may be manufactured with a resilient rubber compound and have carry handles fitted. Filling caps may be of an anti-spill design. These days, batteries are of a similar design, with very little to distinguish marine batteries from the automotive types except the label. In many cases you are paying a premium for a label.

5.3 Battery Rating Selection. This chapter covers the important task of selecting suitable batteries for use in service (house power) roles. Most problems arise from improper battery selection. Battery bank capacities are either too small, with resultant power shortages, or so large that the charging system cannot properly recharge them, resulting in premature battery failure due to sulfation. Initially, it is essential to list all equipment on board along with power consumption ratings. Ratings can usually be found on equipment nameplates or in equipment manuals. It is recommended that the ratings, usually expressed in watts, be converted to current in amps. To do this, divide the power by your system voltage. Calculate the current consumption for a 12-hour period while in port or anchored. The calculation assumes that the engine will not be operated, and no generator with battery charging will be operational. While motoring, all power is being supplied from engine alternators, and when batteries are charged the alternator effectively supplies all power. The table illustrates the typical power consumption, with space for you to insert and calculate your vessel data.

a. **Load Calculation Table.** To calculate the total system loading, multiply the total current values by the number of hours to get the amp-hour rating. If equipment uses 1 amp over 24 hours, then it consumes 24 amp-hours.

b. **Capacity Calculation.** Select the column that matches the frequency of your charging periods. The most typical scenario is one of the boat at anchor, or on a mooring and operating the engine every 12 hours to pull down refrigerator temperatures with an engine driven eutectic refrigeration compressor.

Eg. Total consumption is 120 Ah over 12 hours = 10 amps/hour

c. **Capacity De-rating.** As we wish to keep our discharge capacity to 50% of nominal battery capacity, we can assume that a battery capacity of 240 amp-hours is the basic minimum level. In a perfect system, this would be a minimum requirement, but certain realities must now be introduced into the equation. The figures below typify a common system, with alternator charging and standard regulator. Maximum charge deficiency is based on the premise that boat batteries are rarely above 70% charge and cannot be fully recharged with normal regulators. There is reduced capacity due to sulfation, which is typically a minimum of 10% of capacity. The key to maintaining optimum power levels and avoiding this common and surprising set of numbers is the charging system.

Nominal Capacity			240	Ah
Maximum cycling level	(50%)	Deduct	120	Ah
Maximum charge deficiency	(30%)	Deduct	72	Ah
Lost capacity (10%)		Deduct	24	Ah
Available Battery Capacity			**24**	**Ah**

d. **Amp-hour Capacity.** It is important to discuss a few more relevant points regarding amp-hour capacity, as it has significant ramifications on the selection of capacity and discharge characteristics:

(1) **Fast Discharge (Peukerts Equation).** The faster a battery is discharged over the nominal rating (either 10 or 20 hour rate), the less the real amp-hour capacity the battery has. This effect is defined by Peukerts Equation, which has a logarithmic characteristic. This equation is based on the high and low discharge rates and discharge times to derive the Peukert coefficient '*n*'. Average values are around 1.10 to 1.20. If we discharge a 250 amp-hour battery bank, which has nominal battery discharge rates for each identical battery of 12 amps per hour at a rate of 16 amps, we will actually have approximately 10–15% less capacity. Battery discharge meters such as the E-Meter incorporate this coefficient into the monitoring and calculation process.

(2) **Slow Discharge.** The slower the discharge over the nominal rate, the greater the real capacity. If we discharge our 240 amp-hour battery bank at 6 amps per hour we will actually have approximately 10–15% more capacity. The disadvantage here is that slowly discharged batteries are harder to charge if deep cycled below 50%.

e. **Battery Load Matching.** The principal aim is to match the discharge characteristics of the battery bank to that of our calculated load of 10 amps per hour over 12 hours. Assume that we have a modified charging system so that we can recharge batteries to virtually 100% of nominal capacity. The factors affecting matching are:

(1) **Discharge Requirement.** The nominal required battery capacity of 240 Ah has been calculated as that required to supply 10 amps per hour over 12 hours to 50% of battery capacity. In most cases, the discharge requirements are worst for the night period, and this is the 12-hour period that should be used in calculations. What is required is a battery bank with similar discharge rates as the current consumption rate. This will maximize the capacity of the battery bank with respect to the effect defined in Peukerts coefficient.

(2) **Battery Requirements.** As the consumption rate is based on a 12-hour period, a battery bank that is similarly rated at the 10-hour rate is required. In practice you will not match the precise required capacity, therefore you should go to the next battery size up. This is important also as the battery will be discharged longer and faster over 12 hours, so a safety margin is required. If you choose a battery that has 240 amp-hours at the 20 hour rate, in effect, you will be installing a battery that in the calculated service has 10-15% less capacity than that stated on the label, or approximately 215 Ah, so you are below capacity. This is not the fault of the supplier, but simply a failure to correctly calculate and specify the right battery to meet system requirements.

5.4   Load Calculations. It is essential to list all equipment on board along with power consumption ratings. Ratings can usually be found on equipment nameplates or in equipment manuals. Insert your own values into the Actual column. Calculate power used for 12 hours. To convert power (in watts) to current (in amps), simply divide the power value by your system voltage. Add up all the current figures relevant to your vessel and multiply by hours to get an average amp-hour consumption rate. Space is reserved to add in specific values. Most of these items will be on when anchored or moored, but many will not be relevant if at a marina connected to a battery charger.

Table 5-1 DC Load Calculation Table

Equipment	Typical	Actual	12 Hours	Other
Radar- Transmit	4.5 A	_____	_____	_____
Radar - Standby	0.5 A	_____	_____	_____
SSB - Receive	0.5 A	_____	_____	_____
VHF - Receive	0.5 A	_____	_____	_____
Satcom	1.0 A	_____	_____	_____
Weatherfax	0.5 A	_____	_____	_____
GPS/LORAN	0.5 A	_____	_____	_____
Navtex	0.5 A	_____	_____	_____
Fishfinder	1.0 A	_____	_____	_____
Instruments	0.3 A	_____	_____	_____
Stereo	0.5 A	_____	_____	_____
Gas detector	0.5 A	_____	_____	_____
Inverter - Standby	1.0 A	_____	_____	_____
Anchor light	1.0 A	_____	_____	_____
Refrigeration	4.0 A	_____	_____	_____
Interior lights	5.0 A	_____	_____	_____
Computer	1.0 A	_____	_____	_____
Television	2.0 A	_____	_____	_____
Video	1.0 A	_____	_____	_____
TOTAL				

5.5 **Additional Load Calculations.** Other basic load characteristics have to be factored in to load calculations. Add up all the current figures relevant to your vessel and multiply by expected run times to get an average amp-hour consumption rate.

    a.   **Intermittent Loads.** It is often hard to quantify actual real current demands with intermittent loads. My suggestion is simply to use a baseline of 6 minutes per hour, which is .1 of an hour.

    b.   **Motoring Loads.** Certain loads are only applicable when motoring. Loads must be subtracted from charge current values, and actually may impact on charging system efficiency at low speeds. Loads include navigation lights, refrigeration clutch, watermaker clutch and ventilation fans.

Table 5-2 DC Load Calculation Table

Equipment	Typical	Actual	12 Hours	Other
Other Loads				
Bilge pump	3.5 A	_____	_____	_____
Shower pump	3.5 A	_____	_____	_____
Water pump	4.0 A	_____	_____	_____
Wash down pump	2.5 A	_____	_____	_____
Toilet	18.0 A	_____	_____	_____
Macerator	15.0 A	_____	_____	_____
SSB -Transmit	15.0 A	_____	_____	_____
VHF -Transmit	4.0 A	_____	_____	_____
Spot light	3.0 A	_____	_____	_____
Extraction fan	1.5 A	_____	_____	_____
Inverter	40.0 A	_____	_____	_____
Cabin lights	2.0 A	_____	_____	_____
Sub Total Table 2				
Sub Total Table 1				
LOAD TOTAL				

5.6 **Lead Acid Batteries**. The fundamental theory of the battery is that a voltage is developed between two electrodes of dissimilar metal when they are immersed in an electrolyte. In the typical lead-acid cell, the generated voltage is 2.1 volts. The typical 12-volt battery consists of 6 cells, which are internally connected in series to make up the battery.

    a. **Cell Components.** The principal cell components are:

        (1) Lead Dioxide (PbO_2) — the positive plate active material.

        (2) Sponge Lead (Pb) — the negative plate material.

        (3) Sulfuric Acid (H_2SO_4) — the electrolyte.

    b. **Discharge Cycle.** Discharging of the battery occurs when an external load is connected across the positive and negative terminals. A chemical reaction takes place between the two plate materials and the electrolyte. During the discharge reaction, the plates interact with the electrolyte to form lead sulfate and water. This reaction dilutes the electrolyte, reducing the density. As both plates become similar in composition, the cell loses the ability to generate a voltage.

c. **Charge Cycle.** Charging simply reverses this reaction. The water decomposes to release hydrogen and oxygen. The two plate materials are reconstituted to the original material. When the plates are fully restored, and the electrolyte is returned to the nominal density the battery is completely recharged.

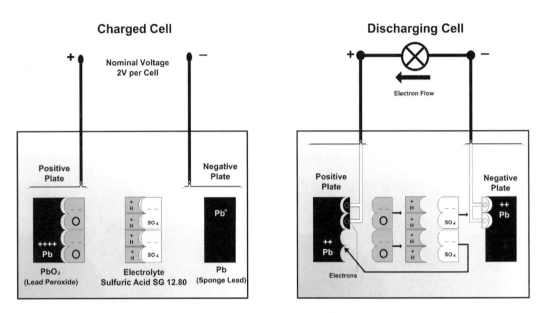

Figure 5-1 Lead Acid Charge and Discharge Reaction.

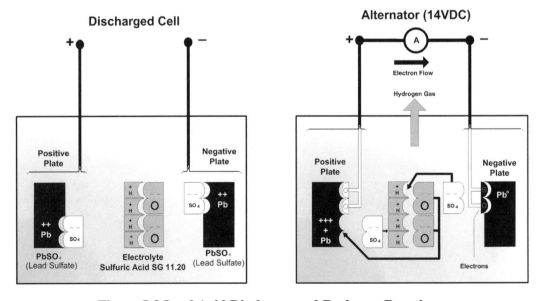

Figure 5-2 Lead Acid Discharge and Recharge Reaction.

5.7   **Battery Electrolyte**. The cell electrolyte is a dilute solution of sulfuric acid and pure water. Specific gravity (SG) is a measurement defining electrolyte acid concentration. A fully charged cell has an SG typically in the range 1.240 to 1.280, corrected for temperature. This is an approximate volume ratio of acid to water of 1:3. Pure sulfuric acid has an SG of 1.835, and water a nominal 1.0. The following factors apply to battery electrolytes.

    a.   **Temperature Effects.** For accuracy, all hydrometer readings should be corrected for temperature. Ideally, actual cell temperatures should be used, but in practice ambient battery temperatures are sufficient. Hydrometer floats have the reference temperature printed on them and this should be used for calculations. As a guide, the following should be used for calculation purposes.

        (1)   For every 1.5°C the cell temperature is *above* the reference value, *add* 1 point (0.001) to the hydrometer reading.

        (2)   For every 1.5°C the cell temperature is *below* the reference value, *subtract* 1 point (0.001) from the hydrometer reading.

    b.   **Nominal Electrolyte Densities.** Recommended densities are normally obtainable from battery manufacturers. In tropical areas it is common to have battery suppliers put in a milder electrolyte density, which does not deteriorate the separators and grids as quickly electrolytes for temperate climate.

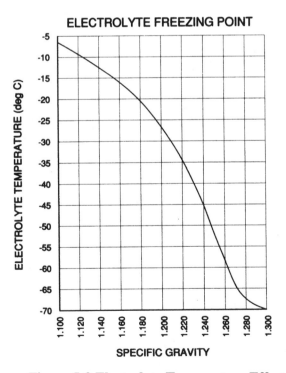

Figure 5-3 Electrolyte Temperature Effects

5.8 **Battery Water.** When topping up the cell electrolyte, always use distilled or de-ionized water. Rainwater is acceptable, but under no circumstances use tap water. Tap water generally has an excessive mineral content or other impurities that may pollute and damage the cells. Impurities introduced into the cell will remain, and concentrations will accumulate at each top up, reducing service life. Long and reliable service life is essential so the correct water must always be used. Water purity levels are defined in various national standards.

Table 5-3 Electrolyte Correction at 20°

Temperature	Correction Value
-5°C	deduct 0.020
0°C	deduct 0.016
+5°C	deduct 0.012
+10°C	deduct 0.008
+15°C	deduct 0.004
+25°C	add 0.004
+30°C	add 0.008
+35°C	add 0.012
+40°C	add 0.016

5.9 **Plate Sulfation.** Sulfation is the single greatest cause of battery failure, and occurs as follows:

    a. During discharge, the chemical reaction causes both plates to convert to lead sulfate. If recharging is not carried out within a couple of hours, the lead sulfate starts to harden and crystallize. This is characterized by white crystals on the typically brown plates and is almost non-reversible. If a battery is only 80% charged, this does not mean that only 20% is sulfating, the entire plate material has not fully converted and subsequently sulfates.

    b. The immediate effect of sulfation is partial and permanent loss of capacity as the active materials are reduced. Electrolyte density also partially decreases, as the chemical reaction during charging cannot be fully reversed. This sulfated material introduces higher resistances within the cell and inhibits charging. As the level of sulfated material increases, the cell's ability to retain a charge is reduced and the battery fails. The deep cycle battery has unfairly gained a bad reputation, but the battery is not the cause, improper and inadequate charging is. As long as some charging is taking place, even from a small solar panel, a chemical reaction is taking place and sulfation will not occur.

5.10 **Efficiency.** Battery efficiency is affected by temperature. At 0°C, efficiency falls by 60%. Batteries in warm tropical climates are more efficient, but may have reduced life spans, and batteries commissioned in tropical areas often have lower acid densities. Batteries in cold climates have increased operating lives, but are less efficient.

5.11 **Self Discharge.** During charging, a small quantity of antimony or other impurities dissolve out of the positive plates and deposit on the negative ones. Other impurities are introduced with impure topping up water and deposit on the plates. A localized chemical reaction then takes place, slowly discharging the cell. Self-discharge rates are affected by temperature, with the following results:

(1) At 0°C, discharge rates are minimal.

(2) At 30°C, self-discharge rates are high and the specific gravity can decrease by as much as 0.002 per day, typically up to 4% per month.

(3) The use of a small solar panel, or regular and *complete* recharging will prevent permanent damage as it can equal or exceed the self-discharge rate.

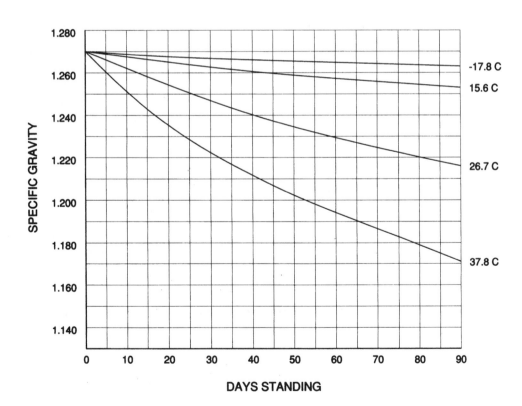

Figure 5-4 Self-Discharge Rates

5.12   Deep Cycle Batteries. Service loads require a battery that can withstand cycles of long continuous discharge, and repeated recharging. This deep cycling requires the use of the suitably named deep cycle battery. Top of the range Surrette (www.surrette.com) and Trojan and Rolls (www.rolls.com) typify the quality deep cycle batteries. The deep cycle battery has the following characteristics.

  a.   **Construction.** The battery is typified by the use of thick, high-density flat-pasted plates, or a combination of flat and tubular plates. The plate materials may also contain small proportions of antimony to help stiffen them. Porous and insulating separators are used between the plates. Glass matting is used to assist in retaining active material on the plates. Plate material can break away as plates expand and contract during charge and recharge cycles. If material accumulates at the cell base, a cell short circuit may occur, although this is less common in modern batteries. If material is lost the plates will have reduced capacity or insufficient active material to sustain the chemical reaction with resultant cell failure. Much has been done to develop stronger and more efficient plates. Rolls have their Rezistox positive plates. The grid design has fewer heavier sections to hold the high density active material. This is due to the dynamic forces that normally cause expansion and contraction with subsequent warping and cracking. Separator design has also evolved and Rolls use double insulated thick glass woven ones that totally encase the positive plate along with a microporous polyethylene envelope. This retains any material shed from the plates than cause cell short circuits.

  b.   **Cycling.** The number of available cycles varies between individual battery makes and models. Typically it is within the range of 800–1500 cycles of discharge to 50% of nominal capacity and *complete* recharging. Battery life is a function of the number of cycles and the depth of cycling. Batteries discharged to only 70% of capacity will last appreciably longer than those discharged to 40% of capacity. In practice you should plan your system so that discharge is limited to 50% of battery capacity. The typical life of batteries where batteries are properly recharged and cycle capabilities maximized can be up to 5–10 years.

5.13   Starting Batteries. The starting battery must be capable of delivering the engine starter motor with sufficient current to turn and start the engine. This starting load can be affected by engine compression, oil viscosity, and engine driven loads. Some loads such as an inverter, thruster or an anchor windlass under full load require similar large amounts of current. Starting batteries have the following characteristics.

  a.   **Construction.** The starting battery is characterized by thin, closely spaced porous plates, which give maximum exposure of active plate material to the electrolyte and offer minimal internal resistance. This enables maximum chemical reaction rates, and maximum current availability. Physical construction is similar to deep cycle batteries.

b.   Cycling. Starting batteries cannot withstand cycling, and if deep cycled or flattened have an extremely short service life. Ideally they should be maintained within 95% of full charge.

c.   Sulfation. In practice, sulfation is not normally a problem, as batteries are generally fully charged if used for starting applications only. If improperly used for deep cycle applications and under charged, they will sulfate.

d.   Self Discharge. Starting batteries have low self-discharge rates and this is generally not a problem in normal engine installations.

e.   Efficiency. Cold temperatures dramatically affect battery performance. Engine lubricating oil viscosities are also affected by low temperatures, and further increase the starting loads on the battery. The reduction in battery capacity in low temperatures, combined with the increased starting current requirements, amplifies the importance of having fully charged batteries. Table 5-4 illustrates the typical cranking power loss when the temperature decreases from 27°C to -18°C using a typical 10W-30 multi-viscosity lubricating oil and the increased percentage of power required to turn over and start an engine.

Table 5-4 Battery Power Table

Temperature	Battery Level	Power Required
+ 27°C	100%	100%
0°C	65%	155%
-18°C	40%	210%

f.   Charging. Recharging of starting batteries is identical to deep cycle batteries. Additional factors to consider are:

(1)   Discharged current must be restored quickly to avoid damage. Similarly temperature compensation must be made.

(2)   Normally after a high current discharge of relatively short duration, there is no appreciable decrease in electrolyte density. The battery is quickly recharged, as the counter voltage phenomenon does not have time to build up and has a negligible affect on the charging.

g. **Battery Ratings.** Starting batteries are normally specified on the basis of engine manufacturer's recommendations, although I have found these to be imprecise. The following is given as a guide only. Table 5-5 shows recommended battery ratings and typical plate numbers for various diesel ratings, as well as typical starter motor currents:

(1) **Start Capability.** Calculate a good safety margin allowing for a multi-start capability. Some classification societies specify a minimum of 6 consecutive starts, and that should be the absolute minimum value.

(2) **Temperature Allowance.** Additional allowances should be made for the decreased efficiency in cold climates as a greater capacity and greater load current is required.

h. **Additional Starting Battery Loadings.** The starting battery should also be used to supply short duration, high current loads. Check with your engine supplier for the recommended battery rating, and then add a margin for safety. Also factor in the following:

(1) **Windlass.** The very heavy current loadings that electric winches demand require a much higher bank rating. The battery banks should be doubled up, so that two identical batteries are then parallel connected.

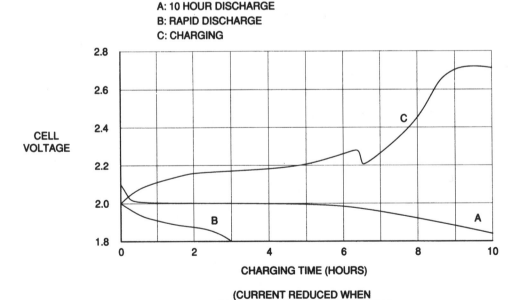

A: 10 HOUR DISCHARGE
B: RAPID DISCHARGE
C: CHARGING

CELL VOLTAGE

CHARGING TIME (HOURS)

(CURRENT REDUCED WHEN
VOLTAGE STARTS TO RISE RAPIDLY)

Figure 5-5 Lead Acid Battery Characteristics

(2)   **Generator.** In some cases the engine battery can be used for starting. Be careful if starting the engine while the generator is running as the small 10- to 15-amp alternators regularly suffer damage from the engine starting motor's high current load.

(3)   **Thrusters.** DC powered thrusters are generally powered directly from engine starting batteries. As the engine should be running much of the load is supplied directly from the alternator. It must be noted that as the engine is in slow or idle, the full output is not available, and considerable load will be taken from the battery.

Table 5-5 Battery Ratings Table

Engine Rating	Current Load	Battery CCA	Voltage
10 hp 7.5 kW	59 amps	375 CCA	12
15 hp 11 kW	67 amps	420 CCA	12
20 hp 15 kW	67 amps	420 CCA	12
30 hp 22 kW	75 amps	450 CCA	12
40 hp 30 kW	85 amps	500 CCA	12
50 hp 37 kW	115 amps	500 CCA	12
100 hp	115/60 amps	500 CCA	12/24
150 hp	150/75 amps	600 CCA	12/24
200 hp	120 amps	800 CCA	24

5.14   **Battery Safety.** The lead-acid battery is potentially hazardous and the following safe handling procedures should be used:

a.   **Gas.** Battery cells contain an explosive mixture of hydrogen and oxygen gas at all times. An explosion risk is always possible if naked flames, sparks or cigarettes are introduced into the immediate vicinity. Always use insulated tools. Cover the terminals with an insulating material to prevent accidental short circuit. Watchbands, bracelets and neck chains can accidentally cause a short circuit.

b.   **Acid.** Sulfuric acid is highly corrosive and must be handled with extreme caution. If you need to refill a battery with new acid on motorboats, observe the following precautions:

(1)   Wear protective clothing and eye protection.

(2)   Avoid splashes or spills as acid can cause severe skin and clothing burns. If acid splashes into the eyes, irrigate with water for at least 5 minutes. Seek medical advice.

  (3) If electrolyte is accidentally swallowed, drink large quantities of milk or water, followed by milk of magnesia. Seek immediate medical attention.

 c. **Manual Handling.** Always lift the battery with carriers if fitted. If no carriers are fitted, lift using opposite corners to prevent case distortion and electrolyte spills.

 d. **Electrolyte Spills.** Electrolyte spills should be avoided, but observe the following measures if a spill occurs:

  (1) Spilling electrolyte into salt water will generate chlorine gas, so ventilate the area properly.

  (2) Neutralize any spills immediately using a solution of baking soda.

5.15 **Battery Voltages and Installation**. Batteries must be installed correctly. There are a number of important criteria to consider when installing battery banks to make up the required voltage and capacity.

 Cell Size. Battery banks may be installed either in cell multiples of 1.2V, 6V, 12V, 24V, 32V, 36V (42V) or 48V. Each configuration has advantages both physically and operationally:

 (1) **1.2 Volts.** This is generally impractical because the batteries take up so much space. The battery plates are generally more robust and thicker. This leads to increased service life, but it is an expensive option.

 (2) **6 Volts.** This is the ideal arrangement. The cells are far more manageable to install and remove (Size GC2 and J250). Large capacity batteries are simply connected in series. Electrically they are better than 12-volt batteries, generally having thicker and more durable plates. Contrary to some opinions, a series arrangement does not necessarily reduce the available power range, nor does it require an equalization network, and these are rarely found. The one proviso is that batteries must be of the same make, model and age. If one battery requires replacement, the other should also be replaced simultaneously.

 (3) **12 (14 Volts).** This is the most common marine battery. Physically batteries up to around 115Ah (Size 27 and 31) are easily managed. They are paralleled in banks of up to three and this is the most practical arrangement. It is not rare to see traction or truck batteries of very large dimensions such as 8D sizes installed, but this is very impractical from any service standpoint. If the battery space is constructed to take a 3-battery arrangement, it is relatively easy to replace one unit. Additionally if you have a multiple bank and lose one with cell failure, two will remain. Charging voltage is 14 volts.

(4)   **24 (28 Volts).** Used in commercial vehicles, it also is prevalent on larger vessels and trawlers. This is a standard voltage in commercial shipping control and backup power supply systems. It is simply any of the above battery or cell sizes connected in series to get the 24 volts. Some boats have series-parallel systems. Charging voltage is 28 volts.

(5)   **32 Volts.** This voltage level has been in service for many years and is comparatively uncommon. The voltage level is made up from 4 x 8 volt batteries, which some manufacturers still make available.

(6)   **36 (42 Volts).** This new automotive voltage requires the connection of 3 x 12 volt cells or 6 x 6 volt cells in series to make 36 volts. The charging voltage is 42 volts.

(7)   **48 Volts.** This voltage level is used for the powering of thrusters. It requires series battery connection of 4 x 12 volt units to get 48 volts. This gives rise to charging problems, which are overcome by use of two 24-volt banks with a series switch when in use so that charging is still only at 28 volts.

5.16   Battery Installation Recommendations. Reference IRBES Chapter 6

Rule 6.1. Batteries should be installed within a separate space or compartment that is located above the maximum bilge water level, and protected from mechanical damage.

The batteries should be installed in a lined box protected from temperature extremes. The preferred temperature range is 10°C–27°C. The box should be located as low down as possible in the vessel for weight reasons, but high enough to avoid bilge water or flooding. Sufficient natural light should be available for testing or servicing. If this is not possible, an ignition-protected light can be installed. Allow sufficient clearance to install and remove batteries. Make sure there is sufficient vertical clearance to allow hydrometer testing.

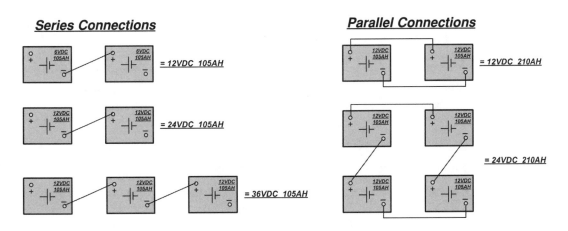

Figure 5-6 Cell and Battery Arrangements

Rule 6.2. Batteries shall not be installed adjacent to any fuel tank, fuel pipe or parts of the fuel system.

The batteries should not be installed close to any source of ignition, such as fuel tanks and parts such as fuel filters, separators and valves. Any leak or accumulation of fuel represents a serious hazard and so any source of ignition should be removed.

Rule 6.3. Batteries should be installed within an enclosure, or have a tray that will contain any spills of electrolyte at all angles of heel or inversion.

The box should be made of plastic, fiberglass or lead lined to prevent any acid spills contacting with wood or water. Boxes should be at least the full height of the battery so that any spills will be contained at all times. PVC battery boxes are acceptable alternatives.

Rule 6.4. Batteries should be secured so that they do not move at any angle of heel or inversion.

Physically secure batteries with either straps or a removable restraining rod across the top. Batteries should be prevented from movement. Insert rubber spacers around the batteries to stop any minor movements and vibrations.

Rule 6.5. Battery terminals and connections shall be installed or protected against any accidental contact with metallic objects. Battery terminals should be coated with petroleum jelly or equivalent compound to prevent corrosion or interaction with electrolyte spray.

Battery box lids should be in place at all times and secured. PVC or other connection covers should be installed where accidental contact by tools or other items can cause a short circuit across the terminals. Terminals should be coated to limit the corrosive effects of acid.

Rule 6.6. Battery compartments shall not contain any electrical equipment liable to cause ignition of any generated gases or vapor.

Do not install any electrical equipment within the compartment or adjacent to batteries. This can cause the generation of sparks and cause ignition of hydrogen gas generated after battery charging.

Rule 6.7. Where batteries are not of the sealed type, the battery compartment should have adequate ventilation to atmosphere of all generated gases.

The area should be well ventilated and vented to atmosphere. The use of an extraction fan is rarely required but should be considered if natural convection methods will be insufficient. If a fast charging device is installed, ensure that the ventilation remains sufficient to remove any generated gasses, and prevent them from accumulating.

Rule 6.8. Where start and service batteries have an interconnecting switch for emergency power supply, the switch should be normally open.

In dual battery systems where an emergency bridging or paralleling switch is installed, it should be always kept at the open position. Many people leave them permanently closed flattening both batteries.

Rule 6.9. Start and service batteries shall be electrically separate and arranged so that service loads cannot discharge the start battery.

In most cases the battery negatives are bridged, and a separate negative for each should be installed. This requires a separate alternator charging negative and grounding negative to the same grounding point as the other battery. Any arrangement should ensure that the starting battery could not be accidentally discharged. Where a solenoid system is used to parallel the batteries for charging, it must always open when the charging ceases.

Rule 6.10. Battery interconnection cables should have the same rating as the main start circuit cables.

In dual battery systems the cables connecting each battery negative or positive should be rated the same as main supply cables. Many are installed in smaller cable sizes.

Rule 6.11. Equipment having high current ratings such as thrusters and windlass systems should be installed to limit the disturbances or effects on the stability of the electrical system. A separate power supply should be considered.

Where high current equipment can cause system disturbances such as large load surges and voltage drops, consideration should be given to installing a separate battery bank with the required characteristics to power the equipment.

5.17   Battery Commissioning. After installation, the following commissioning procedures should be carried out:

    a.   **Battery Electrolyte Level.** Check the electrolyte level in each cell:

        (1)   Cells with separator guard — fill to top of guard.

        (2)   Cells without guard — fill to 2mm above plates.

    b.   **Battery Electrolyte Filling.** If the level is low, and evidence suggests a loss of acid in transit, refill with an electrolyte of similar density. Specific gravity is normally in the range 1.240 to 1.280 at 15°C. If no evidence of spillage is apparent, top up electrolyte levels with de-ionized or distilled water to the correct levels.

    c.   **Battery Terminals.** Battery terminals are a simple piece of equipment, yet they cause an inordinate amount of problems:

        (1)   **Terminals.** Install heavy-duty marine grade brass terminals. Do not use the cheaper plated brass terminals, as they are not robust and fail quickly.

        (2)   **Clean Terminals.** Make sure that terminal posts are clean, that they do not have any raised sections, and are not deformed, or a poor connection will result.

        (3)   **Replace Connections.** Replace the standard wing nuts on terminals with stainless steel nuts and washers. The wing nuts are very difficult to tighten properly without deformation and breakage. I have encountered many installations where the wings and the casting are broken.

(4) **Coat Terminals.** Coat the terminals with petroleum jelly.

d. **Battery Cleaning.** Cleaning involves the following tasks:

(1) **Clean Surfaces.** Clean the battery surfaces with a clean, damp cloth. Moisture and other surface contaminations can cause surface leakage between the positive and negative terminals.

(2) **Grease and Oil Removal.** Grease and oil can be removed with a mild detergent and cloth.

e. **Battery Charging.** After taking delivery of a new battery, perform the following:

(1) **Initial Charge.** Give a freshening charge immediately.

(2) **Routine Charging.** Give a charge every week if the vessel is incomplete or not in service.

5.18 **Battery Routine Testing**. The following tests can be made on a weekly basis to monitor the condition of the battery. Battery status can be measured by checking the electrolyte density and the voltage as follows.

a. **Stabilized Voltage Test.** Voltage readings should be taken with an accurate voltmeter. Switchboards should incorporate a high quality meter, not a typical engine gauge charge indicator. The difference between fully charged and discharged is less than 1 volt, so accuracy is essential. A digital voltmeter is ideal. Battery voltage readings should only be taken a minimum of 30 minutes after charging or discharging. Turn off all loads before measuring. Typical values at 15°C are shown in Table 5-6. Manufacturers have slightly varying densities so check with your supplier.

Table 5-6 Typical Open Circuit Voltages and Densities

Charge Level	SG Temperate	SG Tropical	Voltage
100%	1250	1240	12.75
90%	1235	1225	12.65
80%	1220	1210	12.55
70%	1205	1195	12.45
60%	1190	1180	12.35
50%	1175	1165	12.25
40%	1160	1150	12.10
30%	1145	1135	11.95
20%	1130	1120	11.85
10%	1115	1105	11.75
0	1100	1090	11.65

b. **Battery Electrolyte Specific Gravity.** A hydrometer should be used weekly to check acid density. The hydrometer is essentially a large syringe with a calibrated float. The calibration scale is corrected to a nominal temperature value, normally marked on the float. The following points should be observed during testing with a hydrometer:

(1) Never test immediately after charging or discharging. Wait at least half an hour until the cells stabilize; this is because it takes some time for the pockets of varying electrolyte densities to equalize. Never test immediately after topping up the electrolyte. Wait until after a charging period, as it similarly takes time for the water to mix evenly.

(2) Ensure the float is clean and not cracked and the rubber has not perished. Keep the hydrometer vertical. Ensure that the float does not contact the side of the barrel, which may give a false reading. Draw sufficient electrolyte into the barrel to raise the float. Ensure that the top of the float does not touch the top. Observe the level on the scale. Disregard the liquid curvature caused by surface tension. Adjust your reading for temperature to obtain the actual value.

(3) Wash out the hydrometer with clean water when finished.

c. **Battery Load Test**. The load test is carried out only if the batteries are suspect. The load tester consists of two probes connected by a resistance and a meter. The tester is connected across the battery terminals effectively putting a heavy load across it. A load of approximately 275 amps at 8 volts is normal. Take your battery to your nearest automotive electrician or battery service center for a test.

5.19   Battery Maintenance. Battery maintenance is simple and is not the tedious chore that it is often made out to be. The following tasks should be carried out:

a. **Battery Terminal Cleaning.** (3-monthly). Remove battery terminals and ensure that terminal posts are clean and free of deposits. Refit and tighten terminals and coat with petroleum jelly, not grease.

b. **Battery Electrolyte Checks.** (Monthly). Check levels along with density. Record each cell density so that a profile can be built up. Record the battery voltage as well. Top up cells as required with distilled or de-ionized water.

c. **Battery Cleaning.** (Monthly). Wipe battery casing top clean with a damp rag. Moisture and salt can allow tracking across the top to ground or negative, slowly discharging the battery. This is a common cause of flat batteries, and the mysterious but untraceable system leak.

Table 5-7 Lead-Acid Battery Troubleshooting

Symptom	Probable Fault
Will not accept charge	Plates sulfated Maximum battery life reached
Low cell electrolyte SG	Cell sulfated
Low battery SG value	Low charge level (regulator failure) Plates sulfated (undercharging problem)
Will not support load	Low charge level (undercharging problem) Plates sulfated
Cell failure	Improperly commissioned Electrolyte contaminated (impure water) Overcharging problem (regulator failure) Undercharging problem (regulator failure) Excess vibration and plate damage Cell internal short circuit
Battery warm	Plates sulfated Excessive charge current (regulator failure) Cells damaged

5.20   Absorbed Glass Mat (AGM) or Valve Regulated Lead Acid (VRLA) Batteries. These batteries are installed on my boat and to date the performance has been excellent. Manufacturers include www.eastpenn-deka.com and www.concordebattery.com

    a.   **Electrolyte.** The electrolyte is held within a very fine microporous (boron-silicate) glass matting that is placed between the plates. This absorbs and immobilizes the acid while still allowing plate interaction. They are also called starved electrolyte batteries, as the mat is only 95% soaked in electrolyte.

    b.   **Recombinant Gas Absorption Principles.** In a normal lead-acid battery, water loss will occur when it is electrically broken down into oxygen and hydrogen near the end of charging. In a battery during charging, oxygen will evolve at the positive plate at approximately 75% of full charge level. Hydrogen evolves at the negative plate at approximately 90% of full charge. In normal batteries, the evolved gases disperse to atmosphere, resulting in electrolyte loss and periodic water replacement. These are the bubbles seen in the cells during charging. During charging the current causes decomposition of the water, and oxygen is evolved on the positive plate. The oxygen then migrates through the unfilled pores of the separator matting to react with the negative plate and form lead oxide, lead sulfate and water. The charge current reduces and does not generate hydrogen. The low maintenance recombinational battery has different characteristics. The plates and separators are held under pressure. During charging, the evolved oxygen is only able to move through the separator pores from positive to negative, reacting with the lead plate. The negative plate charge is then effectively maintained below 90% so inhibiting hydrogen generation. They emit less than 2% hydrogen gas during severe overcharge (4.1% is flammable level).

c.   **Plate Construction.** There are variations to flat plate manufacturing techniques. The Optima(r) AGM batteries have a spiral cell, dual plate construction. Another important feature is a greater shock and vibration resistance than gel or flooded batteries. They also have extremely high CCA values of up to 800 amps at 0°F.

d.   **Charging.** Charging of AGM cells have few limitations, and no special charge settings are required. Typical charge voltages are in the range 14.4 to 14.6 volts at 68°F (20°C). The batteries have a very low internal resistance, which results in minimal heating effects during heavy charge and discharge. They can be bulk charged at very high currents, typically by a factor of five over flooded cells, and a factor of 10 over gel batteries. They also allow 30% deeper discharges. They recharge 20% faster than gel batteries, and have good recovery from full discharge conditions. Self-discharge rates are only 1%-3%. If you are a weekend, harbor or river cruiser, who does limited motoring periods, or leave the boat unattended for long periods, the AGM battery is a viable proposition. It has very low self-discharge rates, and very high recovery rates from deep discharges. If a small solar panel is left on with a suitable regulator, they will recoup the annual costs of replacing deep cycle batteries by lasting several seasons, with the more important improvements in reliability. Typical charge voltage levels are 100% is 12.8–12.9 volts, 75% is 12.6 volts, 50% is 12.3 volts, 25% is 12 volts and 11.8 volts is flat. At high temperatures AGMs (and gel cells) are unable to dissipate the heat generated by oxygen and hydrogen recombination and this can create thermal runaway. This will lead to gassing and the drying out of cells. A premature loss of capacity can occur when the positive plate and grids degrade due to higher operating temperatures. This is caused by the exothermic recombination process and higher charge currents. In addition negative plates also degrade due to inadequate plate conversion. The main failure modes are cell shorting and pressure vent malfunctions caused by manufacturing faults.

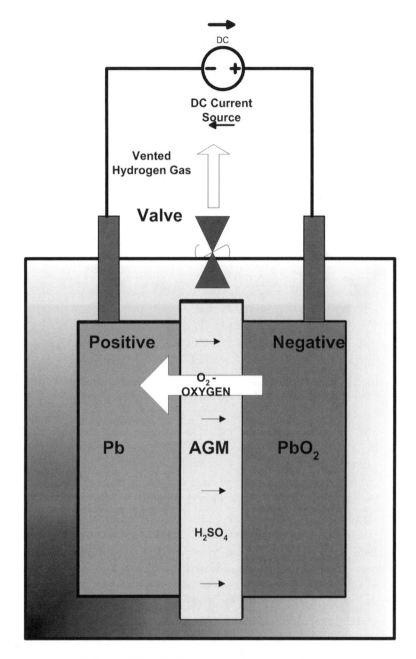

Figure 5-7 AGM Battery Characteristics

5.21 **Gel Cell Batteries**. These battery types are known as Dryfit from Sonnenschein (www.sonnenschein.org) or Prevailer batteries. A quality deep cycle lead acid battery can have a life exceeding 2500 cycles of charge and discharge to 50%. A gel cell has a life of approximately 800–1000 cycles. They do have a much greater cycling capability than normal starting batteries, but not of good deep cycle or AGM batteries.

    a. **Electrolyte.** Unlike normal lead-acid cells the gel cell has a solidified thixotropic gel as an electrolyte, which is locked into each group of plates. The gel electrolyte has a high viscosity and during the charge and discharge process develops voids and cracks. These can impede the flow of acid and cause capacity loss. During charging the gel also liquifies due to its thixotropic properties. Solidification after charging can exceed an hour as thixotropic gels have a reduced viscosity under stress. The newer types use

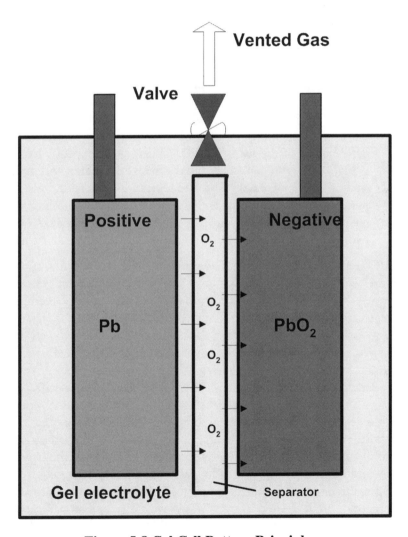

Figure 5-8 Gel Cell Battery Principles

phosphoric acid in the gel to retard the sulfation hardening rates. Water loss can occur in VRLA batteries, and the oxygen recombination cycle is used to minimize electrolyte loss. Sources of water loss are small for each source, however cumulatively they can cause failure, and the process is called dry-out. Water loss causes include reduced recombination efficiency, high charge voltages and corrosion of the positive grid. Transpiration through the cell casing also can occur, typically in temperatures exceeding 40°C. Batteries should be installed in cool areas wherever possible.

b. **Construction.** The plates are reinforced with calcium, rather than antimony, which reduces self-discharge rates, and they are relatively thin. This facilitates gel diffusion and improves the charge acceptance rate as diffusion problems are reduced. The separator provides electrical and mechanical isolation of the plates, and must have a high porosity to facilitate ion migration and electrolyte acceptance. Each cell has a safety valve to relieve excess pressure if the set internal pressure is exceeded. Typical values are 114 psi (100mbar). The valve recloses tightly to prevent oxygen from entering the cell. Lead-acid batteries suffer from corrosion of the current collector grid. Typical grids in VRLA batteries are manufactured from lead-calcium-tin, lead-tin-alloys or lead-antimony-cadmium. Positive plate grids corrode due to the conversion of lead to lead dioxide. This corrosion effect doubles for every 10°C, as well as charge voltages and electrolyte density. As the lead dioxide requires a substantially higher volume, this causes mechanical stressing and deformation of the grid. The effects can cause capacity loss, internal short circuits and even cell case ruptures, which increases with length of service. The process consumes water reducing the electrolyte, and causes lowered performance. VLRA cells are also prone to chemical degradation of the negative plate lugs and strap surfaces and this is called sulfate rot. This is caused by the oxygen recombination reaction and electrolyte inorganic sulfate salts.

5.22 Gel Cell Charging. Batteries have a much higher charge acceptance rate, and therefore a more rapid charge rate is possible. A gel cell cannot tolerate having any equalizing charge applied and this overcharge condition will seriously damage them. The illustration shows the oxygen recombination cycle. During charging the current causes decomposition of the water and the evolvement of oxygen at the positive plate. The oxygen diffuses through the unfilled glass mat separator pores to the negative plate, and chemically reacts to form lead oxide, lead sulfate and water. The charge current then reduces and does not evolve hydrogen gas. The end of charge voltage is typically 2.22 to 2.28 Vpc (volts per cell). If recombination of hydrogen is incomplete during overcharge conditions, the gases may vent to the battery locker causing an explosion risk. Although accepting a higher charge rate than a lead-acid deep cycle battery, and consequentially charging to a higher value, there is at a certain point the problem of attaining full charge, and therefore capacity usage of the battery bank. As no fast charge devices can be safely used, a longer engine run time is required for complete recharging. While these batteries will accept some 30-40% greater current than an equivalent lead-acid battery, they are restricted in the voltage levels allowed, so you cannot use any fast charging system. Typical open circuit voltages are 100% charge is 12.85–12.95 volts, 75% is

12.65 volts, 50% is 12.35 volts, 25% is 12 volts and 11.8 volts is flat. Gel cells are intolerant to over voltage charge conditions and can be damaged in over charge situations. The normal optimum voltage tolerance on Dryfit units is 14.4 volts. There are some minimal heating effects during charging, and this is caused by the recombination reaction. Where batteries are not kept within reasonable temperature ranges thermal runaway can occur. This normally occurs during charging when the temperature of the battery and charge current create a cumulative increase in temperatures and leads to battery destruction. Continuous over or undercharging of gel cells is the most common cause of premature failure. In many cases this is due to use of imprecise automotive type chargers.

5.23 **Alkaline Batteries.** Alkaline cells are typified by the nickel cadmium (NiCad) and nickel iron (NiFe) batteries. The principal factors are cost (typically 500% greater), greater weight and physically larger bank size. Normally these batteries will only be found in larger motor vessels for those reasons. They have completely different operating characteristics to the lead-acid cell. The obvious difference is the use of an alkaline electrolyte instead of an acid. Unlike lead-acid cells, plates undergo changes in their oxidation state, altering very little physically. As the active materials do not dissolve in the electrolyte, plate life is very long. The electrolyte is a potassium hydroxide solution with a specific gravity of 1.3. The electrolyte transports ions between the positive and negative plates and the alkaline solution is chemically more stable than lead-acid cell electrolytes. Unlike lead-acid cells, the density does not significantly alter during charge and discharge and hydrometer readings cannot be used to determine the state of charge. Electrolyte loss is relatively low in operation. Lead-acid and NiCad batteries should never be located in the same compartment as the cells will become contaminated by acid fumes causing permanent damage

a. **Cell Components.** The components of the NiCad cell are as follows:

(1) Nickel Hydroxide ($2Ni(OH)_2$) — the positive plate.

(2) Cadmium Hydroxide ($Cd(OH)_2$) — the negative plate.

(3) Potassium Hydroxide (KOH) — the electrolyte.

b. **Discharge Cycle.** Cells are usually characterized by their rate of discharge characteristics, such as low, medium, high or ultra high. Classification UHP is for starting applications and VP for general services. There is also a category for deep cycle applications. Discharge ratings are given at the 5-hour rate and typically they will deliver current some 30% longer than lead-acid equivalents. The amp-hour capacity rating remains stable over a range of discharge currents values. An over-discharge condition can occur when the cell has been driven into a region where voltage has become negative. A complete polarity reversal takes place. No long-term effects occur on occasional cell reversal at medium discharge rates. Discharge current reduces cell voltage from 1.3 volts to 1.0 volt over 10 hours.

c. **Charge Cycle.** During charging, the negative material loses oxygen and converts to metallic cadmium. The positive material gradually increases in the state of oxidation. While charging continues, the process will continue until complete conversion occurs. Approaching full charge gas will evolve and this results from electrolysis of the electrolyte water component. NiCad cells can be charged rapidly with relatively low water consumption. The disadvantages are that cell imbalances may occur and this can cause thermal runaway. The NiCad cell will generally absorb maximum alternator current for about 85% of the cell charge period, so the alternator must be capable of withstanding this load and have adequate ventilation. Typical voltage regulator settings for a nominal 12-volt battery bank of 10 cells over a 2–4 hour period should be in the range of 15 to 15.5 volts. A NiCad battery accepts high charge currents and will not be damaged by them. At 1.6 volts per cell, a NiCad can absorb up to 400% of capacity from a charging source. In most cases it will accept whatever the alternator can supply. The problem with normal alternator regulators is that they fix the output at only 14 volts, which is far too low for proper charging. Absolute maximum charging rates require 1.6 to 1.8 volts per cell, which is 16-18 volts on a typical 10-cell battery bank. The typical 14-volt output of an alternator is a float charge voltage level only for a NiCad battery. Constant voltage charging is the only practical method of charging on vessels. The regulator setting should be around 15.5 volts for a 2–4 hour charge period. Higher voltages will increase current. The charging cell voltage is 1.5 times the 10-hour discharge current. Water additions should be made immediately after charging, and never after discharging.

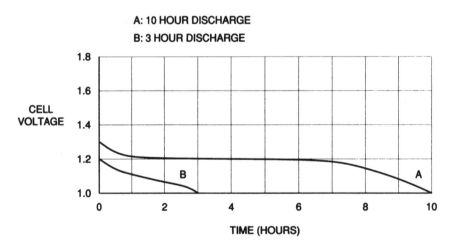

Figure 5-9 NiCad Battery Discharge Characteristics

5.24 **NiCad Battery Characteristics.** The open circuit voltage of a vented cell is around 1.28 volts. This depends on temperature and time interval from last charge period. Unlike a lead-acid cell, the voltage does not indicate the state of charge. The nominal voltage is 1.2 volts. This voltage is maintained during discharge until approximately 80% of the 2-hour rated capacity has been discharged. This is also affected by temperature and rate of discharge. The closed circuit voltage is measured immediately after load connection. Typically it is around 1.25–1.28 volts per cell. The working voltage is that observed on the level section of the discharge curve of a NiCad cell, voltage plotted against time. Typically the voltage averages 1.22 volts per cell. Capacity is specified in amp-hours. Normally it is quoted at 5-hour rate. The nominal rating is the amp-hour delivery rate over 5 hours to a nominal voltage of 1.0 volt per cell. Internal resistance values are typically very low. This is due to the large plate surface areas used and is why the cells can deliver and accept high current values.

5.25 **Small Appliance Batteries**. Standard disposable batteries are zinc carbon, long life alkaline, and super alkaline, lithium, silver-oxide and zinc-air batteries. Rechargeable batteries are far more economical. The small nickel cadmium (NiCad) can be recharged several hundred times. A rechargeable battery should be completely discharged before recharging. The nickel metal hydride (NiMH) cell used in many cellular phones is an example of more recent battery technology. These cells can withstand recharging up to 1000 cycles. They do not suffer with partial discharge and charge, although it is still good practice.

Battery Charging Systems

6.1   Charging. The recommended charging rate for a deep cycle battery is often given as 15% of capacity. In vessel operations it is not possible to apply these criteria accurately. Essentially the charge voltage corrected for temperature should be used. Deep cycle battery charging characteristics are:

   a.   **Counter Voltage.** During charging a phenomenon called "counter voltage" occurs. Primarily this is caused by the inability of the electrolyte to percolate at a sufficiently high rate into the plate material pores and subsequently convert both plate material and electrolyte. This causes the plate surface voltage to rise. The battery will resist charging and deceive the regulator by indicating an artificially high voltage with the recognizable premature reduction in charging.

   b.   **Charge Voltages.** To properly charge a deep cycle battery a charge voltage of around 14.5 volts is required, corrected for temperature. Contrary to some opinions, a charge level of approximately 80% does not represent a fully charged battery, and is not acceptable if you want a reliable electrical power system, and reasonable battery life. If you do not fully recharge the battery, it will rapidly deteriorate and sustain permanent damage.

   c.   **Equalization Charge.** An equalization charge consists of applying a higher voltage level at a current rate of 5% of battery capacity. This is done to reactivate the plates. There is a mistaken belief that this will also completely reverse the effects of sulfation. There may be an improvement following the process, but it will not reverse long-term permanent damage. Equalization at regular intervals can increase battery longevity by ensuring complete chemical conversion of plates, but care must be taken. Equalization charges are typically set at 16.5 volts so it is essential that all circuits be off at the switchboard so that the higher voltages cannot damage equipment power supplies.

6.2   Battery Charging Systems. An efficient battery charging system is essential for optimum battery and electrical system performance. I received many e-mails from motorboat owners who are very confused by conflicting information and simply want a reliable system. The principal charging systems on boats consist of the following:

   a.   **Alternators.** The alternator is the principal charging source on the majority of boats. In many cases it is the only source utilized, even at the dock, due to the higher available charging currents.

   b.   **Alternative Energy Systems.** Solar panels and wind generators are the only alternative systems available, as an option to augment charging while the boat is unattended. Small wind generators are useful for boats left on more exposed moorings.

c.   **Battery Chargers.** The average motorboat spends much time in port. When a boat is at the dock, or with larger vessels where a diesel generator is installed, the battery charger has an important role in the power system.

6.3   Charging System Configurations. There are three principal charging systems in use: the changeover switch, the relay and the diode isolator. The charging system on most engines uses the same cabling as the engine starter circuit. Basically, it consists of a switch with three positions and off. The center position parallels both battery banks. It is not uncommon to see both batteries left accidentally parallelled under load with flattening of both. Parallelling of a heavily discharged battery and a fully charged one during charging can also cause some instability in the charging as they both equalize.

a.   **Switch Operation under Load.** If a changeover switch is operated under load, the surge will probably destroy the alternator diodes. Most switches incorporate an auxiliary make before break contact for connection of field. This advanced field switching disconnects the field and therefore de-energizes the alternator fractionally before the opening of the main circuit. In reality this is rarely connected as most alternators have integral regulators and it is difficult to connect the switch into the field circuit.

b.   **Surges.** If both batteries are parallelled during an engine start, sensitive electronics can be damaged by the surge.

c.   **Circuit Resistance.** In most cases, the cables must run from the batteries to the switch location and back to the starter motor introducing voltage drops. Switches are notoriously unreliable and can introduce voltage drops into the circuit and total alternator or switch failure.

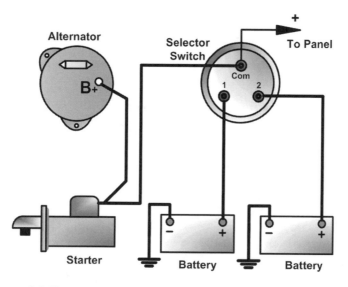

Figure 6-1 Single Engine Changeover Switch Charging System

6.4 **Relay/Solenoid Configuration.** This system improves on the switch system, by separating the charging system from starting circuits. The relay or solenoid does offer a point of failure if incorrectly rated for the task. The relay connects both batteries during charging, and separates them when off, preventing discharge between the batteries. The relay-operating coil is interlocked with the ignition and energizes when the key is turned on. When modifying the system, it is necessary to separate the charging cable from the alternator to starter motor main terminal where it is usually connected. A cable is taken directly from the alternator output terminal to the relay, as illustrated. Relay ratings should at least match the maximum rated output of the alternator. It is prudent to over-rate the relay. Relays are marketed in various forms, the most common being automotive solenoid types. Another system is the Voltage Sensitive Relay (VSR) from BEP Marine (www.bepmarine.com). The relay is open when the engine is started, and when the voltage rises to 13.7 volts it closes to parallel the two batteries, which then charge together. When the engine stops the relay opens to split the two batteries again. The AutoSwitch from PowerTap is also a similar device. The Isolator Eliminator from PowerTap (www.pwrtap.com and www.amplepower.com) has a similar function. It is a multi-step device; however it does not connect battery banks but charges from the higher housed bank under charge. It is temperature compensated like an alternator regulator.

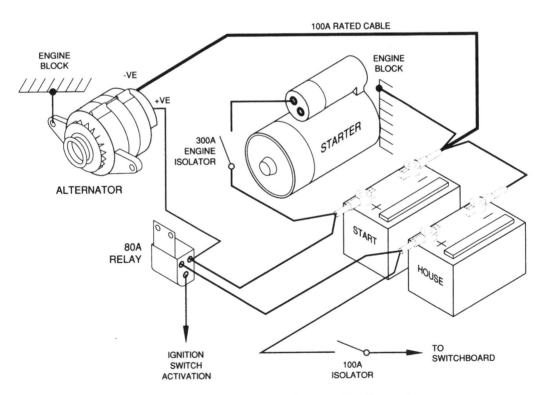

Figure 6-2 Relay Charging System Configuration

6.5 **Diode System.** The diode system is the simplest configuration and the most reliable. A diode has an inherent voltage drop of typically 0.7–0.8 volts. This is unacceptable in a normal charging circuit. If the alternator is machine sensed and does not have any provision for increasing the output in compensation, the diode should not be used. Essentially, a diode isolator consists of two diodes with their inputs connected. They allow voltage to pass one way only, so that each battery has an output. This prevents any backfeeding between the batteries. They are mounted on heat sinks specifically designed for the maximum current carrying capacity and maximum heat dissipation. The diode isolators must be rated for at least the maximum rating of the alternator, and if mounted in the engine compartment, must be over-rated to compensate for the de-rating effect caused by engine heat. Heat sink units should have the cooling fins in the vertical position to ensure maximum convection and cooling. Do not install switches in the cables from each output of the diode to the batteries. A variation on this is the Cross Charge Diode from PowerTap, which uses a Schottky diode. These diodes have low voltage drops in comparison with normal diodes.

Diode Isolator Testing. With engine running, the diode output terminal voltages should be identical, and should read approximately 0.75 volt higher if a non-battery sensed regulator is being used. The input terminal from the alternator should be zero when the engine is off. Test with power off and batteries disconnected.

(1) Set the meter scale to Ohms x 1, and connect red positive probe to input terminal. Connect black negative probe to output terminals 1 or 2.

(2) If it is good, the meter will indicate minimal or no resistance.

(3) Reverse the probes, and repeat the test. The reading should indicate high resistance, or over range.

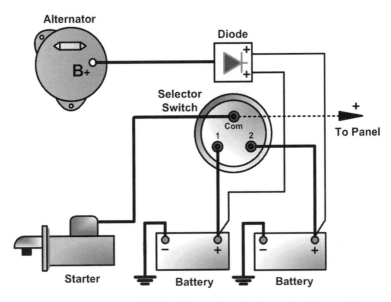

Figure 6-3 Single Engine Diode Charging System Configuration

6.6 **Electronic Battery Switches**. These are also known as charge distributors or integrators and characterized by the following systems:

(1) **NewMar Battery Bank Integrator (BBI).** When a charge voltage is detected that exceeds 13.3 VDC the unit switches on. The unit consists of a low contact resistance relay that closes to parallel the batteries for charging. When charging ceases and the voltage falls to 12.7 VDC, the relay opens isolating the batteries. The unit also incorporates a voltage comparator and time delay circuit. This prevents the unit cycling in the event of a voltage transient or load droop on the circuit dropping voltage below the cutout level.

(2) **PathMaker (Heart Interface).** These devices allow charging of two or three batteries from one alternator or battery charger. The units use a high current switch rated at 800 and 1600 amps for alternator ratings up to 250 amps. The unit has an LED status indicator.

(3) **Isolator Eliminator (Ample Power).** This is a multi-step regulator that controls charge to the second battery bank, typically used for engine starting. It is temperature compensated like an alternator control system.

(4) **Battery Mate (Mastervolt).** This is a charge splitter that can supply three batteries, without voltage drop.

6.7 **Failure Analysis and System Redundancy.** After considering the previous chapters on engines, batteries, control systems etc., it is time to review either the existing system or proposed system. I am actively involved in large ship systems, and carrying out what is called a Failure Mode and Effects Analysis (FMEA), and subsequent trials. This principle can be also adapted to smaller motorboats. The exercise is to analyze the starting and charging systems, as both are critical to propulsion or power, and identify single point failures. In a dual engine vessel there is inherent redundancy as there are two separate systems. In a single engine vessel there is virtually none. It is necessary to first identify all of the points that upon failure will also fail the system, and then devise methods to improve redundancy. It is important when assessing risk to consider the following factors and statistics:

a. A failure in the battery charging system means no charging of batteries and therefore an eventual loss of all electrical power, and possibly propulsion starting.

b. A failure in the engine starting system means no propulsion and no charging of batteries, and eventual loss of all electrical power.

c. Approximately 80% of all electrical system circuit failures are due to faulty or failed connections and this is crucial to this exercise.

d. Approximately 70% of equipment and machinery failures are attributable to poor or improper maintenance.

6.8 **Failure Analysis and Risk Assessment.** A charging system must not be viewed as simply a collection of series connected components, but as a system. The typical charging system comprises a considerable number of elements:

a. **The Charging System.** It is a good idea to trace out each circuit on your boat, and draw in each component and mark each connection on it. As a minimum, you will have 4 main positive circuit connections; 4 main negative circuit connections; 4 control circuit connections; 2 changeover switch contacts; a meter shunt; the alternator; the regulator and the battery.

    (1)   The alternator (includes several components such as brushes, brushgear, sliprings, bearings, diodes and windings).

    (2)   The regulator (may be integral or separate).

    (3)   The DC positive circuit (includes connections at alternator and battery, and the changeover switch).

    (4)   The DC negative circuit (includes connections at alternator and battery, the cable back to the battery, and the meter shunt if fitted). In addition, the engine block also becomes part of the negative circuit, along with the alternator bracket, holding bolts etc.

    (5)   The battery.

b. **Charging System Failure Mode Analysis.** There are a total of 14 connection points plus the alternator, regulator and battery that can impact on the starting system. Each point represents a single point failure with subsequent total system failure, with no apparent redundancy. For this exercise wind, water and solar panels are considered extra or supplementary charge sources, as are generators with AC mains chargers. These however can be factored into redundancy provisions. The operational factors also must be considered. If a changeover switch is opened or fails during operation, the alternator diodes can be destroyed.

c. **Engine Starting System.** A starting system must also be viewed as not simply a collection of series connected components, but as a system. The typical starting system includes the following elements:

    (1)   The DC positive circuit (includes connections at the battery, the isolator or changeover switch, the solenoid connection, and solenoid contacts, the starter motor (which includes several components such as brushes, brushgear, commutator, bearings, windings).

    (2)   The DC negative circuit (includes connections at the battery, engine block, the cable back to the battery, the engine block, and the meter shunt if fitted).

    (3)   The engine control system (includes key switch, stop and start buttons, wiring harness, connectors and fuses etc).

    (4)   The preheating system (includes heating elements and interconnections, relays and connectors).

    (5)   The battery.

d. **Starting System Failure Mode Analysis.** There are a total of 14 connection points plus the solenoid coil, the starter motor, the battery, and the key switch that can impact on the starting system. Each point represents a single point failure with subsequent total system failure, with no apparent redundancy. If someone persists with turning over an engine that will not start, he may also burn the starter motor out. There are other less common scenarios.

e. **Auxiliary Systems Failure Mode Analysis.** A similar analysis should be carried out on air start systems, fuel supply and filtering systems, the engine cooling water system, both salt and fresh water. The engine air system should be examined for failure modes, and that may include ventilation and fans. The final key area is the propulsion system, that is shaft, gearbox, stern tubing, propellers and related equipment.

6.9 **Systems Redundancy.** The key to minimizing failure or mitigating its effects is the provision of redundancy. In the average single engine motorboat, systems do not incorporate any redundancy on charging, power or starting systems. In most commercial shipping, this is a basic premise in all systems design. The only trawler yacht manufacturer advertising essential equipment redundancy is Pacific Motoryachts (www.realtrawlers.com) and it should be a central philosophy to all boat manufacturers. There are several methods for improving redundancy; the following are the easiest and most economical to carry out. While not easy on motorboats, some measures can be implemented. Redundancy is the process of having backup systems. This includes carrying appropriate critical equipment spares.

6.10 **Charging Systems.** There are relatively simple modifications that can be carried out on the charging system to improve efficiency and reliability:

a. **Second Alternator.** Installing a second alternator on the engine will require adding a second pulley. The second alternator is for the house battery charging circuit, with the existing alternator being used for charging the start battery. Each alternator will have a separate positive circuit without any switches or other devices in it. This will eliminate changeover switch problems on alternators that commonly destroy the alternator rectifier diodes. This reduces connections to just 2. It also eliminates accidental switch operation under load, or switch contact failures, which are very common. Each alternator will have a separate negative circuit cable running back to the respective battery from the alternator. This provides separation from the starter motor to battery negative, with the main starter negative serving as a backup. This reduces connections to just 2. It also takes the engine block out of the circuit, and generally reduces voltage drop. There is anecdotal evidence that current flow through a bearing also results in reduced engine bearing life.

b. **Separate Charging System.** Separate the charging system from the starting circuit. Previous illustrations show how these various methods can be done, and in the long term, will considerably reduce problems and increase reliability. This process entails the deletion of battery selection changeover switches. It requires the installation of a separate charging circuit, which may include charge splitting diodes or relays. An emergency crossover switch between battery banks can be installed; however this does not affect the circuit during operations.

c. **Install Separate Negative Cables.** Install a separate negative conductor of at least 6 AWG (15mm^2) from each alternator case or negative terminal directly back to the corresponding battery negative. This bypasses the engine block and all the cumulative resistances of mountings and brackets. This provides a good low resistance path and reduces stray currents through the block, which can cause pitting of bearings. It also eliminates a single point failure of the main negative connection to the engine block.

d. **Replace Positive Cable.** Most installed positive cables are too small, especially if a fast charge device is installed. The cable size should be doubled. Install a minimum cable size of 6 AWG (15mm^2). An additional cable rating problem that compounds maximum charge current and heavily discharged batteries can occur. The heat of the engine compartment also de-rates the current capacity of the cable when hot. In most cases a significant voltage drop develops across the cable under full output conditions.

e. **Starting Circuit.** Relocate and connect the main negative cable to, or as close as possible to the starter motor. This maintains 2 connections but takes the engine block out of the circuit, and generally reduces voltage drop in the circuit.

6.11   Maintenance Philosophy. Commercial ships and offshore-based rigs follow a number of maintenance philosophies. The traditional and most accepted is the Planned Maintenance System (PMS). The maintenance tasks are based on time intervals, either set periods or operational hours. The previous exercise allows the implementation of Risk and Criticality Based Maintenance and Inspection. We have evaluated all the areas most critical to boat operation, so the maintenance strategy should be centered on this. Integration of condition monitoring is also a valuable tool and use of oil sampling on engines and hydraulics, or vibration monitoring allows maintenance decision making based on the results.

6.12   Maintenance Factors. Perform the recommended maintenance on all critical equipment and systems.

a. **Starter Motors.** Starter motors have low failure rates, as actual operating hours are relatively low. Failures depend on operational frequency with seized bearings or stuck brushgear being the major failure causes. Regular operation reduces failures. In addition this generates heat, which assists in displacing moisture within the windings. Starter motors should be cleaned or overhauled on a regular basis, at least every two years.

b. **Alternators.** Alternators have a relatively low failure rate, as actual operating hours are relatively low. Failures are generally caused by diode failures, or overheating, in particular with fast charge regulators and oversized battery banks. Alternators should be cleaned and overhauled on a regular basis, at least every two years. Consider a higher rated alternator to reduce overloading and heating.

c.   **Batteries.** Batteries have the highest failure rate. This is generally due to either inadequate charging with resultant sulfation, lost capacity and failure, or flattening of the battery with subsequent damage. The second highest failure is inadequate inspection and topping up of electrolytes, with resultant plate damage. Consider different batteries such as AGM types with lower failure rates.

d.   **Connections.** All connections on alternators, starters, engine blocks and batteries should be checked and tightened every six months. It is an easy task and results in fewer intermittent and complete failures.

e.   **Spares.** It is rare to see a boat with a spare starter motor or alternator and these should be a prerequisite on an extended voyage. While some boats may carry spare bearings, diode plates, brushgear etc, it is easier and quicker to change out the entire alternator. Invest in a spare starter motor and alternator.

6.13   FMEA Results. There is now a significant reduction in exposure to single point failures. With two separate charging circuits there is full redundancy. There are only a total of 4 connections in both the positive and negative circuits, the negative having a backup with the starter motor negative. In a typical system using a changeover switch, that is a reduction of up to 75% in possible failure points. There is a significant improvement in charging efficiency. This is a gain of up to or exceeding 0.5 VDC due to lower circuit resistance in both positive and negative circuits. This reduces alternator loads, and can shorten charging time, reduce charge current and extend alternator life. The starting system is more efficient with the negative at the starter reducing voltage drops, lowering current, reducing run time, and improving starting times. Coupled with a spare starter motor/solenoid, there is a reasonable chance of being operational within an hour. Separation of start and charging systems eliminates the many problems of voltage surges and transients. There are now two redundant power systems, each one capable of powering the vessel, and any single failure of one system will not affect the other. The alternator negatives provide some redundancy to the main starter negative. As critical equipment has been evaluated and appropriate maintenance strategies implemented there is increased Mean Time Before Failure (MTBF) rates.

6.14   Multiple Alternator Charging System Configurations. In twin engine vessels there is by default two charging systems. In single engine boats, the option of fitting a second alternator is a useful option where redundancy is required. There are a number of different system configurations for multiple alternator installations.

a.   **Discrete Systems.** These systems usually have the original engine alternator charging the engine start battery only. The additional alternator, usually a higher rated type of 80 amps or greater charges the house batteries only. If there is more than one bank, this may be split through either a diode isolator or a switch. Ideally the start battery alternator should be used to charge a third battery bank as the alternator is under utilized given that start batteries require very little charging.

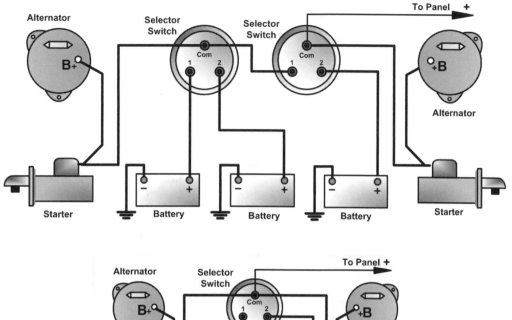

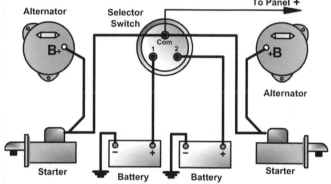

Figure 6-4 Two Engine Changeover Switch Charging Systems

b. **Cross Feed Systems.** These systems usually have each alternator charging a primary battery bank except that each alternator cross feeds to the other battery bank via a diode isolator. A fast charge device should still be used. Although initially this looks complicated, it is in fact simple and the advantages of such a layout are:

(1) **Alternator Redundancy.** The arrangement allows charging of both battery banks even if one alternator should fail.

(2) **Load Balancing.** It is easier to balance loads between battery banks in order to achieve similar discharge levels of the same periods. This allows both batteries to be charged at a similar rate, which overall is faster, assuming that alternators and regulators are the same.

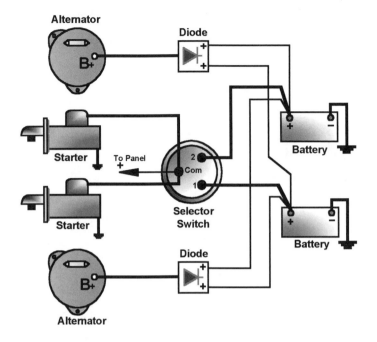

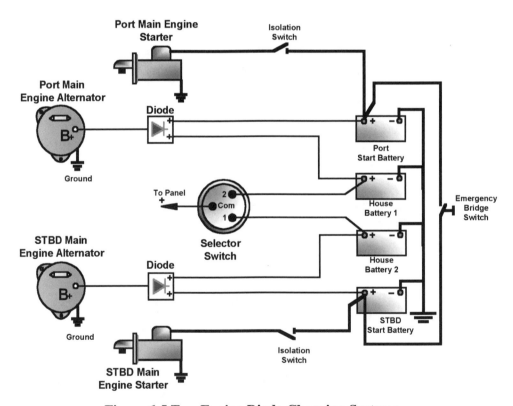

Figure 6-5 Two Engine Diode Charging Systems

6.15 **Battery Charging Cycles**. There are four recognized parts of any charging cycle, and understanding these parts is crucial to understanding charging problems.

a. **Bulk Charge**. The bulk charge phase is the initial charging period before the gassing point is reached. This is typically in the range 14.4 to 14.6 volts, corrected for temperature, though with a traditional alternator and regulator, output is fixed at 14 volts. The bulk charge rate can be anywhere between 25% and 40% of rated amp-hour capacity at the 20-hour rate, as long as temperature rises are limited.

b. **Absorption Charge**. After attaining the gassing voltage, the charge level should be maintained at 14.4 volts until the charge current falls to 5% of battery capacity. This level normally should equate to 85% of capacity. In a typical 300 amp-hour bank, this is 15 amps.

c. **Float Charge**. The battery charge rate should be reduced to a float voltage of approximately 13.2 to 13.8 volts to maintain the battery at full charge.

d. **Equalization Charge**. A periodic charge rated at 5% of the installed battery capacity should be applied for a period of 3-4 hours until a voltage of 16 volts is reached.

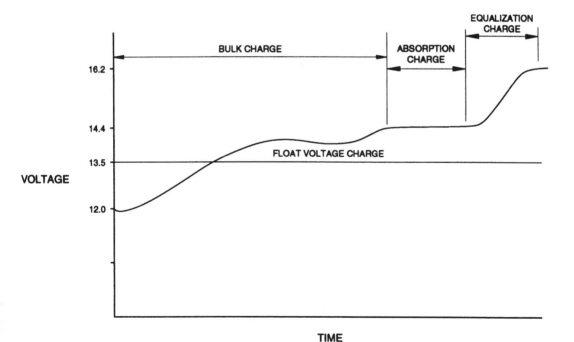

Figure 6-6 Charging Cycles

6.16   Charging Efficiency. Before any charging systems can be considered, a number of factors must be summarized and taken into account. Manufacturers specify nominal capacities of batteries, and the total capacity of the bank must be taken into consideration. Older batteries have reduced capacities due to normal in-service aging, and plate sulfation. Sulfation increases internal resistance and subsequently inhibits the charging process. The electrolyte is temperature dependent, and the temperature is a factor in setting maximum charging voltages. The state of charge at charging commencement can be checked using the open circuit voltage test and electrolyte density. The level of charge will affect the charging rate. Also critical to the state of charge is the temperature. It has a dramatic effect on charge voltages as indicated in the curve below. Charging voltage is defined as the battery voltage plus the cell voltage drops as follows:

a.   **Cell Volt Drops.** Cell volt drops are due to internal resistance, plate sulfation, electrolyte impurities and gas bubble formation that occurs on the plates during charging. These resistances oppose the charging and must be exceeded to effectively recharge the battery. Resistance to charging increases as a fully charged state is reached and decreases with discharge.

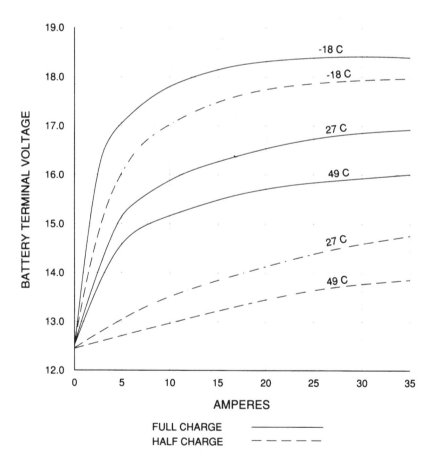

Figure 6-7 State of Charge/Temperature Relationship

b. **Charge Regulation.** A battery is self-regulating in terms of the current it can accept under charge. Over-current charging at excessive voltages (which many so called fast charging devices do) simply generates heat and damages the plates, which is why those types are not recommended (see cycle regulators).

6.17 **Alternator Charging**. The alternator is the principal charging source on most powerboats. The basic alternator consists of several components, which are described below. The typical automotive type alternator generates a 3-phase AC alternating current, which is where it derives its name. This is then rectified to produce a DC output for charging via the full wave bridge rectifier. There are variations in design, and some 12 pole units are rated to run at speeds up to 20,000 rpm, with modified cooling arrangements. There are vehicle derived units that have no brushes or windings. The excitation winding is fixed and pre-excitation is not required. Although water cooled alternators are common in vehicles they are not on boats. They use a windingless rotor and connect into the engines cooling water system, which maintains operating temperatures and reduces overheating.

a. **Stator.** The stator is the fixed winding. It consists of a three phase winding that is connected in a "star" or a "delta" arrangement. The windings are formed onto a solid laminated core. They supply three phases of alternating current (AC) to the rectifier.

b. **Rotor.** The rotor is the rotating part of the alternator. The shaft has the pole or claw shaped magnet poles attached, the excitation winding, the cooling fan at one end, the bearings, and the collector sliprings.

c. **Rectifier.** The rectifier consists of a network of six diodes, which are connected across the positive and negative plates. These plates also function as heat sinks to dissipate the heat from power generation. This rectifies the three generated AC phase voltages into the DC output for charging. Two diodes are used on each winding to provide full wave rectification. In some alternators Zener diodes are used to limit voltage peaks that arise during sudden load changes.

d. **Exciter Diodes.** The exciter (D+) or pre-excitation diodes consist of three low power diodes which independently rectify each AC phase and provide a single DC output for the warning light or auxiliary control functions. They are required as the residual magnetism (or remanence) in the iron core is insufficient at low speeds and starting and cannot initiate the self-excitation required to build up the magnetic field. This only occurs when the alternator voltage is higher than the voltage drop across the two diodes. The warning lamp functions as a resistor and provides pre-excitation current, which generates a field in the rotor. In this respect the power or watts rating of the lamp is important and 2 watts is typical.

e. **Brushgear.** The brushes are normally made of copper graphite. The brushes are spring-loaded to maintain correct slipring contact pressure and are soldered to the terminals.

f.   **Voltage Regulator.** The voltage regulator is usually combined with the brushgear or mounted adjacent to it. The field control output of the alternator is connected to one of the brush holders, which then supplies the rotor winding though the slipring. Regulator sensing is normally connected to the D+ output circuit. The regulator maintains a constant voltage output over the entire operating range of the alternator. Earlier electro-magnetic contact type regulators are relatively uncommon now with most being electronic types with no moving parts. The electronic regulator allows precise control with short field switching periods.

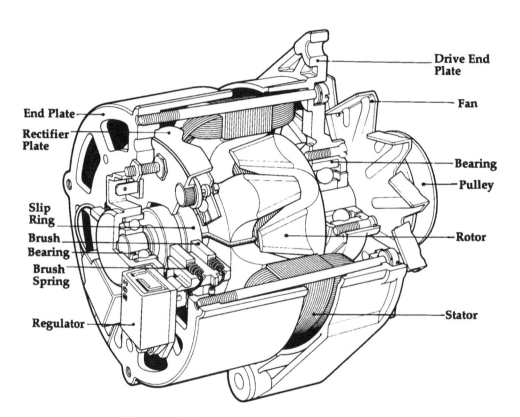

Figure 6-8 Bosch Alternator, *Courtesy of Bosch*

6.18   **Field Circuits**. The field circuit is used to vary the output of the alternator, and can be simply defined as the alternator "controller" because all alternator output is controlled by the field current level.

a.   **Warning Light.** The light circuit is not simply for indicating failure. The lamp provides excitation to the alternator. In many cases an alternator will not operate if the lamp has failed and this is because the remanent voltage or residual magnetism has dissipated. Ideally a lamp should be in the range of 2-5 watts. Undersized lamps are often characterized by the need to rev the engine to get the alternator to kick in. This is often highly visible with alternator driven tachometers. Many newer engine panels have a printed circuit board type of alarm panel.

b.   **Advanced Field Switching.** This method is comparatively rare in modern integral regulator alternators. The field is taken through the changeover switch auxiliary contacts, so that the field circuit is broken, de-energizing the alternator immediately before the main output contacts break. This will prevent any accidental circuit interruption and subsequent diode destruction through generated surges.

c.   **Oil Pressure Switch Control.** This method, which can still be found, may be of two configurations. The first senses battery voltage through an oil pressure switch on the engine. The alternator does not commence generating until after engine oil pressure has built up. The second method takes the field directly through an oil pressure switch.

d.   **Field Isolation Switch.** This circuit is common in small engines or where small output auxiliary engines drive more than one piece of equipment. This

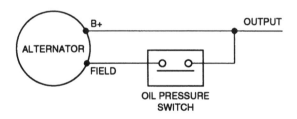

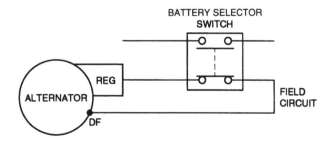

Figure 6-9 Field Circuits

125

enables the alternator to be switched off to reduce engine loadings so that other equipment such as refrigerators or watermakers can operate. It is advisable to operate the switch before or after charging.

6.19   Battery Charging Recommendations. Reference IRBES (See Chapter 7).

Rule 7.1. The primary battery charging source should be calculated with a minimum output of 30% of the total installed battery capacity.

From the power analysis table we have calculated the maximum current consumption. Added to this is a 20% margin for battery loss giving a final charging value. A battery requires the replacement of 120% of the discharged current to restore it to full charge. This value is required to overcome losses within the battery due to battery internal resistances during charging. A popular benchmark is that alternator rating should be approximately 30% of battery capacity. An 80-amp alternator is recommended, which is approximately the largest rating possible without advancing to high priced or exotic high output alternators. I avoid where possible installing a battery bank in excess of 300 amp-hours and usually fit a bank of two six-volt cells rated at 230 amp-hours. With a suitable regulator system, this is generally adequate for most charging and load requirements. As a battery is effectively self-limiting in terms of charge acceptance levels, we cannot simply push in the discharged value and hope that it will recharge. The battery during charging is reversing the chemical reaction of discharge, and this can only occur at a finite rate. The alternator therefore must be selected if possible to recharge at the battery optimum charge rate as specified. Charging by necessity has a tapered characteristic, which is why start and finishing rates are specified. These ratings are largely impractical in marine installations. The required charging current is the sum of the charge rate plus anticipated loads during charging.

Rule 7.2. Alternative charging sources such as wind, solar and water should not be included within power calculations. These systems are to be classified as supplementary charging sources.

Other charging sources should be viewed as additional and not be used in the primary calculations, as they are reliant on weather.

Rule 7.3. Where two alternators are installed, one alternator should be dedicated to the starting battery. The two alternators should not be connected in parallel to a single battery.

Where two alternators are installed to provide redundancy or improved charging capability, one should be dedicated to starting. Both alternators should not be charging in parallel to the same battery bank. In most cases, one will act as a slave and be very inefficient.

Rule 7.4. The positive cable from the alternator to the battery, or charge distribution device (diode, relay) should be rated at the maximum rated alternator current and for a maximum voltage drop of 5%.

All charge circuit cables must be rated for maximum current capacity of the alternator, with minimal voltage drop and allow for high ambient temperatures. Many installations are under-rated.

Rule 7.5. A negative cable should be installed equivalent in size to the positive cable, from the negative terminal or case of the alternator to the battery. Where more than one alternator is installed the negative cables should be connected to the respective battery negatives.

To maintain system separation and minimize voltage drops in the charging circuit, which normally includes the engine block, a separate negative should be installed for each alternator. These should go to the correct battery under charge, and crossovers are frequent.

Rule 7.6. All charging system cable terminations and connectors shall be rated for the maximum alternator current. All charging system cable connectors shall be crimped.

Many charging system terminations are under-rated for the current capacity of the cable. Ensure that crimp connections of the right capacity are used with rings of the correct size for the termination bolts on alternator and battery. Many are over-sized and make poor contact. Soldered connections frequently fail or are high resistance points in the circuit. After charging, touch the alternator output terminal; if it is very hot, the connection is probably undersized and therefore overheating causing charging system power losses.

Rule 7.7. No alternator output cable shall have any isolation switch or fuse installed within the circuit so that opening of the circuit during operation could cause damage or failure of the alternator.

Switches and fuses should not be installed in any alternator output circuit. Alternator failures caused by inadvertent operation of changeover switches are common. When a switch is opened, the spike normally destroys the alternator diodes.

Rule 7.8. Where a fast charging regulator or similar device is installed, they should not increase voltages to a level liable to cause excess gas generation from the batteries. Maximum voltages should not exceed installed equipment ratings or be able to cause damage.

The majority of alternators have a fixed output of 14 volts, with some makes having the option of regulator adjustment up to around 14.8 volts for isolation diode voltage drop compensation. The regulator should not be able to cause high voltages that cause excessive gassing of batteries or in excess of normal equipment voltage input ranges.

6.20 Alternator Selection. The alternator probably has the highest onboard equipment failure rate. This includes the regulators, and careful selection is required. The majority of motorboats run engines for excessive periods attempting to recharge batteries. The maximum run time goal is one hour in the morning and one hour in the evening. Diesel engines should not be run with light loads as unloaded engines suffer from cylinder glazing. A high output alternator can provide loads of up to 1.5 hp if at rated output. The engine should be able to charge at maximum rates at relatively low speeds. The most preferred speed is a few hundred revs/min above idle speed. The alternator speed is dependent on the drive pulley ratio and the alternator cut-in speed.

    a.   **Marine Alternators.** Marine alternators are essentially enclosed, and ignition protected with a UL listing to prevent accidental ignition of hazardous vapors. Windings are also protected to a higher standard by epoxy impregnation and output characteristics are generally similar to automotive types. Manufactured marine units have a corrosion resistant paint finish and are designed for higher ambient operating temperatures. An alternator can be marinized to a reasonable degree. Bearings should be totally enclosed. Replace if they are not. Windings should be sprayed or encapsulated with a high grade insulating spray. The back of the diode plate can also be sprayed with an insulating coating, preventing the ingress of moist salt laden air and dust which can short out diodes and connections.

b. **Water Cooled Alternators.** These are available from Bosch and are used on motor vehicles. They will ultimately appear in boat systems for the same reasons and advantages and will be standard for 42-volt systems.

c. **High Output Alternators.** Many people choose to install a high output alternator, typically in the range from 90 to 130 amps at 12 volts and up to 150 amps at 24 volts. While this will solve battery charging problems, it is an expensive option and, in many cases, masks the more common problems of poor circuit design and installation, and regulation. In most cases an alternator rated at over 80/90 amps is not required. The real solution is in the regulator, which is considerably cheaper and more reliable. If you choose to upgrade your alternator, install a quality alternator such as Silver Bullet, Lestek, Balmar, Niehoff, Powerline or Mastervolt. This will require the addition of a second pulley to match the dual pulley on most high output alternators. Beware of rewound standard units; they are notoriously unreliable.

6.21   Alternator Installation. Optimum service life and reliability can only be achieved by correctly installing the alternator. The following factors must be considered during installation.

a. **Alignment.** It is essential that the alternator drive pulley and the engine drive pulley be correctly aligned. Misalignment of pulleys can impose twisting and friction on the drive belts and additional side loading on bearings. Both can cause premature failure.

b. **Drive Pulleys.** Drive pulleys between the alternator and the engine must be of the same cross-section. Differences will cause belt overheating and premature failure. Solid pulleys of the correct ratio should replace slit automotive type pulleys on some alternators.

c. **Drive Belt Tension.** Belts must be correctly tensioned. Maximum deflection must not exceed 10 mm. When a new belt is fitted, the deflection should be re-adjusted after 1 hour of operation and again after 10 hours. Belts will stretch in during this period.

(1) **Under-tensioning.** This causes belt overheating and stretching, as well as slipping and subsequent undercharging. The excess heat generated also heats up pulleys and the high heat level conducts along the rotor shaft to the bearing, melting bearing lubricating grease and increasing the risk of premature bearing failure.

(2) **Over-tensioning.** This causes excessive bearing side loads which leads to premature bearing failure. Signs of this condition will be characterized by sooty looking deposits around the belt area, and wear on the edges of the belt.

d. **Drive Belts.** Belts must be of the correct cross section to match the pulleys. Notched or castellated belts are ideal in the engine area as they dissipate heat easily. If multiple belts are used, always renew all belts together to avoid varying tensions between them. In any alternator over 80 amps in rating, a dual belt system should be used, as a single belt will not be able to cope with the mechanical loads applied at higher outputs.

e. **Ventilation.** Engine compartments offer very few ventilation options. Ideally, a cooling supply fan should be fitted to run when the engine is operating. An alternator, similar to electrical cable, is de-rated in high temperatures. The fan outlet should be directed to the alternator. Many alternator failures occur when boost-charging systems are installed because they run at near maximum output for a period in high ambient temperatures. Always ensure when fitting an additional alternator that the fan is rotating in the correct direction.

f. **Mountings.** Mountings are a constant source of failure.

(1) **Tensioning.** When tensioning the alternator, always adjust both the adjustment bolt and the pivot bolt. Failure to tighten the pivot bolt is common and causes alternator twisting and vibration. Vibration fatigues the bracket or mounting and causes it to fracture. Additionally, this can cause undercharging and radio interference.

(2) **Adjustment Arm.** Ensure that the slide adjustment arm is robust. Most marine engines have a level of vibration that will fatigue the slide and break it. The arms should be upgraded. Take off the old one and have another one custom made.

6.22 **Alternator Drive Pulley Selection.** Ideally, maximum alternator output is required at a minimum possible engine speed. This is typically a few hundred revs/min above idle speed. Manufacturers install alternators and pulleys based on the premise that the engine is only run to propel the vessel, when in fact engines spend more time functioning as battery chargers, at low engine revolutions. Alternators have three speed levels that must be considered and the aim is to get full output at the lower speeds.

a. **Cut-in Speed.** A voltage will be generated at this speed.

b. **Full Output Operating Speed.** This is the speed where full rated output can be achieved.

c. **Maximum Output Speed.** This is the maximum speed allowed for the alternator, otherwise destruction will occur.

d. **Pulley Selection.** An alternator is rated with a peak output at 2,300 revs/min. At a typical engine speed of 900 revs/min and a minimum required alternator speed of 2,300, a pulley ratio of approximately 2.5:1 is required. The maximum speed in this case has a 10,000-rev/min rating. Maximum engine speed is 2,300 in this case, so 2,300 multiplied by 2.5 = 4,000 revs/min. This falls well within operating speeds limits and is acceptable. A pulley giving that ratio would suit the service required.

e. **Selection Table.** Table 6-1 gives varying pulley ratios with an alternator pulley of 2.5 inches.

Table 6-1 Drive Pulley Selection Table

Engine Pulley	Pulley Ratio	Engine RPM	Alternator RPM
5 inch	2:1	2000	4000
6 inch	2.4:1	1660	4000
7 inch	2.8:1	1430	4000
8 inch	3.2:1	1250	4000

6.23 **Low Speed (Trolling).** It is important to understand the speed and output relationship in alternators. In large powerboats and trawlers used for fishing, trolling speed entails very low engine speeds. The result is almost no charging for several hours as the available output is used to supply boat electrical equipment and is generally insufficient so there is a net current discharge situation. Table 6.1 and table 6.2 give typical specifications for a range of Bosch alternators and other makes are similar in performance. They illustrate the outputs available at different speeds. The methods to overcome this are not easy. The first method is to place a larger pulley on to gain maximum alternator speed. The first speed level is the cut-in speed where the alternator is turning sufficiently to allow a voltage to be generated. In many trolling situations, the speed is often around this point. For boats with charging problems, there are few options and variable pitch propellers may be an option where the problems are critical.

6.24 **Overvoltage and Surge Protection.** Some alternators are provided with separate surge protection units. Overvoltage protection comprises several methods.

a. **Zener Diodes.** The rectifier diodes are Zener diodes that limit the high voltage spikes or peaks that arise below a safe value, which can damage the regulator. The typical limiting voltages of Zener diodes in use are 25–30 volts for 14-volt alternators and 50–55 volts for 28-volt alternators.

b. **Surge-proof Alternators.** Some alternators are equipped with high specification components. The components are rated up to 200 volts for 14-volt systems and 350 volts for 28-volt systems. This is supplemented by the installation of a capacitor across the alternator output and ground. Lucas/CAV alternators incorporate a surge protection avalanche diode within the alter-

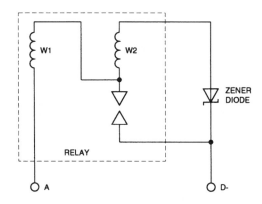

(a) LUCAS SURGE PROTECTION UNIT

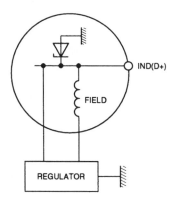

(b) LUCAS AVALANCHE DIODE REGULATOR PROTECTION

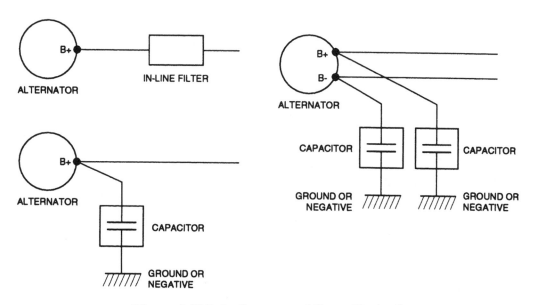

Figure 6-10 Interference and Surge Protection

nator (ACR and A115/133 range). This protects the main output transistor in the regulator.

c.   **Overvoltage Protection Devices.** Often these are only installed in 28-volt alternators. These electronic semi-conductor devices are connected across the alternator output. They operate by short-circuiting the alternator through the excitation winding when peaks rise over a set value. Some alternators use what is called a freewheeling diode, anti-surge or suppressor diode. This is connected in parallel with the excitation winding of the alternator.

d.   **Zap Stop (Cruising Equipment Co.)** This device is a high voltage spike suppressor that shunts excess voltages to ground. The device is connected across the main alternator output and ground.

e.   **NewMar Filters.** The 80-A and 150-A are designed for installation in the alternator output lead adjacent to the alternator. They will reduce noise in the 70kHz to 100 MHz range that commonly affects GPS, and radios. They are relatively heavy and large so they will require careful fastening on the engine, or on an adjacent bulkhead if close.

f.   **Additional Protection.** A Metal Oxide Varister (MOV) installed across the B+ and negative terminals will provide additional surge protection. Another good method is to solder a capacitor rated at 0.047F /250 V across each of the AC windings.

g.   **Interference Suppression.** Alternator diode bridges create noise (RFI) that can be heard on communications or electronics equipment. Always install an interference suppression capacitor. As a standard, install a 1.0-microfarad suppressor. In some cases, a suppressor is required in the main output cable.

6.25   Alternator Characteristics. The graph shows the relationship between output current, efficiency, torque and HP against rotor revolutions. The optimum speed can be selected from these characteristics. The curves illustrated are for a Lestek high output alternator, and for a 9135 series 135-amp alternator.

Table 6-2 Alternator Test Specifications

Model	Output	Speed	Stator Ohms	Rotor Ohms
14V 35A Bosch	10 A	1300 rpm	0.24	4.0
	23 A	2000 rpm		
	35 A	6000 rpm		
14V 55A Bosch	16 A	1200 rpm	0.14	4.0
	36 A	2000 rpm		
	55 A	6000 rpm		
12V 130A Mastervolt	30A	1000 rpm		
	115A	2000 rpm		
	130A	3000 rpm		

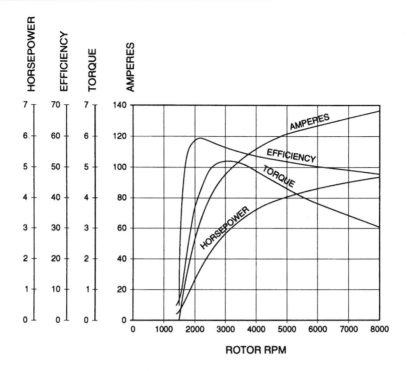

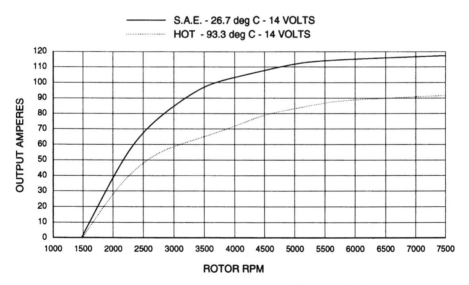

Figure 6-11 Alternator Output Characteristics

133

6.26   **Alternator Maintenance**. Many alternator failures can be avoided by performing basic maintenance tasks.

   a.   **Drive Belts.** Check monthly as follows:

   (1)   Check and adjust tension. Deflection is 10mm maximum.

   (2)   Examine for cuts, uneven wear or fatigue cracks.

   (3)   Ensure belts are clean, with no oil or grease.

   b.   **Connections.** Check monthly as follows:

   (1)   Clean and tighten all alternator terminals.

   (2)   Check cable and connectors for fatigue.

   c.   **Vibration.** Check monthly as follows:

   (1)   Check alternator for vibration when running.

   (2)   Examine mounts for fatigue cracks.

   d.   **Bearings.** Check every 1500 operating hours as follows:

   (1)   Remove alternator and turn rotor. Listen for any bearing noises.

   (2)   Renew every 3000 hours or at major overhaul.

   e.   **Brushes.** Check every 1500 operating hours as follows:

   (1)   Check brushes for excess or uneven wear.

   (2)   Check sliprings for scoring.

   f.   **Cleaning.** Clean yearly as follows:

   (1)   Wash sliprings, diode plate and brushgear with electrical solvent. Do not use any abrasives on sliprings; they must be cleaned only to preserve a film that is essential for brush contact.

   (2)   Wash out windings and dry.

   g.   **Pre-cruise.** Take alternator to a quality marine/auto electrical workshop. Request the following tests:

   (1)   Test alternator output for maximum current.

   (2)   Check diodes.

   (3)   Clean windings, sliprings and brushgear.

   (4)   Renew bearings and brushes.

6.27   **Alternator Faults and Failures**. Failures in alternators are primarily due to the following causes, many of which are preventable with routine maintenance.

   a.   **Diode Bridge Failures.** Diode failures are generally attributable to the following causes along with simple overheating and the inability for the heat sinks to dissipate properly.

   (1)   **Reverse Polarity Connection.** This is a common occurence. Reversal of the positive and negative leads will destroy the diodes.

   (2)   **Short Circuiting Positive and Negative.** A short circuit will cause excess current to be drawn through the diodes and the subsequent failure of one or more of diodes; the most common cause is reversing the battery connections.

   (3)   **Surge.** This occurs if the charge circuit is interrupted, most commonly when an electrical changeover switch is accidentally opened. A high voltage surge is generated by the inductive effect of the field and stator windings. There is an alternator spike reducing device that connects across the alternator output which consists of an avalanche diode to maintain voltage at 16 volts.

   (4)   **Spikes.** Short duration, transient voltages several times greater than the nominal voltage can be caused by high inductive loads when starting up, say, a pump. Most spikes, however, are caused by lightning strikes. Countermeasures are covered in the lightning protection chapter.

   b.   **Winding Failures.** Stator winding failures are usually due to the following causes:

   (1)   **Overheating.** Normally due to insufficient ventilation at sustained high outputs, this causes insulation failure and intercoil short circuits.

   (2)   **Stator Winding Short Circuit.** Shorts are due to mechanical winding damage, overheating or ingress of moisture.

   (3)   **Rotor Winding.** Short circuit or ground fault due to overheating or over voltage if the voltage regulator fails.

   c.   **Brushgear.** Brushgear failures are not that common in a properly maintained alternator but they are generally due to:

   (1)   **Brushes.** Brushes worn and sparking, and characterized by fluctuating outputs and radio interference.

   (2)   **Sliprings.** Scoring and sparking due to build-ups of dust, also causing radio interference.

   d.   **Bearing Failure.** The first bearing to fail is normally the front pulley bearing. Rotation by hand will usually indicate grating or noise.

6.28 **Alternator Terminal Designations**. Alternators have a variety of different terminal markings and these are listed in Table 6-3.

Table 6-3 Alternator Terminal Markings

Make	Output	Negative	Field	Auxiliary	Tacho
Bosch	B+	D-	DF	D+/61	W
Ingram	B+	B-	F	IND/AL	W
Lucas	BAT	E	F	L	
Paris-Rhone	+	-	DF	61	W
Sev Marchal	B+	D-	DF	61	
Motorola	+	-	F	AUX	AC
CAV	D+	D-	F	IND	
AC Delco	BAT	GND	F		
Niehoff	BAT+	BAT-	F	D+	X
Valeo	B+	D-		D+	W
Mitsubishi	B+	E	F	L	
Nippon Denso	B+	B	F	L	
Prestolite	POS+	GND		IND LT	AC TAP
Motorola/Prestolite	B+			D+	AC TAP
Silver Bullet	+	-	F		R
Mastervolt	B+	D-	DF	D+/61	W

6.29 **Alternator Troubleshooting**. Troubleshooting should be carried out in conjunction with charging system troubleshooting as described in Table 6-6.

   a.   **Check Output.** This initially depends on the lamp and the regulator. Using a voltmeter, check that the output across the main B+ terminal and negative rises to approximately 14 volts. No output indicates either total failure of alternator or regulator. Partial output indicates some diodes failed or a regulator fault.

   b.   **Regulator Check.** If there is no output, either the alternator is faulty or the regulator is failing to excite the alternator. This is not difficult with external regulators but if an internal regulator is fitted, the alternator will need to be opened and a wire attached to the brush-holder. Switch off all electrical and electronic equipment at the switchboard circuit breaker before commencing test. *If in doubt, don't try it.* Check that the alternator gives full output by shorting the wire to negative in negative type machines or positive in positive types. If the alternator gives full output voltage, the regulator is probably faulty.

   c.   **Alternator Test.** The other components are tested after confirming the function of the regulator. I recommend first that you remove the alternator, and take it to any good automotive electrician with a test bench if in port. This saves a considerable amount of time and effort. If you don't carry spares, you can do little. To get home with partial diode failure, you can disconnect the regulator and apply a full field voltage to get maximum output.

d.   **Auxiliary Diode and Warning Light Tests.** On some occasions, the auxiliary diodes may fail. Put your multimeter on the 20-volt range and connect across 61/D+ and negative. If there is any reading, the diode may be faulty. Turn on the ignition key without starting. The reading should be around 1-2 volts. If lower, the wiring may be faulty, if higher, the diode may be faulty; or there is excessive rotor resistance or a bad connection. Check that the warning light is operating and on when the ignition switch is turned on. If not the lamp may be faulty, or seating badly if a replaceable lamp, or there is a lamp connection fault. Check that the wire is not off the D+ terminal, or connection is loose.

e.   **Rotor Testing.** If a regulator has failed, particularly in an overcharge condition, prior to replacing the regulator, the rotor should be checked for damage. The test is as follows:

(1)   **Test Insulation Resistance.** Place one multimeter probe on a slipring, and the other on the rotor core. Resistance should be infinite or over-range.

(2)   **Test Winding Resistance.** Place the multimeter probes on each slipring. Resistance should be around 4 ohms. If it is very high, an open circuit may exist, and if very low, a coil short circuit may exist.

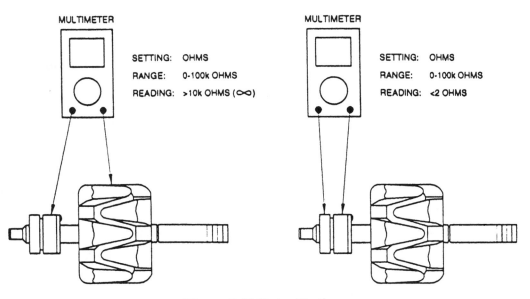

Figure 6-12 Rotor Testing

6.30 **Alternator Remagnetization.** After dismantling or stripping down an alternator, it is not uncommon to find it simply won't work at all, so perform the following checks before dismantling the alternator.

a. **Field Disconnect.** Disconnect the regulator field connection (assuming you have installed a separate regulator or controller).

b. **Manual Field Activation.** With the engine running at idle speed, and all electrical and electronics equipment off, temporarily touch the field connection to the following:

(1) **Positive Control.** (Bosch, Paris-Rhone, Motorola, new Sev-Marchal) If the field control is on the positive side, touch the lead to main alternator output terminal B+, or if a diode is fitted then to the diode battery output terminal.

(2) **Negative Control.** (Lucas, CAV, Hitachi) If the field control is on the negative side, touch the lead to the negative terminal or to the case.

c. **Output.** The alternator should immediately give a full output, you will hear the engine load up, and voltage will rise to 16 volts. Do this for 1-2 seconds. Reconnect the regulator back to normal. In many cases, this will restore magnetism to the alternator and it will operate normally. If there is no or a low output after this test, it generally indicates a fault in the alternator. Normally this is caused by a faulty diode bridge, or the brushes not seating on sliprings.

6.31 **Emergency Repairs.** The following gives basic survival methods where an alternator or regulator has failed and you have neglected to carry spares. In some cases, it may not work, but it may get you home.

a. **Regulator Failure.** This may be either no or full output voltage:

(1) **No Output.** To overcome this it is necessary to apply full field voltage as described in 6.30. For sustained motor sailing in this condition, place a spare navigation or bunk light lamp in the field circuit to limit field current value.

(2) **High Voltage Output.** Run the engine for limited periods to avoid excess gassing of the battery. Disconnect electronics to avoid damage. The internal regulator should be disconnected and a lamp placed in a temporary circuit if motoring for extended periods. Periodically it should be disconnected to prevent serious overcharging.

(3) **Alternator Diode Failure.** This is characterized by low charge voltage. In many cases, only a few diodes may have failed. To get some charging capability, reduce battery capacity to one battery to prevent overloading of the diode bridge.

b. **Warning Light Failure.** In many cases, an alternator will not operate without it. Place any small lamp in series with the lead off the auxiliary output

(D+), and touch it to battery positive. Excitation is usually immediate. Remove straight away.

6.32 **Alternator Regulators.**The regulator is the key to all alternator-charging systems. The function of the regulator is to control the output of the alternator, and prevent the output from rising above a nominal set level, typically 14 volts. Higher voltages would damage the battery, alternator and other electrical equipment.

a.   **Principles.** An alternator produces electricity by the rotation of a coil through a magnetic field and varying the level of the field current controls the output. This is achieved by applying the field current through one brush and slipring to the rotor winding, and completing the circuit back through the other slipring and brush. Essentially the regulator is a closed loop controller, constantly monitoring the alternator output voltage and varying the field current in response to output variations.

b.   **Regulator Operating Range.** A regulator does not control the charging process significantly until battery charge level is approximately 50%. When the voltage of the battery rises to this threshold, the regulator starts limiting the voltage level. The charge current levels off as the voltage level rises, and this is called the regulation zone.

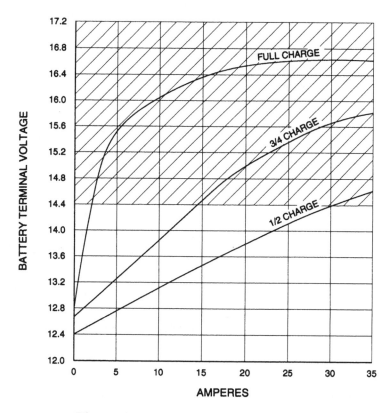

Figure 6-13 Regulator Operating Range

6.33 **Alternator Regulator Sensing.** With any type of charging system, there is a voltage drop between the alternator output terminal and the battery. With a nominal alternator output of 14 volts, it is not uncommon to have a very inadequate 13 volts at the battery. This voltage drop increases with an increase in current. Regulator sensing consists of the following configurations.

a. **Machine Sensed.** The machine-sensed unit simply monitors the output terminal voltage and adjusts alternator output voltage to the nominal value, which is typically 14 volts:

(1) **Charge Circuit Voltage Drops.** The machine-sensed regulator makes no compensation for charging circuit voltage drops. Voltage drops include inadequately rated terminals; cables and the negative path back through the engine block.

(2) **Diode Isolators.** If a diode isolator, charge distribution system is installed this will also contribute a further drop, typically 0.75 volt.

b. **Battery Sensed.** The battery-sensed unit monitors the voltage at the battery terminals and adjusts the alternator output voltage to the nominal voltage:

(1) **Charge Circuit Voltage Drops.** The battery-sensed regulator compensates for voltage drops across diodes and charge circuit cables. By sensing the battery terminal voltage, the regulator varies the output from the alternator until the correct voltage is monitored at the battery. Some alternator manufacturers such as Bosch, Lucas, Prestolite and Sev-Marchal are introducing modifications so that regulators can be compensated with a separate sense connection that goes directly to the battery. Always install battery sensing if possible.

(2) **Caution.** In some cases, the voltage drop between alternator terminals and battery may be considerable, and figures of 1.5 to 2 volts and above are not uncommon. With a multimeter, check the output and battery voltage to find out the drop, ideally at full rated output current. An excessive voltage drop is a fire risk. Excessive current can flow, and along with high ambient engine space temperatures, literally melt and ignite the cable insulation, or typically first burn off the terminals. Check output terminal to see if it is hot.

c. **Temperature Compensation.** Very few alternator manufacturers incorporate temperature compensation. An electrolyte is affected by temperature. In hot climates charge voltages should be marginally decreased, and in cold climates voltage should be increased. Regulators with compensation usually have it sensed at the regulator. In most vessels, the batteries are not always located near the engine so the regulator senses the engine compartment temperature and reduces charging output in compensation. Compensation should be based on the ambient temperature of the batteries.

6.34 **Alternator Regulator Types.** It is extremely important to distinguish between a regulator and a controller. Some new devices do not fit the regulator definition.

a. **Regulator Function.** A regulator is a fully automatic device that ensures a stable output from the alternator. What follows is crucial to understanding what a regulator does, as this is frequently forgotten with disastrous results. The primary function of a regulator is to prevent overcharging of the battery and damage to the alternator and this point should be considered when selecting a controller.

b. **Alternator Control Devices.** There are five main categories of alternator control devices:

(1) **Standard Regulators.** These are factory fitted to alternators. The standard alternator regulator is a simple and inexpensive electronic device. The contents are a simple voltage regulator device with associated circuitry. They are normally installed as an integral part of the alternator, or incorporated with the brushgear as a removable module, or located externally on the engine or an adjacent bulkhead. The typical scenario is one of a high charge at initial start-up and then a rapidly decreasing current reading on the ammeter. One of the many undesirable effects of standard regulators is that when a load is operating on the electrical system, charging current also decreases. Based on tests I made with an alternator with a total output of 30 amps at 14 volts and a vessel electrical load of 24 amps, I found that only 6 amps was flowing into the battery with a terminal voltage of only 13.2 volts.

(2) **Cycle Regulators.** These devices use a cyclic regulator control principle that is microprocessor controlled such as the Adverc.

(3) **3-Stage Stepped Cycle Regulators.** These use a timed cycle of voltage steps that use bulk, absorption and float charge steps.

(4) **Regulator Controllers.** These devices either parallel connect or override existing standard regulators with manual settings.

(5) **Manual Controllers.** These devices have no regulator function and control alternator output manually by operator control.

6.35 **Regulator Polarity.** Regulators and field windings have two possible field polarities. It is important to know the difference when installing different regulators or testing regulator function. The two types are as follows.

a. **Positive Polarity.** The positive regulator controls a positive excitation voltage. Inside the alternator, one end of the field is connected to the negative polarity. Alternators with this configuration include Bosch, Motorola, Ingram, Sev-Marchal, Silver Bullet, Lestek, and Balmar:

(1)   **Polarity Test.** To test, use a multimeter on the ohms x 1 range and connect across the field connection to an unpainted part of the alternator case or negative output terminal.

(2)   **Meter Reading.** The reading should be in the range of 3 to 8 ohms.

b.   **Negative Polarity.** The negative regulator controls a negative excitation voltage. Inside the alternator, one end of the field is connected to the positive polarity. Alternators with this configuration include Hitachi, Lucas A127, ACR 17-25 and AC5, CAV, Paris-Rhone, New model Sev-Marchal and Valeo, AC Delco, Mitsubishi:

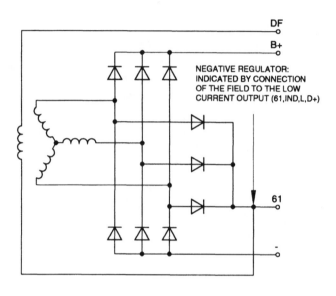

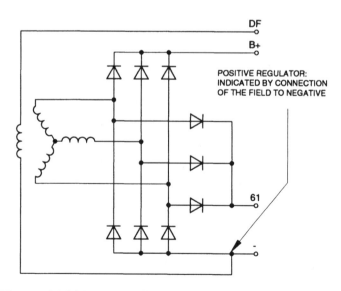

Figure 6-14 Alternator Regulator Field Polarity

142

(1)   **Polarity Test.** To test, use a multimeter on the ohms x 1 range and connect across the field connection to the alternator's positive terminal.

(2)   **Meter Reading.** The reading should be in the range of 3 to 8 ohms.

6.36   Regulator Removal. If a regulator must be removed or checked, certain procedures should be used to avoid damage. The following diagrams illustrate various alternators for the main engine groupings and disassembly procedure. Mounting a separate regulator on the engine bulkhead makes replacement simple and inexpensive, and facilitates testing.

a.   **Bosch (K1/N1 Series).** Dismantle as follows:

(1)   Unscrew the two screws retaining the regulator.

(2)   Carefully lift the regulator up and out. Be careful not to damage the brushes.

(3)   Disconnect the (D+) lead from the back of the regulator.

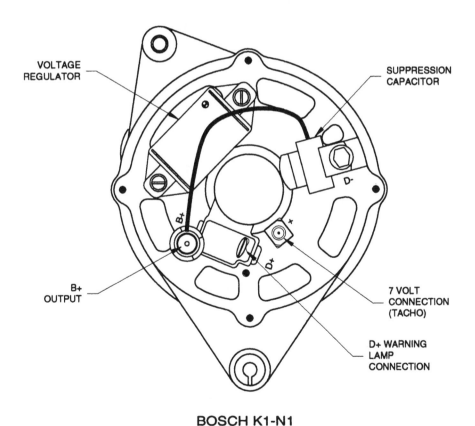

BOSCH K1-N1

Figure 6-15 Bosch Series K1/N1 Alternator

b. **Paris-Rhone/Valeo.** Usually a standard type fitted to Volvo engines, Paris-Rhone and Valeo are now all the same as Valeo alternators, though there are some differences in the design. Use the following procedure to disconnect and install a new external regulator system, or replace the existing one:

(1) Unscrew and remove the 4 screws securing the regulator to the casing.

(2) There are 4 cables leading from the regulator (5 on the new Valeo). If you are replacing the regulator with an external type, cut the cables at the regulator, as the regulator and housing acts as a spark arrestor cover for the brushgear.

(3) Remove the negative cable to the regulator entirely.

(4) The cable running internally under the plastic cover to terminal 61 should be soldered to one of the brush-holder connections. This cable was initially connected to the regulator until cut off.

(5) Solder a wire to the remaining brush-holder and run it out through the cover for connection to the new regulator. This is the field control connection.

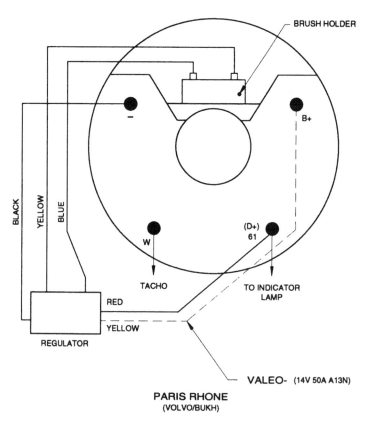

Figure 6-16 Paris-Rhone/Valeo Alternator

144

c. **Hitachi.** This is a standard alternator type fitted to Yanmar engines (models LR 135-74 35A, LR 155-20 55A and LR 135-105 35A):

    (1)   Remove the rear casing from the alternator. The screws are generally torqued extremely tight; use the correct screwdriver size.

    (2)   Carefully cut off the connections to the existing regulator. There are 5 in total.

    (3)   Solder a 1.5 mm bridging wire between the R and F terminals, as illustrated.

    (4)   Replace the rear casing.

    (5)   Connect the external field connection to the socket at the rear of the alternator. A cable and plug is normally fitted and can be removed.

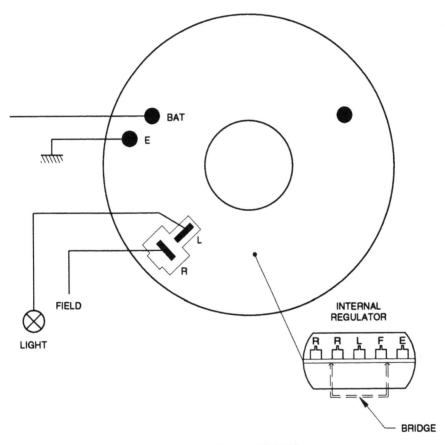

HITACHI (YANMAR)

LR 135-74 35A
LR 155-20 55A
LR 135-105 35A

Figure 6-17 Hitachi Alternator

145

d. **Motorola.** Usually a standard alternator type fitted to Nanni and Universal engines and is a Model 9AR. Remove as follows:

(1) Unscrew and remove the 2 retaining screws holding in the existing regulator.

(2) Either cut, or remove the 2 cables connecting the regulator to the alternator.

(3) Fit a new wire to the vacated lower terminal and run it out through the cover for connection to the new regulator. This is the field control connection.

(4) Refit the old regulator and housing which acts as a spark arrestor cover for the brushgear.

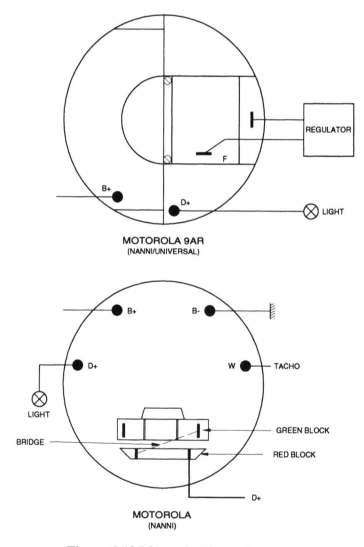

Figure 6-18 Motorola Alternator

6.37 **Adverc Cycle Regulator**. A cycle program is the basis of the charging system. The regulator also is designed for parallel connection to the existing regulator, giving some redundancy should failure ever occur. Temperature compensation also takes place; the Adverc has a linear one. The Adverc system has a light warning system, with indication given for low and high voltage conditions or a loss of sensing leads. Adverc regulators are designed with value engineering principles, and components are over rated by 400%. This of course is important where robust construction is a key consideration. Latest versions have had circuit enhancements that attenuate RFI and smoother control outputs. I have an Adverc installed and the system has proven itself. See www.advercbm.co.uk.

a. **Cycle Period.** The cycle periods on the Adverc system consist of four 20-minute intervals followed by a one-hour rest period. Voltage levels within the charging cycle are a normal charge rate of 14.0 volts, and a high level of 14.5 volts. To check operation, always connect a digital meter across the battery and observe the cycles.

b. **Adverc Regulator Color Codes.** The following are color codes for Adverc (and TWC) regulators:

(1) **Green.** Connects to the field connection of the alternator.

(2) **Brown.** Connects to the auxiliary D+ output terminal.

(3) **Yellow.** Connects to alternator warning light, taken off the D+ terminal of the alternator at installation. Splice them together.

(4) **Black.** Connects to the alternator negative or case.

(5) **Blue.** This is a sense wire that connects to the alternator main output B+, but note that where a diode isolator is used, it must be connected to the house battery side of the diode isolator. This may entail lengthening the blue wire. The lead also has a 0.5 "clamp" applied to the circuit protect against high output voltages.

(6) **Red.** This is the sense wire that connects to the house battery or changeover switch common terminal.

6.38 **Balmar.** Balmar have a range of regulators (See www.balmar.net)

a. **Max Charge MC-612 Regulator.** This is microprocessor-controlled unit with several user selectable multi-voltage variable-charge time programs for six battery types. The settings are via dipswitches. The principle is the use of an automatic absorption time program, alarm outputs, LED status and alarm indicators. The amp manager function has a remote controlled power reducer if required. The unit has a data output port, and the option of a soft start and ramp up function; this is to save belt wear. There is an optional battery compensation sensor and alternator temperature sensor for over-temp protection.

b. **Max Charge MC-412 Regulator.** This is microprocessor-controlled unit with several user selectable multi-voltage variable-charge time programs for four battery types. It also has an LED display for program mode indication, and self-diagnostics. It has connections for warning light and electrical tachometer output. The amp manager function is included along with a data port. There is an optional battery compensation sensor and alternator temperature sensor for over-temp protection.

c. **BRS-2 Regulator.** This single stage regulator has a nominal setting of 13.7 volts, and has a range of settings for various battery types. It has connections for warning light and electrical tachometer output.

d. **ARS-4 Regulator.** This is a 3-step controller with user settings for Deep Cycle, Gel, AGM and Optima batteries; it uses bulk, absorption and float charge principle. It also has an LED display for program mode indication, and self-diagnostics. It has connections for warning light and electrical tachometer output.

6.39 Heart Interface Alpha (InCharge) 3-Stage Charge Regulator. This is a 3-stage regulator that has user definable settings for Accept, Float and Time. The first step is the bulk charge phase, where voltage rises steadily up to approximately 14.2–14.4 volts, and maximum current output occurs up until approximately 80% charge level. The second step is the acceptance phase where the voltage is maintained constant and the current slowly reduces. The third step is the float phase where voltage reduces to approximately 13.8 volts and maintains a float charge to the battery. See www.heartinterface.com.

6.40 PowerTap. PowerTap has a range of regulators:

a. **Smart Regulator SAR-V3.** The regulator uses a microprocessor controlled cycle type program. It has no operator adjustable functions with respect to the charging cycle, and operates based on 12 programmed charging cycles. Battery temperature compensation is incorporated and it is for use with P-type alternators only. An alarm function uses a coded flash system. An over-voltage runaway circuit detects over-voltage conditions that occur when regulator output has a short circuit and runaway. This is indicated via the alarm lamp circuit. Current limiting is via a user adjustable function that requires connecting an externally operated switch. The switch will reduce output to a relatively low level to avoid overheating of an alternator or to remove load off a smaller engine. The equalization function is a user adjustable feature that requires connection of an externally operated switch. The function enables an equalization current to be applied until battery voltage reaches 16.2 volts. The regulator has some very commendable features. The field output driver protects the regulator from damage in the event of a field circuit failure. Additionally, all inputs are voltage transient protected, although normal precautions should still be installed. The lamp circuit is also over-rated to provide alarm buzzer load capability as well. In addition, a voltage limit function enables charge voltage to be held at 13.8 volts to prevent halogen light damage during long night motoring passages.

b. **3-Step Deep Cycle Regulator.** The 3-step device uses a step type program, that is fully automatic, and operates based on the charging cycles of absorption and float. The unit consists of a timer circuit rather than an intelligent program chip, and has simple battery and ignition inputs. Users are able to manually alter absorption and float voltage settings which is useful in applications such as NiCad cells that require different charging voltage levels. The manufacturer states that due to full alternator output requirement in step 1, many alternators may not be able to cope, and may suffer failure. This is generally due to windings overheating and diode failure. The regulator is suitable for P-type alternators only (i.e. Bosch, Prestolite, Motorola, Valeo/Paris-Rhone etc). The regulator has the following control steps:

(1) The alternator is controlled to give full output until the absorption set point is reached. The time required to reach this level depends on the initial battery level and output speed of the alternator.

(2) The absorption set point (14.5 volts) is maintained for a period of 45 minutes.

(3) The charge level reduces to the float voltage set point (13.8 volts).

c. **Next Step Regulator**. The Next Step deep cycle regulator is an improved version of the 3-step unit. The unit is microprocessor-controlled and incorporates temperature compensation. Due to full alternator output requirement in step 1, many alternators may not be able to cope, and may suffer failure. This is generally due to windings overheating and diode failure. Users are able to manually alter both absorption voltage and time as well as float voltage settings. The regulator has the following control steps:

(1) The alternator is controlled to give full output until the absorption set point is reached. The time required to reach this level depends on the initial battery level and output speed of the alternator.

(2) The absorption set point (14.5 volts) is maintained for a period of 45 minutes.

(3) The charge level reduces to the float voltage set point (13.8 volts).

6.41 **Ideal Regulator**. This regulator is different in that current is a factor in the charging process, not just voltage. I have not seen this in any other regulator types I have come across. The regulator is used in conjunction with a digital circuit monitor. The regulator has the following control steps:

(1) **Delay Period.** A 20-second delay period after voltage is applied from ignition allows engine speed to rise to normal running speed.

(2) **Ramping Up Period.** This allows a controlled increase of alternator output over a 10-second period until the default current limiting value is reached. This reduces shock loadings, allows belts to warm up, and reduces powerline surges that occur when full outputs are applied.

(3)   **Charge Cycle.** The charge cycle allows full alternator output until the battery voltage reaches 14.3 volts.

(4)   **Acceptance Cycle.** Charging continues at 14.3 volts until charge current decreases to a default value of 2% of capacity. Once the 2% level is reached, the acceptance hold cycle begins.

(5)   **Acceptance Hold Cycle.** Charging is held at 14.3 volts and the charging current is monitored and continues for a minimum of 10 minutes. A maximum of 20 minutes is imposed on this cycle.

(6)   **Float Ramp Cycle.** This is a transition phase between charged and float cycles. Voltage is reducing to the float setting of 13.3 volts during the cycle.

(7)   **Float Cycle.** Voltage is held constant at 13.3 volts.

(8)   **Condition Cycle.** This is a manually activated function. Current is held at 4% of battery capacity, until 16 volts is attained. Once voltage reaches 16 volts, it is maintained until charge current falls to charge current percent setting. The cycle then automatically terminates. On termination, it reverts to the float ramp cycle to bring the voltage down.

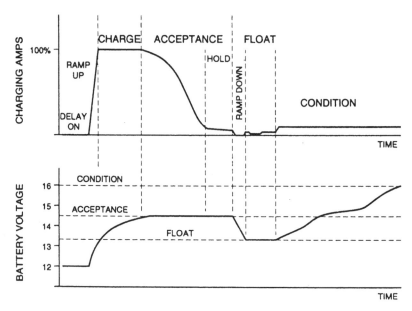

Figure 6-19 Quad Cycle & Ideal Regulator Characteristics

6.42 **Battery Charge Settings.** Different battery types require different charge voltages, and regulator systems should be adjusted to suit the installed batteries.

Table 6-4 Battery Regulator Charge Levels

Temp	Flooded Hi/Float	Gel Hi/Float	AGM Hi/Float
90°F	14/13.1	14.0/13.6	14.4/13.9
80°F	14.3/13.3	14.0/13.7	14.5/14.0
70°F (20°C)	14.4/13.5	14.1/13.8	14.6/14.1
60°F	14.6/13.7	14.3/13.9	14.7/14.2
50°F	14.8/13.9	14.2/14.0	14.8/14.3

6.43 **Alternator Manual Control Devices**. Manual devices are those that require total operator control of the alternator output without regulation. Some handbooks give information on how to make your own controllers. From personal experience, I can say that, once these homegrown controllers and circuits are installed, the charging system, batteries and alternator will be burned out not too far into the future. There is no such thing as a cheap solution, and if you really care about your power system, don't risk it. There is no sense in having and relying on electronics worth thousands only to balk at paying relatively small sums to improve charging. Use the following control methods at your own risk. While there are many around who boast how reliable and cheap these devices are, I do not mind making a very nice living off the majority who have subsequent problems. The savings initially achieved on these methods are more than negated by one mishap which often shortens battery life through overcharging and plate damage.

a. **Field Switches.** A typical manual method is to connect the switch directly to the field connection. It simply puts on a full field voltage resulting in maximum alternator output. The results can be quite spectacular and very damaging to both battery and alternator. Once, while his boat was crossing a dangerous bar, a friend casually flicked a switch, which was followed by sparks and smoke curling out of the engine compartment. After investigation, I found this same set-up, which nearly led to a disaster.

b. **Field Rheostats.** The most common type of control is the rheostat. A rheostat is simply a variable resistance rated for the field current. The term rheostat is still in common usage and low value variable resistances are generally termed potentiometers. Rheostats are totally reliant on operator control, with no safety cutouts or regulation. As a general alternator charging control, it is not recommended, as both alternator and battery are easily and commonly damaged.

6.44 **Alternator Controllers.** Controllers are devices that require the motorboat owner to manually select or partially over-ride the existing regulator to fast charge. It is important to remember the basic phases of charging a battery, i.e. bulk, absorption, float and equalization and that at no stage does battery voltage exceed gassing level. In most cases, controllers do not adhere to these basic charging principles.

    a. **Operating Principles.** Controllers are either direct regulator replacement units or are connected in parallel to the existing regulator. Some units have an ammeter to monitor output and require continual adjustment of field current to maintain required charge current level, but they do not monitor or take into account the high and damaging system voltages that are imposed while maintaining the initial high charging currents.

    b. **Precautions.** All controllers will have some beneficial outcome, and can improve the charging process to varying degrees. There are however serious risks that must be considered to avoid damage:

        (1) **Power System Disturbances.** If you apply excessive voltages or full alternator outputs, spikes and surges can arise on the system that will damage regulators and electronics equipment.

        (2) **Battery Damage.** Forcing current into batteries above the natural ability to accept charge will simply damage plates, heat the battery up, and generate potentially explosive gases. Failure of automatic cutouts, or forgetting about the regulator may cause all of the mentioned problems.

    c. **Performance and Efficiency.** There are some important factors to consider before purchasing controllers.

        (1) **Efficiency.** At best, these types of units can offer a 10-15% improvement that brings charge levels up to approximately 85% of nominal capacity.

        (2) **Performance.** It is interesting to note that virtually none of the controller manufacturers can offer any verifiable proof or independent testing to support claims that they in fact improve charging.

    d. **Controller Types.** Some of the more common controllers on the market include the AutoMAC. This controller is parallel connected to the existing regulator. A potentiometer is used to adjust alternator current in conjunction with an ammeter. When a predetermined voltage is reached the unit automatically cuts off and existing regulator takes over.

6.45 **Diesel DC Charging Systems.** An alternative or addition to main propulsion energy charging systems is a dedicated engine powering an alternator, with possibly extra power take-offs for compressors, pumps or desalinator high-pressure water pump. These can be either diesel or gasoline driven. A traditional method has been the use of lay shafts, but they are often complicated and cause some difficulties. Systems are as follows:

a. **Balmar.** Balmar in the US has a unit driven by a FW cooled 13 hp Yanmar diesel. It is installed with a 310 amp brushless alternator, Max Charge regulator, and small start battery alternator. Optional equipment is a 20 or 40 gph watermaker. It is an efficient charging solution and consumes around 0.25 gph, which is economical.

b. **Ample Power Genie.** This unit uses a seawater cooled Kubota diesel fitted with a 120-amp alternator and Smart regulator system.

c. **Stirling Cycle Machine.** This new system is known as the WhisperGen. It is based on a principle developed in 1816, which uses a continuous combustion process with no noise as the motor/generator is hermetically sealed, requires no oil lubrication as there are no moving parts, and no exhaust fumes. Maintenance requirements are also low with burners requiring cleaning every 2000 hours and a low fuel consumption of 0.7l/hr. The DC output is from a permanent magnet DC generator. Ratings are in the 4–6 kW range. Log on to www.victronenergie.com.

6.46   AC Battery Chargers. Battery chargers are generally used as a primary charging source in motorboats that are at the dock continuously or have AC generators on board. Many vessels have had batteries ruined by poor quality chargers due to a marginal overcharge voltage level. The basic principles of most battery chargers are as follows.

a. **Transformation.** The AC mains voltage, either 230 or 110 volts AC is applied to a transformer. The transformer steps down the voltage to a low level, typically around 15/30 volts depending on the output level.

b. **Rectification.** A full wave bridge rectifier similar to that in an alternator rectifies the low level AC voltage. The rectifier outputs a voltage of around 13.8/27.6 volts, which is the normal float voltage level.

c. **Regulation.** Many basic chargers do not have any output regulation. Chargers that do have regulation are normally those using control systems to control output voltage levels. These sensing circuits automatically limit charge voltages to nominal levels and reduce to float values when the predetermined full charge condition is reached.

d. **Protection.** Battery chargers have a range of protective devices that range from a simple AC input fuse to the many features that are described as follows:

(1) **Thermal Overload.** These devices are normally mounted on the transformer, or rectifier. When a predetermined high temperature is reached, the device opens and prevents further charging until the components cool down.

(2) **Input Protection.** This is either a circuit breaker or fuse that protects the AC input against overload and short circuit on the primary side of the transformer.

(3)   **Reverse Polarity Fuse.** A fuse is incorporated to protect circuits against accidental polarity reversal of output leads.

(4)   **Current Limiting.** Limiting circuits are used to prevent excessive current outputs, or to maintain current levels at a specific level.

(5)   **Short Circuit Protection.** Usually this fuse protects output circuits against high current short circuit damage.

e.   **Interference Suppression.** Most chargers have an output voltage ripple superimposed on the DC. This is overcome by the use of chokes and capacitors across the output. This ripple can affect electronics and cause data corruption on navigation equipment.

6.47   Battery Charger Types. There are a number of charger types and techniques in use

a.   **Constant Potential Chargers.** Chargers operate at a fixed voltage. The charge current decreases as the battery voltage reaches the preset charging voltage. Unsupervised charging can damage batteries as electrolytes evaporate and gas forms. Additionally such chargers are susceptible to input volt-

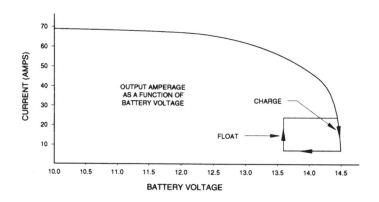

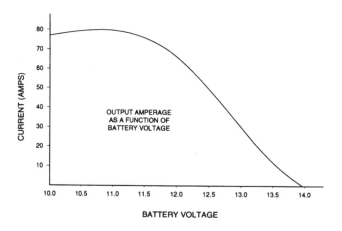

Figure 6-20 Newmar Battery Charger Characteristics

age variations. If left unattended, the voltage setting must be below 13.5 volts, or batteries will be ruined through overcharging. This type of charger must be used for gel batteries.

b.   **Ferro-Resonant Chargers.** These chargers use a ferro-resonant transformer, which has two secondary windings. One of the windings is connected to a capacitor, and they resonate at a specific frequency. Variations in the input voltage cause an imbalance, and the transformer corrects this to maintain a stable output. These chargers have a tapered charge characteristic. As the battery terminal voltage rises, the charge current decreases. Control of these chargers is usually through a sensing circuit that switches the charger off when the nominal voltage level is reached, typically around 15% to 20% of charger nominal rating.

c.   **Switch-Mode Chargers.** Compact switch-mode chargers are becoming increasingly popular due to their compact size and low weights. These charger types convert the input line frequency from 50 to 150,000 hertz. This reduces the size of transformers and chokes used in conventional chargers. An advantage of these chargers is that line input and output are effectively isolated,

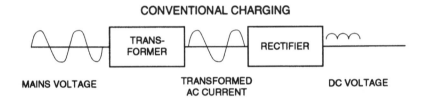

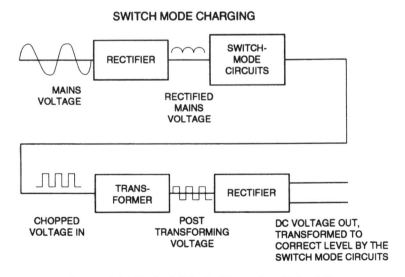

Figure 6-21 Switch Mode Charging Principles

eliminating the effects of surges and spikes. These chargers are my personal choice and I have one installed. The chargers are battery-sensed, temperature-compensated, have integral digital voltmeters and ammeters, and are very compact. The illustration below shows the principle of operation and the various waveform conversions from the AC input to a stable DC output.

d. **Automatic Chargers.** This term covers a large range of electronic controlled charging systems. These include chargers that have SCR or Triac control, a combination of current and voltage settings, with appropriate sensing systems and control systems, as well as overvoltage and overcurrent protection. The ideal charger characteristic is one that can deliver the boost charge required and then automatically drop to float charge levels so that overcharging does not occur.

6.48   **Battery Charger Installation**. Chargers should be mounted in a dry and well-ventilated area. Always switch off battery charger during engine starting if connected to the starting battery. The large start load can overload the charger. Proper bolt on terminal lugs should be used on cables if the charger is permanently installed, not clips. Switch off the charger before connecting or disconnecting cables from battery, as sparks may ignite gases. Do not operate a large inverter off a battery with a charger still operating. The large load can overload the charger and may damage circuitry.

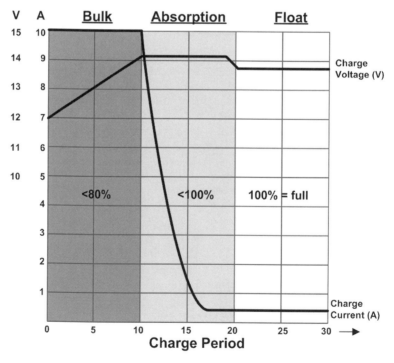

Figure 6-22 Automatic Charging Characteristic

6.49 **Multiple Battery Charging.** Most marina-based boats have a charger connected permanently to charge a single house battery bank. Many boats also have multiple house banks and twin engines with separate batteries. A separate battery charger is required or a method of splitting the charge to each battery. The two or more batteries under charge should also have bridged negatives if the two systems are electrically isolated. Remember that gel cells or AGM batteries may have different requirements and this should be checked prior to using any system, as batteries when fully charged can loose water rapidly if charging is imprecise.

a. **Multiple Output Chargers.** Install a battery charger with multiple outputs, such as those from NewMar. Each battery bank has its own isolated charging outputs, which prevents any interaction and is an efficient way of having two or more separate chargers.

b. **Diodes.** A diode isolator can be used to split the charge between the two or three battery banks. For three battery banks use 2 diode isolators, and link the diode isolator inputs. There are problems of voltage drop across the diode that have to be considered, and battery chargers with battery sensing are required to compensate for this. The typical voltage drop is around 0.7 volts so the charger outputs without sensing will require adjustment of output voltage to an additional level equivalent to the drop.

c. **Relay/Solenoid.** A relay or solenoid can be used to direct the charge current to each battery bank. This is activated either with the monitored charging voltage or via a manually operated switch. The configuration effectively parallels all of the batteries to form a single battery bank. Possible systems include the NewMar Battery Bank Integrator (BBI). When a charge voltage is detected that exceeds 13.3 VDC, the unit switches on. The unit consists of a low contact resistance relay that closes to parallel the batteries for charging. When charging ceases and the voltage falls to 12.7 VDC, the relay opens isolating the batteries. The unit also incorporates a voltage comparator and time delay circuit, which prevents the unit cycling in the event of a voltage transient or load droop on the circuit dropping voltage below the cut-out level. Another similar device is the PathMaker from Heart Interface. These devices allow charging of two or three batteries from one alternator or battery charger. The units use a high current switch rated at 800 and 1600 amps for alternator and charger ratings up to 250 amps.

d. **Smart Devices.** These are intelligent charge distribution devices such as the Ample Power Isolator Eliminator. This is a multi-step regulator that controls charge to the second battery bank, typically the one used for engine starting. It is temperature compensated like an alternator control system and is effectively a secondary charger. Another system is the AutoSwitch from Ample Power, which is a smart solenoid system. An electronic sensing circuit will enable the setting of the different modes. One mode is a timed function that terminates the charging to the second paralleled start battery once the period expires. There is also a voltage mode, which disconnects the second battery after the preset voltage is reached. Other devices such as Charge-Link and Echo-charge perform a similar function. These smart devices reduce the chances of overcharging secondary batteries such as the start or generator battery.

6.50   Solar Energy Systems. Many canal boats, barges and houseboats use solar panels and wind generators to trickle charge batteries when anchored or moored. Solar energy concepts are not new, and date back to 1839 when the French scientist Becquerel discovered the photovoltaic phenomenon. Solar systems are the most commonly used alternative energy sources and offer a renewable and nearly maintenance-free energy source. The fundamental process of a solar cell is that when light falls onto a thin slice of silicon P & N substrate, a voltage is generated. This is called the photovoltaic principle. Cells consist of two layers, one positive, and one negative. When light energy photons enter the cell, the silicon atoms absorb some photons. This frees electrons in the negative layer, which then flow through the external circuit (the battery) and back to the positive layer. When manufactured, the cells are electronically matched and connected in series to form complete solar panels with typical peak power outputs of 16 volts. There a number of solar cell types and this is based on the cell material or structure used:

a.   **Mono-crystalline.** Pure, defect-free silicon slices from a single grown crystal are used for these structures. The cell atomic structure is rigid and ordered and unlike amorphous cells cannot be easily bent. The cells are approximately 12%–15% efficient. The thin pure silicon wafers are etched within a caustic solution to create a textured surface. This textured surface consists of millions of four-sided pyramids, which act as efficient light traps, reducing reflection losses. Panels are made by interconnecting and encapsulating 34–36 wafers onto a glass back.

b.   **Polycrystalline.** These cell types use high-purity silicon 0.2mm wafers from a single block, and are high power output cells. The wafers are bonded to an aluminium substrate. Solarex cells are covered with a tempered iron glass, and a titanium dioxide anti-reflective coating to improve light absorption. The polycrystalline cell has better low light angle output levels and is now the most commonly used.

c.   **Amorphous Silicon.** These cells are formed from several layers applied to a substrate. They have a characteristic black appearance. Solarex cells have a tin oxide coating to improve conductivity and light absorption. Unlike crystalline cells, these thin film panels have a loosely arranged atomic structure and are much less efficient. They do have the advantage that the cells can be applied to flexible plastic surfaces and as such flexible panels are made. Additionally they are capable of generating under low light conditions. Crystalline cells won't do this. The big disadvantage is that power outputs are nearly a quarter of crystalline cells of the same size.

6.51   Solar Ratings, Efficiency and Regulation. Efficiency is at an optimum when a solar panel is angled directly towards the sun and manufacturers rate panels at specific test standards. The most effective panels are rigid units while the flexible units have significantly lower outputs. Output ratings are normally quoted to a standard, typically 1000W/m² at 25°C cell temperature. The level of irradiance is measured in watts per square meter. The irradiance value is multiplied by time duration to give watt-hours per square meter per day. Location and seasonal factors affect the amount of energy available. Cells are approximately 15% efficient and start producing a voltage as low as 5% of full sunlight value. Solar angles are important to the efficiency of panels. With the sun at 90° overhead, panels give 100% output. When angled at 75°, the output falls to approximately 95%. At 50°, the output falls to 75%, and a lower light angle of 30° reduces output by 50%. Many panels now will give some output on dull days, The table shows typical seasonal hours and yearly averages based on solar array tilted towards the sun at an angle equal to latitude of the location +15°.

Table 6-5 Peak Solar Level Table

Location	Winter Hours	Summer Hours	Average
California	4.0	5.0	4.5
Miami	3.6	6.2	4.9
Central Pacific	4.5	6.0	5.3
Caribbean	5.5	5.5	5.5
Azores	2.2	6.0	4.1
Northern Europe	1.5	4.0	2.7
Southern England	0.6	5.0	2.8
South France	2.5	7.5	5.0
Greece	2.4	7.4	4.9
SE Asia	4.0	5.5	4.7
Cape Town	4.0	5.0	4.5
Red Sea	6.0	6.5	6.3
Indian Ocean	5.0	5.5	5.3
Eastern Australia	4.5	5.5	5.0

a.   **Charging System Interaction.** There is often an interaction between solar panels and alternator charging regulators during engine charging periods. In many installations, solar panels are not regulated, and it is quite common to see a voltage of up to 16 volts or more across the battery. Not withstanding the damage to batteries that can occur, when an alternator regulator senses this high voltage level, it simply registers this as a fully charged battery, and as a result, the alternator does not charge the battery, or does so at a minimal rate. When installing panels and regulators, consider installing an isolation switch on the incoming line to the panel so that it can be switched out of circuit. Alternatively, you can automatically disconnect the solar panel via a relay so that the solar panel output does not impress a higher voltage and confuse the alternator regulator.

b. **Panel Regulation.** In any panel over a small 12-15 watt unit, a shunt regulator is required to restrict the voltage to a safe level. It is not uncommon to have voltage levels rise to 15–16 volts, and the boiling dry of batteries over any extended and unsupervised period. The external regulator functions simply to limit panel output voltage to a safe level and prevent damage to a battery. Units may be simple and limit voltage to 13.8 volts, the maximum float level, dissipating heat through a heat sink. More sophisticated units incorporate an automatic boost level of 14.2 volts and a float setting of 13.8 volts. The regulator will float charge the battery until a lower limit of approximately 12.5 volts is reached before switching to boost charge. The regulator eliminates the need for an additional blocking diode.

6.52 **Solar Panel Diodes.** Most panels have diodes. While a diode can reduce the voltage by approximately 0.75V, if you are installing a couple of three amp panels which is typical, you will require a regulator to reduce the voltage to avoid overcharging and damaging your batteries. If the regulator is a good unit, the control will float between 14.5 and 13.8 volts, so this voltage drop will not be a major problem. If the regulator has reverse current protection such as a diode, then the panel-installed unit can be removed to increase the input voltage to the regulator, which will give a marginally higher output. If you are not going to regulate the solar supply, failure to install or leave the diode installed may result in a flat battery overnight. There are two functional uses of diodes: By-pass diodes are normally factory installed within solar module junction boxes. By-pass diodes are used to reduce power losses that might occur if a module within the array is partially shaded. For 12-volt systems, these offer sufficient circuit protection without the use of a blocking diode. In 24-volt systems with 2 or more modules connected in series, the solar modules should be connected in individual series circuits. To obtain the required total array current, the circuits should then be paralleled. If one module of a parallel array is shaded, reverse current flow may occur. Blocking diodes are often connected in series with the solar panel output to prevent discharge of the battery back to the array at night, but not all manufacturers install them as standard. If the panels do not have a diode, then a diode rated to 1.5 times the maximum output (5 amps) should be installed at the regulator input. Most solar regulators will often have the diode incorporated. Panels with a by-pass diode installed in the connection box do not require any further diode.

6.53 **Solar Panel Installation.** Solar panels are manufactured in either rigid or flexible form. Cabling should be properly rated to avoid voltage drop. A 15 amp cable is the minimum size for two 65-watt panels. Use only tinned copper marine cable. Most panels have weatherproof connection boxes and connections should be simply twisted and terminated in terminals. Do not use connectors or solder the wire ends. Manufacturers also specify grounding of array or module metallic frames. I have heard concerns over vessels that have automatic bilge pump arrangements with a solar panel charging the battery. If the pump cable develops a fault, once the battery is flat, a serious electrolytic corrosion problem may develop and corrode skin fittings and hull as a voltage is being applied directly to them. Although theoretically possible, I have never heard of this occurring and it would be extremely rare. Always cover solar panels to prevent a voltage being generated during installation or removal so that accidental short-circuiting of terminals or cables cannot occur. Each panel should be

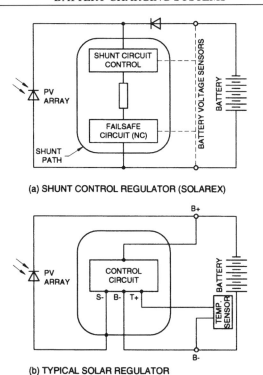

(a) SHUNT CONTROL REGULATOR (SOLAREX)

(b) TYPICAL SOLAR REGULATOR

Figure 6-23 Typical Solar Regulator Systems

securely mounted and able to withstand mechanical loads. Ideally, they should be oriented to provide unrestricted sunlight from 9 to 3 pm solar time. Allow sufficient ventilation under the panel. Most panels in frames have sufficient clearance incorporated into them. Excessive heat levels will reduce output and damage cells.

6.54   Solar Panel Maintenance. Maintenance requirements of solar panels are minimal:

   a.   Cleaning. Panels should be cleaned periodically to remove salt deposits, dirt and seagull droppings. Use water and a soft cloth or sponge. Mild, non-abrasive cleaners may be used, do not use scouring powders or similar materials.

   b.   Connections. Check that the terminal box connections are secure and dry. Fill the box with silicon compound.

6.55   Solar Panel Troubleshooting. Faults are normally the result of catastrophic mechanical damage. A single cell failure will not seriously reduce performance as multiple cell interconnections provide some redundancy. Reliability is very high and manufacturers give 10-year warranties to support this. Faults can be virtually eliminated by proper mounting and regular maintenance. As with all electrical systems, the most common faults are cable connections. Panels are de-rated for several conditions, such as high temperatures, a panel operates 20–25° higher than ambient. The following checks should be carried out if charging is not occurring:

a. Check regulator output for rated voltage, typically 13.2 VDC.

b. Check regulator input, voltage will be typically 14+ volts. Disconnected from battery, it can be up to 17-18 volts.

c. Check panel junction boxes for moisture or corroded connections.

d. Check that panels are clean.

e. Check for shadowing.

f. Check azimuth and tilt angles.

6.56 **Wind Charging Systems.** Wind generators are the second most used alternative source. As with all charging systems, important factors must be considered when deciding whether to install a unit as part of a balanced power system. The following chapter outlines the various factors to consider.

a. **Locations.** Wind generators appear more effective in some areas than others. In the Caribbean they are very effective, and in the Mediterranean, solar power is considered more efficient. If your cruising lifestyle also takes you primarily to sheltered anchorages, they may not be an economical or practical proposition. It is however at anchorages that wind generators are the most useful and give 24-hour charging. The average wind generator typically produces anything from 1 amp to 15 amps maximum depending on the wind speed. Ratings curves are always a function of wind speed and are quoted at rated output voltages. Check each model to suit your particular requirements.

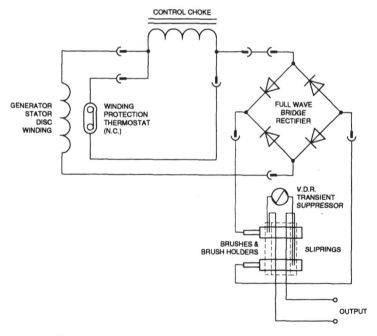

Figure 6-24 Rutland Wind Generator Circuit

> **b.   Generator Types.** Essentially, a wind generator is either a DC generator or alternator driven by a propeller. In the US, the trend is normally for large two- or three-bladed DC generator units. The UK/European trend is for smaller diameter multi-bladed AC alternator units. These units incorporate a heavy hub that acts as a flywheel to maintain blade inertia. Many units have a permanent magnet rotor, with up to 12 poles. A three-phase alternating current is generated and rectified to DC similar to engine driven alternators. The aerodynamically shaped AeroMarine is a three-bladed unit and has a brushless permanent magnet alternator with internal regulator. From many observations in protected marinas and bays, the Rutland is spinning away with the AeroMarine stopped. Log on to www.marlec.co.uk.

6.57   Wind Generator Regulators. A regulator is required to limit normal charging voltages to a safe level (14.5 volts) and to limit output at high wind speeds. Normally, a shunt regulator is preferred over a normal solar panel regulator as it is more suited to constant loads. Shunt regulators divert excess current to a resistor which functions as a heater and dissipates heat through a heat sink. If series regulators are used, a power zener diode should be installed to provide some load when the battery is fully charged. 12-volt systems should use an 18-volt zener diode. The zener must be rated for at least half rated generator output. Like solar panels installations, interaction may occur with alternator charging systems. The charging should be either switched out of circuit or diverted to a battery other than the sensed one (eg start battery). Some units incorporate a choke to limit the charge produced at high wind speeds. A number of generators incorporate a winding embedded thermostat which opens in overload conditions, when the winding overheats. Some units incorporate a transient suppressor, installed to minimize the effects of intermittent spikes being impressed on the charging system, which would otherwise damage the rectifier and onboard electronics. The suppressor is usually a voltage dependent resistor (VDR).

6.58   Wind Generator Installation. The ideal arrangement is on a post, which keeps the blades clear of crew. One of the major complaints is that under load the wind generator creates vibration. It is essential that the post be as thick as possible and well supported. Mountings can also be cushioned with rubber blocks or similar material to reduce the transmission of vibrations.

6.59   Wind Generator Troubleshooting. Always secure the turbine blades when installing, servicing or troubleshooting a wind generator. If no ammeter is installed on the main switchboard, install an ammeter in line and check the charging current level. If there is no output, check the system according to the manufacturer's instructions. If there is no output and the generator has brushes, check that they are free to move and are not stuck. Many generators do not have brushes and commutators, but a set of sliprings are installed with brushes to transfer power from the rotating generator down through the post to the battery circuit. They can jam and on rare occasions cause loss of power. Some generators have a winding imbedded thermostat. Check with a multimeter that it is not permanently open circuited. If it is open circuited, the generator will not charge. The thermostat will open in high wind charging conditions. If the thermostat has not closed after these conditions and the generator case is cold, the thermostat is defective. Regrettably it cannot be repaired unless a new winding is installed. To get the generator back into service, connect a bridge across the thermostat terminals.

a.   Bearing wear will cause excessive vibration. If the unit is a few years old, renew the bearings. Vibration can also be caused by damage to one or more blades, and these should be carefully examined for damage.

b.   Check the rectifier to ensure that it is not open or short-circuited. If the generator output is correct, check the regulator is not malfunctioning. The voltage input may be in the range 14-18 volts, and the output approximately 13-14 volts.

c.   Ensure all electrical connections are secure and in good condition.

Table 6-6 Charging System Troubleshooting

Symptom	Probable Fault	Corrective Action
Reduced charging	Drive belt loose	Adjust to 10 mm
	Oil on belt	Clean belt
	Loose alternator connection	Repair connection
	Partial diode failure	Repair alternator
	Suppressor breaking down	Replace suppressor
	Regulator fault	Replace regulator
	Diode isolator fault	Replace diode
	Negative connection fault	Repair connection
	Solder connection fault	Re-solder connection
	Under-rated cables	Uprate cables
	In-line ammeter fault	Repair connections
	In-line ammeter fault	Replace ammeter
	Ammeter shunt fault	Repair connections
Over charging	Regulator fault	Replace regulator
	Sense wire off	Replace wire
No charging	Drive belt loose	Re-tension belt
	Drive belt broken	Replace belt
	Warning lamp failure	Replace lamp
	Auxiliary diode failure	Repair alternator
	Regulator fault	Replace regulator
	Diode bridge failure	Repair alternator
	Jammed brushes	Clean brushgear
	Stator winding failure	Repair alternator
	Rotor winding failure	Repair alternator
	Output connection off	Repair connection
Negative connection off	Repair connection	
Fluctuating ammeter	Alternator brushes sticking	Repair alternator
	Regulator fault	Replace regulator
	Loose cable connections	Repair connections
High initial start current, low charge current	Ammeter fault/overcurrent	Replace ammeter
	Batteries sulfated	Replace batteries
	Battery cell failure	Replace batteries
	Battery charge very low	Recharge extended time

DC Systems, Installation and Wiring

7.1   Introduction. Approximately 85% of vessel failures can be attributed to improper connections, terminations or incorrectly installed cables. Using accepted wiring practices can eliminate these failures. Unfortunately the common attitude is to treat vessel low voltage systems like automotive installations, and the high failure rates on boats reflect this attitude. Exposure of DC systems to water may cause fire, shock and catastrophic damage. All DC electrical system equipment must be rated for the DC rated voltages, and not AC. Log on to www.ancorproducts.com, www.indexmarine.co.uk, www.newmar.com for quality products.

7.2   Electrical Standards. Electrical systems should be installed to comply with one of the principal standards or recommendations in use, and most standards are similar. The following are what I consider the most recognizable, and for the purposes of this chapter, all references will quote the International Standards Organization (ISO) Standard as applicable. Rules are relatively expensive, and many people are intimidated by the complexities. Many rules are difficult to interpret, as they are not written in plain language, and consist of technical jargon. To make readers aware of typical requirements I am using and quoting a set of recommendations called *The International Recommendations for Boat Electrical Systems (IRBES)* that encompass or exceed many of the provisions of the various standards listed below. They will not cover all of the provisions but they use best practice and will assist in getting your installation to a similar level. Where you are required to use standards, a copy of the relevant standard should be used.

- **European Recreational Craft Directive.** These include EN ISO 10133 Electrical systems—Extra-low-voltage DC installations. EN ISO 13297 Electrical systems—Alternating current installations (revision of ISO 13295, 1995. EN 60092-507 Electrical installations in ships, pleasure craft (Note: for 3-phase systems only). EN 28846, 1993 (ISO 88460, 1990) Electrical devices—Protection against ignition of surrounding flammable gas. EN 28849, 1993 ISO 8849, 1990) Electrically operated bilge pumps. EN ISO 9097, 1994 Electric fans. PrEN ISO 16180 Electric navigation lights. PrEN ISO 16147 Inboard diesel engines—Engine-mounted fuel and electrical components.

- **NFPA 302**, *Fire Protection Standard for Pleasure and Commercial Motor Craft*, 1994 Edition. This standard is approved by the American National Standards Institute and is applicable to motorboat installations. The technical committee includes representatives from ABYC, USCG, Underwriters Laboratories (UL), and others such as the National Association of Marine Surveyors.

- **Lloyd's Register of Shipping.** *Rules and Regulations for the Classification of Yachts and Small Craft.* Normally used when a vessel is to be built to class, it serves as a very high benchmark. Commercial vessels, trawlers and large super yachts may fall under other large ship Rules.

- **American Boat and Yacht Council (ABYC).** *Standards and Recommended Practices for Small Craft.* (www.abycinc.org) These are voluntary standards and recommendations that are widely used by many US boat builders.

- *The International Recommendations for Boat Electrical Systems© (IRBES).* These rules and recommendations cover most of the provisions in the various other recommendations and standards. They are generic in nature and incorporate best installation practice. I developed them over several years in consultation with several marine electrical engineers. Wherever your vessel must comply to Class (Lloyd's, DNV, Bureau Veritas, ABS) survey or other requirements and provisions, such as the USCG in the United States, the European Recreational Craft Directive (RCD) or others, the Rules should be obtained and referenced for the particular installation.

7.3   DC System Voltages. It is quite common to see vessels having both 12- and 24-volt systems in use; 42 volt will also have the same factors. They should be treated as two entirely separate entities. In polarized ground systems the negatives will be at the same potential. This will mean two alternators and two battery banks. The merits of 24 volts for heavy current consumption equipment such as inverters and windlasses are obvious. The cables are half the size and weight of 12-volt systems. In many cases electronics will be able to operate on 24 volts without modification.

a.   **12 (14) Volt Systems.** The 12-volt system is the most common system. This is because of automotive influences, which have led to a large range of equipment being available. 12 and 24 volts are used to power most boat electrical and electronics equipment. It is also possible to purchase virtually any appliance rated for 12 volts.

b.   **24 (28) Volt Systems.** This system is prevalent, especially in commercial applications. It has the advantage of lower physical equipment sizes, cabling, and control gear. Additionally, voltage drops are not as critical. Because much equipment is commonly 12 volts, a DC-DC converter must be used to step down to 12-volt equipment. Although complicating the system, this does isolate sensitive electronics equipment from the surge- and spike-prone power system.

c.   **32 Volt Systems.** This is an old system voltage still found on some vessels.

d.   **36 (42V) Volt Systems.** A new automotive standard voltage to be introduced in 2002 and which may eventually transfer to boats.

e.   **48 Volt Systems.** This system is now starting to become more prevalent, in particular for powering thrusters.

7.4   DC Voltage Conversion. In many vessels, a mix of voltages requires the use of DC converters to step down from 24 to 12 volts. The same will be required for 42 volt systems, if implemented on boats. There are a number of technical points that must be considered when selecting converters.

a. **Power Input.** Converters may be either galvanically isolated or only isolated in the positive conversion circuit. Galvanically isolated units will totally isolate input and output providing protection to connected loads. Good quality converters have a stabilized output of around 13.6 (27.2) volts. Stability is typically about 1% between line and load at rated output voltage. Typical power consumption of a converter without a load connected is approximately 40 to 50 milliamps, so there will always be a small battery drain. The converter should ideally have an isolation switch on the input side. Most converters are installed with automatic thermal shutdown, short circuit fuse protection, current limiting and reverse polarity protection.

b. **Power Output.** Converters are able to withstand a short surge current. Normally a 50% over current can be applied for intermittent surges, and approximately 70% for a very short duration of up to 30 seconds for peak loads. Some high power units can withstand peak overloads of 200% for up to 30 seconds. Duty cycle ratings are also applicable to converters. Intermittent overloads can only be sustained on a cycle of 20 minutes every hour, and peaks for 30 to 60 seconds per hour. Failure to observe these duty cycles will result in a burned-out converter. Converters in common with most electrical equipment are designed to provide an output at a specific temperature range, typically 0–40°C. At 50°C, converters should be de-rated to 50%.

c. **Installation.** Good ventilation is essential. Converters should be mounted so that fins are vertical for convection cooling. Sufficient clearance must be allowed between top and bottom.

7.5 **How to Wire and Rewire Your Boat**. The average motorboat has many systems installed. Equipment is often purchased before the actual impact on the system is considered. Planning the installation requires a carefully considered systems approach. In the majority of cases, systems are over complicated and follow no accepted electrical practice. They have inherent problems that are only overcome with costly total rewires. Do it once and do it right!

Wiring Plan. References are to IRBES Section 1, Chapter 4.

Rule 4.1. Each boat shall have a complete wiring diagram showing all the wiring and systems installed. The diagram should include Equipment Identification, Equipment Current Rating, Cable Sizes, Circuit Breaker and Fuse Ratings, and Circuit Identification.

Perform the following planning tasks.

(1) Make a plan of your vessel and locate every item of equipment on it. Write down the equipment identification name.

(2) Write down the current draw for each item of equipment. Enter these into the battery calculation Table 5.1 and 5.2. This will allow calculations to be made on required battery capacity and charging requirements.

(3)   Draw in the proposed cable route for each item of equipment. Show all bulk-heads, decks or other obstructions. Where the cable will be routed within bilge areas or exposed to mechanical damage, use an alternative route.

(4)   Determine the cable size by using the current draw and calculating the voltage drop within the circuit. It is best to standardize on 15–16 amp cables for most applications, as it is economical to buy cable by the roll. It also elimi-nates the selection exercise based on lowest cable size to achieve specific volt drop values for most, but not all circuits.

(5)   Enter the circuit breaker or fuse rating for the circuit and assign a circuit number. Use a logical sequence, such as switchboard left hand vertical row is No. 1 downwards and so on.

7.6   Wiring Considerations. There are a number of important considerations.

a.   **Hull Material.** The hull material has important implications with respect to wiring systems as well as grounding and corrosion. This is important if you are building a boat, as you can purchase an engine with a fully isolated elec-trical system for a steel or alloy boat.

b.   **Boat Size.** This affects the length of cable runs, with consequentially greater cable weights and voltage drop problems. It is an important factor on canal boats, barges and on catamarans. This affects voltages, and large boats have a real case for selecting 24 volts as the voltage drop problems are reduced. The battery weight and sizes for a given capacity are less, and the equipment weight and size is generally reduced. Larger powerboats have a greater level of accommodation, and therefore more people are often aboard, with longer parties! This places greater demands on the batteries for lighting, electric re-frigeration, with increased requirements on the charging system. Boat builders largely overlook this simple lifestyle factor, but it is significant.

7.7   Wiring Configurations. References are to IRBES Section 1 Chapter 8 and 9.

Rule 8.1. The two preferred systems for distribution are:

Rule 8.1.1. The two-wire insulated system. This system is preferred for all steel and alloy vessels.

All steel and alloy vessels should use the two-wire insulated return system. This configura-tion has no part of the circuit, in particular the negative, connected to any ground or equip-ment. The system is totally isolated, and this includes engine sensors, starter motors and alternators.

Rule 9.17. In two-wire, insulated systems, each outgoing circuit positive and negative supply circuit shall have a double pole short circuit protection and an isolation device installed. This may be incorporated within a single trip free circuit breaker. The isola-tor shall be rated for the maximum current of the circuit.

In this configuration, a short circuit between positive and ground will not cause a short circuit or system's failure. A short circuit between negative and ground will have no effect. A short between positive and negative will cause maximum short circuit current to flow.

Rule 8.1.2. The two-wire with one pole grounded system. This system is preferred for GRP and timber vessels.

This is also called a polarized system. It is the most common configuration, and holds the negative at ground potential by connection of the battery negative to the mass of the engine block.

Rule 8.2. The main negative cable is considered to be the grounded negative conductor in two-wire grounded circuit arrangements.

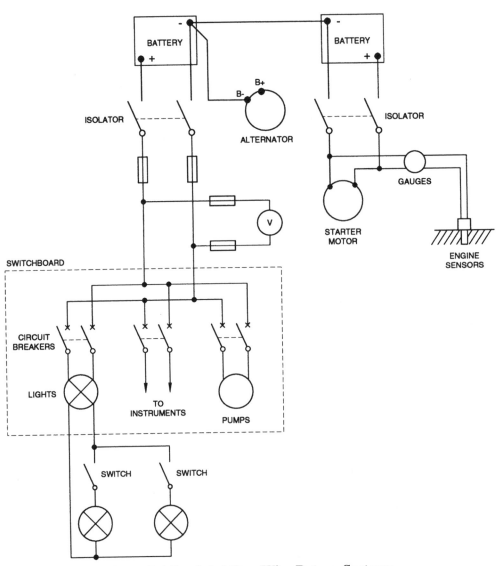

Figure 7-1 Insulated Two Wire Return Systems

In most installations, the main negative to the engine polarizes the system, as the engine mass and connected parts such as shaft provide the ground plane. There should only be one ground conductor.

Rule 9.18. In a two-wire, one-pole grounded system, each outgoing circuit positive supply circuit shall have a short circuit protection and an isolation device installed. This may be incorporated within a single trip free circuit breaker. The earthed pole should not have any protective device installed.

In this configuration, a short circuit between positive and ground will cause maximum short circuit current. A short circuit between negative and ground will have no effect. A short be-

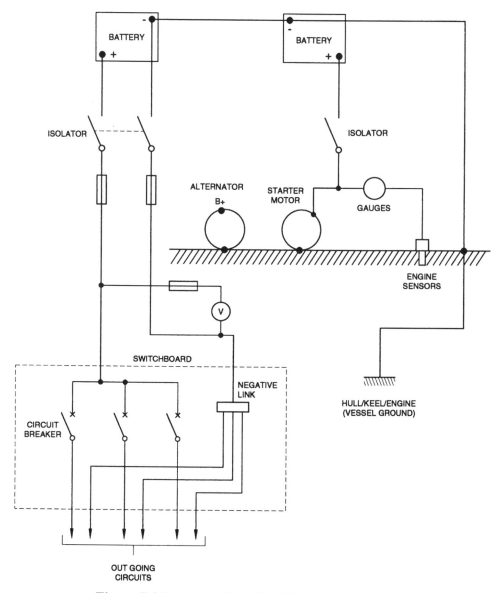

Figure 7-2 Insulated One Pole Grounded Systems

tween positive and negative will cause maximum short circuit current to flow. The single pole circuit breaker will break positive polarity only.

7.8   Distributed Systems. These systems are typically broken down into a system of sub-panels. They are becoming increasingly preferable on larger motorboats. There are a number of significant advantages over a centralized system, including the separation of potentially interactive equipment such as pumps and electronics. Other options include intelligent control systems that have remote control of circuits, and systems such as those from Axon have touch screens to switch circuits. The circuit control boxes have 16 circuits with ratings up to 70 amps.

     a.   Separation enables a reduction in the number of cables radiating throughout the vessel from the main panel to areas of equipment concentration. This is a cause of RFI interference and requires a greater quantity of cable. Most distributed systems run all the sub-circuits from the central panel, with each circuit having a circuit breaker to protect it.

     b.   The illustration below shows the preferable breakdown of sub-circuits and panels. It is based on successful installations on a number of vessels. Only essential services are kept with the metering on the main panel. Lighting panels can be located anywhere practicable; once the circuits are on, lights are switched locally.

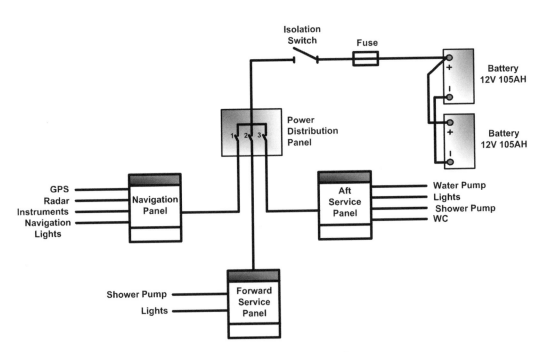

Figure 7-3 Distributed Power Systems

7.9   42-Volt Power Systems. These will require a two-voltage system in a distributed configuration. If such systems are used with motorboats, the following would be a typical arrangement. The higher voltages and lower currents will allow for elimination of relays with solid state switching.

a.   **High Current Consumers.** The 42-volt system will be supplied by a high output water-cooled alternator rated at up to 4kW, which is around 100 amps. Vehicles may use an integrated crankshaft starter alternator. The alternator output will charge a 36-volt battery bank, and a high current consumer panel. This panel will supply the thrusters, hydraulic power unit (HPU), anchor windlass, winches, and possibly autopilots drives and radars. As these consumers are normally powered up when an engine is running, the full 42 are available for use offering significant reductions in weight and size along with reduced cable sizes, and no voltage drop. This will typically give a net saving of 25% in total. A power management system will be also be integrated to manage power within the electrical network.

b.   **Low Current Consumers.** Low power consumers will be supplied from the 36-volt battery bank, or a separate 12 or preferably a 24-volt battery system. These consumers will include the lighting loads, electronics and auxiliary power circuits. Voltage reduction to this equipment would be via a DC-DC converter.

7.10   Circuit Control and Protection. The heart of all electrical systems is the switchboard or panel, which allows control, switching and protection of circuits. The purpose of protection systems is to prevent overload currents arising in excess of the cable rating. They also protect the cables and equipment from excessive currents that arise during short circuit conditions. Circuit protection is not normally rated to the connected loads, although this is commonly done on loads that are considerably less than the cable rating, such as VHF radios or instrument systems. The two most common circuit protective devices are the fuse and the circuit breaker and these are described in the next entries (7.11 and 7.12). The references are from IRBES Section 1 Chapter 9.

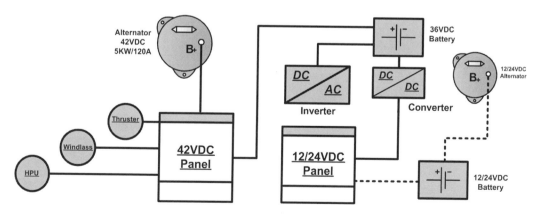

Figure 7-4 42-Volt Power Systems

a. **Short Circuit Current.** A short circuit is where two points of different electrical potential are connected, that is positive to negative.

b. **Overload Current.** An overload condition is where the circuit current carrying capacity is exceeded by the connection of excessive load. Excessive load can come from too many devices or equipment such as pumps with higher than normal load.

Rule 9.1. The switchboard or panel shall be constructed of non-hygroscopic and fireproof material. The panel should be rated to a minimum of IP44.

Switchboard panels are normally made from aluminum, or plastic based materials. Ideally panels should be non conductive; however, many are made of etched aluminum. They should be rated to meet either an IP or NEMA standard against the ingress of water.

Rule 9.2. The switchboard interior shall be fireproof or incapable of supporting combustion.

Survey authorities specify that the internal part of the switchboard should be lined with a fire resistant lining. Line all interior walls with appropriate sheeting.

This will help in containing any fire that may arise in severe fault conditions.

Rule 9.3. The switchboard shall be located in a position to minimize exposure to spray or water.

All switchboards should be installed in a location that is protected from seawater, spray or moisture. Where occasional spray is possible, some protection is recommended, which may be a clear PVC cover or similar measure.

Rule 9.4. DC systems should not be located or installed adjacent to AC systems. Where DC and AC circuits share the same switchboard, they should be physically segregated and partitioned to prevent accidental contact with the AC section. The AC section must be clearly marked with Danger labels.

The DC switchboard should not be integrated with the AC system. Where possible, the AC panel should be located in a different location. This eliminates the chances of accidental contact with live circuits, or confusion between wiring systems. Where systems are integrated, physical separation should be used to prevent contact. The barriers should be well marked warning of the danger.

Rule 9.5. A voltmeter shall be installed to monitor the voltage level of the start battery.

A good quality voltmeter is essential for properly monitoring battery condition. A voltmeter will also indicate if the battery is charging at the correct voltage level. As a battery has a range of approximately one volt from full charge to discharge condition, accuracy is essential. Analog voltmeters are the most common. The sense cable should go directly back to the battery. On service battery connections, most connect directly to the switchboard busbar. Direct connection gives greater accuracy and less influence from local loads. Voltmeters should be of the moving iron type and have a fuse installed on the positive input cable. Half a volt error is quite common. Switch off the meter after checking.

Rule 9.6. A voltmeter should be installed to monitor the voltage level of the service battery. A switch may be installed to enable monitoring of the service and start batteries from the same meter.

The same provisions apply as for start battery voltage monitoring. In practice more attention is given to house battery monitoring. Some switchboards also use LED voltage level indicators, and these devices are often used as a voltmeter substitute. They are not recommended, as they do not give the precise readings required. Digital voltmeters are relatively common and are far more accurate. They are susceptible to voltage spikes and damage; and many have maximum supply voltage ranges of 15 volts. There are a number of types, including Liquid Crystal Displays (LCD) and Light Emitting Diodes (LED). LED types consume power, a LCD meter consumes much less power and is more practical. Where one voltmeter is used to monitor two or more batteries, switching between batteries to voltmeter is through a double pole, center off toggle switch or a multiple battery rotary switch.

Rule 9.7. Voltmeters should have fuses installed within the meter circuit to provide short circuit protection.

A voltmeter is connected across the supply, that is positive and negative, and protection against short circuit is required.

Rule 9.8. An ammeter should be installed to monitor the discharge current rate from the service battery. An ammeter is not required for the starting battery. The installation of an ammeter in the primary charging circuit to monitor the charging current is recommended.

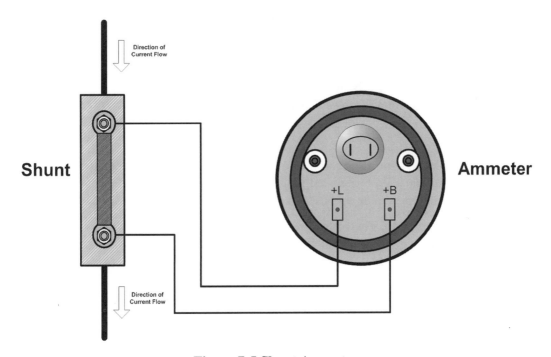

Figure 7-5 Shunt Ammeter

175

Ammeters are essential on the switchboard's input positive to monitor service battery discharge levels. Analog ammeters should be selected for the calculated operating range. Shunt ammeters are also used in these applications. An ammeter installed in the charging system can indicate that current is flowing. Cheaper ammeters are of the series type with the cable under measurement passing through the meter. The major failing of these is that often very long cable runs are required with resultant voltage drops, and if the meter malfunctions damage can occur. Preference should be given to a shunt ammeter. A shunt allows the main current to flow while monitoring and displaying a millivolt value in proportion to the current flowing. The advantage is that only two low current cables are required to connect the ammeter to the shunt, and the risk of damage is reduced. Do not run the main alternator charging cables to the meter location and connect it. This can insert excessive voltage drop into the charging circuit. Install a shunt in the line wherever practical and run sense wires back to the panel mounted meter. The digital ammeter often uses a different sensing system. Instead of a shunt the digital ammeter has a Hall Effect sensor on the cable under measurement. The Hall Effect sensor generates a voltage proportional to the intensity of the magnetic field it is exposed to. For vessel applications, a 0–10 volt transducer output corresponds to a 0–200 amp current flow. Sensitivity is increased, and range reduced by increasing the number of coils through the sensor core.

Rule 9.9. An integrated monitoring device that measures and displays all values is accepted as an alternative to separate meters.

Unlike starting batteries, house battery charge levels cycle up and down, and power level information is critical in determining charging periods. Typical of integrated monitors is the E-meter (Link 10). I have installed one of these on my own boat. These are "intelligent" devices in that they monitor current consumption and charging current. They also have a range of monitoring functions that includes voltage, high and low voltage alarms, amp-hours used and amp-hours remaining. This allows the battery net charge deficit to be displayed. The system also maintains accuracy by taking into account charging efficiency. The charging efficiency factor (CEF) is nominally set at 87%, with the factor being automatically adjusted after each recharge cycle. A falling CEF is indicative of battery degradation. In addition the E-meter also contains a 'n' algorithm for the calculation of Peukerts coefficient. These meters offer a simpler diagnosis of battery power status without trying to guesstimate the actual level based on voltages.

  a. **Shunt.** A meter shunt (500A/500mV) is installed in the negative load line. It is connected by twisted pair wires to prevent noise from induced voltages being picked up and carried into the meter, and corrupting data.

  b. **Protection.** The battery sense lead and DC meter power supply have fuses installed, and these should be checked if the meter fails to function.

Rule 9.10. All protection and switchboard devices shall be clearly marked to properly identify them.

All circuits should be properly labeled to allow easy identification. This should also include the circuit number if practicable.

Rule 9.11. All circuit isolation and protection devices should have visual status indication.

Circuit breaker status indicators consist normally of LED lights, filament lights, or backlit nameplates. Generally Green indicates off and Red is on. An LED requires a resistor in series and this is typically valued at 560 ohms for 12-volt systems. Red filament lamps are also commonly used. The one disadvantage of these is the power consumption, typically around 40 mA. If there are 20 circuits on, this can add up to a reasonable load or drain on the system. If you have a very large switchboard, allow for the current drain. In many cases boaters assume they have a current leakage problem when in fact it is the switchboard indicators causing the drain.

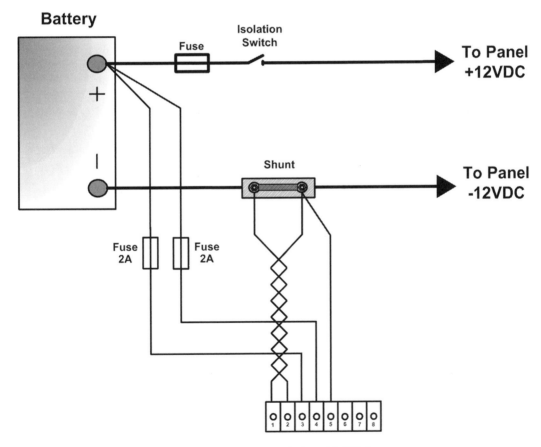

Figure 7-6 E-Meter/Link 10 Wiring

Rule 9.12. All cables and cable looms to switchboard panels shall permit opening of the panel without placing strain on connections or cables.

In many installations, cable looms are too short to allow easy opening of panels for inspection or installation. It is common to have the connectors pulled off the rear of circuit breakers due to the strain on conductors or wiring looms. Looms should be neatly tied in 2 or 3 separate looms. They should have sufficient length to allow complete opening of the switchboard, and the circuit cables should be secured so as to prevent undue mechanical stress on the connectors.

Rule 9.13. All protection and isolation devices shall have an assigned DC fault rating and be approved by a relevant national or international standard. Such standards may include NEMA, UL, CSA, Lloyd's Register and others.

Install only circuit breakers that are approved by UL, CSA or Lloyd's. Approvals for small vessel breakers categorize them as supplementary protectors. I normally use ETA, Ancor and Carling circuit breakers. They must be approved for DC operation and be marked with the rating.

Rule 9.14. The power supply to the switchboard shall have short circuit protection and circuit isolation installed as close as practicable to the battery in both the positive and negative conductors. The isolator should be accessible. This may be incorporated within a single trip free circuit breaker. The isolator shall be rated for the maximum current of the starting circuit.

A circuit breaker rated for the cable should be installed as close as possible to the battery, and be accessible. Fuses can be used, but it is better to combine isolation and protection within one

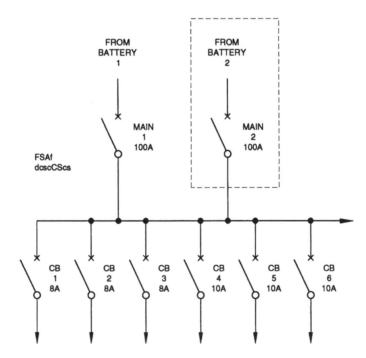

Figure 7-7 Supply Circuit Isolation

device that can easily be reset. They should also be mounted as high as possible above potential bilge and flooding levels. This recommendation does not allow changeover switches.

Rule 9.15. The power supply to auxiliary equipment connected directly to the battery shall have short circuit protection and circuit isolation installed as close as practicable to the battery in both the positive and negative conductors. This may be incorporated within a single trip free circuit breaker.

These auxiliary supplies generally include high current equipment such as thrusters, electric windlasses, winches, toilets, etc connected directly to a battery. A circuit breaker rated for the cable should be installed as close as possible to the battery, and be accessible. They should also be mounted as high as possible above potential bilge and flooding levels.

Rule 9.19. Each navigation light circuit shall have a short circuit protection device installed.

A circuit breaker supplying all navigation lights has the risk of a single fault tripping the breaker and all lights become unavailable until the fault is cleared. This may not be possible in adverse weather conditions. Where possible, separate circuit breakers should be used. Alternatively where a single breaker is used, each circuit should have a replaceable fuse installed. This may be a multi-circuit fuse block or the rear of the switchboard, carrying fuses or circuit breakers for all circuits.

Rule 9.20. Circuits for power and lighting shall be separate.

Circuits should not have mixed consumers, such as power to outlets or motors also connected to lighting equipment.

Rule 9.21. The main bilge should have a separate visual and audible alarm to indicate levels above the normal operating range of automatic systems.

Most boats have automatic bilge pumping systems. If the pump is running and cannot keep up with the water, an additional alarm will indicate the high bilge level. If the float does not operate and the bilge starts to fill, a separate alarm will also indicate the condition. I have experienced both conditions and additional protection is prudent.

Rule 9.22. Where bilge pump control circuits incorporate automatic operation (e.g float switch), caution should be given to the risks of pollution by uncontrolled or unmonitored discharge of oily bilge water.

The majority of bilge pumps have a float switch incorporated to enable automatic unattended operation. Where pumps are running in this mode, you should be aware that uncontrolled discharges of oily bilge water into the water might render you liable for stringent penalties and fines. Consideration should be given to installing suitable filtering equipment.

Rule 9.23. All fuses, distribution busbars, and terminals shall be covered.

Covers should be fitted over all positive and negative busbars, distribution busbars and fuse holders such as slow blow ones used with anchor windlasses. This is a also a requirement of ABYC and protects against accidental contact and water.

7.11   **Fuses.** Fuses are still widely used, and although cheaper than circuit breakers, they have many disadvantages. Control and DC circuit fuses are ceramic or glass type. There are either simple fuse holders or a combination fuse switches. Fuses are either fast acting or dual-element time-delay types. Fast blowing current-limiting fuses, also known as High Rupturing Capacity (HRC) fuses are found in many AC machinery installations. The advantages are a lower initial capital cost. The disadvantage is that when you're in trouble you can't find a spare fuse.

    a.   **Rating Variations.** The typical glass fuse is not always accurate and can rupture as much as 10–50% above or below nominal current rating.

    b.   **Service Fatigue.** Fuse elements fatigue in service with the fuse element properties altering. Vibration also commonly causes failure.

    c.   **Voltage Drop.** There is added contact resistance in the fuse holder between each contact and the fuse ends which commonly causes voltage drops, intermittent supply and heating, and increases with corrosion.

    d.   **Troubleshooting.** Problems are amplified when a circuit has a fault and you go through a box of fuses on a trial and error troubleshooting exercise. A circuit breaker allows simple resetting.

7.12   **Circuit Breakers.** Circuit breakers are the most reliable and practical method of circuit protection. They are manufactured in press button aircraft, toggle, or rocker switch type. They are used for circuit isolation and protection, combining both functions, which saves switchboard space, costs and installation time as well as improves reliability. Single-pole circuit breakers are normally fitted to most vessels; however, classification societies only allow these in grounded pole installations. This is because a fault arising on the circuit will provide a good ground loop and the large current flow will ensure proper breaker interruption. Double-pole breakers are recommended for all circuits, as they will totally isolate equipment and circuits. This is a requirement of many classification or survey authorities.

    a.   **Circuit Breaker Selection.** Circuit breakers must be selected for the cable size that they protect. The rating must not exceed the maximum rated current of the conductor. The cable sizes in Table 7-3 give recommended ratings for single cables installed in well-ventilated spaces. Bunching of cables and high ambient temperatures require de-rating factors. Ratings are given according to IEC Standard 157.

Table 7-1 Circuit Breaker Selection

Wire mm²	AWG	Circ Mils	Current	CB Rating
1.5 mm²	15	3260	7.9–15.9 A	8 Amps
2.5 mm²	13	5184	15.9–22.0	16
4.0 mm²	11	8226	22.0–30.0	20
6.0 mm²	9	13087	30.0–39.0	30
10.0 mm²	7	20822	39.0–54.0	40
16.0 mm²	5	33088	54.0–72.0	60
25.0 mm²	3	52624	72.0–93.0	80
35.0 mm²	2	66358	93.0–117.0	100
50.0 mm²	0	105625	117.0–147.0	120

b. **Discrimination.** The principle of discrimination in both DC and AC circuits is extremely important, but is rarely considered on motorboat electrical systems. A circuit normally should have two or more over-current protective devices, such as the main and auxiliary circuit breakers installed between the battery and the load. The devices must operate selectively so that the protective device closest to the fault operates first. If the device does not operate, the second device will operate protecting the circuit against over-current damage and possibly fire:

(1) Use circuit breakers with different current ratings. This effectively means that at a point on the time delay curve, the first breaker will trip. If it does not and the current value increases, the next will. A point is reached called the limit of discrimination. At this point the curves intersect and both breakers will trip simultaneously.

(2) Use circuit breakers with different time delay curves to achieve the same result.

(3) Use circuit breakers with different time delay curves, current ratings and different breaker types. This enables using all of the above to ensure discrimination.

c. **Tripping Characteristics.** Characteristics are normally given by the manufacturer of the breaker in a curve of current against time:

(1) The greater the current value over the nominal tripping value, the quicker the circuit breaker will trip. In cases of short circuit, tripping is rapid due to the high current values.

(2) Slower tripping characteristics are seen where a small overload exists and tripping occurs some seconds or even minutes after switch on. This happens as the current levels gradually increase.

181

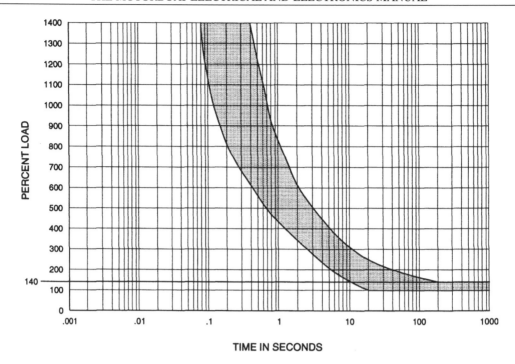

Figure 7-8 Circuit Breaker Time Delay Curve

7.13   **Switchboard Troubleshooting.** There are a number of faults that routinely occur on switchboards and their protective devices. The following faults and probable causes should be checked first. It is assumed that power is on at the switchboard.

a.   **Circuit Breaker Trips Immediately at Switch On.** In most cases, the ammeter shows an off-the-meter, full-scale deflection that indicates a high fault current:

(1)   **Load Short Circuit.** Check out the appropriate connected load and disconnect the faulty item before resetting.

(2)   **Connection Short Circuit.** If after disconnecting the load the fault still exists, check out any cable connections for short circuit, or in some cases cable insulation damage.

b.   **Circuit Breaker Trips Several Seconds After Switch On.** The ammeter shows a gradual increase in current to a high value before tripping off, and is typically an overload condition.

(1)   **Motor Seizure.** This fault may arise if the electric motor has seized or, more probably, the bearings have seized.

(2)   **Load Stalling.** This fault is usually due to a seized pump.

(3)   **Insulation Leakage.** This fault is usually due to a gradual breakdown in insulation, such as wet bilge area pump connection.

182

c. **There is No Power After Circuit Breaker Switch On.** If power is absent at the equipment connection terminals, check the following:

(1) **Circuit Connection.** Check that the circuit connection has not come off the back of the circuit breaker. Also check the cable's connection to the crimp connection terminal.

(2) **Circuit Breaker Connection.** On many switchboards, the busbar is soldered to one side of all distribution circuit breakers. Check that the solder joint has not come away. In some cases, breakers have a busbar that is held under breaker screw terminals. Check that the screws and connection are tight.

(3) **Circuit Breaker.** Operate the breaker several times. In some cases the mechanism does not make proper electrical contact and several operations usually solve the problem by wiping the contacts.

(4) **Circuit Negative.** If all tests verify that the positive supply is present, check that the circuit negative wire is secure in the negative link.

d. **Circuit Power On But No Indication Light.** The LED may have failed, and in some cases the resistor. Also check the soldered connection to the circuit breaker terminal.

7.14 **Conductor Selection.** This chapter references IRBES Section 1 Chapter 10.

Rule 10.1. Conductors shall be selected based on the maximum current demand of the circuit. Ambient temperatures exceeding the rated temperature of the cable should be de-rated by a factor of 0.05 for each 5 °C above.

All cables have nominal cross-sectional areas and current carrying capacities. The *ISO-10133* standard specifies nominal capacities for a range of cross-sectional areas and temperature ranges. Temperature reference is typically 25°C. Table 7-1 illustrates typical current ratings for equivalent cable sizes. Standard cable sizes are used, which is cheaper and simpler to calculate. All cable current carrying capacities are subject to de-rating factors. In any installation where the temperature exceeds the nominal value, the continuous current carrying capacity of the cable is reduced. This is important in engine spaces. Where the temperature exceeds 50°C, the de-rated capacity is the nominal capacity multiplied by 0.75. Consult actual cable manufacturers' ratings for accuracy.

Table 7-2 Typical DC Cable Nominal Ratings

Size AWG	Size mm²	PVC Insulation (Heat Resisting)	Butyl Rubber (Lloyds 100A1)	Resistance Ohms/100m
17	1.0	11 amps	12 amps	1.884
15	1.5	14	16	1.257
	1.8	15		1.050
14	2.5	20	22	0.754
12	4.0	27	30	0.471
10	6.0	35	38	0.314
8	10.0	49	53	0.182
6	16.0	64	71	0.1152
4	25.0	86	93	0.0762
2	35.0	105	119	0.0537
1	45.0	127	140	0.0381
0	50.0	150	160	0.0295
2/0	70.0	161	183	0.0252

In the US the more common method of calculating cable current ratings or ampacity is the use of tables and the following formula.

CM = K x I x L/E

Where CM = Circular Mil area of the conductors

K = 10.75 (a copper resistance constant per mil-foot)

I = Current in amps

L= Conductor length in feet

E = Voltage drop at the load in volts

Rule 10.2. Conductor size shall be selected with a maximum allowable voltage drop of 5% for all circuits. The voltage drop can be calculated using the formula in ISO Standard 10133, Annex A.2.

Voltage drop must always be a consideration when installing electrical circuits. Unfortunately, many voltage drop problems are created by the poor practice of trying to install the smallest cables and wiring sizes possible. The maximum acceptable voltage drop in 12-volt systems is 5% or 0.6 volt. The voltage drop problem is prevalent in starting and charging systems, thrusters, windlasses, and in long runs to equipment. The following formula is that specified in ISO Standard 10133, Annex A.2.

$$\text{Voltage Drop at Load (volts)} = \frac{0.0164 \times I \times L}{S}$$

S is conductor cross-sectional area, in square millimeters

I is load current in amperes

L is cable length in meters, positive to load and back to negative.

Example: Anchor Windlass. These cable sizes must be calculated at working and peak loads. As the calculations show, a larger cable size ensures less voltage drop and fewer line losses. Working-load current = 85 amps, cable run = 12 meters, CSA = 35 mm², rating = 125 amps.

$$\text{Drop at 85 amps} = \frac{0.0164 \times 85 \times 24}{35}$$

$$= 0.96 \text{ V } (35\text{mm}^2) \text{ } 0.67 \text{ V } (50 \text{ mm}^2)$$

$$\text{Drop at 125 amps} = \frac{0.0164 \times 125 \times 24}{35}$$

$$= 1.41\text{V}(35 \text{ mm}^2) \text{ } 0.98 \text{ V } (50 \text{ mm}^2)$$

Rule 10.4. Conductors should be insulated and sheathed (double insulated).

Double insulated cables should be used on all circuits to ensure insulation integrity. Additionally, insulation is temperature rated which has important implications with respect to ratings. In most vessels PVC insulated and PVC sheathed cables rated at 75°C are used. For classification societies, ship wiring cables that use Butyl Rubber, CSP, EPR or other insulating materials are specified. They have higher temperature ratings and subsequently also have higher current carrying capacities.

Rule 10.5. Conductors should be identified as red for the positive conductor, and black for the negative conductor. Numbered cores are an acceptable alternative; the numeral 1 shall be positive and numeral 2 negative.

This is the common system worldwide. Many years ago, AC systems moved to IEC standards to avoid confusion, leaving black and red for DC, and brown and light blue for AC. This did not take place in the US and recently this was further complicated with the ABYC nominating yellow as a negative polarity color. Yellow is also a primary AC phase, switching or control circuit color so exercize care. Some ship wiring cables often have only white cores, with numbering imprinted on the insulation. Ensure that AC and DC are not in proximity to avoid any possible confusion.

Rule 10.6. Conductors shall be of stranded and tinned copper.

When untinned copper is exposed to saltwater spray or moisture, it will very quickly degrade and fail. The argument used against the installation of tinned copper is cost. The price differential is typically 30% greater and the reliability (and vessel resale increase) advantages far outweigh the lower priced plain copper conductor.

Rule 10.7. All conductors shall have a minimum cross-sectional area of 1.0mm².

The minimum conductor size to be used shall be 1.0mm² (16 AWG). It is recommended that conductor sizes be standardized to 2.5 mm² (13 AWG).

Rule 10.8. Where cables are bunched the cables should be de-rated.

When several (6-8) cables are bunched in a large loom, the current capacity of the cable is reduced. The factor is typically around the nominal rating multiplied by 0.85. This may become an issue in very large boats only.

Rule 10.9. Where cables carry large currents for short time durations, they should be used subject to duty cycles.

Heavy current carrying cables such as those used on windlasses, winches, thrusters and starter motors are in fact only used for short durations. As there is a time factor in the heating of a cable, smaller cables can be used. The table shows battery cable ratings that are rated at 60% duty.

Table 7-3 Battery Cable Ratings

Size AWG	Size B & S	Size Mm²	Current Rating (60% Duty)
8	8	8	90 amps
6	6	15	150 amps
4	3	26	200 amps
2	2	32	245 amps
1	0	50	320 amps
00	00	66	390 amps

7.15   Conductor Installation. This chapter references IRBES Chapter 11.

Rule 11.1. Cable runs should be installed as straight as practicable. Cable bend radii shall be a minimum of 4 x cable diameter.

Cables should be neatly installed in as straight a run as practicable. Tight bends should be avoided to reduce unnecessary strain on conductors and insulation. The minimum cable bend radii are applicable to all cables. Particular care should be taken with larger and more inflexible cables, and x 6 is a better target radius.

Rule 11.2. Cables should be accessible for inspection and maintenance.

The emphasis must be on accessibility, both for initial installation, maintenance and for the addition of circuits. Under no circumstances should you fiberglass in cables. All cables, in particular those entering transits, should be capable of routine inspection.

Rule 11.3. Cables shall be protected from mechanical damage, either where exposed, or where they are within compartments.

All cables should be installed to prevent any accidental damage to the insulation, cutting of the conductors, or place undue strain on the cable. Even though cables are routed through lockers, machinery spaces and cupboards, the cables require protection. In many cases, faults are traced to what are considered safe areas. Objects and equipment are thrown into the space, and sharp edges damage the cable or insulation. In machinery or engine spaces, cables are often damaged during engine repairs.

Rule 11.4. Cables passing through bulkheads or decks shall be protected from damage using a suitable non-corrosive gland or bushing. Cables transiting decks or watertight bulkheads should maintain the watertight integrity.

Cable glands are designed to prevent cable damage and ensure a waterproof transit through a bulkhead or deck. A significant number of problems are experienced with the ingress of water through deck fittings and I have seen a variety of methods used. Running cables through GRP with some sealant invariably results in chafing and cable failure. Use circular multi-core cables if possible to ensure proper gland sealing is possible. The purpose designed Index (Thrudex) types are recommended. The structural material of a deck has to be considered before selecting glands. A steel deck requires a different gland type to a foam sandwich boat.

Rule 11.5. Cables shall be supported at maximum intervals of 200mm. Supports and saddles are to be of a non-corrosive material. Where used in engine compartments or machinery spaces, these should be metallic and coated to prevent chafe to the cable insulation. Cable saddles should fit neatly, without excessive force onto the cables, or cable looms, and not deform the insulation.

Cables can be neatly loomed together and secured with PVC or stainless saddles to prevent cable loom sagging and movement during service. While the recommendation is 450mm apart in *ISO 7.3,* the closer support distances secure the cables more efficiently. I prefer standard electrical PVC conduit saddles, which come in a variety of sizes. It is important to have a neat fit, and not force saddles over cables or looms so that insulation is deformed. In machinery spaces metal saddles are often used; however, they should have a plastic sleeve placed on them to prevent the sharp edges chafing the cable insulation.

The PVC cable tie or tie-wrap is universal in application. It should be used where looms must be kept together, or where any cable can be securely fastened to a suitable support. Do not use cable ties to suspend cables from isolated points, as this invariably causes excessive stress and cable fatigue. For internal cable ties, you only require the white ones, and any external cable ties should be the black UV-resistant type.

PVC spiral wrapping is an extremely useful method for consolidating cables into a neat loom. If a number of cables are lying loose, consolidate them into some spiral wrap, and then fasten the loom using cable ties.

A hot glue gun is often used to fasten small or single cables above headliners, or in corners behind trim and carpet finishes. It is useful where there is no risk of cables coming loose. Do not use on exposed cable runs.

Rule 11.6. Cables shall be as far as practicable separated into power, signal, data and heavy current carrying groups. Instrument and data cables should be installed as far as practicable from power cables, and communications aerial cables. A minimum distance of 300mm (12") is recommended. AC cables shall not be run within DC system cable looms, and shall be kept separate.

Cables should be separated into signal, instrument cables or DC power supply cables. Where space allows, also separate heavy current carrying cables such as windlass or thrusters. This is to minimize induced interference between cables, in particular on long, straight parallel runs. All data and instrument cables should be routed as far as practicable away from power cables. Aerial cables should also be routed well way from power cables. AC and DC cables must be kept separated *(ISO 7.7)*.

Rule 11.7. Where cables may be exposed to heat, they should be installed within conduits or otherwise protected from the heat source.

Cables installed with machinery or engine spaces should be rated for the maximum heat of the space. In addition, where cables may be exposed to heat sources, such as exhaust manifolds or piping, they should be protected.

Rule 11.8. Where cables are installed within conduits, they should be supported within 75mm (3") of both entry and exit points. Conduit ends should be treated, or otherwise protected to remove sharp edges and prevent chafe to cable insulation.

Conduits are often installed during the construction phase, and this allows cables to be easily pulled in, replaced, or added. Conduits offer good mechanical protection to cables. In many cases, single-insulated cables are run in conduit back to the switchboard. As the cables are single insulated, they are exposed where they enter or exit the conduits, and should be supported by saddle or clamp to prevent excessive movement. Avoid installing large bunches of cables in flexible conduits as they tend to move around and chafe. PVC conduits should not be used in machinery spaces. Where cables exit conduits, the exit should have a bushing installed to prevent chafing. During installations when pulling in cables, insulation is frequently damaged as insulation rubs against sharp edges.

Rule 11.9. All externally installed cables should be protected against the effects of ultraviolet (UV) light.

Continued exposure to UV on external equipment cables will result in insulation degradation and failure. Small cracks in the insulation allow water to penetrate the conductor and subsequently degrade the copper. This is common on navigation lights, GPS aerial cables, radio aerial cables and other equipment. All exposed cables should be covered in black UV resistant spiral wrapping to prevent rapid degradation of insulation. Cable ties should also be of the black UV resistant type. Use tinned copper conductors on all external wiring to navigation lights, spotlights, and cockpit lights.

Rule 11.10. Connections should be minimized within any circuit between the power supply and the equipment.

Connections and joins in cables should be avoided. Any connection adds resistance to a circuit and introduces another potential failure point.

Rule 11.11. Equipment grounds should be made to the same point as the battery negative ground point.

Equipment grounds, such as pump casings, are usually connected to the boat ground. In many cases, a ground terminal block is installed close to instruments. A large ground conductor is taken to the same point as the battery negative connection point. This is not the battery but actual termination point.

Rule 11.12. Electrical equipment and cables should not be installed within any compartment or space that may contain equipment or systems liable to emit explosive gases or vapors. This may include spark ignition engine fuel systems, LPG installations or flooded cell battery installations. Where any equipment or fittings are to be installed, they shall be ignition protected in accordance with the appropriate national standards.

No cables, connections or equipment should be installed in any space subject to gas or vapors. Equipment or fittings must be classified as ignition proof by an appropriate organization, such as UL.

7.16   Instrument and Data Cable Installation. This chapter references IRBES Section 1, Chapter 14.

Rule 14.1. Instrument and data cables should be installed as far as practicable from power cables and communications aerial cables. Long parallel runs close to power cables should be avoided.

Cables should be separated as far as possible from power supply cables, and heavy current carrying cables such as the windlass or thruster. This is to minimize induced interference between cables, in particular on long, straight runs. Cables should also be routed well away from aerial feed cables.

Rule 14.2. Where instrument and data cables cross power cables, this should be done as close to an angle of 90° as practicable.

This is to prevent induced interference with right angle crossovers.

Rule 14.3. Navigation, autopilot and position fixing equipment shall be located as far as practicable from radar, satellite communications equipment, VHF, HF, HAM and cellular telephone equipment, tuners and control units, cables, aerials, antennae and related components. A minimum clearance distance of 1m is recommended.

Where practicable, electronics equipment, control modules, processors, etc., should be located clear of cable looms and aerial cables to prevent interference. This should include all satellite communications and television systems, and cellular telephones. Autopilots are prone to interference causing major uncontrolled course alterations.

Rule 14.4. Screens should be grounded at one end only, or in accordance with specific manufacturers recommendations.

Conductor screens should be grounded as recommended by the equipment manufacturer. The termination is normally at the equipment end.

Rule 14.5. Electronic equipment grounds should be made to the same point as the battery ground, or in accordance with specific manufacturer's recommendations.

Equipment grounds are usually connected to the boat ground. In many cases, a ground terminal block is installed close to instruments. A large ground conductor is taken to the same point as the battery negative connection point. This is not the battery but actual termination point.

7.17   Grounding Systems. The following chapters on lightning, corrosion, AC power systems, radio systems will all make reference to grounding systems. It is crucial to understand what the various grounds are and their importance within respective circuits as well as to each other. Confusing the functions is a principal cause in system problems.

a.   **DC Negative.** The DC negative is not a ground. It is a current carrying conductor that carries the same current that flows within the positive conductor. In a single-circuit wiring configuration, it may be bonded to a grounded point, usually the mass of the engine. The engine is connected to an immersed item such as the steel hull or prop shaft. This is used to polarize the system and does not actually carry current.

b.   **Lightning Ground.** A lightning ground is also a point at ground potential that is immersed in seawater. It only carries current in the event of a lightning strike and the primary purpose is to ground the strike energy. It is not a functional part of any other electrical system, and should not be interconnected.

c.   **Cathodic Protection System Ground.** The cathodic protection system ground is effectively the sacrificial anode that is connected to protected underwater items via bonding wires.

d.   **AC Ground (or Earth).** The AC ground is a point at ground potential that is immersed in seawater. Under normal operating conditions, it carries no voltage or current. The primary purpose is that, under fault conditions, it will carry fault current to ground and hold all connected metal to ground potential. It will ensure operation of protective equipment, and protect against electric shock from exposed metal parts. In most cases where it is connected, it is to the same point as the DC negative. The main stated justification is that where the DC negative and AC ground are not connected, and a short circuit condition develops between the AC hot conductor and a DC negative or bonding system, this would result in the AC protection not tripping. This may cause energization of these circuits up to rated voltage, creating a risk to persons in contact. There are other stated risks of potentially fatal shock risks to swimmers. A separate ground plate is a good option to ensure total isolation from other systems, as is the proper separation of DC systems. The practice of bonding DC and AC has created much controversy due to well documented cases of corrosion.

e.   **Radio Frequency Ground.** The radio frequency ground is an integral part of the aerial system and is sometimes termed the counterpoise. The ground only carries RF energy and is not a current carrying conductor. It is not connected to any other ground or negative.

f. **Instrument Ground.** The instrument ground, which most GPS and radar sets have, is nominally vessel ground. In many cases, a complete separate ground terminal link is installed behind the switchboard, and to which the screens and ground wires are connected. A separate large low resistance cable is then taken to the same ground point as other grounds. Do not simply interconnect the DC negative to the link as equipment may be subject to interference.

7.18 **Conductor Terminations.** This chapter references IRBES Section 1, Chapter 12.

Rule 12.1. All conductors should be terminated where practicable using crimped connectors. Where cables are terminated within terminal blocks, they should be secured to prevent contact with adjacent terminals.

The most practical and common method of cable connection are the tinned-copper, crimp terminals or connectors. These are color coded according to the cable capacity that can be accommodated. Terminals are usually designed and manufactured according to NEMA standards, which cover wire pullout tension tests, and voltage drop tests. Where possible, select double crimp types, which should be used in high vibration applications.

When crimping use a quality ratchet-type crimping tool, not a cheap pair of squeeze types. These do not adequately compress and "capture" the cable subsequently causing failure as the cable pulls out of the connector sleeve. A good joint requires two crimps. Always crimp both the joint and the plastic behind it. Ensure that no cable strands are hanging out. Poor crimping is a major cause of failure. A crimp joint can be improved by lightly soldering the wire end to the crimp connector, but excessive heat must be avoided. After crimping, give the connector a firm pull to ensure that the crimp is secure.

Table 7-4 Standard Cable Connectors Table

Color	AWG	Cables Sizes	Current Rating
Yellow	12-10	3.0 to 6.0 mm^2	30 amps
Blue	16-14	1.5 to 2.5 mm^2	15 amps
Red	22-18	0.5 to 1.5 mm^2	10 amps

Quick-disconnect (spade) connectors are commonly used, particularly on switchboards. When using, always select the correct quick-disconnect (spade) terminals for the intended cable size. Female connectors are easily dislodged, and there is a tendency for these types to slip off the back of circuit breaker male terminals, so ensure they are tight to push on. Ensure that the terminal actually goes on the CB terminal, and not in between the insulation sleeve and the connector. For heavy duty, look at using heat-shrink fully insulated types. It is important not to apply too much strain on the cables.

Ring terminals are used on all equipment where screw, stud, bolt and nut are used. They should also be used on any equipment subject to vibration, or where accidental dislodging can be critical, particularly switchboards. Always ensure that the hole is a close fit to the bolt or screw used on the connection, which ensures a good electrical contact and use spring washers. One practical method used to prevent nut or screw creep is to dab on a spot of paint.

In-Line Cable (Butt) Splices. Where cables require connection and a junction box is impracticable, use insulated in-line butt splices. This is more reliable than soldered connections, where a bad joint can cause high resistance and subsequent heating and voltage drop. Use heat shrink insulation over the joint to ensure waterproof integrity is maintained. When heated, some connectors form a watertight seal by the fusing and melting of the insulation sleeve. These are ideal for bilge pump connections.

Pin Terminals. Pin terminals can make a neat cable termination into connector blocks; however, I have found these to be unreliable simply because vibration and movement work them loose. In most cases they do not precisely match the connector block terminal and make an inadequate electrical contact.

Snap Plug (Bullet) Terminals. These are useful where used in cabin lighting fittings. I often use these on all cable ends, female on the supply and male on the light fitting tails. This makes it easy to disconnect and remove fittings.

Wire Terminations. Cable ends should have the insulation removed from the end, without nicking the cable strands. The bare cable strands should be simply twisted, and inserted in the terminal block or connector of a similar size. Ensure there are no loose strands. If you are terminating into an oversize terminal block, twist and double over the cable end to ensure that the screw has something to bite on.

Rule 12.2. Conductor terminations shall not be soldered.

Do not solder the ends of wires prior to connection. In most cases, this is done to make a good low resistance connection and prevent cable corrosion. In my experience, soldered connections cause many problems, with the solder traveling up the conductor causing stiffness. This creates greater vibrational effects at the terminal with resultant fatigue and failure. In most cases, the soldering is poorly done, making a high resistance joint. A soldered cable end also prevents the connector screw from spreading the strands and making a good electrical contact, causing high resistance and heating. Use connectors of the correct size for the cable.

Rule 12.3. Conductor terminations shall be marked with a number. The negative and positive cable should be marked with the same number. Identification shall be consistent with the wiring diagram.

Always mark cable ends to aid in reconnection and troubleshooting. The numbers should match those on the wiring diagram. A simple, slide-on number system can be used. The stick-on adhesive types should be avoided as they generally unravel and fall off. If wires are color-coded, use additional numbers, as they are easier and much quicker to identify. Commercial shipping use numbers.

The circuit positive should sequentially match the supply source such as the circuit breaker. The circuit negative should match the positive, and be placed in the same sequential order on the negative link. The numbering convention if unmarked is left to right.

Rule 12.4. Where connections are made within any area subject to water or moisture, such as bilges, the terminations should be made as far as practicable near the top of the bilge. Connections should be suitably protected against water ingress.

Connections should be made above the maximum bilge water level. Joints should be finished with self-amalgamating tapes, or heat shrink tubing. I have frequently seen connections permanently immersed and fail. In automatic bilge circuits, the live connection also contributes to corrosion problems in some boats.

Rule 12.5. Plugs and sockets where used for the connection of cables or equipment should incorporate screw retaining rings, and protective caps to prevent the ingress of water when not in use. They should be rated to a minimum of IP54.

Deck plugs and sockets are often used instead of deck glands and junction boxes at a mast base or as outlets for hand spotlights. Many are of inferior quality and prematurely fail. Do not use the cheap chrome plugs and sockets, as they are not waterproof. The best units on the market are either the Bulgin type units from Index or those from Dri-plug. When using deck plugs, ensure that the seal between the deck and connector body is watertight. Leakage is very common on wet decks up forward where they are usually located. Make sure that the cable seal into the plug is watertight. It is of little use having a good seal around the deck and plug to socket, if the water seeps in through the cable entry and shorts out terminals internally as is often the case. Most connectors have O-rings to ensure a watertight seal. Check that the rings are in good condition, are not deformed or compressed, and seat properly in the recess. A very light smear of silicon grease assists in the sealing process. Ensure that the pins are dry before plugging in and that pins are not bent or show signs of corrosion or pitting. Do not fill around the pins with silicon grease, as this often creates a poor contact. Keep plugs and sockets clean and dry.

Rule 12.6. Where connections are made, they should be protected within a suitable junction box, and installed in a protected area.

Junction boxes are the most practical way to terminate a number of cables, especially where access is required to disconnect circuits. To reduce the number of cables radiating back to the switchboard and minimize voltage drops, I use one junction box forward and one aft to power up lighting circuits. Terminal blocks are usually used, and in many cases, the box is too small for the quantity or size of cables. In these cases, the box lid is forced on, applying pressure to the cables. This should be avoided as unnecessary stress is applied to terminations.

Rule 12.7. Cables terminated within a junction box should enter from the bottom, and be looped to prevent water entering the box and connections.

All cables should enter from the bottom. Junction box upper surfaces should have no openings that permit the entry of water. Cables looped in at the bottom will allow water to drip off, and prevent surface travel to the connections.

Rule 12.8. Cables within junction boxes should be marked with numbers that correspond to circuit numbers used at the main switch panel.

Cable ends should be numbered to aid in reconnection and troubleshooting. The numbers should match those on the wiring diagram.

Rule 12.9. The main negative cable should be secured on the engine using a spring washer, to prevent the connection becoming loose from vibration.

The main engine negative cable is prone to vibration from the engine. It frequently comes loose causing starting problems, intermittent equipment operation, interference, and in some instances alternator failures. In most cases, it is simply fastened to a convenient bolt. The mating surface must be cleaned to ensure a good electrical contact, and a spring washer used to maintain tension.

7.19   Circuit Testing. This chapter references IRRBES Section 1, Chapter 13.

Rule 13.1. The insulation resistance between conductors, or conductors and ground of all circuits or the complete installation shall be greater than 100,000 ohms. All fuses, circuit breakers and switches are to be closed. A low voltage test instrument (50 to 100 VDC) should be used. Tests shall be made with all equipment, lamps and electronic equipment disconnected.

All circuits should be tested to verify the levels of insulation are satisfactory on the entire system, and on each circuit. When testing, power should be disconnected, and a minimum test voltage of twice the rated voltage, i.e. 12 VDC requires minimum of 24 VDC test voltage, and 24 VDC requires 48 VDC. Supply circuit breakers should be switched on so that the switchboard is included within the test. A multimeter set on the resistance range should be used between the positive and negative conductors. If readings are low, check that a load is not connected.

7.20   Auxiliary DC Equipment. Motorboats have several auxiliary electrical systems and equipment:

    a.   **Horns.** Most motorboats have horns, and larger ones must meet IMO COLREG's standards. These are exposed to weather, so corrosion of parts and failures of connections due to water ingress are common. Horns may have an integral motor driving a rotary air compressor. Like all rotating equipment, these can seize up. Many horns are also air powered and electromagnetically operated, and the air solenoid valves often corrode and seize. Vessels larger than 75m have to have horns with outputs in the 130-350 Hz, 135dB range in single, two or three tone outputs. Units may also have integral heating for cold climate use.

    b.   **Davits/Passerelles/Gangways.** Many boats have powered systems, either DC or AC motorized through gearboxes or hydraulic. Motorized units often suffer from seizure due to corrosion as they are exposed to the elements. Regular operation, and wrapping with Denso grease tape or other sealing method is a good preventive measure for motors and control boxes. Some davit systems will also have micro-switches and these should be inspected regularly. If they jam and don't operate when recovering a boat, you may end up damaging or breaking the fall wires and damaging the boat. Outside control stations also require regular inspection.

c.   **Pilot Chairs.** Some vessels have pilot chairs with electric servo adjustment of lumbar and seat back; at the luxury end heating and ventilation are possible. The chairs have an integral control panel for all functions. Common faults are mechanical damage to the panel and wiring. Regular inspection of wiring looms is recommended for chafe and wear. Powered systems such as those from Recaro and Stidd (www.stidd.com) are powered by a 12 VDC permanent magnet motor operating at 7500rpm through a 30:1 reduction gear. Motors have a duty cycle of 60% and this should be remembered when adjusting the seat. Some chairs such as the Norsap 1500 have armrest-mounted joysticks and maneuvering controls, and these are generally installed on larger vessels.

7.21   Elevators. Some of the larger vessels may have small passenger, galley or dumb waiter elevators installed. These may be traction-geared types or hydraulic systems. Many newer systems also use PLC control systems. There are strict rules regarding elevators defined by ABS, LRS, DNV and others. Elevators have defined operational conditions for rolling and pitching, Lutz systems are typically up to 30° roll and 15° pitching. The typical problems include sensors on doors, limit switches, and brake operation.

a.   **Car will not move after request or command.** Check that doors are closed and switches activated, or obstruction sensors are not activated. Check that the overload has not tripped. Check that car has not gone too low or high and activated the safety cutouts. Check that motor fuses have not blown. If the fuse ruptures, check the load with an ammeter. This can be caused by excess weight in the car, seizing of the drive motor or high hydraulic pump loads. Where variable voltage variable frequency (VVVF) drives are used, check that they are operational. Where PLCs are used check that they are operational, in most cases inputs may be absent preventing the system from starting.

b.   **Car stops in high, or low position.** This is often caused by overloading of the car, brake problems or misalignment of limit switches. Do not lower the car using emergency release with people inside.

c.   **Hydraulic ram systems.** Check system for leaks, also that oil reservoirs are full. Check that directional control valve solenoids are operating.

7.22   Window Systems. Most boats have bridge and windshield wiper systems, washer systems and some have heating systems.

a.   **Windshield Wipers.** Most power and motorboats have wipers and they tend to have the high failure rates due to corrosion and seizure of the pantograph arm mechanisms. Marine grade systems have marinized components such as Exalto (www.imtra.com) and have sealed heavy-duty motor units. They come in various configurations, either fan or parallel type, with either single or dual wiper motors. Choose the inside motor versions if at all possible. Most have variable speed functions, which are generally reliable. On DC units, this is a variable resistance. Some units also have the option of a heater to prevent freezing. Power supplies are either 12/24 VDC or 115/220 VAC; the typical power consumptions are in the range 26W to 96W depending on the motor torque which can range from 23Nm up to 80Nm. Some systems can cause RFI interference problems and this should always be checked if there is a problem. Heaters should also be routinely operated and moisture ingress is the most common problem. The rubber blade inserts can suffer degradation due to ultra violet exposure and should be checked and replaced if deteriorating to maintain wiping efficiency. Protection is typically a 3–4 amp fuse and spares should be carried.

b. **Washing Systems.** It is not always easy to access bridge windows to clean salt off. In many boats, jet-washing systems are installed, and these are supplied either directly off the boats freshwater system, or from refillable reservoirs. The washing jets are mounted either on the wiper arms or on the bulkhead. Systems supplied with water off the pressurized water system have a switch operated solenoid valve on the water supply. These are simple systems that are energized from a switch. Reservoir systems have integral pumps; these should be operated regularly to avoid seizure, they also allow use of antifreeze solutions to be added. Common problems are switch contacts, loose connections and seizure of the solenoid through lack of use. It is good practice to operate on a regular basis. Always use caution when operating wipers, as hard salt crystals are very abrasive. The window should be wet before operation. Some water jet systems may also incorporate heating, and typically these are rated at 115W.

c. **Wiper Speed Control.** Wiper systems usually have a variety of control options, ranging from simple push-pull switches to touch pad control that uses relays for switching. The basic systems offer 2-speed operation for single or dual motors, and self-parking of arms when switched off. More sophisticated systems also incorporate intermittent wipe action, while electronic controlled systems offer more intermittent speed options, and synchronization of multiple wipers. The function relays are generally reliable and, where microprocessor controlled synchronization units are installed, they are generally resilient to voltage spikes; however, failure can be often attributed to such faults.

d. **Clearview Screens.** Rotating clearview screens are popular on many boats, such as ocean going workboats prone to heavy spray, ice and snow which wipers cannot cope with. The optically ground armored glass screens are dynamically balanced and rotate at high speeds, in the range of 1600-1900 rpm and centrifuge the water off instantly. Normal speeds take approximately 25–50 seconds to reach. Units may have a center mounted drive motor or be belt-driven types. The rotating glass is also relatively heavy to provide inertia and maintain the high speeds. Typical power consumption is 2.5–3.5 A for

12 VDC systems. Some systems, such as those from Speich and Wynn Kent are available in all DC and AC voltages up to 3 phases. Some units may also have an optional heating element and demisting; these typically consume 40W at 12 volts, and 60–150W for 24 VDC. Systems also have inbuilt radio interference suppressors. The main failure areas are the motor drives, normally because of bearing seizure. The screens should be run up to speed regularly, and idle time during wet weather is a good test opportunity.

Corrosion and Lightning Protection

8.1 **Corrosion.** Corrosion with respect to motorboats and basic electrical systems falls into two main categories: *galvanic corrosion* and *electrolytic corrosion.* Corrosion is often improperly called electrolysis.

> **Galvanic Corrosion.** Galvanic corrosion is the process that occurs when galvanic cells form between two pieces of metal with different electrochemical potential which come into contact. The difference in electrical potential between the two pieces of metal generates a measurable current flow between the metals. The metal with the lowest potential will corrode and is called the anode. The metal with the higher potential is called the cathode. Corrosion will occur in either salt- or freshwater and the principles are the same.
>
> **(1)** **Corrosion Process.** When two different metals with differing potential are interconnected and placed within close proximity in seawater a galvanic cell is created. This will significantly accelerate the corrosion of the base metal. The result is pitting and corrosion of propellers, split pins, stern tubes, shafts, shaft struts, rudders and hangings, rudder stocks and any other incompatible underwater metallic items. This can also occur underneath the paint coatings. The anodic corrosion current level, the water temperature and salinity levels significantly influence corrosion rates. A basic parameter is derived from Faradays' Law, which states that a known current

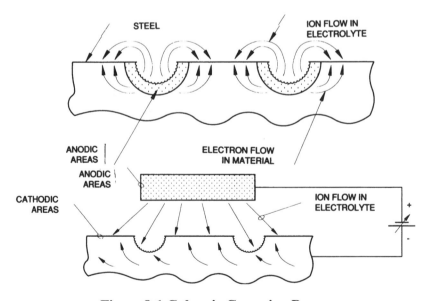

Figure 8-1 Galvanic Corrosion Process

acting for a known time will cause a predictable weight loss of metal. For example, 1 amp applied for 1 year will cause a loss of 10kg of steel. The size of the exposed area of cathodic metal relative to the anodic metal will also affect the corrosion rate.

(2)   **Portable Testers.** Portable digital and analog corrosion meters are available. These effectively involve the use of a reference cell that is dropped into the water around the hull, with the circuit completed to the steel hull. The potential differences can then be measured. I have used similar devices on oil rigs and found them very useful. Corrosion monitors from MG Duff have an onboard corrosion monitoring system and monitor the voltage on the hull relative to seawater using a reference cell.

(3)   **Metal Nobility.** All metals, both ferrous and non-ferrous, can corrode, Base metals such as steel and aluminium corrode more readily than the noble metals such as stainless steel and bronze. All metals can be classified according to molecular structure and these characteristics are listed in a metallic nobility table. The base metals at the top of the scale conduct easily, while the noble metals at the bottom do not. The materials with the greatest negative value will tend to corrode faster than those of a lower potential. The voltage difference between metals will drive current flow to accelerate corrosion of the anodic metal.

Table 8-1 Metal Nobility Table

Metal	Voltage
Magnesium and alloys	- 1.65 V
Zinc plating on steel	- 1.30 V
Zinc	- 1.10 V
Galvanized iron	- 1.05 V
Aluminum alloy castings	- 0.75 V
Mild steel	- 0.70 V
Cast iron	- 0.70 V
Lead	- 0.55 V
Manganese bronze	- 0.27 V
Copper, brass and bronze	- 0.25 V
Monel	- 0.20 V
Stainless steel (passive)	- 0.20 V
Nickel (passive)	- 0.15 V
Silver	- 0.00 V
Gold	+ 0.15 V

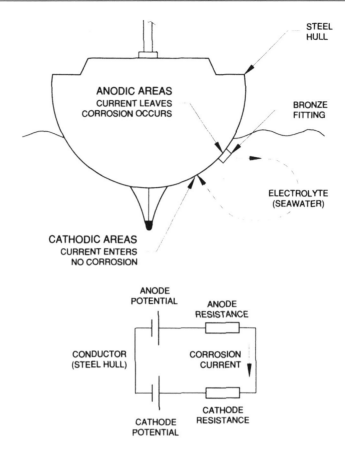

Figure 8-2 Vessel Galvanic Corrosion

8.2   Galvanic Protection. The British Admiralty introduced anodic protection back in 1824 on copper clad timber men-of-war sailing ships. A vessel should be constructed so that most metallic items are galvanically compatible. If they are, there are no potential differences, so no current will flow and there will be no corrosion. If the materials in contact are different, they must be isolated with physical barriers between the dissimilar metals, or be protected. This chapter references IRBES Section 1, Chapter 16.

Rule 16.1. All vessels should be assessed for potential corrosion sources. Galvanic compatibility and protection of all immersed metal components should be considered.

All boats should assess the various underwater metal components with respect to metal compatibility, possible interaction and corrosion. This should be based on drawing of all items, listing the materials in a table, and making calculations.

Rule 16.2. All cathodic protection systems shall use anodes with approved metal purity standards.

The average vessel uses zinc sacrificial anodes for corrosion protection. They are called sacrificial because they are sacrificed instead of the item they are attached to, such as the hull, shaft, rudder or trim tabs. As zinc is high on the nobility scale and has a higher electrical potential, they will corrode faster than other items such as mild steel. Pure zinc anodes are good conductors and are affixed below the water line. Zinc alloy anodes should conform to US Mil Spec MIL-18001J or Australia AS2239-1979. If they do not have a purity standard quoted, exercise caution before installing them. The zinc anode generates an electric current, and as the hull has a higher potential the anode allows current flow through it and bonded items to the seawater and back to the hull. Figure 8-3 illustrates the process along with the galvanic corrosion process. The process corrodes the anode proportional to the level of current flow present, while preserving the base metal such as the hull. Canal boats, barges and other vessels on freshwater rivers and canals follow the same criteria as boats in salt water. The difference is that the anodes may be made from magnesium, zinc or aluminum. Freshwater has a much greater insulation value than salt, so anodes such as magnesium and aluminium with a higher driving voltage than zinc anodes are required. When a boat moves into seawater or water of a higher salinity, anodes will become more active and should be inspected after only just 14 days.

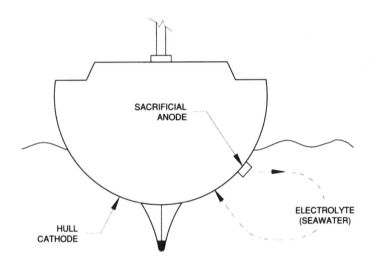

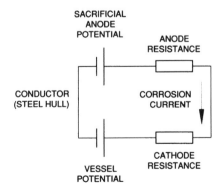

Figure 8-3 Galvanic Protection

Rule 16.3. Anodes should be fixed in view of the parts and areas they protect, and be bonded to the parts under protection.

Anode positioning is not critical but they must be able to "see" the parts to be protected. When a zinc anode is 50–75% wasted, it must be replaced. White or green halos around zincs or metals indicate stray current is affecting them. Bright zincs indicate excess current flow. A small amount of current also causes paint reactions. Rapid zinc wastage and degree of paint reaction indicate problems that are more serious. Where a boat has moved into freshwater and back to salt, the anode will become coated with a white crust. This will stop it from functioning and it must be cleaned off.

Rule 16.4. Equipotential bonding conductors shall be green in color. The conductor shall be identified with the letters EB to avoid confusion with any AC ground.

Many recommendations nominate green to identify bonding cables. Caution should be used, as this is an AC safety ground color in the US. Identifying each termination with the sleeved letters EB (Equipotential Bond) will reduce chances for accidental disconnection. This is a real possibility as the bonds go to the common ground point. Disconnection of an AC ground can cause shocks, so this is for clear safety reasons. While some standards allow bare conductors, this can lead to early conductor deterioration and is not recommended..

Rule 16.5. All cathodic bonding system cables shall be run clear of bilges or other wet areas.

Al bonding cables should be installed above the bilge line, or any other area that may be subject to water. They should interconnect only the items to be protected, and not indiscriminately bond all other items. All interconnections must be of at least a 12 AWG (4.0 mm^2) tinned copper conductor and be bolted to the main bonding connection.

Rule 16.6. The total resistance of any cathodic bonding circuit should not exceed 0.02 ohms.

The purpose of bonding is to equalize the electric potential of the underwater metals being connected. It is not to dissipate stray currents on the 12-volt system and increase the surface areas. It is critical that bonding cables be resistance free and the use of a heavy gauge conductor is recommended. When the vessel is hauled out, use a multimeter set on the x 1 ohm range and check the resistance between the anode and propeller. The maximum reading must be 0.02 ohm. The current flow in a bonding circuit is very small and any resistance introduced into the circuit from bad connections and cable resistances creates a difference in potential. This will cancel any protective measures and may actually create corrosion problems.

Rule 16.7. No grounding connections shall be made to any skin fittings.

Do not indiscriminately bond skin fittings and seacocks to the system. Only parts being protected should be bonded. This is at variance to ABYC, but I have come across many cases of degraded fittings directly caused by this practice to recommend it. Bronze fittings and seacocks do not generally require bonding.

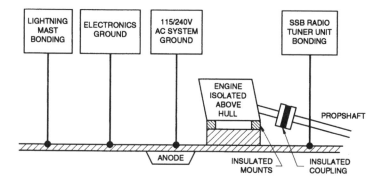

(a) STEEL/ALLOY BONDING CONNECTION

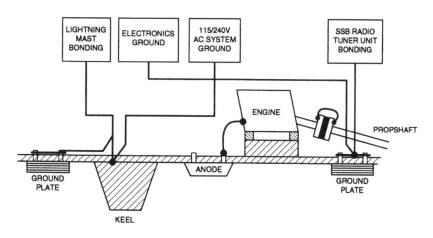

(b) GRP/TIMBER HULL BONDING CONNECTION

Figure 8-4 Corrosion Bonding Arrangements

Rule 16.8. The bonding system shall not be connected to the lightning protection system.

Do not bond the lightning ground system or the down conductor to the anode bonding system. This is at variance to ABYC; however there have been several well-documented cases of skin fittings being blown out in a lightning strike and the vessel subsequently sinking.

Rule 16.9. Ferrous and non-ferrous metals shall not be bonded to the same anode.

Do not bond ferrous and non-ferrous metals to the same anode, otherwise you effectively create a cell or battery.

8.3   Aluminum Boats. It is essential that hulls be correctly protected. Insulate or use compatible through-hull fittings. Insulate any equipment made of differing metals above aluminium on the nobility scale. Many boats use Lloyd's approved plastic (Marelon) through-hull valves and fittings, which solves many problems. Do not use bronze fittings if at all possible. Avoid mooring next to steel or copper sheathed vessels for extended periods. The interaction problem can be very severe with aluminium. Unlike steel vessels, an over-protected aluminium hull does not simply lose paint, but the hull is corroded by a caustic attack. The recommendations for steel hulls are also valid. An insulated two-wire electrical system is recommended.

8.4   Stern Gear Bonding. The usual method, both commercially and in small vessels, is the installation of a brush system. The company M.G.Duff has a system specifically designed for this called the Electro Eliminator. The system is illustrated below. It is a simple brush system connected to the cathodic bonding system, or on steel boats grounded directly to the hull or central bonding point. The systems use copper graphite brushes; the quoted service life is about 2000 hours. If the system is used the shaft must be kept clean and free of oil, grease and water. Sliprings are not the ideal solution for short length shafts. It is better to bridge the coupling to the engine block and use a collar anode or separate anode directly bonded to the engine block. Many engine installations incorporate flexible couplings on the propeller shaft. The coupling must be electrically bridged to ensure proper electrical continuity of the shaft system when the engine is not maintained electrically isolated above the bonding system.

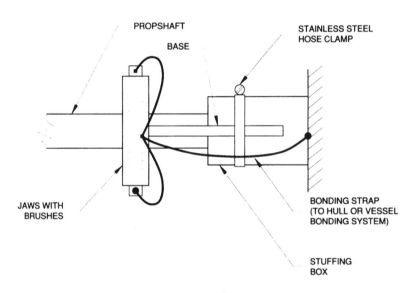

M.G. DUFF "ELIMINATOR"

Figure 8-5 Propeller Shaft Bonding

8.5   **Timber and Fiberglass Boats.** These recommendations are based on those from a leading corrosion specialist for fiberglass and timber vessels. Consult your zinc supplier for boat specific applications. These anode sizes are based on propeller sizes and are approximate only.

    a.   **Type A Vessels.** Single-screw boats with a short propeller shaft length in contact with seawater. They generally have wooden or fiberglass rudders. Normally only one anode is required for propeller and shaft protection. The main anode should be located on the main hull below the turn of the bilge equidistant from the gearbox and the inboard end of the stern tube.

    b.   **Type B Vessels.** Single- or twin-screw boats with long exposed propeller shafts, supported by a shaft strut and in contact with seawater. One anode is required for each propeller and shaft assembly. Separate anodes are required for mild steel rudders. Bronze or stainless steel rudders with bronze or stainless steel rudder stocks must be bonded to the same anode.

    c.   **Type C Vessels.** Single-screw boats with long exposed propeller shafts supported by a shaft strut and in contact with seawater. They have fiberglass rudders and bronze or stainless steel rudder stocks. Normally only one anode is required for propeller and shaft protection. If there are mild steel bilge keels they should have separate anodes affixed.

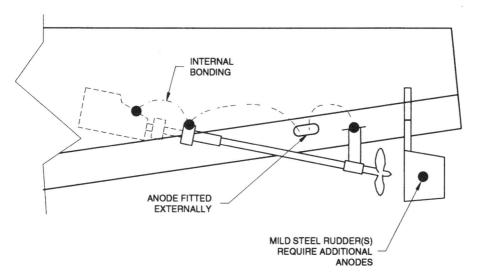

Figure 8-6 Anode Arrangements

Table 8-2 Anode Mass Table (Salt and Fresh Water)

Prop Size	Type A	Type B	Type C
10" SW Zinc	1.1 kg	2 x 1 kg	1.1 kg
FW Magnesium	0.3 kg	2 x 0.3 kg	0.3 kg
14" SW Zinc	1.1 kg	2 x 1 kg	1.1 kg
FW Magnesium	0.3 kg	2 x 0.3 kg	0.3 kg
19" SW Zinc	2.2 kg	2 x 1 kg	2.2 kg
FW Magnesium	0.4 kg	2 x 0.4 kg	0.4 kg
21" SW Zinc	2.2 kg	2 x 2.2 kg	2.2 kg
FW Magnesium	0.7 kg	2 x 0.7 kg	0.7 kg
26" SW Zinc	2.2 kg	2 x 2.2 kg	2.2 kg
FW Magnesium	0.7 kg	2 x 1.0 kg	0.7 kg
30" SW Zinc	2.2 kg	2 x 2.2 kg	2.2 kg
FW Magnesium	0.7 kg	1 kg	1 kg
36" SW Zinc	4.5 kg	2 x 4.5 kg	4.5 kg
FW Magnesium	1 kg	1 kg	1 kg
40" SW Zinc	4.5 kg	2 x 4.5 kg	4.5 kg
FW Magnesium	1 kg	2 x 1 kg	1 kg
48" SW Zinc	4.5 kg	2 x 4.5 kg	4.5 kg

d. **Type D Vessels.** These are stern drive boats fitted with outdrive units. Outdrive units normally have manufacturer designed and supplied anodes. Where no anodes are installed, a small round anode is installed to the hull and bonded to the leg.

e. **Fiberglass/Timber Anodes.** The principal anode installation factors are:

   (1) **Location.** The anode fixing studs must be above the bilge line internally. There must be a minimal internal bonding cable installation length. The anodes must not be installed forward of the log and depth transducers as the flow will cause problems. Ensure that you can access the bolts internally.

   (2) **Anode Backing Sheets.** An anode backing sheet must be installed behind each anode when installed against the hull. The sheet helps control the anode wastage.

   (3) **Seal Anode Bolt Holes.** Always seal the timber both in and around the anode securing boltholes with silicon sealant. This will ensure it is well sealed and reduce wood decay and corrosion.

   (4) **Connection.** Fan disc washers are used under the anode securing nuts to ensure a good low resistance contact. These require replacement when the anode is replaced.

8.6 **Steel Boats.** Corrosion risks are significantly increased on a steel vessel. The following precautions must be observed to reduce galvanic and electrolytic corrosion. It cannot be overstressed that good protection on a steel hull is a function of a properly planned and applied paint program. Use the technical services of your paint supplier in addition to the protection measures described.

    a. **Anode Number Calculations**. Calculations are normally based on wetted surface area calculations. The main vessel dimensions used are water-line length, breadth and mean loaded draft. Area is calculated using the formula:

    Length Water Line (LWL) x (Breadth + Draft)

    This formula will suit most motor cruisers, canal boats and barges. For medium density vessels multiply the calculated sum by 0.75. For light displacement vessels multiply by 0.5. Based on this calculation look at the anode selection table. Protection for a 2-year period has approximately 50% greater anode quantities. Anodes are either welded on, or are bolt-on stud mounted.

Table 8-3 One-Year Anode Selection Table

Wetted Area	Hull Anodes	Rudders
Up to 28 m^2 (300ft^2) SW	2 x 4.0 kg zinc	2 x 1.0 kg zinc
Up to 28 m^2 (300ft^2) FW	4 x 1.5 kg mag	2 x 0.3 kg mag
28.1 - 56 m^2 (>600ft^2) SW	4 x 3.5 kg zinc	2 x 1.0 kg zinc
28.1 - 56 m^2 (>600ft^2) FW	4 x 3.5 kg mag	2 x 0.3 kg mag
56.1 - 84 m^2 (>900ft^2) SW	4 x 4.0 kg zinc	2 x 1.0 kg zinc
56.1 - 84 m^2 (>900ft^2) FW	4 x 3.5 kg mag	2 x 0.3 kg mag
84.1 - 102 m^2 (>1100ft^2) SW	4 x 6.5 kg zinc	2 x 2.2 kg zinc
84.1 - 102 m^2 (>1100ft^2) FW	6 x 4.5 kg mag	2 x 0.7 kg mag
102.1 - 148 m^2 (>1600ft^2) SW	6 x 6.5 kg zinc	2 x 2.2 kg zinc

    b. **Shaft Collar Anodes.** When fitting collar anodes, make sure that the shaft is clean, and the anode is not placed over an antifouled shaft. The collars must be mounted as close as possible to the shaft support strut, typically the clearance is 4–10 mm. Do not antifoul the anode!

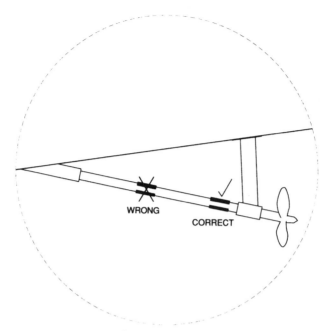

Figure 8-7 Shaft Anode Installation

8.7   Galvanic Isolators. These devices are designed to provide galvanic isolation of the AC shore ground from a DC bonding system when they are connected. Small stray DC currents may flow from the AC ground to the DC bonding system and may increase anode corrosion rates. When a boat is at the marina connected to shore power, it effectively has the same AC ground plane as all other connected boats. In boats without inverters or generators, the main ground is the shore ground, as there is often no on-board grounding installed. In effect, the vessel is simply an appliance on the end of an extension cable, much like a trailer. In this mode, any DC currents imposed on the AC system will not affect the boat. When the boat has an AC system that is grounded through an inverter or generator installed on board, the AC ground will be connected to the DC ground point. This provides a path for DC stray leakage currents to the DC power system, the immersed parts of the boat such as the propeller, and the cathodic protection system. Depending on circumstances a significant current can flow.

a.   The isolator is normally installed as close to the shore power inlet as possible. Space must be allowed for ventilation and access.

b.   The units should be tested every month to ensure that they are functioning.

Caution. It must be clearly stated that no electrical standards, recommendations or classification society rules, with the exception of ABYC, allow any device to be inserted within any grounding or earthing conductor. It is not allowed ashore in any place in the world that I am aware of. Any person having an isolator installed may be in breach of local and international rules. If the isolator is faulty or not working, the boat may be left without an AC ground if an onboard ground is not used.

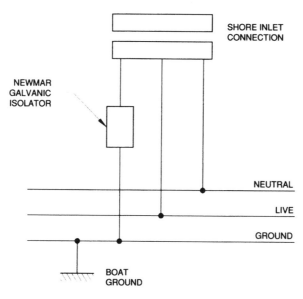

Figure 8-8 Galvanic Isolator System

8.8 **Impressed Current Cathodic Protection (ICCP)** . These systems are installed on larger steel and alloy vessels. Protection is based on the compensation of corrosion currents by the use of a counter current using an on-board power source. The reference anode senses the electrical potential of the seawater and sends a signal to the control unit, which then outputs an appropriate current to the active anode. The protective current is transmitted through the seawater electrolyte to the areas under protection. The area under protection is converted into a cathode preventing metal corrosion. Zinc anodes have very low and non-variable driving voltages with reduced effectiveness. The varying combinations of water temperature, chemical composition and exposed surface require monitoring and different current levels. The anode is made of a relatively inert material such as silicon iron, silver/lead alloys, tantalum or platinum. The driving voltage and current outputs are adjusted at the power source to enable precise control. Corrosion will be inhibited as long as the protective potential is applied. In normal operation, mechanically damaged or porous hull areas will have an insulation layer form over them, caused by salts and the current flow.

a. **Cathodic Protection Problems.** It is important not to overprotect using too high a potential. Traditional paint systems will soften and blister as hydrogen bubbles form under the paint surface. Chlorinated rubber paint systems are used to counter this characteristic.

b. **Stern Drives.** Some drives such as Volvo and Mercury (MerCathode) have an active electronic anti-corrosion system. They use a reference anode and active anode. The reference senses surrounding seawater potential, and the control unit sends a current to the active anode. These anodes emit varying levels of ions into the water surrounding the drive. They complement the zinc anodes and do not replace them.

c.   **Electrical Antifouling Systems.** Units such as those from Cathelco and Jotun are used for protecting sea chests and seawater inlets against fouling by marine growth. These use a copper anode, which releases copper ions into the system, which then acts as an antifouling.

8.9   **Corrosion System Maintenance.** Corrosion systems require maintenance:

a.   **In Water Inspections.** Perform the following basic inspections:

(1)   **Main Anodes.** Do an underwater check of anodes after 6 months and check for increased corrosion rates. If the vessel has moved into warmer or more saline conditions, the rates increase. Rapid zinc loss and shiny zincs indicate a possible stray current problem.

(2)   **Shaft Anodes.** Check that shaft anode is still on the shaft, as they may loosen and fall off. Check the anode corrosion rates.

b.   **Haul-out Inspections.** Perform the following inspections:

(1)   **Anode Replacement.** Replace anodes if they are more than 75% reduced and check the connections.

(2)   **Shaft Anodes.** Replace the anode if necessary. Check the mating surface of the shaft anode. Check that it is correctly located on the shaft.

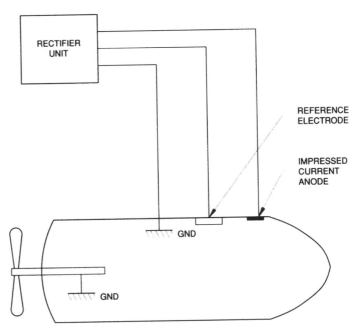

Figure 8-9 Impressed Current Protection Systems

(3)   **Bonding Connections.** Inspect the bonding system interconnections to see that they are tight and clean. Remove connections and clean, so that contact resistance is zero.

(4)   **Check Bonding System Resistances.** Check bonding resistances between the anodes, propeller and the hull.

Table 8-4 Corrosion System Troubleshooting

Symptom	Probable Fault
Anode corroded 80%	Replace anode
Rapid anode corrosion	Hull electrical leakage Increased water salinity Increased water temperature Degraded bonding system Moored adjacent to vessel Marina electrical problems No isolation transformer on boat
Paint stripping off keel and hull	Hull over protected (too many anodes) Severe hull leakage (electrical problem)
Paint stripping around studs	Anode stud connection defective
No anode corrosion	Anode hull connections defective Bonding wires broken Impure zinc anode
Propeller and shaft pitted	Inadequate protection Degraded bonding system Shaft anode missing Shaft anode fitted over antifouled shaft Cavitation corrosion

8.10   Electrolytic (Stray Current) Corrosion. A number of factors must be considered. Electrolytic corrosion has different principles from galvanic corrosion; protective measures for galvanic corrosion do not protect against electrolytic corrosion. Stray current corrosion will however dramatically increase corrosion rates on underprotected hulls and anodes, degrading the galvanic protective system. If the faults are undiagnosed, the anodes will rapidly degrade, followed by stripping of the paint and antifouling. This will often require the complete repainting of the hull from the metal primer upwards. References are to IRBES Section 1, Chapter 16.

> **Electrolytic Corrosion Sources.** Electrolytic corrosion is caused by an external DC current source. This may be from electrical faults on the boat or from shore sources:
>
> **(1)   Leakage Currents.** Leakage currents are caused by surface voltage leakages across condensation. They are also caused by conductive salt deposits at DC connections in junction boxes, or tracking from main starter motor terminals. 24 and 48-volt systems have higher risks then 12-volt systems given the higher potential differences. In some cases, they may also be caused by damaged insulation. In a properly installed electrical system, there are relatively few opportunities for the situation to arise.
>
> **(2)   Ground Faults.** Ground faults on AC and DC conductors occur where the cable insulation has been damaged and contact is made with the hull or connected metalwork. In many cases, the fault may not be sufficient to operate protective devices and remains unnoticed for a considerable and damaging period. The most common areas causing faults are where cables enter grounded stainless steel stanchions, alloy masts, engine charging and starter cables. In any area where a cable can contact grounded metal, leakage or fault currents can flow. Install a leakage test lamp unit such as a Mastervolt that handles both AC and DC. This allows the hull to be monitored continuously and any problems can be rectified promptly.
>
> **(3)   Shore Power.** The electrolytic corrosion problem is due to interaction between shore and the vessel. When the two grounds develop an unequal potential, a DC component flows to the vessel.

Rule 16.10. Boats should consider the installation of an isolation transformer in the shore AC power circuit to minimize the effects of electrolytic corrosion.

Install an isolation transformer on the shore mains supply. This will provide galvanic separation between the shore and vessel power systems, and the ground systems. Refer to the shore power chapter for details. The isolation transformer can also be used on GRP and timber boats as well as steel and alloy ones where problems exist.

8.11   Steel/Alloy Hull Leakage Inspections. It is difficult to maintain a steel or alloy hull above ground. Moisture and oil residues mixed with salt lower the isolation level. It is important to regularly examine isolation values to ensure that it is maintained. These tests are based on an electrical system with an insulated two-wire above hull configuration. The galvanic bonding system is also an independent system.

a. **Passive Insulation Test.** This test measures the level of resistance between the hull and the positive and negative circuits. A multimeter set on the resistance x 1 ohm scale is required. Perform the test as follows:

  (1) Turn main power switch off.

  (2) Turn on all switches and circuit breakers to ensure that all electrical circuits are at equal potential or connected in one grid.

  (3) Connect the positive meter lead to the positive conductor, and the negative to the hull. Observe and record the reading.

  (4) Connect the positive meter lead to the negative conductor, and the negative to the hull. Observe and record the reading.

b. **Passive Test Results.** The test results can be interpreted as follows:

  (1) A reading of 10 k ohms or above indicates that isolation above hull is acceptable.

  (2) A reading in the range of 1k ohm to 10k ohms indicates that there is leakage, and the isolation is degraded. While not directly short circuited to the hull, leakage can occur through moisture or a similar cause. With meter connected, systematically switch off each circuit to localize the fault area and rectify. A common area is the starter motor connections.

  (3) A reading less than 1k ohm indicates a serious leakage problem that must be promptly localized and rectified or serious hull damage can result.

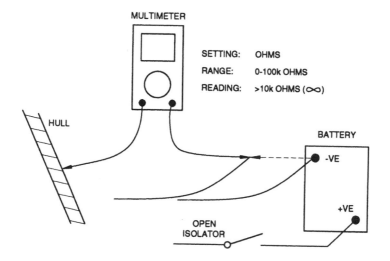

Figure 8-10 Passive Testing

c. **Voltage Insulation Test.** As a system is not passive, a voltage and a difference in potential exists. While a passive meter test can show all is satisfactory, a voltage can break down the resistances and cause leakage. To properly test the electrical isolation, a voltage test should be performed. With 220/115-volt mains systems, this test must be performed using a 500-volt insulation tester and all results must exceed 1meg ohm. This is not recommended for low voltage installations, as the insulation values of cables are not rated this high. A low voltage DC tester set at 100 volts DC should be used. Another easier test is as follows:

(1)   Turn on all electrical circuits so that all are "alive."

(2)   With a digital multimeter set on the DC volts scale, place the positive probe on the supply negative. Place the negative probe on the hull.

(3)   There should be no voltage at all. If there is a small voltage, a leakage may exist on the negative.

(4)   With a digital multimeter set on the DC volts scale, place the negative probe on the supply negative. Place the positive probe on the hull.

(5)   There should be no voltage at all. If there is a small voltage, a leakage may exist on the positive.

(6)   Systematically turn off electrical circuits to verify that there is a leakage, and that, with all power off, the difference in potential is zero.

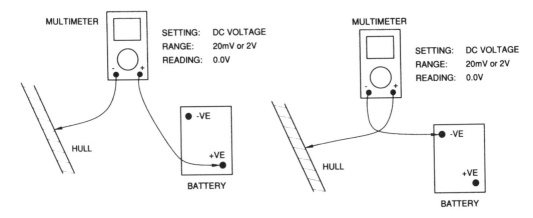

Figure 8-11 Insulation Testing

214

8.12 **Lightning Physics.** Within the cloud formation, strong updrafts and downdrafts generate high electrical charges. When the voltage reaches a sufficiently high level both cloud to cloud and ground discharges occur.

    a. **Negative Cloud to Ground.** These strikes occur when the ground is at positive polarity and the cloud's negative region attempts to equalize with ground.

    b. **Positive Cloud to Ground.** The positively charged cloud top equalizes with the negative ground.

    c. **Positive Ground to Cloud.** The positively charged ground equalizes with the negative charge cloud.

    d. **Negative Ground to Cloud.** The negatively charged ground equalizes with the positively charged cloud top.

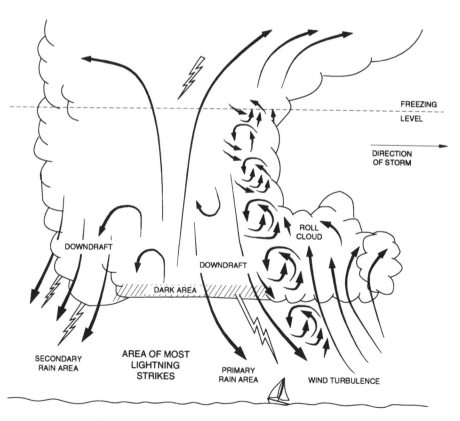

Figure 8-12 Cumulo-Nimbus Storm System

215

8.13 **Lightning Components.** Lightning consists of a number of components that form a multidirectional flow of charges exceeding 200,000 amperes at over 30,000°C for a matter of milliseconds. The positively charged ions rise to the cloud top, and the negative ions migrate to the cloud base. Regions of positively charged ions also form at the cloud base. Eventually, the cloud charge levels have sufficient potential difference between ground and another cloud to discharge.

    a. **Leader.** The leader consists of a negative stream of electrons comprising many small forks or fingers that follow and break down the air paths offering the least resistance. The charge follows the fork, finding the easiest path. Each successive layer is broken down and charged to the same polarity as the cloud charge.

    b. **Upward Positive Leader.** This positive charge rises some 200 feet (50 meters) above the ground.

    c. **Channel.** When leader and upward leader meet, a channel is formed.

    d. **Return Stroke.** This path is generally much brighter and more powerful than the leader. It travels upwards to the cloud, partially equalizing the potential difference between ground and cloud.

    e. **Dart Leader.** In several milliseconds after the return stroke, another downward charge takes place along the same path as the stepped leader and return stroke. This is sometimes followed by multiple return strokes. The movements happen so fast that it appears to be a single event. This sequence can continue until the differential between cloud and ground has been equalized.

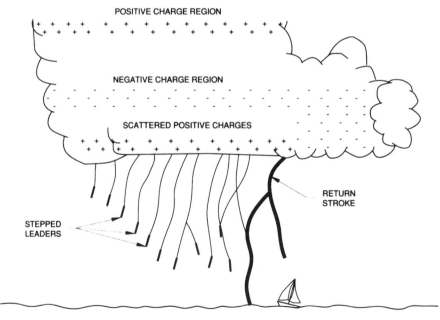

Figure 8-13 Lightning Process

8.14   Lightning Safety and Protection. All Class societies, Lloyd's, ABYC, NFPA, etc. make similar recommendations, but very few boats adhere to them. The emphasis has always been on sailing boats, but there are many instances of power vessels also being hit with equally catastrophic results. Many motorboats have prominent mast structures to carry radar, navigation lights and large whip aerials. Fly bridges have extensive stainless steel tuna tower structures, with trawler yachts and motor sailing vessels also often having small masts, so protection should be considered. More than a 1,000 people are killed worldwide annually by lightning strikes. In the US, damage from lightning voltage transients on transmission systems exceeds 1 billion dollars. In an electrical storm, stay below decks at all times. Take a position and plot it prior to shutting down, or in case of all electronics equipment being blown. Turn off all electronic gear and isolate circuit breakers if at all practicable. Disconnect aerials also if possible. Do not operate radios until after the storm unless in an extreme emergency. Compasses should be rechecked and deviation corrections made after a strike, and in some cases, complete demagnetization may occur.

8.15   Lightning Protection. This chapter references IRBES Section 1, Chapter 15. There are a few basic elements in any protection system and they must be done correctly. A range of dissipation devices has come onto the market. These devices are typically brush or "bottle brush" type arrangements. The principle is that all the spikes "bleed" off or dissipate electrons or ions, reducing the differential that may cause a lightning strike. They do not protect the boat in the event of a strike, and safely carry strike energy to ground.

Rule 15.1. A lighting conductor shall be installed at the masthead. This should consist of a turned copper spike of at least 12mm (½") in diameter, and projecting at least 150mm (6") above the highest point.

The first element is the air terminal; it should be a copper rod with pointed tip. To avoid metal interaction, stainless rods are commonly used but should be of a thicker section than the more conductive and lower resistance copper. The spike should be at least six inches higher than any other equipment, including VHF aerials; this requires a terminal 12–24" in height. Many commercial units (Dynarod and Seaground) have an offset in the rod which, although not being the the required straight section, would be satisfactory. The purpose of the point being sharp is that it facilitates what is called point discharge. Ions dissipate from the ground and effectively cause a reduction in potential between the cloud and the sea. In many cases, the strike may be of lower intensity or not occur at all. A stainless steel VHF whip aerial does not constitute any protection. The air terminal is mounted clear of all other equipment and gives a cone of protection below it, to capture the strike. This protective cone prevents strikes to adjacent areas and metalwork, which in a motorboat can mean rails or other items lower than the air terminal. Typically these may be on navigation equipment Christmas trees, and fly bridge or tuna tower stainless steel structures.

Rule 15.2. The total resistance of the grounding circuit from the lightning conductor to the ground plate or hull grounding point shall not exceed 0.02 ohms.

A low resistance grounding circuit is critical to the performance of the protection system. Any resistance will cause significantly greater heating effects and strike energy will seek shorter and lower resistance ground paths. High resistance circuits contribute to side strike activities.

Rule 15.3. In vessels with alloy masts, the base of the mast should be bonded to the deck and mast step, or compression post. This should then be bonded to the ground plate or keel. Boats with a timber mast should have a separate down conductor fastened to the mast.

It is often easier to bond the base of an alloy mast to the mast step, and then bond this to the compression post. The bottom of the compression post is then bonded to the ground plate or keel. Keel-stepped masts can be directly bonded to the ground plate or keel with a short and heavy gauge conductor. Timber masts ideally should have a conductor fastened externally to the mast. Some use a flat copper strip rather than a thick conductor, also bonding the external sail track. There is a view that requires the secondary bonding of the stays and chainplates to the ground point. This creates a higher impedance parallel path down the stays and chainplates, which can result in crystallization of the stainless steel and possible loss of the tensioned rig. One major spar manufacturer voids all warranty on masts if they are struck by lightning as the heat can alter the metallurgical properties of the mast section. It is imperative that a single, low resistance grounding system is installed, then relatively dangerous alternative methods are not required.

Rule 15.4. Lightning down conductors shall be of at least 100mm^2 (4 AWG) cross sectional area. Conductors should be run as straight as practicable without sharp bends. Where down conductors are of standard battery cable, they should be enclosed where possible in an additional insulated conduit to increase the insulation values.

The purpose of the down conductor is to safely conduct the strike current through a low impedance circuit. This conductor must be rated to carry the strike current to the ground point and to eliminate side flash dangers. It must minimize induction into other conductors, and assist in keeping the strike period to the lowest time possible. Much of the damage in a strike can result from heat, as the large current flow into even a low resistance down conductor cable makes the cable act like a large heating element. The chapters on voltage drop are relevant here. It is essential that the cable has a sufficient cross sectional area, at least 4 AWG but preferably larger. The overall resistance of the cable must not exceed 0.02 ohms maximum. Electricity follows the path of least resistance, and this reduces side flash dangers if energy looks for alternative paths. This means that if a ground circuit is 2 ohms overall and a communications ground 1 ohm, the energy will divert through the communications ground. Welding cable is best as it has high quality insulation in comparison to battery cables. In shore installations special purpose tri-axial cables are used. The multiple screens reduce the large radiated fields that are generated. However, this is an expensive option, valid only on large super yachts. The bonding cable to the ground plate should be as straight as practicable without sharp corners, as side discharges called corona discharge will occur. It is also useful to enclose the conductor internally with PVC flexible conduit normally used in shore electrical systems to increase the insulation levels, as DC battery cable insulation will break down under high voltage conditions.

Rule 15.5. The lightning conductor shall be terminated at the hull, keel or an immersed ground plate with a minimum area of 0.2 m^2 (2 ft^2).

In any boat, the ground plane is seawater. Strike energy must be dissipated to ground with a minimal rise in ground potential through a low impedance grounding system. Steel and alloy boats use the hull as ground. In GRP and timber sailing boats, conductors are grounded on keel bolts. On most boats, you will have to install a large separate ground plate, or a radio ground shoe (Dynaplate, Wonderbar or Seaground), preferably the largest ones in the 50-100 sq.ft range. NewMar states that its ground shoes are not intended for lightning protection. Some quality shoes use a gold-based grease that is applied under the bolt heads to ensure a good low resistance connection. Do not use the radio RF ground plate as the lightning ground. An innovative and portable device that incorporates all of the correct lightning protection elements is the Strikeshield (www.strikeshield.com). A clamp is connected to the mast or other conductive down conducting item such as the tuna tower stainless structure, and this is connected to a 1/0 or 2/0 AWG shielded and tinned copper cable. The cable is terminated with a specially designed dissipation electrode that is dropped into the water.

Rule 15.6. A bridge or link should be installed between ground plate bolts or at least two keel bolts to distribute current evenly. A grounding system may have more than one grounding plate connected to the down conductor.

Bridge out the two terminal bolts with a stainless steel link to spread the contact area. In other cases, a large ground shoe can be used, or up to three smaller ground shoes can be configured in what is called a crow's foot principle. This radial system lowers the overall impedance to allow energy to diverge as each conductor and ground shoe takes a share of current. In a strike, the water permeating the sintered bronze ground shoe will literally boil, increasing local resistance, so any increase in surface areas will reduce this effect. The voltage gradients around the shoe will also be lower. The ground point must have sufficient area to adequately dissipate the strike energy. Links can also be drilled and used to bolt the ground cable connector, as many ground shoes have relatively small bolts designed for RF grounds only.

Rule 15.7. All connections shall be crimped and soldered joints shall not be used.

Never use soldered joints alone, as they will melt during a strike causing further destruction. It is very difficult on large cables to ensure a good low resistance solder joint. After crimping, solder can be run in to enhance the joint, but this is not really necessary. Always crimp the connections and ensure that all bonded connections are clean and tight. All connections must be bolted to the ground point.

Rule 15.8. All metallic items within 2 meters (6 ft) of the mast base or ground point shall be bonded to the ground plate.

Some recommendations call for bonding of rails, stanchions and all large metallic equipment such as stainless water tanks be bonded to the lightning ground. It is only necessary to bond internal metallic equipment within six feet of the down conductor and bonding point. The bonding should be made at the point closest to the main conductor. The ground plane potential equalization bonding between systems is designed to eliminate earth loops, differentials and reduce the level of potentially destructive transient currents that can flow when potential differences exist between unbonded grounding systems. In practice there have been incidents caused by the bonding of the cathodic protection system to power supply negatives, grounds and RF grounds. This has resulted in the vessel sinking as the skin fittings have been blown out, and all the electrical and electronics systems destroyed. Dissimilar metals such as aluminum, copper strap, and steel must be interconnected to ensure no galvanic corrosion can occur.

Rule 15.9. The lightning protection system shall not be connected to the DC negative, boat ground point, RF ground or cathodic protection bonding system.

The lightning ground system should not be bonded to the corrosion system bonding, machinery or electrical system negatives or radio grounds. No interconnection should be made to through hull fittings.

8.16 Surge, Transient (and Static) Protection. All electrical systems should have surge suppression devices fitted. It is common to have high levels of static build up on fiberglass decks in hot, dry, low humidity wind conditions. This causes significant static electricity shocks, so they require dissipation. The condition is common in the Mediterranean. Surge protection methods are described:

a. **Radio Antennas.** Aerials can draw a strike or have an induced current flow through the coaxial conductor to the radio. All antennas should have arresters fitted, although this is rarely done on boats. Antenna cables can be fitted with a two-way switch, one side to the radio, one to ground. You can buy remote and manual coax switches from NewMar. During a storm or if the vessel is left unattended, place the switch to ground position. Ideally an arrestor (Hy-Gain or Dynapulse), or a spark gap device can also be used. Coaxial cable surge protectors (Dynadiverta or Polyphase Corp) can also be used. Coaxial cable surge protectors via RF feeders are used even in shielded cables and tri-ax cables, which will confine most current. Some induction can still occur due to magnetic and capacitive coupling.

b. **DC Power Supplies.** Power supplies should have double pole isolation on both positive and negative supplies. Surge suppression units can be installed which will clamp any overvoltage condition to a safe value, typically around 40 volts. All equipment can have what is called a transient protection device installed across the input power supply connections. These are generally metal oxide varistors (MOVs), and are available from electronics suppliers.

c. **AC Power Supplies.** Efficient clamping and filtering at the power supply point requires surge diverters. The purpose is to limit residual voltages to a level within the immunity level range of the equipment. In 230VAC RMS systems, damage can occur with just 700-volt peaks. Typical tolerances of battery chargers are under 800 volts. Some shunt devices can clamp the voltage at less than these voltages but they do not limit the fast wave front of the strike energy (dI/dt) before clamping action starts. In a lightning strike, the rate of current rise can exceed 10kA/μsec, and this can be greater in multiple strikes and re-strikes. Low pass filter technology primary shunt diverters will reduce the peak residual voltage and reduce rate of current and voltage rise reaching equipment. Surge Reduction Filters (SRF) will provide multi-stage surge attenuation by clamping and then filtering the transients on power input circuits, and these include MOV's. Look at www.yachtguard.com.

d. **St.Elmo's Fire (Brush Discharge).** This phenomenon is more common on steel vessels. When it occurs, it may precede a strike, although the effect does not occur all the time. The vessel in effect becomes a large ground mass. The discharge is characterized by ionised clouds and balls of white or green flashing light that polarize at vessel extremities. The discharge of negative ions reduces the potential intensity of a strike. Damage to electrical systems is usually induced into external wiring, as the steel hull acts as a large Faraday cage.

e. **Electromagnetic Pulse**. A vessel can have damaged equipment from a strike within a few hundred yards. Insurance companies do not like to accept claims on damage unless you can show total damage to external masthead or other strike damaged systems. A strike sends out a very large electromagnetic pulse, which is a strong magnetic field. This field induces into wiring and systems a high voltage surge, doing just as much damage as a direct hit. If you suspect damage from an induced electromagnetic pulse, check with all the vessels adjacent to your boat and obtain statements to support your contention. Generally, all the electronics will be out if this is the case since the external wiring acts as a large aerial.

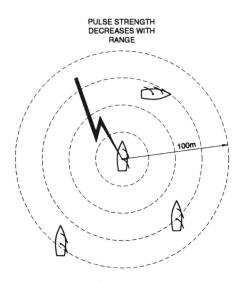

Figure 8-14 Electromagnetic Pulse Effect

Deck Equipment and DC Motors

9.1 **Anchor Windlass.** The anchor windlasses are as important as the main engine and it is crucial that they are properly selected and installed. Unfortunately, they are rarely maintained properly and subsequently fail at critical periods. This chapter explains the process and the factors to consider.

    a. **Windlass Selection.** Choose the windlass based on the vessel length and displacement, length of anchor rode, weight of anchor chain. Choices on whether horizontal or vertical are related to space and anchor chain fall.

    b. **Electrical Installation.** Install the correctly rated cables and protective systems.

    c. **Electrical Control.** Install a reliable control system.

9.2 **Anchor Selection.** If it is a new system, the correct anchor for the vessel must be selected. The CQR is one of the most useful and common anchor types and this will be used as a yardstick. Simpson-Lawrence are the manufacturers of this anchor type and their selection chart should be used as correct weight selection is critical. Other anchor types such as the Delta, Claw, Plough and Bruce also can be considered.

9.3 **Anchor Windlass Selection.** Windlass selection is based on the weight of an anchor and the chain weight. Table 9.1 illustrates a selection of short link chain sizes for a variety of vessel lengths.

Table 9.1 Anchor Chain Weight Selection Table

Vessel Size	10 Meters	12 Meters	14 Meters	16 Meters	18 Meters
Chain Size	8 mm	10 mm	10 mm	13 mm	13 mm
All Chain	40 m	50 m	70 m	80 m	90 m
Rope/Chain	12 m	14 m	16 m	18 m	20 m
Chain Wt	1.42 kg/m	2.22 kg/m	2.22 kg/m	3.75 kg/m	3.75 kg/m

    a. **Winch Loading Calculation.** The minimum anchor winch capacity is derived from the following formula, after working out the chain weight or chain/rope weight from the table for your vessel size. The x 3 factor covers windage, tidal current and safety margin.

Windlass Capacity = (Anchor Weight + Chain Weight) x 3

Eg. 12-meter vessel has CQR of 35 Kg.

Chain Weight 111 kg + 35 kg = 146 kg x 3 = 438 kg

b. **Rated Output.** The windlass must have a rated pull of at least 438 kg. Manufacturers have selection charts to assist in selection. Add in an additional safety margin of 15–25%.

c. **Anchor Loading.** A windlass is not designed to take the entire load when riding to anchor, especially in large swells or heavy conditions. As a safety precaution, always transfer the load to a bollard or load bearing point using a rope snubber or use a chain stopper.

d. **Anchor Retrieval.** Speeds are typically designed around a figure of 10 meters/minute at 100 kg loading. Higher loads cause a slower anchor retrieval rate. Windlasses therefore do not have a constant load during anchor recovery. When operating the windlass, observe the following:

(1) **Motoring.** The first phase involves slowly motoring towards the anchor. Load will slowly increase and without high loads the recovery rate will be maximum. The alternator supplies part of the motor load and keeps the motor from impressing a large voltage surge on the electrical system, and more importantly keeps the voltage from dropping too low. The windlass should never be used without motoring; the voltage drop is so severe that a drop in windlass power occurs after a few minutes.

(2) **Recovery.** The load will increase as tension increases towards the anchor breakout point. At the breakout point, maximum current will be drawn for a brief period, and this current peak may be 2–3 times rated current. Once the anchor is broken out, the load drops as the windlass hauls the anchor vertically back to the boat. If you are having a problem with anchor retrieval, do not continue to load the anchor windlass to stall conditions without stopping every few minutes, and allowing the motor to cool down. The motor may overheat due to the lower voltage causing damage or even burnout.

9.4 **Anchor Electrical Installation**. Anchor windlass performance is frequently reduced by the installation of incorrectly rated cables. Anchor windlass electrical supplies should run the most direct route to the engine starting battery, via the appropriate isolator and protective devices. At full rated load, significant voltage drops can develop with a corresponding decrease in rated lifting capacity. The following system components must be specified and installed correctly. The practice of installing a separate battery at either the machinery space or forward adjacent to the windlass is not recommended. Use the engine starting battery as it has a high cranking amp rating and is more able to deliver the currents required by a windlass at maximum loads. A deep-cycle service battery cannot cope with these loads without possible damage.

a. **Cabling.** Cabling must be able to cope with the large current consumption over an extended distance. Voltage drop should not exceed 5%. Table 9-2 gives cable sizes for length of cable run, not the vessel length.

Table 9-2 Windlass Cable Rating Table

Cable Length	Current Rating	AWG	Metric	B & S
up to 6 meters	200 amps	4/0	25 mm^2	3
up to 8 meters	245 amps	2/0	35 mm^2	2
up to 10 meters	320 amps	1/0	50 mm^2	0
up to 12 meters	390 amps	0	65 mm^2	00

b. **Circuit Protection.** Current ratings vary depending on the manufacturers. Many windlasses have converted DC starter motors. Simpson-Lawrence uses permanent magnet motors, typically in the range 600–1,000 watts. Typical working current loadings are given as 55 amps at no load, 110 amps half load, and 180 amps full rated load.

(1) **Circuit Breakers.** A slow-blow circuit breaker should be installed on the supply reasonably close to the battery, and easily accessible. Typically, these range for 400 watt motor at 40 amp current with 50 amp breaker, 600 watt at 55 amp with 70 amp breaker, etc. Use DC rated circuit breakers, not AC ones as many people do. Windlass makers stock the correct circuit breakers.

(2) **Automatic Thermal Cutouts.** I would caution against using automatic thermal circuit breakers. They trip automatically in overload conditions and reset. The problem is that you have to wait until they reset, which is usually when you desperately need the windlass.

(3) **Slow Blow (Time Delay) Fuses.** ABYC and USCG require the installation of a Slow-Blow type fuse on the system, and many manufacturers integrate this within the control box. The fuses are normally rated above the windlass rated working current, typically 200 amps for 12-volt systems. They delay opening on low-level overloads, and trip only on sustained over-currents. Make sure you carry a spare fuse.

c. **Connections.** Connections are a common cause of failures. The following points should be observed:

(1) **Connector Types.** Always use heavy-duty crimp connectors. Do not solder connections as dry joints are commonplace and solder can melt under maximum load. Soldered joints also stiffen up the cables, causing fatigue.

(2) **Insulation.** Put on a section of heat shrink tubing over the entire crimp connector shank and cable to prevent the ingress of moisture.

(3) **Connections.** The lug terminal hole should always fit neatly to ensure maximum contact. Use a spring washer on the nuts to prevent loosening and subsequent heating and damage under load. Coat the battery terminals with a light layer of petroleum jelly.

d. **Performance Curves.** The following curves for Lewmar windlasses graphically illustrate the effect load has on power consumption and hauling speed.

(1) The higher the load, the higher the current until a point is reached where the motor will overload and stall. The higher the load when the windlass is operated, the shorter the operation time allowed on the electric motor.

(2) The higher the load, the slower the recovery speed. Any anchoring process can be shortened with less wear and tear on the windlass by motoring up over the anchor. This removes chain tension, makes recovery quicker and imposes less load on the electric motor.

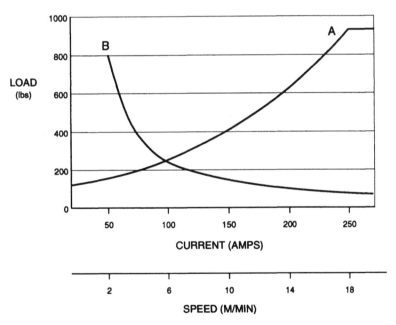

Figure 9-1 Anchor Windlass Performance Curve

225

9.5   **Anchor Windlass Electrical Control.** One of the most common failure points is the control system. Controls consist of the following configurations:

    a.   **Single Direction Footswitch.** A footswitch is connected directly in the positive supply to the windlass motor. Footswitches are notorious for filling with water. In this type of control, a short-circuit develops, or the contacts and spring corrode. Short-circuiting can result in a brief uncontrolled operation of the windlass and a burned-out switch.

    b.   **Single Direction Solenoid/Footswitch.** The footswitch is used to control a heavy-duty solenoid located below decks, which supplies the main power supply to the electric motor.

    c.   **Pneumatic Deck Footswitch.** These units have a PVC tube from the switch to the control solenoid box. Air pressure from the switch operates a microswitch. There have been several reports of spontaneous start-ups or shutdowns in extreme heat conditions. In one case this caused serious injuries. The problems are caused by pressure build-up in the air system in high heat conditions. Earlier units are the most prone and major suppliers already have a safety air bleed to avoid the problem. Carefully follow the correct depressurizing procedures when installing switches.

    d.   **Chain Counters and Controllers.** Companies such as B & G have controllers that enable programmed anchor control for precise lengths in or out,

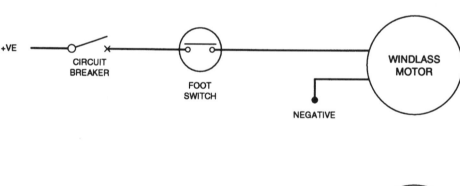

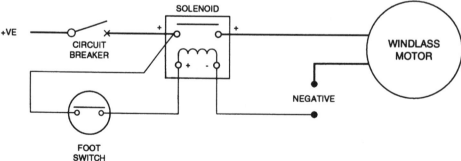

Figure 9-2 Windlass Control Systems

and automatic slow down when approaching the stemhead fitting. The display also shows actual chain out. The system connects to the solenoid control system for directional commands, and has a simple power input.

e.   **Dual Direction Solenoid Control.** A control box consisting of two or four solenoids is used for reversing the motor for both hoisting and lowering. Two footswitches and a remote panel are used for control.

(1)   **Power Consumption.** Solenoids typically consume 1 amp each.

(2)   **Caution.** Never operate both footswitches together; in fact many manufacturers specify only the up foot control be fitted.

(3)   **Protection.** Some control boxes incorporate fuse protection. Failure of the fuse is rare, but make sure that a spare is in the box for emergencies.

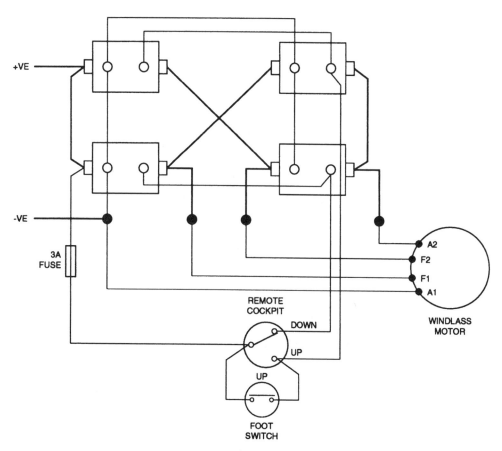

Figure 9-3 Windlass Control Systems

227

f. **Remote Controls.** There are several remote control devices:

(1) **Portable Controls.** These are weatherproof hand-held control modules that can be plugged into pre-wired socket outlet stations. Ensure that the socket remains watertight.

(2) **Radio Controls.** These devices are relatively new and innovative, and work like TV controls.

(3) **Touchpad Panels.** These are waterproof membrane touch panels. They have low reliability and a high failure rate. Control is achieved through the positive side of relays or solenoids. Many touchpad controls switch the negative so that other footswitch controls on solenoids must be converted also to negative or have relays inserted in the circuit.

(4) **Switch Panel.** The basic weatherproof rocker, or toggle switch remote system, has proved to be the most reliable remote station system. The switches must be waterproof and be spring loaded to off.

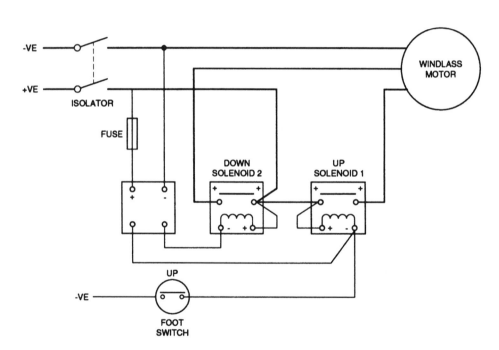

Figure 9-4 Windlass Remote Control Systems

Table 9-3 Anchor Windlass Troubleshooting

Symptom	Probable Fault
Windlass will not operate	Footswitch fault (most common cause)
	Circuit breaker switched off
	Isolator switch off
	Footswitch connection loose
	Solenoid connection fault
	Solenoid fault
	Solenoid fuse blown (if fitted)
	Motor connection loose
	Motor fault (sticking brush is common)
	Motor fault (winding failure)
	Motor internal thermal cut-out tripped
	Slow blow fuse ruptured
Windlass stalls under load	Excessive load
	Low battery voltage
	Motor connection loose
	Motor fault (brushes sticking)
	Battery terminal loose
Windlass operates slowly	Excessive load
	Low battery voltage
	Motor connection fault (hot)
	Motor fault (brushes sticking)
	Battery terminal loose
Circuit breaker trips during operation	Motor fault
	Windlass seizing
	Windlass overloading
Circuit breaker trips at switch on	Motor fault
Control fuse ruptures	Fault in solenoid
	Fault in control circuit
	Fuse fatigue
Solenoid "chatters"	Low voltage
	Fault in control switch
	Control switch connection loose
	Solenoid connection loose

9.6   Electric Furlers and Winches. Deck winches and furling gear on larger boats are rapidly being electrically and hydraulically powered. They are generally treated in the same way as anchor windlass circuits and require good circuit protection and correctly sized cables. Winches may be powered from an electric motor or a hydraulic power pack. Most furlers operate from a hydraulic power pack. Electrical loads are quite considerable and for 12-volt systems the following cable sizes are required. Electric winches generally consume more power than windlasses and careful power supply planning is required. The power source should be off a starting battery, and the engine start battery can be paralleled with another of equivalent size. Install the largest cold cranking rating possible.

Table 9-4 Winch Cable Rating Table

Cable Length	Current Rating	AWG	Metric	B & S
up to 10 meters	320 amps	1/0	50 mm^2	0
10 to 15 meters	390 amps	00	65 mm^2	00
15 to 20 meters	500 amps	000	85 mm^2	000

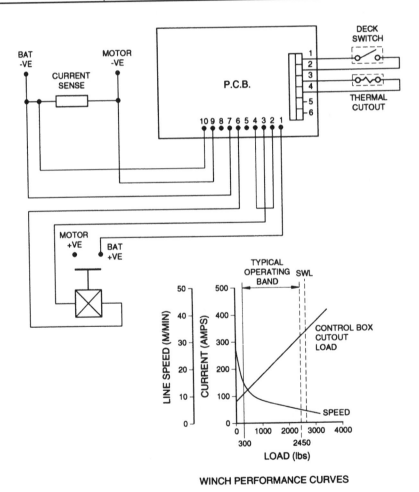

WINCH PERFORMANCE CURVES

Figure 9-5 Lewmar Winch Control

9.7 **DC Motors.** Most installed pumps and machinery have DC motors installed, and most are low maintenance. Where larger motors (thrusters, windlasses, winches, refrigeration compressor drives, starter motors and motor driven generators) are in use, the question of proper maintenance becomes critical. My commercial seagoing career started on 220-volt DC systems, and the first lesson I learned was that DC motor performance and reliability is directly related to effective preventive maintenance. Routine inspection of DC motors on thrusters, furlers, starters, windlasses and propulsion systems consists of rigorous and thorough inspection. This should be performed every 6 months.

    (1)   Inspect the carbon brushes for chipping, grooving, uneven wear and loose or frayed wire connectors. Compare the length of brushes and replace the entire set of brushes if worn.

    (2)   Check that brushes move freely within the brush-holders. Check that spring pressure is correct by simply pulling the brush back and snapping it against the commutator.

    (3)   Ensure the wire brush connectors are clear of any moving parts. Check that brush tail connections are tight.

    (4)   Inspect the commutator.

    (5)   Inspect electrical connections and mechanical fasteners inside the motor and connection box.

    (6)   Inspect the field winding connections.

    (7)   Inspect the motor interior for condensation, access covers and gaskets.

9.8 **Commutators.** The condition of a DC motor can be determined by observing the condition of the commutator.

    a.   **Good Commutator Surfaces.** Good commutator conditions can be found by observing the copper surface patina or surface markings. The skin that develops is made up of oxide and graphite.

        (1)   **Light Tan Film.** This condition indicates a machine is performing correctly.

        (2)   **Mottled Surface.** This condition is characterized by random film patterns on commutator segments and is normal.

        (3)   **Slot Bar Marking.** The film is slightly darker, and occurs in a definite pattern that relates to the number of conductors per slot.

        (4)   **Heavy Film.** This condition is acceptable if uniformly found over the entire commutator.

b. **Commutator Deterioration Signs.** The following signs and causes indicate degrading motor performance and require attention:

(1) **Streaking.** Commutator surface streaking indicates the start of metal transfer from commutator to brush. Light brush pressures, a light electrical load, an abrasive or porous brush in use or dust contamination can cause the condition.

(2) **Threading.** Fine line threading on the commutator surface happens when an excessive quantity of copper transfers to the brushes. If severe, the commutator will require resurfacing and brush wear will be rapid. Light electrical loads, light brush pressures, porous brushes, or dust contamination can cause this condition.

(3) **Grooving.** Grooves in the brush path are caused by abrasive brushes and dust contamination.

(4) **Copper Drag.** A build-up of copper material at the trailing edge of a commutator segment is caused by light brush pressures, vibration, abrasive brushes and contamination.

(5) **Pitch Bar Marking.** Low or burn spots on the commutator surface are caused by poor armature connections, unbalanced shunt fields, vibration or abrasive brushes. The number of marks equates all or half the number of poles.

(6) **Heavy Slot Bar Marking.** Etching of the commutator segment trailing edges is caused by poor electrical adjustment, electrical overloads or dust contamination. The pattern relates to the number of conductors per slot.

9.9 **DC Motor Cleaning.** Regular cleaning of DC motors is essential to reliability and long service life. Use a portable vacuum cleaner and soft bristle brush to dislodge dust and other material.

(1) Disconnect the power.

(2) Clean the brush boxes and brushes, and ensure brushes move freely within the brush holders.

(3) Clean the accessible field and armature windings.

(4) Clean the commutator and commutator risers. Use a small soft brush and clean out any build-up of dust in between commutator segments. Build-ups have the effect of shorting out the insulation between the commutator segments. *Do not polish or clean commutator with emery paper.*

(5) Clean the lower part of the motor.

9.10   Carbon Brushes. The carbon brush must have good commutating and contact characteristics, good mechanical strength and wear properties, a resistance to sparking and a suitable contact voltage drop. Brushes are normally manufactured from hard carbon and natural or electrical graphite. Metal graphite brushes are used for slipring applications as they have lower contact voltage drops. If brush wear is abnormal, this may be caused by very low humidity, abrasive dust or intermittent loads. The commutator surface may not have a properly developed skin, or have incorrect brush grades, jammed brushes and excess sparking. Sparking is caused by poor machine commutation, and this may be due to wrong brush types and grades, incorrect brush pressures, badly undercut commutators, or excessive vibration or overloading. Typical brush pressure is in the range 170-210 g/cm^2. If the brush pressure is too low, the contact voltage drop increases and brush wear will increase due to burning. If the pressure is too high there will be increased friction and increased mechanical wear. Check the pressure on all brushes using a small spring balance. The wear surface of the brush can also indicate performance. A very shiny surface indicates excessive friction or brush movement. A brush should always be semi-bright and have a surface covered with small pores. If brush replacement is required, it must be done correctly or considerable damage will be done to the commutator.

(1)   Ensure that you use the correct brush for the machine.

(2)   Use a very fine grade strip of sandpaper slightly wider than the brush. Reverse it so abrasive surface is under the brush. Move it back and forth around the commutator so that the carbon brush is shaped to that of the commutator.

(3)   Use a vacuum cleaner and extract all the dust out of the machine to prevent accumulations of abrasive materials. Never use emery cloth; it will scratch the commutator surface, and shed the conductive particles that lodge in the commutator segments, causing shorts and arcing.

Table 9-5 DC Motor Troubleshooting

Symptom	Probable Fault
Windings overheating	Motor overloading
	Run time excessive
	Ventilation insufficient
	High ambient temperature
Excessive commutator sparking	Motor overloading
	Oil on commutator
	Brushes sticking
	Brush pressure too low
	Brushes worn
	Commutator dirty
	Commutator damaged
	Excessive brush dust buildup
Motor overloading	Excessive mechanical load
	Bearings binding
Excessive current draw	Excessive mechanical load
	Bearings binding
	Valve closed (if a pump load)
	Electrical connection fault
Excess motor noise and vibration	Bearing failure
	Motor hold down bolts loose
	Motor load transmitting vibration
	Misaligned coupling
	Coupling damaged, out of balance
	Brushes bouncing on commutator

Lighting Systems

10.1 **Lighting Systems.** Boat lighting systems are important. Installing the right light for the right function is often a problem. The aesthetic considerations are of obvious importance but there are also a number of technical factors. Many motorboats have large saloon and external areas. Illumination areas, power consumption, numbers of lights and cabling to them are factors to be considered.

    a. **Illumination Area.** The size of the area to be illuminated is an important consideration. In most vessel applications, specific areas are illuminated. Consider the following:

        (1) **Spot Lighting.** Spot lighting is generally used in areas such as main saloon areas, bunk reading lights and main deck areas. Projected lights generally require a fitting with a reflector or a special lamp. Factors such as beam power and beam angle are important.

        (2) **Large Area Illumination.** Many motorboats, in particular those with large saloon areas or bridge deck areas such as power cats, present lighting problems. Unlike in houses, the deck head is lower than ceilings, which limits the effectiveness of lights. Consideration must be given to beam angles and light output power.

    b. **Illumination Level.** The level of light reaching the working areas on the deck, or the overall light levels below must be sufficient to safely perform tasks. The term lumens per watt is used to measure how much light in lumens is produced for each watt of energy. The following factors must be considered:

        (1) **Background Lighting.** This lighting is generally low power and uses interior surfaces and upholstery to reflect light for unobtrusive and shadowless lighting.

        (2) **Low Level Lighting.** This is localized illumination that does not require levels sufficient to perform work. Typical are night lighting, courtesy lights and general saloon lighting.

        (3) **High Level Lighting.** This lighting is used in deck spotlights, handheld spots, saloon lights, bunk lights, engine space and transom lights to name a few. These lights should give as far as possible shadowless illumination without excessive glare.

    c. **Light Colors.** The color rendering properties of the light play a significant part in effective lighting. Using lights of the right color rendering properties can significantly alter the richness of woods, for instance.

(1) **Warm or Soft Colors.** Fluorescent tubes are generally warm soft. The newer, low energy lights have a softer light that strikes a balance between good illumination levels and good color rendering.

(2) **Cold or Hard Colors.** Halogen lamps and some fluorescent tubes have a very cold, hard and intense white light.

d. **Power Consumption.** Electrical power consumption is the very first factor to consider. Compare the main light types, and make a decision based on the most satisfactory light for a given power consumption. Low energy tube lights offer the best light per amp output and I have had great success with them. A mixture of light types will be required to obtain the required results.

10.2   AC Fluorescent Lights. The majority of AC powered vessels have extensive lighting circuits. These primarily consist of fluorescent lights, which are 3–4 times more efficient than incandescent lights. They operate at lower temperatures and have significantly longer life spans than normal incandescent lights, typically around 15,000 hours compared to 1,000 hours for the incandescent lamp. The life span of fluorescent lights is affected by factors such as the frequency of switching and the voltage levels. The main fluorescent light types in use are the Preheat, Slimline Instant Start and the Rapid Start. A fluorescent light requires several other circuit components to function.

a. **The Starter.** The starter or the glow tube starter is used on preheat type lights. Many new lights such as instant and rapid start types do not require starters. Starters consist of a small gas filled tube, which incorporates a switch. When the power is switched on, a glow discharge occurs to heat the bimetallic switch and the contacts then close to supply current to the tube filament electrodes. The glow discharge ceases and the bimetallic switch cools and opens to interrupt the current to the ballast. The current supplied by the switch to the ballast opens to provide a high voltage (400-600 V) inductive surge at the filament. This ionizes the mercury to form a vapor, which initiates the discharge and emits the UV light, causing the phosphor coating to emit visible light. Once the light is on, a lower voltage of around 100–175 volts is required to maintain discharge. Pulse starters are an electronic version that interrupts the filament supply to generate the inductive kick at the correct instant.

b. **The Ballast.** The ballast, sometimes called the inductor, is used to assist in the starting process by generating the high voltage inductive surge and to limit current flow as the tube has a very low resistance. A Slimline Instant Start fitting requires a high open circuit voltage 300% higher than normal operating voltages to initiate an arc. To achieve this, an autotransformer is used as part of the ballast unit, along with a choke coil or reactor to reduce starting voltage to the rated lamp voltage. These ballast types are either Lead Lag or Series Sequence. In Series Sequence lights, the two tubes are connected in series and the lamps are started in sequence. Rapid Start lights are the most common types; they use low voltage cathodes that are preheated by heater windings that are incorporated into the ballast. Ballasts are generally electromagnetic "core and coil" types, which function as a transformer and as a choke to limit current. Electronic ballasts have a high frequency output up to 20 kHz, using electronic conversion circuits. They consist of a high frequency inverter and switch with current limiting from a small inductor that has a high impedance at high frequency. This has resulted in a reduction in size, weight and noise as well as increased efficiency. Hybrid electromagnetic and electronic units are also available. Ballasts and fixtures must be properly grounded as an electric shock risk exists. These ballast types generally eliminate the 100–120kHz flicker that is common on iron type ballasts as they incorporate rectification and filtering circuits. The ballasts have been known to cause radio interference, although European ones must be RFI free.

c.   **Capacitors.** Capacitors are used to correct voltage and current back in phase. In large installations every third fitting may have a capacitor installed across the ballast to improve power factor. Some circuits also incorporate a capacitor for suppression of RFI, which is generated by radiation from the lamp to aerials and aerial feed lines, or fed back into the supply. Fluorescent lights should be kept as far as possible from aerials to reduce interference.

d.   **Troubleshooting.** When a light is faulty, always check the lamps first. Check all lamp sockets for good pin contact, check that the starters are functioning. Check and tighten all wiring connections, and check the ballasts. The most common faults are:

    (1)   **Iron Ballasts.** The main cause of failure is deterioration of the ballast secondary insulation, mainly because of incorrect wiring polarity connection. If a new lamp is installed and lights, the ballast is good. A power off test with a multimeter set from each winding to ground should be high resistance; be careful as lights may have charged capacitors. Ballasts that have failed generally have burns, an acrid smell, or hum and buzz loudly. Ballasts may have an overheat switch which opens when overheating, and this cycling may open and close as ballast heats and cools down. Ballast faults can damage other components and should be rectified promptly.

    (2)   **Tube Faults.** Blackened ends on tubes often indicate a faulty tube in 30–40W rapid start light fittings. Electrode and filament failure is usually indicated by a low level glow or flickering at the tube ends, and sometimes there is no light at all. Tube replacement is the easiest way to test the fitting. Tube swirling indicates possible low voltage levels, or incompatibility between lamp and ballast.

    (3)   **Tube Fittings.** Faulty or fractured BiPin tube sockets are a common fault. In boats, this is often caused by vibration, subsequent overheating and arcing. The other main cause is the forcing in of tubes damaging the end caps and contacts.

10.3   Internal Lights. Internal DC lighting systems consist of several light types. Different lights are used for different functions, and one of the main criteria is gaining maximum light output for a given power consumption. There are several light types available and, before deciding on lights for below, consider light reflectivity.

a.   **Reflectivity.** The level of brightness and the contrast with the background must be considered. In a full timber cabin, reflected light will be minimal while a cabin with painted surfaces, or light timbers, will increase the overall illumination levels. I have seen some beautiful wood-lined cabins, with large numbers of lights fitted in the headliner, or additional corner spots. Yet, even with many lights on, they are still gloomy with low light levels. Interior schemes that are efficient mean fewer lights with less cable, and much less electrical power consumption for a given light level. Reflectivity is usually expressed as a percentage. Maple and birch is 60%; light oak 40%; walnut and teak 15–20%: white and light cream paint is 70–80%; sky blue/pale grey 40–45% and beige is 25–35%.

b.   **DC Fluorescent Lights.** This is one of the most common light types, but they do have drawbacks. DC fluorescent tubes have an integral inverter that raises the voltage to a higher AC value. The elongated shape provides a good lumen/watt ratio and relatively low power consumption, approximately 80% less for the same output. Typical output is 65–90 lumens. They also withstand vibration and shock well. The working life is 5–8 times longer than incandescent lights. Log on towww.thinlight.com, www.aquasignal.net. The main components are:

(1)   **Inverter.** The inverter in low voltage DC fittings is generally the main cause of failure. In most cheaper light fittings, the quality of the electronics is poor. They also fail in relatively small overvoltage conditions such as when charging voltages rise to 14 volts. Always install fluorescent lights with a voltage input up to 15 volts.

(2)   **Tube.** The fluorescent tubes for household use function quite satisfactorily if the inverter quality is good. If the electronics are of poor quality, the tube will show blackening in a very short period. The output of a tube varies with temperature. Peak output is normally at 25°C; if hotter or colder, the light output is reduced.

(3)   **Ballasts.** In AC fluorescent lights, older ballast types are now replaced with low energy units. Ballasts can be electromagnetic, electronic, rapid start or instant start. Units are designed for single or dual tube installations. Ballasts provide the high start voltage required to initiate tube conduction. Starters also preheat the tubes.

(4)   **Radio Frequency Interference.** Fluorescent lights have a reputation for radio frequency interference. This is due to the quality of the inverter electronics. High quality inverters, such as those from

Aquasignal, are suitably suppressed to international standards. Fluorescent units with high quality inverters are far more reliable.

c. **Incandescent Lights.** Incandescent lights are the oldest and most common light types. The following factors should be considered:

(1) **Power Consumption.** When switched on, power consumption can be 15 times normal hot power consumption. The basis of the incandescent lamp is the heating of a filament, and much of the energy is dissipated as heat.

(2) **Life Expectancy.** They consume high power for the available light output and are subject to damage by vibration, over voltage, and reasonably rapid filament degradation. Most AC lamps can be replaced by compact fluorescent tubes for big energy savings.

(3) **Voltage Limitations.** Overvoltage conditions significantly reduce incandescent lamp life expectancies. Running at lower voltages extends life, but seriously reduces light output. For every 5% of voltage drop, light output reduces by 20%. The familiar yellow glow as the battery voltage decreases is common. The key to operating incandescent lamps, especially navigation lamps, is to keep voltage drop to a minimum.

d. **Halogen/Xelogen/Xenon Lighting.** Halogen lights were the first high output lights in common use, as they have higher outputs, typically around 20 lumens. They have been supplemented and, in some cases, replaced by Xenon and Xelogen lamps. The halogen lamp base is designated as G4 and Xelogen G5. Many powerboats use light rails that incorporate 1, 2 or 3 lamps and produce about 100–200 lux. Log on to www.cantalupi.it.

(1) **Life Expectancy.** Halogen lights are categorized as incandescent lights. They are designed for use in commercial installations on a stable 12/24 volts AC power source. When used in DC installations, the life expectancy is significantly reduced, and the higher voltages generated during battery charging also reduce life. Xelogen lamps have a service life 10 times that of a halogen lamp, and should last for 20,000 hours. They have a lower operating temperature and while the glass can be handled, it is still better not to. The Xelogen lamp is also dimmable.

(2) **Voltage Limitations.** Vibration resistance is relatively poor. Resistance to overvoltage situations is also poor. Normally a halogen lamp is operated in commercial applications with a very stable 12-volt AC supply, with maximum life being at around 11.8 volts. When operating on DC, and at charging voltages up to 14.5 volts, bulb life can be seriously reduced.

239

(3)   **Installation.** The pure silicon glass used in halogen lamps can degrade with salt air interaction. Under no circumstances should the glass be handled as salts and impurities from the fingers will degrade the silicon glass and shorten life. Allowances must be made for the high temperatures generated that can reach 700°C in normal operation. Good ventilation is required to prevent the lamp holder or wire from reaching a maximum of 250°C. Most halogen fittings also have high temperature wiring.

e.   **Low Energy Lighting.** Low energy lights are now commonly installed on many vessels both AC and DC. They operate on a similar principle to fluorescent lights in which an electrical arc is generated between two electrodes, located at each end of the tube. These lights give a very high output for a relatively small power draw. They produce a light only marginally less than a 60-watt household bulb, and have a power consumption of just 16 watts. Most vessels I have installed these on run just one light for the entire saloon area. Life expectancy is greater than for standard fluorescent lights. Similar to halogen or fluorescent lights, they are intolerant to overvoltage conditions, most accept voltages up to 17 volts. In AC lighting, the Compact Plug-in Fluoro Tubes have an average rated life of around 10,000 hours. These include 2D (square fluoro), short twin-tube, quad-tube and triple-tube. There are screw-in Edison Screw (ES) types that do not require adapters including twin and quad tube types. Quality light fittings have a PCB with integrated circuit operating at 35khz suiting lamps in the 5–11 watt range. Typical life expectancy is around 8,000 hours. Typical outputs and equivalent light outputs are for 12 volt units 5W/520mA for 25W, 7W/680mA for 40W, 9W/850mA for 60W and 11W/1000mA for 75W. Log on to www.marlec.co.uk for Leisurelights.

f.   **Red Night Lights.** Red lights are very useful in strategic locations. It can take up to 45 minutes for normal night vision to return if the eye is subject to a white light. The typical locations for night lighting are at the helm and in the pilothouse. Some fluorescent lights have dual tube fittings, and the use of LED cluster lights is effective. Some manufacturers make fittings with red diffusers.

10.4   Dimmers and Voltage Stabilizers. Many boats incorporate dimmers on lighting circuits, and many have halogen lamps.

a.   **DC Dimmers.** Earlier types were variable resistance rheostat types; new technology systems use electronic pulse width modulated (PWM) control. PWM units' features are no heat, high outputs of around 100W at 12 volts, and high efficiency with minimal losses of only round 2%. Control modules are also overload and reverse polarity protected. One feature on some models is a soft-start function that limits the initial inrush current, which can improve the life of bulbs. Some modules also have a no-load consumption, typically around 10mA, so light circuits must be isolated or switched off when boats are unattended. Modular dimmers such as the Cantalupi types, have short circuit and thermal protection. When installing, the correct output rating must be used, overloading will lead to early failure. Ratings are 2 amps = 12V/24W or 24V/48W; 5 amps = 12V/60W or 24V/120W; 10 amps = 12V/120W or 24V/240; 20 amps = 12V/240W or 24V/480W; 30 amps = 12V/360W or 24V/720W. Dimmers often create electrical noise, and a filter capacitor should be installed as close as possible to the dimmer. Dimmers are reliable; in case of failure, always check the module power input and connections first. When more than one push button is used, check all first. If all are out, the module is the cause. The push buttons and connections are the most common failure point.

b. **AC Dimmers.** Larger vessels having AC lighting systems use different dimmer types. Toroidal transformer units are being used. Unlike normal transformers, there is virtually no mechanical vibration noise or any magnetic hum. The no-load power consumption is around 80% less than standard transformers, and overall efficiency is around 95%. The transformers have primary voltages of 120 volts with a secondary of 12 or 24 volts. Capacity ratings are quoted in VoltAmps (VA) and can be in the range of 60 up to 600 VA. Units typically include overload, thermal and short circuit protection. If a unit suddenly stops, the thermal protection is the first possible cause. Some lighting systems also use electronic transformers such as the Aurora types which offer full dimming and a soft start function. The transformers have AC input voltages of 120 volts 50/60 Hz with stable output voltages on 11.5 volts. These supply low voltage AC lighting such as halogens, and an output frequency of typically 30kHz, and power outputs of 20–75 VA. Some units have a soft start feature, which ramps up the voltage from zero to full output current, as well as the usual thermal and short circuit protection. The units also use toroidal transformers instead of ferromagnetic ones to reduce heat and increase efficiency. Like all AC powered equipment, caution must be used when installing and troubleshooting, and they must be switched off when working on equipment.

c. **Lamp Voltage Stabilizers.** Lamps are affected by higher voltages reducing life expectancy. Light manufacturer Cantalupi has developed a voltage stabilizer that can accept a variable input voltage in the range 12.5 to 16 volts at 12 volts or 24.5 to 29 volts at 24 volts. The output is stable at 12 or 24 volts over all voltage ranges up to maximum power rating of 25W to maximize lamp life by at least 200-400%. It is a good investment in vessels with large halogen light installations. Devices have short circuit, thermal, overload and reverse polarity protection. A similar device is the IML Bulb Saver which reduces lamp voltage by 1.5 volts, and has a 15 amp rating in the range 10–40 VDC. Always mount in an area with good ventilation to reduce the heat. Units should be mounted on a heat sink.

241

10.5   **Deck Lights.** There is a range of lights with different functions that must be installed properly and maintained.

      a.   **Courtesy Lights.** The installation of courtesy lighting in the cockpit, flybridge, stairs and transom areas is very useful but there are points to consider. Many of the lights available are of very poor quality and quickly degrade, so select quality fittings. A newer development are the LED types, which consist of high output LEDs such as the Hella units that have 10 LEDs. This is equivalent to a 20-watt incandescent bulb using just 0.16 amps. The cheaper fittings that use festoon bulbs are a constant cause of problems, including poor bulb contacts. Similar LED fittings such as bait well lamps in amber color also serve well as courtesy lights.

      b.   **Safety and Working Lights.**

          (1)   **Deck Lights.** Deck lights are essential for everything from fishing, entertainment, security and boarding at night, to name a few important reasons. Halogen and Xenon lamps have now replaced incandescent sealed beam types, with increases in efficiency and light outputs. Xenon lamps have working lives up to 2,500 hours and have internal Xenon ballast modules. Anchor area spotlights are typically fixed on the flybridge or motorized spotlights are used to illuminate the area. Where stainless steel pulpits are installed, I often install small white navigation lights on the pulpit facing down to illuminate the anchor well. The lights can be switched from the steering station. The light is not too bright but it is practical.

          (2)   **Docking Lights.** Many motorboats have recessed sealed beam spotlights in the bows. It is important to ensure that the seals are in good condition, as failures are caused through corrosion of the connections. 35-watt Xenon lamps, with a service life that is 500% longer than a halogen and consume less than 3 amps, are being used.

          (3)   **Fiber Optic Lighting.** Fiber optics are used to direct lighting to steps and deck areas. The light sources have a long life expectancy at around 3,000 hours average. The Fondle company has Edgepoint for toerails, Deckpoint for winches and cleats, Specpoint for chart tables and engine bays and Navpoint for navigation light systems. Light source reliability is quoted as 3000mtb. www.fondle.co.uk

          (4)   **Helideck Lighting.** Some super- and mega-yachts have helidecks. It is important to regularly inspect fittings as they are prone to water ingress. Similarly, any floodlights on the perimeter also require inspection. Red hazard obstruction lights on high points near the helideck require inspection and maintenance to remain in good working order.

c.   **High Intensity Discharge Lights.** Many larger motorboats, tugs, workboats and trawlers have AC powered mercury vapor, metal halide and high-pressure sodium spot and deck lights. High-pressure sodium lights have a characteristic orange color, very high light outputs (2,500–140,000 lumens), and are very energy efficient, with an average life of around 24,000 hours. Power consumption depends on light types and sizes and ranges from 35 watts to 1kW. Metal halides are marginally behind these, followed by mercury vapor in terms of efficiency and light outputs. Lights require discharge ballasts to start and limit starting or ignition currents. Some mercury vapor bulbs are self-ballasted.

10.6   Lamp Bases. Lamp bases are extremely varied and the designations are often confusing. The following are the more common lamp base types and their designations:

a.   **Halogen Lamps.** Lamp socket types include E14, E27, E40, R75, BA95, B15D, G4, G6, and 35.

b.   **Incandescent Lamps.** Lamp socket types include E14, E27, E40, B15D, B22D, P28, Candle base E12, and Medium Base E26.

c.   **Fluorescent Lamp.** Lamp socket types include G5, G13, G23, G24 and G32. AC fluorescent lamps are undergoing change with newer more energy efficient tubes,

10.7   Spotlights. Spotlights are generally confined to foredeck spot lighting. The very severe environment they are subject to requires careful selection. Always get the best quality available because when you need them, it is always under difficult conditions. Usually ratings are given in Candlepower or Lux, with Lux being the amount of light at a nominated target distance, typically 100 and 500 yards. A rating may be given then as 330,000 candlepower or 52 Lux at 100 yards and 2.1 Lux at 500 yards. Many powerboats have remote controlled spotlights mounted on foredecks and fly bridge fronts. Some units use Xenon lamp systems, and have outputs of 1.5 million Candelas, and with a 24-volt supply consume 8 amps. The biggest failure area on spotlights is poor wiring and connections. Make sure that cables are rated for the power of the unit. As they are exposed to weather, keep them covered when not in use, and operate them regularly through complete rotations, as well as pan and tilt to prevent seizing. If fuses blow, it is generally due to seizing and overloading. Deck spotlights have more concentrated beams that are around 6–8 degrees compared to general floodlights of around 3–40 degrees. Light output must be sufficient to ensure good illumination at deck level and typically this is the anchor windlass area. When there is a problem with anchors, you really need good illumination, and most vessels mount quite inadequately rated fittings. Spotlights should have a clearly defined beam pattern without scattering at the sides. The illustration below shows the different beam distributions and light ranges for Optronics Blue Eye spotlights. The range is for clear conditions and a reflective target. Always select a light with a switch for signaling.

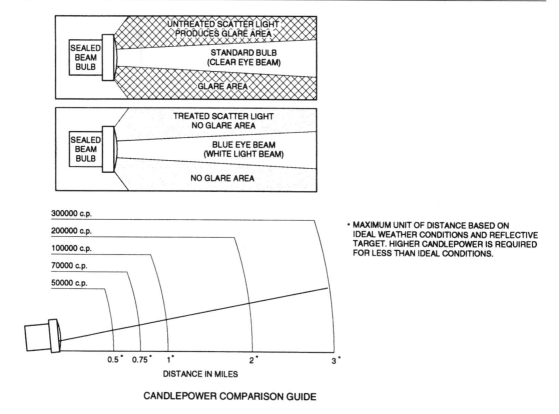

CANDLEPOWER COMPARISON GUIDE

Figure 10-1 Spotlight Characteristics

10.8 **Navigation Lights**. Navigation lights are of critical importance, both for safety and for legal, rules-of-the-road reasons. It is not sufficient to simply say you have lights installed, and even on correctly. They must be mounted at the correct locations. It is all very well to blame merchant ships for running pleasure craft over, but if the correct lights are missing, they are unable to identify your vessel. Special incandescent lamp types are almost standard; LED-based lights are now appearing on the market, such as those from Hella.

> **a.** **Legal Requirements.** All vessels are required by the International Regulations for Preventing Collisions at Sea to display the correct lights. Failure to comply may void insurance policies in the event of a collision:
>
> > **(1)** **Navigation Lights.** Lights should be displayed in accordance with the provisions of Part C, Lights and Shapes.
> >
> > **(2)** **Lights.** Lights should be of an approved type and conform to the provisions of Annex I with respect to positioning and technical details of lights and shapes.

b.   **Navigation Light Monitoring.** Larger vessels under survey or class will be required to have primary and backup navigation lights. In addition they need to have light circuit monitoring for failures. Aquasignal makes off the shelf control panels. These units are reliable, but connections again must be secure.

c.   **Anchor.** The anchor light is an all-round white light. It should not be masked at any point. Reference Annex I. 9(b) with respect to horizontal sectors. Always use it if you are anchored where traffic is possible. If you do not and a vessel collides and sinks you, it's your fault.

d.   **Port and Starboard Lights (Sidelights).** The port light (red), and the starboard light (green) must display an unbroken light over an arc of 112½°, from dead ahead to 22½° abaft the beam. In a vessel under 20 meters, the light can be combined into a bi-color fitting. These lights are usually mounted on the pulpit in many powerboats, but often a stainless steel section of the pulpit will partially obscure the light. Ensure that it is visible over the prescribed arc, otherwise you are technically displaying an illegal light.

e.   **Stern Light.** This is a white light placed at or near the stern, preferably on the centerline. It must display an arc of visibility totalling 135°, from dead astern to 67½° each side:

    (1)   **Display.** It must always be displayed when vessel is under power, along with the sidelights and masthead light.

    (2)   **Mounting.** Do not mount the lights on angled transoms without mounting plates to ensure that they are vertical. Lights angled skywards are very difficult to see and technically illegal.

f.   **Masthead Light (Steaming Light).** This is a white light that must be visible over an unbroken arc of 225°, from dead ahead to 22½° abaft the beam on each side. The light must be fixed on the centerline of the vessel. There are also vertical mounting requirements for the masthead light. Reference Annex I.2 Vertical Positioning and Spacing of lights:

    (1)   **Vessels 12 meters LOA or less.** A minimum of 1 meter above the sidelights.

    (2)   **Vessels 12 to 20 meters LOA.** A minimum of 2.5 meters above the gunwale.

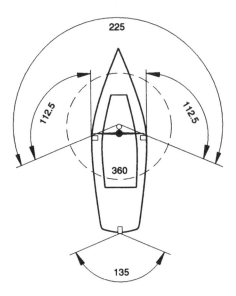

STARBOARD LAMP	112.5 DEGREES
PORT LAMP	112.5 DEGREES
MASTHEAD LAMP	225 DEGREES
STERN LAMP	135 DEGREES
ANCHOR LAMP	360 DEGREES

Figure 10-2 Navigation Lighting Plan

10.9   Navigation Light Technical Requirements. Navigation lights have legal requirements regarding (chromacity) color. Reference Annex I.7 Color specification of lights and
Annex I.8 Light intensities www.aquasignal.net:

    a.   **Color.** Color or chromacity are defined by the International Collision Regu-
lations. By purchasing approved light fittings, you know that they meet the
requirements.

    b.   **Lamp Ratings.** Lamp ratings are generally given by the manufacturers and
are designed to give the required range and luminosity of the granted ap-
proval. Do not increase the lamp rating to increase the brightness, or decrease it to save power. If you do alter the lamps and you have an accident,
your insurance may be invalidated and you could be sued for damages, as
you are technically not displaying approved navigation lights:

        (1)   **Sockets.** Special sockets are used to ensure that filaments are cor-
rectly aligned to the lens and horizontal shades systems.

        (2)   **Light Outputs.** Light output and wattage are designed for a high
lumen per watt ratio.

        (3)   **Light Consistency.** Light emission gives an equal output through a
360° azimuth.

c. **Visibility.** The required minimum ranges of visibilities are as follows:

    (1)   **Stern Light.**   <12m = 2 nm, 12-20m = 2 nm.

    (2)   **Sidelights.**   <12m = 1 nm, 12-20m = 2 nm.

    (3)   **Masthead Light.**   <12m = 2 nm, 12-20m = 3 nm.

    (4)   **Anchor Light.**   <12m = 2 nm, 12-20m = 2 nm.

d. **Approvals.** Navigation lights should all be approved. Most manufacturers will issue a certificate with each fitting.

    (1)   **National Approvals.** It is important to note that some fittings are only approved by a national port or marine authority (ABYC or USCG) and may technically be illegal in another country.

    (2)   **Approval Certificates.** Always keep the numbered approval certificate with your vessel files.

e. **Maintenance.** It is important to check lights regularly, as any defects may cause failure or be illegal. Check the following:

    (1)   **Moisture.** Check the light's interior for moisture that can degrade lamp contacts or cause a short circuit. Remove and replace the lamp a few times to exercise the spring. Ensure a good contact on the lamp base contact. Operate light for an hour to dry it out.

    (2)   **Diffuser.** Check the light diffusers for small surface cracks that will alter the light characteristics or let water in.

Water and Sewage Systems

11.1   Pressurized Water Systems. The modern motorboat has several water systems that must be properly planned and maintained. A failure in the freshwater or sewage system can make life uncomfortable; a failure in the gray water systems such as the shower drain and sink units inconvenient; a failure in the bilge pumps systems is dangerous and can render the boat unseaworthy. Freshwater is essential, and having the capacity to make it rather than find ports and marinas to refill offers more options, including longer voyages. Watermakers can pay for themselves with reduced marina fees, fuel for return to port and loss of time. A typical arrangement is illustrated below. Look at Jabsco (www.jabsco.com) who also own FloJet and Rule.

11.2   Water Tanks. It is good practice to have two separate tanks for water stowage. Before filling a tank, transfer the remaining water to one tank. The new water can be put in the tank without contaminating water you know to be good. If the new water is found to be of poor quality and you have to dump it, you do not lose the whole lot. Toxic by-products from bacteria are characterized by unpleasant smells. Cleaning regimes should be undertaken at least twice a year to ensure the integrity of the water.

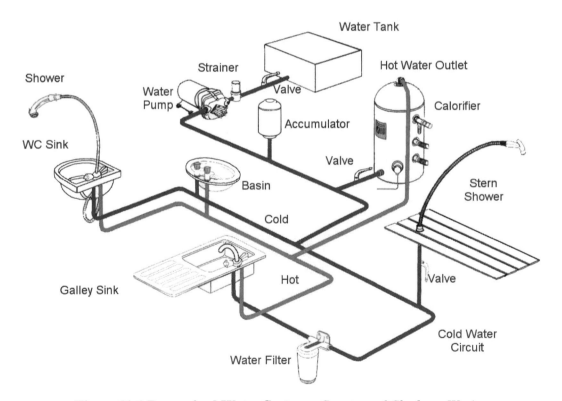

Figure 11-1 Pressurized Water System , *Courtesy of Cleghorn Waring*

a. **Cleaning.** The tank should be scoured by hand with a brush, but do not use excessive quantities of detergent.

b. **Flushing.** Fill the tank and flush out at least three times.

c. **Disinfection.** The new water and tank must be disinfected to prevent bacterial growth. Water chlorination is easily accomplished by adding a solution of household bleach in the quantities of 5 to 100 of tank contents. Let a certain amount run through all outlets to disinfect all parts of the system. Top off the water tank and allow to stand for four hours. Re-flush the system another three times. Pour in a quantity of vinegar in the ratio of 1 liter to 50 liters of system capacity and allow to stand for 2 days. Refill with freshwater and flush 3 times again. The tank is then ready for use and will maintain potable water quality for several months. An easier and quicker way is to use Puriclean or Aquatabs or similar brand sterilizing solution. This will clean and purify the tank. After filling the tank and adding the cleaning solution, let it stand for a few hours before flushing.

11.3   Water Pressure Pumps. The primary purpose of the pump is to supply and pressurize the water from the tank. A pump is selected based on the number of outlets to be supplied and the flow rate required. If the pump is incorrectly rated for the system, the flow will drop off when another outlet is opened. The Sensor-Max VSD (Variable Speed Drive) water pump from Jabsco offers a significant development. The pump unit has a Hall Effect pressure sensor for the water flow and varies the motor speed to maintain constant pressure. This dispenses with the requirement for an accumulator and pressure switches. The VSD controls the motor speed using a PWM DC motor controller.

a. **Diaphragm Pump.** These units are the most robust and are designed for multi-outlet systems. They are self-priming, relatively quiet in operation, more tolerant to dry running conditions, and have built-in hydraulic pulsation dampening.

b. **Impeller Pump.** These units normally have a pump with bronze casing and a nitrile or neoprene impeller. They are self-priming, and less tolerant to running dry.

Table 11-1 Water Pump Data Table

Model	Current	Flow l/min	Max. Head	Cut-in	Cut-out
Jabsco					
44010	4.0 amps	9.5	1.2 m	10 psi	20 psi
36800	6.0 amps	12.5	1.5 m	10 psi	20 psi
Flojet					
143-12 V	3.9 amps	12.5		20 psi	35 psi
143-12 V	6.0 amps	17.0		20 psi	35 psi
Whale					
EF 2.0612	3.9 amps	7.0		16 psi	32 psi
EF 2.1012	4.2 amps	10.0		16 psi	32 psi

11.4   Pump Wiring. There are a couple of installation points to observe when installing water pumps.

   a.   **Cable Sizes.** Ensure that the cable is rated for maximum current draw and voltage drop. Voltage drop problems are very common, and oversizing the cable is a good practice.

   b.   **Connections.** Connections are normally made directly to the pump motors, and the crimps must be done properly. Also put some Vaseline over the connection to stop moisture getting to the connection lugs. Where wire tails require a butt splice, make sure that they are crimped properly. Some pumps with integral pressure switches require connection directly to one side, and this must properly done.

   c.   **Bonding.** Some metal cased pumps, such as wash down pumps must be bonded. This should be taken to the negative polarity of the supply. In the event of a positive short the case, this will ensure circuit breaker trips.

11.5   Water System Strainer. The strainer is installed in the water suction line to the pump. Its purpose is to protect the pump from damaging sediment and particles from the storage tank. Observe the following:

   a.   **Element Cleaning.** It is essential to clean regularly the stainless steel element. Blockages are most frequent when commissioning a new vessel, or after refilling an empty tank. I have seen a number of vessels where the element has been removed because the owners were tired of cleaning blockages. The result will be early pump failure. It is good practice to clean the system and eliminate the cause.

   b.   **Bowl Seals.** After cleaning the element, make sure that a good seal is made with the transparent inspection cover. Imperfect seals can cause air being drawn into the system. Ensure that the seal is in good condition; a smear of Vaseline or silicon grease often helps.

11.6   Water System Accumulators. An accumulator is an essential part of any water system. The basic principle is that air will compress under pressure and the water will not. The accumulator is a tank filled with air that fills to approximately 50% with water when the pump operates. After the pump stops running, the compressed air provides pressurized water, which is stored within the accumulator. It serves two functions, the first being to create a pressure buffer or cushion which absorbs fluctuations in pressure. The effect is to operate quietly, and the pump pressure switch is able to reach the cut-off pressure, which increases the life of the pump, motor and the pressure switch. The life of the pump is extended, as the accumulator will prevent the pump operating as soon as the water outlet is opened. If a large accumulator is installed, the pump will operate less, and where large demand systems are installed, larger accumulators are required. Accumulators come in two main types:

a.   **Non-pressurized.** These units are typically plastic cylinders, which are installed upright within the system. These also have a cock at the top to vent off air within the water system. With tanks that do not have bladders to separate the air and water, the tank must be drained every few months. The air gradually disappears, and the tank no longer functions as an accumulator as there is air inside.

b.   **Pressurized.** These accumulator types have an internal membrane or bladder that can be externally air pressurized with a bicycle pump, or are factory pre-pressurized with nitrogen. At installation, the following procedure must be performed:

   (1)   Turn pump off.

   (2)   Open outlets and release system pressure.

   (3)   Using a car tire pressure gauge, release nitrogen until pressure falls to 5 psi below pump cut-in pressure.

   (4)   If too much pressure is relieved, use a bicycle pump to increase to correct pressure.

11.7   Water Filters. Filters should be fitted to all drinking water outlets. A filter will remove small particles, off tastes and smells caused by tank water purification chemicals, as well as some bacteria. This will form in pipes and tanks during extended periods of inactivity. You can use the tank sterilization procedure to flush the system out. Always install a filter with easily replaceable filter elements and replace promptly at the end of stated service life. The Whale types are a unit replacement. Jabsco have the Aqua Filter. Always cleanse the water system before installing a new filter. Filters are generally manufactured of activated carbon. Improved water quality is possible from filters that use porous ceramic, which removes all particles and detectable bacteria. A good filter should always come with a test report issued by an appropriate authority. It should be rated for the expected flow rate, in gallons or liters, and should be renewed at the due date. A filter is never a substitute for clean tanks. If you rely on the filter, (and many do), you risk the safety and health of all on board. One high quality filters system is the Seagull IV-X-1FP from General Ecology.

11.8   Hot Water Calorifier. The calorifier or hot water system is becoming one of those hard-to-do-without luxuries. It is not difficult to install or incorporate into a system, and it will even function as an additional water reserve. The term *calorifier* is still used as most marine hot water systems heat from built-in coils (calorific transfer) supplied from heated engine cooling water or on the old tramp ships I once served on, steam. It makes sense to utilize all the available energy consumed by the engines. The following should be noted:

a.   **Heating Coils.** The majority of units are fitted with a single copper heating coil. Beware of the cheaper imported units, as the coils are very small and have only one or two turns. Quality calorifiers will have several turns installed to ensure good heat transfer rates. I have a preference for C-warm units from Cleghorn-Waring as they incorporate all the required safety features.

b.   **Electric Elements.** Calorifiers should also incorporate an auxiliary electric heating element for AC mains power heating capability.

(1)   **Ratings.** Element ratings should not exceed 1200–1800 watts due to electrical supply limitations of shore power and small generators, unless high output generator set is installed.

(2)   **Thermostats.** A thermostat is essential for controlling temperature and preventing overheating and therefore over pressure conditions.

c.   **Pressure Relief Valves.** All calorifiers should have a pressure relief valve. The valve should be regularly operated manually to ensure that it is not seized, and to eject any insects or debris from the overflow pipe.

d.   **Valves.** The inlet of a calorifier should always have a non-return valve fitted to prevent the heated and expanding water in the tank from back flowing into the cold water system and pressurizing it.

e.   **Insulation.** Ensure that the calorifier has a good insulation layer or cover to avoid wastage of heat. If the engine is run every alternate day, good insulation will keep it warm over the extended period.

f.   **Mounting.** The calorifier must be mounted with the coil on the same level as, or below, the engine cooling water source. This is because the engine pump must circulate water through a longer system, which introduces resistance and could overload the pump.

g.   **Air Locks.** There must be no air locks in the system as these also go through the engine cooling system and affect cooling efficiency. The calorifier must always be installed lower than the engine water filling point.

h.   **Hose Connections.** Use heat resistant rubber hoses to connect up the heating circuit. Ensure that air locks cannot form in the hoses. Ensure that all hose connections have double hose clamps installed.

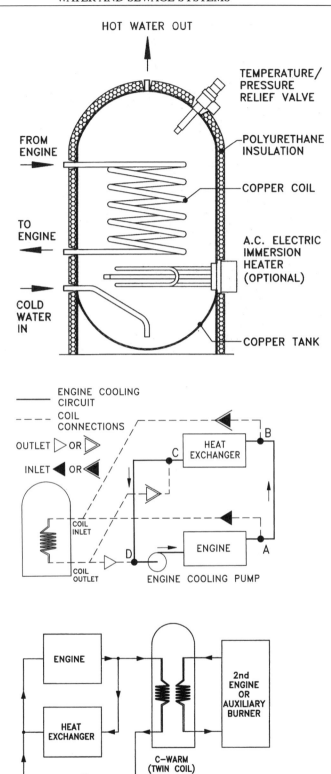

Figures 11-2a and 11-2b Calorifier Hot Water Systems, *Courtesy of Cleghorn Waring*

11.9 **Water Piping and Fittings.** Piping should be of high quality material suited to both hot and cold water. The following should be observed when selecting and installing piping. Look at www.cleghornwaring.co.uk and www.whaleusa.com.

    a. **Pipe Standard.** The piping should be non-toxic, suitable for potable water system use, and must not be able to support microbiological growth. Piping is of two types:

        (1) **Semi-Rigid Piping.** Whale has a color-coded, semi-rigid pipe system. Ensure that pipe is not kinked. Where tight bends are required, install a bend. The system is excellent and I have used this on my own boats. You require a special pipe cutting tool.

        (2) **Flexible Hose.** The most common is flexible hose. Ensure that it meets required standards and, as it is prone to kinking, installation should be done with care.

    b. **System Pressures.** Piping must be capable of withstanding the water system pressures. Whale piping is rated at 60 psi and 90°C. When installing piping, the longer the run, the larger the pipe required in order to reduce the friction losses. Table 11-2 illustrates pipe diameters.

    c. **Fittings.** Fittings must be able to withstand pressures in the system. Nuisance leakage can be avoided. Where plastic hoses are used, generally PVC tee-joints are installed with clips. An excellent system is the Whale system which is easy to install and service.

    d. **Outlets.** There are many different taps, valves and showerheads on the market. Always choose good quality items, and choose only those that are compatible with the whole plumbing system. This makes finding spares easier. Reputable names include Whale and Jabsco. If you are using a non-flexible and permanent showerhead, choose one of the domestic low water conservation types.

    e. **Connections.** Ensure that all piping or hose connections are double clamped. Whale fittings should be firmly tightened.

Table 11-2 Recommended Pipe Diameters

Pump Port Diameter	Hose Diameter
6 mm	13 mm ID
10 mm	13 mm ID
13 mm	16 mm ID
19 mm	25 mm ID
25 mm	25 mm ID
38 mm	38 mm ID
50 mm	50 mm ID

Table 11-3 Water System Troubleshooting

Symptom	Probable Fault
Will not prime (No discharge)	Restricted inlet or blockage in pipe Restricted outlet Air leak in suction or discharge line Pump diaphragm ruptured Debris under flapper valves Pump housing fractured Strainer clogged Valve closed Kink in water pipe or hose No water in tank Clogged one way valve Discharge head too high Low battery voltage (pump slow) Pump housing fractured Pump seized, or debris in same
Pump will not operate	Circuit breaker tripped or fuse failed Pump connection loose or broken Pressure switch fault Motor fault Pump seized, or debris in same Wiring/connection failure
Pulsating water flow	Restricted pump delivery, filter blockage No accumulator installed Suction pipe too small
Pump cycling on and off excessively	System or pipe pressure leak Water outlet leaking Accumulator problem
Pump will not switch off (will not reach cut-off pressure)	Water tank empty Pump diaphragm ruptured Discharge line/pipes leaking Pressure switch fault Debris under valves
Low water flow and pressure	Air leak on pump inlet Strainer clogged (common) Pump diaphragm/impeller/valves worn Pump diaphragm ruptured Pump motor fault Low voltage to pump High discharge head Pump improperly rated Debris or scale in pump/pipes

11.10   Water System Maintenance

    a.   **Winterizing.** For those in colder climates, proper winterization is essential to prevent freezing and damage. Perform the following protective measures:

        (1)   **Remove Pump.** If possible, remove the entire pump and store in a dry place.

        (2)   **Drain System.** The most practical precaution is to totally drain the water system, including the pump and accumulator. Do not use anti-freeze solutions in the potable water system.

    b.   **Maintenance.** Opening the faucets or outlet and depressurization of the system when the power is turned off can increase the life of the pump. This reduces unnecessary wear on pump diaphragms and valves.

11.11   Shore Water Systems. Marina facilities have expanded and have become very sophisticated. Many boat owners take the opportunity to connect to electrical power, telephone, cable TV, Internet, water, and sewage. In many cases, a permanent water connection is made, however this can pose some problems. The normal shore water pressures are usually significantly higher than on board system pressures. Where regulation units are installed, they filter the water, and then regulate down to onboard system pressure. The system can incorporate a solid-state bilge sensor that will automatically close an inlet solenoid, and activate an alarm as well as the bilge pump, should the bilge water level rise. This is to ensure that should the system leak there is minimal flooding. The system is illustrated below.

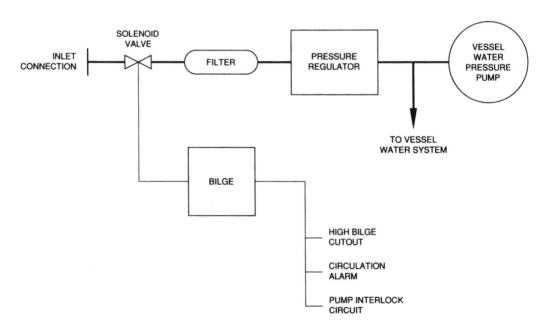

Figure 11-3 Shore Water Systems

11.12   Watermakers. On board water resources are generally limited, and this affects the maximum cruising ranges. There are a number of factors to consider when specifying a watermaker. The most practical system is the reverse osmosis system, although evaporative systems are economical when used with long-term engine use in ocean going passage makers. It must be stressed that water should not be made within 10 miles of a coastline. These waters are often polluted to levels well above World Health Organization (WHO) recommendations and this can be carried into the tanks with product water. Look at www.searecovery.com www.villagemarine.com and www.seafresh.co.uk The operating principles are as follows:

a.   **Reverse Osmosis Principles.** When a semi-permeable membrane separates fresh and salt water, the natural osmosis is for the freshwater to flow through to the salt-water side. To reverse this process, salt water is pressurized to force the freshwater through the membrane out of the salt water. Seawater is pressurized by a priming pump and filtered to remove particles and the high-pressure pump then increases pressure. The high-pressure water is then forced through the membranes. The membranes are housed in a high-pressure casing. The illustration below shows the basic principles of operation.

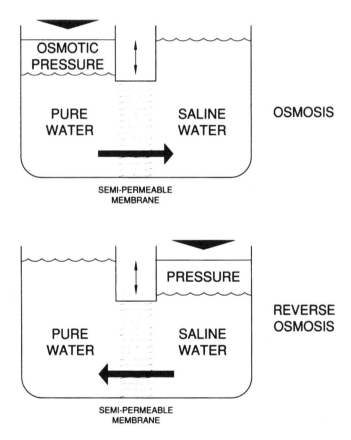

Figure 11-4 Reverse Osmosis Process

b. **Monitoring and Control.** The Sea Recovery (www.searecovery.com) system is a typical system:

(1)   Raw seawater is supplied through the seawater inlet valve and sea strainer to the booster pump suction.

(2)   The seawater is then pressurized to 20 psi by the booster pump and supplied to the media filter. The 5 micron pre-filter and oil water filter remove sediments, suspended solids, silt and oil. This water is pressure monitored with a gauge and low pressure switch, which stops the system when low pressure is detected.

(3)   The water is pressurized to around 900 psi by the high-pressure pump and regulated by a valve. This is also monitored and controlled by a high pressure switch.

(4)   The pressurized water enters the reverse-osmosis membrane, which forces out the salt and minerals. A salinity probe monitors the product water quality, which also adjusts for water temperature. The brine flows through a monitor and then is dumped through a discharge valve.

(5)   The product water is monitored, passed through a charcoal filter and UV sterilizer, and is then piped to the potable water tanks.

(6)   The system also has an automatic freshwater flushing system, which flushes the system to reduce membrane fouling.

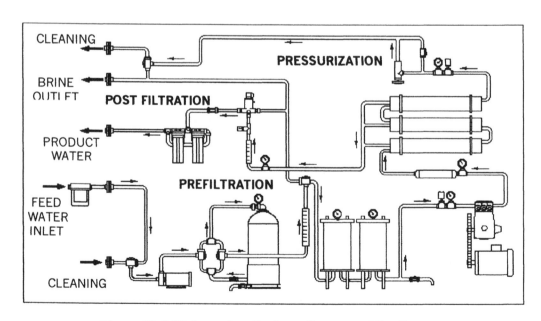

Figure 11-5 Watermaker System, *Courtesy of Sea Recovery*

c. **Installation.** Space considerations are always of critical importance, and many systems such as Sea Recovery, Spectra, SeaFresh and Pur have solved this problem. Through-hull fittings are required for raw seawater intake and the overboard brine discharge. It is not good practice to take the input from the propulsion engine or generator water inlets as this may starve those systems of water.

d. **Outputs and Membrane Correction Factors.** In a good system, salt rejection rates are typically 99% in the pH ranges 4 to 11 at operating pressures of 700–900 psi. In these conditions, the output is unaffected by pressure and temperature. Where temperatures and pressures change, correction factors must be applied to ensure improved production rates.

e. **Water Treatment.** Membrane fouling is a common problem, caused by organic molecules, suspended solids, bacteria and algae, as well as minerals. Pre-filters take out only partially some of the material. Cleaning is time consuming and requires the use of chemicals. The Zeta Rod system (www.zeta-copr.com) significantly increases the intervals between cleaning and increases the permeate rates, lowers feedwater pressure and transmembrane pressure drops. This entails the use of an electrode in the feedwater line. The

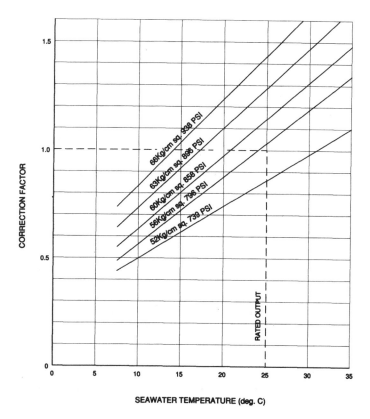

Figure 11-6 Desalinator Temperature Correction Factors

rod forms a capacitor with the water and any impurities, and the piping and vessel walls. The system charges particles that ultimately form sludge and scale to the same polarity. This causes repulsion and prevents bonding and formation of deposits in the piping and membranes. The units use a high voltage to generate the electrostatic field, and current consumption is low. Systems reduce the output to zero if a short circuit develops.

f. **Maintenance.** These are typical maintenance procedures:

(1)   Clean inlet strainer at the same time as the engine strainer.

(2)   Pre-filters can be washed 5–6 times before replacement. This equates approximately 80 hours operation in clean waters.

(3)   Disinfect membranes to prevent biological fouling for any shutdown period exceeding 14 days using recommended biocides. Failure to do this will significantly reduce output and damage membranes. Never allow membranes to dry out.

(4)   Check pressure pump oil levels and renew every 500 hours.

(5)   Check and re-tension rubber drive belts every 6 months.

(6)   Clean membranes when output drops below 15% of rated output or when product salinity increases. This is due to the build-up of grime, biological material and mineral scale. Do not open the pressure vessel to do this. Clean according to the manufacturer's recommendations. This usually entails the use of alkaline and detergent cleaning for removal of organic material, and acidic cleaning for removal of mineral scale.

11.13   Bilge Pump Systems. Bilge pumps play a critical safety role in any vessel. The tendency is to buy the cheapest unit available and install it improperly. Bilge pumps should be of the highest possible quality, be correctly installed and maintained. The following factors should be considered when selecting and installing electric bilge pumps. There are two basic types, the submersible pump and the centrifugal pump. Submersible pumps cannot be maintained or repaired:

a.   **Head.** Head pressure is related to the height that the water must be lifted to. All pumps have maximum head figures for a particular model. The higher the head, the lower the flow rate; in submersible pumps the flow rate drops very quickly.

b.   **Flow Rate.** Most bilge pumps are listed with flow rates, which are designated as liters or gallons per/hour or minute. Electric impeller pumps with bronze housings are rated up to about a maximum of 50 l/min (11 gal/min).

c.   **Impellers.** Bilge pump flexible-blade impellers come in a number of different compounds. Choose the correct type for optimum life and efficiency. In operation, the impeller blades rotate away from a cam to create a vacuum that draws liquid in. On the discharge side the blades bend against a cam to

Table 11-4 Desalinator Troubleshooting

Symptom	Probable Fault	Corrective Action
Low water flow	Blocked strainer Blocked pre-filter Membranes fouled Pump belts loose	Clean strainer Clean or replace filter Clean membranes Tension belt correctly
No product water flow	Pump stopped Circuit breaker tripped	Check circuit breaker Check drive belts Clutch wire broken Clutch coil fault
Circuit breaker tripping	Pump clutch coil failed Clutch wire grounding out Pump seizing	Replace winding Repair connection/wire Repair pump Overhaul valve Overhaul pump
Low working pressure	Relief valve leaking Pump fault High pressure loss Dump valve jammed open	Examine for leaks Repair valve
Product water salty	Fouled membranes Excess working pressure	Clean membranes Decrease pressure

squeeze liquids out. Impeller pumps should never be operated dry for more than a maximum period of 30 seconds, if at all. The pumped liquid lubricates the pump, and failure to operate with liquid will generally ruin the impeller. They do have long service lives compared to other pumps. They are self-priming and can be mounted clear of the bilge, with suction via a strainer. The maximum pressures are around 20psi. Impeller types are as follows:

(1)   **Neoprene.** These are typically found in bronze pumps (Jabsco) and are suitable for bilge pumping duties. Temperature range is 4°C to 80°C. If used at the outer temperature limits, the performance and service life are reduced. They must not be used to pump oil-based fluids as the impeller compound will absorb oil compounds and expand. The result is that on the next start-up the impeller will bind and be destroyed. Always flush out a line if oily fluids are used.

(2)   **Nitrile.** These are designed for pumping of fuel but are also suited for pumping oil- and fuel-contaminated engine bilges in temperatures from 10°C to 90°C. Use at the upper temperature limits reduces

performance and service life. Nitrile impellers have a flow rate 30% lower than neoprene impellers, so should not be used in any high temperature applications.

d. **Submersible Pumps.** These centrifugal pumps are by far the most common. It is important to always buy and install the very best quality you can. Pumps have the following general characteristics:

(1) **Motor Rating.** Motors should be rated continuously; some are not, so check the pump data sheet. One model I had recently was not recommended for anything but standing water, and not for coping with serious water ingress. It failed within 9 months.

(2) **Motor Type.** Motors generally use a permanent magnet motor, which means no brushes.

(3) **Dry Running.** Dry running does not damage the pump impellers, though motors require water to cool them.

e. **Diaphragm Pumps.** These are self-priming and can be mounted clear of the bilge, with suction via a strainer. They can be operated dry without damage, and tend to suit shallow bilges. A diaphragm membrane moves in alternate directions, creating liquid suction and pressure.

f. **Automatic Systems.** Automation of bilge pumps is very common. There are a number of important factors to consider when putting in any automated control:

(1) **Pollution.** There are very heavy penalties for the willful or accidental discharge of oily wastes into harbor and coastal waters. It is the environmental responsibility of all boat owners not to discharge any waste into the sea. Any bilge, which is capable of having oil in it, must never be fitted with an automatic pumping system. All vessels have obligations under MARPOL and filter systems are a good investment.

(2) **Controls.** Automatic switches are notoriously unreliable. If the float switch stays on, the bilge pump may burn out, and probably ruin a set of batteries by totally flattening them. There are a number of activation devices, which are explained below.

g. **Float Switches.** Float or level switching devices are now available in a number of different operational principles:

(1) **Mechanical Float.** This is the most common device and probably the most reliable if the float switch is of high quality. The bilge switch must be free of debris or cannot be fouled by the pump cable. A circuit diagram is illustrated for a steel boat that enables isolation of positive supply to the float switch, minimizing the common risk of serious corrosion problems if a leakage occurs.

(2) **Solid State.** Solid-state devices include ultrasonic, conductive probes, and capacitive units. While some appear to work well, there are a great number of failures. Some cheaper units can cause electrolytic corrosion problems. If the probes are fouled or coated with oil, they often do not work. Some units have a delay feature that requires the presence of water for 15–20 seconds before they activate. This prevents the pump from start-and-stop cycling in rough water. I have not found any device to be too reliable.

(3) **Optical Devices.** These devices solve many of the problems normally encountered with units using probes. They operate on a rather innovative principle. The pump units are controlled by an optical fluid switch. The unit emits a light pulse every 30 seconds. If the lens is immersed in water, the light beam refracts. The change in direction of the beam is sensed by a coating inside the lens, and triggers the pump control circuit. The units also have time delay circuits that can be adjusted for periods of 20–140 seconds so that the pump will drain the bilge after water clears the sensor.

(4) **Air Devices.** These are relatively old but simple, reliable devices. They depend on the pressure of water in a tube to activate a switch via a diaphragm.

(5) **Ultrasonic Devices.** These devices are not that reliable and I would suggest keeping to more proven systems.

h. **Manual Bilge Pumps.** One hand pump should be operated from the cockpit or deck. The manual bilge pumps are usually large bore units with a single diaphragm. It is important to choose a unit that can be operated for significant periods and location is a consideration.

i. **Centrifugal Clutch Pumps.** Centrifugal pumps are often required under Class and survey rules. They give a high and smooth output at low pressure. As liquid enters the pump, the rotating impeller creates a vacuum to force liquid out of the discharge. The pumps are not cheap to install but they pump large volumes, pass bilge debris and double as fire fighting or deck wash pumps. As with all flexible impeller pumps, they are easy to service but must not be run dry as they do not self-prime and the seals will be damaged. They can be belt driven from your engine, and are available with either manual or electromagnetic clutches for remote control. The circuit is similar to a refrigeration electric clutch circuit, and after use, the supply must be switched off to avoid burning out the coil.

11.14   Bilge Pump Installation. Bilge pumps must be properly installed if they are to operate correctly and reliably. Always mount the pump or suction line in the lowest part of bilge and keep this a short distance from the bottom to avoid drawing in bilge sediments. Always install a strainer on the suction side of centrifugal pumps. Submersible pumps have a strainer as an integral part of the base, but these are rather coarse and ingress of bilge debris and jamming of the impeller is quite common. Select flexible discharge hoses that will not kink, as many pumps are ineffective due to kinks or constriction of the discharge line. Always use two hose clamps on every hose connection as a safety precaution.

a.   **Electrical Connections.** If the cable is long enough, make the connections above maximum bilge water levels. Ensure that any automatic float switch is rated for the maximum pump current, otherwise serious voltage drops can cause pump problems. I would advise that each connection be soldered, the joint covered with heat shrink insulation and the overall cable also covered in heat shrink or wrapped in self amalgamating tape. This will generally prevent the joint interacting with salt water and failing.

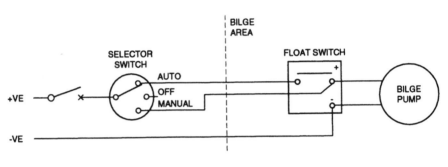

STANDARD BILGE CONTROL

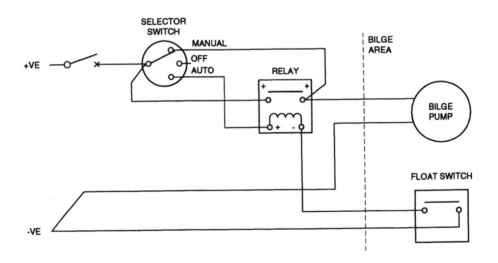

ISOLATED SYSTEM FOR STEEL/ALLOY VESSELS

Figure 11-7 Bilge Control Schematics

b. **Protection.** The ABYC requires that the circuit be fused or has a circuit breaker rated for the cable size. This requirement has been disputed and has been wrongly blamed as a cause of a boat sinking in the event of a failure. If the pump fails, it is generally because the cable, connections or the pump are dysfunctional. The most common fault is a seized impeller caused by bilge debris, which causes maximum current. The pump will be stalled and should trip the breaker or fuse, otherwise the cable will overheat and possibly cause a fire. If there is concern, install a separate backup small bilge line and automatic pump. Run the pump after installation and ensure that pump rotation is correct.

11.15   Bilge Pump Maintenance. Regular maintenance is essential for reliable pump operation. Regularly clean bilges of sediment and debris. Operate pumps on a monthly basis with water in the bilges. Many bilge pumps are found to be seized after months or even years of non-operation. Some submersible pumps have the impeller attached via a screw. From personal experience the low grade stainless screw on my pump corroded, the impeller came off and the boat nearly sank.

Table 11- 5 Bilge Pump Troubleshooting

Symptom	Probable Fault
Low water flow	Strainer blocked with debris Pump impeller fouled Suction hose is kinked Suction hose is blocked with debris Suction line has air lock
Pump will not operate	Circuit breaker tripped Float switch fouled (usually with debris) Float switch connections corroded off
Pump will not switch off	Float switch jammed Float switch fouled by debris Float switch mounted too low Float switch connection short circuited
Circuit breaker tripping	Pump impeller seized Bilge area connections short circuited Pump winding fault

11.16   Shower Drain and Sink Systems. Shower drain systems and sinks require specific pumps. The common pumps in use are:

a. **Diaphragm Pumps.** Jabsco has a range of purpose designed shower diaphragm pumps such as the Par Max 3 (170 gph) and Par Max 4 units (190 gph) that eliminates the sump pump and float switch. The pumps are self-priming and have four chambers connected directly to the drain outlet, and a strainer installed in-line on the suction side. The pumps have power consumption rates of around of 5–8 amps at full load. The Whale Gulper 220 is also very reliable and effective and I have installed these on my own boats. They can also run dry, and strainers are recommended to prevent blockages. Pumps are also generally repairable with the appropriate spare parts kit.

b. **Submersible Pumps.** These plastic units are common. Rule and others manufacture fully integrated sump, suction filter, pump and float switch. The sump pump units usually have a check valve to prevent back siphoning and a clear cover for inspection.

c. **Centrifugal Pump.** Some manufacturers such as Flojet recommend a centrifugal self-priming pump. These have a flow rate of around 12 L/min and use 3.6 amps at full load. This offers the chance to match all the pumps, so that bilge, wash down and shower pump motors are all interchangeable. You can do this with Whale diaphragm pumps.

d. **Electrical.** Par Max pump motors have an integral thermal overload trip protection. If they trip on internal overload, determine the cause of the trip. Typically the cause is overloading due to seizing bearings or the pump is jammed with debris and overheating.

e. **Maintenance.** Shower and sink drain pumps are prone to rapid filter clogging due to hair, soap residues and other debris. In automatic float switch units, hair and solidified soap often causes the float to stick. The filters should be checked and cleaned weekly.

11.17   Sewage Systems. Many sewage systems are being altered from hand pump toilets to electric operation. The stringent requirements for holding tanks and pump-out systems require careful consideration in system planning. In the US, the Clean Vessel Act of 1992 is the primary legislation. In many countries, similar legislation is being introduced. It is important to comply with laws pertaining to illegal discharges. A marine sanitation device (MSD) is any equipment for installation on board the vessel that is designed to receive, retain, treat or discharge sewage, and any process to treat the sewage. Politics and confusion are prevalent in many places relating to the use of devices, and boaters should make sure they understand the legal requirements. The USCG certifies MSDs, which fall into 3 categories:

a. **Type I MSD.** This device uses chemicals to disinfect sewage. The discharge must be free of visible solids and meet standards for bacterial content. The sewage must be macerated to break up solids. The fecal coliform bacteria output must be at least 100 colonies per 100 milliliters or less. A system that meet this standard is the Raritan Lectra/San. It operates using both salinity and electric current that consists of electrodes to break down the seawater to form chlorine (hypochlorous acid), a chlorinating agent that kills bacteria and disinfects the sewage. After treatment, the acid recombines to reform as salt water. The Raritan PuraSan MSD uses a solid tablet made of chlorine that produces a halogen solution to treat waste. Both systems draw around 45 amps for 3 minutes on each flush, which has considerable impact on the electrical system power requirements. These units cannot discharge into No-Discharge zones. The SeaLand SanX can be used in all waters but the installation requirements are considerably more than the others and may suit larger vessels. The SanX injects a chemical disinfectant agent into the treatment tank to mix with the macerated waste.

b.   **Type II MSD.** This is a device similar to the Type I device with a higher level of treatment and higher quality discharge. The fecal coliform bacteria output must be at least 200 colonies per 100 milliliters, with suspended solids of less than 1,000 parts per 100 milliliters. The best-known devices are those from Microfors and Galleymaid. Cost and installation are considerably greater than Type I devices.

c.   **Type III MSD.** This is a holding tank. This means no discharges within nominal limits. Emptying is usually via a deck fitting and tanks have a vent line overboard.

11.18   MSD Systems. MSD systems have several process components and various sensors and electrical elements. Some MSD units are PLC controlled, and correct operation of all input sensors and output devices is critical for proper operation. The first stage treatment tanks contain level sensors. The second stage sedimentation tanks do not have any components. The macerator pump, sludge pump and discharge pump all require routine maintenance. Backwash systems have both a water pump and solenoid valves. The disinfection system has a flow control system with chemical feed pump, and chlorination units have a power supply. Ensure that no toilet chemicals incompatible with sodium hypochlorite are being used on the boat. Normal troubleshooting principles apply, so check the power supply, auto and manual selections which may be wrong. The PLC may require resetting, and check inputs and outputs to level switches or solenoids. Operational checks include the following:

a.   **Daily.** Check macerator pumps, discharge, backwash and sludge pumps and electric motors for unusual noises and vibration. Check all hose and pipe connections for leaks. Check that the chlorination liquid (bleach) reservoir is full. Check pump pressures are normal where they are installed.

b.   **Bi-annually.** Check control panel for moisture ingress and corrosion, and ensure cover is tightly closed. Check and tighten all connectors every year. Replace the desiccant crystals if installed.

c.   **Annually.** Check treatment and sediment tank anodes if installed. Check that solenoid valves are operating correctly, and remove to check and clean. Grease bearings only in accordance with operating hour requirements, typically every 10,000 hours.

11.19   Toilet Systems. Toilets come either as a manual system, or an electric unit with integral macerating function. Manual systems use a piston rod type pump to pump out the combined sewage and seawater. Electric pumps replace the piston rod pump with an impeller type pump and macerator that effectively liquefies waste. These systems use a lot more water to ensure all materials are flushed out properly. Many power vessels have vacuum flush systems such as the VacuFlush (www.sealandtechnology.com) and Environvac. They use small water quantities, and operate with a vacuum pump. These units have vacuum ejector pumps or generators and discharge pumps that require routine inspection and maintenance. The automatic valves, vacuum and level sensors, and the control system with alarms also require regular inspection. 12-volt vacuum pumps have typical power consumptions of 4-6 amps and large boat systems have pumps up to ½ hp. Discharge pumps consume around 6 amps. Look at www.leesan.com for details.

a.   **Electrics.** One of the biggest problems with toilets is the failure to install adequately sized cables to the units or allow for voltage drop. The PAR unit consumes 18 amps and requires a heavy-duty cable rated at around 30 amps. As toilets are always located in a wet shower area, ensure that all electrical connections are covered with waterproof self-amalgamating tapes. Always allow sufficient cable length to pull the toilet out, as it will be difficult to disconnect the motor. Check the motor connections monthly to ensure no corrosion is occurring. Lightly coat the terminals with silicon grease or Vaseline. I have resprayed motors with an additional paint layer to seal and prevent water seeping into the motor housing flanges, as corrosion starts here. Before installation, remove each bolt and apply anti-seize grease.

b.   **Waste.** It is essential that only normal waste be put through the toilet. To quote that readily available plaque for marine heads, "Don't put anything in the bowl that you haven't eaten and already digested". Macerator cutter plates are easily jammed or damaged by cigarette and cigar butts, rags and sanitary towels. Cleaning macerators is the most unpleasant task on a vessel, so it is well worth making the effort.

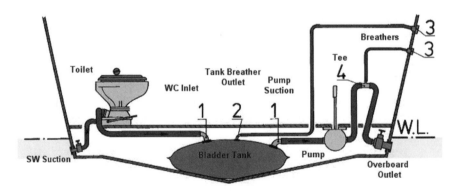

Figure 11-8 Typical Sewage System, *Courtesy of Vetus*

c.   **Macerators.** Macerator pumps are usually connected to the holding tank discharge and are used to pump out waste to shore facility tanks or overboard. Units grind waste to 3mm size, and are self priming. Remember that pumps are not rated continuously, and run times should not exceed approximately 10 minutes. Heavy-duty models are available for larger systems and greater pump-out capabilities. Jabsco Models are given in Table 11-6. Flow rates are given at maximum and normal heads. After pumping out tanks, flush out macerator pump with clean water to expel any debris that may cause bacterial build-ups.

d.   **Troubleshooting.** Noisy or vibrating pumps or low pump discharge pressures and volumes have a number of possible causes. Pump or pipe may be clogged, or the impeller or cutter may be worn. Reduced pump speeds can be due to wiring and connection faults. High viscosity liquids and altered pump axial clearances affect flow rates and pressures. Noises are often caused by water damaged bearings, pump cavitation and loose impellers.

Table 11-6 Jabsco Macerator Pump Specifications

Pump Type	Port Size	Current	Flow Rate
21950–1603 (12 mins rated)	Inlet 1½–2" Outlet 1"	10 amps	36 l/min @ 1.5m 19 l/min @ 6.1m
22140–1421 (60 mins rated)	Inlet 1½–2" Outlet 1"	25 amps	40 l/min @ 1.5m 30 l/min @ 9.8m

Heating, Ventilation and Air Conditioning (HVAC) Systems

12.1   Diesel Heater Systems. Power consumption figures, heat outputs and fuel consumption rates for typical Eberspacher models are illustrated in Table 12-1. Log on to www.espar.com; ww.wallas.fi; www.webasto.com; www.dickinsonmarine.com. Heaters have the following operational cycles:

> **a.**   **Starting.** An electric fan draws in cold air to the exchanger/burner. In most systems there is an air purge period.

> **b.**   **Ignition.** Fuel is drawn at the same time by the fuel pump, mixed with the air, and ignited in a combustion chamber by an electric glowplug.

> **c.**   **Combustion.** The combustion takes place within a sealed exchanger and gasses are exhausted directly to atmosphere.

> **d.**   **Heating.** Heat is transferred as the main air flow passes over a heat exchanger to warm the air to the cabin. A thermostat in the cabin shuts the system down and operates to maintain the set temperature.

Table 12-1 Diesel Heater Data Table

BTU Output	Fuel (liters/hour)	Power Draw
6100	0.21	40 watts
11000	0.38	45 watts
15000	0.57	70 watts
28000	1.05	115 watts
41000	1.40	190 watts

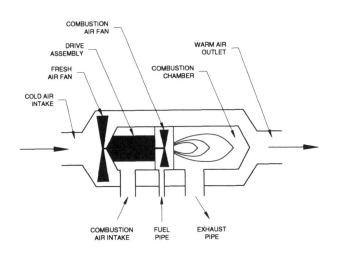

Figure 12-1 Diesel Heater System

e. **Power Consumption.** Typical power consumption is 40 watts (3.33 amps) during running. At start up, the draw can be up to 20 amps for a period of 20 seconds during the glowplug ignition cycle.

f. **Heater Maintenance.** The following maintenance tasks should be carried out to ensure optimum operation:

(1) Check that all electrical connections are tight and corrosion free.

(2) Check exhaust connections and fittings for leaks. Leakages can cause dangerous gases to vent below deck.

(3) Remove and clean the glowplugs. Take care not to damage glowplug spiral and element. Use a brush and emery cloth, and ensure all particles are blown out afterwards.

(4) At 2,000 hours take the unit to the dealer and have the heat exchanger decoked and the fuel filter replaced.

Table 12-2 Diesel Heater Troubleshooting

Symptom	Probable Fault
Heater will not switch off	Temperature switch fault
Heater smokes and soots	Combustion pipe clogged Fuel metering pump fault Blower speed too low
Heating level too low	Hot air ducts clogged Fuel metering pump fault Blower speed too low Temperature switch fault
Heat will not start	Supply fuse blown Low battery voltage Blower not operating Fuel metering pump fault Thermal cut-out tripped Fuel filter clogged No fuel supply Glowplug fault Control unit fault
Heater goes off	Fuel metering pump fault Thermal cut-out tripped Fuel filter clogged Fuel supply problem Control unit fault

12.2 **Diesel Hot Water Boilers.** Some larger boats have a more substantial oil-fired boiler system, and steam boilers have similar principles. The Kabola (www.kabola.nl) and Hurricane (www.kurandamarine.co.uk) are typical units. Boilers provide hot water for air conditioning heating, hot water, and central heating. The Hurricane unit can burn No.1 and 2 diesel, kerosene, and furnace oil. Installation is critical; the exhaust system must be properly specified and installed. Good combustion depends on good air drafting, so the length, diameter and limited bends all affect this. Typical operation cycles are:

(1) **Temperature Control.** The thermostat is the set-point and is used to set the required temperature setting. The power switch is turned on starting the ignition cycle.

(2) **Ignition.** The oil burner unit fan starts and purges the boiler of fumes. Oil is then injected from the boiler nozzle, and ignited using a piezo ignition device. If the flame stops, the system is shutdown by a flame-failure device for safety. Exhaust gas is taken outside via the flue. Electric ignition current draw is typically around 2 amps for 30 seconds. Kabola units on 24 VDC have a jet atomizing burner unit with an oil preheating element and a typical start-up power consumption of 4 A and 5-7 A during operation.

(3) **Water Control.** Depending on which service is selected, Hot Water, Central Heating, etc., the inlet water solenoid valve opens, and the circulating pump starts operating. The cold water inlet is solenoid controlled and regulated by a flow valve. The system has a pressure relief valve installed.

(4) **Water Heating.** The hot water is heated via a heat exchanger. When the set-point temperature is reached, the thermostat controls burner operation to maintain it. This should be around 180°F (82°C). Overheat cut-outs should be set at approximately 195°F (91°C).

(5) **Troubleshooting.** The usual problems on any oil burner system are the burner ignition points or glowplugs. Burners tend to require regular cleaning as they can clog or soot up, and atomization affects the efficiency. Flame-failure devices also require cleaning. Solenoid valves can stick and should be checked. The usual electrical faults of poor connections may occur, as maintenance tends to be low because people avoid the boiler. An oil filter unit should be installed, and checked regularly. High temperatures or failure to ignite often indicate thermostat failures, so check this before going into burner control circuits. If the central heating radiators are not getting warm, check the circulation pump supply first, and if pump is functional, check heating and control circuits.

12.3   Diesel Hot Water Heaters. The compact diesel hot water system is now becoming commonplace on vessels. This unit can also be part of a central heating system. Companies such as Eberspacher, Mikuni, Webasto and Hurricane have very efficient systems. The Webasto is illustrated below. The typical operational cycle is as follows:

> a.   **Starting.** An electric fan draws in cold air to the heat exchanger/burner. This is normally from the engine area.
>
> b.   **Ignition.** Fuel is drawn in at the same time by the fuel pump from the main tank and mixed with the air. The fuel is ignited by an electric glowplug in a combustion chamber.
>
> c.   **Combustion.** The combustion takes place within a sealed exchanger and the exhaust gases are expelled to atmosphere.
>
> d.   **Heating.** An integrated water pump circulates the water through the heat exchanger and subsequently to the calorifier and heating radiators. A thermostat in the cabin shuts the system down and operates to maintain set temperature. Eberspacher has developed an automatic quarter heat control to reduce unnecessary cycling, which improves the fuel economy.

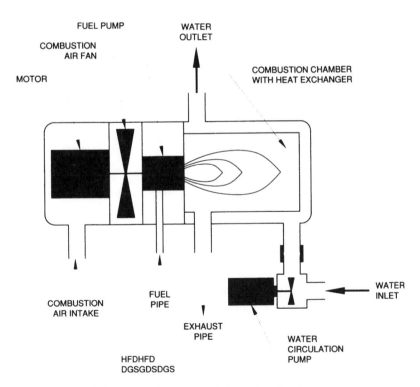

Figure 12-2 Diesel Hot Water System

12.4   Ventilation Fans. Good ventilation is essential in many areas of the vessel, especially the galley, machinery space, and the cabins. There are a number of ventilation fan options, and all have uses in particular applications. Fans can be classified either as extraction or supply (blowers) fans.

a.   **Extraction Fans.** Extraction fans take air out of a space, either to increase natural ventilation flow rates and air changes, or to remove excessive heat or fume concentrations.

(1)   **Solar Fans.** Solar fans are an excellent ventilation option. They simply have a small solar cell powering the fan motor. Some models have a small battery so that the fan can continue at night after being charged by the solar module.

(2)   **Engine Extraction Fans.** These are used to extract heat from engine spaces. In warmer climates, it is preferable to leave the fan operating for half an hour after the engine stops to reduce heat and stop lower deck temperatures increasing from radiated heat.

(3)   **Ventilators.** The most common of these types are the Ventair and Ventilite static ventilators. The latter allows natural light from the outside to come into the cabin. These units have two speeds and are reversible, which allows adaptation to the conditions inside. Air displacement is very good at 25 cfm (cubic feet per minute), which suits normal cabin environments. Power consumption is also relatively low at only 1.7 amps on the fast setting. The 2 speed VETUS units are a more economical option; they utilize an electronic brushless motor with a current draw of only 0.2 amps. Air extraction rates are a reasonable 36 cfm.

b.   **Blowers.** Blowers push air into a space, and are used to either displace existing air such as in bilge blower applications, or to direct air in large volumes over specific areas. Ratings are either in m^3/min or cubic feet per minute with $7m^3$/min = 250 cfm.

(1)   **In-Line Blowers.** In-line blowers are commonly used in bilge blower applications. These types simply install directly into the ventilation ducting tubes. Air flow rates are typically around 4-8 m^3/min and have a power consumption of around 4 amps.

(2)   **Bilge Blowers.** Blowers used in area where hazardous vapors are concentrated must be ignition proof. They are often used to ventilate engine spaces. Typical air flows are in the range of 150-250 cfm. Power consumption is in the range of 4 to 10 amps, which is quite high. In most cases, they are run with the engine operating. It is a good practice to interlock the fan to the engine start with a relay to ensure that it always operates and switches off at engine shutdown.

12.5   Air Conditioning. Air conditioning is possible on even small boats and is virtually standard on larger vessels. Like refrigeration, air conditioning cools a cabin by transferring heat out. In most marine installations, seawater is used generally for condenser cooling although fan cooled systems are available and are less effective. There are two types of marine air conditioning system: the single stage direct expansion and the tempered (chilled) water two-stage type. Manufacturers such as Cruisair, HFL, Climma all offer extensive ranges with options. Under the Montreal Protocol, Freon 12 has been replaced by Freon 22. Systems are generally rated in British thermal units (BTU), which is the energy required to heat or cool an area. In metric this is Kilo calories (Kcal). The conversion is approximately 4 BTU = 1Kcal. Systems requiring gas charging must be performed by certified technicians using approved (EPA) equipment.

    a.   **Self Contained and Remote Condensing Systems.** These single stage direct expansion units may be either self-contained or have a remote condensing unit installed within the machinery space. The self-contained reverse cycle system is normally a relatively compact module, such as the Cruisair StowAway, that can be installed under a bunk or locker. The modules are rated between 5000–24000 BTU/hr. They are pre-charged with R-22 refrigerant at the factory, are seawater cooled from a remote pump, and have integral reciprocating, rotary or scroll compressor depending on the model. Units also have integral condenser, evaporator, blower and safety switches. Many systems have a remote condensing unit installed within the machinery space, adjacent to the seawater supply. Refrigerant is carried to the air-cooling unit. These units have cooling capabilities in the range 5,000 to 60,000 BTU/hr. Look at www.cruisair.com and www.veco.net.

    b.   **Tempered (Chilled) Water Systems.** Tempered water systems are used on larger boats and commercial vessels. A chiller refrigeration unit is used to chill (or warm in reverse cycle systems) water. This is then circulated around the vessel by a freshwater circulating pump through insulated piping in a closed loop to the fan coil air-handling units. A seawater system is also used

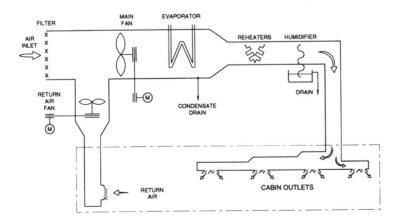

Figure 12-3 Air Conditioning Schematic

275

to cool the condenser. Modular installation materials from companies such as Climma have special purpose color-coded flexible piping, valves and fittings that simplify installation. Systems such as those from Cruisair have modular control systems, which incorporate temperature control, control circuits to pumps and refrigeration compressors, fault alarm indicators, and systems monitoring. Chilled water systems have water flow loss alarms and shutdowns, and high and low temperature limits, that prevent either freezing or overheating of the water. A time delay relay for the compressor contactor may also be installed to prevent all auxiliaries such as water pumps and air handling units powering up together, which reduces electrical load surges. Tempered water systems should be checked regularly for leaks and ensure that water level is adequate to prevent air in the system. Air handler motorized valves should be checked for corrosion and lubricated periodically. Cruisair has programmable control systems, which use a replaceable plug-in EPROM for the program. The system has a non-volatile memory to retain settings when switched off. System controls offer various features that include automatic dehumidification, intermittent or continuous fan operation, low and high fan speeds and operating temperature differentials. The air handlers require a power/logic module and temperature sensing elements. The controllers also have integral LED digital displays that also show fault codes,

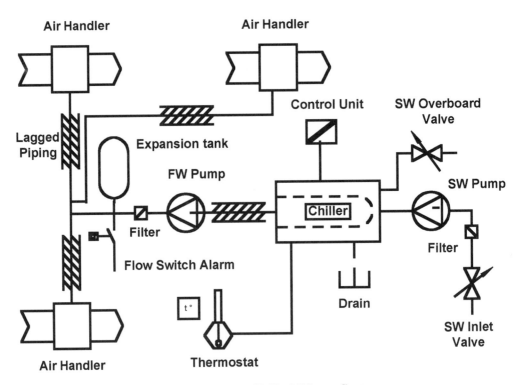

Figure 12-4 Climma Chilled Water System

program prompts and temperature information. Common faults on chilled water systems are as follows:

(1) **Low water flow.** The circulation pump is either faulty or has tripped off. If the pump is operating, check that the pump has not become air locked. This may require the opening of the system at the fill valve point and bleeding the system. If pressures are normal, the flow switch may have failed.

(2) **Compressor not running.** Check power supply and circuit breakers. Check control devices such as thermostats, and the liquid line solenoid valves. Check HP and LP cut-outs are not activated. LP faults can be caused by reduced refrigerant; gas pressures should be checked and leak points identified.

(3) **High discharge pressure.** The condenser is the usual cause; it may be plugged, or have insufficient cooling water passing through it. Usually the strainer is clogged with debris. Systems with air cooled condensers may have be clogged or the fan is not operating.

(4) **Low suction pressure.** It may be due to low water flow, as well as a clogged filter/dryer, and this requires replacement. A dirty evaporator or low refrigerant charge levels can also be a cause and the system should be checked for leaks. Expansion valve problems may also create the problem.

(5) **Freeze protection activates.** This is due to a faulty or incorrectly set freeze thermostat. Low chilled water flow can also cause this and should be checked. Check that any strainers within the system are not clogged. The other possible cause is low suction pressure.

(6) **Compressor loading and unloading not operating properly.** The main cause is a faulty or an incorrectly set thermostat. Another cause is a flow switch fault or low water flow. The capacity controller may also be at fault, or the unloading mechanism.

c. **Electrical Power Requirements.** Air conditioning system power requirements are as follows:

(1) **AC Systems.** A system normally requires a constant AC power source to operate, so the generator must run continuously. Cruisair quotes as a guide, 1 amp per 1000 BTU/hr, however 1.3 is closer for 177 VAC systems. If an air conditioning system is to be installed on the vessel, the generator must take account of the maximum loads. As systems use AC induction motors on the compressor, there is a significant start-up current surge that must be allowed for in generator load calculations, typically 3–4 times full-load amps. Hermetically sealed compressors have high starting currents that are reduced by capacitors to around 3–5 times running current.

(2) **Seawater Pumps.** Electrical load calculations should also factor in the seawater pump. Pumps are generally not self-priming and must be positioned at or below the waterline. Like all seawater pumps they are prone to corrosion. Self-priming impeller pumps should be installed where possible. Refer to the chapter on AC motor maintenance. The seawater pump is generally controlled via a relay box, and this should be mounted in a dry location. Pump capacities are typically 100gph for a 5,000 BTU unit up to 250gph for a 12,000 BTU system.

(3) **DC Systems.** HFL Marine International has a 12 or 24-volt DC system in the "Ocean Cool" series. It has a hermetically sealed compressor and draws 44 amps for a 6,000 BTU/h (1,500Kcal/h) unit so the engine may have to run to supply the power, and an additional alternator is a good option. The quoted battery capacity is a minimum of 160 Ah.

(4) **Control Systems.** Controls range from simple on and off switches, speed control and thermostat to programmable controllers. These offer timing functions; high and low temperature settings, systems monitoring, fan speed controls and compressor restart time delays, including fault condition automatic shutdown and even automatic dehumidification. Protection and control systems are similar to those in refrigeration systems. There are also variable speed fan controllers that use small variable frequency drives.

d. **Maintenance.** There are a number of maintenance tasks to perform:

(1) Weekly. Check the seawater inlet strainer and clean.

(2) Monthly. Filters on air cooling units should be checked and cleaned.

(3) Bi-annually. Seawater cooling condensers should be cleaned if possible. Where systems have anodes in the cooler, they should be checked and replaced.

e. **Troubleshooting.** Air conditioning systems have many faults similar to refrigeration systems.

(1) Check external control equipment such as thermostats.

(2) Check system HP and LP cut-outs where installed.

(3) Make sure the evaporator cooling systems are clean and functioning.

f. **Capacity Calculations.** The capacity of the system must be calculated by determining the volume to be cooled. The following are guidelines used by HFL. For ambient temperatures exceeding 30°C, add 20%, and for water temperatures exceeding 25°C, add a further 20%. This is to maintain 16–22°C. The estimated seawater cooling requirement is for 3.5 gallons per minute for each self-contained unit.

(1) For below decks cu.ft x 14 = BTU. (m^3 x 504 = BTU).

(2) For above decks cu.ft x 17 = BTU. (m^3 x 612 = BTU).

Table 12-3 Air Conditioning Capacity Table

Capacity (BTU/hr)	Below Deck Sq. Ft	Mid Deck Sq. Ft	Above Deck Sq. Ft
6000	90	60	45
7000	115	75	55
9000	165	110	85
12000	200	150	100
16000	267	178	135
20000	335	250	167
24000	405	300	200

Refrigeration Systems

13.1   Introduction. Refrigeration plays a central role in any well-found galley. On fishing and shrimp trawlers the proper functioning of the refrigeration system is critical. The refrigeration system must be properly installed, selected and maintained. This chapter illustrates the basic principles of refrigeration and the most common systems found on motorboats. I served on some of the most automated and advanced refrigerated cargo ships afloat as a Chief Electrical Officer/Engineer. We were carrying beef, lamb, frozen chicken, bananas, apples, grapes. The multi-compressor refrigeration and computerized control systems required a great deal of maintenance. Log on to www.glacierbay.com; www.seafrost.com; www.technautics.com; www.kenyonmarine.com; www.frigoboat.com.

13.2   Refrigeration Principles. The fundamental principle is that when a high-pressure liquid or gas expands, temperature reduces. A compressor pumps the refrigerant fluid, normally Freon, around the system. The typical cycle of a system is as follows:

    a.   **Compression.** The compressor increases the refrigerant gas pressure, which becomes hot. The high-pressure hot gas then passes through to the condenser.

    b.   **Condensation.** The condenser is a heat exchanger, either air cooled by natural convection, a fan, or by water passing through coils. The hot gas passes through the condenser, condenses into a hot liquid, and passes through to the expansion valve.

    c.   **Dryers.** A small amount of water vapor will remain in a system, regardless of purging and evacuation. Water causes ice formation at the expansion valve creating either total blockage or incorrect operation. The dryer is installed in the liquid line between the receiver and expansion valve serving as both a filter and removing water. Flared units enable easy change-out when saturated rather than soldered ones, and the removable cartridge type are even better. Internal corrosion begins at above 15ppm, also causing oil breakdown making it acidic, and contributing to motor burnouts in hermetic systems. In Glacier Bay systems a module concept is used incorporating a receiver, accumulator and dryer. The suction accumulator is used to prevent liquid slugging to the compressor.

    d.   **Sight Glass.** The sight glass allows visual inspection of the liquid. Bubbles indicate low refrigerant levels. All indicators incorporate a moisture indicator. The site glass will show bubbles if refrigerant levels are low; often this is seen at start-up and stop. It will also show restrictions or blocked filter dryers ahead of the sight glass.

    e.   **Refrigerant Control.** The thermostatic expansion valve (TX valve) regulates the rate of refrigerant liquid flow from the liquid receiver high side into the evaporator low side. It maintains the pressure difference and therefore expansion into the evaporator in exact proportion to the rate of liquid leaving the evaporator. Flow is regulated in response to both pressure and temperature within the evaporator. The thermal sensing element is placed on the outlet end of the evaporator, and where installed also a motor thermal sensing element, which consists of a bulb and capillary. Valves can normally be adjusted for optimum temperature. This pressure reduction causes a fall in temperature of the liquid. The cold liquid then passes to the evaporator. The thermostatic TX valve is controlled by two conditions, the temperature of the control element and the evaporator pressure. The automatic TX valves allow refrigerant flow only if evaporator pressure falls when the compressor operates. The single greatest cause of TX valve failure is dirt, acids, moisture and sludge in the system. All of these will freeze up or jam the valve.

f.　**Evaporator.** The cold liquid passes through to the evaporator cooling surfaces (or eutectic tanks). Heat within the refrigerator space is absorbed by the cold refrigerant, causing the air to cool. The absorption of the heat causes the refrigerant liquid to evaporate into a gas.

g.　**Recycle.** The cooled gas is suctioned back into the compressor to repeat the cycle.

h.　**Refrigerants.** The most commonly used refrigerant was Freon 12 (R12). As it is harmful to the ozone layer, and like all CFC gases it is being replaced by Freon R22. HFC-134a is also becoming a new standard refrigeration sys-

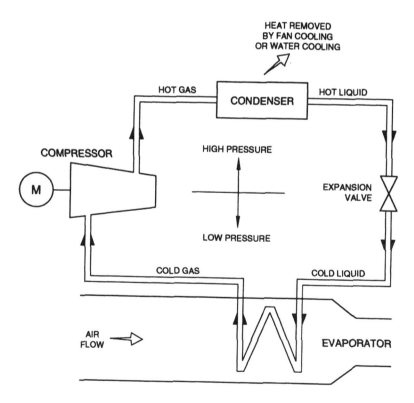

Figure 13-1 Basic Refrigeration Cycle

tem gas. This gas type is an obvious choice as auto air conditioning systems will all use the same gas, having already made the conversion. You cannot use HFC-134a in an existing Freon 12 system as virtually all the system components are incompatible and will require renewal. Glacier Bay and SeaFrost already have efficient HFC-134a systems on the market.

13.3   Eutectic Refrigeration Systems. This is the most common and efficient method of vessel refrigeration. The evaporator is replaced by a eutectic plate or tank. Operation is as follows:

> **a.   Eutectic Principles.** A eutectic system uses brine or a fluid that freezes at what is called eutectic temperature. Originally brine solutions were used but systems now have an ethylene glycol/water mixture or similar. The mixture has a much lower freezing point than water. Once the mixture is frozen completely (eutectic point) and refrigeration is removed, the tank will cool the refrigeration space, gradually thawing out as it absorbs heat.

> **b.   Holdover Period.** The period of time that the space will remain within required temperature ranges before refrigeration is required is called the holdover period. When specifying a system, the holdover time and the temperature required are critical to the size of the plates or tanks and the type of eutectic solution required.

13.4   Compressors and Motors. There are five compressor types in common use, the reciprocating, rotary, scroll, screw and centrifugal. Many systems use an engine driven reciprocating compressor, or either DC or AC motor powered compressors with a belt drive. Engine powered units have a belt drive off the engine and the drive pulley has an electromagnetic clutch for operation of the compressor. The most common compressors in use are the reciprocating and swash plate types.

> **a.   DC Drive Motors.** Glacier Bay DC motor systems have quoted figures for power consumption over 24 hours at 20.5 amp-hours and 39.5 amp-hours for refrigerator and freezer respectively. DC drive motors are typically rated at ½ hp, and Leeson is the most common. Glacier Bay has developed a new low speed motor which operates at the lower speed of 675 rpm rather than the 1800 rpm Leeson. With 300% greater torque it is nearly 80% heavier. Unlike the Leeson unit with 2 pole magnets and 2 brushes it has 6 poles and 4 brushes and is designed to have an increased service life of 500%. Other features are the ventilated commutator and significantly reduced running temperatures.

> **b.   Swash Plate Compressors.** These are typified by automotive air conditioning compressors, satisfactory where temperatures down to approximately minus 15°C are required. For most average applications these are suitable. These compressors are not really designed for eutectic refrigeration systems and although they work well, failure rates are higher than reciprocating units. They are ideal in air conditioning applications.

c.   **Reciprocating Compressors.** The reciprocating compressor consists of cylinders, piston intake and exhaust valves, and connecting rods to the crankshaft similar to an engine. The compressors are driven by belts from the drive motors.

    (1)   **Daily.** Check operating pressure gauges, temperatures, compressor oil levels, and abnormal noise or vibration.

    (2)   **Weekly.** Check evaporator and defrost if necessary. Make sure all valve covers are on and tight.

    (3)   **Bi-annually.** Check operation of high and low pressure cut-out switches. Perform oil sample test. Inspect and clean condenser. Check V-belts and adjust.

d.   **Lubrication.** Lubricants in refrigeration systems are miscible, wax free oils. These do not degrade under low temperatures or high pressures. Lubricating oils are carried around the system with the refrigerant and eventually return back to the compressor sump. Only reciprocating compressors have an oil sump, while swash plate units do not. The oil should be shiny and clear, have no visible particles, and feel smooth and greasy when rubbed between the fingers. Samples will help determine internal component condition and wear. Wear particles should not exceed in ppm the following; Lead (10); Copper (10); Silicon (25); Iron (100); Chrome (5); Nickel (5); Aluminum (10) and Tin (10).

e.   **Reciprocating Compressor Servicing.** Perform the following:

    (1)   **Condenser Pressure and Temperature.** High pressures indicate reduced cooling or air in the condenser. Low pressures indicate that refrigerant may be restricted to the evaporator.

    (2)   **Filters.** Liquid line, oil return, suction line and TX valve require cleaning, as clogged filters will cause restrictions in evaporator supply.

    (3)   **Moisture Indicators.** If these alter from green to yellow, moisture is in the system and filter dryer requires replacement.

    (4)   **Leak Detection.** Regular checks should be made on new installation every month until joints and flanges settle and are retightened. Refrigerant should be recharged.

    (5)   **Pressure Switches.** These should be checked and adjusted.

    (6)   **Condensers.** Open and clean tubes. Check and replace anodes.

    (7)   **Belts.** Rubber V-belts should be checked and re-tensioned.

13.5   **Auxiliary Refrigeration Controls.** A few different control devices are essential for safe and efficient operation.

    a.   **High Pressure Cutout.** The purpose of the high pressure cutout is to protect against high pressures, caused by loss of cooling water, a plugged condenser, or in the worst case, serious contamination of the refrigeration system with water and air. The cutout is usually wired in series with the compressor contactor or clutch. Typically this is above 75psi in the condenser. To test operation, close the cooling water off and wait until head pressure builds up and activates it. High pressures can seriously damage refrigeration compressors.

    b.   **Low Pressure Cutout.** The low-pressure switch monitors suction line pressure. The cutout operates when gas discharge from the evaporator is too low. Operation of the cutout is indicative of a low refrigerant charge, typically below 30psi. To test the switch, slowly close in the suction valve to activate the switch. Low suction pressures increase compression ratios and can cause compressor damage.

    c.   **Thermostatic Control.** This is used to set required temperatures. To test, vary settings and observe cut-in and out. Many are now microprocessor controlled and the temperature sensor is located at the holding plate, although some use the general box cooling space.

    d.   **Defrost Timers.** This is used only on larger vessels where the evaporator has heating elements, and is activated for 1 hour or more every 24 hours. They can malfunction.

    e.   **Clutch Engine Interlocks.** Many electromagnetic clutches are operated from a dedicated circuit breaker on the main switch panel, giving protection on the clutch coil and cabling. It is common for the switch to be inadvertently left on causing the batteries to flatten, as the typical current draw is around 3–4 amps. On some occasions the operating coil can burn out. To prevent this, an interlock should be installed into the ignition system so that the clutch is de-energized when the engine is shut down.

    f.   **Reduced Holdover Times.** A common complaint is that holdover times have reduced for the following reasons:

        (1)   **Warm Foodstuffs.** A refrigeration or freezer system is often pulled down to the required temperature. Then a full load of unfrozen food or warm drinks such as a case of beer is dumped into it with the expectation that they will be cooled rapidly.

        (2)   **Climate Change.** More often than not the system worked well in a temperate climate, but the first extended cruise in tropical waters results in a dramatic reduction in apparent efficiency. The refrigerator should be opened sparingly. Keep access down to the minimum.

(3)   **Mechanical Causes.** Engine drive belts are not re-tensioned and as such belt slip under load causes decreased refrigeration.

(4)   **Seawater Temperatures.** In many cases, a voyage to warmer waters also causes changes in condenser cooling efficiency. In many cases the eutectic plate takes longer to pull down, and refrigeration operation times need to be extended.

13.6   Electric Refrigeration Systems. These systems are typically self-contained. Electric refrigeration requires either AC or DC battery power for operation. The average power consumption is approximately 50 amp-hours for a refrigerator, and approximately100 amp-hours for freezers operating on a 50% duty cycle. To restore battery capacity there is a far greater run time involved than an equivalent engine driven system, and the installation of either a higher output alternator, and a fast charging device should be considered.

a.   **Free Standing Electric.** There are a number of freestanding, or self-contained refrigerators in use. These are DC powered and have eutectic holdover plates. Insulation on the units is reasonable but where installed, the surrounding area should be insulated further. Sizes of these units tend to be in the range of 40 to 120 liters. Power consumption of these units average around 35Ah per day, depending of course on ambient temperatures, and frequency of opening. As many units are built in, good ventilation must be provided to carry away heat from compressor unit. Many units do not function properly as a result of this omission, and a fan and ducting makes a difference.

b.   **Energy Utilization.** Some manufacturers have introduced circuitry that enables over-riding the thermostat during engine run periods. If temperatures are down, the alternator can supply loads for an additional pull down period that reduces electrical consumption later. A similar function is used on Isotherm automatic start up (ASU) systems. The controller senses the raised system voltage from the alternator and operates at double the speed to pull down temperatures and maximize the energy available. Another feature of

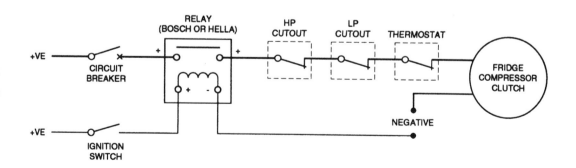

ELECTRIC FRIDGE COMPRESSOR INTERLOCK

Figure 13-2 Refrigeration Clutch Interlock

Isotherm (www.isotherm.com) systems is the control of compressor speed with respect to refrigeration requirements. The new Danfoss hermetically sealed compressors are used with electronic control on the 3-phase motor supply. In addition, there are also twin compressor models.

13.7   Hermetic Compressors. The majority of electric systems use hermetically-sealed Danfoss type compressors. The electric motor is sealed within a domed housing along with the compressor. The motor and compressor assembly is supported on a spring suspension system to absorb vibration. Lubrication and cooling come from oil and refrigerant flowing over the windings. The most common AC motor used in hermetic compressors is the capacitor type. These vary but typically are the capacitor start, induction run type. Condenser and evaporator fans use capacitor and shaded pole type motors.

a.   **Capacitor – Start, Induction – Run Motors.** These are used as the starting torque characteristics are very good. The motor has two windings, one for start and one for running. The motor also has a capacitor, which is the black cylinder on the unit, wired in series with the motor start winding. A starting relay is also used, which may be a current or potential relay switch, and is located on the outside of the compressor unit. When power is switched on, current passes through the start and run windings. The capacitor alters the phase angle and effectively converts the motor to a two-phase motor. When the motor speed increases and start current decreases at approximately

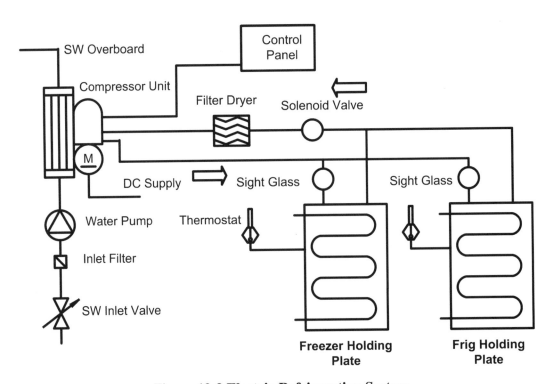

Figure 13-3 Electric Refrigeration System

60–75%, the switch opens and the start winding and capacitor are disconnected. Many motors have a thermal overload protector. Motor connections and terminals are normally as follows:

(1) **Start Winding** connected between S and C (common).

(2) **Run Winding** connected between R and C (common).

(3) **Capacitor** connected between R and S via start relay.

(4) **Supply** connected across R and C.

b. **Compressor.** Hermetic units are typically twin-piston reciprocating compressors with a valve plate assembly. Units with fan driven condenser cooling should be cleaned every 3 months. Tube flare nuts and service valve caps should be tight to prevent leaks.

c. **Troubleshooting.** Motor failures are usually due to external causes. Continuity and resistance checks will indicate status of windings. Start winding C to S resistance is approximately 5 ohms. Run winding C to R resistance is approximately 2 ohms. Both windings R to S resistance is approximately 7 ohms. Megger R or S to case is at least 1 meg ohm. Testing of both open circuit voltage and on-load voltage also will indicate problems. A difference exceeding 10 volts indicates an overload or motor winding fault. Use a clamp ammeter to check operating current. If the compressor current draw exceeds 7 amps it is close to failure. Check all external control devices first before assuming compressor failure. Discharge the capacitor first, use an ohmmeter and test across the capacitor terminals. A short circuited capacitor will indicate zero ohm. A high reading indicates an open circuit. If the capacitor is good the reading will initially go to zero then slowly rise. Regular failures in capacitors are usually caused by slow starts, too many starts, low supply voltages or the starting switches are faulty.

13.8   **Refrigeration System Installation.** There are kits for refrigeration installations, however I would recommend to get a good refrigeration mechanic to install the system. A number of factors can be controlled:

a. **Insulation.** If a refrigeration system is to be effective and reliable, it must be of sufficient size to meet the expected needs, and be well insulated. The insulation thickness should be at least 4 inches or greater. Inadequate insulation is a primary cause for inefficient boat refrigeration systems. As much insulation as possible should be installed. The ideal insulating material is urethane foam, followed closely by fiberglass wool and polystyrene foam. In many installations, foaming is done in place using a two-part mix. Failure to have the mix correct will produce inadequate results. The foam must have a good closed cell finish for good insulation qualities. The use of preformed slabs is much more reliable, and any outstanding voids can be filled with foam mix. The whole insulation block should be surrounded with plastic to prevent the ingress of moisture. A layer of reflective foil such as that used in

Table 13-1 Hermetic Compressor System Troubleshooting

Symptom	Probable Fault
Compressor fails to start (No hum sound)	Power supply failed or tripped Motor overload device (bridge and check) Relay defective Compressor fault Thermostat fault (bridge and check) Connection fault Capacitor failure
Compressor fails to start (Makes humming sound)	Low voltage to compressor motor Start relay faulty Compressor internal fault Defective start capacitor Motor winding fault
Compressor trips overload	Low voltage to compressor motor Motor winding fault Compressor seizing Start relay not opening
Capacitor failure	Start relay faulty Excessive start period, due to relay fault Excessive start load current Excessive short cycling on overload
Compressor cycle on and off	Low refrigerant charge Refrigerant leak
Compressor runs continuously	Low refrigerant charge Refrigerant leak Thermostat fault Condenser is dirty
Compressor stuck	Valve broken or defective Compressor overheated Low oil levels
Compressor short cycles	Overload protector faulty Thermostat faulty Low refrigerant charge Air in system
Excess noise levels	Loose parts, fan or motor vibration Copper tubing touching case Compressor or valve failures

domestic house construction will minimize heat radiation. A two-layer system of foam slabs and foil is the ideal combination. Vacuum insulation panels are expensive but give very high insulation values.

b. **Refrigeration Size.** Do not build refrigeration spaces greater than the actual requirements. Many boat owners build oversized boxes that remain half empty. This is a waste of energy and results in greater installation costs for a system that will not be used efficiently.

c. **Compressor Brackets.** The engine compressor mountings and brackets must be extremely robust to prevent vibration. Make sure that vibration will not fracture any part of it.

d. **Compressor Drive Belts.** Alignment of the compressor and engine drive pulleys is essential to ensure proper transfer of mechanical loads. Belts are usually dual pulley arrangements. Ensure that both belts are tensioned correctly.

e. **Energy Saving Measures.** Energy conservation and efficiency improvement measures can be implemented. Fill any empty spaces in the refrigerated compartment with blocks of foam, or inflated empty wine cask bladders. This will decrease the refrigerator space and reduce energy requirements. Place all frozen goods at the bottom of the refrigerator and cover the food with a mat to retain the cold air.

f. **Battery Voltages.** Ensure that battery voltage levels are maintained. Low battery levels will cause inefficient compressor operation. Do not let the battery level sink to the normal minimum level of 10.5 volts. It takes far more energy and engine run time to charge a nearly flat battery than one half charged.

g. **Ventilation.** Make sure the compressor unit is well ventilated. Install an additional fan and ducting to ensure positive ventilation on non-water cooled units.

13.9 **Refrigeration System Troubleshooting.** Vacuum pumps, bottles of refrigerant, gauge sets and spare parts are rarely carried. To carry out refrigeration work may be a breach of environmental laws if you are not certified. Knowingly releasing Class I (CFC) and Class II (HCFC) substances into the atmosphere can result in severe penalties and imprisonment. Besides working on refrigerated cargo ships, I used to also work for a period as a refrigeration mechanic repairing shipping container systems. Repairs were done in filtered clean areas. It is highly unlikely that conditions will be suitable for you to properly overhaul and repair compressors. The first way to avoid problems is to have the system properly installed in the first place. This chapter does not include procedures for the disassembly and checking of compressors, purging and recharging, as you are more likely to do further damage. If after checking the control systems you are unable to rectify problems, call in a licensed refrigeration technician. It is important to determine what is going on in the system. Pressure gauges are used to check system pressures, and thermometers are used to measure evaporator, line and condenser temperatures.

a.   **Condensers.** If a condenser is undersized or dirty, internal and external, the head pressure and condensing temperature rise. The higher temperature will make the compressor pump to this higher pressure and temperature. It is important to check and clean condensers regularly.

b.   **Refrigerant Loss.** Refrigerant loss is a common fault that causes a gradual reduction in cooling efficiency, and eventual tripping of the low-pressure cutout. Low refrigerant levels can be observed in the sight glass and bubbles will be seen. An empty sight glass indicates no refrigerant at all. If all the gas has escaped, after the leak has been located the system must be purged of air and moisture before gas recharging. A qualified refrigeration mechanic will be required to do this. A frost-covered evaporator generally signals that gas levels are satisfactory. If the system is undercharged, refrigerant does not properly liquefy before passing through the TX valve, the effective latent heat is reduced so refrigeration is poor. Some vapor will pass through the TX valve reducing refrigeration control capacity, and the vapor passing at high velocity will increase the wear on the TX valve needle and seat. Air in the system will increase total head pressure. The refrigerant will then have to condense to a higher temperature and pressure. The cylinder head and exhaust on the compressor and top tube of the condenser will all be at higher temperatures. This will also then affect the oil quality. It is also important to ensure that the caps on the service valves are replaced and tight to reduce leaks.

c.   **Leak Detection.** Perform leak detection by pressurizing the system and then check all possible leakage points at connections and fittings. Do not use a torch with HFC-134a refrigerants.

   (1)   **Halide Torch.** The most common test will require the use of a halide torch. Air is drawn to the flame through a sampling tube. Small gas leakages will give the flame a faint green discoloration, while large leaks will be bright green.

   (2)   **Soapy Water.** A simple method is to use soapy water, generally dishwashing liquid, and apply it to all piping joints with the system running. If a pressurized leak is in the joint, a bubble will form.

13.10   Domestic Refrigerators. Many boats have domestic freestanding type refrigerators installed. Maintain by keeping clean and deodorized to avoid smells.

a.   **Refrigerator not cooling or not coming down to temperature.** The thermostat is set incorrectly or is malfunctioning. Check that the hermetic compressor is actually operating. If it is running, then there may be a compressor fault, or a loss of gas in the system. Heavy ice or frost build up on the evaporator coils will also seriously affect cooling and require defrosting, and this may indicate an automatic defrost problem. Condensers must be kept clean, as dust accumulates when fan cooling is used, and heavily clogged condensers will require cleaning. If a fan is installed, always check that the fan is operating. If the refrigerator is badly ventilated this can also affect cooling function. In some cases the refrigeration does not start after a defrost cycle.

b. **Refrigerator builds up with frost.** Most units have automatic defrost systems. If the defrost timer is malfunctioning, or the defrost heater or thermostat is not functioning correctly, frost will build up. If after manual defrosting the system cools correctly, then the auto defrost system has failed.

13.11 **Freezers.** Upright and top loading freezers are often installed in vessel galleys. Symptoms and failure causes are similar to those in refrigerators.

a. **Freezer not functioning.** The most common causes are the power is off, the thermostat is faulty, the defrost timer is malfunctioning, or the compressor is faulty. If the compressor is running, this may also be due to refrigerant loss.

b. **Cooling is reduced.** Check the condensers, which must be kept clean. Ensure that the fan is running. Check for excess ice build up on the evaporator. If the thermostat is faulty it may cycle off too early.

13.12 **Ice Makers.** Many motor and power boats carry ice makers. Typical are those from U-line and the Raritan Icer-ette. Systems are available in 12 volts and others 110/220 volts AC. The refrigeration system principles remain the same and systems should be maintained. Water filters should be installed and regularly checked and cleaned.

a. **No ice production or ice production has stopped.** Check that the machine power is on, if the wire adjacent to the ice maker is raised, lower the wire to restart. Check that fill tube is not blocked with ice; a hair dryer is useful in defrosting this. Check that the water filling valve and shutoff valves are functioning.

b. **Small ice cubes.** The most common cause is a clogged water inlet pipe, or the water inlet valve is faulty. The next probable cause is the thermostat is faulty. If the refrigeration is not functioning correctly this will also affect ice production.

Table 13-2 Refrigeration Troubleshooting

Symptom	Probable Fault
Compressor abnormal noises	Low oil pressure Oil foaming Liquid in suction line Coupling misalignment Oil pump faulty Piston rings or cylinder wear Discharge valves faulty Solenoid valve oil return faulty Oil filter clogged Compressor mounting loose Low cooling water flow High water temperature
High condenser pressure	High pressure cutout activated Refrigerant overcharged Cooling water loss High cooling water temperature Condenser clogged Inlet water valve closed
Low condenser pressure	Low refrigerant charge Excess cooling to condenser Piston rings or cylinder wear
Low oil pressure	Oil pressure switch has activated Oil level low Oil pressure too low at regulator Oil foaming in crankcase Liquid in suction line Oil pump defective Bearing worn out Oil filter clogged
Oil level falling	Oil foaming in crankcase Poor oil return Liquid in suction line Piston rings or cylinder wear Solenoid on oil return faulty Oil filter clogged
Reduced or no cooling	Leak in system Clutch connection broken Clutch coil failure High pressure cut-out activated Low pressure cut-out activated Low refrigerant level Drive belt slipping Thermostat faulty

Table 13-3 Refrigeration Troubleshooting

Symptom	Probable Fault
Slow temperature pull down times	Drive belt slipping
	Low refrigerant level
	Compressor fault
	High cooling water temperature
	Condenser plugged
	Low battery voltage
	Frig space seals damaged
	High ambient temperature
	Insulation failure
	Thermostat faulty
Clutch circuit breaker tripping	Clutch coil failure
	Clutch cable shorting out
	Compressor bearing failure
Expansion valve icing up	Dryer requires replacement
	Low refrigerant charge
High discharge pipe temperature	TX valve fault
	Discharge valves leaking
Low oil temperature	Oil level low
	Oil is foaming in crankcase
	Oil pump defective
	Bearings worn
	Oil filter clogged
Low suction pressure no cooling water	Oil in evaporator
	Low refrigerant charge
	TX valve frozen up
	TX valve not operating
	Liquid line filter clogged
	Liquid line solenoid valve
Moisture in system	Condenser leaking
	Compressor gasket failure
	Compressor bearing failure
Refrigerant gas leakage	Pipe compression fitting
	Condenser leak
	Isolation valve leak
	Damaged piping
	Valve caps off

Table 13-4 Ice Maker Troubleshooting

Symptom	Probable Fault
Ice maker not starting	Power supply off Circuit breaker tripped Loose connection or switch fault Refrigeration controller faulty Compressor relay faulty or not operating Icemaker module faulty
Insufficient cooling to make ice cubes	Refrigerant leakage Condenser clogged Refrigeration compressor faulty Fan motor faulty or jammed Icemaker control module faulty
No water supply to make ice cubes (but freezing)	Water filter clogged or water off Water inlet solenoid faulty Mold heater assembly faulty Icemaker module faulty Refrigeration controller faulty
No ice cube ejection	Ice mold thermostat faulty Icemaker module faulty Ice ejection relay faulty
Machine stops in mid-ejection cycle	Icemaker control module faulty Electrical connection fault Ice ejection relay fault Electrical power supply fault
Slow ice production rate	Ice mold thermostat fault Condenser clogged Fan motor fault Ice ejection relay fault
Excess water and ice accumulations	Water inlet solenoid valve fault Icemaker control module fault Ice mold thermostat faulty Water filling assembly misaligned

AC Power Systems

14.1 **AC Power Safety.** AC is potentially lethal, and systems and equipment must be correctly selected, installed and maintained. The following safety precautions must be undertaken at all times when carrying out work.

$$\boxed{\textbf{WARNING}}$$

a. **Never work on "live" equipment. Always isolate and lock out equipment before opening. Attach a Danger Tag.**

b. **Never work on AC equipment alone, always have someone ready to assist if you accidentally receive a shock.**

c. **Always remove the shore power plug, inverter or any automatic changeover system before checking anything on the switchboard so that no power source remains connected to the system.**

d. **Learn artificial respiration and CPR techniques.**

14.2 **Shore Power Systems.** The increasing use of appliances such as air conditioning, washing machines, stoves, microwaves, hot water, TVs, power tools and other devices requires more power both on and away from the marina. The AC power systems on many motorboats now consist of several elements that include shore power installations, inverters, generators, AC motors and starters, and AC installations with grounding and circuit protection. The following basic recommendations are advisory and should be used in conjunction with the relevant national or other standard. References are to IRBES Section 2, Chapter 1.

Rule 2.1. Any boat that is connected to a marina or any other shore power circuit is generally required to comply with the relevant provisions of local and national electrical codes. Recommendations contained within this section are advisory only, and do not override the legal responsibilities of boat owners to meet specific requirements.

Connection of the vessel to a marina power system imposes certain obligations on the boat owner. A vessel must comply with national or other electrical standards. Acceptable standards are:

(1)   US National Electrical Code (NEC).

(2)   NFPA 302, Fire Protection Standard for Pleasure and Commercial Motor Craft.

(3)   Regulations for the electrical and electronic equipment of ships (Institution of Electrical Engineers-UK) BS7671:2001.

(4)   Lloyd's Register of Shipping (LR). Rules and Regulations for the classification of ships.

Rule 2.2. All boat AC electrical systems should be installed and tested by an AC qualified and appropriately licensed electrician.

Where possible, always use a qualified and AC licensed marine electrician, or a shore based AC licensed industrial electrician. An accident caused by a fault in the system due to incorrect wiring may void your insurance policy and expose you to criminal and civil liability. Many marine electricians have automotive backgrounds and are not AC qualified, so check up first.

Rule 2.3. Shore power inlet sockets shall be of the self closing type and rated to IP56. All inlet sockets shall have a means for locking in the plug when inserted.

Inlet sockets should be weatherproof in accordance with international protection standards, IP56 or equivalent NEMA rating, which require protection against heavy seas. Inlet sockets must have spring-loaded, self-closing and locking covers. The inlet sockets must also be of a male type connector only. Do not use inlet sockets that are designed for caravans, trailers or recreational vehicles, as they are not of the standard required. The plug should have a screw locking-ring that prevents the plug from being pulled out with boat movement. Suppliers such as Marinco (www.marinco.com) and Hubble (www.hubble.com) can supply good quality equipment. Ratings of inlet sockets and plugs are 15 amps for 240-volt systems. Domestic extension cables when used are often 10 amps only. 30 amps is the nominal rating for 115 volts systems. Check that the O ring seals are always in good condition as the seal will also fail.

Rule 2.4. Shore power inlet sockets shall be mounted at a position and height that prevents mechanical damage and immersion.

The sockets should be in an accessible location and as high as possible above the deck line. They must be located so that there is no mechanical damage risk. They should also be shielded from rain so that driving rain at a 45° angle will not enter the plug and socket.

Rule 2.5. The vessel should not be connected to any marina power supply outlet that is damaged.

Inspect the conditions at the marina before you connect your boat. Look for damage to outlets and tracking on pins, wires and damaged conduits. If the marina systems are degraded, this represents a risk to you, your crew and boat, and possible nuisance tripping of GFCI units. Check the dock supply voltages with a multimeter, If they are low (more than 5%), this is not good for on board electric motors. Some battery chargers will also have lower outputs. Start your largest appliance, plus operate all the systems proposed and see whether the circuit will withstand it, in many cases it does not. You must check and report deficiencies, as you may become liable. If they are not reported, they do not get fixed.

Rule 2.6. Shore power leads shall be weatherproof, and have a high visibility outer sheath.

Shore cables should be suitable for outdoor use. The cable must be heavy-duty rated, which is typical of most outdoor rated extension cables and special shore power lead suppliers. High visibility outer sheaths are yellow or orange; they are also UV stabilized unlike standard duty domestic leads, which should not be used. It is good practice to have a strain relief grip over the cable to prevent unnecessary strain on the cable, particularly where the plug into the supply pedestal has a screw locking ring fitting. The flexible cable should permit normal movement of the vessel without stress in the full predicted tidal range. It also must prevent water travelling along the cable to the inlet receptacle and be secured so that immersion in the water is not possible. Provision must be made to prevent the plug falling into the water if it is accidentally disconnected. Plugs should be double insulated and be made of impact resistant material. If a plug has accidentally been immersed in water, do not use it. Disconnect and dismantle for cleaning and drying first. Cables should be regularly inspected, and the outer insulation checked for cuts or other damage. Do not repair or join a damaged cable, it must be replaced. Cables should always be run from the pedestal to minimize exposure to damage, or present tripping hazards to other people on the marina.

Rule 2.7. No shore power ground conductor should be disconnected as a method for reducing corrosion.

Some boat owners disconnect the shore power ground connection either in the plug or at the socket inlet to open the ground path ashore. This should never be done; in many cases it removes the safety ground of equipment, and creates serious electric shock risks.

Rule 2.8. The AC power panel should have a polarity indicator and reversal switch.

Switchboards should incorporate a reverse polarity indicator, and have a changeover switch. It is quite common to find marina supplies with the neutral and active (hot or live) conductors reversed. This condition is indicated and the switch simply reverses to the correct polarity. Most marina supply outlets are protected by a circuit breaker or a GFCI, which may trip on connection of the boat if ground and active are wrongly connected.

Rule 2.9. The AC power panel shall have power input isolation, power source selection and short circuit protection.

The switch panel should have input isolation and short circuit protection. The input isolation can be a trip free circuit breaker rated at the maximum power input of the panel. The selection switch is for switching of each input source (shore power, inverter, generator) without paralleling. Parallel connection of an inverter will destroy it.

14.3   115VAC 60Hz Single Phase System. This voltage (also stated as 117 or 120 V) is primarily used in the United States and Canada, Brazil and most South American countries. Normally a 30-amp supply requires a supply cable of 12 AWG (4.0 mm^2). The following circuit illustrates a typical shore power system. In this configuration, only one wire in the power inlet is "hot" or energized.

(1)   Black wire is "hot".

(2)   White wire is neutral.

(3)   Green wire is ground or earth.

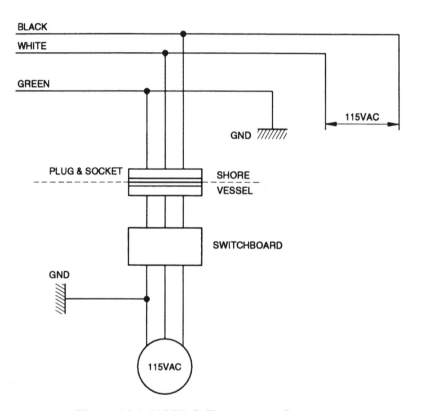

Figure 14-1 115 VAC Shorepower Systems

14.4 **115/230 Volt Systems.** The following circuit diagrams and color codes are for typical American dual voltage shore supply systems. Observe the following:

(1)   Red wire is "hot".

(2)   Black wire is "hot".

(3)   White wire is neutral.

(4)   Green wire is ground or earth.

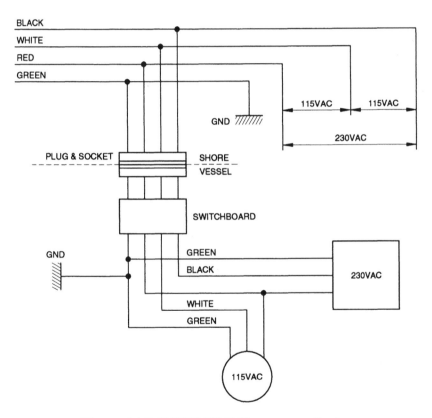

Figure 14-2 115/220 VAC Shor power Systems

14.5   220/240 Volt Systems. *220/230/240VAC 50Hz Single Phase System.* This voltage is the IEC standard and used in the UK, Europe, Australia, New Zealand, South Africa, Fiji, New Caledonia and most other countries. The IEC is standardizing most countries at 230 VAC. The following circuit diagrams are for typical systems using IEC standard color codes, and incorporating an isolation transformer. Normally a minimum 15-amp supply rating requires supply cable of 2.5 mm². Many marina supplies only have a 10-amp supply. The cable should be approximately 45 feet; anything over this will start to introduce volt drop problems at rated load.

(1)   Brown wire is "hot" (used to be red).

(2)   Blue wire is neutral (used to be black).

(3)   Green/yellow stripe wire is ground or earth (used to be green).

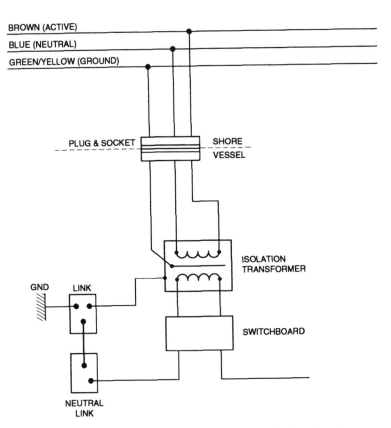

Figure 14-3 220/240 VAC ShorePower Isolation Systems

14.6   440/460VAC 60Hz 3 Phase System. This arrangement is more commonly used on larger vessels, such as trawler yachts, tugs, super yachts and larger motorboats. In vessels having 3-phase power supplies, connection to shore power is less common or unavailable. Few normal marinas are able to offer power supplies. 3-phase offers equipment 20% lighter and smaller than single-phase, and 150% greater efficiency. In a 3-phase vessel, power is usually generated in a three phase, star or wye configuration. This means that the center point is grounded. In a 208 VAC 3-phase wye system, you get 208 V between phases, and 120 VAC phase to ground. Connected loads are usually symmetrical with electric motors, however where loads are connected to each phase, unacceptable imbalances can occur. Single-phase loads must be evenly distributed across phases. In some instances 115/220V transformers are used to power lower voltage systems.

Delta connected systems are relatively rare, although recently they are being used on large DP offshore drilling rigs. In an ungrounded Delta system, a grounding of any one phase will not stop the whole system. Ground fault monitoring is used to monitor the insulation levels of the Delta systems, and faults must be rectified quickly. Delta systems normally have double pole isolation and protection. In Star systems, any phase to ground short circuit will trip the protection. In Delta systems problems arise where equipment such as UPS units have a grounded neutral rather than a floating live neutral. This has undesirable performance affects on the equipment circuits. This is often resolved by the use of a Delta/Star isolation transformer to provide a grounded neutral configuration. Quality UPS units such as those from Energy Technologies Inc. (www.powersource.net) incorporate isolation transformers for galvanic separation, and much development has resulted from work with the US Navy.

a.   **Phase Marking.** Circuit designations are R, S and T for each phase, also it may be R, Y and B to represent the phase cable colors. In the US this may be L1, L2 and L3. Secondary motor circuits may be also called U,V and W or U1, V1 and W1.

b.   **Phase Colors.** The phase colors are black, white and red in the US. In most other parts of the world they are red, yellow and blue, although yellow may be replaced by white.

c.   **Phase Sequencing.** Phases must be connected in the correct sequence for a motor to run in the correct direction. If a motor is running in reverse rotation, then reverse any two phase cables to reverse the direction.

d.   **Phase Current Loads.** In any 3-phase motor, each phase should have the same current. An imbalance indicates a high resistance in the connections or in some cases a failing motor winding.

14.7   Transformers. Transformers are used to lower voltages, either in electronics equipment power supplies, in starters for control voltages, and in isolation transformers for shore power supplies. Larger motorboats transform 3-phase from 480VAC to 208/120VAC for power and lighting circuits. It consists of a primary winding and a secondary winding on an iron core. Power applied to the primary magnetizes the core and induces a voltage into the secondary winding. The most common type is the isolation transformer, which electrically separates input and output. Autotransformers are lighter and cheaper, with connected primary and secondary windings. Transformer maintenance consists of a simple cleaning of dust and insulation test every year. Visually check windings and wire insulation for heat damage. The cycle "hum" can cause vibration, which can loosen screws and all connections should be tightened. At switch on there are high inrush currents, up to 25 times the rated current, and these must be considered when selecting protection devices. There are also booster transformers available that also act as isolation devices, and are used to boost lower dockside supply voltages.

14.8   Domestic Plugs. The following is additional information on power plugs, as the various plug types required when travelling can be confusing. It is recommended that you acquire an international adapter kit.

> **(1)**   US Type—2 parallel pins (US, Canada and South America).
>
> **(2)**   Australia Type—2 and 3 pins (Australia, Fiji, New Zealand).
>
> **(3)**   European Type—2 pins round (all of Europe, South Africa).
>
> **(4)**   UK Type—3 pins square (UK, South Africa, Portugal).

Rule 2.10. Isolation transformers shall be rated for the maximum current rating of the shore supply inlet.

By eliminating the ground path ashore, isolation transformers galvanically isolate the vessel from the shore power system, reducing electrolytic (stray current) corrosion. Most marina outlets rarely exceed a maximum of 15 amps/240-220 volts or 30 amps/115 volts. Some transformers are dual input with inputs of 120/240 or 480/240 and this gives some flexibility. Transformers do not alter frequency. Frequency may be different in some places, and this affects motor speeds (50 Hz is slower than 60Hz), for battery charging, domestic appliances and resistive loads, this is not a major problem. Victron (www.victron.nl) has also incorporated a Soft Start unit, which manages high start currents that would otherwise trip the marina supply breaker, and short circuit protection.

Table 14-1 Isolation Transformer Rating Table (0.8 pf)

Output (kW)	Output (kVA)	Current 120 V	Current 240 V
3	3.74	34 amps	17.0 amps
4	5.00	45 amps	22.7 amps
5	6.25	57 amps	28.4 amps
7	8.75	80 amps	39.8 amps

14.9   Shore Power Inverters. A relatively new development from Atlas Energy, Mastervolt and Asea Power, shore power inverters use frequency conversion and control technology to output a stable AC voltage to the boat. In many marinas and other AC power supplies, the shore voltage is low, fluctuating in voltage levels or generally unstable. The shore inverter accepts all input ranges and frequencies, and will always output a stable waveform and voltage level irrespective of the input variations. The units operate similarly to UPS units and use inverters and pulse-width-modulation techniques that allow wide input voltage ranges and ensure stable, good waveform outputs. These units will suit the larger boats as they are relatively expensive, but for boats at the dock for long periods, many power problems of computers and other sensitive equipment will be solved. The systems also allow parallel connection of two shore leads in their Smart Box unit. Atlas also have their new ShorPOWER converter supply onboard 3-phase power from a single-phase power inlet. Log on to www.mastervolt.com and www.aseapower.com.

14.10   Power Management. Victron makes a system called Mains Manager. It is a combination transfer switch and switchboard. Loads are grouped into heavy, medium and light. The power input groups such as shore power, generator and inverter are supplied to the panel. When the major power supply source such as the generator is supplying the board, all load groups are available. If a limited shore power source is connected, heavy load groups are inhibited so they cannot operate. As the system has input voltage monitoring, when the voltage drops, the system will switch off equipment to prevent damage and overloads. The system transfer switch operates in 200ms. Another automatic device from Victron is the Filax transfer switch unit. It allows changeover from shore, generator or inverter in just 20ms, which stops computers rebooting, video and microwave clocks resetting.

14.11   Uninterruptible Power Supplies (UPS). In commercial and offshore environments, all key equipment is powered through UPS units; in any computer control applications they guarantee power supply quality. The UPS serves as a stabilized power supply, as it filters out transients. Many are quite sophisticated units with integral systems monitoring and control, and many computer UPSs are relatively simple. The main power supply is filtered before input to an IGBT full wave rectifier, where it is converted using pulse-width-modulation techniques. The DC output is used to charge the integral battery bank, and then to the inverter. An oscillator controls the inverter output frequency, and the clean sinusoidal AC output passes through a static switch. The static switch transfers load to the bypass line when the inverter is overloaded or unable to feed the load. The output is filtered and then goes to the load via a maintenance bypass switch. Systems that rectify AC to DC and invert an AC output are commonly called voltage and frequency independent (VFI) systems. When the AC main power fails, the output is still maintained by conversion of the DC battery output to the inverter. Every 6 months, switch the power supply off and monitor the battery discharge. Monitor the voltage across the battery when you switch off, and then at 15 and 30 minutes. The UPS should shutdown when battery voltage drops to nominal values so as to prevent complete battery discharge. Power on will switch the UPS back to normal and recharge the battery bank.

Rule 2.11. The switchboard shall be of the dead front type, and constructed of non-hygroscopic and fireproof material. The panel should be rated to a minimum of IP44.

Open dead front type switchboards must be of a non-conductive and non-hygroscopic material. If protective and isolation devices are not to be integrated into the main electrical panel, then consider an industrial or domestic consumer distribution panel or module as an alternative. These panels are made of plastic with a splash-proof cover, and have all earth and neutral conductors, main switch or RCD and MCB's within one compact unit.

Rule 2.12. The switchboard shall be located in a position to minimize exposure to spray or water.

Locate the switch panel or distribution unit in a dry place such as a cupboard or other suitable and safe area.

Rule 2.13. DC systems should not be located or installed adjacent to AC systems. Where DC and AC circuits share the same switchboard, they should be physically segregated and partitioned to prevent accidental contact with the AC section. The AC section must be clearly marked with Danger labels.

Where DC and AC are installed on the same panel, which is common on boats, cover the exposed AC connections at the rear of the panel, or preferably enclose them in a separate compartment.

14.12   AC Circuit Protection Principles. In any AC system, there are several control and protection devices. It is normal to have these co-ordinated; this is called discrimination or selectivity. The principle is that a fault appearing in any part of the system is cleared or disconnected by the protection device immediately upstream of the fault. Discrimination should be full ideally, but in most cases is only partial. Partial discrimination may be achieved up to a current level, and any fault current levels above that will cause all breakers to trip. This is achieved by having different current settings, with a motor thermal overload set, a switchboard distribution breaker, and generator supply breaker set at different levels. Tripping times are dependent on the rate of current increase. If a fault such as an overload arises up to a level of 0.75 above normal current, the thermal relay will trip. If the current continues to rise such as in an impedant short-circuit, the magnetic circuit breaker supplying the circuit should trip. If the fault is a full short circuit current, the supply breaker also should operate very fast. If there is no discrimination, all circuit breakers will open up to the generator supply. Merlin-Gerin has designed this into circuit breakers; the compact NS devices provide discrimination on current, time and energy. GFCI or RCD devices installed on marina supply pedestals and in vessel circuits detect and isolate earth leakage conditions only.

14.13   What is an AC Short Circuit? Short circuits are relatively rare in boat electrical systems, and are not that common on big ships or ashore. A short circuit is where two points of different electrical potential are connected, that is live to neutral, live to ground, phase to phase, and phase to ground. A short circuit causes a very rapid rise in current which can reach several hundred times the nominal value in milliseconds, and causes high thermal and mechanical stresses which can destroy the cables, and the busbars which feed the fault. There are two thresholds in short circuits. The first is where electrical arcs commence, insulating materials start to breakdown and parts start to deform. The second level is where contacts melt and weld together, electrical arcs continue and insulators start to carbonize. Short circuits can be either a lower level condition called an impedant or intermediate short-circuit, usually caused by deterioration in insulation. A full short-circuit is usually caused by directly connecting two phases or a similar connection fault.

14.14   What Causes a Short Circuit? Typically short circuits are caused in order of probability by loose connections, insulation damage or failure, metallic bodies or conductive deposits on terminals within junction boxes and motor terminals, broken conductors within a cable, dust and moisture gradually tracking and burning across to create a short, and after new installations or repairs there are connection or crossover errors.

14.15   Short Circuit Calculations. Prospective short circuit current (Isc) can be calculated for circuits although this is often only done in larger super yachts and motorboats with large power systems and built to survey or Class. This is defined as the calculated RMS value of short circuit fault current at any point in the system, should a conductor of negligible impedance replace the protection device. Values depend on the supply voltage and line impedance.

14.16   What is a Short Circuit Protective Device (SCPD)? Typically this is either a fuse or a circuit breaker. Fuses are devices whose conductors melt to break the fault current. Circuit breakers detect short circuit current and open the poles to clear the fault. An SCPD must detect and break high fault current levels quickly before reaching peak current values. Given the high rise times and magnitude of currents, this must be fast to be effective. Speed of the SCPD is determined by the peak current and breaking capacity of the contactor thermal device to withstand overload. A DOL starter has a start curve of approx 7.2 x current for 10 seconds. Thermals must protect against low-level faults but allow for machine start-up times and current. An MCB combines the action of an isolation switch, overload protection, and short circuit protection.

 a.   **Overload Protection.** This function is a thermally operated one. Tripping values are normally to hold 110% of rated value and trip at 137% of rated value at 25°C.

 b.   **Short Circuit Protection.** This function is a magnetic one. A solenoid coil within the breaker trips when the factory set short circuit current value is reached. Under short circuit fault conditions a large arc can be generated, and breakers use the generated magnetic field to direct and quench the arc in a chute.

14.17   Selecting Protection Equipment. Equipment must be selected properly if it is to perform properly under fault conditions.

Rule 2.14. The main switch or protection circuit breaker shall be rated for the maximum current capacity of the circuit.

The MCB must be selected to protect the cable, not the equipment. The MCB must be rated to hold at the maximum demand, such as motor starting loads, which can be 4 to 6 times rated load. The device voltage must suit the system voltage. The interrupting capacity must be able to cope with any prospective fault current levels. The MCB current rating must hold at 100% of operating current, and trip at 125% at 40°C.

14.18   Cable Installation. The cabling installation requirements for AC systems are virtually the same as those defined for DC systems. These are briefly redefined.

Rule 2.15. Conductors shall be selected based on the maximum current demand of the circuit. Ambient temperatures exceeding the rated temperature of the cable should be de-rated.

Conductors should be selected based on the maximum current of the connected load. Where cables are to be installed in hot machinery spaces, consideration should be given to de-rating if the ambient temperature exceeds the cable rating temperature.

Rule 2.16. Conductor size shall be selected with a maximum allowable voltage drop of 5% for all circuits.

The maximum acceptable cable voltage drop is 5% in all circuits. The voltage drop problem can be prevalent in high starting current equipment, and where equipment may be running at maximum load a larger cable size may be a good option.

Rule 2.17. Conductors shall be stranded, insulated and sheathed (double insulated) and where possible of Ship Wiring standard. All conductors shall have a minimum cross-sectional area of 1.0mm^2.

Cable ratings and insulation materials should conform to recognized national standards. Where possible, cables classed as "Shipwiring Cables" should be used. 3 Core (2 core and Ground) cables should be used and typical ratings are given in Table 14-2. Shipwiring cable is expensive. If you do not want to pay the costs of such cable, and do not have to meet Class requirements, install 15/30-amp heavy duty outdoor rated, orange or yellow-sheathed extension cable. Do not install domestic triplex single strand type cable under any circumstances.

Rule 2.18. Conductor color codes shall conform to either IEC or US standard codes.

IEC: Brown wire is active "live or hot"; blue wire is neutral; ground (earth) is a green/yellow stripe wire. Three-phase systems should consist of the primary color red, yellow and blue for each phase, and in some cases white is used for the yellow phase. Switching and control circuit wires may be any other color that cannot be confused or mistaken.

US: Red wire is hot "active"; black wire is hot "active"; white wire is neutral; ground is green wire.

Rule 2.19. Cable runs should be installed as straight as practicable. Cable bend radii shall be a minimum of 6 x cable diameter.

Cables should be installed in as straight a run as practicable. Tight bends should be avoided to reduce unnecessary strain on conductors and insulation. The minimum cable bend radii is 6 x the diameter.

Rule 2.20. Cables should be accessible for inspection and maintenance.

All cables must be accessible for maintenance and inspection. All cables, in particular those entering transits, should be capable of access for routine inspection, and adding other circuits.

Rule 2.21. Cables shall be protected from mechanical damage, either where exposed, or installed within compartments.

All cables should be installed so as to prevent any accidental damage to the insulation or application of excessive stress on the cable.

Rule 2.22. Cables passing through bulkheads or decks shall be protected from damage using a suitable non-corrosive gland, bushing or cable transit. Cables transiting decks or watertight bulkheads should preserve or maintain the watertight integrity.

Cable glands are designed to prevent cable damage and ensure a waterproof transit through a bulkhead or deck. They should be installed properly and not degrade watertight bulkhead integrity.

Rule 2.23. Cables shall be supported at maximum intervals of 200mm. Supports and saddles are to be of a non-corrosive material. Where used in engine compartments or machinery spaces, these should be metallic and coated to prevent chafe to the cable insulation. Cable saddles should fit neatly, without excessive force onto the cables, or cable looms, and not deform the insulation.

Cables should be neatly loomed together and secured with PVC or stainless saddles to prevent cable loom sagging and movement during service. In machinery spaces metal saddles are often used; however, they should have a plastic sleeve placed on them to prevent the sharp edges chafing the cable insulation.

Rule 2.24. Cables shall be run as far as practicable from DC power cables, network, data and signal cables.

Cables should be run separately from DC cables and should never be within the same loom or cable bundle. They should also be run clear of any data cables, network or signal cables.

Rule 2.25. All neutral conductors terminated in a neutral link shall be identified to correspond to the marked circuit number.

When connecting AC circuits, the neutral should be marked and connected to the same numbered terminal in the neutral terminal block. Similarly if an earth or ground terminal block is used to collect the grounds, the ground for the circuit should have the same terminal number. For example circuit 1 has neutral 1 and ground number 1.

Rule 2.26. The ground conductor shall not have any switch, fuse or other device installed.

The ground conductor should not have anything connected in line to it that may cause opening of the circuit. See notes on galvanic isolators.

Rule 2.27. All ground connections shall be mechanically secured, and be protected against mechanical damage or corrosion.

Ground connections must be mechanically secured so that they cannot come loose. The ground connection point should be protected from mechanical damage or any accidental disconnection. The connection should be clear of water or moisture so that corrosion cannot occur. The connection should be coated for protection.

Table 14-2 AC System Cable Ratings

Cable Size	PVC	Butyl Rubber	EPR
1.0 mm^2	8 amps	12 amps	13 amps
1.5 mm^2	11 amps	16 amps	17 amps
2.5 mm^2	14 amps	22 amps	23 amps
4.0 mm^2	19 amps	31 amps	32 amps
6.0 mm^2	25 amps	39 amps	40 amps
10.0 mm^2	35 amps	53 amps	57 amps
16.0 mm^2	40 amps	70 amps	76 amps
25.0 mm^2	60 amps	93 amps	102 amps
35.0 mm^2	73 amps	115 amps	120 amps
50.0 mm^2	85 amps	135 amps	155 amps

Rule 2.28. Equipment shall be grounded and the maximum resistance between any ground point and the boat ground shall be 1 ohm.

The maximum resistance of the grounding (earthing) system shall be 1 ohm between the main ground terminal block and the boat ground. It should also be less than 1 ohm between any grounded point and the boat ground. Any fault arising on an ungrounded or inadequately grounded item of equipment may cause exposed metal to be "alive" up to rated voltage. Accidental touching and grounding by a person may cause serious electric shock, injury and death. Grounding provides a low resistance path for any fault arising on exposed and bonded metal. During fault conditions, extremely large current levels of several hundred amps may flow. This high current usually ruptures fuses or trips circuit breakers. Improper or degraded grounding or a high resistance ground may cause circuit conductor heating and fire. Corrosion protection is an important consideration, but it is both misguided and dangerous to consider the corrosion risk ahead of the safety factor. In multiple grounded systems ashore, any current flowing in the grounded neutral conductor will also cause a voltage rise on that conductor above the mains supply voltage. This will also be impressed on the grounding system, and this is typically a few volts above ground potential. In a fault on the mains, the supply neutral voltage on the installation grounding system will rise in proportion to the load, and the value will depend on the impedance of the main ground system. Some rules specify that the AC ground and DC negative are bonded to reduce stray current corrosion. The chapters on corrosion should be read on this subject. In a lightning protection context there is a view put forward that failure to bond AC and DC to the lightning ground will allow a build-up of high voltages in both circuits and that equipotential bonding will minimize that. In a properly installed lightning protection system with a suppression device to clamp the voltage to a safe value, that prospect is significantly reduced. If an AC system is interconnected with the vessel corrosion bonding system, RF aerial and lightning ground risks are introduced. In the event of an AC fault, and where a faulty main ground connection also exists, all other systems may become alive up to rated AC voltage (115V, 230V or 480V). This imposes a serious risk to life. Equipotential bonding works both ways: while normally meant to hold at an equal ground potential, take away that ground bond and apply a fault and you have a very lethal environment.

14.19   Ground (Earth) Leakage Protection. The most reliable and accepted method for personal protection is the installation of earth leakage protection devices. Many marinas now install these on each circuit. The new devices are considerably more advanced; they include residual current devices (RCD), ground fault current interrupters (GFCI), or residual current circuit breakers (RCCB).

Rule 2.29. Ground fault protection devices should be installed on all boat power outlet circuits.

GFCI/RCCB/RCD units should protect all power outlets on a boat. This may be on the entire circuit or integral to the power outlet. They are not required on water heating or electric cookers as element leakages will cause nuisance tripping. This also can occur in clothes washers and dishwashers with water heating elements.

Rule 2.30. Where earth leakage protection devices are installed such as RCD (Residual Current Devices) and GFCI (Ground Fault Current Interrupters), they should be tested monthly to verify operation.

All RCD/GFCI units should be tested every month using the integral test facility. The GFCI has an integral test button that simulates a ground fault to test the tripping function, and a reset button. Devices also require checking with a special test unit, as the self-test button is not always a reliable function test.

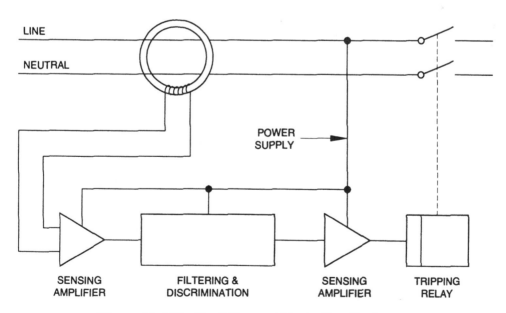

Figure 14-4 Residual Current Protection Devices

a. **Installation Requirements.** The selection and installation of an GFCI is based on the tripping values, and therefore the level of protection. The values are as follows and tripping times are around 25ms:

(1) **5-30 mA Value.** These values are used for quick tripping and protection against personal shock. Many GFCI are set at 5mA.

(2) **100 mA Value.** This level is designed to give fire protection.

b. **GFCI Tripping.** Due to the environment, earth leakages are commonplace, and nuisance tripping is common at marina berths. The principal causes of tripping are as follows:

(1) Connection of a neutral and ground (earth) connection downstream of a GFCI.

(2) A crossed neutral between protected and unprotected circuits.

(3) Deterioration of cable insulation.

(4) Water and moisture in terminal boxes, and cumulative leakages from a number of sources with small leakage paths.

(5) Absorption of moisture into heating elements including steam irons, refrigeration defrost elements, stove and hot water elements and electric kettles. This problem disappears if element operates for half an hour or more.

(6) Tracking across dirty surfaces to ground.

(7) Intermittent arcing internally in appliances.

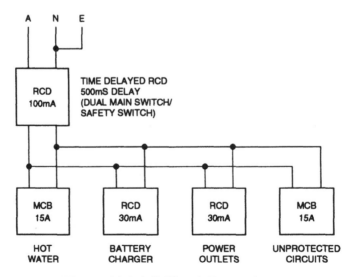

Figure 14-5 AC Circuit Protection

(8) High voltage impulses caused by switching off inductive motor loads.

(9) High current impulses caused by capacitor start motors.

c. **GFCI (RCD) Operation.** The GFCI/RCD units work on an electromagnetic principle as illustrated below:

(1) A toroidal transformer detects magnetic fields created by current flow in the active and neutral conductor of the protected circuit.

(2) Under normal conditions, the vector sum of the currents, known as residual current, is effectively zero and the magnetic fields cancel.

(3) If a condition arises where current flows from active or neutral to ground, the residual current will not be zero and the magnetic field will send a tripping signal to the protected circuit.

d. **Installation Checks.** Installation should be performed by an AC licensed electrician and tested using test equipment made for the purpose. The following tests must be performed using a 500-volt (Megger):

(1) Disconnect supply, neutral and earth. Test between active and earth. On new installations readings must exceed 1 meg ohm and a minimum of 250k ohms on existing systems.

(2) Test between neutral and earth. Readings must be a minimum of 40k ohms.

14.20 **Circuit Testing.** The following *must* be tested before putting any circuit into service, and as part of routine inspection and testing:

Rule 2.31. The insulation resistance between all circuit insulated poles and ground, and between poles shall exceed 1 meg ohm.

A 500-volt DC insulation Megger tester should be used. Disconnect all electronics and appliances, turn power off and disconnect the main grounding conductor. All switches should be in the on position. Insulation resistance between ground and live conductors must be a minimum of 1meg ohm. Water heater elements must be at least 10k ohm. An ohmmeter should be used to check between all active and neutral poles on each circuit to ensure that only load resistances are present, and with all switches on, there is no short circuit through either cable damage or incorrect equipment connection.

Rule 2.32. The insulation resistance between all switchboard busbars, and between busbar and ground shall exceed 1 meg ohm.

A 500-volt DC insulation Megger tester should be used. Disconnect all electronics and appliances, turn the power off and disconnect the main grounding conductor. All switches should be in the on position. Insulation resistance between busbars and ground must be a minimum of 1 meg ohm.

Rule 2.33. The insulation resistance of all generator and motors, cables, windings and control gear and ground shall exceed 1 meg ohm.

A 500-volt DC insulation Megger tester should be used. Insulation resistance between all parts and ground must be a minimum of 1 meg ohm. Where possible the tests should be made on hot machines.

Rule 2.34. There shall be no transposition of active and neutral conductors.

All switches, circuit breakers, outlet live pins, equipment terminals must be checked and be of the same polarity. No transposition of neutral and actives (crossed connections) is allowable.

Rule 2.35. There shall be no transposition of ground and neutral conductors.

All equipment and outlets must be checked to ensure that there are no crossed connections.

14.21   Generators. The majority of generators are single phase, with three phase machines being used on larger vessels. The majority of units come complete with optional sound shields and only require external connection of cooling water, fuel, electrical and exhaust systems. Important factors are the stability of the output voltage, the stability of the frequency, the quality of the output waveform, and the ability to withstand high starting currents. Most manufacturers have significantly reduced weight, physical size, noise emission and vibration levels. Diesel generators generally have the same principles and requirements as those for main propulsion diesels and in practice they operate longer hours than main engines. A number of alternators driven off main propulsion engines have been developed, and are common on canal boats and barges which have long motoring periods when in transit. Typical of these are the Auto-Gen unit which has a sine wave output unit of 4.5 KW, (19.6 A). This type of unit is belt coupled to a main crankshaft pulley, and requires up to 9 HP at full rated output. The units use a clutch and control system to compensate for engine speed variations and ensure frequency stability. Other types use an alternator to feed an inverter system with fixed stable frequency. Earlier units had a modified sine wave output. A Northern Lights generator is illustrated below with various systems. Log on to www.northerns-lights.com; www.kohlergenerators.com; www.onan.com; www.hflgen.com; www.masegenerators.it; www.fischerpanda.com

> a.   **Installation.** The basic installation factors are as follows:
>
> > (1)   **Fuel Systems.** Clean fuel is essential and the installation of a separator system such as a Racor is essential. Check them regularly and drain off any accumulated water.
> >
> > (2)   **Exhaust System.** Improperly installed exhaust systems are a major cause of failure. The seawater inlet should not be fitted with a scoop type inlet. It can pressurize the water and subsequently force water past the pump impeller, which can cause the muffler to fill. In the worst case this can flow into the exhaust manifold and engine cylinders. The exhaust outlet should be installed above the loaded waterline; the transom is the best location. Ensure that the vented loop (siphon break) is installed where required and regularly check that it

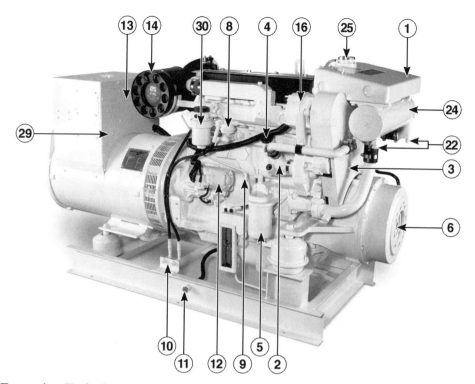

1: Expansion Tank; 2: Injection Pump Drive; 3: Drive Belt Cover; 4: Lub Oil Filler;
5: Lub Oil Filter; 6: Power Take Off; 8: Fuel Lift Pump; 9/10: Fuel Manifold;
11: Lub Oil Drain; 12: Starter; 13: DC Circuit Breaker; 14: Air Cleaner; 16: DC Alternator;
22: Heat Exchanger Zincs; 24: Heat Exchanger; 25: Coolant Filler; 29: AVR Fuse
30: Fuel Filter

Figure 14-6 Northern Lights Generator, *Courtesy of Northern Lights-Lugger*

operates. Ensure that exhaust lines are properly installed with respect to loops, and slope, and that there are no points where water
can be trapped. As with all engines use caution when cranking over
the generator as water can fill the muffler and back up into the engine. When bleeding the fuel system, Northern Lights recommends
closing the seacocks, and removing the water pump impeller during
the process. A new innovation from Northern Lights is the Gen-Sep
which separates the water from the exhaust gas and drains it via a
through-hull fitting.

(3)   **Seawater Systems.** Ideally a separate water system supply and strainer should be used. Ensure that the strainer is cleaned regularly, which is often forgotten until a high temperature occurs. Where the generator has anodes, check these regularly.

b.   **Control Systems.** Generators are generally remote start and stop with automatic engine protection systems. In most generators, all shutdown functions are suppressed for 10–20 seconds at start-up, and this may include low water pressure and low oil pressure. Some larger generators on large trawler yachts and super yachts will have generator units that have a pre-lubrication pump operating when the engine is stopped, and a failure in pre-lube pressure will inhibit the start. On vessels with multiple generators and automatic stop and start functions, all systems must be selected to Auto. In any system it is important to know what interlocks are in the start ready chain. Most generators will trip automatically on overspeed, high crankcase pressure, high temperature, low oil pressure, and low oil levels.

c.   **Governor.** The mechanical governor controls the fuel rack and maintains constant speed. When the engine starts, it runs up to nominal speed and then the governor maintains it. Many now have electronic governors.

14.22   Generator Fuel Consumption. Table 14-3 gives approximate fuel consumption rates at full rated load for a number of engine (not electrical) output ratings. These will act as a general guide in working out similar on-board consumption values.

Table 14-3 Generator Fuel Consumption

Cylinders	Capacity	Speed	Output	Fuel Rate
2	0.5 liter	3000	7.5 kW	1.5 l/hr
3	1.0	1500	7.7	2.5
4	1.3	3000	9.8	3.2
4	1.3	1500	19.4	5.9
4	1.5	1500	11.9	2.6
4	1.8	1500	13.0	4.5
3	2.5	1500	21.0	6.1
4	3.9	1500	34.0	10.2

14.23   AC Alternators. Alternators are generally robust and constructed to marine standards. The alternator consists of the main stator winding, the exciter stator winding, the main wound rotor, the rotor exciter winding, the cooling fan, terminal box, the bearings and the rotating rectifier.

a.   **Single Phase Alternators.** The single-phase 2 or 4 pole alternator is the most common configuration and may be either brushless and self-excited or brush with sliprings and externally excited. Alternators may be single bearing and directly coupled to the engine, or dual bearing machines driven by coupling.

(1)   **Operation.** At initial start-up, there is sufficient remanent voltage (residual magnetism) left in the machine to establish the main field. Once rated speed and output are reached, the automatic voltage regulator (AVR) controls the output voltage in response to system variations. Frequency is a function of speed and the engine governor maintains speed and therefore frequency stability.

(2)   **AVR Operation.** The AVR controls the excitation voltage level. The control voltage is applied through the brushes and slip rings to the rotor-mounted excitation winding and the diode rectifier. The rectifier DC output then goes to the main rotor excitation winding rotating field and controls the field strength.

14.24   **AC Alternator Parameters.** The alternator has the following parameters:

a.   **Voltage.** The typical rated output voltages are 115/230, or 220/240 volts for single-phase machines, and 440/480 volts for three-phase machines. The automatic voltage regulator (AVR) maintains nominal output. The AVR is an electronic regulator that senses output terminal voltage and varies the field strength to maintain correct value. Regulation is typically within 2% of nominal rating. The AVR must be able to control the output rapidly in response to large load fluctuations. Recovery in good machines is typically 3% of rated output within 0.25 seconds when full load is applied. Voltage is not a function of speed or frequency when an alternator is running at or near rated speed.

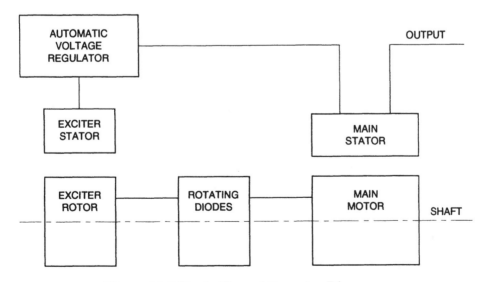

Figure 14-7 Single Phase Alternator Diagram

b. **Frequency.** Frequency is specified in hertz, the number of alternating cycles per second. Output frequency is a direct function of speed and varies in response to speed fluctuations. Stability depends on the ability of the machine to maintain nominal frequency over the complete power output range; this is typically within 1%. The engine governor controls engine speed. When a large load is applied, such as a motor starting, the generator loads the engine, causing it to slow momentarily. The governor reacts by increasing fuel flow and speeding the engine up. When the load is removed, the reverse occurs. Stability depends on response time, and governors are factory set. A small time lag is inherent in the system and helps minimize hunting, caused by continual alterations based on small load fluctuations. Frequency and specified engine speed depend on the number of poles within the alternator. Two-pole machines generate one cycle per revolution, and require an engine speed of 3000 rev/min for 50 hertz. Four-pole machines generate two cycles per revolution, and only require 1500 rev/min for 50 hertz.

c. **Power.** Power output is stated in either kVA or kW ratings. These are defined as follows:

(1) **kVA Rating.** The KVA rating is the power output, which is the current multiplied by voltage to give volt amps, and divided by 1000 to give a KiloVoltAmp rating.

(2) **kW Rating.** Kilowatt rating is the kVA rating multiplied by a power factor, typically 0.8. This is the actual power output.

14.25   AC Alternator Rating Selection. Rating selection must consider a number of factors. A total expected load analysis must also be undertaken to calculate the peak loads that might be encountered:

a. **Starting Currents.** Starting current values may be as high as 5–9 times that of actual normal running current. The in-rush current at starting causes these high currents, and the energy required to overcome bearing and load inertia. Duration of the peaks is typically less than one second, and most alternators can withstand 250% overloads for up to 10 seconds.

b. **Power Factor.** In simplified terms, Power Factor (PF) is the ratio of useful power in watts to the apparent power (volt amps) of the circuit. Power (watts) = Volts x Amps x Power Factor. In a purely resistive circuit such as a heater, the alternating current and voltage are said to be in phase. The average power over a complete cycle is the product of the voltage and current in volt amps. When reactance is introduced into the circuit, the voltage and current become out of phase, so that during any cycle the current is negative, and the voltage positive. The resultant value is less than the volt amp value. Inductive reactance causes current to lag the voltage. This will be an electrical angle between 0 and 90°. Resistive loads are said to be in phase, with no angle of difference and these are termed unity power factor. In electrical circuits, capacitive reactance cancels out inductive reactance. The use of capacitors can improve low power factors, and this is generally limited to fluorescent lighting systems. Most machinery nameplates specify power factor ratings. Available alternator output power decreases with any reduction in system power factor values so the higher the better.

14.26   Generator Rating Calculation. From a load analysis, the following calculations can be performed to estimate required minimum alternator size:

a.   Generator to run at 80% maximum load with 20% reserve.

Largest Single Load Value   =   2400 watts

Max. Start Current (Ir)   = $\dfrac{\text{Power (watts)}}{\text{Volts x PF}} = \dfrac{2400}{240 \text{ x } 0.8} = 12.50$ amps

Max. Start Current (Is)   =   Ir x 4 = 50 Amps

b.   If alternator can withstand overloads of 250% for 10 sec., the starting current (Is) must be divided by 2.5 = 20 Amps.

c.   Rating is therefore 20 x 240 = 4.8 kVA or 0.8 x 22.8 x 240 = 3.8kW. Adding a 20% minimum margin to operate at 80% = 4.5kW.

d.   In selecting an output rating, an estimate must be made of the maximum load likely to be applied. Some loads are resistive and do not have large starting currents, such as kettles and heaters. If the device having the startup current is to operate simultaneously with other equipment, the other loads need to be added. So if an air conditioner with 3.8 kW rating is to be run with hot water, then add 2.4kW, and for a kettle 1.8 kW then a figure of 7 kW, plus a margin for other small loads such as lights, TV etc, you require 8.4kW. The higher the rating, the higher the initial capital cost, the greater the weight and space required. A decision must be made about how the equipment will be used in order to reduce the generator to the lowest suitable size. A generator should be loaded to at least 35% and ideally operate at 75–80%. The running of gensets diesels on light loads causing cylinder glazing will increase maintenance costs.

14.27   AC Equipment Ratings. Many of the generator over-rating problems can be solved by carefully choosing appliances for use on board. Inductive loads such as coils, solenoids, motors and fans have "inrush" currents when starting, several times the normal running current. Resistive loads such as toasters and kettles do not. Many fast boil kettles have an element rated at 2.4 kW (240 VAC). On a 4 kW generator that is more than half load. Buy a lower rated kettle around 1200 watts. Most automatic toasters have large current consumptions. The older type fold down side toasters have a lower current draw, and are more reliable. Microwaves should be a simple and compact unit with a relatively low power rating. Some regular size microwaves on high have ratings of around 1600 watts. Many fan heaters on high setting are also rated at 2.4 kW, and place a significant load on a generator. Hot water heating elements should be 1.2 kW instead of a 2.4 kW unit. High current AC motors can be fitted with soft-start starters that reduce or limit starting currents. This will depend on the load attached. Refer to Chapter 15.

Table 14-4 AC Load Analysis Table

Equipment	Typical Rating	Actual Rating
Inductive Loads		
Air conditioner	3600 watts	_____
Washing machine	1800	_____
Hydraulic pump	3600	_____
Water pump	2400	_____
Fluoro lights	40	_____
Pressure cleaner	2400	_____
Refrigerator	500	_____
Washing machine	1200	_____
Hand tools	650	_____
Microwave	1200	_____
Food processor	1200	_____
Battery charger	1200	_____
Dive compressor	3600	_____
Resistive Loads		_____
Toaster	1000	_____
Kettle	1200	_____
Incandescent light	60	_____
Water heater	2400	_____
Television	100	_____
Video player	200	_____
Hair dryer	500	_____
Iron	1200	_____
Fan heater	2400	_____
Low energy light	60	_____
Coffee maker	750	_____
Total Load	_____ W	_____ W

14.28   Generator Systems. The following covers some well known generators. Most have optional sound shield options, with very low noise and low vibration levels. Also all use good design practices by having items that need servicing, such as oil filters, all accessible on one side. A few also have viable power takeoffs driven off the engine to power hydraulic pumps or watermaker pumps, usually having an electric clutch system.

    a.   **Northern Lights.** Northern Lights (www.northern-lights.com) generators have always had a reputation for being rugged and commercial grade. These generators operate at a lower speed of 1800 rpm with 4-pole brush and brushless synchronous wound rotor alternators, with Class H rated winding insulation. The generator prime mover is a Lugger diesel engine. Most generators have an alternator rated at up to 40 amps that can be used as house battery charge source in addition to the AC charger. Voltage regulation is rated at just +/- 1% RMS for the 8–99 kW range, while units in the 104 to 520 kW range are rated at +/- 0.5%. The 5 and 6 kW machines are rated at +/- 5%, and have a special dedicated auxiliary winding to power the AVR which improves starting performance. Excitation uses shaft-mounted diodes, which are sensibly made accessible although failures are very rare. Fuel consumption for the 32kW units is typically 2.6 gph (9.8l/hr) at full load. The units also have zinc anode corrosion protection, which must be checked. Control systems use relays and the engine stop is an electric operated solenoid.

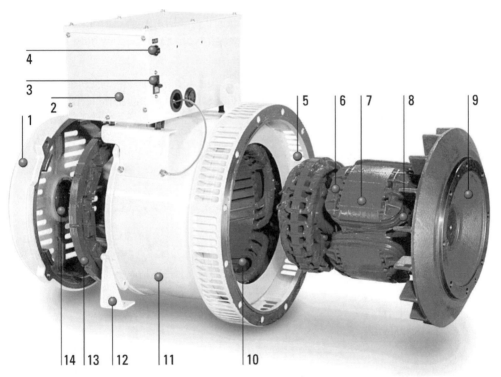

1: Bearing Housing; 2: Junction Box; 3: AVR AC Circuit Breaker; 4: DC System Circuit Breaker; 5: Cast Iron Housing; 6: Exciter Rotor; 7: Main Rotor 8: Cooling Fan; 9: Mounting Ring; 10: Skewed Stator; 11: Frame; 12: Mounting Foot; 13: Exciter Stator Bolts: 14: Bearing Carrier.

Figure 14-8 Northern Lights Alternator, *Courtesy of Northern Lights-Lugger*

b. **Mase Generators.** Unlike many alternators, these brushless machines do not use a voltage regulator, and are self-regulating and self-exciting, with a capacitor connected across the auxiliary winding of the stator. While rotating, the residual magnetism and permanent magnets induce a voltage into the auxiliary winding for excitation. This voltage is fed to the capacitor, which generates a capacitive current in the circuit. The capacitive current creates a magnetic field, which is rectified by the diode, supplying a DC current to the induction winding. This generates a rotating magnetic field for generation of output. A varistor is connected across the diode to absorb transient spikes.

c. **Onan.** These come in the output range of 4 to 95kW. The latest e-QD systems include digital controls with integral diagnostics. Speed control has an electronic governor with close isochronous regulation to maintain output frequency stability under heavy loads typical of high current equipment starting. The engine has an automatic glowplug pre-heat system to ensure good starting.

d. **Kohler.** The units are available in the 4–65 kW range. Kohler uses its own AVR called PowerBoost for very good regulation characteristics, and the alternators are brushless.

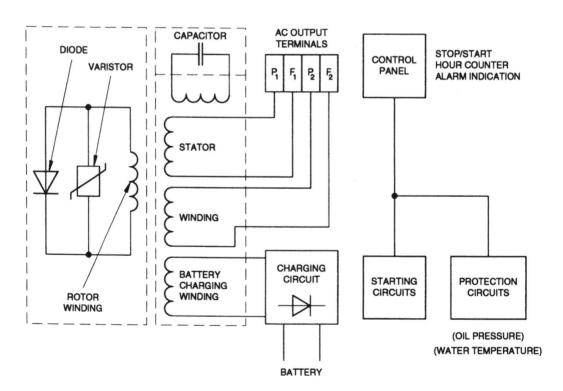

Figure 14-9 Mase Generator System

e.   **Fischer Panda Generators.** These are regulated asynchronous generators running at 3,600 rpm with 2 poles. An asynchronous alternator has a rotor of highly magnetic material without windings. This allows the smaller generator sizes to be realized, however the higher speeds also emit more noise, and efficient sound shields are essential. The smaller units retain heat and water cooling is used. Regulation is achieved using a voltage control system (VCS) which governs engine speed of the diesel with respect to load in the range +/- 3 volts at 80% of maximum load. The system also incorporates an integrated start booster (ASB) that minimizes the droop caused by heavy current consumers such as electric motors at start up and can withstand 300% overloads. In conventional machines the voltage level drops below rated value. The asynchronous generator is different in that it does not have rotating windings, diodes, brushes or a wound rotor. One model has both a three-phase and single-phase windings for dual operations, which has advantages where single-phase loads would create phase load imbalances. The units also have another feature with automatic negative pole uncoupling via a relay, which minimizes corrosion, and all sensors are isolated as well. These units have water-cooled alternators via a copper/nickel/bronze heat exchanger that minimizes corrosion. Diesel units in use are Farymann and Kubota units on smaller units and Mercedes, MTU, MAN, Yanmar on larger units. One additional useful feature is the ability to install on the Panda 10 HTG-Duo model, a high output 230 amp DC alternator system, and where AC is not required to also then run at lower speeds.

14.29   Generator Protection. Diesel generators have several protection systems.

a.   **Low Oil Pressure Shutdown.** Most generators have automatic shutdowns on low oil pressure to protect the engine. This is usually a pressure switch activated function.

b.   **Low Oil Level.** This activates when oil level in the sump falls; it is a level switch.

c.   **High Water Temperature Shutdown.** Generators will shutdown on detection of a high jacket cooling water temperature.

d.   **Low Water Level Shutdown.** This is activated when expansion tank level falls.

e.   **Low Seawater Flow Shutdown.** Loss of seawater cooling, either due to plugged strainer or impeller failure, will initiate an automatic shutdown.

f.   **High Exhaust Temperature.** A high exhaust temperature will initiate an automatic shutdown.

g.   **Over-speed Shutdown.** If the generator over-speeds, an automatic shutdown is initiated. This can be caused by governor failure.

h.   **Over-voltage Shutdown.** If the AVR malfunctions and the voltage fails to high the generator will be shutdown.

14.30   Alternator Protection. The alternator system requires the following protection:

a.   **Protection.** Protection of generator electrical circuits consists of one or more of the following, which may be integral to the main circuit breakers for larger vessels, or be part of a separate protection system:

(1)   **Overload.** Some gensets have an overload circuit breaker fitted at the genset control box. Reset if tripped; if repeatedly tripping, fault find the system and remove the cause of the overload. In many cases the problem may simply be too many appliances operating and overloading. Overloads are characterized by time delays between reset and tripping. If a major motor is installed and it is seized or has a locked rotor, tripping may be immediate due to high current.

(2)   **Short Circuit.** This generally is a circuit breaker, which is mounted at the genset control box. If it trips immediately after initially resetting, troubleshoot and correct the fault first.

(3)   **Reverse Current.** This protection is generally only seen on larger installations or where two units are parallelled. If the load sharing function fails, or when manually taking a generator off the board, the load is taken to zero, this will trip.

(4)   **Low Frequency.** Not all generators have this protection, adjust only according to manufacturers' instructions.

(5)   **Undervoltage.** Undervoltage trip relays are used in larger installations and are normally interlocked with main circuit breakers. It usually indicates an AVR fault.

b.   **Grounding.** All exposed metal capable of carrying a voltage under operating or fault conditions must be grounded to an equipotential point. The generator frame should be securely connected to the boat ground system. In most generators the starter negative is also bonded locally to the AC ground. This will require bonding to the main boat ground. In single-phase installations, the neutral is connected to the distribution system neutral at the main switchboard. Connection should be in accordance with installation instructions.

c.   **Parallelling of Machines.** In larger vessels with more than one generator, parallelling of the units onto the main switchboard busbar may be necessary. To do this a frequency meter will be required to correctly synchronize the machines, or lights are used. The engine speed is controlled using the manual speed control. When the synchroscope is moving very slowly clockwise and nearly stopped, and is approaching the 11 o'clock position, close in the circuit breaker. Some vessels will have an automatic phasing and synchronizing module.

14.31   Alternator Maintenance. Alternator maintenance is simple and easily carried out.

a.   **Alternator Inspection.** Carry out the following tasks:

(1)   Remove the alternator access covers, and check the gaskets and seals. Connection boxes should be clean and dry.

(2)   Inspect the interior for dirt, dust, oil, and water. Clean all accessible surfaces and windings with a vacuum cleaner.

(3)   If the generator has a brush excitation system, check the excitation brushes for breaks, chips and make sure they move freely in the holders. Check brush springs and shunts.

(4)   Make sure the sliprings are smooth. They should not have any scoring and have a shiny surface patina. Do not polish or use emery paper.

(5)   Check for loose electrical and mechanical connections.

b.   **Insulation Test.** Use a 500-volt Megger to test all active conductors to ground. Measure and record the temperature of the alternator stator circuit insulation resistance in the boat maintenance log. Isolate the exciter and measure the rotor insulation resistance and record. Any reading less than 1 meg ohm should be rectified.

14.32   Generator Troubleshooting. Faults within generators are normally confined to bad connections at the alternator. In rare cases the cables may chafe causing insulation damage. The main faults that may arise on the alternator are:

a.   **Over Voltage.** This condition arises when the voltage regulator is faulty.

b.   **Under Voltage.** This condition arises when the voltage regulator or excitation circuit is faulty.

c.   **Voltage Fluctuation.** This occurs when a voltage regulator is faulty. In brush machines this occurs when a brush sticks, or the sliprings are dirty and there is arcing.

d.   **Current Pulsation.** This is indicated as oscillation of the ammeter needle. It is caused by diesel problems such as a faulty injector.

e.   **Unable to Sustain Load.** This fault typically occurs with a faulty regulator, or where a rotor diode is breaking down or has failed. In units with capacitors, faulty capacitors, or transient suppressors can also cause this.

14.33   Inverters. Inverter technology has advanced considerably in the last few years. They range from small portable units of just 150W up to large fixed systems rated at 5kW with some units that can be paralleled with an automatic synchronization module. The combination charger/inverter is also very common. The latest units use isolated gate bipolar transistors (IGBT) which provide precise output control and waveforms, over MOSFET type systems. Transformers have been reduced in size and weight as conversion is done at high frequencies. Reliability on most systems is greatly increased over earlier generation units that unfairly gave inverters a bad reputation. Units use fans to assist in heat dissipation.

a.   **Output Waveforms.** Output waveforms are an important consideration when looking at proposed applications:

(1)   **Trapezoidal.** The majority of inverters have a trapezoidal waveform. This is suitable for most equipment, but microwaves and some inductive loads do not operate at full output, dropping efficiency by some 20% or more in some cases. Fluorescent lights may also be less efficient at starting and a 3-microfarad capacitor across input will improve starting characteristics. Interference is possible on these waveforms.

(2)   **Modified Sine Wave.** Some units have what is called a modified or quasi sine wave output, which resembles a pure sine wave. It is not exactly the same and offers slightly reduced performance. Interference is possible on these waveforms. Appliances and equipment such as microwaves and VCR units with clocks often run either slow or fast. Battery chargers for cordless portable drills are susceptible to early failure. If a charger gets excessively warm or hot turn it off as some incompatibility may exist. There is a ferro-resonant line conditioner called a Line Tamer, Model PCLC, which can improve performance. These are available from Shape Electronics in Illinois (tel. 708-629-8394).

(3)   **Sine Wave.** Sine wave output units are preferable and offer improved quality but are more expensive. Where sensitive equipment is used then the sine wave unit is preferable. They are available in most ratings up to 1,800W in 12-volt systems, with outputs at 230V RMS +/- 5%. Frequency stability is typically +/- 0.05%. Quality units have low harmonic distortion, typically less than 3%, and low electromagnetic interference (EMI) levels.

b.   **DC Loads.** The typical inverter is capable of drawing large DC current loads from the battery. It is essential for battery capacity to be able to support these loads without affecting the existing electrical system and connected loads, particularly electronics equipment. A simple method of calculation is to divide the power in watts by 10 for 12-volt systems or 20 in 24-volt systems. It should be noted that some manufacturers offer inverters for 12, 24 and 48 volts input depending on the system voltage. The minimum battery capacity required for an inverter is 20% of the inverter capacity, ie 2,000 watts 400 Ah capacity.

Table 14-5 Inverter 12 VDC/220 VAC Current Loads

AC Load	DC Current Draw	Peak Overload
200 W (0.8 amps)	18 amps	42 amps
400 W (1.6 amps)	37 amps	100 amps
600 W (2.4 amps)	56 amps	145 amps
900 W (3.6 amps)	84 amps	180 amps
1200 W (4.8 amps)	120 amps	290 amps
2400 W (9.6 amps)	240 amps	580 amps
3000 W (12 amps)	300 amps	750 amps

c. **Transfer Systems.** If another AC power source is connected across the inverter output, the inverter electronics will be seriously damaged. Shore power supplies, generator and inverter outputs must not be paralleled.

    (1) **Rotary Switches.** The normal selection system is a rotary cam switch. The switch should be a center-off type with the inverter to the side opposite the generator and shore power.

    (2) **Automatic Transfer Systems.** Many units are also able to automatically switch the supply from shore power or generator to the inverter on supply loss giving the same features as a UPS. Freedom series inverter/chargers have an automatic "load sharing" feature that offers protection to the connected AC loads from variations in shore power or generator power. When the shore or generator power is connected, the unit transfers the power to any connected AC loads and some power is used to charge the batteries. When in the charge/transfer mode, the incoming AC power is monitored and when the voltage decreases, or increases longer than 8 milliseconds, charging ceases, load transfer ceases and the inverter mode starts.

d. **Efficiency.** The typical inverter is now approximately in the range of 85% to 95% efficient at rated output. This efficiency level has evolved with new electronic switching technologies such as MOSFET and IGBT. The illustration below shows the various output characteristics of inverters.

e. **Combination (Combi) Units.** Most of these units have a modified sine wave output. The chargers can be set for various battery types such as flooded cell, Gel or AGM batteries, and those from Heart use a 3-stage microprocessor charging process. An automatic transfer switch and relay transfers between charger mode and inverter mode when AC power is off. As a note of caution, always remember that combi units may automatically supply AC so proper isolation from the battery source is essential before opening or working with the unit.

f. **Input Cables.** Always install the maximum size cables possible as considerable volt drop problems are possible at peak loads. Ensure cable connections are tight.

g. **Inverter Grounding.** Inverters must be grounded. There are documented cases of fatalities where this has not been done. Grounding introduces a number of factors that require consideration. The corrosion aspects must never compromise the safety requirements. Most standards or recommendations (ISO, ABYC, USCG) specify that the AC ground be connected to the DC negative. This requirement has raised considerable controversy in shore power installations as well as inverters. Many do not do this to reduce the risks of corrosion. The ABYC recommends that the inverter chassis be bonded to the DC negative, although this is doubling up the grounding as the AC ground and DC are already bonded. Refer to chapters on isolation transformers and galvanic isolators.

h. **Ground Fault (GFCI) Protection.** It is normal to install a GFCI on the AC output of the inverter. Heart interface uses the Pass and Seymour/Legrand unit, although any make will be satisfactory. As indicated, the GFCI must be tested regularly (refer to chapter on GFCI). The GFCI should be function tested when inverting or when transferring generator or shore power supplies. Do not test when the inverter is in idle mode, as the unit may not trip, and the GFCI electronic circuits could be damaged by the inverter idle mode sense pulses. Nuisance tripping does occur on inverters, and this is generally caused by neutral to ground leakages, usually from surge suppression circuits which contain capacitors connected across active and ground or neutral and ground. This is attributed to waveform harmonics on modified sine wave outputs. Another cause of GFCI tripping is due to the improper connection

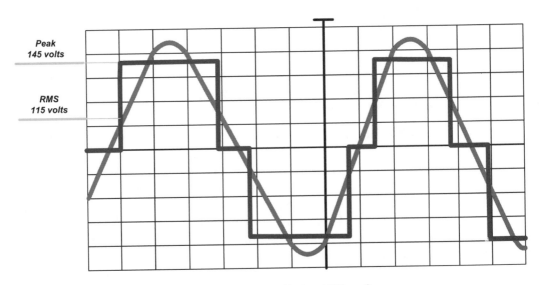

Figure 14-10 Inverter Output Waveforms

of the inverter AC output neutral to the main neutral bus. Inverters such those from Heart ground the output neutral when in the OFF mode or in inverting mode. If the output neutral is connected to the main neutral, the main neutral will also be grounded, the GFCI will detect this and trip out before the inverter is able to disconnect the ground from the output neutral during shore power and generator transfers.

i.   **Interference.** The control electronics, such as logic circuits and memory circuits in inverters can be corrupted. This may be from lightning strike surges, onboard electrical power system surges, voltage dips and spikes. In many cases the unit may simply require resetting if no signs of catastrophic failure have been detected such as smoke or burning smells. Try the following procedure before calling in technical assistance.

(1)   Switch off power at remote panels if fitted.

(2)   Switch off inverter main power switch.

(3)   Disconnect the AC input power source.

(4)   Disconnect the DC negative cable for at least 5 minutes.

(5)   Reconnect the DC negative cable, sometimes a small spark will be seen as filter capacitors start charging.

(6)   Switch on the inverter power switch and switch on an AC load to ensure inverter has a load. Check that inverter supplies AC power.

(7)   Reconnect the AC input power source and check that automatic transfer functions.

(8)   If this does not restore operation, check that fuses have not blown or circuit breakers have tripped. Check that all connections are secure.

j.   **Auto Start.** Most units have an auto start capability. This means they remain in a standby or idle mode until a load is switched on.

(1)   **Idle Mode.** Input current in idle mode is typically around 10–50 mA (1.5W). This load value must always be included in DC load calculations.

(2)   **Activation Load.** The load required to activate most inverters is approximately 6–10 VA or greater. If the vessel is to be left unattended for an extended period, the DC supply should be switched off. In some cases loads such as fluorescent lights or electronics equipment may not activate, and another load should be momentarily switched on to cut the inverter in.

k.   **Protection.** Most inverters have an under voltage cutout that is typically set at around 10.5 V. Units also have overload protection and a high voltage cutout, thermal overload protection that will shut down the inverter if an over-temperature condition is reached. Units also have reverse polarity indication and protection, short circuit protection of the output, and input voltage ripple too high. Some units have AC backfeed protection and a GFCI on the output.

l. **Ventilation.** Good ventilation is essential for reliable operation and full rated outputs.

(1) Install the unit in a dry, well-ventilated area.

(2) Allow sufficient vertical clearance for natural convection of heat from unit. De-rating factors are illustrated in efficiency Table 14-6.

Table 14-6 Temperature De-rating Factors

Temperature	Output Rating
+40°C to +50°C	80% Rated Output
-10°C to +40°C	100% Rated Output
-10°C to -20°C	140% Rated Output

m. **Ratings.** Units generally have an output rating based on a resistive load for a nominal period, typically 30 minutes. (Eg. 1,600 watts). The continuous rating is the normal continuous operation rating. (Eg. 1,000 watts). The peak or maximum rating is the maximum short duration load that the inverter can withstand (Eg. 3,000 watts). Most units are capable of withstanding the short duration and intermittent overloads that are required, especially with motor starts. The surge rating enables them to withstand short time overloads of up to approximately 200% over the continuous rating for 5 seconds.

AC Power Equipment

15.1   AC Motors. The most common type of AC machinery is the electric motor. Motors are generally very robust and give years of trouble-free service. The fixed-speed and constant torque squirrel-cage, single-phase motor is the most common in use. Larger boats have three-phase motors, with higher starting torques and efficiency with lower power consumption. Motors should be selected with the right rating for the load, and the right degree of protection (NEMA and IP ratings). Insulation ratings also should be as high as possible, with Class B the most common; however on ships Class F at the top is the most common. Totally enclosed fan cooled (TEFC) motors should be used in marine environments. Motor failures are primarily caused by bearing failures, often due to over- and under-greasing. Sealed bearings offer a good maintenance free solution. It is also important for connected loads such as compressors and pumps to be properly aligned so that vibrations do not transmit through to the bearings and cause early failure. Nameplate data is important to understanding the motor ratings. When replacing motors, this is essential for ordering. Ratings are typically NEMA ones.

a.   **Output Ratings.** The following are typical nameplate ratings:

   (1)   **Torque.** The force or turning effort applied to the shaft, given in inch pounds, or ft. pounds.

   (2)   **Starting Torque.** The force produced when starting from stationary to normal run speed.

   (3)   **Full Load Torque.** The force produced at normal operating speed and rated power output (kW or HP).

   (4)   **FLA is Full Load Amps.** This is at rated load, speed, voltage and frequency.

b.   **Insulation Class.** Each 10°C rise above the Class ratings will give an approximate 50% reduction in service life.

   (1)   Class A = 105°C (221°F)

   (2)   Class B = 130°C (266°F)

   (3)   Class F = 155°C (311°F)

   (4)   Class H = 180°C (365°F)

c.   **Service Factor.** The Service Factor (SF) is the capacity of the motor to operate without overload or damage at rated voltage, frequency, current, speed and ambient temperature. This is derived by multiplying the rated output (in HP or kW) by the service factor to obtain the maximum service loads.

d.   **Explosion Proof Ratings.** The classes are as follows relating to possible hazardous gases and vapors on a boat. Class II relates to combustible dust. The rules and requirements for these types of equipment are complex and extensive and beyond the scope of this manual. In the offshore oil industry and on oil and gas tankers, such equipment is rigidly controlled, inspected and maintained.

Class I. Gases and Vapors. Group A includes acetylene (in cutting equipment storage areas); Group B includes hydrogen (in battery compartments); Group C includes ethylene; Group D includes butane, acetone, gasoline, methane, propane (in propulsion and cooking fuels).

e. **Motor Enclosure Types.** This is based on both protection and cooling.

(1) **Drip Proof.** This rating must prevent any liquids falling into the motor at an angle of 15 degrees of vertical.

(2) **Totally Enclosed Air Over (TEAO).** The motor must be mounted within the airflow of the shaft-mounted fan airflow.

(3) **Totally Enclosed Non Ventilated (TENV).** These have no air ventilation openings. They do not have cooling fans and cooling is from air convection.

(4) **Totally Enclosed Fan Cooled (TEFC).** These have external cooling fans integral to the motor and cool by forcing air over the motor frame.

15.2 Protection Codes (NEMA and IEC). Motors, generators and alternators, junction boxes, light fixtures and other equipment will normally have a NEMA protection or IP number on it. This defines the levels of protection provided by electrical enclosures in regard to persons, the equipment within the enclosure and the ingress of water, dust etc. The IP number consists of a two number code and a third number is often added giving the degree of mechanical protection. The first numeral is for protection against contact and solid bodies and the second numeral is protection against the penetration of liquids.

Table 15-1 IEC Protection Table.

No.	Protection – Solids	No.	Protection – Water
0	Non Protected	0	Non protected
1	Solid objects > 50 mm	1	Dripping water
2	Solid objects > 12 mm	2	Dripping water tilted to 15°
3	Solid objects > 2.5 mm	3	Rain
4	Solid objects > 1 mm	4	Splashing water
5	Dust protected	5	Water jets
6	Dust tight	6	Heavy seas
		7	Effects of immersion
		8	Submersion

NEMA Protection Codes. These are similar to IEC codes. The NEMA classes of protection for enclosures with corresponding IEC ratings are as follows:

NEMA Type 1. For indoor use and to protect against falling dust and dirt and to provide protection against contact with the enclosed equipment. (IP10)

NEMA Type 2. For indoor use to protect against limited quantities of falling dust and water.

NEMA Type 3. For outdoor use to protect against rain, sleet and dust. (IP54)

NEMA Type 4. For outdoor and indoor use to protect against dust and hose directed water. (IP65)

NEMA Type 5. For outdoor and indoor use to protect against dust and dripping non-corrosive liquids.

NEMA Type 6. For outdoor and indoor use to protect against limited submersion and hose directed water. (IP67)

NEMA Type 12. For indoor use to protect against circulating dust, falling dirt and non-corrosive liquids. (IP52)

NEMA Type 13. For outdoor use to protect against dust, lint, water spray and non-corrosive coolant.

15.3   AC Motor Starters. Most single- and three-phase starters have a direct-on-line (DOL) starting system. Other starting configurations in use on smaller HP motors are split phase, with moderate starting torques:

a.   **Capacitor Start - Induction Run.** The capacitor assists in increasing starting torque up to 400% of rated load. An electrolytic capacitor is connected in series with the start winding. The centrifugal switch disconnects the auxiliary winding and start capacitor when the motor is close to normal rated speed.

b.   **Capacitor Start - Capacitor Run Motor.** A second run capacitor is permanently connected in series with the auxiliary winding when the motor is operating at rated speed and load.

c.   **Permanent Split Capacitor Motor.** The motor has an auxiliary winding and a run capacitor and both are connected when operating at rated load and speed. This is for low torque loads.

15.4   DOL Motor Starters. In DOL starters, voltage is fed to the starter via a panel-mounted isolator switch that may incorporate links or fuses. When the switch is closed, it supplies power to one side of the contactor, and also via a fuse to a control transformer, typically 220 to 24 volts. The output of the transformer then feeds the control circuit. Either a panel mounted or remote start/stop button activates the starter. When the start button is depressed, a control voltage is applied to the contactor operating coil. The coil energizes, and the contactor closes. An auxiliary contact supplies a voltage to the coil to maintain voltage when the start button is released. The power is then fed to the motor from the other side of the closed contactor via a thermal overload unit. Control power is supplied through the stop circuit and the normally closed contacts of the stop button. If the stop button is depressed, the circuit opens removing control voltage to the contactor coil, which then de-energizes and opens the contactor. The thermal overload has auxiliary control circuit contacts that are normally closed. If an overload causes the thermal overload to trip, the control circuit opens and de-energizes the coil. Thermal overloads have a manual reset, normally a small red push button. Some motors also have an integral thermal reset switch on the motor so a circuit may have two devices that require checking.

The main problem with AC motors is the starting current, which may be 2–5 times rated load at start-up. Thermal overloads are usually adjustable within a range. The thermals will withstand the short motor start overloads. Starter ammeters are supplied via a current transformer (CT). The ratios vary but typically may be 30:5 which means that 30 amps through the CT will give a 5-amp output. The meter is scaled to read actual current. These are black cylindrical devices, and either the active or a phase is passed through the center of the CT. The output is connected to the ammeter. Some meters are set at zero and have a small adjustment screw; others may have a small dot that is used for zero calibration. Some may also be star-delta starters. These consist of two contactors, the star connection contactor is controlled by a time relay, and when this times out changes over the connection to delta. The following table shows 3-phase motor ratings at 400V, 1500 rpm.

Table 15-2 Three-Phase AC Motor Ratings

Rating (kW)	HP	Rated Current	Fuse Rating
1.1	1.5	2.6	6
3.0	4.0	6.6	16
5.5	7.5	11.3	25
7.5	10	15.2	32
11	14.75	21.7	40
15	20	29.3	63
22	29.5	41	80
30	40	55	100

15.5   Motor Circuit Protection. AC squirrel cage motors have a high in-rush current at starting, caused by the high inductance of the copper stator winding, and the magnetization of the stator iron core. A motor supply circuit may have up to four control devices. Short circuit protection, such as fuses and circuit breakers, are to protect the motor and cables from large overcurrents. Control devices, such as contactors and drives, give control over starting and speed. Overload protection, such as thermal overloads, provide protection against small overcurrents. Supplementary protection, such as winding cutouts, provide additional overload protection, and RCD devices for monitoring insulation leakages to ground. Overloads are caused by mechanical overloads on the load or bearings, and electrical ones are low voltages or loss of a phase. Major short circuits are usually due to connection errors, minor short circuits are usually caused by motor winding faults. Simple DOL starters usually consist of a contactor and a thermal overload relay. There is a trend to install more sophisticated devices. These units have separate protection circuits for overload (adjustable), short circuit (14 x Iu), current limiting, undervoltage release and phase failure.

15.6   AC Variable Speed Drives. Where the electrical supply system cannot sustain the starting currents, Soft Start units are used. They are only suited to low torque applications, such as fans and pumps. Typically they control starting in the range 40-100% over time ranges of 0.5 to 60 seconds. The units also have adjustable current limitation that prevents excessive start current values. The units also often have integral motor protection. Variable speed drives (frequency inverters) are occasionally found on larger boats, usually for fans, pumps, and some loads with high starting torques where soft start systems are not suitable. They will have full torque outputs from as low as 1.5 Hz and the inverter has IGBT transistor bridges.

15.7   AC Motor Connection. Most motors have connection terminal diagrams inside the terminal box. Many 3-phase machines have 6 winding terminals and a ground connection. The windings are connected in delta for 380 volts, and star (Wye) for 660 volt. In 3-phase machines, to reverse rotation, reverse any two-phase leads in the terminal box. Depending on the motor and application, the terminal box may also have standstill heating terminals which may be alive and must be isolated before working. Also some motors may have PT100 temperature probe and thermistor connections. In single-phase motors, the capacitors can retain a charge across the motor terminals even when stopped and cause an electric shock.

15.8   AC Motor Starter Inspection. On larger boats with AC installations and AC powered machinery, motors and starters require inspection every 6 months.

(1)   Isolate electrical power, lock out, and danger tag it. Test the starter incoming supply to ensure circuit supply is dead.

(2)   Inspect the starter interconnecting bus bars and tighten. Look for signs of overheating on the insulation and connections. Examine all control wiring for insulation damage or signs of overheating.

(3)   Check and tighten all connections, including the control circuit terminal block connections.

(4)   Remove any dust from the starter interior using a non-metallic vacuum cleaner extension.

(5)   Inspect the contactor magnetic seating surfaces. Operate manually and ensure that moving contactor part is mechanically free.

(6)   Check the condition of contacts on larger contactors, and if there is serious contact erosion from arcing, replace the contacts. Examine the contactor coils for signs of swelling caused by overheating.

(7)   Check that overload settings are correctly set. Check fuses are tight.

(8)   Check that auxiliary relays where fitted are seated in bases correctly and that retainers are in place.

(9)   Connect the Megger and measure insulation resistance between ground connection and active. In 3-phase systems, check phase to ground. Record the insulation resistance reading in boat machinery maintenance file. Readings should be a minimum of 1 meg ohm.

15.9   Bearing, Coupling, Pulley Installation and Alignment. The proper alignment of electric motors and the connected loads is critical to the long term performance of the motor. Misalignment causes premature bearing failures and excessive vibration. Couplings must be properly aligned, and to do this the shafts must be parallel. The maximum clearance allowed between coupling halves and parallel misalignment is 0.002 in. (0.05mm). A pair of dial gauges should be used, one placed axially and the other radially. Replacement or installation should be done using bearing pullers or special tools. A good bearing puller set is necessary; I would recommend a set from Proto, my set has successfully completed many pulling tasks. Use the right tools, and never use a hammer to install coupling halves or pulleys on a shaft.

15.10   Bearing Failures. More damage is done to motors and rotating machinery because of improperly installed bearings than nearly any other cause. The most common causes of bearing failures are:

a.   **Contamination.** The majority of bearing failures (over 90%) are caused by contamination introduced at installation. It is essential that bearings are handled using clean hands and tools. Don't unwrap the bearing until you are ready to install it. When regreasing, using a grease gun, clean the grease nipple properly first so that dirt is not pumped in with the new grease.

b.   **Incorrect Installation.** Improper mounting is the other major cause of premature bearing failures. Bearings are normally installed with a press fit on the shaft and the outer ring being either a press or interference fit. If a bearing is mounted using hammer blows or pressure to the outer race, it will cause dents. A loose fit on the shaft or housing will cause rotation, generate heat and metal particles that will also cause damage. Where the fit is too tight, the rings may be stressed causing cracking and internal preloading deformation leading to high temperatures and failures. The most common installation method on smaller bearings is the use of a tubular dolly that matches the inner ring. This is tapped using a metal mallet. Where heating is used, this typically raises the bearing temperature to 60–70°C, using an oil bath or oven, then pressed on using a dolly. Motor end shields may also be heated to around 40°C. Running a motor with roller bearings and no radial force applied to the shaft may damage bearings. Motors with angular contact bearings should not be run without axial force applied in the right direction to the shaft.

c.   **Misalignment.** The main causes are due to bent shafts, out of square shaft shoulders, clamping nuts and spacers, which leads to overheating and failure of separators.

d. **Lubrication.** The purpose of bearing lubrication is to minimize friction at the various contact points within the bearing, the protection of the finished surfaces from corrosion, the dissipation of heat generated within the bearing and protection from particles and dirt. The choice of lubricant depends on the bearing temperature, the size of the bearing, the operational speed, the load, the service conditions, the method of re-lubrication and the method of sealing. Bearings with the notation Z, ZZ or 2Z are sealed and cannot be greased. If a greasable bearing is removed and cleaned, use kerosene to wash out the bearings. Repack to only 50% with new grease.

e. **Electrical Damage.** Electric currents can pass through motor shafts and the bearings, causing arcing at the contact points between balls and races. This leads to pitting and cratering resulting in spalling and vibration with failure. The typical maximum voltage drop across a bearing is 0.4 volt.

f. **High Temperatures.** If motors are run within nominal ambient temperatures of 25°C, the operating life of bearings is typically around 16,000–26000 hours for 2 and 4 pole machines. Vertical machines should have this reduced by 50%. Where temperatures increase, the heat will transfer from the shaft to the bearing and cause breakdown of the grease. The grease may liquefy and bleed off, or cause oxidation and carbon formation, and this may cause a jamming of the balls. Heating also alters the metal temper characteristics and reductions in metal hardness, as well as changes to internal clearances and preloading.

g. **Bearing Fatigue.** The metal components in the bearing can fatigue due to the rotational forces and dynamic impacts between balls and races. The constant flexing and loading of the components eventually causes flaking of the metal and wear with bearing failure.

h. **Corrosion.** This is caused by moisture, acids, lubricant breakdowns, condensation and water ingress. The finished surfaces when corroding create abrasive particles which causes excess wear, pitting and vibration. The particles are often absorbed into the grease and the wear rate is increased.

i. **Vibration.** Motors that are not turned over regularly can suffer bearing damage called the vibration or false Brinell effect. This is caused by the rapid movement of balls within the bearing race. As there is no rotation, the balls are not properly lubricated which causes wear and indentation on the metal contact points. If a motor is stationary for much of the time, the bearings should be maintained by turning the shaft by hand monthly.

15.11 **Bearing Lubrication.** Grease is composed of oil and an oil carrier such as soap and thickeners.

a. **Bearing Regreasing.** Bearings on new motors that can be regreased should have the specified quantity of grease applied before starting. When regreasing, remove the grease outlet plug if fitted. Insert grease until old grease is coming out. Allow the motor to run for at least an hour until excess grease is forced out, and then replace the plug. If the motor is stationary, insert only half the amount of grease, run for several minutes, then insert the remainder. Re-greasing intervals are determined by the motor duty. This includes the operating hours, the speed at which the motor runs, and the temperature at which it operates. The following table is based on ABB recommendations and gives common frame sizes, operating speeds and lubrication intervals in hours for roller bearings, and quantity of grease in grams per bearing. This is for horizontal motors; the intervals should be halved for vertical motors. Roller bearing intervals are reduced by approximately 60%.

b. **Bearing Temperatures.** The operating temperature of bearings has a direct impact on lubrication. The higher the temperature, the more often a bearing must be regreased. This is due to an increase in the grease oxidation rate; a rise in temperature of 25°F will double the oxidation rate. The recommendations are based on 25°C ambient with bearing temperatures of 80°C. For an increase of 15°C the values are reduced by 50%. The greasing of bearings on most boats is a minimal requirement as the operating hours are relatively low. Quality grease is also essential, Sodium soap greases are used in anti-friction bearings as they have good mechanical stability and wide operating temperature range. Lithium soap greases are used in most multi-purpose greases as they have good high and low temperature characteristics, good water resistance and mechanical stability. Use greases such as Shell Albida RL2, BP Energrease LC2, Esso N2 or N3, or Mobil Mobilith SHC 100. Oil bearings are also used in rotating equipment, and are suited for high speeds and temperatures. They enable easier oil and bearing cooling and are simpler to keep clean. The most common method is an oil bath arrangement, although other methods include oil mist, drip feed and pressurized circulation systems. The oils must have a minimum viscosity at normal operating temperature, and most oils include additives such as oxidation, corrosion and wear inhibitors, as well as viscosity index enhancers.

Table 15-3 Typical Bearing/IEC Frame Size Lubrication Intervals

Frame	Kw/hp	Gm/brg	1000	1500	1800	3000
112	4/5	10 g	25000	21000	18000	13000
132	12/15	15 g	23000	19000	17000	11000
160	20/25	25 g	21000	17000	14000	9500
180	30/40	30 g	20000	16000	13500	8000

15.12 **Bearing Noises.** You can check the operation of bearings by creating a stethoscope from a large screwdriver. Place the tip on the bearing housing and then place the handle to the ear. The vibration will pass up the screwdriver shaft.

(1) Low noise or rumble sound. Damage due to poor installation.

(2) Irregular rasping sound. Balls and races are damaged.

(3) High-pitched shrill sound. Clearance problems or bearing running dry.

(4) Intermittent sounds. Bearing grease is contaminated with dirt.

(5) Abnormal temperature rise. Overload, lubrication failure.

(6) Subdued humming sound. The bearing is good.

15.13 **AC Motor Inspection.** Do this with the motor power still isolated.

(1) Open terminal box cover, and check seals and gaskets.

(2) Inspect for evidence of connection overheating. Check and tighten the connections, including the ground wire if internal.

(3) Inspect the cable for clearances from terminal box sides and any insulation chafing.

(4) Check that cable glands are properly tightened.

(5) Check that the ground-bonding strap is secure if externally connected.

(6) Put the motor back in service and operate until normal operating temperatures are attained.

(7) Lubricate bearings if required.

(8) Listen for bearing noise and vibrations.

(9) Check operating loads using a clip-on ammeter.

15.14 **Repairs and Maintenance.** Repairs are generally limited to bearing replacement only, while rewinding and similar repairs will be undertaken by a shore repair facility. On many occasions an AC motor may have a very low winding insulation value, due to moist air, or if it is becoming flooded. To dry out the winding, dismantle the motor completely. If the motor has been immersed in seawater it should be rewound. This is a temporary repair measure.

(1) If motor has been immersed in seawater, wash stator out with fresh water.

(2) Place the stator in the oven at approximately 90°C for at least 12 hours and then 105°C for 6 hours.

(3) Check insulation value to case with 500 volt Megger tester, reading should be at least 1 meg ohm.

(4) Recheck insulation reading after 4 hours to ensure that the reading remains high.

15.15 **Rubber Belts.** Many loads are driven via pulleys and rubber belts. The following are primary belt troubleshooting areas.

a.   **Slipping Belts.** The main cause is incorrect tensioning. If the load is too high, the pulley and belt design should be assessed, but check that oil and other contaminants are not causing slip. If the drive pulley groove is shiny or belts are bottoming out in the groove, the pulley may be worn.

b.   **Noisy Belts.** The main cause is incorrect belt tension, or excessive load. If the pulley size is too small, this will cause reduced contact area.

c.   **Cracked Belts.** This is caused by slipping belts due to heat from slipping. This is also caused by mismatched pulleys and belts.

d.   **Rapid Belt Wear.** This is caused by belt slipping, or mismatch of pulley and belts, so check that the right belt matches the pulley grooves. Worn pulleys will also cause rapid deterioration, as will misalignment. If excessive abrasive material or dust is present this can contribute to wear rates. Always check that no other parts are rubbing on belts.

e.   **Belt Swelling.** This is caused by oil or other liquids contaminating the belt.

f.   **Belts Turning.** A belt may turn over within the pulley groove. This is caused by misalignment, overloading of belts and under-tensioned belts. In some cases the belt may have suffered partial mechanical failure.

15.16 **AC Appliances.** Many vessels have AC appliances installed, some marine units are manufactured in stainless steel, but many are just commercial or domestic grade. In commercial installations, keeping galleys and laundries running is a major task, and carrying out basic maintenance and prompt troubleshooting is essential. I have spent more hours in commercial ship and oil rig laundries and galleys than I would care to do again. The following describes the basic maintenance and troubleshooting tasks for the main equipment installed. As appliances are powered from 110/220/440 Volts AC, always switch off and remove the plug before opening up or checking control systems. Galleys also include food processors, mixers, tilting kettles and more. Keep them clean, and ensure leads and sockets are in good condition.

15.17 **Washing Machines.** Washing machines are common on many barges, canal boats, workboats, trawlers and super-yachts. They become essential items of equipment as they cater for relatively large crews. The best maintenance is keeping the machine clean, with the inlet water filters and lint filters being cleaned. Always check hoses, seals and fittings for leaks, and repair. Also ensure machines are properly levelled. Where centrifuges are used after washing and prior to drying, the main fault area is the lid interlock switch. Clothes can also be a problem and distributing clothes will prevent violent drum imbalance vibration.

a.   **Machine will not operate.** Make sure the power is on, and indicator light will indicate this. The door or lid interlock switch is the most common cause of non-operation, and opening and closing the door will usually clear the problem if it is just sticking. Ensure that water inlet faucets are open, and if water is not filling, the inlet valve may be faulty. In some rare cases the cycle timer or program circuit board may be faulty and inlet valve does not open.

Table 15-4 AC Motor Troubleshooting

Symptom	Probable Fault
Motor will not start	Fuses blown or breaker tripped Winding open circuit, connection broken Stator winding short circuited (fuses blown) Motor mechanically overloaded Bearings seized Rotor failed (very rare)
Motor stalls	One phase winding open Mechanically overloaded Low terminal voltage
Motor overloaded	Stalled load Seized bearings Terminal connection loose or hot
Motor high current	Mechanically overloaded Terminal voltage too low High resistance joints, volt drops
Motor overheating	Mechanically overloaded Fan broken or loose Fan inlet blocked Stator winding short circuit One phase open Ground fault on one winding Terminal voltage imbalance, connections
Ground fault	Insulation resistance broken down (moisture, overheating, aging or mechanical damage to winding) Stator winding short circuit One phase open Ground fault on one winding Terminal voltage imbalance, connections
Circuit breaker tripping	Ground fault Mechanical overload, high current Winding intercoil short circuit Terminal box cable fault Stalled load, seizing bearings

Table 15-5 AC Motor Troubleshooting

Symptom	Probable Fault
Bearings hot	Bearing lubrication failure
	Drive belts over tensioned
	Bearings worn
	Misalignment of couplings
	Under or over greased
	Bearings overloaded
	Shaft bent
	Pulleys too small
Vibration	Coupling out of balance
	Motor base holding bolts loose
	Motor or coupling misaligned
	Bearing failure
	Unbalanced load
	Motor rotor balance altered
	Loss of one phase in 3-phase machine
	Shaft bent
Phase currents imbalance	Stator windings fault–intercoil short
	Ground on phase
	High phase resistance connection
	Contactor pole high resistance fault
Wrong direction of rotation	Reverse phase sequence
Loss of motor phase	One fuse failed
	One isolator pole failed
	One contactor pole failed
	One starter phase connection burnt off
	One terminal phase connection filed
	One winding failed

    b.   **Machine fills but does not start cycle.** If the float switch is faulty, the unit may not start the cycle; in pressure tube sensing types the tube may be kinked causing the problem. If the filling is very slow, the inlet water filters may be clogged or the water supply pressure is low.

    c.   **Machine overfills with water.** This is caused by a faulty level switch, or an inlet valve remaining jammed open.

    d.   **Machine will not agitate or drum rotate.** Always check the door or lid interlock switch first. If the water level has not come up to correct level, the unit may not start. In some cases the belt or motor couplings may be defective.

e.   **Machine will not drain.** If the machine drum spins and water does not drain, the lint filter on the pump suction may be clogged. This is a common problem. The pump impeller may also be clogged; I have found underwear and socks in them as the filters are sometimes removed. The drain valve may also be jammed or clogged. In some cases the drain pipe may be clogged for the same reasons. Pump impellers do fail but this is less common. If the motor is turning but the spin function is not operating, the pulley on the pump may be the problem.

f.   **Machine will not spin.** The usual cause is a belt problem, either broken or slipping. In some cases it may be either the motor pulley or a motor fault. On some occasions the door or lid switch may be intermittent and this stops the entire machine. Some machines have clutches and motor couplings that also may fail and should be checked. Top of the range models may have an AC variable speed motor drive unit, and this can be a cause. Motor centrifugal switches may also be faulty.

g.   **Machine cycles slowly.** The most common causes are heaters and thermostats being faulty and the machine takes a long time to come up to cycle program set temperatures. Check the drain valves and filters as very slow draining also causes slow cycling. The water filling may also be slow due to blocked inlet filters or low pressure. Inlet valve solenoids may also be a cause and hum when partially open. In some cases the cycle timer or program circuit board may be at fault and either the cycle stops at one point or doesn't advance, and may require replacement.

h.   **Water temperature does not rise or is too hot for setting.** The heating element or thermostat may have failed, and element failures often cause tripping of the supply circuit breaker. Over temperature is caused by faulty thermostats, and where hot water filling is used, a partially jammed hot water inlet valve is the cause and usually this causes overfilling.

15.18   Clothes Dryers. Always check and clean the lint filters; overheating and fire are common on commercial vessels. Always listen for unusual noises, often due to a loose screw or coin in the drum; failing drum bearings, blowers, rollers and idler pulleys make very severe and worrying noises.

a.   **Machine will not operate.** Check that the power is on, and indicator light will indicate this. The door interlock switch is the most common cause of inoperation, and opening and closing the door will usually correct this.

b.   **Dryer will not heat up.** Check all fuses and circuit breakers first. The usual fault is a heating element failure or a thermostat fault. Check the element continuity to confirm failure. In some units, an overheat switch may also trip out and in some machines there is a replaceable thermal fuse.

c.   **Dryer overheats.** This is caused by a thermostat failure or clogged vent ducting.

d. **Drum will not rotate.** Always check the door switch first. Drive belt failure is another common fault and you will hear the motor turning. In less common cases the drive motor may burn out. Motors usually burn out due to bearing failure, and you will hear unusual noises from the motor and idler pulley before failure. The drum should rotate easily by hand with the belt removed and this should be checked for seizure.

e. **Dryer has slow drying times.** Usually this is caused by faulty cycle timers or thermostats. With multiple heating elements the failure of one can decrease heating effect, also partial element failure can occur. Always check that the outlet vents are clear and unobstructed.

15.19   Dishwashing Machines. These are generally installed in large vessel galleys and they do cause problems. Maintenance consists of keeping them clean. Smells can be avoided by deodorizing the machine. Rusting of the coated plate racks is a common problem along with corroding screws. The filters do become clogged with debris and must be cleaned regularly, to prevent damage to pumps and seals. Spray arms also can clog up and need regular cleaning, it's a fiddly job but worth the effort. Always check for leaks that indicate gasket and seal failure. Door mechanisms if treated roughly also get misaligned and cause leakages. Listen for abnormal noises, which may be due to loose components, failing motor bearings on the main motor and drying heater fan. Pumps with damaged impellers or objects caught up also can cause noise.

a. **Machine will not operate.** Check that the power is on, and the indicator light will indicate this. The door interlock switch is the most common cause of non-operation, and opening and closing the door will usually start things. If it is regular problem, a new switch is required. Timers and selection switches can fail but this is the least likely cause.

b. **Machine does not wash properly.** The most common cause is a faulty water inlet valve, and some installations will have a water filter that is clogged with sediment. This causes water starvation and you will sometimes hear a water hammer sound. The internal filters in some machines also can clog, and these filter material from the pump inlet. Drain valves also cause problems and if jammed up with debris they will affect the cycle by allowing water to drain out when it does not close properly. The inlet hot water must be up to temperature and on boats this is a common problem. Units with an integral heating element may have a faulty thermostat or heating element, in these cases the cycle never proceeds past this stage. The cycle timer is the last possible cause. A fault in the detergent dosing system also causes washing problems. These may have a bimetallic switch or a wax motor to initiate opening and if faulty will stop detergent being inserted.

c. **Washer has no water supply.** Water inlet valves can fail, either the valve is mechanically faulty or the coil has failed. Another possible cause is a jammed water level float switch, so always check this out. Machines with a seized water overflow valve will also prevent water filling.

d. **Washer will not drain.** A clogged drain pipe is a common cause, usually at a bend or where the pipe discharges. The second major cause is the drain pump, and the operation should be checked but the spray arms and assembly will have to come off first. The drain valve also may jam or the solenoid coil has failed. If the machine uses a belt drive, check the belt condition. The motor also may be seized up, and on boats this is common due to lack of use, so manually rotate the motor and try again. Control faults such as the timer are less common.

e. **Washer drying cycle is not working normally.** The usual cause is either the thermostat or the heating element. Element failure may cause the circuit breaker to trip. A drying fan if installed may also cause problems.

15.20 **Galley Ranges.** These are integral to the feeding of the crew, and failures cause serious morale problems. Maintain ranges by keeping clean, use appropriate cleaners on solid elements and ceramic hob surfaces. Check interior oven lights and have a spare on hand. Check error codes on displays and if one appears check the equipment manual for a description.

a. **Range fails completely.** Check power supply and fuses, in some cases I have found burned-off wiring at connection points.

b. **Oven (or broiler/grill) will not heat up.** Check that the element is working. Elements can be removed as they are normally plug-in items. The element resistance can be checked using a multimeter. The element receptacles burn out and should be checked. If the elements are found to be good, the thermostat or control switch may be faulty. Check that the timer settings are correct or the timer is switched off. Incorrect setting is a common cause of problems. Clock failure can also shut down the whole oven function.

c. **Oven heats but is either too high or too low.** This indicates a faulty thermostat. Some oven types may require recalibration of the thermostat.

d. **Stovetop heating elements do not work.** The element may have failed, and sometimes a surface blistering can be seen. Another common fault is the element plug-in receptacle or the wires and connections to the socket are faulty and intermittent. This is characterized by pitting, corrosion and burning. The element control can also be faulty along with the sensing circuit. The entire control will require replacement.

15.21 **Microwaves.** The microwave converts the input voltage into a high voltage and then supplies the magnetron which emits radio waves. These vibrate food molecules to heat and cook the food. The best maintenance is to keep the internal parts clean and the interior dry.

a. **Microwave will not operate.** Check the power supplies. Check that the door switch is operating by opening and closing a few times. An internal fuse may also fail. If no heating is occurring, the unit may have an internal control fault. If there has been a high voltage transient condition on the boat such as a lightning strike, the surge may have damaged the control circuits. If a loud buzzing or humming is heard but no heating, this indicates a magnetron fault, or a capacitor or power diode problem.

b.   **Carousel will not rotate.** The small drive motor may have failed or the linkage to the carousel has broken.

c.   **Internal arcing during operation.** The wave guide may have burn spots and require replacement.

d.   **Cooking power level cannot be adjusted.** This is usually a problem on the electronic control board or output circuits.

15.22   Trash Compactors. Before troubleshooting always switch off and unplug the unit. The best maintenance is keeping the unit clean and hygienic. Where filters are installed, these should be checked and replaced regularly.

a.   **Compactor will not operate.** Check the power supplies. Check the operation of the door interlock switch, and the ram limit switch.

b.   **Compactor ram is jammed.** Check the drive chains, gears or belts. The second possible cause is a control fault and the outputs may require checking.

15.23   Waste Disposal Units. Always switch off and unplug the unit before troubleshooting. Routine problems such as leaks are due to damaged gaskets. In some cases the entire unit will require replacement as it cannot be repaired. Maintain by rinsing well with water after use and deodorizing regularly.

a.   **Disposal unit will not operate.** The reset button is tripped out or the power is off. Tripping is caused by overheating and overloading. There may also be a motor failure. Check the stopper switch if one is installed.

b.   **Disposal unit hums but will not grind the waste.** This may be instantaneous or occur after a few seconds of loud whirring. The macerator plates are probably clogged or jammed up with non-food waste. Don't keep trying to operate as the motor can burn out through overheating while in a stalled condition. Plastic debris and bones are the most common cause of jamming. Most units have a " Allen wrench" port at the bottom that is used to move the macerator plates and free them up when jammed. Some units also may have a reversing switch.

c.   **Disposal unit hums but is not jammed.** The electric motor has failed or is about to fail. Seized bearings may also be a cause.

d.   **Excessive noise.** This can be caused by loose components, such as macerator plates, bearings, or metallic objects caught in the unit.

e.   **Disposal unit does not macerate waste properly.** The macerator plates are worn and the disposer will require replacement.

f.   **Disposal unit drains down slowly.** The drain line may be clogged with grease so run very hot water through it. Run more cold water through when grinding waste. Macerator plates may be worn and grinding inadequate with larger particles causing blockage.

SECTION TWO

ELECTRONICS SYSTEMS

Electronics Systems

16.1   System Basics. There have been significant advances in marine electronic systems within recent years. Boat systems are now at levels of sophistication that can exceed even those on commercial vessels. The following chapters cover most electronics systems found on motorboats, including selection, installation, maintenance and troubleshooting information. Good planning is essential, and reliability depends on a stable electrical power system.

    a.   **Power Supplies.** The power supply is a fundamental part of any electronics equipment. Power supplies are a common cause of failure or source of interference. Typical power supplies are designed to withstand supply variations of 5–10% over the whole load range and maintain a stable output voltage. The principal power supply in use is the filtered and rectified DC supply type. It has been replaced in recent years by regulated switch mode power supplies. Switch mode supplies have the advantage of low weight, minimal interference, improved performance and lower costs.

    b.   **Filtered Rectified Power Supplies.** These consist of the transformer, the diode bridge rectifier and the filter capacitor. The output voltage contains an AC component, ripple and voltage fluctuations. Some equipment is tolerant of these components. A voltage regulator is required to maintain the output voltage at a stable level through all input voltage levels and load current demands.

    c.   **Regulated Switch Mode Power Supplies.** These systems offer weight and size savings and the ability to withstand wide variations in the input voltage. They incorporate filters to eliminate noise. The switching regulator rectifies the line voltage, and then converts the DC into a high frequency square wave using transistor and diode switching. This is transformed and then rectified for output, and the output is maintained by pulse width modulation. Transformer sizes are reduced by the use of high frequencies for the switching, typically in the range of 10–100 kHz.

    d.   **Processors.** All systems incorporate microprocessor-based signal and data processing circuits. These are typically on printed circuit boards and not user serviceable. They are static sensitive and care should be taken in handling circuit boards.

16.2   Navigation Stations. There is a certain amount of satisfaction in having an attractive looking navigation station. It attests to a seamanlike attitude that is not lost on the more informed guests. However, a well-presented navigation station is worthless if the equipment malfunctions or is unreliable because of lack of planning or a failure to consider the technical requirements of the equipment. Make it look good, but above all make sure it works. Before starting the installation of navigation equipment, or fitting out a new vessel, consider carefully the following requirements that ensure reliable performance.

a. **Location.** Navigation stations are invariably located at the front of pilot-houses, and in many boats there are dual station arrangements such as fly bridges with radar, chart plotters, radios and fishfinders located in positions exposed to spray. Select equipment rated as waterproof or at least splash proof, so it can withstand intermittent spray. Standards of waterproofing are to USCG CFR-46 and many instrument displays are IP55, IP56 and IP67. Ensure that instruments are mounted to prevent water from getting to the data and power connections. In exposed positions, additional protection should be considered.

b. **Ergonomics.** Instruments should be positioned so that they are easy to operate and monitor. They should be grouped into functional blocks where possible. Keep communications equipment in one block, position-fixing equipment in another. Equipment must be fitted so that access is unobstructed. Many navigation stations consist of various equipment items installed into any available space. Important considerations are as follows:

(1) **Display Visibility.** Position the displays at an angle that is normal for observation. Many instruments are mounted vertically for observation when seated. When at sea in normal operations they are generally monitored when standing up. Difficulties are more pronounced with LCD displays.

(2) **Accessibility.** Make sure you can easily reach and operate controls. On some badly designed stations, you either have to stretch awkwardly, or a knob is placed in such a tight corner you cannot access it properly.

(3) **Lighting.** Make sure that there is adequate lighting with a good dimmable light at the chart table.

c. **Electrical Factors.** Consider the effects the instruments can or may have on each other.

(1) **Cable Routing.** Route all radio transmission cables clear of signal cables. Where cable crossovers are required, make sure they are at 90°. Properly space out and secure power, radio and signal cables with the required separation distances. Position electronic equipment so that aerial cables and inputs are exiting the navigation station area directly, without being routed behind other instruments, or close to other cables.

(2) **Electrical Equipment Location.** Where possible, do not locate the main electrical switchboard next to the electronic equipment. In most cases, this can be very difficult. The trend now is to install small sub-boards containing circuit breakers for the electronic equipment. This has the advantage of removing a great deal of interference caused by electrical equipment from the adjacent area.

(3) **Accessibility.** Make sure you have easy access to rear connections. In many cases the rear fuse holders in power leads or the equipment casing may require access.

16.3   Notebook Computer Systems. The laptop/notebook computer is now a powerful mobile office work tool to incorporate major vessel management systems. There are several companies that specialize in mobile computing as well as a full range of options and marine software. I would recommend that you contact them and discuss the options. Mobile Computing Magazine (www.mobilecomputing.com) is a good start, also Home Office Computing Magazine (www.smalloffice.com or www.marinecomputing.com). The criteria in selecting a suitable computer are the same as for any other environment and makers such as Toshiba, Sony, IBM and Compaq all have good machines. Machines continue to get smaller, lighter and slimmer. This is often due to the miniaturization of components, such as CD ROM, or smaller battery or floppy, and a reduction in the display size. Decisions require compromise and for boat applications the fully integrated machine is probably the best way to go. There are computers available for marine use, and they are of good quality. I have successfully carried notebooks on and off planes, helicopters and done most of my professional work on oil rigs and ships. I wrote this book and others aboard my own boat using a Toshiba Tecra and an IBM Thinkpad. The Toshiba finally died with a motherboard failure, and the Thinkpad is proving very reliable, and both are off the shelf Circuit City models. In the end if you treat them roughly or soak them with water, they will fail, and budget is a primary consideration. If you are doing serious offshore boating, a rugged version may be ideal. Many motorboats and commercial ships have desktop PCs with a UPS and they work reliably.

a.   **RAM and Processor.** Each notebook manufacturer has different processors, all of which affect the price. Whether it is an Intel Pentium II, III, IV or Celeron, AMD or Cyrix, they are designed along with associated circuitry to maximize power efficiency and minimize heat dissipation. When selecting RAM (Random Access Memory) go for as much as you can afford. The more RAM you have, the faster applications will operate, in particular some powerful graphics packages and chart plotting software, so 64K is a start; 128K or more is far better.

b.   **Hard Drive and Data Storage.** I would select the largest hard drive possible within budget, as so many software packages soon absorb capacity. For data storage and backups, I opted to have an Iomega Click drive with removable 40 MB disks. I had previously an Iomega ZIP drive but it was an extra piece of kit to carry and plug in. I have also invested in a travel-size CD burner. Other developments include the LS-120 SuperDisk drive which is identical to standard 3.5" floppy disks, but can store up to 120MB of data.

c.   **Communications Ports and Modems.** Communications is a key function in mobile computing and most notebooks come with a 56K modem as standard. The modem along with the installed Internet browser and a mobile phone allow web access and e-mail. I have an infrared port and also communicate with my Palm Pilot. Additional modems can be plugged into the PCMCIA slot, along with the Digital Camera, network Interface cards, etc. Selecting a machine with USB ports and facility to plug in PCMCIA PC cards is important. I have a 40 MB Iomega Click Drive that simply slides in. Many packages also have plug in modems for NMEA interfacing, Weatherfax and e-mail interfaces for SSB/HF radio.

d. **CD ROM and Writer.** The majority of notebooks have integral CD-ROM drives, and newer models have integral CD writers and DVD. The CD is the primary program-loading source, and is also used for many other applications such as plotter charts, reference disks, etc. The drive speed is important and the higher the better. My own CD is used for music, and the DVD is a great advantage for boats over standard videocassettes.

e. **Displays.** Desktop PCs use cathode ray tube screens, and the notebook uses an LCD. The two main LCD display types available are the TFT Active Matrix (Thin Film Transistor) and the DSTN Passive Matrix (Dual Scan Twisted Neumatic). There are several variations on these types called HCAD, HPA and CB-DSTN. For performance the TFT has a sharper and brighter image with better color. If you view graphics, video and DVD it will refresh faster, and it allows wide angle viewing. The downsides are that TFT consumes more power than DSTN screens, and DSTN units are cheaper. For chart plotting applications TFT is the better choice. Screen technology and operating software have improved graphics and video quality of LCD screens dramatically and on DVD applications I find them more than adequate.

f. **Power Supplies and Battery Life.** This is an important selection point for anyone considering boat applications. I get around 3 hours on my IBM Thinkpad in economy mode, which is far from ideal. The two principal battery types are the LiON (Lithium-Ion) or the NiMH (Nickel Metal Hydride). The LiON batteries weigh less and hold charge for a longer period, with less memory effect than the NiMH, but they do cost more. Carrying a spare battery is a good option, and also a battery conditioner will restore batteries suffering from memory effects. Cycling the computer down to full discharge and recharge is also a good practice. I have the Targus DC travel and car charge kit, which includes a variety of other plugs including ones for aircraft. The computer is plugged into a cigarette lighter outlet on board, and like the cellular phone my battery appears to recharge more fully when plugged into my boat DC supply.

g. **Keyboard and Mouse.** The smaller notebook keyboard will never be as good as a full size desktop one, however you get used to it. The notebook keys have a different feel, and the key locations vary, requiring adaptation. My IBM has a pointing stick type mouse located in the center of the keyboard and it is easy to use. It takes practice to move the cursor around the screen when using a pressure sensitive touch pad. The decision will depend on personal preferences.

16.4 **Computer System Options.** The following show some options.

    a. **Printers.** The usual printer will be an inkjet. If there is the room and you operate an office, a small laser is probably a better choice. There are small and compact printers, and it will depend on the quantity and quality of printing planned.

    b. **Acoustic Couplers.** Units such as that from Konex allow access to the Internet via shore telephones.

    c. **Scanners.** The scanner may suit those who file everything they get, and is a realistic option for quite a lot of paper-based information storage.

16.5 **Software Options.** The following will help memory size planning.

    a. **Standard Software Packages.** This manual was written on an IBM ThinkPad, in MS Word while afloat on my own boat and on a couple of offshore oilrigs. The CD player was usually on, with the integral speakers or headphones to provide soothing tones. Many illustrations were done using Visio 2000. I run Microsoft Office 2000, which caters for most needs. I write professional manuals and help systems using RoboHelp and DocToHelp, and both require considerable memory. Other packages I use are Adobe Acrobat, Adobe Illustrator, and AutoCad LT. Of course I also have a CD ROM interactive sailing package, and run a few other demo packages from various marine electronic equipment manufacturers.

    b. **Electronic Charting.** Refer to Chapter 20.

    c. **Entertainment.** In addition to games packages, the computer can be used with the CD player for music, and the DVD for movies. It is also possible to watch television on the laptop using the TV-to-Go package. This has a PCM-CIA Card to plug in, with integral antenna or a connection to an external one. It requires a Zoom Video (ZV) PC Card port.

    d. **Weather Information.** There are many weather software options, and many are listed in Chapter 18.

    e. **Photographs.** The digital camera (I use a Fuji model) and software allow easy image storage and e-mail of pictures to friends and relatives.

    f. **Tides.** Many packages are available, including Tide Wizard, for UK, Europe or worldwide. This package allows tidal predictions using the simplified harmonic method. Claimed accuracy is 0.1 meter. Results are tabulated or graphical. Another package is Tides and Currents, which uses the full harmonic method and data from the UK Hydrographic Office. A North American Region version is available.

    g. **Astro and Celestial Navigation.** I have used DOS versions for years, however the Windows packages are really easy to use. More for sailors than motorboats, the Win Astro package, a sight reduction program, typifies them. It has a perpetual almanac for the sun, moon, planet and stars. The DOS packages I have used are AstroNav and Polystar.

h. **Boat Management.** There are electronic log packages that collect data via a NMEA interface to the GPS, log, and depth, etc., and automatically maintain the vessel log.

i. **E-mail.** There are a variety of methods, as discussed in the e-mail chapter, in particular for HF radio. There are also packages to assist in other systems. For those with INMARSAT-C there is a package called WordSat, which is a Windows based package that allows message management and compression to 50%. Read and prepare in MS Word.

   (1) In US and Caribbean waters JUNO offers a free e-mail service 800-654-5855, or alternatively call 1-800-419-0093 for subscription service.

   (2) AOL has many local access numbers for e-mail and Internet. The Earthlink Network on 800-395-8425 and at www.earthlink.net is cited as superior to all major ISP in document download speeds.

j. **Internet.** Access can be difficult when on the move, but changes are occurring rapidly. The options should improve when Teledesic finally starts, and Ku band satellite allows access to the Internet.

16.6 Computer Maintenance. The following basics will improve reliability:

a. **Disc Drive.** All hard disc drives are sealed and are maintenance free. Ensure that dust is vacuumed out regularly. Floppy disc head cleaning kits are also available.

b. **Printer.** A small inkjet printer is the most commonly used printer, and a few basic maintenance tasks are required to maintain optimum performance. Ensure you carry spare ink cartridges.

   (1) Clean out the interior using a soft brush.

   (2) Outside casings should be wiped using a damp cloth. Do not use solvents or abrasive cleaners. Never apply lubricants or electrical cleaners into mechanisms.

c. **Keyboard.** Brush out dust and particles regularly, and wipe the board with a slightly damp cloth. Keep wet fingers, coffee mugs, etc., well away. Small purpose-made, battery-powered vacuum cleaners are available to extract dust and particles.

d. **Battery Packs.** All systems have battery packs. The major problem is that battery packs are not properly cycled and some can develop what is called memory effect. Discharge them properly on a regular basis and then recharge completely. In the US visit website www.1800Batteries.com. Charging is also an issue, some opt for the use of a small inverter; I use a Targus DC car charge kit that works very well.

16.7   Computer Troubleshooting. There are a few basic checks to make.

    a.   **Power Supply.** The majority of problems on computers on boats can be attributed to poor quality power supplies. Both AC and DC supplies can carry damaging voltage transients. Most externally powered laptops have a 15-volt maximum. If using an alternator fast charge device, disconnect the computer from the vessel DC system during charging.

    b.   **Printers.** The most common problems are:

        (1)   **Paper Feed Jams.** In most cases it is caused by moisture being absorbed into the paper. Use only as much paper as required in sheet feeders, keep the rest packaged and dry.

        (2)   **Printer Communication Error Messages.** Use self-test functions first. Check that cables are properly inserted into sockets. Check that the correct default printer is selected.

Figure 16-1 Computer and Weather Modem , *Courtesy of ICS Electronics*

GMDSS Communications

17.1   Global Maritime Distress and Safety System (GMDSS). GMDSS was fully implemented in 1999 for all commercial vessels exceeding 300 GRT. In many areas VHF Channel 16 or 2182 kHz is not monitored and requirements will be dropped by 2005. The primary function of GMDSS is to coordinate and facilitate Search and Rescue (SAR) operations, by both shore authorities and vessels, with the shortest possible delay and maximum efficiency. It also provides efficient urgency and safety communications, and broadcast of Maritime Safety Information (MSI) such as navigational and meteorological warnings, forecasts, and other urgent safety information. MSI is transmitted via NAVTEX, International SafetyNet on INMARSAT C, and some NBDP radio telex services.

17.2   GMDSS Operational Details. Worldwide communications coverage is achieved using a combination of INMARSAT and terrestrial systems. All systems have range limitations that have resulted in the designation of four sea areas, which defines communications system requirements.

a.   **Area A1.** Within shore-based VHF radio range. Distance is in the range of 20–100 nm. Radio required is VHF operating on Channel 70 for DSC, and Channel 16 radiotelephone. EPIRB required is 406 MHz or L-band unit (1.6 GHz). After February 1999 a VHF EPIRB is required. Survival craft require a 9-GHz radar transponder and portable VHF radio (with Channel 16 and one other frequency).

b.   **Area A2.** Within shore-based MF radio range. Distance is in the range of 100–300 nm. Radios required are MF (2187.5 kHz DSC) and 2812 kHz radiotelephone, 2174.5 NBDP, and NAVTEX on 518 kHz. Also needed are the same VHF requirements as Area A1. EPIRB required is 406 MHz or L-band (1.6 GHz). Survival craft requirements are the same as in Area A1.

c.   **Area A3.** Within geostationary satellite range (INMARSAT). Distance is in the range of 70°N–70°S. Radios required are MF and VHF as above and satellite (with 1.5-1.6 GHz alerting), or as per Areas A1 and A2 plus HF (all frequencies). Survival craft requirements are the same as in A1.

d.   **Area A4.** Other areas (beyond INMARSAT range). Distance north of 70°N and south of 70°S. Radios required are HF, MF, and VHF. EPIRB required is 406 MHz. Survival craft requirements are the same as in Area A1.

17.3   GMDSS Radio Distress Communications Frequencies. The frequencies designated for use under GMDSS are as follows:

a.   VHF   DSC Channel 70, Channel 16, Channel 06 intership, Channel 13 intership MSI.

b.   MF   DSC 2187.5 kHz, and 2182 kHz.

c.   HF4   DSC 4207.5 kHz, and 4125 kHz.

d. HF6 DSC 6312 kHz, and 6215 kHz (CH421).

e. HF8 DSC 8414.5 kHz, and 8291 kHz (CH833).

f. HF12 DSC 12577 kHz, and 12290 kHz (CH1221).

g. HF16 DSC 16804.5 kHz, and 16420 kHz.

17.4 Digital Selective Calling (DSC). DSC is a primary component of GMDSS and is used to transmit distress alerts and appropriate acknowledgments. DSC will improve accuracy, transmission, and reception of distress calls. VHF Channel 70 is the nominated DSC channel.

a. DSC has the advantage that digital signals in radio communications are at least 25% more efficient than voice transmissions, as well as significantly faster. A DSC VHF transmission typically takes around a second, and MF/HF takes approximately 7 seconds, both depending on the DSC call type.

b. DSC requires the use of encoders/decoders, or additional add-on modules to existing equipment. A dedicated DSC watch receiver is required to continuously monitor the specified DSC distress frequency. Affordable VHF DSC radio equipment is a priority for small vessels and Class D controllers are now available, in the US these are from Horizon and Icom. In Europe there are units from ICS and Simrad. Class E DSC MF/HF receivers are now available for A2 areas.

c. DSC equipment enables the transmission of digital information based on four priority groupings, Distress, Urgency, Safety, and Routine. The information can be selectively addressed to all stations, to a specific station, or to a group of stations. To perform this selective transmission and reception of messages, every station must possess what is called a Maritime Mobile Selective-call Identity Code (MMSI). Note that Distress "Mayday" messages are automatically dispatched to all stations. A DSC Distress alert message is configured to contain the transmitting vessel's identity (the MMSI nine-digit code number), the time, the nature of the distress, and the vessel's position where interfaced with a GPS. After transmission of a distress alert, it is repeated a few seconds later to ensure that the transmission is successfully transmitted.

17.5 GMDSS Distress Call (Alert) Sequence. It is important to explain the various elements of GMDSS in an emergency situation.

a. Distress Alert. This is usually activated from a vessel to the shore. For motorboats this is usually via terrestrial radio, and larger vessels use satellites. Ships in the area may hear an alert, although a shore-based Rescue Coordination Center (RCC) will be responsible for responding to and acknowledging receipt of the alert. Alerts may be activated via an INMARSAT A, B, or C terminal, via COSPAS/SARSAT EPIRB (243/406 MHz), or via an INMARSAT E EPIRB. DSC VHF or MF/HF can also activate alerts.

b.   **Distress Relay.** On receipt and acknowledgment of alert, the RCC will relay the alert to vessels in the geographical area concerned. This targets the resources available and does not involve vessels outside the distress vessel area. Vessels in the area of the distress can receive appropriate alerts via IN-MARSAT A, B, or C terminals, DSC VHF or MF/HF radio equipment, or via NAVTEX MSI. On reception of a distress relay the vessels concerned must contact the RCC to offer assistance.

c.   **Search and Rescue.** In the SAR phase of the rescue, the previous one-way communications switch over to two-way for effective coordination of both aircraft and vessels. The frequencies used are as outlined previously.

d.   **Rescue Scene Communications.** Local communications are maintained using short-range terrestrial MF or VHF on the specified frequencies. Local communications take place using either satellite or terrestrial radio links.

e.   **Distress Vessel Location.** A Search and Rescue Transponder (SART), and/or the 121.5MHz homing frequency of an EPIRB assist in determining the precise location of the vessel in distress.

17.6   False Alerts and System Coverage. GMDSS is relatively new, and currently the false alert rate is around 95%. False alerts are not desirable simply because of the load placed on SAR services. False alerts are generally caused by operator errors and incorrect equipment operation. Another cause of false alerts is the improper acknowledgment of distress alerts

Figure 17-1 GMDSS Radio Station, *Courtesy of ICS Electronics*

leading to excessive DSC calls. Training and experience of equipment operation is essential to solve these problems. Coverage is not global at this time. While Europe is covered, the USCG will not have capability at the 44 group command stations and rescue craft until 2006. As all commercial vessels have DSC under GMDSS you will get some coverage.

17.7   GMDSS and Motorboats. The installation of GMDSS is not compulsory for pleasure boats. Due to universal implementation on commercial vessels, boats will be forced to install partial GMDSS equipment simply to remain "plugged in" to the system. GMDSS will certainly maximize SAR situations for boats, and in most cases it will enhance offshore safety. GMDSS equipment will accurately identify your own boat, current position, and type of emergency, and this information will be broadcast automatically. What you get is automatic activation of alarms at coast stations and on other vessels simply by pushing one button. Just as GPS, electronic charting, and the EPIRB have opened up the world to cruisers, so will GMDSS significantly improve sea safety. As a minimum the following equipment is required for an offshore trip. Few will be able to invest in full INMARSAT terminals. A more advanced training course and operation certificate is also required and is being run in many locations.

    a.   NAVTEX receiver (ICS, Alden, Furuno, PC Navtex).

    b.   406 EPIRB (correctly registered).

    c.   VHF DSC (Class D controller: Icom, Raymarine, Standard Horizon).

    d.   VHF (approved handheld type, i.e., Simrad Axis range).

    e.   SART (optional but desirable).

    f.   MF/HF Class E DSC (optional but desirable).

17.8   Satellite Communications Systems. Under GMDSS, satellite systems play a major role and prices are becoming more affordable for pleasure boats. INMARSAT was established by the IMO to improve distress and safety of life at sea communications and general maritime communications. INMARSAT is based on satellites placed in geostationary orbit. Under GMDSS all commercial vessels operating in areas outside designated areas of International NAVTEX coverage require a receiver for reception of INMARSAT SafetyNET Maritime Safety Information (MSI). The Standard-C SES is a GMDSS-compliant system that offers compact and lightweight terminals. These systems are designed to support data-only services, not voice. Services are telex, e-mail, Internet access, and computer database access.

17.9   COSPAS/SARSAT System. GMDSS incorporates the COSPAS/SARSAT system as an integral part of the distress communications system. The acronym is based on the former Soviet "Space System for Search of Distress Vessels" and the American "Search and Rescue Satellite Aided Tracking." Under GMDSS if a vessel does not carry a satellite L-band EPIRB in sea areas A1, A2, and A3 (described earlier), then a 406 MHz EPIRB is required. This unit must have hydrostatic release and float-free capability. The system is a worldwide satellite-assisted SAR system for location of distress transmissions emitted by EPIRBs on the 121.5/243 MHz and 406 MHz frequencies. 121.5 kHz is an aircraft homing frequency and 243 MHz is a military distress frequency that enables military aircraft to assist in SAR operations. The Emergency Position Indicating Radio Beacon (EPIRB) is an essential item of safety equipment for any offshore vessel. Earlier EPIRB units relied solely on over-flying aircraft for detection of signals and relay of the position to appropriate SAR authorities; the new systems utilize satellites. The satellite-compatible system relies on satellites inserted in near polar orbits with orbit times of approximately 100 minutes. Accuracy of the system improved from approximately 10 nm for 121.5/243 MHz units to 3 nm for a 406 MHz unit. Note that the 406 MHz units are far more effective at lower latitudes than the 121.5/243 MHz units, and the latter are being phased out. These were not useful in mid ocean and had a high false alarm rate so it was usual to wait for two separate satellite hits before activating SAR, there was no vessel specific identification, and error was around 20km. 121.5 kHz is now primarily used on personal locator beacons (PLB) only.

17.10   Satellite (L-Band) EPIRBs. This system, developed by the European Space Agency, will alert rescue services in distress within 2 minutes, rather than in hours as with current systems. The new system combines position determination along with a distress signal using the INMARSAT geostationary satellites. The system uses special EPIRBs that incorporate GPS receivers and ensure a position fix within 200 meters. The distress signal transmits via one of four Land Earth Stations (LES) and landline links with appropriate rescue coordination centers. Recent testing shows an average 5-minute delay from activation to reception by rescue services.

17.11   406 EPIRBs. The 406 MHz units have a unique identification code, and information is usually programmed at time of sale, with MMSI or registered serial numbers. Some units also have integral strobes and all incorporate 121.5 MHz for aircraft homing signal purposes. Float-free units are called Category 1; manual bracket units are Category 2. Orbit time is 100 minutes using COSPAS satellites so a delay in transmission up to 4 hours near the equator can occur. Accuracy is 2km and uses the Doppler effect, and usually requires 2 satellite passes. The system uses a store and forward system so the satellite stores and downloads distress data when in view of a LUT. Log on to www.acrelectronics.com, www.pwss.com, www.profind406.com.

17.12   406 MHz EPIRB Registration. If you acquire a vessel with a 406 MHz EPIRB, you must register the EPIRB unit properly and provide all of the appropriate data, including its unique identification number (or MMSI). Registration should be done immediately upon purchase. Failure to do this can cause absolute havoc if you use it, because a vessel may be incorrectly identified or, worse still, not identified at all, which could seriously jeopardize your rescue. Bad information means very bad rescue problems for everyone. If you have not registered, contact the organizations listed:

(1)   United States of America. NOAA/NESDIS. Tel +1-301-457-5428. Additional information on registration. Tel +1-302-763 4680.

(2)   United Kingdom. EPIRB Registry, Marine Safety Agency, Tel +44-1326 211569 (www.msa.co.uk).

(3)   Canada. Canadian EPIRB Registry Director, Search and Rescue, Canadian Coastguard, Tel +1-613-990 3124.

(4)   Australia. Maritime Rescue Co-ordination Center, Australian Maritime Safety Authority. Tel +61-2-6230 6811. (rrcaus@amsa.gov.au and www.amsa.com.au).

(5)   Netherlands. Ministry of Transport Tel +31-50-222111.

(6)   New Zealand. CAA. Tel +64-4-5600400.

17.13   EPIRB Activation Sequence. On activation of an EPIRB the following sequence of events occurs:

(1)   A satellite detects the distress transmission. With 243/121.5 MHz units a satellite and the EPIRB must be simultaneously in view of the Local User Terminal (LUT).

(2)   The detected signal is then downloaded to a LUT. (In 406 MHz units the satellite stores the message and downloads to the next LUT in view.)

(3)   The LUT automatically computes the position of the distress transmission. The distress information is then passed to a Mission Control Center (MCC) before going to a Rescue Control Center (RCC) and then to SAR aircraft and vessels.

17.14   EPIRB Operation. Do not operate an EPIRB except in a real emergency, because you could initiate a rescue operation. Do not even operate it for just a short period of time and then switch it off, because authorities may assume your vessel went down quickly before circumstances stopped transmission. With current attitudes changing toward false alarms, it may reflect very badly on boaters as a whole in terms of wasting taxpayers' money. If you activate your EPIRB during an emergency, once rescued, do not leave the EPIRB in the raft or floating as the beacon may continue to transmit for some time.

17.15   Rescue Reaction Times. There is a mistaken belief that rescues are instantaneous after activation of an EPIRB. The reality, however, is a time lag that can average up to 6 hours or more from detection of a signal and physical location, although position is usually confirmed in less than 2 hours. This is dependent on suitable aircraft, weather conditions, and SAR coordinator response times. Every LUT has a "footprint" coverage area, and the closer you are to the edge of that footprint, the longer the delay. Time lags depend on intervals between satellite passes over a given location. There are six polar orbiting satellites and, although random in orbit, their tracks are predictable. If you have to activate, be patient and wait. Remember, you are not a survivor until you're on the deck of a rescue vessel or in the helicopter. Priority one is a survival training course. Have you done one? Have you evaluated and planned a helicopter evacuation procedure?

17.16   Battery Life and Transmit Times. Much concern has been raised over battery transmit life after activation. Always ensure that the battery pack is replaced within the listed expiration date. Nominally a lithium battery has a life of 4 to 5 years depending on the manufacturer. Typical transmit times are 80–100 hours at 5W output. Standards require a minimum of 48 hours.

17.17   EPIRB Maintenance. The only maintenance required is to test the EPIRB using the self-test function every six months in accordance with the manufacturer's instructions. Do not self-test by activating the EPIRB distress function. Do not drop the unit unless it is in the water or damage may occur.

17.18   Personal Locator Beacons (PLBs). The PLB is essentially a miniature EPIRB. They operate on 121.5 MHz, which is the frequency used for homing in by SAR vessels and aircraft. Due to their small size they can be attached into wet weather gear, or carried in a pocket or panic pack. It is not as accurate as other units and will localize your position to around 12 nm, because the transmitters are line of sight only. Some units are configured to activate in water, and most operate for at least a 24-hour period and some work up to 48 hours. The PLB is not a substitute for a 243/121.5 MHz or 406 MHz EPIRB.

17.19   Radar Target Enhancers (RTEs). The operation of these devices works by the reception of an incoming radar signal, the amplification of that pulse, and the retransmission of the pulse back to the radar signal source. This has to occur simultaneously and at the same frequency. The returned signal is displayed in enhanced form, with the relatively small return of the boat appearing significantly larger than it actually is. The recently introduced Mc-Murdo Ocean Sentry RTE claims a target enhancement factor of eight times greater than actual reflected image. This obviously has the advantage of displaying strong and consistent echoes on radar screens. Effectiveness depends on the incoming radar signal strength, the height at which the RTE is installed, and the height of the other vessel's radar above sea level. The Ocean Sentry unit operates either in standby or transponder modes. In standby mode, the unit is activated only when a radar signal is present. These units operate in response to 3-cm X-band radars only, not S-band. The effective range is typically around 12 nm, but not less than around 3 nm.

17.20   Search and Rescue Transponders (SARTs). Under GMDSS these units are required on all vessels over 300 GRT. These devices are designed for use in search and rescue, and are different from the RTE. An EPIRB will put potential rescue vessels in the area, but the transponder will accurately localize your position to search radars. The transponder is similar to an RTE in operation. Units typically have the following characteristics:

  a.   **Signal Transmission.** The transponder responds automatically and emits a 9200–9500 GHz high-speed frequency sweeping signal which is synchronous with the received scanning radar pulse.

  b.   **Signal Reception.** On reception of the signal, the position is indicated on radar screens as a line of 12 blips giving range and bearing.

  c.   **Transponder Receiver.** The transponder gives an audible alarm when the radar emission of a search and rescue vessel is detected.

17.21   NAVTEX. NAVTEX is an integral part of GMDSS as well as the Worldwide Navigational Warning Service (WWNWS). It is an automated information system providing meteorological, navigation, and maritime safety information (MSI). Messages are broadcast in English on a pretuned and dedicated frequency of 518 kHz with an additional frequency of 590 kHz now being implemented within UK/Europe in local languages. Range is typically around 250 nm, sometimes more or less. INMARSAT enhanced group calling (EGC) provides long-range information. Each of the 16 Navarea are divided into four groups. Each has up to 6 transmitters with 10-minute transmission times within each four-hour period. This is time shared to prevent interference on adjacent areas, and they have limited power outputs. Message reception requires a dedicated receiver. Broadcast times are included within frequency listings. Dedicated units such as those from ICS and Furuno have LCD display units, and ICS also have printer versions. PC Navtex is a PC version.

a. **Message Priorities.** Prioritization is used to define message broadcasts. Vital messages are broadcast immediately, usually at the end of any transmission in progress. Those classed as important will be broadcast at the first available period when the frequency is not in use. Routine messages are broadcast at the next scheduled transmission time. Those messages classified as vital and important will be repeated if still valid at the following scheduled transmission times. Messages incorporate a subject indicator code (B2 character), which allows acceptance and rejection of specific information. Navigational and meteorological warnings and SAR information are non-selective so that all stations receive important safety information. B2 codes include Nav warnings (buoy positions altering, wrecks, floating hazards, oil rig moves, naval exercises), meteorological warnings such as gales, ice reports, SAR and anti-piracy info (cannot be rejected), weather forecasts shipping and synopsis, pilot service messages, Loran messages, OMEGA messages, GPS messages, other NAVAID messages, Nav warnings additional to A. (cannot be rejected). (A = Nav warnings, B=Gales, D=Distress information, E=Forecasts.)

b. **Station Identification.** Navigation information is broadcast from a number of stations located within each NAVAREA. Broadcast times as well as transmitter power outputs are carefully designed to avoid interference between stations. Each station is assigned an identification code (B1 character). This is essential so that specific geographical region stations can tune in.

c. **Operation.** Stations are selected by letter designation such as M-Casablanca, I-Las Palmas. The letter Z indicates there are no messages to transit, checks the system and is an operational check message.

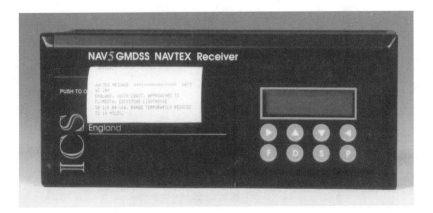

Figure 17-2 Navtex Receiver with Printer, *Courtesy of ICS Electronics*

Format nine characters, header code followed by technical code

ZCZC B1 (transmitter ID) B2 (subject ID), B3, B4 (consecutive number)

Time of origin

Series ID and consecutive number

The message text

NNNN (End of message group)

17.22   VHF Radio. VHF is probably the most useful radio system available. It allows easy ship-to-ship, or ship-to-shore communications. The disadvantage is that the range is line of sight, typically around 35 miles. All countries have licensing regulations that must be adhered to. Failure to comply may result in prosecution and fines. Log on to www.standardhorizon.com.

a.   **Ship Station License.** All VHF installations must possess a station license issued by the appropriate national communications authority, i.e. FCC. On issue of the first license, a call sign is also issued.

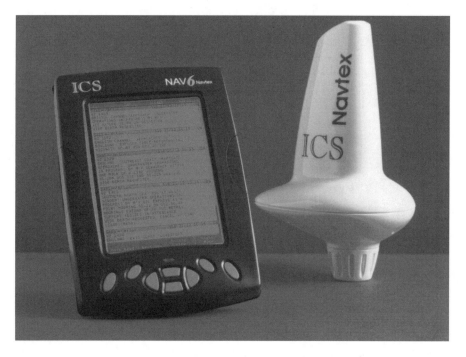

Figure 17-3 Dual Frequency Navtex with LCD Display, *Courtesy of ICS Electronics*

b. **Operator License.** At least one operator, normally the person registering the installation should possess an operator's license or certificate. Under GMDSS and DSC this has changed. In the UK, it is the Short Range Certificate (SRC), similarly the requirements have changed in the US, Canada and Australia. It requires a short one-day course.

17.23 **Theory.** The spectrum consists of 55 channels in the 156-163 MHz band.

a. **Range.** As VHF is line of sight, the higher the two antennas are mounted, the greater the distance. There are theoretical ways to work out the range, but for simplicity I will leave them out. Atmospheric conditions and the installation itself also affect the actual range. Typical range with a coast station is approximately 35–40 nm.

b. **Power Consumption.** Typical units consume 5–6 amps when transmitting. Reception-only consumption can add up as the set is on for 24 hours. This is in the range of 1 to 7 amps. In a day, that can add up to 12–17 amp-hours depending on the set. VHF, however, should be left on regardless of power consumption. The merchant ship that sights you and tries to communicate will do so well before you may be aware of it.

17.24 **VHF Propagation.** VHF signals penetrate the ionosphere rather than reflect. In some circumstances VHF signals can reflect back from the ionosphere to give "freak" long distance communications such as during very strong solar cycles. This occurred during cycle 19 in 1957/58, cycle 21 in 1980 and cycle 22 in 1990. During these peaks, the monthly sunspot average rose to extremely high values and the ionosphere reflected higher frequencies than normal. VHF can also be reflected from clouds of increased ionization in the E layer of the ionosphere, and during auroras, which are the light curtains caused by charged particles from the sun.

17.25 **VHF Operation.** As VHF is widely used by official and commercial operators, it is essential to use your set properly for optimum performance.

a. **Power Setting.** Always use the 1-watt low-power setting for local communications, and the 25-watt high-power for distance contacts.

b. **Squelch Setting.** Squelch reduces the inherent noise in the radio. Do not reduce the squelch too far.

c. **Simplex and Duplex.** Simplex means that talk is carried out on one frequency. Duplex is where transmit and receive are on two separate frequencies.

d. **Dual Watch.** This facility enables continuous monitoring on Channel 16 and the selected channel.

e. **Talk Technique.** Hold the microphone approximately 2 inches from the mouth and speak only slightly louder than normal. Be clear and concise and don't waste words. Many newer sets also incorporate noise-cancelling microphones, which are a good development.

17.26   **Radio Procedure.** After selecting the required channel, use the following procedures. Procedures are valid for coast stations or other vessels:

a.   **Operating Procedure.** Wait until any current call in progress is terminated.
Even if you do not hear speech, listen for dial tones or other signals. Do not
attempt to cut in or talk over conversations. Sometimes traffic may be busy
and patience is required.

(1)   Always identify your vessel and call sign both at the beginning and
end of transmission.

(2)   Keep conversations to a minimum, ideally less than 3 minutes.

(3)   After contact with other vessels, allow at least 10 minutes before
contacting them again.

(4)   Always observe a 3-minute silence period on the hour and half hour.
While it is not essential it is good practice.

b.   **Coast Station Calls.** Operate your transmitter for at least 7-8 seconds when
calling and use the following format:

(1)   Call the coast station 3 times.

(2)   "This is <vessel name & call sign>" and repeat 3 times

(3)   Response will be "Vessel calling <station name> this is <station
name> on Channel <No>." This is usually on VHF 16 or the nominated call channel.

(4)   Response "This is <call sign> my vessel name is <name>."

(5)   State purpose of business, link call, request for information or advice. "Good evening Sir, I wish to make a transfer charge call". "
The number I require is (number)."

(6)   On completion of business, "Thank you <station> this is <vessel
name> over and out, and listening on Channel 16 or <No>."

17.27   **Distress, Safety and Urgency Calls.** Channel 16 should only be used for the following.

a.   **Mayday.** Use of this distress call only under the direst of circumstances,
"grave and imminent danger". Use of the call imposes a general radio silence
on Channel 16 until the emergency is over. Use the following procedure, and
allow time before repeating:

   (1)   "MAYDAY, MAYDAY, MAYDAY."

   (2)   "This is the vessel <name>."

   (3)   "MAYDAY, vessel <name>."

   (4)   "My position is <latitude and longitude, true bearing and distance from known point>."

   (5)   State <Nature of Distress> calmly, clearly and concisely

   (6)   State type of assistance required.

   (7)   Provide additional relevant information including number of people on board.

b.   **Pan-Pan.** (Pronounced pahn-pahn) Use this call to transmit an urgent message regarding the immediate safety of the vessel or crewmember. It takes priority over all traffic except Mayday calls. The call is used primarily in cases of injury or serious illness, or man overboard:

   (1)   "<All Ships>."

   (2)   "PAN PAN, PAN PAN, PAN PAN."

   (3)   "This is the vessel <name>."

   (4)   Await response and transfer to working channel.

c.   **Security.** (Pronounced say-cure-e-tay). For navigational hazards, gale warnings, etc. as follows:

   (1)   "SAY-CURE-E-TAY, SAY-CURE-E-TAY, SAY-CURE-E-TAY."

   (2)   "This is the vessel/station <name>."

   (3)   Pass the safety message.

d.   **Medical Services.** Use this call to advise of an urgent medical emergency. It takes priority over all traffic except Mayday calls.

   (1)   "PAN PAN, PAN PAN, PAN PAN."

   (2)   "RADIOMEDICAL or MEDICO."

   (3)   "This is the vessel <name, call sign, nationality>."

   (4)   "My position is "latitude and longitude. Diverting to <location>."

   (5)   Give patient details, name, age, sex, and medical history. Give present symptoms, advice required, and medication on board.

e.   Phonetic Alphabet

A.	ALFA	N.	NOVEMBER
B.	BRAVO	O.	OSCAR
C.	CHARLIE	P.	PAPA
D.	DELTA	Q.	QUEBEC
E.	ECHO	R.	ROMEO
F.	FOXTROT	S.	SIERRA
G.	GOLF	T.	TANGO
H.	HOTEL	U.	UNIFORM
I.	INDIA	V.	VICTOR
J.	JULIETT	W.	WHISKEY
K.	KILO	X.	X-RAY
L.	LIMA	Y.	YANKEE
M.	MIKE	Z.	ZULU

f.   Phonetic Numbers.

1.	WUN	6.	SIX
2.	TOO	7.	SEVEN
3.	THUH-REE	8.	AIT
4.	FO-WER	9.	NINER
5.	FI-YIV	0.	ZERO

17.28   VHF Frequencies. Rapid growth in cellular phone use has significantly reduced link call activity resulting in the closure of many coast stations. In the US, the Maritel Company (www.maritelusa.com) has bought and opened a private network, and in the future there will be substantial US coastal VHF coverage with automated link call capabilities. This has been a reality for many years in countries such as Australia. In Europe, Channel 06 is used for intership business, Channel 77 is for intership chat only. Where the boat is navigating within Vessel Traffic System (VTS) zones, make sure you have the correct frequencies for contacting control stations. The following are public correspondence channels and weather broadcast information.

    a.   USA GREAT LAKES – CANADA ST. LAWRENCE. The Great Lakes and approaches operate on various frequencies. Call on Channel 16. Channels 24, 26, 27, 28 and 85 are the most often used. Traffic, harbor, port and bridge control usually 11, 12, 13 and Channel 14 for locks. Weather is broadcast continuously on WX1, WX2, WX3. **Buffalo** (Weather 22 0255, 1455); **Rochester** 25, 26; **Ripley** 17, 84, 86; **South Amherst/Lorain** (Weather 17 0002, 1102, 1702, 2302); Erie 25; **Cleveland** 28, 86, 87; **Oregon/Toledo** 17,

Table 17-1 United States & Canada VHF Channels

Channel	Channel Designation
01	Harbor – Ship-to-Ship
02	Harbor – Ship-to-Ship
03	Harbor – Ship-to-Ship
04	Harbor – Ship-to-Ship
05	Harbor – Ship-to-Ship
06	**SAFETY - SAR Communications – Ship-to-Ship**
07	Commercial ship-to-ship
08	Ship-to-Ship Commercial
09	**US Calling Channel (Ship-to-Ship)**
10	Commercial ship-to-ship
11	Harbor – Ship-to-Ship
12	Port operations, traffic advisory, USCG Coast Stations
13	**Bridge and Locks, Ship-to-Ship (1 watt only) Intracoastal Waterway (ICW)** Commercial vessels. No call signs, abbreviated operating procedures only. Maintain dual watch 13 and 16
14	Port Operations - Bridge and Lock Tenders
16	**DISTRESS, SAFETY and CALLING**
18	Commercial ship-to-ship and harbor
19	Commercial ship-to-ship and harbor
20	Port Operations (Duplex)
22	USCG and Marine Information Broadcasts
24	Public telephone – Marine Operator (Duplex)
25	Public telephone – Marine Operator (Duplex)
26	Public telephone – Marine Operator (First priority) (Duplex)
27	Public telephone – Marine Operator (First priority) (Duplex)
28	Public telephone – Marine Operator (First priority) (Duplex)
60-62	Harbor, Public (Duplex)
63	Harbor, ship-to-ship
64	Harbor, Public (Duplex)
65	Port operations ship-to-ship
66	Port operations ship-to-ship
67	(1 watt only)
68	Ship-to-ship and harbor
69	Ship-to-ship and harbor
70	**DIGITAL SELECTIVE CALLING ONLY (DSC)**
71	Ship-to-ship and harbor
72	Ship-to-ship (Non-commercial)
73	Port Operations
74	Port Operations
77	Ship-to-ship
78, 79,80	Ship-to-ship and harbor
81-83	USCG Auxiliary
84	Harbor – ship-to-ship - Public telephone (Duplex)
85	Public telephone (Duplex)
86	Public telephone (Duplex)
87	Public telephone (Duplex)
88	Ship-to-ship
WX1-10	NOAA Weather broadcasts – Receive Only

Table 17-2 International VHF Channels

Channels	Channel Designation
1,2,3,4,5, 7	Public correspondence, port operations, ship-to-ship, movement
6	**SAR,** Ship to ship, movement, public, port operations
8	Public correspondence, port operations, ship-to-ship, movement
9	Public correspondence, port operations, ship-to-ship, movement
10	**SAR,** Ship to ship, movement, public, port operations
11, 12	Public correspondence, port operations, ship-to-ship, movement
13	**Navigation Safety Communications,** ship-to-ship
14	Public correspondence, port operations, ship movement
15	Public correspondence, port operations, ship movement
16	**DISTRESS, SAFETY and CALLING**
17	Public correspondence, port operations, ship movement
18 to 22	Public correspondence, port operations, ship movement
23	Public correspondence, port operations, ship movement
24	Public correspondence ship movement
25 to 28	Public correspondence
60 to 66	Public correspondence
67	**SAR,** ship-to-ship
68, 69	Ship movement, ship-to-ship
70	**DIGITAL SELECTIVE CALLING ONLY (DSC)**
71, 74	Port operations, ship movement
72, 77	Ship to ship
73	**SAR,** Ship to ship, port operations
78, 81	Public correspondence, port operations
79, 80	Ship movement, public correspondence, port operations
82	Public correspondence
83	Public correspondence
84	Public correspondence
85 to 88	Public correspondence

25, 84, 87; **Detroit** 26, 28 (Weather 22 0135, 1335); **Port Huron** 25; **Grand Haven** (Weather 22 0235, 1435); **Harbor Beach** 17, 86, 87; **Bath City** 28; **Spruce** 17, 84, 87; **Frankfort** 28; **Milwaukee** (Weather 22 0255, 1455); **Michigan City** 25; **Chicago** 26, 27; **Port Washington** 17, 85, 87; **Sturgeon Bay** 28; **Hessel** 17, 84, 86; **Sault Sainte Marie** 26 (Weather 22 0005, 1205); **Grand Marais** 28; **Marquette** 28; **Copper Harbor** 86, 87; **Duluth** 28. **ST LAWRENCE:** Most stations 16 and primary channels 24, 26 or 27.

   b.   **GULF of MEXICO:** WLO on Ch 25, 28, 84, 87 with Traffic Lists on the Hour. **St. Petersburg** (Weather 22 1300, 2300); **Marathon** 24; **Naples** 25; **Cape Coral** 26; **Venice** 28; **Palmetto** 25, 27; **Tampa Bay** 86; **Clearwater** 24, 26; **Crystal River** 28; **Cedar Key** 26; **Panama City** 26; **Mobile**

(Weather 22 1020, 12220, 1620, 2220); **Pensacola** 26; **Pascagoula** 27; **Gulfport** 28; **New Orleans** 24, 26, 27, 87 (Weather 22 1035, 1235, 1635, 2235); **Venice** 24, 27, 28, 86; **Leeville** 25, 85; **Houma** 28, 86; **Morgan City** 24, 26; **Lake Charles** 28, 84; **Port Arthur** 26, 27; **Galveston** 25, 86, 87 (Weather 22 1050, 1250, 1650, 2250); **Port Lavaca** 26, 85; **Corpus Christi** 26, 28 (Weather 22 1040, 1240, 1640, 2240); **South Padre Island** 26.

c. **ATLANTIC COAST: Southwest Harbor** 28 (Weather 22 1135, 2335); **Camden** 26, 27, 84; **Portland** 24, 28 (Nav 22 1105, 2305); **New Hampshire** 28; **Gloucester** 25; **Boston** 26, 27 (Weather 22 1035, 2235); **Hyannis** 28, 84; **Nantucket** 27, 85, 86; **Woods Hole** (Weather 22 1005, 2205); **New Bedford** 24, 26, 87; **Providence** 27, 28; **Bridgeport** 27; **Riverhead** 28; **Long Island Sound** (Weather 22 1120, 2320); **Bay Shore** 85; **Moriches** (Weather 22 0020, 1220); **New York** 25, 26, 84 (Weather 22 1050, 2250); **Sandy Hook** 24 (Weather 22 1020, 2220); **Bayville** 27; **Atlantic City** 26; **Cape May** (Weather 22 1103, 2303); **Philadelphia** 26; **Wilmington** 28; **Dover** 84; **Delaware Bay** 27; **Salisbury** 86; **Cambridge** 28; **Baltimore** 24 (Nav 22 0130, 1205); **Point Lookout** 26; **Norfolk** 25, 26, 27, 84; **Hampton** 25, 26, 27, 84; **Georgetown** 24; **Charleston** 26 (Weather 22 1200, 2200); **Savannah** 27, 28; **Brunswick** 24; **Jacksonville** 26; **Daytona Beach** 28; **Cocoa** 26; **Vero Beach** 27; **West Palm Beach** 28, 85; **Boca Raton** 84; **Fort Lauderdale** 26, 84; **Miami** 24, 25 (Weather 22 1230, 2230); **Miami Beach** 85; **Homestead** 27, 28; **Key West** 24, 84 (Weather 22 1200, 2200).

d. **PACIFIC COAST (CANADA –CG)): Vancouver** 26; **Van Inlet, Barry Inlet, Rose Inlet, Holberg, Port Hardy, Alert Bay, Eliza Dome, Cape Lazo, Watts Pt., Lulu Is., Mt. Parke, Port Alberni** 26 Dundas; **My Hayes, Klemtu, Cumshewa, Naden Harbour, Calvert, Nootka, Mt Helmcken, Mt. Newton, Bowen Is., Texada, Discovery Mt** 84. Weather continuous broadcast on WX1, WX2, WX3, 21B.

e. **PACIFIC COAST (USA): Bellingham** 28, 85; **Camano Is.** 24; **Seattle** 25, 26 (Weather 22 CG 0630, 1830); **Tacoma** 28; **Cosmopolis** 28; **Astoria** 24, 26 (Nav 22 CG 053, 1733); **Portland** (Nav 22 CG 1745); **Newport** 28; **Coos Bay** 25; **Brookings** 27; **Humboldt Bay** (Weather 22 CG 1615, 2315); **Casper** 28; **Point Reyes** 25; **San Francisco** 26, 84, 87; **Santa Cruz** 27; **Monterey** 28 (Weather 22 CG 1615, 2345); **Long Beach** (Weather 22 CG 0203, 1803); **Santa Barbara** 22, 86; **Avalon/San Pedro** 24, 26; **San Diego** 28, 86 (Nav 22 CG 0103, 1703).

17.29 CARIBBEAN

a. **MEXICO. Chetumal** 26, 26; **Cozumel** 26, 27; **Cancun** 26, 27; **Veracruz** 26, 27. Channel 68 is for local cruiser nets.

b. **BERMUDA.** 27, 28. Coastal forecasts on Channels 10, 12, 16, 27, 38 at 1235 and 2035.

c. **BAHAMAS. Nassau** 16, 27; **8 Mile Rock** 27; **Exuma** 22 CG; **Marsh Harbor** 16. Forecasts every odd hour Channel 27. Cruisers Net operates on Channel 68 at 0815 with weather forecasts, etc.

d. **CAYMAN ISLANDS.** Radio Cayman 1205, 89.9, 105.3 at 0320, 1130, 1220, 1230, 1330, 1710, 2320.

e. **JAMAICA. Kingston** 16, 26, 27. Forecasts for SW, NW, and Eastern Caribbean, and Jamaica coastal waters forecast at 0130, 1430, and 1900 on Channel 13.

f. **PUERTO RICO (USCG).** 16 **Santurce** 16, 26. NOAA forecasts broadcast continuously on VHF WX2 and VHF 22 at 1210 and 2210.

g. **VIRGIN ISLANDS (US). St. Thomas** 16, 24, 25, 28, 84, 85, 87, 88. Forecast West North Atlantic, Caribbean and Gulf of Mexico on Channel 28 at 0000 & 1200. Channels 16, 24, 25, 28 (Traffic Lists), 84, 85, 87 and 88.

h. **VIRGIN ISLANDS (UK). Tortola** 16, 27. Weather on ZBVI Radio 780 at 0805, and every H+30 0730-1630, 1830-2130 LT.

i. **WINDWARD ISLANDS. Martinique (Fort-de-France), Guadaloupe** 16, 11. Warnings on receipt odd H+33 and VHF 26 and 27 every odd H+30. Weather messages VHF 26 and 27 at 0330 and 1430.

j. **BARBADOS.** 16, 26. Forecasts at 0050, 1250, 1650, 2050. Warnings on receipt and every 4 hours for Caribbean, Antilles, Atlantic waters on Channel 26.

k. **GRENADA. St. George's** 16, 06, 11, 12, 13, 22A. Forecast on request.

l. **TRINIDAD and TOBAGO.** 16, 24, 25, 26, 27. Forecast at 1340 and 2040.

17.30 EUROPE, UK, MEDITERRANEAN

a. **UK.** Gale and strong wind warnings on receipt and every 2 hours. Local nav warning on receipt. Shipping forecast times are in brackets and italics. MSI transmitted for Southern Region at 0733 and 1933 on **N.Foreland, Humber, Start Point** 26; **Orfordness, Pendennis** 62; **Thames** 02 *(0810, 2010);* **Hastings, Bacton,** 07; **Niton** 28; **Weymouth, Ifracombe** 05; **Lands End, Grimsby** 27; **Lands End (Scilly Is.)** 64; **Celtic** 24. Northern Region at 0703 & 1903 for **Wick, Cromarty** 28; **Shetland, Portpatrick** 27; **Orkney, Stonehaven, Cullercoats, Anglesey, Clyde** 26 *(0820, 2020)*; **Buchan, Whitby, Islay** 25; **Forth, Skye** 24. HMCG broadcast MSI on 10 & 73 after call on 16. This is changing (2000/2001) to Channel 26 and 83; HMCG **Falmouth** 26, 83 (0940, 2140); **Dover** 26, 83 (0940, 2140); **Solent** 26, 83 (0840, 2040).

b. **UK Weather – BBC Radio 4.** 24 hr forecast for coastal areas at 0048, 0535, 1201, 1754 on 198kHz. Also 92.4–94.6 MHz 0556; Sundays at 0542 after shipping forecast. Forecasts long wave for **Trafalgar, Finisterre, Biscay** on 198khz at 0048, 0555, 1201, 1750.

c. **NETHERLANDS.** VHF 13 is for intership communications. 24 hour watch on **Schiermonnikoog** 5; **Brandaris** 5; **Den Helder** 12; **IJmuiden** 88; **Scheveningen** 21; **Hoek van Holland** 1, 3; **Ouddorp** 74; **Vlissingen** 14, 64. Weather forecasts for Dutch Coastal Waters and IJsselmeer at 08.05, 13.05 and 23.05 local time. (Local Time is UTC + 2 hrs March to October and UTC +1 October to March). Gale warnings and safety messages are on Channel 23 and 83, after prior announcements on Channel 16. Scheduled broadcast times are at 03.33, 07.33, 11.33, 15.33, 19.33 and 23.33 UTC.

d. **IRELAND.** Forecast on **Valentia** at 0103 and every 3 hours to 2203 on Channel 24. **Malin Head** on Channel 23 for **Fastnet, Shannon** and Irish coastal waters. Valentia MF on ITU Channels 278 and 280, Malin Head on ITU Ch 244 and Ch 255.

e. **CHANNEL ISLANDS (Jersey).** Weather at 0645, 0745, 1245, 1845, 2245 on Channels 25, 82.

f. **FRANCE.** Weather bulletins all in French. Storm, Gale and Nav Warnings (times in brackets) in English and French. **Gris-Nez 79** (H+03); **Jobourg** 80 (H+03); **Corsen** 79 (H+03): **Etel** 80 (H+03), **Soulac** 16, 15, 67, 68, 73; **Agde, LaGarde, Corsica** 16, 11, 67, 68, 73; Monaco 16, 20, 22, 23, 86. Weather 0903, 1403, 1915.

g. **SPAIN.** Weather channel and time in brackets. **Bilbao** 26 **Santander** 24 (Ch11 @ 0245, 0645, 1045, 1445, 1845, 2245; **Cabo Peñas** 26 **Coruña** 26 (Ch26 @ 0803, 0833, 2003, 2033); **Finisterre** 01, 02 (Ch11 @ 0233 every 4 hrs); **Cádiz** 26 **Tarifa** 82 (Ch10, 74 @ 0900, 2100); **Málaga** 26 **Cabo Gata** 27 **Almeria** (Ch10, 74 @ every H+15); **Cartagena** 04 **Alicante** 01 **Valencia** (Ch10 @ every even Hr +15); **Algeciras** (Ch15, 74 @ 0315, 0515, 0715, 1115, 1515, 1915, 2315; **Ibiza** 03 **Palma** 07 **Menorca** 87 **Las Palmas.** Weather Forecast on 04, 05, 26, 28 at 0903, 1203 and 1803. **Arrecife** 25 **Fuerteventura** 22, 64 **Tenerife** 27 **La Palma** 22.

h. **PORTUGAL: Arga** 25, 28, 83; **Arestal** 24, 26, 85; **Monsanto** (Ch11 @ 0250, 0650, 1050, 1450, 1850, 2250); **Montejunto** 23, 27, 87; **Lisboa** 23, 25, 26, 27, 28; **Atalaia** 24, 26, 85; **Picos** 23, 27, 85; **Estoi** 24, 28, 86; **Sagres** (Ch11 @ 0835. 2035); **Acores.** Forecast on 16, 23, 26, 27, 28 at 0935 & 2135. **Madeira** 25, 26, 27, 28.

i. **ITALY: (Sardinia) Monte Serpeddi** 04 **Margine Rosso** 62 **Porto Cervo** 26; (West Coast): **Monte Bignone** 07 **Castellaccio** 25 **Zoagli** 27 **Gorgona** 26 **Monte Argentario** 01 **Monte Cavo** 25 (West Coast/Sicily): **Posillipo** 01 **Capri** 27 **Sera del Tuono** 25 **Forte Spuria** 88 **Cefal** 61 **Ustica** 84 **Erice** 81 **Pantelleria** 88 **Mazarra del Vallo** 25 **Gela** 26 **Siracusa** 85 **Campo Lato Altoi** 86 **Lampedusa Ponente** 25 **Crecale** 87 **Capa Armi** 62 **Ponta Stilo** 84 **Capo Colonna** 88 **Monte Parano** 26 **Abate Argento** 05 **Bari** 27 **Monte Calvario** 01; (Adriatic). **Silivi** 65 **Monte Secco** 87 **Forte Garibaldi** 25 **Ravenna** 27 **Monte Cero** 26 **Piancavallo** 01 **Conconello** 83. (Weather bulletins on Channel 68 @ 0135, 0735, 1335, 1935; Nav and gale warnings on receipt and H+03 & H+33, continuous broadcast in Northern Adriatic).

j.   **CROATIA. Senj, Pula, Zadar** 10, 16 **Rijeka** 04, 16, 20, (24) 0535, 1435, 1935; **Split 16**, 21 (0545, 1245, 1945); **Dubrovnik** 07, 63, (04) (0625, 1320, 2120); Channels 67, 69, and 73 have continuous weather forecasts for Northern and Central Adriatic Sea updated three times per day in English.

k.   **GREECE. Kerkyra** (02) 03, 64; **Kefallinia** 26, (27), 28; **Koryfu** 87; **Petalidi** 23, (83), 84; **Kythira** (85), 86; **Poros** 27, 28, 88; **Gerania** 02, 64; **Perama (Piraeus)** 25, 26, 86, 87; **Parnis** (25), 61, 62; **Lichada** 01; **Pilio** 03, (60); **Sfendami** (23), 24; **Tsoukalas** 26, 27; **Thasos** 25, 85; **Limnos** (82), 83; **Mytilini** (01), 02; **Chios** 85 **Andros** 24 **Syros** 03, (04) **Patmos** 84 **Milos** 82 **Thira** 26, 87; **Kythira** 85, 86; **Astypalea** 23 **Rodos** 01, (63) **Karpathos** 03 **Sitia** (85), 86; **Faistos** 26, 27; **Moystakos** 04 **Knossos** (83), 84. Hellas Channels in parentheses at 0600, 1000, 1600, 2200. Hellas Channel 86 has Wx Bulletin from Perama.

l.   **TURKEY. Akcakoca** 01, 23 **Keltepe** 02, 24, 82 **Sarkoy** 05, 27 **Camlica** 03, 07, 25, 28 **Mahyadagi** 04, 26 **Kayalidag** 01, 23 **Akdag** 02, 24, 28 **Izmir** 16, 04, 24 **Antalya** 25, 27 **Dilektepe** 03, 07, 25 **Palamut** 04, 05, 26 **Yumrutepe** 01, 23 **Anamur** 03, 25 **Cobandede** 02, 26 **Markiz** 02, 24.

m.   **CYPRUS. Olympos** 16, 26, 24, 25, 26 **Kionia, Pissouri, Lara** 25, 26, 27.

n.   **MALTA.** 01, 02, 03, 04, 16, 28. Traffic Lists on 04.

17.31   AUSTRALIA AND NEW ZEALAND. VHF coast stations and supplementary safety channels. Primary channels are given first. The asterisk denotes Autocall channel only. All stations monitor 16 and 67.

a.   **New Zealand. Kaitaia** 71 **Whangarei** 67 **Great Barrier Is.** 68, 71 **Auckland** 71 **Plenty** 68 **Runaway** 71 **Tolaga** 67 **Napier** 68 **Taranaki** 67 **Wairarapa** 67 **Wellington** 71 **Picton** 68 **Farewell** 68 **D'Urville** 67 **Kaikoura** 67; **Westport** 71; **Greymouth** 68; **Akaroa** 68; **Fox** 67; **Waitaki** 67 **Fiordland** 71 **Chalmers** 71 **Bluff** 68 **Puysegur** 67.

b.   **Australia**

    (1)   **Darwin Radio (VID). Darwin** 23, 2 **Gove** 28.

    (2)   **Townsville Radio (VIT). Darnley Is.** 60 **Torres Strait** 26 *23 **Thursday Is.** *66 **Cooktown** 61 **Cairns** 27, 24 **Townsville** 26,23 **Ayr/Home Hill** 60 **Whitsunday Is.** 26, 28, *25, *83, 86 **Shute Harbour** 66 **Mackay** 65 **Yeppoon** 61.

    (3)   **Brisbane Radio (VIB). Port Clinton/Keppel Is.** 01, *04 **Gladstone/Bundaberg** 27, *24 **Fraser Is.** 62 **Sunshine Coast** 28, *25 **Brisbane** 02 **Gold Coast/Tweed Heads** 26, 87, *23, *84 **Coffs Harbour** 27, *24.

(4) **Sydney Radio (VIS). Camden Haven** 62 **Port Stephens/Newcastle** 28, *25 **Newcastle/Lake Macquarie** 01 **Hawkesbury River** 02, 60, 05, 66 **Sydney** 26, *23, *63 **Sydney Sth/Wollongong** 88, *86 **Nowra** 27 **Eden** 86.

(5) **Melbourne Radio (VIM). Lakes Entrance** 27, *24 **Wilsons Prom** 60 **Westernport/Port Phillip Bay** 26, *23 **Adelaide** 26, *23 **Kangaroo Is.** 61 **Pt. Lincoln** 27, *24. Tasmania: **Devonport** 28 **Hobart** 07 **Bruny Is.** 27, *24 **St Mary's** 26.

(6) **Perth Radio (VIP). Perth** 26, 23 **Rottnest Is.** 60 **Jurien Bay** 62 **Geraldton** 28, 25 **Dampier** 26 **Broome** 28.

17.32   SOUTH AFRICA and NAMIBIA. Capetown. Forecasts at 1333, 0948, 1748, on Channels 01, 04, 23, 25, 26, 27, 84, 85 and 8. **Kosi Bay** 01 **Sodwana Bay** 03 **Cape S Lucia** 25 **Richards Bay** 28, 24 **Durban** 01, 26 **Mazeppa Bay** 28 **East London** 26 **Port Elizabeth** 87 **Kynsna** 23 **Albertinia** 86, 03 **Capetown** 01, 25 **Saldanha** 27 **Doringbaai** 87 **Port Nolloth** 01 **Alexander Bay** 04 **Walvis Bay** 16, 23, 26, 27.

17.33   VHF Aerials. The majority of motorboats use whip aerials. Trawler yachts and motor sailing vessels may use a masthead-mounted aerial to achieve maximum height. The aerial length is directly related to the aerial gain, and the higher the gain, the narrower the transmission beam. A high gain antenna has a greater range, but during vessel rolling and pitching the lower gain antenna is more reliable with a greater coverage pattern. Half-wave whip aerials are typified by the stainless steel rod construction. The radiation pattern has a large vertical component, which suits boats under heel conditions. These antennas can also come in the form of a whip with lengths varying between 1 to 3 meters. The fiberglass whip effectively increases the height, and therefore the range of the radiating element. The gain is typically 3 dB. Helical aerials have a gain slightly less at 2.5 dB, but do have a characteristically wider signal beamwidth. The higher the gain, the more directional the emitted signal becomes. Motorboats usually have 6 dB aerials as they are more directional. The vessels and the aerials are normally vertical as there is roll and pitching, but not a permanent heel as in sailing boats.

17.34   Aerial Cables and Connections. Cables and bad connections are the principal causes of degraded performance. Avoid using thin RG58U coaxial cable where possible as the attenuation is increased and large signal losses can occur. The amount of signal that is transmitted depends on low losses within the cable and the connections. For cabling aerials always use RG213/U or RG8/U 50 ohms to minimize attenuation. Ensure that the cable has no sharp bends that may affect the attenuation of the cable. The typical cable attenuation of both types for a 100-foot run is:

a. **RG58/U.** This is a nominal 7.1 dB, a signal loss of approximately 75-80%.

b. **RG8/U and RG8/X (RG213/U).** This is a nominal 2.6 dB, a signal loss of approximately 45%.

17.35   VHF Installation Testing. Many vessel VHF installations operate poorly, with often undiagnosed problems. Many boaters install their own cables, connectors, and aerials, but in the majority of cases the installation is never tested. If the maximum range is to be realized, then the installation requires proper testing. With the increasing reliance on new technology, in particular, with DSC type VHF units, reliability is of critical importance. In an earlier chapter I highlighted the importance of installing the correct coaxial cable to reduce losses. The attenuation inherent within the cable is only part of the loss equation, and the following should be observed.

Voltage Standing Wave Ratio (VSWR). When a signal is transmitted via the cable and aerial, a portion of that signal energy will be reflected back to the transmitter. The effect is that coverage is reduced due to the reduced power output. Measure the VSWR with a meter. Up until recently you had to hire a technician to bring along an expensive meter (I am fortunate to possess a Bird meter), but you can now use a Shakespeare meter, the ART-1. This allows easy fault diagnosis and timely repairs, and is highly recommended. A number of problems can reduce the VSWR. Regular testing of reflected power and detection of excessive values will alert you to potential installation problems. It may even save your life.

(1)   **Damaged or Cut Ground Shields.** This is common where the cable has been jointed, or improperly terminated at the connector. Make sure the shield is properly prepared and installed.

(2)   **Dielectric Faults.** This common problem occurs when cables are run tightly around corners, through bulkheads, and through cable glands. Make sure that cables are bent with a relatively large radius. The tighter the bend the more dielectric narrowing will occur with increased reflected power.

(3)   **Pinched Cable.** This common problem occurs where a cable has not been properly passed through a bulkhead with the gland or connector. This impinges on the cable and reduces the dielectric diameter. Radio waves pass along the outside of the central core and along the inner side of the braiding, so any deformation will alter the inductance and reduce power output.

(4)   **Connector Faults.** The most common problem is that of connectors not being installed or assembled correctly. Ensure that connectors are properly tightened. Pins must be properly inserted, and the pin-to-cable solder joint must be good and not a dry joint. Ensure that shield seals are properly made. Many connectors appear good at the time of assembly, but deteriorate very quickly when exposed to rain, salt spray and corrosion. Check the status with a multimeter between the core and screen for short circuits.

(5)   **Antenna Faults.** If an antenna is out of specification or suffered storm damage, or if a new antenna has been damaged in transit, the functional efficiency will decrease and losses increase. Inspect the antenna and connectors regularly. I always wrap the aerial connection with self-amalgamating tape to reduce ingress of moisture and salt air.

Communications

18.1   Cellular Telephones. The rapid development of the mobile cellular telephone has made personal communications in coastal waters much easier. Many of us are fortunate to be able to utilize GSM technology. I can use my phone offshore and in more than 30 countries. This technology has not been without a price. The rapid drop in placement of link calls has meant the closure of many coastal stations and repeaters. I have received some interesting calls: on one occasion I had a call from a motorboat regarding a charging problem. After enquiring about the boat location, I was informed that it was 2000 miles to the north, and 10nm offshore. On another occasion a skipper in a major offshore yacht race called me during the race and described his problem; we nursed him to the finish line. More recently there have been text message SOS calls from Indonesia to the UK setting off SAR via Australia, and people in life rafts calling for help. The cell phone must be put into perspective and it must be emphasized that it is not a substitute for VHF or HF marine communications systems.

18.2   Distress and Cellular Phones. There are many reasons why cell phones are not good for distress. A vessel in distress cannot communicate with other potential rescue vessels in the area. This has the effect of delaying rescues considerably, it uses greater resources and increases the risks to all involved. If you are in distress, you simply may be placed on hold and not get through to an appropriate authority, or you may be at the outside of the cell range and drop out repeatedly. Vessels in distress who cannot provide exact position information cannot be located using VHF direction-finding (DF) equipment. Vessels in distress cannot activate priority distress alert using cell phones. Rescue scene communications can be severely disrupted because normal cell phone communications can only occur between two parties. Most rescue vessels and SAR aircraft do not have cellular phones. These communication problems and resulting message exchanges have the potential to cause disruptions or delays to the extent that a safe rescue opportunity is lost with catastrophic results. It is worth noting that a number of system operators have introduced services for vessel cellular phone users. Bell Atlantic in the US offers direct contact with the Coast Guard (press star key followed by "C" and "G").

18.3   Coverage. If you use your cellular phone on coastal trips, you will have a few problems with dropouts. The problems will occur at the outer range of the transmission cell, and this is more pronounced at sea. Range is typically 8 miles, which is a lot less than VHF. If you really need to use a cellular phone regularly, install an external aerial for maximum range. Many lament the passing of analog to digital, as range was better. If you wish to install a set on board, it is worth considering buying a higher 8-watt set such as that from Motorola. Install it to the vessel power supply and add an external whip aerial to maximize range and power. It is also worth considering a dual or tri-band phone to maximize operational range.

18.4   SIM Card Change Outs. Global roaming rates are not cheap. If you are in one place for any length of time, and make lots of local calls, consider buying a pay-as-you go SIM card and number. This offers real long-term savings in most countries. I have found it the ideal solution in Europe.

18.5   Text Messages. For locations within reach of GSM, short text messages are a useful low-cost way of staying in touch. Make sure you can both send and receive text messages if you intend using this method. I have had problems in some European areas. In some cases the memory will fill quickly, so messages must be deleted to ensure you don't lose the new ones.

18.6   SSB/HF Radio. While HF is part of GMDSS, a number of boaters keep using sets without the capability, in particular for e-mail and weatherfax. Long-range radio communications depend on radio frequencies in the High Frequency (HF) spectrum of 2 to 24 mHz. Log on to www.sea-dmi.com, www.icomamerica.com.

> **a.   Signal Propagation.** Skywaves travel up until they reach the ionosphere and are bent and reflected back over a wide area. The ionosphere exists at a height of 30 to 300 miles (50km–500km) above the earth, and is formed by the ionization of air atoms by incoming UV ionizing radiation from the sun. The ionosphere is a weakly ionized plasma that is constantly changing and these changes alter the propagation characteristics of the radio waves. This is typified by the differences in night and day time transmission characteristics. Good HF communications depend on the utilization of these changing conditions with use of optimum frequencies. The ionosphere structure is divided into layers which are D, E, F1 and F2 in order of increasing height. There is a software package called HFProp, which is useful for predicting optimum transmission times worldwide.
>
> > **(1)   F Layer.** The main reflecting layer is called the F layer and is approximately 200 mile (320 km) high. The layer is permanently ionized but, during daylight hours, energy from the sun causes the intervening layers E and D to form, and at night these reflects the highest radio frequencies in the HF bands.
> >
> > **(2)   E and D Layers.** The signals reflected from these layers have lower ranges. Frequencies of 3 mHz or less are absorbed by the D layer, eliminate skywave propagation, and therefore 2 mHz is not favored.
> >
> > **(3)   Ground Wave.** Ground wave signals travel along the earth's surface but are absorbed or masked by other radio emissions.
> >
> > **(4)   Skip Zone.** The skip zone is the area between the transmission zone and zone where the signal returns to earth. The skip zones generally have negligible signal.
>
> **b.   Propagation Changes.** The ionosphere will affect each frequency differently. Extreme Ultra-Violet EUV radiation is responsible for forming and maintaining the ionosphere and depends on solar sunspot activity. When sunspot activity is lowest, the solar cycle EUV radiation is also weak and the density of charged particles in the F region is also lowest. In this state, only lower frequency HF signals can be reflected. At sunspot cycle peaks, the EUV and ionosphere density are high and therefore higher frequencies can be reflected. The season, time of day, and the latitude also affect HF radio

communications. Solar flares produce high levels of electromagnetic radiation, and the X-ray component increases the D layer ionization. As HF communications use the F layer above, they must transit the D layer twice during any signal skips. During a major solar flare, the increased ionization results in a higher density of neutral particles and absorption of signal in the D layer. This is called sudden ionosphere disturbance (SID). It is characterized by increased attenuation of HF signals at lower frequencies. The disturbance is called short wave fadeout, SSWF for a sudden fadeout and GSWF for a gradual one. These events are synchronized with solar flare patterns. They are characterized by rapid onsets of just several minutes and declines of up to an hour or greater.

18.7   Space Weather Effects and HF Radio. Space weather has become very important in the satellite communications age. The underlying factor ruling space weather, at least in this end of the galaxy, is our sun. The sun is by nature prone to dramatic and violent changes with events such as solar flares. The results are blast streams of radiation and energized particles that stream towards earth. Space weather is caused by changes in the speed or density of the solar wind, and this is the continuous flow of charged particles that flow from the sun past the earth. The flow tends to distort the earths' magnetic field, compressing it in the direction of the sun and stretching it out in the opposite direction. The solar wind fluctuations cause variations in the strength and direction of the magnetic field near the earth's surface. Sudden variations are called geomagnetic disturbances. The electrical layers of the ionosphere are disrupted.

18.8   Solar Cycles. Space weather depends on an 11-year solar cycle. Cycles vary in both intensity and length, and the solar activity is characterized by the appearance of sunspots on the sun. Sunspots are regions of stronger magnetic field, and the solar maximum is the time when maximum spot numbers are visible. Sunspot numbers are quoted for average numbers over a 12-month period, and are the traditional measure of solar cycle status. Peak sunspot like highest rainfall is that for recorded worst cases, and 5 of the last 6 have been of high magnitudes. Cycle 19 in 1957 peak had a sunspot number of 201, and was largest on record. Cycle 21 in 1979 had a peak sunspot number of 165 and was the second largest. Cycle 22 in 1989 was the third largest. At present it is in a rising phase, with Cycle 23 predictions of a large amplitude number in 2000 of 165 or greater. This means a 5-year period of disruption.

Frequency Preferences. The best ocean frequencies are on 4 mHz with ranges of up to 300 miles in day conditions, and thousands of miles at night without static at 2 mHz. The principal characteristics are:

(1)   **Sunset.** At sunset, the lower layer ionization decreases, and the D layer will disappear.

(2)   **Dusk.** At dusk, range increases on 2 mHz over thousands of miles, almost instantaneously. The interference levels are dramatically reduced.

377

(3) **Night.** The reflecting layer of the ionosphere rises at night, increasing the ranges for 4–6 mHz so lower frequencies are best at night. High frequencies are not good at night.

(4) **Day.** Low frequencies are weak during daytime. High frequencies are used in the daytime.

Table 18-1 SSB Optimum Transmission Times

Frequency (MHz)	Sunrise 0600	Noon 1200	Sunset 1800	Midnight 2400
22000	Average 100-2000 nm	Good 2000 nm plus	Good 2000 nm plus	Average 100-2000 nm
12000	Good 2000 nmplus	Good 2000 nmplus	Good 2000 nmplus	Good 2000 nmplus
8000	Good 2000 nmplus	Average 100-2000 nm	Average 100-2000 nm	Good 2000 nmplus
6000	Good 2000 nmplus	Average 100-2000 nm	Average 100-2000 nm	Good 2000 nmplus
4000	Average 100-2000 nm	Bad 50 nm	Bad 50 nm	Good 2000 nmplus
2000	Good 2000 nmplus	Bad 50 nm	Bad 50 nm	Good 2000 nmplus

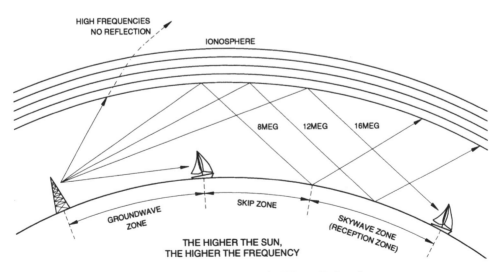

Figure 18-1 HF Radio Wave Behavior

18.9 **Operation Requirements.** There are certain legal requirements and operational procedures to observe.

  a. **Ship Station Licensing.** Every vessel must have a license issued by the relevant communications authority. Transmitters must also be of a type approved by the appropriate authority. The issued call sign and vessel name must be used with all transmissions.

  b. **Operator Licensing.** An operator's certificate is required and a test is given that covers knowledge of distress and safety procedures, as well as related marine communications matters.

18.10 **HF Radio Frequencies and Bands.** Always consult a current list of radio signals. The UK Admiralty List of Radio Signals (ALRS) is by far the most accurate, so invest in the relevant volume for any world location.

  a. **Listen to Station.** If you can hear traffic clearly on the band, you will probably have relatively good communications on that band.

  b. **Monitor Bands.** Monitor the various bands and channels and determine the best peak period for communications. If the signal strength is good but the channel is busy, use a second channel if available, or wait. Do not tune equipment while a call is in progress.

  c. **Station Identification.** Have name, call sign, position, and accounting code ready for the operator if required.

18.11 **United States SSB Weather Frequencies.** USCG CAMSPAC (Master Station Pacific) Honolulu (NMO) and Point Reyes (NMC) have very good weather transmissions.

Table 18-2 US Coast Guard Channels

ITU Channel Number	Receive Frequency	Transmit Frequency
	2182.0	
424	4426.0	4134.0
601	6501.0	6200.0
816	8764.0	8240.0
1205	13089.0	12242.0
1625	17314.0	16432.0

18.12   US, Canadian and Caribbean Frequencies. Weather and working frequencies with Navtex transmissions with the B1 Character in brackets.

a.   UNITED STATES

(1)   Point Reyes (NMC) (MMSI 003669905)

Frequencies	4426, 8764, 13089, 17314.
Weather	0430, 1030 on 4426 and 8764. 1630, 2230 on 13089 and 17314.
Navtex (C)	0000, 0400, 0800, 1200, 1600, 2000.

(2)   Mobile (WLO) www.wloradio.com

Frequencies	2182, 2572, 4343, 4369, 6416, 8514, 8713, 13179, 17380. ITU Channels 405, 836, 829, 1235, 1647, 2246.
Weather	Forecasts at 0000, 0600, 1200, 1800.
Navtex (G)	0300, 0700, 1100, 1500, 1900, 2300.

(3)   Miami (NMA)

Frequencies	2670 and VHF 22A.
Weather	Forecasts at 0350, 1550.
Navtex (A)	0000, 0400, 0800, 1200, 1600, 2000.

(4)   Boston (NMF)

Frequencies	2670 and VHF 22A.
Weather	Forecasts at 1035, 2235.
Navtex (F)	0445, 0845, 1245, 1645, 2045, 0045.

(5)   Charleston (NMB)

Frequencies	2670 and VHF 22A.
Weather	Forecasts at 0420, 1620.
Navtex (E)	0040, 0440, 0840, 1240, 1640, 2040.

(6)   Galveston (NOY)

Frequencies	2670 and VHF 22A.
Weather	Forecasts at 1050, 1250, 1650, 2250.

(7)   Honolulu. (USCG) (MMSI 003669990)

Frequencies	2182, 6501, 8764, 13089 ITU 424, 601, **816, 1205.**
Navtex (O)	0040, 0440, 0840, 1240, 1640, 2040.
Weather	0600, 1200, (6501, 8764), 0005, 1800 (8764, 13089) 0330, 1730 (8416.5, 22376).

b. **CANADA**

(1) **Prince Rupert (VAJ)**

Frequencies   2054.

Weather   0105, 0705, 1305, 1905.

Navtex (D)   0030, 0430, 08030, 1630, 2030.

(2) **Tofino (VAE)**

Frequencies   2054, 4125.

Weather   0050, 0500, 0650, 1250, 1730, 1850, 2330.

Navtex (H)   0110, 0910, 1310, 1710, 2110.

(3) **St. Lawrence (St Johns, Halifax, Sydney Placentia, Port Aux Basques, Riviere-au-Renard, S.Anthony)**

Frequencies   1514, 2538, 2582. Traffic lists on 2749, 2582.

(4) **Fundy (VAR) (MMSI 003160015)**

Frequencies   2182, 2749.

Weather/Nav   0140, 1040, 1248, 1625, 1730, 1948, 2020.

Navtex (U)   0320, 0720, 1120, 1520, 1920, 2320.

(5) **Sydney (VCO)**

Frequencies   2182, 2749.

Weather/Nav   0033, 0733, 1433, 1503, 2133.

Navtex (Q)   0255, 0655, 1055, 1455, 1855, 2255.

(6) **Riviere-au-Renard (VCG)**

Frequencies   2182, 2598, 2749.

Weather/Nav   0437, 0847, 0937, 1407, 1737.

Navtex (C)   0020, 0420, 0820, 1220, 1620, 2020.

c. **CARIBBEAN**

(1) **Bermuda (Bermuda Harbor) (MMSI 003100001)**

Frequencies   2182, **2582** (ITU 410, 603, 817, 1220, 1618).

Weather   Coastal forecast 1235, 2035 on www.weather.bm.

Navtex   0010, 0410, 0810, 1210, 1610, 2010.

(2)   Bahamas (Nassau)

Frequencies   2182, *2522*, *2588*, **2522**/2126.

Weather   Forecasts every odd hour on 2522, storm and hurri-cane warnings are issued on receipt. Radio Bahamas 1540/1240/810, and 107.9-MHz broadcast detailed shipping weather reports M-F at 1205 hrs. Daily weather messages/synopsis 0815, 1315 and 1845 hrs.

(3)   Jamaica (Kingston)

Frequencies   2182, 2587, *2590*, 3535 ITU 405, 416, 605, 812, 1224.

Weather   Coast Guard on 2738 kHz at 1330, 1830 hrs for SW, NW, and Eastern Caribbean, and Jamaica coastal waters forecast. Radio Jamaica on Montego Bay 550/104.5. Weather messages M-F 0015, 0340, 1104, 1235, 1709, and 2004 hrs. Jamaica B.C. on 560/620.700/93.3 MHz, fishing and weather fore-cast M-F 2248 hrs.

(4)   Puerto Rico (USCG) San Juan

Frequencies   2182, *2670* (Santurce) 2182, 2530.

Weather   Forecast at 0030, and 1430.

Navtex (R)   0200, 0600, 1000, 1400, 1800, 2200.

(5)   US Virgin Islands (St Thomas)

Frequencies   2182, **2506**/2009 ITU   401, 604, 605, 804, 809, 1201, 1202, 1602, 1603, 2223.

Weather   Forecast West North Atlantic, Caribbean and Gulf of Mexico on 2506 at 0000 and 1200. Also at 1400, 1600, 1800 and 2000 forecasts for Virgin Islands Eastern Caribbean. Virgin Islands Radio on VHF 28, 85 at 0600, 1400, 2200. Detailed Caribbean Weather reports. WIVI FM 99.5 MHz 0730, 0830, 1530 and 1630.

(6)   Curacao (Netherlands Antilles)

Frequencies   2182, 8725.1.

Weather   Forecast at 1305.

Navtex   (H)   0110, 0510, 0910, 1310, 1710, 2110.

(7) **Barbados**

Frequencies 2182, *2582*,2723, 2805. ITU 407, 816 (Traffic Lists), 825, **1213**, and 1640.

Weather Forecasts at 0050, 1250, 1650, 2050. Warnings on receipt and every 4hrs for Caribbean, Antilles, and adjacent Atlantic waters. **Caribbean Ham Weather Net (8P60M).** Broadcasts out of Barbados on 21.400 MHz daily at 1300 hrs. Receives positions 1300-1330. Translates RFI WFs 1330-1400.

(8) **Martinique (Windward Islands)**

Frequencies 2182, **2545**.

Weather Warnings odd H+33. Weather messages 2545 at 1333.

(9) **Grenada (Windward Islands)**

Frequencies 2182, 1040, 3365, 5010, 1508, 7850.

Weather Forecast at 2100-0215 (1040), 2230-0215 (3365), 2100-2230 (5010), 2100-0215 (15085). GBC Radio on 535 and 15105. Hurricane Warnings on receipt and every H+30 after news 0200, 1030, 1130, 1630, 2030, 2230.

(10) **Trinidad and Tobago**

Frequencies 2182, 2735, 2049, 3165.

Weather 1250 and 1850.

(11) **Caribbean SSB Weather Nets.** Synoptic forecasts and analysis including hurricane information and tracks for all of Caribbean. Times are all UTC. Frequencies 4003 kHz at 1215 to 1230, 8104 kHz at 1230 to 1300, in the hurricane season also 8107 kHz at 2215 to 2245.

18.13 English Channel and Atlantic. The following are selected frequencies for navigational warnings, weather forecast and working frequencies.

a. **NETHERLANDS** **(CG Radio) (MMSI 002442000)**

Frequencies 2182, MF DSC 2187.5, 3673.

Weather North Sea forecasts at 09.40 and 21.40 hrs UTC on 3673 kHz. Gale warnings are made on receipt. Scheduled broadcast times at 03.33, 07.33, 11.33, 15.33, 19.33 and 23.33 UTC.

Navtex (P) 0230, 0630, 1030, 1430, 1830, 2230.

b. **BELGIUM (Oostende Radio) (MMSI 0020050480)**

Frequencies	2182, *2761.*
Weather	Forecast at 0820 and 1720.
Navtex (M)	0200, 0600, 1000, 1400, 1800, 2200 (for Dover Straits).

c. **UNITED KINGDOM**

(1) **Lands End Radio (MMSI 002320014)**

Frequencies	2182, *2670.*
Weather	0803, 0903, 1503, 2003, 2103.

(2) **North Foreland Radio (MMSI 002320010)**

Frequencies	2182, *1848.*
Weather	0303, 0803, 0903, 1503, 2003, 2103.

(3) **Niton Radio**

Frequencies	2182, *1834.*
Weather	0303, 0803, 0903, 1503, 2003, 2103.
Navtex (S)	0300, 0700, 1100, 1500, 1900, 2300.
Navtex (I)	(490kHz) 0120, 0520, 0920, 1320, 1720, 2120.

d. **CHANNEL ISLANDS**

Jersey Radio

Frequencies	2182, *1726.*
Weather	0645, 0745, 1245, 1845, 2245.

e. **IRELAND**

Valentia Radio (MMSI 002500200)

Frequencies	2182, *1752.*
Weather	0233, 0303, 0633, 0903, 1033, 1433, 1503, 1833, 2103.
Navtex (W)	0340, 0740, 1140, 1540, 1940, 23403.

f. **FRANCE**

(1) **Boulogne-sur-Mer Radio**

Frequencies	2182, *1770, 1692, 1694.*
Weather	1770 - H + 03 and H + 33 and 1692 @ 0703, 1833.

(2) **Gris-Nez (Cross) (MMSI 002275100); Jobourg (Cross) (MMSI 002275200); Corsen (Cross) (MMSI 002275300)**

Frequencies	1650, 2182, 2677.

Etel (Cross) (MMSI 002275000); Soulac (Cross) (MMSI 002275010)

Frequencies	2182, 2677.

(3) **Brest Radio**

Frequencies	1635, 1671, 1876, 2691, 1862.
Weather	1635 - H + 03 and H + 33 and 1671, 1876, 2691, 1862 @ 0733, 1803 and 1671, 1876 @ 0600.

(4) **St. Nazaire Radio**

Frequencies	2182, 1671, 1876, 1722, 2691, 2740.
Weather	0333, 0733, 0803, 1133, 1533, 1833, 1933, 2133.

g. **SPAIN** (Port operations on Channels 18, 19, 20, 21, 22, 79, 80).

(1) **Coruna Radio (MMSI 002241022)**

Frequencies	2182, *1698.*
Weather	0803, 0833, 1233, 1733 (Bay of Biscay), 2003.
Navtex (D)	0030, 0430, 0830, 1230, 1630, 2030.

(2) **Finisterre Radio**

Frequencies	2182, *1764.*
Weather	0803, 0833, 1203, 1703 (Bay of Biscay), 2033.

(3) **Tarifa Radio**

Frequencies	2182, 1704.
Weather	0803, 0833, 1233, 1733, 2003.
Navtex (G)	0100, 0500, 0900, 1300, 1700, 2100.
Navtex (X)	0350, 0750, 1150, 1550, 1950, 2350 (Valencia).

(4) **Islas Canarias (Las Palmas Radio) (MMSI 002240995)**

Frequencies	2182, *1689*, 2045, 2048, 2114, 2191. ITU 406, 604.
Weather	Gale warnings and forecast on 1689, 2820, 4372, 6510 at 0903, 1203 and 1803.
Navtex (I)	0120, 0520, 0920, 1320, 1720, 2120.

h.   PORTUGAL

(1)   Lisboa (MMSI 002630100)

Frequencies	2182, ITU 802, 813, 1203, 1207, 1615, 1632, Traffic lists on 13083 at even H +05.

(2)   Apulia Radio

Frequencies	2182, *2657*.
Weather	0735, 1535, 2335.

(3)   Sagres Radio

Frequencies	2182, 2657.
Weather	0835, 2035.
Navtex (R	0250, 0650, 1050, 1450, 1850, 2250.

(4)   Acores (Faial) Horta Radio

Frequencies	2182, 1663.5, *2657*, 2742, 2748, 4434.9/4140.5.
Weather	Warnings and forecast 0935 and 2135.
Navtex (F)	0050, 0450, 0850, 1250, 1650, 2050.

(5)   Madeira Radio

Frequencies	2182, 2843, *2657*.
Weather	0905, 2105.

18.14   Mediterranean Radio Frequencies and Weather Forecasts. The following frequencies are for principal Mediterranean areas.

a.   SPAIN

(1)   Tarifa   2182, 1704/2129.

(2)   Malaga   2182, 1656/2081.

(3)   Cabo de Gata Radio

Frequencies	2182, *1767*.
Weather	0803, 0833, 1233, 1733, 2033.

(4)   Palma Majorca (Palma Radio) (MMSI 002241005)

Frequencies	2182, *1755*.
Weather	0803, 0833, 1203, 1703, 2033.

b.   FRANCE

(1)   Nice Radio

Frequencies   1350.

Weather   0725, 1850.

(2)   Marseille Radio

Frequencies   675.

Weather   0725, 1850.

(3)   Monaco (UTC + 1)

Frequencies   2182, *4363*, 8728, 13146 (ITU Med - Ch 403, 804, 1224, 1607, 2225; Atlantic 403, 830, 1226, 1628, 2225).

Weather   On receipt and at H+03. Forecast at 0903, 1403, 1915. On 8728 @ 0715 and 1830, 13146 on request, Atlantic Bulletin on 8806, 13152, 17232 and 22846 @ 0930. Coastal continuous on 161.750M. Nav info at 0803 and 2103.

c.   ITALY

(1)   Cagliari

Frequencies   2182, *1722* (Traffic list on 2680, 2683).

Weather   0125, 0725, 1325, 1925.

Navtex (T)   0310, 0710, 1110, 1510, 1910, 2310.

Navtex (V)   0330, 0730, 1130, 1530, 1930, 2330 (Augusta)

(2)   Porto Torres (*2719*) **Genova** (1667, 2642, *2722*) **Livorno** (1925, *2591*) **Civitavecchia** (*1888*, 2710, 3747) **Napoli** (1675, *2632*, 3735) **Palermo** (*1852*) **Mazara** (1883, *2211, 2600*) **Lampedusa** (*1876*) **Augusta** (1643, *2628*) **Crotone** (1715, *2663*) **S.Benedetto** (*1855*).

(3)   Messina Radio

Frequencies   2182, *2789*.

Weather   0135, 0233, 0633, 0735, 1133, 1335, 1533, 1933, 1935.

(4)   Roma

Frequencies   *4292*, 8520, 13011, 17160.8.

Weather   0348, 0948, 1518, 2118; Fleet Wx 0830, 2030.

Navtex (R)   0250, 0650, 1050, 1450, 1850, 2250

(5)   Bari Radio (Adriatic)

Frequencies   2182, *2579*.

Weather   0125, 0725, 1325, 1925.

(6)   Ancona Radio (Adriatic)

Frequencies   2182, *2656*.

Weather   0148, 0748, 1348, 1948.

(7)   Trieste Radio

Frequencies   2182, *2624*.

Weather   0848, 1218, 1648, 2048.

Navtex (U)   0320, 0720, 1120, 1520, 1920, 2320.

(8)   Venezia Radio

Frequencies   2182, *2698*.

Weather   0135, 0403, 0735, 0903, 1303, 1335, 1935, 2103.

d.   CROATIA (Adriatic)

(1)   Rijeka   (MMSI 002387010)

Frequencies   2182, 1641, 1656.

(2)   Dubrovnik Radio

Frequencies   160.95M.

Weather   0625, 1320, 2120.

(3)   Split (MMSI 002380100)

Frequencies   160.95M.

Weather   0545, 1245, 1945.

Navtex (O)   0240, 0640, 1040, 1440, 2240.

e.   GREECE (Hellas Radio MMSI 002371000)

(1)   Kerkyra (MMSI 237673190)

Frequencies   2182, *2830* (Traffic 2607, 2792, 3613).

Weather   Forecasts at 0703, 0903, 1533, 2133.

Navtex (K)   0140, 0540, 0940, 1340, 1740, 2140.

(2)   Limnos

Frequencies   2182, *2730*.

Weather   Forecasts at 0033, 0633, 1033, 1633.

Navtex (L)   0150, 0550, 0950, 1350, 1750, 2150.

(3)   **Rodos (MMSI 237673150)**

Frequencies   2182, *2624.*

Weather   Forecasts at 0703, 0903, 1533, 2133.

(4)   **Iraklion Kritis (MMSI 237673180)**

Frequencies   2182, **2799,** 1742, 3640.

Weather   Forecasts at 0703, 0903, 1533, 2133.

Navtex (H)   0110, 0510, 0910, 1310, 1710, 2110.

(5)   **Athinai**

Frequencies   2182, 1695, 1767, *2590*, (8743).

Weather   Forecasts at 0703, 0903, (1215), 1533, (2015), 2133.

f.   **TURKEY**

(1)   **Izmir (MMSI 002716000)**

Frequencies   1850, 2182, *2760.*

Weather   0333, 0733, 1133, 1533, 1933, 2333.

Navtex (I)   0120, 0520, 0920, 1320, 1720, 2120.

(2)   **Antalya (MMSI 002713000)**

Frequencies   2182, *2187.5*, 2670.

Navtex (F)   0050, 0450, 0850, 1250, 1650, 2050.

g.   **CYPRUS (MMSI 002091000)**

Frequencies   2182, *2187.5*, 2670, 2700, 3690. ITU 406, 414, 426, 603, 807, 818, 820, 829, 1201, 1208, 1230, 1603.

Weather   2700 kHz @ 0733, 1533.

Navtex (M)   0200, 0600, 1000, 1400, 1800, 2200.

h.   **MALTA**

Frequencies   2182, *2625.* ITU 410, 603, 832, 1216, 1233.

Weather   0103, 0603, 1003, 1603, 2103.

Navtex   0220, 0620, 1020, 1420, 1820, 2220.

18.15   South Africa and Namibia

    a.   SOUTH AFRICA (Cape Town) DSC: MMSI 006010001

Frequencies	2182, *1764, 4435,* 2191, 17338, 22711. ITU 405, 421, 427, 801, 805, 821, 1209, 1221, 1608, 1621, 1633, 2204, 2206, 2221. Weather at 1333, 0948, 1748.
Navtex (C)	0020, 0420, 0820, 1220, 1620 and 2020 UTC.

    b.   NAMIBIA (Walvis Bay) DSC: MMSI 006010001

Frequencies	2182, *1764,* 2191, 2783, 4125, *4357*, ITU 401, 602, 801.

18.16   Australia and New Zealand. The following are the main frequencies.

    a.   NEW ZEALAND (Taupo Maritime Radio) MMSI 005120010

Frequencies	2182, 2207, 4125, 6215, 8291, 12290, 16420.
Weather	0133, 0533, 1333, 1733 on 2207, 4146, 6224. Ocean and Islands at 0303, 0903, 1503, 2103 on 6224, 12356.

    b.   AUSTRALIA

        (1)   Darwin (VID)

Frequencies	2182, *2201*, 4125, 6215, 8291. ITU Radphone 415, 424, 603, 811, 1227, 1622.
Weather	0233, 0833, 1233, 2233 and 12365 @ 2100-0900 hrs. NT/WA coastal waters and Nav Warnings, High Seas (Northern) and Navarea X warnings.

        (2)   Townsville (VIT)

Frequencies	2182, *2201*, 4125, 6215, 8291, 12290, 16420.
Weather	0003, 0603, 1203, 2003 and 12365 @ 2100-0900 hrs. Qld/NSW coastal waters and Nav Warnings, High Seas (North Eastern) and Navarea X warnings.

        (3)   Brisbane (VIB) DSC: MMSI 005030330

Frequencies	2182, 8291, 12290, 16420. ITU Radphone 405, 607, 802, 817, 829, 1203, 1231, 1602, 1610.

        (4)   Sydney (VIS)

Frequencies	2182, *2201*, 4125, 6215.
Weather	0703, 1903 and 12365 @ 2100-0900 hrs. NSW/Qld coastal waters and Nav Warnings, High Seas (South Eastern) and Navarea X warnings.

(5)   **Melbourne (VIM)**

Frequencies   2182, *2201*, 4125, 6215, 8291, 12290, 16420. Radphone 404, 607, 811.

Weather   0148, 0348, 0948, 1348, 2148 and 12365 @ 2100-0900 hrs Vic/Tas/SA coastal waters and Nav Warnings. High Seas (South Eastern) and Navarea X warnings.

(6)   **Perth (VIP) MMSI:005030331**

Frequencies   2182, *2201*, 4125, 6215, 8291, 12290, 16420. Radphone 427, 424, 603, 806, 1226, 1604.

Weather   0118, 1118, 1518, 2318and 12365 @ 2100-0900 WA/SA coastal waters and Nav Warnings, High Seas (Western) and Navarea X warnings.

(7)   **Penta Comstat (VZX) – Firefly (Private Station).** Times are local EST. E-mail pentacom@ozemail.com.au.

Frequencies   2182, *2524*, 4483, ITU 608, 836, 1234, 1642.

Weather   Warnings at 0525, 1925, 2325 on 2524, 4483, Ch 836; 0535, 1935 on 4483, 836, 1642; Weather Gabo Is. to NSW/Qld border at 0225, 1725, 2125 on 2524, 4483, Ch 836. NSW/Qld to Bowen at 0235 on 4483, Ch 608, 836. High Seas forecast, synopsis, warnings. Equator to 50°S and 142°E and 170°E at 0535, 1935 on 4483, 836, 1642. Bowen to Torres Strait gale warnings Ch 836 and Ch 1234 at 0700 and 2200. Long-range navigation warnings. Equator to 50°S and 142°E and 170°E on 2524, 4483, Ch 608 and Ch 1234 at 0935 and 4483, Ch 836 and Ch 1642 at 2335.

18.17   HF Radio Tuner Units. The tuner unit's function is to match the antenna length to the frequency being used:

a.   **Manual.** There are still manual tuner units around, although they have been largely phased out by fully synthesized systems with automatic tuner units. These require matching the antennas by adjusting tune and load controls using a built-in tune meter.

b.   **Fully Synthesized Units.** The new synthesized radio sets with automatic tuner units allow non-technical oriented boaters to communicate easily. Units consist of a full range of ITU EPROM controlled frequencies. The tuner unit essentially consists of inductors and capacitors that are automatically switched in series or parallel with the antenna to achieve the correct tuned length.

18.18   HF Radio Aerials. The aerial is critical to proper performance of the HF radio. On motorboats, the whip is the most practical. The whip generally operates over a wider frequency range than the wire line aerials seen on sailing boats. Manufacturers are Shakespeare in the US and V-Tronics in the UK.

a.   **Loaded Whip.** These aerials have loading coils, and are generally very long.

b.   **Unloaded Whip.** These whips have a similar performance to long wire backstay aerials. The ATU provides the required aerial length. The voltage and currents can be significant at the base. It is essential to use high quality insulators and insulated feed line cables to minimize losses. A very low resistance ground system is required.

c.   **Backstay.** The insulated backstay is the most common on sailing boats. They do find some use on trawler motor yachts as well, often in a triatic stay arrangement and they are most efficient in the 2–8 meg range. Losses can occur here as well, as signal radiates into the mast and rigging. It should be at least 11 meters long for an effective aerial. The insulators should be free of chips and have long leakage paths.

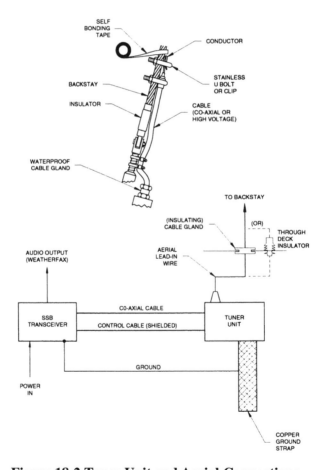

Figure 18-2 Tuner Unit and Aerial Connections

d. **Aerial Feed Line.** The feed line to the aerial is very important as resistance degrades the transmission signals.

(1) **Feed Line Cables.** Thin conductors and bad joints result in conductor heating and losses. Ideally the cable should not run close to metal decks or hull.

(2) **Insulation Quality.** Insulation losses also occur through conductors and deck feed insulators. Use cables with good insulation values, such as silicon insulated high voltage cable.

(3) **Deck Transits.** Poorly insulated leads close to metal decks and hull can cause arcing or induction losses. External cables can also leak when the insulation cracks due to UV rays. The best system in steel vessels is the use of through deck insulators. These offer long leakage paths and less signal loss. Insulators must be kept clean.

(4) **Backstay Connections.** It is imperative that the feed line to aerial connection be made properly.

18.19 **HF Radio Grounds.** The HF radio problems of transmission and reception are often caused by inadequate grounding systems. Remember that the ground plane is an integral part of the aerial system. If it is inadequate, you may not be able to tune properly to required frequencies.

a. **Ground Shoes.** Ground shoes are the most effective method of providing an RF ground plane on fiberglass and wooden boats. They provide half of the required aerial length and are an integral part of the signal radiating system.

b. **Internal Copper Mesh.** Glass and timber vessels may avoid the installation of ground shoes by glassing in a large sheet of copper mesh which is available from Newmar.

c. **Copper Straps.** The interconnecting copper strap from the tuner unit to ground plane is essential. It must be a strap, not cable and the surface area is the critical factor. To be effective, a low resistance is required and is the cause of many performance drops and interference. The ground strap should be at least 2" wide. The copper strap should be installed clear of bilge areas.

18.20 **HF Radio Maintenance.** There are regular maintenance tasks that will ensure good radio performance.

a. **Aerial Connections.** The lead wire aerial connections should be regularly checked for deterioration. If exposed, the wire may degrade, and introduce resistance into the circuit. Always tape the connection with self-amalgamating tape.

b. **Insulators.** Always clean the insulators to remove salt deposits that encrust and cause surface leakages. This should include the upper insulator on the wire antennas. A damp rag is the best tool.

c. **Ground Connection.** Check the RF ground connections. Clean and tighten the bolts and connection surfaces. After this, apply a light smear of petroleum jelly to prevent deterioration in the bilge area. It is advisable to always check and keep this area clean and dry if in a bilge area, as reaction between the copper strap and metalwork can cause corrosion problems.

18.21 **HF Radio Troubleshooting.** Basic HF troubleshooting faults are:

Table 18-3 HF Radio Troubleshooting

Symptom	Probable Fault
No reception	Wrong channel selected Propagation problems Aerial lead wire broken Aerial connection corroded Tuner unit fault
Poor reception	Propagation problems Aerial connection corroded Insulators encrusted with signal leakage Aerial grounding out
No transmission	Tuner unit fault Aerial connection corroded Insulators encrusted with signal leakage Aerial grounding out Aerial lead wire broken Ground connection corroded Low battery voltage Transceiver fault
Poor transmission	Propagation problems Aerial connection corroded Insulators encrusted with signal leakage Aerial grounding out Tuner unit fault Ground connection corroded

18.22 **Standard Time Frequencies.** A useful function is the ability to accurately fix time, plus weather data; it is available from the following stations:

a.   **WWV (Fort Collins).** Times are announced at the 8th and 9th minute past the hour on 2.5, 5, 10, 15 and 20 mHz. Information is given on weather, location and movement of storm centers, wind speeds and propagation data.

b.   **WWVH (Kekaha, Hawaii).** Times are announced at the 48th, 49th and 50th minute past the hour respectively on 2.5, 5, and 10mHz. Information is also given on weather; location and movement of storm centers; wind speeds and propagation data.

c.   **VNG (Llandilo, Australia).** Times are announced continuously on 5.000, 8.638, 12.984 mHz. 2200-1000 UTC on 16 mHz. Voice broadcasts on 5 and 16 mHz on the 15th, 30th, 45th and 60th minute.

18.23 **Amateur (Ham) Radio.** Ham radio is the realm of a worldwide group of radio enthusiasts. Ham operators have been involved in many life saving efforts with sailors, but ham operators and the system have been badly abused. Ham radios are a major communication source in the cruising world. In the US, about 70% of cruisers sail with ham radio, while in the UK and Australia it is probably around 10%. There are a number of important factors to consider.

a.   **Operator Licensing.** It is the operator, not the station, that is licensed. There are a number of levels that give either partial or full access to frequencies. Levels require examination in Morse code, radio theory, rules and regulations with respect to operations. Fear of technical matters and theory as well as the Morse test deters many amateurs. A general class license will be required for access to Maritime Mobile Nets in the 15, 20 and 40-meter bands.

b.   **Penalties.** You must be licensed for the country of operation. Be aware that in some third-world countries where communications are controlled, jail and vessel loss can occur if it is used in port without authorization. In many cases you will not be acknowledged on ham bands unless you are licensed and have a call sign.

c.   **SSB vs. Ham.** This argument is never ending, with both systems having their use. Carry both or a combined unit such as those from SGC.

(1)   **SSB Radio.** Radio sets are generally easier to operate and, with automatic tuning, it is simple to enter in a channel number and talk. Radios have automatic emergency channel selection, and are type-approved for marine communications. Only a restricted license or permit is required. You are allowed to operate a SSB radio on amateur frequencies if you have a ham licence. One of the disadvantages of SSB on ham frequencies is that synthesizers are programmed in 0.10 kHz steps. Ham communications may be at frequencies outside of these so that SSB sets can be marginally off frequency. Most SSB sets operate on upper side band (USB) while most frequencies below 40 meters are lower side band (LSB).

(2) **Ham Radio.** The ham operator must have a license appropriate to the frequency band being worked. Access to GMDSS emergency frequencies is illegal except in emergencies. It is illegal to operate non type-approved radios such as ham radios on marine frequencies. Ham allows the use of casual conversation which marine SSB does not. Ham allows full access to information-packed nets, and a worldwide communications network. Ham does not readily allow access to telephone networks, although some stations and net controllers may offer phone patches.

18.24   Ham Nets. A good receiver allows listening to ham nets and valuable information as marine SSB sets cannot access them. The following maritime mobile net times could vary an hour either way depending on summer time changes in respective countries. Frequency 14.314 is monitored virtually 24 hours, and is the de facto maritime mobile international calling frequency.

Table 18-4 Atlantic/Caribbean/Mediterranean Nets

UTC	Frequency	Call Sign	Net Name and Area
0100	3.935		Gulf Coast hurricane net
0230	14.313	K6QTR	Seafarers net
0530	14.303		Sweden net
0645	12.353		Greece net
0530	7.088		Eastern Med net
0700	14.313		German MM net
0700	14.303		International net
0800	14.303		UK net
0900	14.313	HP3XWB	Mediterranean net
0900	7.080		Canary Island net (Atlantic)
1000	14.303	G3TJY	German net
1030	3.815		Caribbean WX net
1030	14.265		Barbados cruising net
1130	3.815		Antilles emergency weather net
1130	14.320		South Africa MM net (South Atlantic)
1230	7.240		Caribbean net
1300	7.268		Waterway net (US East Coast/Caribbean)
1300	21.400		Transatlantic net (operates in crossing season)
1400	7.292		Florida Coast net
1600	14.313		US Coast Guard net
1700	7.240		Bejuka net (Central America)
1800	14.303		MM net (Atlantic weather forecast)
2030	14.303		Sweden net
2300	7.190		Admirals net (US West Coast)

Table 18-5 - Pacific/Asia/Indian Ocean Nets

UTC	Frequency	Call Sign	Net Name and Area
0100	21.407	W6BYS	MM net (Pacific/Indian Ocean)
0200	7.290	KH6B	Hawaii Interisland net (MF)
0220	14.315	VK9JA	John's weather net (Norfolk Is and Pacific)
0230	14.313	K6QTR	Seafarers net (Also operates Atlantic)
0300	14.106		Travelers net
0300	14.313	VE7CEM	DDD (Doers, Dunners and Dreamers) net
0400	14.318		Arnolds net (Weather Pacific)
0500	21.200	VK3PA	Aus/NZ/Africa net (Indian and Pacific Ocean)
0530	14.314	WH6ANH	Pacific MM net (covers all Pacific via relay stations)
0630	14.330	255MU	Durban net (Indian Ocean)
0630	14.180	VR6TC	Pitcairn net
0700	14.220		Pacific net
0715	3.820	ZL1BKD	Bay of Islands net (South Pacific/Australia)
0800	14.315	P29JM	Pacific Interisland net
1000	14.320	HG3BA	Dixie's net MM (Philippines, Weather NW Pacific)
1000	14.330		Pacific Gunkholers net
1200	14.320	WB8JDR	SE Asian net
1430	3.963	WA6VZH	Sonrisa net (Baja California)
1545	14.340		Marquesas net
1600	7238.5	W6IM	California Baja net
1630	21.350	VR6TC	Pitcairn net
1700	14.329	KH6FWV	MM Hawaii net
1700	14.115	VR6TC	Pitcairn net
1700	14.329	KH6OE	Skippers net
1700	14.340	K6VDV	California Hawaii net
1730	14.115	VE7CEM	Jerry's net
1800	14.282	KH6S	South Pacific net
1800	7.197	WA2CPX	South Pacific Sailing net
1900	21.390		MM's Pacific net
1900	7.285	KH6BF	Shamaru net (Hawaii)
1900	14.329	ZL1BKD	Bay of Islands net
1900	14.340	KA7HYA	Manana net (Mexico)
1900	7.288		Friendly net (Hawaii)
1900	3.990		Northwest MM net (NW Pacific)
2000	12.359		Pacific Cruisers net (Herb Hilgenberg)
2000	14.305	N6GYR	Confusion net (Pacific)
2030	7.085		Sydney/New Caledonia net
2100	14.315	ZL1ATE	Tony's net (South Pacific MM's Only)
2100	7.060	VK4LZ	Coral Coast net (Airlie Beach, Australia)
2130	14.318		Daytime Pacific net
2200	21404	KH6CO	Pacific Maritime net (2300 in winter)
2300	28.300	VK4ACZ	10 Meter net (Cairns, Australia)
2300	21.325		Cal-Sth Pacific net
2400	14.320	VS6BE	SEA MM net (Rowdy's net, SW Pacific/ SE Asia)

18.25   Short-Wave Radio Frequencies. Regular monitoring of the news services can often inform you of changes or other factors that may affect your plans. Frequencies are valid for up to 6 months and may alter marginally. Contact the broadcasters for free schedules and frequency information.

a.   **Voice of America (VOA).** VOA broadcasts worldwide. Times are UTC. In many cases you may be able to tune into broadcasts to other areas for limited periods. Frequencies are subject to variation.

(1)   **Caribbean Service.** Broadcasts 0000-0100 on 5995, 6130, 7405, 9455, 9775 and 11695; 0100-0130 on 5995, 6130, 7405, 9455, 9775, and 13740 kHz; 0130-0200 5995, 6130 and 9455; 0200-0500 1530 and 1580; 1000-1100 on 6165, 7370 and 9590.

(2)   **Far East/Pacific Service.** Broadcasts on 1143, 1575, 6160, 7115, 7125, 7215, 9635, 9645, 9760, 9770, 9775, 11705, 11760, 15185, 15290, 17740, 17820 kHz.

(3)   **Europe/Mediterranean.** 792, 1197, 1260, 1548, 6040, 6160, 9530, 9680, 9700, 9760, 9770, 11805, 11965, 15205, 15255 kHz.

b.   **British Broadcasting Corp. (BBC) World Service.** The BBC World Service is the news service most commercial mariners tune in to, and considered the most accurate world news information provider. **Time** (Frequencies), and time is in UTC.

(1)   **Caribbean Service.** Antigua 98.1MHz @ 00.00-2400.

(2)   **Mediterranean Service.** 0200-0400 (9410); 0400-0600 (1323, 6195, 7115, 9410); 0600-1900 (1323, 9419, 12095, 15070, 17640); 1900-2230 (1323, 6180, 6195, 7325, 9410, 12095, 15070).

(3)   **North America.** 000-0230 (5975, 6175, 9590); 0230-0330 (5975, 6175, 9895); 0330-0700 (5975, 6175); 0900-1000 (6195); 1200-1300 (5965, 6195, 9590, 15220); 1300-1400 (5965, 6195, 9515, 9740, 11865, 15220); 1400-1600 (6195, 9515, 9740, 11865, 15220, 17840); 1600-1800 (17840); 2200-2400 (5975, 6175, 9590).

(4)   **Pacific SE Asia Service.** This covers Papua New Guinea, Radio Fiji, Radio Tonga, Solomon Islands, Western Samoa, Radio Tuvalu, Radio Kiribati, Radio Vanuatu and Radio Niue. Times are GMT. World News is broadcast at 0100, 0130, 0300, 0600, 0700, 0800, 0900, 1200, 1400, 1500, 1600, 1700, 1900, and 2100. Newsdesk is broadcast at 0000, 0400, 1000, 1800, and 2200. Newshour is broadcast at 1300 and 2200. Mornings tune to 5975, 9740, 11955 kHz. Daytime tune to 6195, 7145, 15360 kHz. Evenings tune to 6195, 7110, 9740, 11955 kHz.

c.   **Radio Australia. Pacific Service.** Radio Australia broadcasts to Asia and the Pacific areas. News is broadcast every hour on the hour. Mornings tune to

9415, 5890, and 5995 kHz. Daytime tune to 1180, 7240, 12080, 15510, 17795, 13755, and 12080 kHz. Evenings tune to 15240, 11880, and 9580 kHz.

18.26   E-Mail Services. For many, "snail mail" is a thing of the past. For most boaters an INMARSAT terminal is not a viable economic alternative, although GMDSS-inspired changes make communications improvements essential. If, like myself, you have a quality SSB radio on board, that valuable piece of equipment is your means to get connected to the world.

    a.   **HF E-Mail System Components.** The basic components are:

    (1)   **SSB Radio.** Not all SSB radios are configured for e-mail and may require modification to operate, with the addition of an audio output jack. This should provide a line level output signal of 100mV RMS. Radios such as the ICOM M710 are e-mail ready. Radios must be able to transmit full power signal without damage, however older sets, including ICOM M700, SEA 235, SGC SG2000, cannot do this so they must be operated at reduced output power levels. A good power supply is essential to maintain constant transmission and battery voltages must be up and power supply connections sound. Aerials and ATU grounds must also be good to ensure optimum transmission and reception.

    (2)   **HF/SSB Modem.** Modems are generally part of the service providers' systems. Those using other non-service company systems such as packet radio enthusiasts, use what is called a Terminal Node Controller (TNC); the most common modems are those from Kantronics such as the KamPlus and the Kam98. A modem has a power input, data port, and radio port, along with operating software. The recommended SailMail modem is the SCS PTC-II: it is compact and has lower power consumption and faster speeds. The audio cable to the SSB consists of 4 wires: transmit audio (TxD); receive audio (RxD), push-to-talk (PTT), and the audio signal ground. The audio cable must be shielded with the shield being connected at both ends. Prewired cables are available from Kantronics. Clip-on ferrites must be fitted at both ends to reduce RF interference, and also coax line isolators (ungrounded T-4 model), and these are available from www.radioworks.com.

    (3)   **Notebook/Laptop Computer.** Many boaters are incorporating this as an essential part of the equipment inventory. The addition of an e-mail function further enhances the investment.

    (4)   **Software.** Software is required and AirMail is a proven Windows-based message package. You prepare messages using the text editor and attach word processing files with point-and-click simplicity, as well as automating the radio link. You can download AirMail for use with SailMail from the SailMail website.

b. **Transmission System Modes and Configurations.** Both the principal service providers and alternative systems utilize different methods for handling e-mail traffic. Although similar equipment is used, the systems cannot communicate with each other.

(1) **Clover.** These modems are used by PinOak and are made by HAL Communications in the US. These modems use a four-tone signal and are used in the PinOak PODLink-e service. Currently Globe establishes a link in SITOR (marine telex) and then switches over to Clover mode. PinOak does not use SITOR but establishes links either in Clover or PacTOR 2.

(2) **PacTOR 2.** These modems are made by SCS in Germany. They use a two-tone signal and are far more effective and reliable with data transfer in noisy environments. Effectively, they are a hybrid Packet/Amtor modem. They are becoming the favored modem type for use in most marine HF e-mail systems. The new PinOak PODLink-f service utilizes PacTOR modems. PacTOR is replacing Amtor communications due to improved capabilities and is supported by many Aplink stations.

18.27 **E-Mail Service Providers.** There are several ways to connect to e-mail via HF, SailMail and WinLink. They have become very popular and two other main service providers and pioneers of this service are listed below. Both offer GMDSS level services that require the installation of satellite systems.

a. **Sailmail.** This system operates using SSB radio. It is a relatively cheap, non-profit group and the best option. Check out www.sailmail.com for complete details on using the system and at www.pentacomstat.com.au. The designated frequencies and SailMail stations are as follows, and in J3E mode with non-automatic tuning you will have to subtract 1.7kHz from the listed frequencies.

(1) **WRD719, Palo Alto, California;** 2661.4, 5881.4, 7971.4, 13971.0, 18624.0 kHz.

(2) **KZN508, Rockhill, South Carolina;** 2656.4, 5876.4, 7961.4, 7981.4, 10331.0, 13992.0, 13998.0, 18618.0, 18630.0 kHz.

(3) **VZX1, NSW, Australia;** 6357.0, 8442.0, 12680.0, 16908.0, 22649.0 kHz.

b. **PinOak Digital.** Stations are located worldwide include Galapagos, Falkland Islands, Cape Town, Cape Verde Islands, Grand Banks, West Greenland, Eastern Mediterranean, Sri Lanka, Hawaii, Tahiti, Wellington, South China Sea, Perth, and others. Coverage varies from 5 hours up to a full 24 hours and it is for commercial vessels. PinOak Digital, P.O. Box 360, Gladstone, NJ 07934; Tel 800-746-6251; Fax 908-234-9685. Users are charged a subscription fee, which allows a specific amount of data transfer, and then a charge per kilobit transferred. Over 4000 worldwide weather forecasts are available, along with e-mail services and Internet access. Log on to www.pinoak.com.

c.   **AMTOR (Amateur Teletype Over Radio).** This is probably the cheapest option that I have seen in wide use. The system uses what is termed Amtor Packet Link (Aplink). These Aplink stations are ham stations configured for automatic reception, storage, and transmission of Amtor messages. Messages are transferred between stations until the designated destination station is reached. Addressing mail requires the recipient MBO (Electronic Mail Box) details. What I found most attractive with on-board systems using this system is the ability to "talk" with other vessels on a chat net. Log on to www.airmail2000.com and www.shortwave.co.uk for useful information and www.win-net.org for ham e-mail shore stations.

d.   **Globe Wireless.** They are not interested in pleasure boats; however, they have stations worldwide in San Francisco, New Orleans, Hawaii, Bahrain, Sweden, Newfoundland, Australia, and New Zealand. Service offered is called GlobeEmail, along with GPS position reporting tied with USCG AMVER system. Users are charged a subscription fee, which allows a specific amount of data transfer, and then a charge per kilobit transferred. Message reception is similar with automatic notification. Log on to www.globewireless.com.

e.   **Alternative E-Mail Systems.** The main systems offer a seagoing system, but there are other useful options.

   (1)   **WinLink.** For licensed ham radio operators using pactor based system, log on for details at www.winlink.org.

   (2)   **Pocketmail.** I have some friends who regularly send me messages from their boat in Europe using this system. I decided to use my Palm Pilot to get connected. This system can be used with the GSM cell phone. As Palm backs up via a cradle to the laptop all messages are prepared using a full size keyboard then downloaded to the Palm. Log on to www.pocketmail.com or www.stargate3.co.uk.

   (3)   **SeaMail.** This Australian system is operated by Penta Comsat and services the Pacific. Log on to www.xaxero.com for details and software downloads.

   (4)   **CruiseEmail.** This is a Florida based service (who has a tie up with SeaMail) to offer Atlantic, Caribbean and Pacific Services.

f.   **Acoustic Couplers.** This system still requires a notebook computer with an appropriate modem card installed, as well as an acoustic coupler. Subscribing to an Internet provider such as Compuserve gives you appropriate e-mail access. Download or send your mail from a phone on land and then you're back off to the boat. It is an economical alternative if you don't mind taking your PC ashore to a phone booth.

g.   **Internet Cyber Cafes and E-Mail Centers.** Many marinas now offer access to e-mail and Internet. Log on to www.ipass.com for information on how to access your ISP back home when you are away by dialing a local telephone number. In most cases, you can find an Internet cafe virtually everywhere, just log on to Yahoo or Hotmail and create an account. I have switched to Yahoo as they have 6 meg accounts compared to the 2 meg Hotmail accounts, with the latter having unsustainable quantities of junk mail and very slow access.

18.28   Satellite Services. There are a variety of services available and these are described along with salient features. The system selected will depend on many factors that include the services required; coverage area; initial installation costs; antenna sizes, and the annual and call costs. Log on to www.heavens-above.com for information on satellite orbits and tracking.

a.   **INMARSAT.** INMARSAT is based on INternational MARitime SATellite Organization. The system comprises four satellites in geostationary orbit 23,000 miles (36,700km) high, and the satellites remain in the same position relative to the earth. There are 4 ocean regions (Atlantic East, Atlantic West, Pacific and Indian). The ship station or Mobile Earth Station transmits and the satellite relays the signal to a Land Earth Station (LES) for routing via terrestrial communications networks. Log on to www.inmarsat.org for details.

(1)   **Standard-A SES.** The first system introduced in 1982 and unlike later systems is analog. New Standard-A systems have dramatically decreased the size of equipment. It supports telephone, telex, fax, e-mail and data transmissions. It also supports GMDSS requirements, but is seen only on large commercial vessels due to the large antenna size.

(2)   **INMARSAT-B.** This was introduced in 1994, and will replace Inmarsat-A by 2010. This is a high-speed digital service that provides high quality data, fax, telephone, telex, video transfer and conferencing. Inmarsat-B HSD (High Speed Data) is a more recent enhancement and transmits data at 64k bits/sec direct to an ISDN line. This system is now a primary one for many commercial vessel operations and complies with all GMDSS requirements.

(3)   **INMARSAT-C.** This was introduced in 1991. It provides reliable text, e-mail and fax messages and is an essential part of GMDSS. It uses small antennas and utilize a laptop computer. It can be programmed to receive enhanced group calls (EGC) and then get SafetyNet broadcasts of Marine Safety Information (MSI). If using e-mail, log on to www.rme.com for compression software.

(4)   **INMARSAT-D+.** This new service provides global 2-way paging services with a limit of 128 characters per message. It is also utilized as a vessel-tracking system.

(5) **INMARSAT-M and Mini-M.** This was introduced in 1992 and enhanced in 1997 with new Series 3 satellites. Services include low speed fax, data (2.4Kbps) and voice. Antennas are small (25cm), gyro-stabilized, and are the most popular system on many powerboats. SIM cards offering pre-paid call billing options are used. The Mini-M systems do not give global coverage and utilize "spot beam" technology. The signal is beamed to specific areas, such as main landmasses and coastlines, typically giving coverage up to 200 nm offshore. Service suppliers include KVH TracPhone, BoatPhone from Thrane and Thrane, and WorldPhone from Nera.

(6) **INMARSAT-P.** Currently under development, it will offer a global handheld system with voice, paging, fax, and data services.

b. **Globalstar.** It consists of 48 low earth orbit (LEO) satellites, which are dual mode satellite and GSM 900 systems. Services include high quality voice, short messaging services (SMS) and roaming. Also dial-up fax and data services are available at 9.6kbps (bits per second). Coverage is limited to coastal areas to around 200nm offshore, which will suit many people. This is not a GMDSS system. The domes are very small. Log on to www.globalstar.com.

c. **Motient/AMSC.** This system has a single geostationary orbit satellite and has a footprint covering North America and Hawaii up to 200nm offshore. It offers voice, fax and e-mail services. Check out equipment on www.wireless.westinghouse.com.

d. **ORBCOMM.** Consists of 26 LEO satellites. The service is digital data only and will offer paging, e-mail, etc. It is not a GMDSS system and details are at www.orbcomm.net.

e. **Iridium.** It consists of 66 satellites in low earth orbit (LEO) and offers global voice, data, fax, and paging services. The system is now operated by Boeing and the US Department of Defense is the largest client. At the time of publication service has resumed and it is becoming a viable alternative system again. This is not a GMDSS system. Iridium offers Enhanced Mobile Satellite Services (EMSS) that gives low rate data and voice, the data rate is at 2.6kbps. They now have a new phone that is smaller and lighter than the previous one, (Motorola Model 9505) which requires an RS232 data adaptor. Log on to www.iridium.com.

f. **VSAT.** (Very Small Aperture Terminals) They use Ku-Band geostationary satellites such as Intelsat and Eutelsat with data rates of 1.5 mbps. They do not have global coverage with any one company, and require more precise antenna tracking.

g. **Thuraya.** This new system has a single geostationary orbit satellite and has a footprint similar to the Inmarsat Indian Ocean unit. The handsets offer phone, SMS, e-mail and fax, as well as GPS positioning.

h.   **Emsat.** This new system also has a single geostationary orbit satellite and the major satellite communications company Eutelsat operates it. Coverage is limited to the Mediterranean and Northern Europe.

i.   **ICO/New ICO.** Intermediate Circular Orbit, uses 10 medium earth orbit (MEO) satellites, it is scheduled to start operations in 2002 offering voice, fax and data.

j.   **Teledesic.** This system will use 288 low earth orbit satellites, and is scheduled to start in 2005. The system is a broadband Internet-in-the-Sky. Ka-Band radio waves uplink 28.6-29.12 GHz at 2 Mbps and 18.8-19.3GHz downlink at 64 Mbps. Bill Gates, Motorola, Boeing and Middle East Investors are developing the system. The system will offer high-speed internet access, interactive multimedia and high quality voice communications. Log on to www.teledesic.com.

18.29   Satellite System Installation. The following is for a Nera Saturn-Bm system, and the criteria apply to all systems. Systems consist of the radome, which encloses a stabilized antenna dish, a pedestal control unit (PCU) and the RF Unit. Follow installation instructions in the user's manual precisely as the warranty may be voided if installation is incorrect.

a.   **Radome Installation.** The radome must be located as far as practicable from any HF and VHF antenna, and preferably a minimum of 5 meters from all other communications and navigation receiver antennas. Avoid locating near any exhaust funnel, as soot will gradually degrade performance. Do not mount the unit in any location subject to vibration. Safe compass distance is a minimum of 1 meter. Systems also require radiation precautions, and should be 5 meters from any accessible area, and 2 meters above to avoid excessive microwave radiation. If at 2 meters vertical clearance the 5 meter rule is not required. The radome should be outside the beamwidth of radar antennas, typically 10 degrees each side of the central plane. The radome should be properly aligned parallel with the boat's axis. As beamwidth is 10°, a clear line of sight is required from 5° elevation and above. Obstructions will create blind spots, and disrupt communications. Obstructions less than 15cm are acceptable within 3m of the antenna, however note that marginal signal strengths are vulnerable to them. The azimuth and elevation angles must be considered at all times. Normal cable installation rules apply, and must be observed to prevent mechanical damage. The antenna unit uses double-screened 50 ohm coaxial cable. This is usually RG223/U and RG214, with maximum lengths of 13m and 25m respectively to achieve 10dB/0.6 ohm maximum losses and attenuation. All cables must be shielded, and the shield grounded. Peripheral equipment must also be grounded. Co-axial connectors must be put on correctly, and this is a frequent cause of problems.

b.   **Operation.** The antenna can be directed accurately at the nominated satellite to optimize signal transmission and reception. In normal operation, the dish auto-tracks the satellite. To do this, the dish must be aligned correctly. The nominated satellite is based on the boat's position, and then selection of a relevant satellite with area coverage. The boat heading is required to give correct azimuth heading, and a gyro or fluxgate compass input provides this. The azimuth angle is the angle from North and horizontal satellite direction. The elevation angle is the satellite height above the horizon in relation to the vessel. At power-up, the system must locate a satellite and synchronize with it. This is either by automatic- or manual-initiated hemispheric scan, manually selected or ocean region satellite. The dish does a search pattern until the satellite signal is located in the relevant ocean region. Systems also carry out a self-test at initialization. Systems default to last settings on gyro, azimuth and elevation, and if the vessel position is lost and the data is required. Under GMDSS the default LES and Distress Alarm address must be configured. During operation, displays on handsets show signal quality, and signal strength Signal/Noise Ratio (S/N). Bit Error rates (BER) decrease with increased signal quality.

18.30   Weatherfax Receivers. Weather facsimile gives access to many stations that transmit weather charts and the charts are much easier to interpret than foreign language voice forecasts. Weatherfax services in the US, UK and Europe are under threat amid cost cutting in the wake of GMDSS implementation. Transmitted data is varied and includes ocean current positions, sea temperatures charts, and current weather charts every six hours. Forecasts for up to five days in advance, sea state, swell forecasts and ionosphere propagation forecasts for areas also available.

a.   **Facsimile Signal Components.** A facsimile transmission consists of a number of distinct components:

(1)   **Continuous Carrier.** This single tone is emitted before the start of any broadcast. It allows the receiver to be tuned to maximum signal strength prior to data reception.

(2)   **Start Tone.** Also called the Index of Co-operation (IOC) select tone, this enables receivers to recognize the start of a transmission and to select the appropriate IOC drum speed.

(3)   **Phasing Tone.** This tone synchronizes the edge of the transmitted image.

(4)   **Scale Tone.** Some systems enable the tone variations within the broadcast to be selected or varied.

(5)   **Body of Transmission.** This characteristic rhythmic "crunching" tone is the facsimile data being decoded into an image.

(6)   **Stop Tone.** The stop tone is similar to a start tone and indicates the end of the transmission.

(7)   **Close Carrier.** This tone follows conclusion of the transmission.

b.   **Decoders.** To obtain weatherfax data, it is necessary to obtain signals via a SSB or short-wave radio, and decode them for display on a laptop computer or printer. The basic function of a decoder is to convert transmitted audio signals into data. The audio signal is taken from the audio jack if fitted or a terminal on the rear of the SSB set.

c. **Printers.** An ink-jet printer can be utilized from the laptop computer. As a plain paper printer, it is significantly cheaper to operate than thermal paper roll types. One of the factors to consider is both the ease of printing and the size and quality required. Make sure you carry enough spare paper and ink cartridges for your trip, as often these items are hard to procure.

d. **Discrete Systems.** On larger vessels an integrated decoder and printer system is often used. The most common are Furuno and the smaller ICS Fax-2. A paper roll lasts a considerable period. The unit also has a number of useful features. An additional aerial can be added for full Navtex reception, marine page can be utilized, and the reception of RTTY and FEC signals is possible. Like most weatherfax units, you can program it to receive at specific times, which takes all the worry out of looking up and catching broadcast times.

e. **Power Consumption.** The power consumption rate is relatively low, although it should take into account SSB consumption as well if a unit is left on permanently to capture programmed transmissions. If power consumption is an issue, you will have to power up before the required broadcast and after receiving shutdown again. The combination of decoder and SSB over 24 hours can be at least 25–30 amp hours, which is considerable. Typical power rates are as follows:

    (1) **Standby Listening Mode.** The ICS Fax-2 unit has a drain of only 2.5 watts. The SEA SSB unit power consumption is 2 amps, while the 322 model is only 1.0 amp.

    (2) **Print Mode.** The power drain increases to approximately 4 amps when printing. The SSB drain remains the same unless the audio is turned up and it can be around another 0.5A.

18.31 Computer Based Weather Systems. The computer offers a range of weather information options:

a. **MeteoCom.** This is an economical and simple package with reception limited to weatherfax, RTTY, CW and Navtex, which suits most users. A useful function is the reception of SYNOP, which is the current weather reports, transmitted over RTTY, consisting of the raw data used by forecasters. It plots observational data as it is transmitted in real time. Data can include wind speed and direction, temperature, barometric pressure and cloud cover. When all information is displayed, the package automatically generates isobars and isotherms on screen. These signals are decoded into text reports and a plot is automatically made to give the very latest weather situations. Automatic tuning of suitable receivers is also possible.

b. **Easyfax.** A simple package, the demodulator is plugged into the serial port, and operation is print and click easy.

c. **ICS Fax-III (UK) and HF Fax (US).** These two leading packages use a demodulator. Auto tuning and signal tracking is possible. Once an image is received, you can zoom in, scroll or save to disc, or print out if required to name a few functions. The programs are also capable of receiving and printing RTTY, FEC and CW (Morse Code) modes, as well as Navtex transmissions. Both systems have mouse control capability, and can automatically control frequency of Lowe and Icom receivers.

d. **WinsatMarine.** This package enables reception of satellite photos from polar orbiting and geostationary satellites. The package also has an image demodulator and requires a quadrifilar antenna and separate receiver to enable reception of US NOAA, Russian and Chinese satellite data.

e. **Computer Fax Problems.** HF reception criteria apply to receiving quality signals. The greatest problem with computer fax reception is noise generated from the computer and picked up through the audio demodulator line.

f. **Troubleshooting.** Ensure that the frequency is tuned accurately, if instability and drifting occur, the signal will also be inconsistent. Often weatherfax reception problems indicate that aerial and earth connections in the SSB system are defective. Check these out first. The frequencies being used may be affected by adverse propagation conditions, which affect all HF transmissions. It is advisable to tune to another frequency and try again, or wait until conditions improve. If this is a regular problem, obtain propagation forecasts. Check all sources of noise that will include fluoro lights and motors.

18.32 **Aviation Radios and Beacons.** Larger super and mega-yachts often have helicopter-landing facilities. Coupled with this are aviation radios, and non-directional radio beacons. Aviation radios operate in the 110-136 mHz band. Aviation beacons operate in the 1500-1800 kHz band. These require routine inspections and maintenance if they are to remain reliable. External aerial connections to whip aerials must be checked, and the whips must be checked for mechanical damage. Where a long wire aerial is installed around helideck perimeters, they should be checked that they are not grounding and insulators are clean of dirt and salt deposits that will track to ground and reduce transmission signal strengths. Beacons are also usually connected to timers.

Table 18-6 Weather Facsimile Frequencies

Station	Frequencies
Kodiak (USA)	2054, 4298, 8459
Point Reyes (USA)	4346, 8682, 12730, 17151.2, 22527
Honolulu (Hawaii)	9982.5, 11090, 16135, 23331.5
Beijing (China)	5526.9, 8121.9, 10116.9, 14366.9, 16025.9, 18236.9
Canberra (Australia)	2628, 5100, 11030, 13920, 20469
Auckland (New Zealand)	5807, 9459, 13550.5, 16340.1
Valparaiso (Chile)	4228, 8677, 17144.4
Tokyo (Japan) (JJC)	4316, 8467.5, 12745.5, 16035, 16971, 17069.9, 17430
Tashkent	3690, 4365, 5890, 7570, 9340, 14982.5, 18680.4
Halifax (Canada)	122.5, 4271, 6496.4, 10536, 13510
Boston (USA)	4235, 6340.5, 9110, 12750
Offenbach (Germany)	3855, 7880, 13882.5
Bracknell (UK)	2618.5, 4610, 8040, 14436, 18261
Northwood (UK)	3642, 4307, 6452.5, 8331.5
Skamlebaek (Greenland)	5850, 9360, 13855, 17510
Cape Naval (Sth Africa)	4014, 7508, 13538, 18238
Rio de Janeiro (Brasil)	12665, 16978
Dakar (Senegal)	13667.5, 19750
New Orleans (USA)	4317.9, 8503.9, 12789.9
Darwin (Australia)	5755, 7535, 10555, 15615, 18060
Bangkok (Thailand)	7396.8, 17520
New Delhi (India)	7403, 14840
Nairobi (Kenya)	7464.4, 9045, 12315, 16186.9, 17445.6, 22867
St Denis (Reunion)	8176, 16335
Ankara (Turkey)	3370, 6790
Cairo (Egypt)	4526.5, 10123
Rome (Italy)	4777.5, 8146.6, 13587.4
Athens (Greece)	4481, 8105

NOTE: In upper side band mode, adjust frequency 1900Hz (1.9kHz) lower, if in lower side band mode adjust 1900Hz (1.9kHz) higher.

Position Fixing Systems

19.1   Position Fixing Systems. The advances in electronic position fixing systems have been very rapid. The fall in GPS prices make them affordable to all boaters and most boaters have one.

    a.   **Repeatable Accuracy.** This is defined as the ability to sail back to a position or waypoint previously fixed by the receiver, and is vitally important with Man Overboard (MOB) functions. If any system is placed in a static situation, and the positions plotted at intervals, there will be a wandering of position. It is important to remember that all displayed positions must be used with the understanding that errors exist. Hitting the rocks and claiming the position fixing system was at fault is not a valid defense.

    b.   **Predictable Accuracy.** This is less concise than repeatable accuracy. This is the difference between the position indicated on your position fixing system and the position indicated on the chart where you are plotting your positions at regular intervals. These errors are often caused by the vagaries of electronic fixing systems such as signal propagation problems. They can be attributed to datum variations, inaccuracies in the electronically derived position, etc.

19.2   Other Systems. Many boaters are curious about the status of the various systems, given the rapid integration of GPS-based systems. Satnav or the Transit Satellite Navigation System was switched off and receivers cannot be converted for use with GPS. Decca has been shut down and receivers cannot be converted for use with GPS. Radio Direction Finding (RDF) is still in limited use, and there has been considerable reorganization and reduction in stations and beacon frequencies, with fewer stations and frequencies now available. RDF is not part of GMDSS. Loran is still operational although there has been pressure to shut down the system, and some chains have been shut down, but some expansion has also occurred.

19.3   Global Positioning System (GPS). The US Dept of Defense (DOD) operates the NAVSTAR system. The system consists of 24 satellites in six polar orbits so that at least four will always be visible above the horizon at any time. There will be 21 satellites in operation with three used as spares. The US has declared a commitment to GPS until at least to 2005 with a second frequency on line in 2004 and maybe a third. There have been rumors of shut down scheduled for 2008 and replacement with a civilian-controlled system with user charges. The Galileo European system is moving ahead as an alternative high accuracy system. GPS position fixing involves triangulation of position from a number of satellites; satellite ranging to measure the distance from the satellites; accurate time measurement; location of all satellites; and correction factors for ionosphere conditions. Operation of a GPS set is as follows when the power is on:

a. **Initialization.** Turning the power on initializes with the closest satellite and ephemeris data being downloaded into memory. A period of at least 20 minutes is often required to stabilize a position and verify the status of satellites, availability, etc. After switching off a GPS, the last position is retained in memory. If your position remains within 50nm, prior to the next power up, a position will generally be available within approximately 3–5 minutes.

b. **Acquisition.** The receiver collects data from other satellites in view. Based on data, it locks on to a satellite to commence the ranging process.

c. **Position Fix.** Based on the data on position and time, the receiver triangulates the position with respect to the positions of satellites. Normally this will be displayed to two decimal places. Some units give three decimal places, but such accuracy is highly suspect and should be treated with caution.

d. **Differential GPS (DGPS).** This system is designed to overcome the position errors with respect to Selective Availability. The illustration below shows the differential system arrangement. DGPS uses a shore-based reference station located in an accurately surveyed location. The position is compared with the

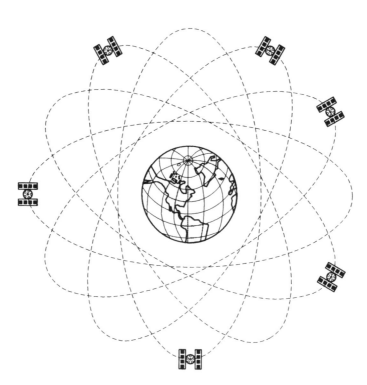

Figure 19-1 GPS Satellite Matrix

GPS derived position to produce an error or position offset. These errors may be due to SA or other causes. A correction signal to satellite range data (pseudorange differential) is then broadcast by radio beacon (285-325 kHz in standard format RTCM SC104) which is then received by a radio beacon receiver. This is then incorporated into the vessel GPS receiver position computation to derive a final and more accurate position. The accuracy has come down to around 2 meters in some instances. DGPS services also use UHF radio correction signals as well as Spotbeam, Inmarsat, Marine Radio Beacon (MRB) and IALA VHF transmitted data.

e.   **Wide Area Augmentation System (WAAS).** DGPS is already being "phased out" in the US with the introduction of WAAS. The system operates by a ground base calculated ionosphere differential correction signal being uploaded to a satellite and rebroadcast back again to WAAS enabled GPS receivers. Systems are known as Satellite Differential GPS (SDGPS). Europe is developing a similar system called European Geostationary Navigation Overlay Service (EGNOS), and in Asia a system called MSAS is under development. Accuracy is typically around 3m against 10m.

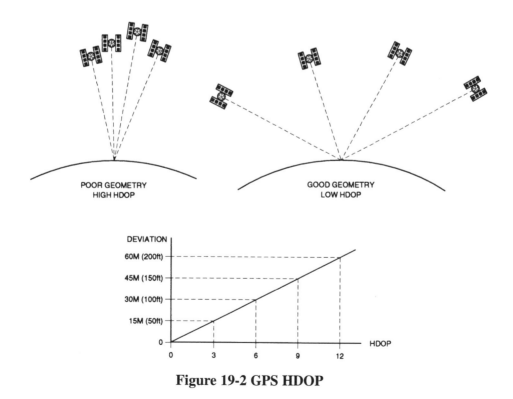

Figure 19-2 GPS HDOP

19.4   GPS Accuracy. GPS accuracy has been the subject of widespread debate and controversy in recent years.

    a.   **Precise Positioning Service (PPS).** This service is primarily for military use and is derived from the Precise (P) code. The P code is transmitted on the L1 (1575.42mHz) and L2 (1227.60mHz) frequencies. PPS fixes are generally accurate within 16 meters spherical error.

    b.   **Standard Positioning Service (SPS).** This service is for civilian use and is derived from the Course and Acquisition (C/A) code. Accuracy levels have been degraded to within 141 meters 95% of the time.

    c.   **Selective Availability (SA).** This is the process of degrading positional accuracy by altering or introducing errors in the clock data and satellite ephemeris data. SA is characterized by a wandering position, and often a course and speed over the ground of up to 1.5 knots is seen while actually stationary. SA has been officially switched off, but it can be activated at times of US defense requirements.

    d.   **Horizontal Dilution of Position (HDOP).** Accuracy is determined by what is called (Geometric) Horizontal Dilution of Precision (HDOP), which indicates the dilution of precision in a horizontal direction. The cause is poor satellite geometry, which is due to poor satellite distribution. It is generally measured on a scale of one to 10. The higher the number, the poorer the position confidence level.

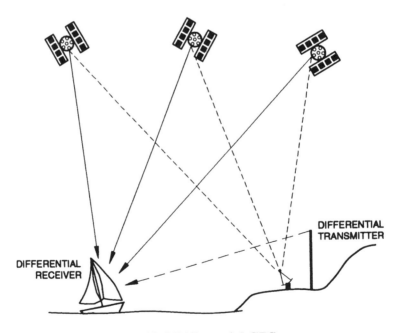

Figure 19-3 Differential GPS

e. **Chart Datum Variations.** Plotting a position on a chart has inherent errors. These errors can be caused by the GPS fix error or the transformation between GPS datum and chart datum. There may be a discrepancy that requires correction, and many charts carry appropriate notes. A wide variety of chart datum are used worldwide. New charts are generally being compiled on WGS84 datum, the same datum used by GPS. Of the 3337 current British Admiralty charts, 65 datums are used, and a typical error is a 140-meter offset in Dover Strait. Recently an official warning was issued not to rely on any position within 3 nm of land in the Caribbean. Note that Datum NAS83 on US charts is the same as WGS84 (GPS) datum on UK charts.

19.5   GPS Error Sources. The GPS that is considered by many boaters to be an accurate navigation source has inherent errors that decrease accuracy. These errors are in addition to the HDOP and SA factors previously mentioned.

a. **GPS Clock Errors.** Each GPS satellite has two rubidium and two cesium atomic clocks. These clocks are monitored against terrestrial atomic clocks. Based on this information, the entire GPS system is continually calibrated against UTC.

b. **Ionosphere Effects.** Like radio signals, both ionosphere and troposphere conditions can affect GPS accuracy. Errors occur in signal transmission times that can impose signal propagation delays. This signal refraction introduces timing errors that cause positional inaccuracies. Like radio propagation it alters with changes in atmospheric conditions, solar activity, etc. Errors can be as great as 20–30 meters during the day and 5 meters at night. See Space Weather for further details.

c. **Multipath Effects.** This occurs when signals from a satellite traveling to a receiver arrive at slightly different times due to reflection or alteration. The effect is that positions may be derived off the "bad" signal, resulting in inaccuracy.

d. **Satellite Integrity.** If the signal being transmitted from a satellite is corrupt due to a malfunction, it will have subsequent effects on position computations and solutions.

19.6   GLONASS Positioning System. The Russian system nominally operates with a 24-satellite system, however this is down to only 7–8. The claims are that the system is more accurate than GPS, and this has been proven in higher latitude locations such as the UK and Europe. There are now dual GLONASS and GPS receivers and the offshore oil industry positioning frequently uses both.

19.7   GPS Satellite Acquisition Modes. The various methods of satellite acquisition are explained below.

a. **Single Channel, Sequential.** A single-channel receiver reduces receiver costs. Position updates are made every 10–15 seconds because a single-channel receiver must search for, interrogate, and acquire satellites in sequential order. This method is slow and in bad weather can cause some problems. In rough weather, when the vessel is subject to considerable movement, the receiver has problems acquiring and locking onto satellites, with resultant position degradation. These types of receivers generally take some time to acquire their first fix, typically from 10 to 20 minutes and longer.

b. **Dual Channel, Sequential.** These common types of receivers use two channels to track several satellites and they process two channels sequentially. Accuracy is very good and the time-to-first-fix (TTFF) is generally very fast, typically around 5 minutes. On some two-channel units, one channel ranges, which speeds up position processing, while the other channel downloads ephemeris.

c. **Multiple Channel, Parallel Processing.** Multiple-channel units are now virtually standard. This powerful processing capability enables the monitoring and tracking of up to 12 satellites and the parallel processing of all those satellites in view simultaneously. These units increase position accuracy, reduce errors, and improve the HDOP. The TTFF in these units is very fast; in fact, TTFF can be achieved in several seconds. Many handheld receivers now incorporate parallel processing, and it is by far the better system to choose. In rough weather conditions, fix integrity and accuracy will generally be very high.

d. **Multiplex Processing.** Multiplex systems use one or two channels to sequentially handle satellites at high processing speeds. They are sometimes referred to as pseudo-multichannel systems because performance under ideal conditions is nearly as fast and accurate as that of true multiple-channel systems. The high speed sampling and processing of ephemeris occurs concurrently with the ranging function.

19.8 Space Weather and GPS Effects. The ionosphere is well known for the effects it has on HF and ham radio. A lot less known are the effects on GPS. It is an important source of range and range rate errors for users of GPS satellites where high accuracy is required. Ionosphere range error can vary from a few meters to tens of meters, with troposphere range error at a peak up to 2–3 meters. The ionosphere has a dispersive effect. It can alter rapidly in value, changing significantly over one day. In practice the troposphere range error does not alter more the + or – 10% over long periods. GPS signals pass through the ionosphere but suffer propagation delays. Ranging errors of tens of meters can occur in extreme ionosphere conditions, and typically it is 5–10 meters. These generally equatorial events are often associated with plasma bubbles that characterize the unstable state of the equatorial ionosphere at night.

a. **Plasma Bubbles.** Ionosphere plasma bubbles are a natural phenomena consisting of wide regions within the atmosphere where there are large depletions of the ionosphere plasma. They were first detected in Brazil in 1976 and continue to be a major problem within their offshore oil industry, and are subject to much research. Plasma bubbles are known to interfere with satellite communications in the frequency range VHF to 6GHz, and are known to interfere with GPS causing position errors. The plasma bubbles are closely aligned with the earth's geomagnetic field lines. They extend along these lines and may extend 1000s of kilometers and across geomagnetic field lines. They occur after sunset and exist at nights only; there is generally more activity during periods of maximum solar activity. The period 2000/2001 is scheduled to be very active and then slowly decreasing.

b. **Scintillation.** Irregularities in the ionosphere produce diffraction and refraction effects. This causes short-term signal fading, which can severely stress the tracking capabilities of the GPS receiver. Signal enhancements also occur, but the GPS user cannot get any benefit from brief periods of strong signal. Fading can be so severe that the signal level will drop completely below the receiver lock threshold and must be continually re-acquired. The effects are called ionospheric scintillations, and the region can cover up to 50% of the earth in varying degrees. Strong scintillation effects in near equatorial regions are observed generally 1 hour after sunset to midnight. Precise measurement using GPS should be avoided from 7 to 12 PM local time during periods of high solar activity and during months of normal high scintillation activity. There are also seasonal and solar cycle effects that also reduce chances of encountering scintillation in near equatorial regions. From April to August, the chances are small of significant scintillation in the American, African and Indian regions. In the Pacific region, scintillation effects maximize during these months. From September to March the situation reverses. The regions where the strongest scintillation effects are observed are Kwajalein Island in the Pacific and Ascension Island in the South Atlantic. The occurrence of strong amplitude scintillation is also closely correlated with the sunspot number; in years with near minimum solar activity, there are little if any strong scintillation effects on GPS.

19.9 **GPS Installation and Troubleshooting.** The reliability and accuracy of your GPS system depends on proper installation. Now that most motorboats have GPS as their primary navigation source, it is essential they be properly installed.

a. **Aerial Installation.** Aerials should be sited so that they are clear of fly bridge frames, spars, deck equipment and other radio aerials. Where possible, the aerial should have as wide a field of view as practicable, while being located as low as possible. In installations that utilize a stern arch or stern post with mounted radar, ensure that the GPS aerial is not within the beam spread of the radar antenna. Ensure that the location is not prone to fouling by ropes and other equipment that may damage the aerial.

b. **Cabling.** Many GPS problems are a result of cabling problems. Power supply cables should be routed as far as practicable from equipment cables carrying high currents. Aerial cables should also be routed well clear. It is extremely important for the aerial cable not to be kinked, bent, or placed in any tight radius. This has the effect of narrowing the dielectric gap within the coaxial cable, which may cause signal problems. Ensure that all through-deck glands are high quality to properly protect the cable and keep water from going below. Thrudex (Index) makes cable glands that enable the plug to be passed through along with the cable. Do not shorten or lengthen an aerial cable unless your manufacturer approves it.

c.   **Connectors.** Ensure that all connectors are properly inserted into the GPS receiver. Ensure that screw-retaining rings are tight, because plugs can work loose and cause intermittent contact. The coaxial connector from the aerial into the receiver should be rotated properly so that it is locked in. External aerial connections should be made water resistant where possible. Use of self-amalgamating tape is a useful method for doing this. If you have to remove and refit an aerial connector, ensure that you use considerable care and assemble the connector in accordance with the manufacturer's instructions. Use a multimeter on the resistance range, and check the center pin to shield resistance. Low resistance generally means a shorted shield strand. Resistance is typically 50–150 ohms.

d.   **Grounding.** The ground connection provided with the system must be connected to the RF ground system or negative supply polarity depending on manufacturer's recommendations.

e.   **Power Supplies.** A clean power supply is essential to proper operation. Use either an in-line filter or install suppressors across "noisy" motors and alternator. The power supply should not come from a battery used for engine starting, or be used with any high current equipment such as an anchor windlass or electric toilet. Note that many cheaper unsuppressed fluorescent lights also cause interference that may cause data corruption.

f.   **GPS Maintenance.** Perform the following routine maintenance checks. Many problems can be identified and rectified before the system fails.

   (1)   Check the aerial to make sure the connections are tight and the plugs in good condition. Ensure that it is mounted vertically and has not been pushed over, a common problem.

   (2)   Ensure that all connectors are properly inserted. In particular, examine the external aerial connector for signs of corrosion, especially the outer shield braiding.

   (3)   Many GPS units have internal lithium batteries with a life span of only around 3 years so ensure that the battery is renewed prior to any voyage.

   (4)   Make a hard copy list of all waypoints for reference and reprogramming if required.

g.   **GPS Troubleshooting.** You should attempt some basic troubleshooting before you call a technician or remove a GPS unit for repair by the manufacturer. Many problems are related to peripheral equipment rather than the unit, and simple checks may save considerable sums of money.

   (1)   **Large Fix Error.** The GPS system may be down, or a satellite may be shut down. Check your NAVTEX transmissions or other navigation information source for news of outages. SA may be activated, or the HDOP may simply be excessive due to poor satellite geometry

in your location. With sequential receivers, loss of signal may be a problem in heavy sea states.

(2) **Small Fix Error.** Errors that are not significantly large but consistently outside normal accuracy levels are attributable to a number of sources. The signal may be subject to an excessive amount of atmospheric disturbances, such as periods of extensive solar flare activity. This may be confirmed by similar HF reception difficulties, which also suffer propagation problems. The aerial connections and part of the installation may have degraded, so check the entire system. Make sure aerial orientation is vertical and not partially pushed over. Check that some aerial shadowing has not been introduced.

(3) **No Fix.** This is often caused in sequential receivers by loss of a satellite view or when a satellite goes out of service. Another common cause is the aerial being pushed over to horizontal, so check that it is vertical. Aerial damage from having been struck by equipment is another major cause of a sudden fix loss. Check all cables and connections. If these show no defects, a check of all initialization parameters may be necessary. If these are found to be good, the receiver and aerial may require shore servicing.

(4) **Data Corruption.** This error is often caused by power supply problems. Check whether the incident coincides with engine or machinery run periods. Radiated interference is also a possibility, often from radio equipment. A lightning strike with resultant electromagnetic pulse can also cause similar problems. Another quite common cause of data corruption is that caused by "fingers." Has another person unfamiliar with operating the GPS altered configuration parameters such as time settings or altitude?

19.10   LORAN-C. Loran-C is a long range pulsed low-frequency hyperbolic radio aid. The system relies on the accurate measurement of the time difference of radio signals received from a master and slave transmitters to derive a hyperbolic position line. With two position lines or more, a position fix can be made based on the intersection on lines of position. Loran-C is prone to a range of errors, which are caused from the following:

a. **Skywave and Groundwave Effect.** Loran signals travel via a ground wave, which is the shortest path. Other paths also occur, including several skywave types. Depending on time of day, skywaves may be even stronger than groundwaves, but they always arrive after groundwaves. At chain extremities the stronger skywaves may be stronger than weak groundwaves giving errors up to 10 nm.

b. **Lightning Impulses.** Pulses from lightning can distort or corrupt signals.

c. **Installation.** Correct installation is the key to optimum performance.

Table 19-1 - GPS Troubleshooting

Symptom	Probable Fault
Large fix error	GPS satellite system down Selective availability switched on High HDOP Severe atmospheric problem Satellite acquisition loss (heavy weather)
Small fix error	Atmospheric propagation problem Aerial shadowing
No fix	GPS satellite system down Aerial fault Aerial cable fault Aerial pushed over to horizontal Aerial "view" obstructed
Data corruption	Power supply interference Radiated interference

(1) **Antenna and Coupler Location.** Correct installation away from electrical equipment and other antennas is necessary. Clearance is ideally a minimum of 6 feet. On motor boats either a separate whip antenna or alternatively an insulated backstay can be used.

(2) **Grounding.** The grounding factor is as important as the antenna. This can be the RF ground plate used by other electronic equipment. The grounding wire should be at least 12 AWG.

(3) **Interference.** Interference is the major cause of fix errors. Loran-C is sensitive to noise in the 90–110 kHz spectrum. Common causes are fluorescent lights, alternators, tachometers, and radars. Suppression methods are outlined in chapter 25, and all should be installed. Generally you can test for noise problems using receiver diagnostics to check Signal to Noise Ratio (SNR). With alternators recommended capacitor is a 10,000-microfarad electrolytic rated at 50V. Datamarine's Dart manual also recommends the installation of a 10A fuse in the capacitor line. Ideally install a Newmar power line filter.

19.11   Radio Direction Finding. RDF has been rapidly consigned to oblivion with GPS. There has been a dramatic reduction in beacons and also beacon frequency rationalization. The call sign of the station must be identified correctly before taking a bearing. Most VHF RDF stations in the UK and Europe are for emergency use only during SAR operations. Use caution with others.

Electronic Charting

20.1   Chart Plotters. Most chart plotters universally now incorporate GPS, or conversely are included within GPS units, and are effectively position fixing devices for many. The chart plotter is essentially a display with processor that decodes the data on the chart cartridges for display on the screen. The information is often layered so that chart areas can be expanded, the lights, buoyage and contours can be called up as required.

a.   **Functions and Features.** There are many functions and stored data available. They can include tidal predictions; sun and moon rise and set, Navaids such as lights and buoys (10,000 plus items is typical), waypoints and routes (1000/20 is typical). DSC radio interfacing is also possible showing the location of a vessel in distress. One important feature is sets that use standard chart cartography as some use proprietary software that may not be easily obtainable. There are many features to consider that include drag and drop waypoints, active route waypoint insertion and deletion, and the ability to store routes, and fast redraw times, typically 0.5 to 3 seconds. Cartography features should include clear chart scale indication, clear direction indication when not in North-up mode, an indication when over-zoomed, good buoy visibility and identification, clearly visible and identifiable land features and contours, the use of standard labelling conventions on features, the display of drying heights, the ability to edit contours and shaded depth contours. One key factor is the ability to update and also some identification when the chart was last updated, similar to paper charts. It is important that any unit be user friendly, has intuitive controls, menus, soft keys and dedicated function keys.

b.   **Displays.** Systems now use high-resolution monochrome (gray) LCD displays, or full color active matrix thin film transistor (TFT) displays. Screen display quality or resolution is determined by pixels, i.e. 480 x 350. The greater the number of pixels, the greater the resolution, and the price also increases. Power consumption is typically 6W (0.5 amps). To get the most from dedicated plotters or computer-based software plotting, make sure you read and understand the manual and practice. Trying to learn while under way is both dangerous and distracting. There is a trend in larger motorboats to have PC based systems with remote sunlight viewable displays, for pilothouse and fly bridge. Many displays are flat screen LCD types with SVGA resolution, and external standard ones are waterproof to NEMA 4 standard and are rated up to a brightness of more than 1,600 nit which is 1000% brighter than a laptop computer.

c.   **Power Supplies.** Most sets have variable voltage inputs up to 50 VDC and consume 0.5 to 1.15 amps, along with NMEA inputs and outputs for interfacing GPS. Most power supplies are resilient to electrical system spikes and surges, and on boats with single battery systems load surges during starting can cause problems.

20.2   **Cartography Systems.** The cartographic chart data systems are based on memory chips or more correctly Electronically Programmable Read Only Memory (EPROM) or CD-Rom. There are many formats that include M-93, S-57, NDI and Navionics.

     a.   **Raster Charts.** A Raster Chart is identical to the paper chart, and originates from original government master charts.

          (1)   Admiralty Raster Chart Service (ARCS) charts are supplied on a CD-Rom.

          (2)   Maptech uses raster scan charts and works with the NOAA to produce official charts. Log on to www.maptech.com.

          (3)   Seafarer are identical to ARCS and are produced by the Australian Hydrographic Office for Australian waters.

     b.   **Vector Charts.** The scanning of paper charts to create a raster image produces a Vector Chart. These are then vectorized to store data in layers, allowing easy zooming in on detail. They do not resemble conventional charts. The advantages over raster charts are much faster screen update rates.

          (1)   C-Map NT uses vector charts. The charts are stored on solid-state memory cards that include C-Cards and PCMCIA cards. Log on to www.c-map.com.

          (2)   Passport uses vector charts based on official charts. Log on to www.nobeltec.com.

          (3)   Garmin G-Charts and G-Map are based on Navionics data for Garmin plotters. G-Map is for the new plotters and is available on CD-ROM also.

          (4)   Navionics Microcharts and Nav-Charts. These credit card sized cartridges use PCMCIA formats. Nav-Charts are contained on very small memory cartridges.

20.3   **Chart Corrections and Updates.** Chart corrections and updates are now part of standard services and are offered by Maptech for NOAA charts. They require up-to-date Notices to Mariners, although you can do that via Internet for free now. Log on to www.nms.ukho.gov.co.uk. Cartridges can be updated every couple of years. This fact must be borne in mind with plotters, where they are used as a substitute for properly corrected charts.

20.4   **Software.** Software developments for electronic charting have been rapid with packages offering very powerful navigation tools; the following are leading software packages and salient features. Typical computing power specifications to run the most powerful packages would be at least 16Mb RAM, Pentium 200MHz or greater, Windows 95/98/NT4, CD ROM and 1 serial port. You should check with software supplier for specific package requirements. There are varying features and capabilities and purchasing decisions will be made on them. Software features include the ability to display multiple chart windows; the ability to rotate charts; passage planning showing hazards; the display of tidal heights and streams and planning; the ability to interface using NMEA to autopilot, radar, GPS and instruments; the ability to overlay radar and display ARPA targets.

a. **dKart.** This new software supports ECDIS vector charts from C-Map, CM-93 and the S-57 format. The charts can be rotated Head-up, North-up or Course-up while maintaining text correctly. When used with passage planning, there is automatic hazard identification within a nominated distance of the track. There is also the facility to show safe depth contour around the boat, with automatic hazard identification on your track.

b. **seaPRO 2000.** This uses several chart formats that include the European Livechart vector charts. In addition ARCS, Seafarer, Maptech and NOAA/BSB raster charts can also be used. SeaPRO Plus offers fuel consumption calculations, and ARPA radar targets. The Network version will suit large powerboats that wish to display the information in cabins.

c. **Chartview.** This is from Nobeltec and supports ARCS Skipper and Navigator raster charts, NDI and Maptech formats. A unique feature when using ARCS charts is the ability to automatically place chartlets in the right geographical location on the chart. Also there is seamless chart quilting and rotation. Tidal streams and currents can be accounted for with the built-in tidal prediction tools.

d. **Raytech.** This is a Raymarine product and had its basis in the New Zealand developed Kiwitech software. It supports Navionics, Maptech and C-Map NT. It will offer additional facilities such as engine monitoring, instrument and radar overlays, and route optimization. It also allows integration with Raymarines' Seatalk system, has touch screen capability, and even Internet access.

e. **Visualseries.** This is from Nobeltec and uses the Passport vector charts (formerly Transas), as well as Maptech and NOAA/BSB raster charts.

Echosounders, Fishfinders and Sonar

21.1   Echosounders. The echo- or depthsounder is very important and indispensable. I have spent considerable time working with underwater acoustics systems in the offshore oil industry, and a couple of years working on a submarine sonar program and I can say that this technology is very complex. Equipment performance depends on the output power of the transmitter, the efficiency of the transducer, the sensitivity of the receiver along with the processing software that filters out the spurious noise. Many fishfinders have user selectable noise filters to enhance noise rejection processing. The price of the equipment reflects all of these elements, with the most expensive systems having the highest performance specifications on all factors. The word SONAR is derived from SOund, NAvigation and Ranging and has its origins in World War II anti-submarine warfare. The depthsounder normally projects the acoustic signal directly downwards at a set beam angle so that a cone of coverage is made with respect to the bottom or contours being passed over. Most depthsounders operate at a frequency of 200 kHz, lower transmission frequencies give greater depth capability, although the EchoPilot operates at 150kHz and B & G at 183kHz.

a.   **Digital.** The most common depth instrument is a vertical unit with a digital or analog display incorporating depth alarms, anchor watch alarm facilities, etc. The information displayed is generally several seconds old due to signal processing times.

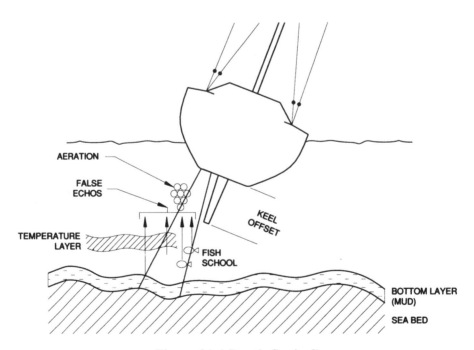

Figure 21-1 Depth Sonic Cone

422

b.   Keel Offset. This adjustment is important so that the depth of the water under the keel is measured; many installations have this inaccurately set. Read the manual and adjust the offset accurately.

c.   Accuracy. Acoustic signals suffer from propagation delays and attenuation as water and various bottom formations cause absorption, scattering, refraction and reflection. Biological matter such as algae and plankton as well as suspended particulate matter such as silt, dissolved minerals and salts can cause this. The water density and salinity levels as well as water temperatures all affect signal propagation. Cold layers of water called thermoclines can affect signal and this is more relevant to deep water. Bottom formations consisting of sand and mud, or large quantities of weed beds will absorb or scatter the signal. Hard bottoms that comprise shale, sand and rock will reflect signal with strong returns. The power output of a unit is also important with respect to range and resolution. The higher the power, the greater the depth range and signal return.

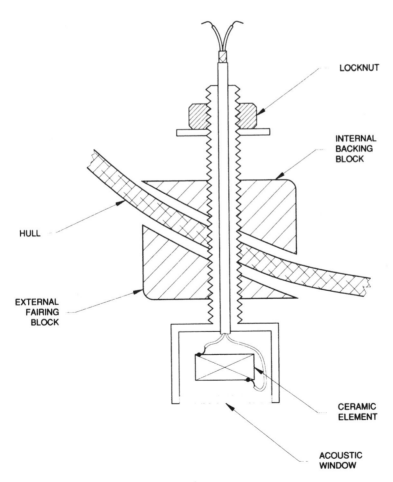

Figure 21-2 Depth Transducer

21.2 **Fishfinders.** Many motor and power boats are used for fishing. A fishfinder is standard on most.

  a.   **Operating Principle.** The basic principle is that an electrical signal is converted to an acoustic signal via a piezoelectric element (crystal) and is transmitted towards the sea bottom. Transducers are typically constructed of a crystal composed of various elements that include lead, zirconate, barium, titanate and conductive coatings. Some fishfinders have transmission power ratings up to 1000W. When the transducer transmits the acoustic signal, it expands to form a cone shaped characteristic. When the acoustic signal strikes a fish or seabed, it is reflected back.

  b.   **Cone Angles.** The shape and diameter of a transducer determines the cone angle. The acoustic signal strength is at maximum along the center axis of the cone, and decreases away from it. The cone angle is based on the power at the center to a point where the power decreases to -3db, with the total angle being measured from -3db point on each side. Most manufacturers offer models with a variety of cone angles. Wide cone angles have less depth capability with wider coverage, and small cone angles give greater depth penetration with reduced area coverage. High Frequency transducers (190 kHz) are available in either wide or narrow cone angles. Low frequency transducers have cone angles in the range 30–45 degrees. The further away from the centerline of the cone, the less strong return echoes are. This can be improved by increasing the sensitivity control.

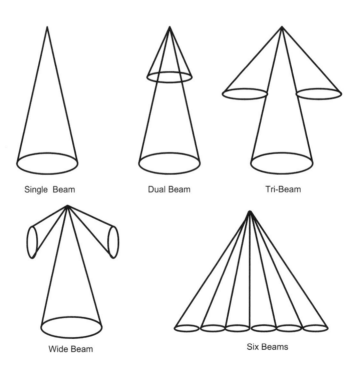

Figure 21-3 Transducer and Beam Angles

c. **Beam Systems.** While most fishfinders have a single beam, manufacturers such as Humminbird (www.humminbird.com) are now introducing multi-beam systems that have several sonar beams ranging from 2 to 6. This subsequently increases the coverage area, and accuracy. The **Single Beam** has a cone angle of 16–24 degrees, which gives a depth of 600-1000 feet. The **Dual Beam** system has ranges up to 2000 feet. The first beam is in the cone center, and a second beam surrounds it to increase the coverage area. The **Tri-Beam** systems have a 90° coverage area with ranges up to 1000 feet. The main beam is directed down, and two beams are configured to each side to give a large coverage area. The **Wide Side** has 3 beams to view bank and bottom contours with the center beam directed down 120 feet and port and starboard to 120 feet. The **6 Beam** system gives a 3D contour display of the sea bottom; Lowrance systems (www.lowrance.com) give a coverage of 53 degrees up to a depth of 240 feet.

d. **Transducer Cavitation.** Cavitation is caused by water turbulence passing over a transducer head and affects transducer performance. At slow speeds the laminar flow is smooth without any interference. At speed air bubbles are created over the transducer face affecting acoustic signal transmission and reception. The effect is to interfere with transmitted acoustic signals that reflect back off the bubbles, which effectively causes noise and masks signals. Turbulence is caused by hull form or obstructions, water flow over the transducer, and propulsion. Transom mounted units must be carefully mounted to avoid turbulence from outboard motors or water flow off the transom. The higher the speed the greater the turbulence; riveted alloy boats create turbulence off each rivet head. Manufacturers are designing transducers that work better at higher speeds, including transducers with improved hydrodynamic shapes. Transducers must be mounted in areas of little turbulence or clear of hull flow areas, which is not always easy.

21.3 **Frequencies and Power Output.** Transmission frequency affects both the depth range and cone angle. The speed of sound in water is a constant of 4800 ft per second, and the time between the transmission and reception of the returned signal is measured to give a range or depth figure. Lowrance has a frequency of 192 kHz and a deepwater one of 50kHz. Simrad units have a user selectable tri-frequency capability of 38/50, 38/200 or 50/200kHz with depth range up to 1800 meters, and a maximum ping rate of 15 per second. Shallow waters less than 300 feet give the best results with high frequency transducers of 200kHz and wide cone angles up to 20 degrees. In depths greater than 300 feet, low frequency transducers of 50kHz with small cone angles of 8 degrees are the best option. Furuno has introduced the Free Synthesizer (FFS) Transceiver on the FCV 1200 Color Video Sounder, with frequency and output power user selectable. The dual-frequency sounder has output settings of 15, 28, 38, 50, 88, 107 and 200 kHz. Power outputs are quoted in watts, some quote peak-to-peak. The use of watts RMS is the more accurate, typically within the range 100–600 watts.

21.4 **Fishfinder Displays.** The most common display type is the Liquid Crystal Display (LCD). Lowrance has what is called Film SuperTwist and Humminbird use FSTN displays that use black and not blue or tan pixels. Displays must be both high resolution and good contrast and are typically in the range of 240 and 320 vertical pixels. Displays are also sometimes quoted in pixels per square inch, i.e. 15,170, and the more pixels the better the resolution. The LCD display includes a complex grid of pixels, small square display elements that comprise a screen image. Pixels are turned on or off to form an image on the screen, and return echoes are processed and displayed as dark pixels. Grayscale displays images in several shades of gray to indicate signal strength variations, with strong signals being very dark and weak ones light gray. Each successive return activates a new column of pixels so that a continuous image is displayed on the screen as each column is replaced. The display resolution quality depends on the number of pixels in each vertical column. The number of horizontal pixels determines the retention period that a displayed image is on the screen. This also determines the ability of a system to support additional image windows in a split screen mode. Some units have high-resolution displays in 8 or 16 colors on a 10.4-inch TFT LCD display. Color displays use up to 16 colors for different signal strengths, the stronger ones are displayed in red, and weaker signals as green or blue, for example baitfish schools are generally in blue or green, with larger game fish being yellow, orange or red. The seabed and wrecks are usually displayed as dark orange or red.

a. **Whiteline Function.** All fishfinders have a feature called grayline or whiteline that assists in discriminating bottom hardness from the bottom contours. The bottom is displayed as a thin dark line with a gray area below it. Thin lines and thick gray areas represent hard bottoms, and a thick black line with no gray represents soft bottoms. This allows targeting of precise bottom formations for specific fish types. The Grayline feature on Lowrance fishfinders allows differentiation between soft and hard bottom types. The feature "paints" gray on bottom targets that have a stronger signal return than preset values. A soft mud type bottom will have a relatively weak return and this is displayed as a narrow gray line. Hard rock bottoms will have a strong return and be represented with a wide gray line, the gray always having the strongest signal.

b. **Zoom Function.** The zoom function allows the magnification of a portion of the depth range to improve analysis and identification of targets in that area. The typical magnification scales are x2 and x4 the normal scale. This allows monitoring of a certain depth range such as 40 to 50 feet, or zooming on the bottom and 10 feet above it. The split screen feature allows tracking of different features simultaneously such as zoom segment and the bottom contour.

c. **Sensitivity.** The sensitivity control enables the receiver to tune in or tune out returns. If the unit is set with low sensitivity, it will not detect bottom details, fish or obstructions. If it is set with high sensitivity, it will return signals on everything and will clutter the screen with spurious returns. Sensitivity should be adjusted so that bottom is clearly defined along with white or gray line and some surface clutter. Most fishfinders have automatic sensitivity adjustment, which compensates for ambient water conditions and depth. Lowrance has Advanced Signal Processing (ASP) which uses complex software to process parameters such as water conditions, noise and interference levels, boat speed to automatically adjust control settings to optimize the images on the display. This entails setting the sensitivity to the highest level possible without allowing noise to be displayed, creating a balance between noise rejection and sensitivity. Submarine sonar systems use extremely sophisticated signal processors and software and this approach is very similar. The sea is a very dynamic environment and sound travels very great distances. The acoustic signals can be absorbed and reflected. The higher the frequencies the greater scattering effects. The lower the frequency the greater the range. Wave actions, microorganisms, varying salt densities and suspended solids further enhance signal scattering.

d. **Water Temperature and Thermoclines.** Water temperature affects fish, as they are cold-blooded animals, and they have the same temperature as the surrounding water. Due to biological factors, fish feeding and spawning behavior is dependent on water temperature, so that fish are generally found at locations where the water temperature suits activities. Any body of water consists of layers, the surface is generally warmer than the middle or bottom layers. The interface between areas of different temperature is called a thermocline. Thermoclines are important to locating fish as they tend to be found either just above or below them. Fishfinders can detect thermoclines; the greater the difference in temperatures the more visible it becomes.

e. **Fish Arches.** The display of fish arches on the screen is directly related to sonar acoustic characteristics. As a fish enters the acoustic cone a display pixel is turned on, and as it moves towards the center of the cone, the distance between the transducer and fish decreases so that pixels are progressively turned on and display a shallower depth and therefore a stronger signal. When the fish reaches the cone center this forms half the arch, and the other half is completed as the fish moves towards the outer edge of the cone. Very small fish probably will not arch at all. Because of water conditions such as heavy surface clutter or thermoclines, the sensitivity sometimes cannot be turned up enough to get fish arches. For the best results, turn the sensitivity up as high as possible without getting too much noise on the screen. In medium to deep water, this method should work to display fish arches. If the fish does not pass through the cone center the arch will either be partial or not be displayed. Arches are not formed in shallower waters as the cone angle becomes too narrow. Arches are not formed when the boat is drifting or anchored. Fish schools vary in displayed shape depending on how much of the school is within the cone. In deeper water each fish if large enough may have an arch displayed. Fish arches are created when the cone of sound passes over a fish. The distance to a fish when the cone first strikes it is shown in Fig A. When the center of the cone strikes the fish, the distance is shorter as shown in Fig B. As the cone leaves the fish, the distance increases again as shown in Fig C. The size of fish arches depends on the sensitivity adjustments, the boat speed, the water depth and cone angle, and location of the fish within the cone.

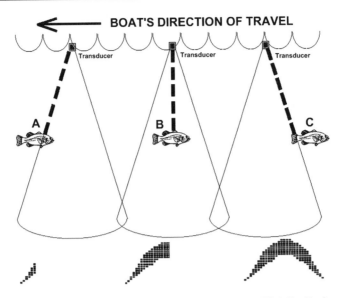

Figure 21-4 Fish Arches (Lowrance Fishfinder)

21.5   Forward Looking Sonar. The most identifiable is the EchoPilot. These systems have benefited greatly from developments in processing power and speed. The units consist of a powerful processing unit, which enables real time processing of data. This is different to the normal depthsounder, which has an inherent delay of typically up to 16 seconds. The transducer head scans from vertical to horizontal with a beam width of 15 degrees and can "see" up to 150 meters forward. Maximum range depends on water depth and seabed contours, with a bottom that is shoaling being easier to see than one that is level or deepening. Like all sonar and depth transducers the head must be clear of turbulence. These units operate at 200kHz; two units operating close together will cause corruption of data. Also it is important to note other depthsounders and fishfinder frequencies; if all three are at 200kHz, problems will arise and only one can be reliably operated and the others switched off.

21.6   Installation. Be very careful not to bump the transducer and possibly damage the crystal element. Most installations are through-hull mounted on a fairing block to ensure that beam is facing directly down on an even keel, and to reduce any water flow turbulence. Locate in an area of minimal turbulence. Water bubbles from turbulence are a common cause of problems. In some cases they are mounted inside the hull within an oil bath or epoxy fastened to the hull on GRP boats. There is a sacrifice in maximum depths, which can reach 60–70% reduction in range and therefore should be avoided where possible.

     a.   **Stern Mounting.** Many powerboats also mount the transducer on a retractable bracket on the stern or transom. This arrangement while effective and less work on smaller vessels is not ideal on bigger ones. Turbulence from the propellers and laminar flow breaking away from the hull generally affect operation and it is only effective at very low speeds.

b. **Cabling.** Always ensure that cables are installed clear of heavy current carrying cables or radio aerial cables. Never install next to log cables as is generally done, as the interference problem can be significant.

21.7   Maintenance and Troubleshooting. The transducer is the only item that can be maintained, and, if not, will dramatically reduce performance. Cleaning is essential, and regular removal of growth off the transducer should be undertaken. Do not bump it or apply any impact to the surface. Avoid applying antifouling to the transducer surface, as it includes small voids and air bubbles, which will reduce sensitivity. If necessary, smear on a very thin layer with your finger. Troubleshooting often entails reading the manual and determining whether settings and operating procedures are correct. Go into the settings or options menu and ensure settings are on auto or defaulting to factory settings.

a. **Connections.** Check all connectors and connector pins for damage, and make sure they are straight and not bent. If straightened the pins might break as they are brittle. Connectors not properly inserted or tightened up are prone to saltwater ingress and corrosion.

b. **Cables.** Check all cables for damage, cuts or fatigue. The transom mounted transducer cables are prone to damage and on some smaller fishing boats the transducer hull cables may be damaged.

c. **Power Supply.** Connection problems are the major cause, either at the supply panel, or at the battery. Check the power at the plug using a multimeter set. If the engine voltmeter shows normal charge voltages, and battery checks out then it is in the intermediate connections.

d. **Interference.** If the fishfinder has interference, turn off all other equipment and then turn engine off. Progressively start up engine and then other equipment to determine the source, and the power supply may require suppression. Check that two fishfinders are not being run at the same time. Two vessels in very close proximity may also cause mutual interference if using similar acoustic frequencies. If the interference is present with all systems off, the fishfinder automatic noise rejection facility may be malfunctioning.

e. **Transducer.** Inspect the transducer for damage, marine growth, antifouling paints, and clean off the surfaces using soapy water. Do not use heavy abrasives or chisels to clean the faces.

f. **Trawler Sonar Systems.** Many trawlers lower transducers using a hydraulic hoist. These are closed systems and oil levels must be monitored. Control systems such as solenoid valves, check and flow control valves and limit switches must also be checked. Also monitor motor insulation values as they are often located in moist areas.

Radar and Radar Reflectors

22.1 **Radar.** RADAR is an acronym for **RA**dio **D**etection **A**nd **R**anging. Radar is a method for locating the presence of a target, and calculating its range and angular position with respect to the radar transmitter. For closing landfalls, navigating channels and poor visibility, radar units make navigation a lot easier. As a navigational aid, radar offers many very useful functions:

(1) Position fixing from geographical points.

(2) Positions of other vessels.

(3) Positions of buoys.

(4) Land formations when trying to make a landfall in poor visibility.

(5) Rain and squall locations.

(6) Collision avoidance at night and in poor visibility.

22.2 **Radar Theory.** Radar transmits a pulse of radio frequency (RF) energy. This is radiated from a highly directional rotating transmitter called the scanner. Any reflected energy is then received and processed to form an image. The time interval between transmission of the signal and reception of reflected energy can be processed to give target distance and bearing. The subject of radar reflection theory is complex and is covered extensively elsewhere. It is essential to understand how radar signals behave on various target materials if radar is to be fully utilized.

22.3 **Radar Scanners.** In practice, the longer the scanner, the narrower the beam width, which gives better target discrimination. Of the two main scanner types, beam widths of enclosed scanners are always larger than open types. This factor is one of the trade-offs that has to be considered when selecting a radar unit. If it can be accommodated, an open scanner performs far better.

    a. **Scanner Types.** The enclosed array scanners are commonly installed. There are two basic types of antenna elements in use:

        (1) **Printed Circuit Board.** Printed circuit board phased antenna arrays are commonly fitted to enclosed scanners. The antenna is on a circuit board instead of the more expensive slotted waveguides.

        (2) **Slotted Waveguide.** Center fed, slotted waveguide arrays are normally used on open array antennas and on larger range radomes.

    b. **Open Scanners.** The traditional open array scanner is more suited to motorboats and offers significant advantages. An open scanner has a beam width nearly half that of enclosed units and as such gives far better target discrimination. If you can tolerate an open scanner, opt for one, the improved performance is worth it. The power consumption is greater which on a motorboat is not a problem. On motorboats the open scanner is far more practicable without the issues that sailing vessels have with weight and snagging of ropes.

c.   **Side Lobe Attenuation.** Beam widths are not precisely cut off. There are zones outside the main beam where power is wasted and dissipated. End slotted waveguides are often used in new radars to suppress side lobes, which generate false echoes. False echoes are more pronounced on short ranges at increased sensitivity.

d.   **Frequencies.** All small boat radars operate on microwave frequencies in what is termed the X band. Frequency ranges are 9200 to 9500 MHz, a wavelength of around 3 cm. Large commercial vessels also have S-band radars.

e.   **Output Power.** Power ratings are given for the actual microwave output power. A 16-mile radar is typically 1.5 kW; 24 nm–2.2 kW; 36 and 48nm – 4kW; 64nm–6kW and 72 nm–12kW. A kitchen microwave operates on a similar principle. Given the effect microwaves have on food, the warning on eye protection should be followed. It is quite common on naval vessels with high power radars to have any bird life in the rigging incinerated when radars are started up.

f.   **Range Discrimination.** Range discrimination or resolution is a function of transmission pulse length. Where the distance between two targets on the same bearing is longer than the pulse length, they are shown as separate. When the distance between targets is less than the pulse length, they will appear as one target. Most radars automatically alter pulse length with a change in range settings.

g.   **Beam Angles.** Radar transmissions are similar to the light beam from a lighthouse, in that a radar's beam has a defined angle in both vertical and horizontal planes. The beam width is normally defined as the angle over which the power is at least half of maximum output.

   (1)   **Horizontal.** Horizontal beam widths open scanners are in the range 1.2° – 2.5° and closed radomes are greater at 3.9° –7°.

   (2)   **Vertical.** Vertical beam widths are all typically in the range 25 to 30°. The larger the width, the better the performance under heeling conditions. It must be remembered that there is always a blind spot around the vessel. Close targets may not be seen as they are inside the minimum range.

   (3)   **Trim Angles.** The trim of a motorboat, and therefore the scanner, has an adverse effect on performance. As most radars have vertical beam angles of around 25°, at any heel angle there will be degradation on the windward side, creating a blind spot. This is common when rolling in a beam sea when there is reflection off the backs of passing waves. Trim both fore and aft also affects performance. When a vessel is up on the plane, a radar installed level when stopped will be virtually useless, as the beam will point skywards when under way. It should be installed so that in normal conditions the beam is 12 ½° above and below the horizon. It should be noted

that at low speeds, the beam will angle downwards significantly affecting range, and may be only useful on short range settings.

h. **Target Discrimination.** Target discrimination or resolution is a function of beam width. A scanner with a narrow beam width is effectively slicing and sampling sectors of approximately 2.5° around the azimuth. Large targets will be sampled a number of times and their size quantified. A wider beam width will sample an area twice that size, and will not always discriminate between two or more targets. If a harbor entrance is narrow, the radar beam may in fact see it as part of the breakwater until the range has closed up. Two targets at the same distance and close together may appear as one at longer ranges.

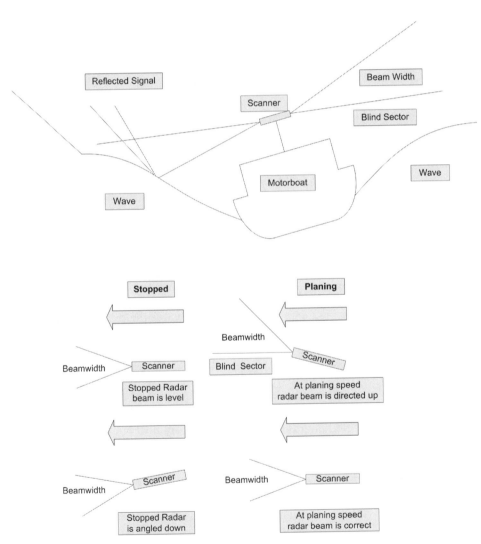

Figure 22-1 Radar Heeling Angles

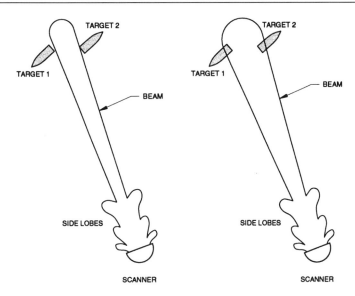

Figure 22-2 Target Discrimination

22.4   Radar Horizons. Maximum radar ranges are a function of both aerial and target height. Radar returns are affected by the target characteristics and also atmospheric conditions. Standard conditions are a pressure of 1013mb, temperature at sea level of 30°C, and a relative humidity of 60%. The formula for 3 cm radars for calculating radar horizon distance is RH in nm = $2.21\sqrt{h}$ where h = height of aerial or target. Radar waves are bent due to refraction, increasing range by about 15% greater than the geometrical horizon which is 1.92 $\sqrt{h}$ to give $2.21\sqrt{h}$. The sea horizon is nm = $2.095\sqrt{h}$ in meters, so the average person at 3 meters can see about 3.6 nm. The sum of the radar horizon distances of the aerial and target respectively gives the maximum distance at which target can return an echo. This is then A = $2.21\sqrt{h}$ (Aerial Height) + B = $2.21\sqrt{h}$ (Target Height). Super-refraction occurs when warm air is located above cold air masses, and with decreased relative humidity. Sub-refraction can also occur. The radar horizon table gives approximate maximum theoretical radar ranges that can be expected for various radar scanner and target heights.

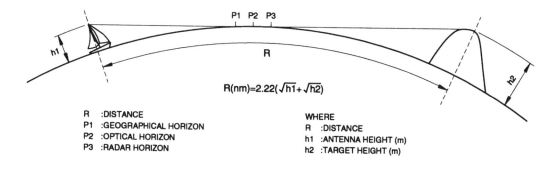

Figure 22-3 Radar Horizons

Table 22-1 Radar Horizon Table

Target Height (Meters)	Scanner Height 5 m	Scanner Height 10 m	Scanner Height 15 m	Scanner Height 20 m	Scanner Height 25 m
Zero	5.0 nm	7.0 nm	8.6 nm	9.9 nm	11.1 nm
5	10.0	12.0	13.5	15.0	16.0
10	12.0	14.0	15.5	17.0	18.0
15	13.5	15.5	17.3	18.5	19.8
20	14.8	17.0	18.5	19.8	21.0
25	16.0	18.2	19.8	21.0	22.3
30	17.3	19.0	20.8	22.0	23.3
35	18.0	20.0	21.8	23.0	24.3

22.5   Radar Displays. There are two display types available on radar systems. The display is also called the Plan Position Indicator (PPI) and this is still used as a term for normal representation. Some new types have a 3D image display of targets.

   a.   **Liquid Crystal Displays.** LCD displays are now found on most new radars. New generation LCD displays have high resolutions and have good direct daylight viewing qualities. Typically this is 232 x 320 pixels on small displays up to 1280 x 960 pixels on large units. These are either color or monochrome. These displays use the same technology as computer monitors. Essentially the screen consists of many dots, which are called pixels. The status of the pixels is installed in the memory and altered in response to signal processing changes, and is updated each antenna scan. Signal processing uses previous scan and current scan to confirm radar returns, and in many cases it takes 3 scans to display a target at full brightness. This allows clutter to be screened out, and low visibility targets that are within clutter to be distinguished. Unlike the CRT display, the rasterscan display is a result of complex digital signal processing of the radar information and allows the use of numerical information on the screen. Digital processing of signals usually has a minimum level that can be displayed, and consequently weak echoes are often rejected. For this reason proper tuning and operation is essential if all targets above that threshold are to be displayed. Manufacturers have introduced a number of processing techniques to overcome these shortcomings.

   (1)   **Single Level Quantization.** This method displays all targets at the same intensity level, regardless of size or strength of return. The main problem is that targets, sea clutter and rain have to be distinguished.

(2) **Multi Level Quantization.** This method of processing assigns echoes into strength categories. The stronger echoes appear bright, while weak echoes appear dim on the screen. Inconsistent or weak echoes may not be displayed. These systems are more expensive as more processing power is required.

b. **CRT Displays.** The cathode ray tube was the primary display type until recent technology advances. The radial display was synchronized with the scanner and effectively displayed every return, the brightness of the target being relative to target strength. These displays were hard to view in daylight. Some new radar still use them, and the images are sharper.

c. **Overlay.** This is a significant technological breakthrough. It enables radar screen images to be directly overlaid onto a chart image. In addition, the screen can share images and windows having chart plotter or fishfinder can be displayed simultaneously. Raymarine uses its HSB data system to allow live transfer of images, and automatic synchronization of chart and radar images is performed.

22.6 Display Orientation. Radar display modes can be made to orient in North-up, Head-up, Course-up and True Motion.

a. **Relative Motion.** The motion of the target is relative to the motion of the boat. Targets all move on the display. Relative vector lines on the display show calculated course and speed of the targets referencing the bow of the boat. Relative bearings reference the boat's heading. Relative target speed is speed referenced to boat's speed and course. Relative target course is referenced to the boat's own bow. A speed log input will allow processing of boat relative speed.

(1) **North Up.** Interfacing of a gyro or fluxgate compass gives the true north at head of screen. One of the advantages of this display is that both chart and display are corresponding and bearings are easily transferred for plotting purposes, which is where many plotting and navigating errors are made.

(2) **Head Up.** The top of the screen is the same as the vessel heading and therefore all bearings are relative.

(3) **Course Up.** The top of the screen is aligned to the selected course using an interfaced gyro or fluxgate compass.

b. **True Motion.** This is the true motion of targets and the boat. This means that land or fixed non-moving targets are stationary while the boat and moving targets are moving. True vectors are lines on the display that show calculated course and speed of the boat and the targets are referenced to true North. True bearings reference true North. True target speed is actual speed made good of the target. True target course is referenced to true North. True motion requires a gyro or fluxgate compass input to measure boat heading relative to true North.

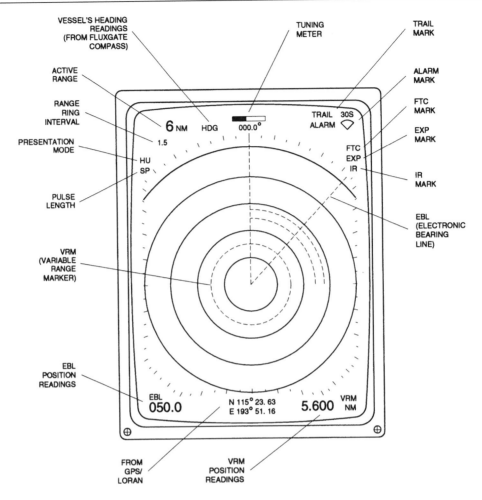

Figure 22-4 Koden 24-nm Radar Display

22.7   **Radar Installation.** Several factors must be considered.

   a.   **Mounting.** There are a number of factors affecting the mounting of the scanner on a fly bridge, or navigation mast:

   (1)   **Radar Range.** The advantage of increased radar range is clearly illustrated in the radar horizon table.

   (2)   **Blind Sectors.** The positioning of the scanner is important. Where scanners are mounted on motorsailer mizzenmasts, you may have a small forward and stern blind shadow sector.

   (3)   **Scanner Leveling.** On powerboats, in particular planing hull vessels, the scanner has to be mounted with respect to level when on a plane. When stopped, the scanner will be angled downwards at the front.

b. **Eye Damage.** Direct exposure to an operating radar transmission can permanently damage retinas or cause blindness. Safe distances are normally given as around 1 meter but recent medical research has recommended an absolute minimum of 2 meters. Scanners mounted very low down where people can pass in front of them represent a very real health hazard, especially with powerful output units.

c. **Cables.** Scanner cables come in a single length and where cutting and joining is required care must be taken. Very few options exist other than multipin plugs or junction boxes available for this purpose. Always ensure that radar cables are well protected from chafing where they enter the mast.

d. **Power Consumption.** Small boat radars generally have power consumption in the range of 3–4 amps. Open scanners typically have a power consumption 50% greater than enclosed types. This is because they have a heavier scanner and the motor required to rotate it is more powerful.

e. **Economy Mode.** This function has been incorporated into a number of new radars and is very useful for power-conscious boaters. The radar can remain operating with guard zones activated and the display off to save power. If any target is detected within the guard zone, the alarm will sound and display can be called up with one button. With a typical power consumption of 3.3 amps, the power saving mode is only 2 amps, which is quite significant in terms of battery power.

f. **Grounding.** Radar as a transmitter requires proper grounding and this is usually at the scanner, and the rear of the display unit.

22.8   Radar Operation. Correct operation of radar is essential if you are to get the maximum benefit from it. You should attend a shore-based course. Don't become one of the very common radar assisted casualties. At first sight, radar has a bewildering array of controls, but they all have clearly defined functions, which can be easily learned. Many adjustments are automatic and Raymarine calls it Auto GST (Gain, Sea-clutter, Tune). Simrad has a useful powerboat function called high-speed mode that doubles antenna rotation speed and therefore image update for high speed target tracking.

a. **Power Up.** At power up, all radars have a magnetron warm-up period. Upon completion, the radar always defaults to stand-by status. When operating a new set, allow it to warm up for at least 30 minutes prior to adjustment and use.

b. **Range Selection.** Always set the range you wish to work on. Typically the 12-mile range is ideal for the average motorboat given the radar horizon. On a scanner mounted high up, a greater range will enable the detection of a large vessel on or just over the horizon. Selecting a range automatically sets the appropriate range ring intervals, the pulse length, and the pulse repetition rate.

c. **Adjust Brilliance.** Adjust the brilliance control to suit your requirements. Do not make it too bright at night, or so dim that targets are not clearly displayed.

d. **Adjust Gain.** Most new radars have automatic adjustment. If manual, adjust the gain control so that screen speckling starts to appear. As this controls the signal amplification, be very careful not to over adjust. Smaller echoes can be masked, or if under the required threshold, they will not appear at all. The gain control is used to remove background noise that appears on the display. Large areas of irregular speckles characterize this across the display. The gain is normally set high for long ranges and reduced for low ones.

e. **Adjust Anti Clutter.** Most new radars have automatic adjustment. This control is often referred to as the sensitivity time constant (STC) control. Clutter is most apparent at the screen center and occurs in that region closest to the vessel. Sea clutter is interference caused by rough seas or wave action where some of the transmitted signal is reflected off the wave faces. Most 3-cm radars transmit a very low signal angle that grazes the water surface. On short ranges, clutter can mask targets, especially weak ones, and the effect decreases at long ranges. Sea clutter always appears stronger on the lee side of the vessel because the vessel heel in that direction exposes the beam to larger water areas or the backs of passing waves.

f. **Tuning.** The majority of radars are self-tuning, and adjustment will be indicated on a small bar readout on the screen. Most radars can be manually tuned, but this should be done carefully.

g. **Pulse Length Selection.** Pulse length selection is automatic with range changes. At short ranges, pulses are at 0.05 microsecond and give better target resolution. At long ranges, they increase to 1.0 microsecond.

h. **Pulse Repetition.** Repetition rates vary across ranges from 200 to 2,500 per second. Rates determine the size of the area around the vessel where there is a dead zone. At 0.05 microsecond, this is around 150 meters. At 1.0 microsecond, this reduces to 30 meters.

i. **Fast Time Constant (FTC).** Most new radars have automatic adjustment. This control is used to reduce rain clutter. Rain clutter is proportional to the density of the rain, fog or snow. Although useful in tracking squalls and rain, caution should be used so that targets are not obscured. Heavy rain may cause total loss of target definition and cannot be adjusted for.

j. **Interference Rejection.** Interference on the display can come from other radars operating in the area. This is particularly apparent near major shipping routes where powerful commercial vessel radars are operating. Use of the IR function will remove these unwanted signals.

22.9 **Radar Plotting.** The whole basis of radar is to detect both stationary and fixed targets. A number of basic features facilitate this:

a. **Range Rings.** The range rings are self-explanatory. They will alter with the selected radar range.

b. **Variable Range Maker (VRM).** This function uses the range rings and the marker, and many types of radar have two VRMs. The readout appears on the screen, but as with all navigation exercises, make sure you are measuring the correct target. Many errors are made this way, which is why radar should be used in conjunction with other position keeping systems, principally the chart and Mark I eyeball.

c. **Electronic Bearing Line (EBL).** The most commonly used function in conjunction with the VRM enables easy plotting of a target, but be careful, many unfortunate incidents occur because a bearing was taken without checking what display is in use, such as true or relative motion.

d. **Target Expansion.** This function on many types of radar allows small- or long-range contacts to be expanded, and can be very useful when making landfalls of low altitude, particularly low atolls and islands.

e. **Off Centering.** A number of radar sets have an offset function which alters the screen center (the vessel) 50% down the screen. This makes forward long-range observation possible in the same radar range.

f. **Guard Zones.** Guard zones offer real safety advantages. They can be set for complete circular coverage or for specific sectors. However, it is wrong to rely on these functions. A proper observation should be made regularly. On some newer radar, an economy or sleep mode saves power by letting the guard zone and alarm function operate without the screen being on.

g. **Target Plotting and ARPA.** This feature comes on most radar and allows a trail to be plotted on targets. Target plotting is time related and can be continuous or set in seconds or minutes. A clear plot of the target is invaluable in ensuring that close quarters or collision risks do not arise. MARPA allows tracking of 10 targets, with selectable target vectors, target risk assessment with alarms, and calculation of target speed, course, CPA and TCPA.

22.10 **Radar Maintenance.** There is not much maintenance required on a radar unit, but undertaking the following will ensure long-term reliability:

a. **Connections.** Once a year, open the scanner and tighten all the terminal screws.

b. **Clean Scanners.** Clean the scanner with warm soapy water to remove salt and dirt. Do not scour or use harsh detergents.

c. **Scanner Bolts.** Check and tighten the scanner holding bolts.

d. **Gaskets.** Check that the scanner's watertight gaskets are in good condition and sealing properly.

e. **Scanner Motor Brushes.** Some scanner motors have brushes. Check these every 6 months. Manufacturers sometimes provide a spare set taped to the motor (such as Koden).

f. **Display Unit.** Clean the screen with a clean cloth soaked with an anti-static agent. Do not use a dry cloth as this can cause static charging that attracts and accumulates dust.

22.11   Radar Troubleshooting. The following table gives typical faults on radar that can be investigated and rectified prior to calling a technician.

Table 22-2 Radar Troubleshooting

Symptom	Probable Fault
Scanner stopped	Motor brush stuck (if fitted)
	Bearing seized
	Scanner motor failure
	Scanner motor control failure
No display	Power switched off
	Brightness turned down
	Fuse failure
	Loose power plug
	Incorrectly tuned
Display on, no targets	Scanner stopped
	Local scanner switch off
	Scanner plug not plugged in
Low sensitivity	Ground connection loose
	Radome salt encrusted
	Open array salt encrusted

22.12   Radar Reflectors. The subject of radar reflection has been one of continuing controversy over the years with a constant stream of so-called reflective safety devices being launched upon unsuspecting boaters. Not to have an effective reflector mounted at all times is, in my judgement, negligent in the extreme. Many motorboats travel at high speeds with significant closing speeds on other motor vessels. There is often little decision-making time available and being visible to other vessels is critical. As many larger commercial vessels have ARPA radar that computes and alarms when on collision headings, this is also important.

a. **Merchant Vessel Visibility.** I have been on the bridge of fast merchant vessels steaming up the English Channel at 24 knots, or through the Caribbean and up the US East Coast dodging motorboats and yachts that are virtually radar invisible. In deep ocean waters, there is still a requirement to be visible. While the shipping lanes may constitute areas of heavy commercial traffic, commercial vessels ply waters everywhere. The commonly adopted view that no one is keeping a lookout and reflectors are unnecessary is fatally flawed. Most vessels have the X and S band radars with ARPA collision avoidance tracking and alarm systems, and if the radar cannot lock on to a good consistent signal, the vessel radar cannot compute and track a target. With large and fast vessels, the earlier you are detected and your course and collision risks assessed, the earlier action can be taken to change course and avoid any close quarters situation.

b. **Search and Rescue.** Besides the collision risk problem, the important Search and Rescue (SAR) benefits cannot be over stated. It never ceases to amaze me how many SAR operations are called off at night. The amount of valuable flying time and fuel that is expended in aerial search patterns under poor conditions and low cloud bases simply because no effective reflector is hoisted is frightening. All that airborne and shipborne high technology equipment is wasted. Reaction times, rescues and survival prospects even in spite of EPIRBs are decreased in the localization and visual identification phase.

c. **Weight, Windage and Aesthetics.** One of the main reasons stated for not having a reflector installed is that reflectors are either too bulky or unsightly. Another cause is windage or they are too heavy on a navigation mast in spite of having a radar and lights up there. Firdell has developed compact, aesthetically acceptable low-profile units specifically for motor- and power-boats.

d. **Mast Shadowing.** Wherever you mount your reflector, there will be some shadowing from the navigation mast. When a reflector such as a Blipper 210-7 is mounted directly to the front of a mast, there is typically a 5–10° blind spot directly aft, the lowest collision risk sector of all. A motorboat's track is far from straight, whether under autopilot or hand steering. Typically variation is in the range of 10° to 25°. Even though some reflective surface will be "seen," this movement will expose a substantial number of reflective corners sufficient to offer a reasonably consistent return at a range of at least 5 miles on a collision course.

22.13   Reflector Theory. To understand reflectors, a basic understanding of the behavior of radar signal is required.

a. **Radar Beam Behavior.** When a radar beam reaches a target, in theory it reflects back on a reciprocal course to be processed into a range and bearing for display on the screen. In practice, a beam does not simply bounce back off an object, as some materials are more reflective than others, while others absorb the signal.

b. **Reflective Materials.** The best reflective structures are made of steel and aluminum. Materials such as wood and fiberglass do not reflect at all. In fact fiberglass absorbs some 50% of a radar signal. There will always be some reflection of most materials, but the direction of the reflected beams will be erratic and so minimal that no consistent return can be monitored.

c. **Reflection Consistency.** Consistency is one of the major requirements of a good reflector. A good reflector consists of a metallic structure, normally aluminum, with surfaces placed at 90° to each other. If a beam is directed to the center of a re-entrant trihedral, parallel to the centerline, it will reflect around and emerge back on a reciprocal course back to the scanner. A re-entrant trihedral is simply a corner with three sides, such as the corner made up of two walls and a ceiling. The basis of understanding radar reflectors comes from a basic principle. The centerline of the corner points in a direction is approximately 36° to each of the sides making up the trihedral. The more the angle increases away from the centerline from a radar beam, the less radar signal returns back.

d. **Radar Reflection Standards.** The basic standards include a number of specifications. Never buy a reflector that does not comply. A peak echoing area of 10m^2 is defined as the equivalent of a metal sphere of approximately 12-feet diameter.

(1) **ISO (8729).** This is an IMO sponsored standard, and specifies an RCS of 2.5 m^2 as the minimum threshold of radar visibility.

(2) **USCG.** A standard is set down for survival craft reflector. Manufacturers are required to demonstrate a range of 4 nm in a calm sea.

(3) **DOT (UK).** Set down in the Marine Radar Performance Specification 197, it requires that reflectors have an equivalent echoing area of at least 10 m^2.

22.14 Reflector Types. There are a variety of reflectors on the market. See the illustrations below. The illustrations are close to scale and show the relative sizes of the devices.

a. **Octahedrals.** The standard octahedral is a structure consisting of 8 re-entrant trihedrals. It was developed in the early 1940s when radar was under development. For optimum effect, they must be mounted in the proper orientation, which is called the "catchrain" position. It is amazing how many are mounted or hoisted up by a corner. One magazine survey gave a figure approaching 70%, and my survey is closer to 80%. The structure, in fact, has only 6 effective corners, pointing alternately up and down, the remaining corners being of little use. The effectiveness of the radar reflector is shown in the polar diagram. On the typical 18-inch octahedral polar diagram, the lobes where peak reflection occurs are clearly visible. The peaks clearly exceed the peak echoing area of 10 m^2. The big problem, however, is the large areas between the lobes, where no reflection occurs, or is so minimal that they are under the minimum standards set down by IMO of 2.5 m^2. The total

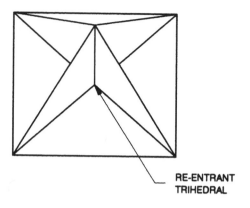

RE-ENTRANT
TRIHEDRAL

18" OCTAHEDRAL IN CORRECT "CATCHRAIN" POSITION

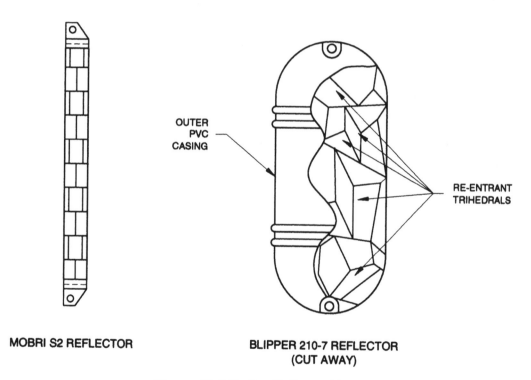

OUTER
PVC
CASING

RE-ENTRANT
TRIHEDRALS

MOBRI S2 REFLECTOR

**BLIPPER 210-7 REFLECTOR
(CUT AWAY)**

Figure 22-5 Radar Reflector Types

blind spots on the correctly hoisted octahedral total nearly 120°, which is not ideal. The small peaks do not affect the result much. The bad news is that, heeled to 15°, the blind spots increase to nearly 180°. Signal return can be further decreased where part of the signal, after reflecting off the sea surface, cancels out another beam traveling directly to the reflector. If you are using an octahedral, anything under 18" is a waste of money.

b. **Optimized Arrays.** The Marconi-Firdell Blipper 210-7 typifies these reflectors. The Blipper consists of an array of precisely positioned re-entrant trihedrals designed to give consistent 360° coverage, and through heel angles up to 30°. As a vessel moves around in a typical 3-dimensional motion, each of the corners moves in and out of 'phase' to the radar signal, with one corner sending back signal directly, and others giving partial returns, resulting in a consistent return at all times. The units are rotationally molded inside a radar-invisible plastic case, and the windage is only 15% of an 18" octahedral. They weigh less than 5 lbs (2 kg). These reflectors have a reputation for meeting and exceeding all published standards, and the numbers mounted on sailing yacht masts attests to this. A survey at a major British marina was marginally over 50%. The Blipper 210-7 has a NATO stock number, which indicates the effectiveness of the unit. They are also commonly seen on trawler yachts, navigation buoys, and small commercial motor vessels such as pilot boats and trawlers.

c. **Stacked Arrays.** Tubular reflectors that resemble a fluorescent tube or rolling pin such as the Mobri units typify these. I have seen boats carrying several of these. They consist of an array of tiny reflectors housed in a transparent plastic case. These reflector types are purchased because they are cheap and small, not for the visibility factor that is the primary requirement. If you analyze the unit, it is hard to see how it can effectively return the amount of signal required. It can only do so in a near perfect vertical position. At any angle of heel, at 1° or more the unit return falls away to virtually nil. At best tabulated positions, at 0° azimuth, the RCS is 6.05; heeled to 1° it falls to 1.46, and to 0.18 at 2°.

d. **Luneberg Devices.** These devices resemble two half spheres mounted back to back and are typified by the Visiball. They are normally fitted to the navigation mast in a fore and aft configuration, but they are very heavy. The main criticism of the reflector is that the returned echo is fore and aft but not athwartships, permitting a large and dangerous blind sector. More importantly the return does not meet the minimum standards of the IMO or RORC having an RCS of around 0.8 m² only.

e. **Foil Devices.** I have read articles, including from responsible merchant marine officers, supporting the concept of hoisting a pair of ladies stockings full of aluminum foil. A case in the UK courts was heard regarding the loss of a catamaran in a collision with a coastal vessel during the 1986 Round Britain Race. The skipper did not hoist a reflector because he feared windage would reduce sailing performance; he inserted instead a foil-filled stocking into the mast. The Admiralty judge in his decision against the catamaran skipper included the following, "To leave an anchorage and proceed without radar into a shipping lane when the visibility is less than 75 yards, so that the navigator is blind, and without a radar reflector so that the boat is invisible, is in my judgement seriously negligent navigation". That statement sums up the issue of radar reflectors and the necessity for having them, and also applies to motor and powerboats.

f. **Others.** Some of these are listed below:

(1) **Cyclops.** This is a more recently launched product that has received some criticism and operates on the Luneberg lens principle. It uses concentric shells of material to reflect and refract radar signal. Two lens assemblies plus an additional two trihedrals are used to give full coverage around the azimuth and at heel. The polar diagram claims RCS of 10.5 m^2 and average of 4 m^2 all round. It is heavy at 4 kg.

(2) **High Gain Rotation.** These devices have been shown to have a best RCS of 3–4 m^2. They are being sold in the US, with claims they are better than all others, but they do not state RCS values or whether it can meet any recognized standards. They claim use by North Atlantic port authorities, but I could not find out which authorities.

22.15 **Liferaft Radar Reflective Devices.** These devices are helium-filled metallized plastic balloons. A 100-foot tether attaches the devices to either a person or a liferaft. The advertised reflective capabilities of the device are up to 14 nm (no doubt in perfect conditions), and an average of 3.3 nm. While the devices meet USCG requirements for lifeboats and liferaft radar reflector requirements, under SOLAS 74/83, they do not meet requirements for vessel radar reflectors.

22.16 **Radar Detectors.** These devices are omnidirectional units that activate an alarm when radar signal is detected in the vicinity. Typical range is approximately 5 nm. When an alarm is activated, the units can be used as a radar direction finder and a plot of the track of a vessel can be made. The disadvantage is that with more than one fast oncoming vessel, it is difficult to plot all targets and make judgements based on the plot. Vessels may have already made collision avoidance alterations, and this only in the case that a good radar reflector is fitted so that you are radar visible. With normal speeds of motorboats, there is little to be done except to make sure you are seen.

22.17 **Radar Reflection Polar Diagrams.** Polar diagrams are the usual way manufacturers represent the performance of radar reflectors. There are two types of polar diagram:

a. **Horizontal Polar Diagrams.** Polar diagrams are essentially signal returns plotted for all points around the azimuth for a reflector in the vertical position. This is crucial in the understanding of test claims and the actual onboard performance of the reflector. The various polar diagrams for the 18" octahedral, the Mobri tubular reflector are illustrated below. The Firdell Blipper

210-7 reflector now only has 3-dimensional polar diagrams and therefore is not included.

b. **3D Polar Diagrams.** The more accurate test of a radar reflector is a 3-dimensional polar diagram, which indicates performance under actual heel conditions. These are illustrated, and are derived from computer-generated results and give a close image of actual performance. The white space is the area of no radar visibility.

22.18 **Radar Fresnel Zones.** in some cases radar signals self-cancel, either in the transmission or return path. This problem is related to a variety of factors that includes radar height, target height, sea and earth surface conditions, and radar range. The regions where cancellation occurs are called fresnel or extinction zones. The regions can be up to a mile in width. In such conditions the radar signal reaching the radar reflector may be relatively weak, with a weak return. The result is no return to the radar, or so weak that it is not processed.

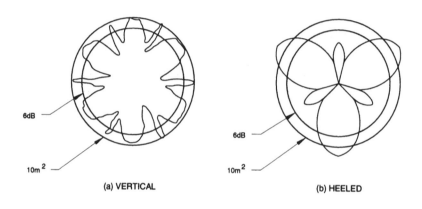

Figure 22-6 Horizontal Polar Diagrams

a. **Reflector Mounting.** It is apparent from the fresnel tables that the masthead is not the ideal place to put your reflector, as a relatively large cancellation zone exists. Reflectors are best mounted around on top of the pilothouse or fly bridge, which is about 4 to 5 meters.

b. **Fresnel Tables.** The following fresnel tables are published courtesy of Marconi-Firdell, and cover the first Fresnel Zone for radar heights 12 and 16 feet, and target heights 4 to 22 feet. The tables are based on a radar frequency of 9.4 GHz and for the range of 0.1 to 10 nm, which is typical for most motorboats.

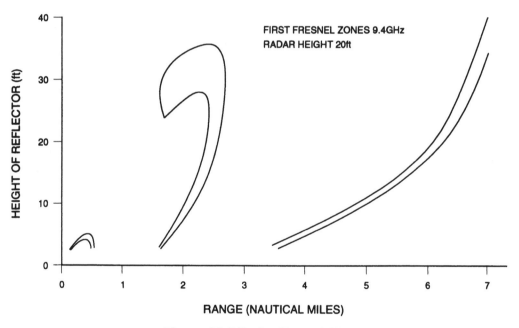

Figure 22-7 Radar Fresnel Zones

Table 22-3 First Fresnel Zone Tables Radar Height 12 Feet

Target Height	Zone (nm)	Zone (nm)	Zone (nm)
4 m	0.140-0.457	1.536-1.578	3.626-3.692
6 m	0.212-0.481	1.692-1.741	4.086-4.166
8 m	0.288-0.487	1.814-1.868	4.440-4.529
10 m	0.393-0.453	1.906-1.965	4.708-4.805
12 m	1.978-2.041	4.915-5.016	
14 m	2.033-2.102	5.078-5.182	
16 m	2.077-2.150	5.209-5.316	
18 m	2.122-2.190	5.318-5.427	
20 m	2.141-2.224	5.410-5.521	
22 m	2.164-2.253	5.492-5.604	
24 m	2.183-2.279	5.565-5.678	
26 m	2.199-2.301	5.632-5.747	
28 m	2.211-2.321	5.695-5.811	
30 m	2.221-2.339	5.755-5.872	

Table 22-4 First Fresnel Zone Tables Radar Height 16 Feet

Target Height	Zone (nm)	Zone (nm)	Zone (nm)
4 m	0.188-0.469	1.626-1.673	3.824-3.891
6 m	0.290-0.473	1.775-1.828	4.271-4.351
8 m	1.898-1.958	4.648-4.740	
10 m	1.997-1.064	4.957-4.058	
12 m	2.077-2.150	5.209-5.316	
14 m	2.140-2.220	5.414-5.526	
16 m	2.189-2.276	5.583-5.700	
18 m	2.227-2.322	5.723-5.844	
20 m	2.256-2.359	5.842-5.966	
22 m	2.276-2.389	5.944-6.071	
24 m	2.288-2.413	6.033-6.162	
26 m	2.292-2.532	6.112-6.243	
28 m	2.288-2.447	6.183-6.316	
30 m	1.574-2.457	6.248-6.382	

Autopilots

23.1   **Autopilots.** The autopilot is one of the few indispensable electronic items. It is often referred to as the non-complaining, non-eating extra crewmember. The real advances in autopilot technology are powerful microprocessors and equally complex software algorithms that give "intelligent" control. Most autopilot problems occur because of incorrect installation, improper selection, or improper operation, rather than crew personality conflicts. The basic function of an autopilot is to steer the vessel on a predetermined and set course, compass heading or to a GPS position or waypoint. The pilot will make course corrections proportional to the course error, and will correct to eliminate any overshoot as the course is met. Virtually all autopilots are microprocessor based, and use the proportional rate system of operation. Correction is based on the amount of course deviation and the rate of change. Autopilots vary depending on the type of steering system used. The factors affecting autopilot selection are:

    a.   **Autopilot Selection.** An autopilot is selected on the basis of a number of important criteria:

        (1)   The steering system installed, which may be wheel hydraulic, wire or direct drive. Also the speed of rudder travel, the rudder size, the required number of turns lock to lock.

        (2)   The loaded vessel displacement, which has wide variations and beam, draft and displacement. Raymarine recommends that 20% be added to design displacement to get realistic cruising displacement.

        (3)   Type of motoring is also important. For motor cruising you must base all factors on worst weather possible, which means power ratings must be capable of coping with prevailing conditions.

    b.   **Power Consumption.** Always compare the current consumption at full rated load, not average consumption. Many find that the pilot consumes far more than expected, although much of the heavy power consumption relates to overworking of the pilot. There is no significant difference between average consumptions of all the drive types for a specific vessel size. Power consumption depends on the pilot efficiency and duty cycle, with efficiency factors being typically around 0.5 to 0.8. Factors that directly affect current draw are the force and speed to turn the rudder and the frequency of operation.

    c.   **Autopilot Torque.** Torque is the force required to hold the rudder in position due to the pressure of water on the rudder, and to overcome the steering gear resistance of bearings and steering system drives. In many cases this is under estimated, and while the pilot is fine in average conditions, it fails in bad weather to keep course. Overstressing an autopilot too small for demand results in premature failure. The forces that must be considered include rudder, speed of turns, speed of boat through water and weight or displacement. Size ideally requires the maximum turning moment or max steering force. The turning moment is the torque applied to the rudderpost needed to turn the boat and is measured in foot/pounds. The steering force is the force required by the helmsman to steer the boat and the maximum is around 50lbs.

d.   **Response Times.** Response time is important, and vessels that track well have faster response times. Lightweight planing hull vessels that have more rapid heading changes due to the effects of wind, wave and swell require faster response times. The use of gyro-stabilized compasses is often required, such as the KVH Azimuth Digital Gyro Compass. Heading data input from NMEA data sentence is typically around 4 secs and real time inputs are much better at maintaining good response times.

e.   **Wheel Drive.** The rotary drive unit is an integrated gearbox and motor, rotating the wheel via a belt. Vessel steering characteristics can be programmed into the control system, and a simple clutch lever enables instant changeover to manual steering. The trend in wheel pilots is now towards an enclosed belt drive system. Belts must be correctly tensioned to avoid premature breakage or wear. Typical units are the Raymarine SportPilot for powerboats, which is installed directly behind the wheel on the steering column. Simrad has a similar unit that installs in place of the steering unit behind the helm console.

f.   **Linear Drive.** The linear drive unit is either an integrated hydraulic ram and pump system or a motor and gearbox drive directly connected to the rudder quadrant.

   (1)   **Advantages.** The linear drive has minimal effect on helm "feel". It is relatively low cost, and the hydraulic units are very reliable. There is also the advantage of a backup steering if some part of the steering drive or pedestal fails. Critical selection criteria are peak thrust, maximum stroke, hard-over times at no-load, hydraulic units are typically up to 12 seconds, and maximum rudder torque, typically up to 3200 Nm.

   (2)   **Power Consumption.** Typical power consumption is relatively low in the range 1.5–3 amps and 2.75–6 amps for larger vessels.

g.   **Rotary Drives.** These drives are usually fitted on vessels where linear drives cannot be installed, or where there are space restrictions, or an inaccessible or small quadrant cannot accommodate any other drive. The motors on these systems consist of an electric motor coupled to a precision manufactured epicyclic gearbox. Some rotary drive units connect to the wheel using chain and sprocket. Power consumption is typically in the range 2–4 amps, and 3–8 amps for larger vessels, and has peak output torques up to around 34 Nm.

h.   **Hydraulic Drive.** Drives suit inboard, outboard and stern drive steering systems. The hydraulic drive consists of a reversible DC pump unit inserted within the system, or constant running with directional solenoid control valves. Units are rated for maximum stall pressure and peak flow rates, and suit single or double-ended rams.

i.   **Sterndrive.** This is an electromechanical drive unit.

23.2   Autopilot Installation. There are a few fundamental points to observe when installing autopilots. The following factors should be considered, as they are the major causes of problems:

a.   **Anchoring.** Always ensure that the drive units are mounted and anchored securely. It is sensible to mount a strong pad at anchoring points, as it is quite common on fiberglass vessels to see the hull flexing because the inadequate mounting points are unable to take the applied loads.

b.   **Wiring.** There are a number of important points to consider:

(1)   **Power Cables.** Make sure that power cables to drive units are rated for maximum current demand and voltage drops, as cable runs are normally long. I install as standard a minimum 6-mm^2 twin tinned copper cable to the motor and computer unit.

(2)   **Radio Cables.** Make sure that all wiring is routed well away from radio aerial cables, as interference is a major cause of problems during radio transmission. Ensure that a ground cable is run from the computer unit to your RF ground. In rare cases you may have to put on a foil shield to SSB tuner unit interconnecting cables as well.

c.   **Fluxgate Installation.** There are a number of important points to remember:

(1)   **Location in Fiberglass and Timber Vessels.** The fluxgate compass should be installed in an area of least magnetic influence, and close to the center of the boat's roll to minimize heeling error. Turning errors can arise if the compass is not properly compensated. The southerly and northerly turning errors increase as distance from the equator increases. This causes slow wandering and slow course correction. Compensation reduces these errors.

(2)   **Location in Steel Vessels.** Steel vessels pose problems due to the inherent magnetic field in the hull. Raymarine recommends to mount the fluxgate sensor at a minimum of 5 feet above the deck.

(3)   **Cables.** Ensure the compass is mounted clear of any cable looms or any other metallic equipment. As fluxgates are invariably installed under bunks, do not store any metallic items such as toolboxes or spares there as often happens.

d.   **Course Computer Location.** This should be located clear of magnetic influences and away from radio aerial cables. While older units were prone to induced interference, newer units are generally made to strict international noise emission standards.

23.3   Autopilot Controls. Many adjustments can be made to achieve optimum autopilot operation. The various controls are as follows:

a.   **Deadband.** This is the area in which the heading may deviate before the pilot initiates a correction.

b.   **Rudder Gain.** This relates to the amount of rudder to be applied for the detected heading error, and must be calibrated. This factor is inextricably linked to proper compass setup and damping. When gain is set too low, the correction response is slow to return to set heading. When the gain is too high, the course oscillates around the set heading. When excessive gain is used, the course is unstable with gradual increases in heading error and course.

c.   **Rudder Feedback.** Rudder feedback or reference provides the precise instantaneous rudder position information to the pilot. It is essential that the feedback potentiometer be properly aligned. Most new pilots have a high-resolution potentiometer that offers more precise feedback than the coarse units of earlier models. Feedback units can be rotary or like the Simrad linear device.

Warning. Do not use autopilot in any channels, confined areas or heavy traffic zones and also use a cellular telephone or handheld VHF as operation can interfere with and cause sudden course changes. There are already fatalities directly attributable to this.

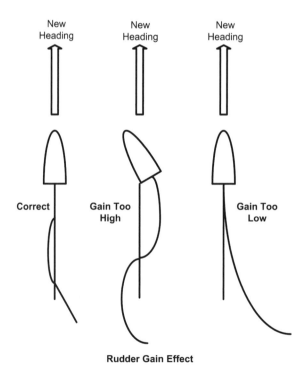

Rudder Gain Effect

Figure 23-1 Rudder Gain Effect

452

d. **Rudder Limits.** This controls the limit of rudder travel. The autopilot must stop before reaching the mechanical stops or serious damage may result.

e. **Rudder Damping.** This calibration is used where a feedback transducer is installed and minimizes hunting when the pilot is trying to position the rudder.

f. **Rate of Turn.** The rate of turn limitation is typically 2° per second.

g. **Dodge and U-Turn Function.** This function usually operates in a 10° step with automatic return to original course, or 180°. The function is useful for dodging containers and debris, or staying out of the way of large ships.

h. **Off-Course Alarms.** All autopilots have an off-course alarm, which activates when the course heading error exceeds typically 15°. Specific alarm angles can be programmed in.

i. **Auto Trim and Auto Seastate.** Many of these small boat systems were pioneered by Autohelm and are as follows:

    (1) **AutoTrim.** (Raymarine) This function automatically compensates for alterations in weather helm, applies the correct level of standing helm, and is a sailboat setting.

    (2) **AutoSeastate.** (Raymarine) This function enables the pilot to automatically adapt to changing sea state conditions and vessel responses. It automatically alters the dead band settings, and is controlled by the pilot software. The pilot does not respond to repetitive vessel movements, but only to true course variations.

j. **Magnetic Variation.** The variation must be entered into the autopilot. Many units have automatic compass compensation to correct for errors.

k. **Compass Damping.** The basis for good autopilot performance is proper setting of compass damping. You should start with minimum damping and increase according to conditions. Failure to get this right will cause either

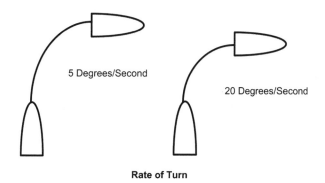

5 Degrees/Second

20 Degrees/Second

Rate of Turn

Figure 23-2 Rate of Turn

453

lagging or overshooting as rudder is applied to maintain course. This of course has detrimental effects on power consumption rates, as well as making you travel a lot farther than you have to. Many lightweight boats may require a rate gyrocompass.

l.   **Heading Error Correction.** This correction compensates for northerly and southerly heading errors. Failure to do this will cause amplification of rudder responses on northerly and southerly headings. Raymarine names this feature AutoAdapt.

m.   **Track Control.** Track control is the function that enables a pilot to steer from waypoint to waypoint in conjunction with a navigation receiver. The autopilot effectively adjusts to take account of tide and current. To do so it takes cross track error (XTE) data and uses it to compute and initiate course changes to maintain the required track.

(1)   **Limitations.** Most pilots will keep within 300 feet of desired track. Track control is less effective at lower speeds, as tidal stream effect has a greater impact. Differences are noticeable where flow speed exceeds 35% of vessel speed, and careful plotting is essential.

(2)   **Waypoint Advances.** Many pilots will advance to next waypoint at a single command. This depends on reception of valid NMEA headers that are the waypoint numbers and bearing to waypoint.

Caution. You must be aware that, if a navigation receiver passes incorrect or corrupt position data, the pilot may alter course and steer the vessel into danger. Never use unsupervised autopilot steering to position or waypoint close to the coast or in enclosed waterways. If a large error occurs on a GPS, by the time you realize it, you are aground.

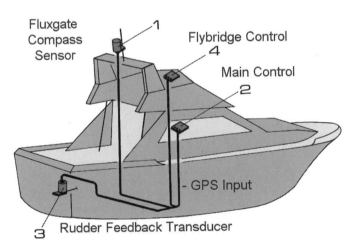

Figure 23-3 Typical Motorboat Autopilot System, *Courtesy of Vetus*

n. **Autopilot Interfacing.** Interfacing of compasses and navigation receivers is now standard.

(1) **Navigation Receivers.** Inputs from GPS enable steering to a position or waypoint. This may be an in-house protocol or NMEA 0183. It is important to remember that position-fixing systems are subject to errors, sometimes extremely large. This will have obvious effects on the steering, so it is important to keep a regular plot, as the autopilot will not be able to recognize the errors.

(2) **Fluxgate Compass.** Inputs from a fluxgate compass provide accurate heading data to the course computer.

(3) **Rate Gyro (GyroPlus).** These allow rapid real time sensing of vessel yawing prevalent in lightweight vessels in following and quartering seas. This data input supplements the fluxgate signal and allows rapid correction to counter the rapidly heading changes that cannot be compensated for by the fluxgate.

23.4 Autopilot Maintenance. A number of basic measures can be undertaken to ensure reliability.

a. **Temperature.** Keep the electronics modules and processors cool. Manufacturers make units with black plastic to facilitate heat transfer from components inside. While the black casing when exposed to atmosphere will dissipate heat generated inside, it will equally absorb heat. Under-rated units that are working hard and under stress will run hot.

b. **Corrosion Control.** Ensure that systems are not exposed to excessive salt water and that seals are intact. Ingress of water is a common failure mode.

c. **Plugs and Sockets.** Regularly check plugs and sockets for water and moisture. Ensure that they seal properly.

d. **Cleaning.** Clean using a damp cloth. Do not use any solvents or abrasive materials. Do not use a high-pressure hose.

Table 23-1 Autopilot Troubleshooting

Symptom	Probable Fault
No rudder response	Loss of power Autopilot fuse failure Rudder jammed Plug/connection fault Control unit fault
Rudder drives hard over	Radio interference (cell phone/VHF) Loss of feedback signal Rudder limit failure Fluxgate compass failure Radio navigation data corruption Control unit failure
Unstable wandering course	Calibration settings incorrect Over damped compass Rudder gain setting incorrect Feedback transducer linkage loose Control unit fault Drive unit fault
North/South headings unstable	Incorrect setup
Display and compass headings different	Deviation correction incorrect Incorrect rudder offset setting
Rudder angle display incorrect	Feedback unit loose or faulty
Condensation in display	Turn on illumination to dry

Instrument Systems

24.1   Instrument Systems. The catalyst for the development of the integrated instrument system is the rapid development of microprocessor computing power, electronics miniaturization and appropriate software developments. Another key development is the low cost fluxgate compasses. The range of parameters available has now reached more than 75 separate measurements. While discrete instrument systems without the ability to either communicate or calculate anything other than the measured function will be around for some years, purchasers will probably have to opt for parts of an overall integrated system. Look at www.kvh.com, www.BandG.com, www.raymarine.com, www.si-tex.com, www.simrad.com.

> **Integration.** Integration can be simply defined in the context of two principal system capabilities. Integrated systems have a great advantage because duplication of equipment such as fluxgate sensors, log and depth transducers are eliminated. The two primary system configurations are as follows:

> **(1)**   All inputs from transducers and information are processed within a single Central Processor Unit (CPU). The information is displayed at the instrument heads and able to communicate freely to external equipment. Data is distributed via a single "daisy chain" network to all instrument heads and connected peripherals such as autopilots and GPS.

> **(2)**   Total integration where all electronics equipment, which includes the instrumentation, position fixing systems, autopilot, chart plotters are both physically matched, with a manufacturer specific interfacing protocol. In some cases engine instrumentation and communications are both physically matched as part of that integration process.

24.2   System Architecture. Basic integrated instrument system architecture varies between manufacturers. The systems in use are:

> **a.   Discrete Instrument Systems.** These systems have a transducer serving each dedicated instrument head. The head processes and displays the information. Data is exchanged between each instrument on a dedicated network for computation of related data.

> **b.   Central CPU (Server) Systems.** These systems have a CPU (server) to which all transducers are connected. External data is also connected direct to the CPU. Instrument displays are connected on a daisy chain. The daisy chain interconnecting cable can convey both data in NMEA sentences or using a manufacturer's protocol along with power to each instrument head.

> **c.   Active Transducer Systems.** This innovation on Corus instrument systems utilizes active transducers. The active transducer has a microprocessor incorporated within the transducer, where all raw input data from depth, wind or log is processed. A single cable network interconnects all the transducers with all data being available to any user definable instrument displays. These

multifunction displays can be configured with simple keystrokes to display required data.

24.3 **Interfacing.** Interfacing is the process of interconnecting various electronic equipment and systems so that digitally encoded information can be transferred between them and used for processing tasks or display. Manufacturers have to consider the type of equipment involved such as the connectors and cables, voltages, impedances, current values and signal timing. At a more technical level, there is the data structure and transfer rate, and the protocol, which determines the information to communicate, the time to communicate, the frequency and error correction. The data messages must also have compatible structures and content. The US National Marine Electronics Association (NMEA) devised the first general digital standard in 1980 (NMEA 0180). This was developed for position fixing systems to autopilot communication to transfer cross-track error. NMEA 0182 followed this up, which was for use with plotting systems. The current and more comprehensive standard is NMEA 0183. A new NMEA 2000 protocol is in the process of rollout.

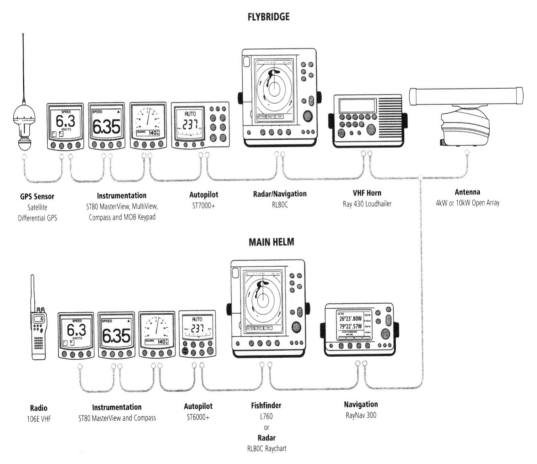

Figure 24-1 Integrated Instrument System, *Courtesy Raymarine*

a. **NMEA 0183.** This standard was designed to enable transfer of a variety of information between position fixing systems, radar, compass, plotters and autopilots as well as any other systems either sending or requiring data. NMEA uses what is called a single-talker, multiple-listener architecture. Compliance with the standards is voluntary, and there are cases where the implementation of the standards has been technically flawed and communication poor or impossible. The NMEA has standard message sentences. They may be divided into input and transmit sentences, where many are simply transmitted as inputs to processors, while other information is transmitted to appropriate systems or display. Message sentences have the following formats, eg. HDM = Compass heading, magnetic, WPL = Waypoint Location, XTE = Cross Track Error. There are as many sentences as there are parameters. One important recommendation was the use of opto-isolation on circuits. The opto-isolator is commonly used in many high noise environments, and an LED and phototransistor are used to provide total electrical or galvanic isolation. This prevents transfer of noise into equipment circuits. A new high-speed version of NMEA 0183 is due for release in 2000/2001.

b. **NMEA 2000.** The NMEA-2000 interface standard has been developed in conjunction with International Electrotechnical Commission (IEC). It is a low cost, bi-directional serial data protocol permitting multiple talkers and listeners to share data. It allows GPS, radar, chart displays, sounders, autopilots, engine monitoring and entertainment systems to exchange digital information over a single channel. NMEA 2000 is based on the Controller Area Network Protocol (CAN) originally developed for the auto industry.

c. **Communications Protocols.** The trend is for implementation of in-house communications protocols. The main reason is that fast broadband data transfer is required to enable transfer of video and graphics images such as radar, plotter and fishfinder screens. NMEA will remain an important data transfer protocol for external communication between peripherals. The major protocols in use are:

(1) **Raymarine SeaTalk and High Speed Bus (HSB and HSB2).** These protocols from the former Autohelm and Raytheon are used for total systems' compatibility between all equipment. ArcNet is used as the backbone for the Pathfinder HSB network. The system allows addition of any equipment, radar, chart plotters, GPS, logs, sounders, etc. NMEA 0183 requires a separate interface.

(2) **Furuno NavNet.** This uses an Ethernet 10BaseT (twisted pair) system, which is common in many shore data systems. Systems have a star topology, with each device having a separate set of wires radiating from the hub. When a fault arises it is contained to that one device or cable. Ethernets have high data rates, and cables must be UTP (unshielded twisted pair) standard to ensure data integrity.

Make sure cables are routed well clear of fluorescent lights, transformers, etc. to avoid interference.

(3) **Controller Area Network (CAN).** This is a fast serial bus designed as an efficient and reliable link between sensors and actuators. CAN uses a twisted-pair cable for communications at speeds up to 1Mbit/s with up to 40 devices connected. Originally, Bosch developed the electronic standard for automobiles. The system requires an interface for NMEA communications. Features include any node access to the bus when the bus is quiet, and use of 100% of band width without loss of data and automatic error detection, signalling and retries.

(4) **B & G NETWORK.** This protocol is also used for total systems communications. NMEA interfaces are provided.

(5) **VDO LOGIC.** This protocol is used for inter-instrument communications, but all instrument heads have an NMEA 0183 output to allow easy connection to other systems.

d. **Interface Installation and Problems.** Virtually all problems with interfacing occur at installation. The majority of faults are related to the following:

(1) **Connections.** Unless an equipment manufacturer supplies the interface cable and connector, make sure that the correct pins are used on the output port connector. These vary between equipment and manufacturers. Check with the supplier, or get them to make up the cable and connector. All connections should observe the correct polarity with respect to ground references. Incorrect connections mean no signals. If the system is fiber optic, ensure the connection is properly inserted, rotate to lock them but do not force them on.

(2) **Grounding.** Ensure screens and reference grounds are properly terminated and connected. In many cases data corruption occurs, or it simply does not work.

(3) **Set-up.** At commissioning, ensure that the appropriate interface output ports are selected with the correct NMEA output format. In many cases problems are directly attributable to this, and many manuals do not clearly explain the process. In most cases carefully go through the set-up procedures.

(4) **Cables.** All cables should be shielded, twisted pair unless stated otherwise. Using other cables may lead to data corruption due to induced "noise" from adjacent electrical cables and radio transmissions. Flat cables are generally untwisted and round ones are. Use only Cat 3, 4 or 5 with data networks. This is usually 100 ohms impedance and 22 to 26 AWG.

e.   **Interfacing Cable Designations.** There are a number of variations in designating interface cable connections. The standard NMEA terminology is signal (positive) and return (negative). NMEA output port variations can be very confusing and obviously lack any standard notation. Equipment NMEA ports are configured in what is termed a "balanced pair", with both wires carrying the signal. The signal level is the difference in voltage between the pair, and is also known as a differential data signal. The connection of wires is simple, the transmitting device has the transmit connected to the receive port of the other. The receive port is similarly connected to the transmit port of the other. No connections should be made to boat ground or the DC negative.

(1)   **Data Signal Output:** Data O/P; Tx; Tx hot; A Line; Positive data; Signal O/P; NMEA O/P; NMEA Sig Out; O/P Sig; Data Out; Tx -ve; Tx Data O/P.

(2)   **Data Return Output:** Gnd; Tx Cold; Ground; Signal Rtn; Return Out; O/P Return; NMEA Rtn; Data Rtn; I/P Gnd; Ref; Negative.

(3)   **Data Signal Input:** Signal I/P; NMEA Sig In; I/P Sig; NMEA I/P; Rx Data I/P.

(4)   **Data Return Input:** Signal Return In; Signal Rtn; I/P Rtn; NMEA Rtn; Gnd; Negative; Reference; Ref.

24.4   Selection Criteria. When selecting a system, consider the following factors:

a.   **Display Types.** Ergonomic design is important, but the major decision is whether you want digital, which is the most common, or analog. You will confront a confusing array of digital displays. The aviation and motor vehicle industries have invested heavily in researching easier assimilation of data as primary safety factor. They still maintain analog data presentations and the display types are:

(1)   **Digital Liquid Crystal Display (LCD).** Most displays use a 7-segment display with chunky numerals. Some displays are difficult to read at wide angles or in bright sunlight, although technology is improving things with higher contrasts and wider viewing angles. All units generally have a multi-level backlit illumination system.

(2)   **Analog Display.** The analog display is still seen on some instruments, and it makes overall instrumentation displays easier to monitor; a changed needle position is easier to see than an altered digit. I personally have a preference for analog displays, particularly on depth displays going into coral reefs with the sun behind, they are easier to see. It is good to see many manufacturers such as Raytheon, Simrad, Silva and VDO making analog repeaters part of the range.

(3)   **LCD Analog Display.** Some manufacturers are incorporating an analog display using the LCD.

(4) **LCD Supertwist Displays.** These displays are relatively new, but allow viewing at much wider angles. The CORUS system has a 14-segment display with increased character sizes and improved visibility.

b. **System Requirements.** How much data do you need and can you use and interpret 75 parameters? Most of these are for use on sailing vessels. System expansion should be considered, and if you want to start with the basics and add as the budget allows, most systems will offer you that. Once you start with one range, you generally will continue. All manufacturers, Raymarine, Simrad, VDO have everything from GPS to autopilots, although if you want to add in other equipment you must ensure that it is compatible.

24.5 Gyro Compasses. The North-seeking action of a gyro is a product of the gyroscope characteristics, the earth's rotation and gravity. In the Simrad Robertson gyro, the gyro rotor is supported inside a horizontal ring on frictionless bearings, and turns at a speed of 12,000 rpm. This is supported within a vertical ring, and there is a stabilizer, which generates the North-seeking action. A 24VDC supply is fed to a DC/DC converter for control power to the CPU, and an inverter, which has an output of 3-phase, 100VAC 400Hz. A single-phase 400Hz supply feeds the rotor excitation. The output after processing drives the compass card and output signals for repeaters, radar and autopilot. Prior to starting up the gyro, get the latitude setting for the area of operation. Normal stabilization settling period is up to 4 hours. Check that the compass card of both master and any repeaters are synchronized with panel gyro readings if fitted. Where installed, check that panel manual speed setting is correct, and adjust if not. Gyro maintenance consists of daily inspection for abnormal noise, vibration and overheating. When needed, get a change in lubrication oil. The electrical connections should be check tightened every year. On gyros with digital displays, always check for any fault codes that have been generated. These are typically abnormalities in control voltage, rotor speed, servo loop, rotor level and main voltage. Makers include Robertson, Anschutz, SG Brown and Sperry (Litton). Power consumption at 24VDC is 4 amps at starting and 2 amps running. New small vessel systems for large motorboats and trawlers are characterized by the DGS Digital Gyro Compass from KVH which uses a gyro stabilized magnetic sensor. These were developed to overcome the problems of northerly turning errors, and also sudden accelerations experienced during roll, pitch and azimuth during various sea conditions or turning.

24.6 Electronic Compasses. The principal compass is the fluxgate, and this is already being surpassed with electronic units.

a. **Fluxgate Compasses.** A fluxgate sensor detects the earth's magnetic field electronically, sampling hundreds of times per second. The sensing part of the compass consists of coils mounted at right angles in a horizontal plane. Each coil is fed a precisely controlled current that is subsequently modified by the earth's magnetic field. The processor compares the signals within each coil, automatically correcting for variation. The resulting analog output is then converted to digital signals for processing.

b. **Electronic Compasses.** These are entirely solid state, and are made by KVH and Ritchie. The purely electronic sensing overcomes the problems of analog-to-digital conversion by the output and processing of a digital signal. KVH has developed a compass called GyroTrac. This combines a digital magnetic compass and a three-axis gyro sensor. These meet more demanding requirements of satellite communications and TV systems, ARPA radars and autopilots. When interfaced with GPS, True North is also available. Displays consist of microprocessor-controlled analog rotating cards (450mA), or analog rotating needle (180mA), or digital supertwist LCD (90mA). Power consumption is with lights on. Unlike gyros with long settling times, these warm up immediately. Interfacing with unit will suit most requirements with NMEA0183, Sin/Cos, Furuno and Stepper.

c.   **Sensor Location.** The sensor must be mounted in the area of least magnetic disturbance, so that no interference is induced into it resulting in errors and degrading accuracy. It must also be positioned close to the center of vessel motion, as errors are caused by vessel heeling and pitching. Remember steel vessels pose problems and it must be at least 5 feet above the deck. Accuracy depends on proper location clear of interference. Accuracy is typically + or - 1°. Although some self compensate to 0.5°, the display accuracy is still 1°.

d.   **Damping.** Typically these can be from 5 to 10 levels for some models. The rougher the sea state, the more damping required. A low damping level will result in erratic or rapidly altering headings.

e.   **Power Consumption.** Current drains are very low, typically around 300-400mA.

f.   **Compensation.** Many have automatic deviation compensation and some will require steering in a circle at commissioning. The compensation takes place with respect to current magnetic deviation. The deviation may vary if you have electrical devices running, but with electronic compasses, re-compensation is simple and quick.

24.7   Speed Logs. The log has the obvious function of indicating speed through the water and distance travelled. Not so long ago, the first merchant vessels I served on in the mid-seventies had a towed Walker's log. As soon as we were clear of port and full away on passage, the turbine was streamed and the mechanical counter was mounted on the poop rail. Logs are now part of the integrated instrument system and normally interfaced to other instruments.

a.   **Paddlewheel Logs.** The common paddlewheel has magnets imbedded in the wheel blades, and a detector giving a pulse that can be counted and processed. Earlier units had a glass reed switch that was prone to fail; new units have a Hall effect device. The signal pulses are normally seen as a voltage change, such as 0 and 5 volts, to give a stepped characteristic that can be counted. The result is directly proportional to the speed and distance travelled. The transducer may count either the pulses per second or the pulse length.

b.   **Ultra Sonic Logs.** B & G, Echopilot and Kaytek have sonic speed sensors, which are significantly more accurate with near linear outputs. The transducer consists of two 2 mHz piezo electric crystals. These transmit short pulse acoustic signals simultaneously and reflect the signals off water particles approximately 6" away, clear of the turbulent boundary layer. The water particles pass through the forward then the aft beam, and the transmission time of the acoustic sound signal between the two crystals is then measured. The time delay is used to determine precise speed based on the known distance between the two transducers.

c.   **Doppler Logs.** These logs operate on the Doppler principle and are used on larger commercial vessels. Like sonic logs, they transmit acoustic pulses into the water that bounce back of particles. They then measure the change in pitch or frequency of the echo return to derive actual speed.

d.   **Installation.** Correct installation is essential if the log is to be accurate and reliable. Observe the following notes:

    (1)   **Location.** The log transducer is normally mounted in the forward third of the hull, and must be in an area of minimal turbulence, called the boundary layer.

    (2)   **Cabling.** Do not run depth sounder and log cables together as interference may result.

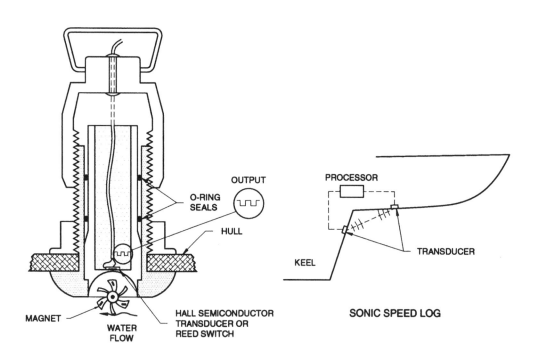

Figure 24-2 Log Transducers

e. **Calibration.** Log calibration normally requires the use of a measured mile. Many new logs are self-calibrating or have an optional manual calibration. The calibration run should be carried out at slack water in calm, wind-free conditions to prevent any inaccuracy. Prior to making a run, check that the correct magnetic course has been worked out to ensure the vessel takes the correct course, and this means making appropriate corrections for variation and compass deviation. Make the runs under power at a constant throttle setting. Ensure that transits used are accurately observed at the start and finish of each run. The formula for determining the log error is as follows:

(1)   Runs 1 & 2 (ground measurement) = Correction K

   Runs 2 & 2 through water

(2)   The resulting figure will show either under or over reading, and this is used either to calibrate log or correct readings.

f. **Transducer Maintenance.** Logs in general need little maintenance, though paddlewheels require more than most.

(1)   Remove and check the paddlewheel for smooth, frictionless rotation. Apply some light oil to the spindle.

(2)   Check that the O-ring seals are in good condition to prevent leakage into the bilge.

g. **Transducer Troubleshooting.** To test whether the paddlewheel transducer or the instrument head is faulty:

(1)   Disconnect the log input cables to the instrument head or processor.

(2)   Using a small piece of wire, rapidly short out the terminals and observe whether a reading is indicated. If there is, the transducer is faulty. If there is nothing, the instrument head is probably at fault.

24.8   Wind Instruments. Motor vessels install wind systems for weather observation rather than for performance-related information, although some motor sailers do. The typical wind system comprises an integral wind speed and direction unit along with instrument head.

a. **Wind Speed.** The anemometer is essentially a rotating pulse counter, similar to the log. The pulses are counted and processed to give speed.

b. **Wind Direction.** This part of the masthead unit consists of a simple windvane, with a number of methods used to measure the angle and transmit the signals to the instrument head or processor. Some units use an electromagnetic sensing system. Other units use an optical sensing system to identify coded markings that relate to the windvane direction.

(1)   **Apparent Wind Direction.** The measured wind direction is apparent wind, which indicates angle relative to boat speed.

    (2)   **True Wind Direction.** The true wind data is a result of the instrument processing vessel course, speed, apparent wind direction and speed.

c.   **Transducer Installation.** The transducer is mounted on the signal mast above the radar and navigation lights.

    (1)   **Fastening.** It is important that the unit be properly fastened down, especially as transducer units are installed into a simple bracket assembly and are removable. Ensure fore and aft alignment is correct to reduce inaccuracies in angle readings. Birds and lightning are the main cause of damage, followed by vibration.

    (2)   **Electrical Connections.** Ensure the cable connector is securely fastened. It is good practice to put a few wraps of self-amalgamating tape around it to prevent ingress of water. If you apply petroleum jelly or silicon grease, do not fill the socket, as it is pushed in with the transducer unit and contributes to a poor electrical contact. Keep the electrical connections dry and tape as suggested. Apply grease to the screw threads to minimize seizing.

d.   **Transducer Maintenance.** There are few tasks and the following should be checked every six months:

    (1)   Check securing bolts and frame, and tighten as required.

    (2)   Check cable connector for moisture and water, as well as for signs of corrosion on the pins. Smear a small amount of petroleum jelly or silicon grease around the threads when replacing it, and rewrap with self-amalgamating tape. Ensure that the cable is not chafing at any access point.

    (3)   Check that the anemometer rotates freely without binding or making any noises that indicate bearing seizure or failure. Check that the cups are not split or damaged, as this is frequently caused by birds.

    (4)   Apply a few drops of the manufacturer's light oil into the lubrication hole, and rotate freely to ensure that it penetrates the bearing.

    (5)   Check the connections in the junction box are tight and there is no corrosion of cable or screw connectors.

24.9   **Instrument Installation.** The following should be observed when installing an instrument system:

a.   **CPU Location.** Always install the CPU or data box if one is used, in a clean, dry area that enables easy access for transducer cables. Ensure that the CPU unit is mounted well away from fluxgate compasses, LORAN, GPS receivers, VHF and SSB radios, satellite radomes, AM/FM radios and cellular phone aerials. The CPU must be a minimum one meter from a magnetic compass.

b. **Transducer Cables.** Transducer cables should not be lengthened or shortened; coil up the extra length at the transducer end.

c. **Instrument Covers.** Do not cover or mount your instruments behind clear plastic covers. This has the effect of magnifying the heat from the sun and burning out the instruments. Always use the covers provided when not in use to prevent UV damage and weathering.

d. **Cables.** Avoid cable stresses and ensure that cables are not bent sharply. All cables must be taken through proper deck transits to connection boxes. Always run cables well away from radio antennas and heavy current carrying cables.

24.10   **Instrument Maintenance.** The following precautions should be followed to ensure maximum reliability:

a. **Check Connections.** Bad electrical connections are the source of many failures, as is moisture in the connection boxes and plugs. When a short circuit occurs, the spike that is generated often causes a failure in the electronics. Ensure that all boxes are dry, well waterproofed and connections tight.

b. **Remove Transducers.** Where possible always remove log or depth transducer while at a mooring or in port and replace with the dummy. Always ensure the paddle rotates freely and is clear of any growth.

Table 24-1 Instrument Troubleshooting

Symptom	Probable Fault
No display	Loss of power Cable connection fault Instrument fault
Partial display	Processor fault LCD fault Transducer fault
Erratic readings	Connection degradation Interference from radios, electrical etc Low battery voltage Transducer fault
No or low boat speed	Transducer not installed Transducer not connected Fouled transducer Transducer misaligned Paddlewheel seizing
High boat speed No wind speed	Electrical interference Mast base connection fault Mast head unit plug fault Anemometer seized Mast head unit fault Processor fault Low battery voltage
Erratic wind angle	Loose connections Corroded mast head unit plug Water in mast head unit plug Mast head unit fault
No depth indication	Transducer damaged Transducer fouled Low battery voltage
Intermittent shallow indication	Weed or fish Water aeration
Shallow readings in deep water	Check your charts! Outside depth range
Inconsistent depth readings	Muddy or silted bottom Low battery voltage Poor transducer interface (in hull only)

Interference

25.1   Interference. Interference is the major enemy of electronics systems. It corrupts position fixes, reduces performance, and is often the cause of electronics damage. Interference and noise superimpose a disturbance or voltage transient onto power or signal lines and this corrupts or degrades the processed data. Look at www.sto-p.com. The following describes problems and some solutions.

    a.   **Voltage Transients.** The voltage transient is the most damaging and comes from many sources. The best known is the corruption of GPS and Loran data where the power is taken off an engine-starting battery. If a significant load is applied, there is a momentary voltage drop (brown out condition), followed by an increase. This under-voltage disturbance can exceed 100 volts in some cases, damaging power supplies, wiping memories, or corrupting data. The same applies to two battery systems where the house bank supplies items such as electric toilets and equipment with large current demand. A starting battery voltage can have a 3–4 volt dip on starting. Transients are also caused by the variation or interruption of current in the equipment power conductor.

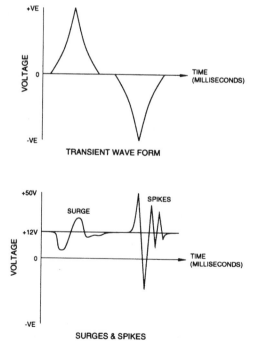

Figure 25-1 Transient Waveforms

b. **Induced Interference.** Electrical fields radiate from cables and equipment and this is induced into other nearby cables or equipment. The most common causes of this are cables running parallel or within the same cable bundle, and is also called mutual coupling. Always run power-supply cables and data cables separately and make sure the cables cross at 90°. In particular run power cables to sensitive equipment separate to main power cables to reduce inductive and capacitive coupling to signal conductors.

25.2   Noise Sources. There are a number of noise sources on motorboats. Noises can be classified as Radio Frequency Interference (RFI) or Electromagnetic Interference (EMI). Noise also occurs in differing frequency ranges, and equipment may only be prone to problems within a particular frequency range. Multiple noise sources can cause a gradual degradation of electronics components and when the cumulative effects reach a certain point, the devices fail.

a. **Arcing Noise.** These are repetitive spikes that are caused by commutators and sparking of brushes. The brushes on any alternator, particularly if dirty, can cause sparking and noise. Charging systems and loose connections commonly cause this. The most common cause is loose or poor engine return paths for alternators, when the negative path arcs across points of poor electrical contact. This is also caused by ignition systems from distributors and spark plugs being impressed on a DC system, often through radiation to adjacent cables.

b. **Induced Coupling Interference.** Wiring that is installed in parallel with others can suffer from inductive coupling interference. This is like a transformer with a single turn primary and secondary coil, with the magnetic effects causing the induction..

c. **Capacitive Coupling Interference.** This is most common in high frequency circuits and in high impedance to ground circuits such as balanced pair systems.

d. **Ripple Noise.** Ripple is created in any rectifier bridges (diode, SCR, etc.) such as alternators, chargers, fluorescent lights and inverters. It is usually a high-pitched whine. Good equipment has suppressed electronics. Ripple badly degrades communications audio quality.

e. **Static Charges.** These have a number of sources:

(1)   **External Charges.** This type of interference can arise due to static build-up in rigging. On reaching a certain voltage level, the static discharges to the ground, causing interference. Another common cause is when dry, offshore winds occur, and a static charge builds up on fiberglass decks. The problem is prevalent on larger fiberglass vessels with large deck areas. A lightning protection system can ground out these charges.

(2) **Engine and Shaft Charges.** This type of interference can arise due to static build-up both induced and due to moving parts in the engine. The static charge discharges to ground and causes interference. Shaft interference can arise due to static build-up on propeller shafts. The static will discharge to ground when it reaches a high voltage level, and cause interference. Typical cures are grounding of the shaft with a brush system.

f. **Surge (Electromagnetic Pulse).** This can be caused by lightning activity, and pulses can be induced into electrical wiring and aerials. The allowable surge is 100 volts for 50ms and 70 V for 100ms.

g. **Spikes.** Turn-on spikes result from the initial charging of input filters on power supplies. Turn-off spikes arise when reactive loads are switched, and the magnetic fields collapse on inductive loads, such as transformers, relay or contactor coils, solenoid coils, pump motors, etc. Spikes can be as much as 500V peak-to-peak. MOV suppressors are often put across the coils.

h. **AC Transients.** Surges and transients on an AC shore power system can be carried through chargers to the boat DC system. Many chargers do not have any power filtering circuits.

25.3   Suppression Methods. There are a number of methods that can be used to reduce or hopefully eliminate interference. The use of shielded cables along with proper grounding is important, but the use of proper equipment enclosures is also critical, as this minimizes electromagnetic radiation.

a. **Filters.** A filter or capacitor installed close to the "noisy" equipment effectively short circuits noise in the protected frequency range. Filters may take a number of forms:

(1) **Filters.** The filter consists of either a capacitor, or a combination of capacitor and inductor connected across the power supply lines. STO-P uses filters with very low ground impedances, typically lower than 20 milliohms at 1 kHz, which cleans our ripple. An option is to supply sensitive equipment through a Navpac from New-Mar. This is a supply-conditioning module that filters out spikes and noise, regulates supply voltage, and has an internal power pack to ensure supply continuity. The StartGuard from NewMar also protects against the surges that occur when the voltage drops when starting engines. This device is connected in parallel with the equipment, and sense circuit is connected with the starter switch or solenoid. The internal battery supplies the load when starting and recharges when in standby mode. The units are rated at 20 amps.

(2) **Suppressors.** Suppression modules from Charles Marine use MOV technology and are available in AC and DC types. Many alternators do not have these fitted, so install them. Normally you will have noticed radio noise or interference on electronics equipment. A 1.0-mi-

crofarad is a starting point, but even experimentation with a couple of automotive types is simple and inexpensive.

(3) **Ferrite Chokes.** Ferrites chokes are sleeves or rings that are placed over cables. They allow differential mode signals through, but block common mode currents by interrupting RF ground loops and prevent RF from coupling into the cables. They are ideal for eliminating problems in e-mail connections to notebook, HF modem and SSB connections and are recommended by SailMail in their installations. They can also be used on any cables such as autopilot cables or others exposed to interference. The Fair-rite chokes are available in the US from Newark Electronics (800-639 2759) and Amidon Electronics (714-850-4660). It is important that when, clipping on ferrites, no air gaps are left between the ferrite halves. Co-axial ferrite line isolators such as the T4 are available from The Radio Works (www.radioworks.com) and are used on the coaxial cable and placed on near the tuner unit. These block the stray RF ground path from the coaxial shield and transceiver grounds.

b. **Power System Stabilization.** In cases of high voltage induction, it is necessary to clamp voltages to a safe level, typically around 40 volts. One of the major causes of lightning strike damage is the failure of equipment power

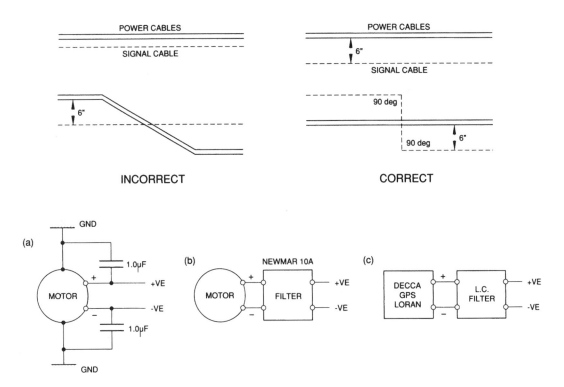

Figure 25-2 Noise Filtering and Stabilization

supplies to cope with high voltage transients. The easiest way of achieving this is to connect a metal oxide varistor (MOV) across the power supply. As the voltage rises, the resistance alters to shunt the excess voltage. A second method is the use of an avalanche diode across the supply. MOVs are designed for AC systems, and DC surges tend to have longer time durations. Also MOVs can be blown without warning.

25.4   Screening. Screening masks sensitive equipment from radiated interference. Common sources include radio equipment, and high current carrying cables. The equipment or cables are covered and grounded by a metal cover or screen (commonly called a Faraday cage). This may be a simple aluminum cover grounded to the RF ground point.

   a.   **Equipment Covering.** A useful product is the Sonarshield conductive plastic sheet. Simply cover the Loran, GPS, radar or radio casing. (Southwall Technologies, 1029 Corporation Way, Palo Alto, CA 94303.) The total metal Faraday shield approach is rarely required.

   b.   **Cable Covering.** Noisy power cables can be wrapped in noise tape, which is a flexible copper foil with an adhesive backing such as that from NewMar. I have used this product and method.

   c.   **Cable Shields.** Shields are designed to protect against interference from unknown or unspecified sources. The effectiveness of shields is measured in terms of transfer impedance. This is a measure of effectiveness in capturing the interference field and preventing it from reaching the conductor pairs inside. Data cables have shields made from a foil/polymer laminate tape or layers of brading. These also may have a drain wire installed to enable termination of the screen. Most manufacturers will also specify the termination of shields. Never ground at both ends, always ground one end only, typically the equipment end. In many cases shields are not connected at all, so check and connect them.

   d.   **Grounding.** The ground must be clean, which means that it should have a ground potential between equipment no greater than 1 volt peak-to-peak. A ground is capable of also conducting transients and emissions so it must be sound. Another grounding source on boats is the grounding of static causing equipment such as shafts and engine blocks. As discussed in alternators, the negative connections to the engine block are a common source of problems. Ensure that the starter motor negative is attached close to the starter itself. Add an additional negative to the alternator. In many cases, interference is caused by arcing and sparking within the engine, as it is effectively part of the negative return conductor. Modifying the negative system eliminates this problem. Ensure that all ground connections are clean and tight.

   e.   **Cancellation.** Twisting together the wires to a piece of equipment effectively causes cancellation as the electrical fields are reversed.

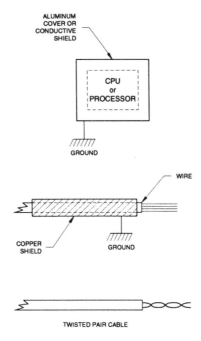

Figure 25-3 Grounding and Screening

25.5   Noise Troubleshooting. Tracing the sources of noise is a matter of logic and systematic switching off the equipment to find the source. In some cases it may consist of two or more sources causing a cumulative effect. Some noise will be simply intermittent, such as static discharges, which may be synchronized with hot dry wind conditions, or lightning pulses, which may not even be visible locally. A cheap, battery-powered AM radio is a good tool for tracking down radiated sources on board, with static being easily picked up. Passing it close to equipment is the method used. Some noise is simply related to time of day. Interference from ionosphere factors on radios is well described in chapter 18. This may affect GPS, HF, and satellite communications all simultaneously, giving the appearance of some greater problem.

25.6   Cable Planning. Cable planning is a major cause of problems. If you have problems, cable routing will have to be assessed and possibly require re-routing of the sensitive cables. This factor is addressed in the wiring sections, and if run properly many problems can be reduced or eliminated.

25.7   Fiber Optics. Fiber optics are now used on many larger vessels and in parts of smaller ones. As they are immune to noise and interference, they are often used in larger vessels and ships, which have high noise electrical environments. They eliminate many of the interference problems that occur in copper based systems. They are immune to EMI, crosstalk, ground loops, have lower transmission losses with higher band widths, and present no electrical hazards. Data control networks are a major area of use and Icom use fiber in HF radio units.

a. **Principles.** Fiber optic transmission works on the principle of internally reflecting a beam of light down the optical fiber. The beam bounces down the inside of the fiber using refraction, which alters the direction. Two types of fiber are used, the graded index and the stepped index, and both determine the light propagation characteristics. Light must enter the fiber within a set angle range, or numerical aperture, so that light transiting the entire fiber is maximized. Propagation modes consist of meridional or skew modes. Meridional modes are where light passes through fiber axis after each rebound, and are the most important. Skew and parallel rays never intersect the axis. This is further classified into high or low order modes, depending on the angle at which the light beam is launched into the fiber. Fiber band width is also affected by either material or modal dispersion. Material dispersion is caused by different wavelengths travelling at different velocities within the same fiber. Different path lengths between low and high order modes cause modal dispersion. Dispersion is generally only a problem in long fiber lengths and not on average boat systems which use stepped index fibers.

b. **Attenuation.** Fiber optic systems suffer transmission losses. These are mainly due to material absorption, scattering caused by core/cladding interface defects, and curvature radiation. The first two are directly related to material quality and imperfections within the fiber. Absorption is caused by molecular impurities, and scattering (Rayleigh scattering) is due to particle impurities scattering the light. The main losses in systems over which some control can be taken are coupling losses, and many on-board installations have preventable losses. Losses are caused by connections, either fiber-to-fiber, fiber-to-bulkhead or fiber-to-emitter/detector. Losses are due to misalignment of connectors with reflection at the mating surfaces and excessive clearances between the mating surfaces. Connectors are high precision items, and must be made properly. Typical attenuation losses should not exceed 2dB. Light emitters are either PIN diodes, PIN photodiodes and lasers, and detectors are Schmitt receivers or pre-amp analog receivers.

c. **Troubleshooting.** Make sure all connections are properly inserted. Check that the cables, in particular those going to connectors, have tight radius bends. Connections are rarely required although few will be able to carry them out. In polymer cables, these can consist of hot-melt connectors, which require polishing and adhesives, crimp ferrules which require no polishing and adhesives.

Fire, Gas and Security Systems.

26.1   Fire Detection Systems. Smaller boats should invest in self-contained units that have an integral battery. Larger vessels may have sophisticated, analog addressable, multi-zone fire systems installed. The control unit processes sensor information and allows the setting of alarm thresholds, and time delays that activate alarms. The sensors or transducers are the detectors and manual call points that are processed. The sensors output analog signals, which are compared with fixed levels in the controller. The controller software program also utilizes processing algorithms when using two or more separate alarms to decide on alarm activation, or to vary threshold compensation for aging or dirt accumulations, which tend to cause nuisance false alarms. A fire system has a combination of sensor types that cover various fire types, risks and characteristics. It is important that you read and understand your own system technical manual, with operational, test and maintenance requirements. Some fire suppression systems also are interfaced with an automatic diesel engine shutdown system, which stops the engine when the extinguisher is activated.

26.2   Smoke Detectors. These are installed in most locations. Modern centralized systems have addressable sensors. Smoke detectors must be located so that the thermal convection of smoke carries to the detector. The various smoke detectors are described and suit various fire types, as this affects the response time of each. The various smoke types are different with respect to the smoke particle sizes. Hot fires tend to have very small and almost invisible particles; low temperature smoldering fires will have larger visible particles. Ion chamber detectors react quickly to small particles, but are slower on larger particles, and the reverse for photoelectric detectors. Aerosol smoke detector testers are used to check units, test notes should be observed.

   a.   **Optical Smoke Sensors.** These detectors are ideal for low levels of smoke. The Raleigh forward scatter principle uses the scattering properties of light from smoke particulates when they enter a light beam. The light sources use a narrow band gallium arsenide (GaAs) emitter and a silicon photodiode photodetector, with a lens installed in front of each. They are aligned so that the optical axes of each will cross in the center of the sampled volume. Baffles are installed within the narrow light beam, so no light reaches the detector. When smoke enters the chamber, some light will get scattered and reach the photodetector, and the quantity of light at the detector is proportional to the smoke density. This is processed within an amplifier and a 0–20mA analog signal is output to the control unit. Units are designed not to activate from insects and background airborne dust particles. Test response time is 6 to 22 seconds.

   b.   **Ion Chamber Detectors.** These operate by the air within a chamber being ionized by a very small radioactive source of americium 241. This allows a small current to flow between the source and a cover, which has a fixed voltage between them. The collector is a perforated electrode with a nominal clean air potential relative to the outer electrode. When combustion particulates enter the chamber, the collector potential increases, and the level of charge can then indicate smoke density. The units operate best with invisible smoke materials released by fast burning fires. Test response time is 6 to 12 seconds.

c.   **Heat Sensors.** There are two types, the first activates when a set temperature is reached; the second activates based on the rate of temperature rise above a threshold level. Many units combine both functions. The heat sensor uses a bridge consisting of two matched thermistors, which are arranged to respond on absolute temperature and rate of temperature change, and are fed to a differential amplifier. The thermistors are negative temperature coefficient types, one is exposed to air and the other is within the detector casing. The bridge voltage will track constant temperatures; when the temperature changes rapidly, the sense thermistor will be unable to follow, and generates an analog output.

d.   **Carbon Monoxide Sensors.** These operate on the principle of oxidation of carbon monoxide gas to carbon dioxide. This conversion process takes place within a catalytic sensing cell. The process requires an exchange of electrons and the flow of electrons generates a small current within the cell. These are suited to slow burning fires. The 0–20mA output is normal at 7.5mA; when the carbon monoxide level increases a proportional output is also generated, and the alarm is activated before reaching the limit of 50ppm.

e.   **Infrared Flame Sensors.** These sensors are used more in industrial environments, and detect flickering infrared radiation emitted by a flame. They use a pyroelectric sensor, and the electrical signal is filtered to remove frequencies outside the required flicker region, and then amplified. It is further analyzed and a signal is output.

26.3   Installation. Installations should conform to I.E.E regulations. Fire alarm system cables should be segregated from other cables. This includes power and signal cables. Typically this is around 0.35 meters for 115VAC and 240VAC, and 0.5 meters for 440VAC in parallel cable runs. Cables also should be routed well clear of interference sources, and this should be at least 0.6 meters from electrical motors and fluorescent lights. Exposed metalwork must be grounded.

26.4   Maintenance and Troubleshooting. All fire systems must be checked regularly to ensure proper and reliable detection and alarm functions. Automatic extinguishing systems (CO2, Halon, Sprinkler and HiFog) must be disabled when testing, along with automatic closing fire dampers or ventilation shutdowns. If a detector does not respond after 60 seconds, it is probably faulty.

a.   **Weekly.** Check the controller unit for line faults and any visual and audible alarms; Sunday at noon is a good time for many ships and boats. Also, check one detector or manual call point within each zone. The control unit internal alarm and indicators should operate. The alarms around the boat also should function. Check internal standby batteries.

b.   **Every 3 Months.** Simulate a fault by removing a detector from a base. Check all sensors for physical damage, look for paint, grease and dirt. Do not open or attempt to clean ion chamber units, they must be returned to the supplier using radioactive materials handling precautions. Check the internal standby batteries.

    c.   **Annually.** Check and tighten all control unit terminals. Check all cables, connectors and mountings. Test all sensors, detectors and call points. Internal standby batteries usually require replacement every 3 to 4 years.

26.5   **Gas Detection.** Any gas is potentially lethal on a boat, either LPG, CNG or other. Leaking gas accumulates in the lowest point, which is the bilge. It only requires a small amount of gas (about a cupful) to completely destroy the vessel if ignited. If gas is installed, a quality gas detector is essential.

    a.   **Theory.** All flammable gases have a lower explosion limit (LEL). As long as the gas/air ratio remains within this range, no explosion can occur. Once this level is exceeded, a significant explosion risk exists. A gas detector must detect gas concentrations before the limit is exceeded, typically 50% LEL. Better units have a sensitivity of 25% LEL.

    b.   **Detector Types.** Two types of gas detectors are in use in detection systems.

    (1)   The main commercial sensor is the catalytic type. On offshore installations, we recalibrated these units on a weekly basis to ensure precise operation.

    (2)   The most common type of sensor on small vessels is the semiconductor type, which consists of a sintered tin oxide element. Upon detection of gas, the resistance alters activating the alarm circuit. It takes several days of operation before the sensor stabilizes and final calibration can be made. Detectors may be subject to temperature drift in the sensing circuit and good detectors incorporate a temperature sensor to correct this and ensure accuracy.

    (3)   Other well known devices use what is called the pellister principle. These devices consist of two heated platinum wire elements. One is coated with gas-detecting material; the other is used for temperature and humidity compensation.

    c.   **Installation.** Sensor elements must be mounted in the areas where gas may accumulate. The problem is that bilge water, or moist salt air can contaminate the element, causing degradation and failure to detect.

    d.   **Testing.** In testing, ideally a precise gas/air mix of the appropriate LEL ratio is used to calibrate the alarm level. In practice, however, this is never done. The simplest method to test whether the system functions is by activating a gas cigarette lighter or even a disposable lighter at the sensor. Activation should be almost immediate.

    e.   **Alarm Outputs.** All detectors should have a gas bottle solenoid interlock. If gas is detected, the solenoid should be closed. This function should be fail safe in operation. An external alarm can be connected, or activate a fan. A typical detector system is illustrated below.

f. **Troubleshooting.** Note the following important factors:

(1) **Alarms.** If an alarm goes off, assume it is real. If the alarm is proven to be false, you can normally readjust the alarm threshold, but do so only enough to compensate for the sensor drift causing the nuisance activation.

(2) **Sensor Element.** The principal cause of problems is invariably the sensor element degrading. Carry a spare sensor for replacement. If after replacing the sensor the alarm still causes problems, have the electronic unit tested.

26.6 **Security Systems.** Keeping the villains out of the boat is always a challenge. You can never keep out a determined thief, but my attitude is always to make the exercise as difficult, uncertain and unpredictable as possible. A variety of detectors and sensors can be coupled with control units and alarms, including:

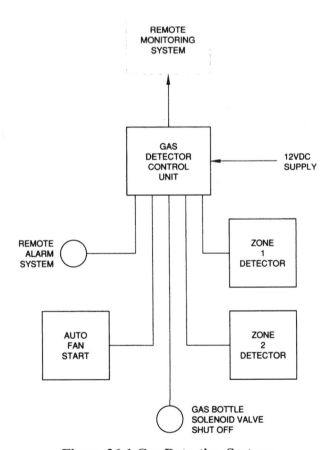

Figure 26-1 Gas Detection Systems

a.   **Ultrasonic Sensors.** These types of sensors are generally unsuited to vessel installation, as they are set off too easily by spurious signals, and they have relatively high power consumption.

b.   **Microwave Sensors.** These are often combined with PIR and use short K-band to reduce false alarm rates.

c.   **Infrared.** Passive InfraRed (PIR) sensors direct a pattern of infrared beams over a set area. When a heat source is detected, the alarm is activated. Some PIR units use pattern recognition to screen out pets. Only one unit properly located is required to cover a typical saloon, but the installation site must be carefully selected so that it is not easily visible. There are also infrared beam detectors. They have relatively low power consumption.

d.   **Proximity Switches.** Magnetic switches are used on hatches and access points and hard wired to the control unit. The magnetic reed switches are N.O. SPST (Normally Open Single Pole Single Throw). The advantages are that the alarm is activated before a thief has broken in or entered the boat, so that an alarm will catch him on deck or in view.

e.   **Pressure Pads.** Pressure-activated pads require installation under carpets and mats. They have a 2 wire N.O. SPST circuit. They can also be placed under a rubber mat in the cockpit to alarm or activate lights before entry.

26.7   CCTV Surveillance Systems. Many larger motorboats in the 50-foot and up range have installed CCTV systems. Cameras need to be properly located for maximum benefit. If used for security, particularly in port, the camera site must ensure there are no blind spots, and be relatively hard to tamper with. Cameras must also suit the environment, outside units having robust and corrosion resistant housings. External units may also have wash and wipe facilities. Units within machinery spaces must be mounted to avoid vibration and excessive heat. Average power consumption is 4 watts plus the monitor.

a.   **Camera Systems.** Systems consist of the cameras, both color and mono-chrome. Monochrome (black and white) cameras use charged coupled de-vice (CCD) image chips, with good resolution in low light conditions. Simple units can have a simple F-stop adjustment with manual or auto iris functions for variable light condition adjustments and field of view selection. Systems also have TV monitors, pan and tilt control panels and sequential switcher units including Quad splitter units to either sequentially show multi-camera images, or simultaneously show images from four cameras.

b.   **Camera Control.** Camera controls should be checked. The auto iris on zoom lenses should be checked in all light conditions, and if an override fa-cility is installed, check control manually. Check that all cable and connec-tors are secure. Switching units such as Quad units that split 4 camera images to a monitor screen should be checked; however, problems are rare, limited to power supplies, operator programming errors, or inputs from a specific camera, usually a cable connection.

    c.   **Maintenance.** Regular cleaning of the glass and refilling of washer reservoirs is required. Do not operate wipers on a dry glass, as scratching and scoring of the glass by hard salt crystals will affect image quality. Cold climates will require automotive grade antifreeze screen washer liquids. The pan and tilt facility should be operated through the entire azimuth range and complete up and down movement. Any vibration and jerking movements will indicate seizing, or fouling of camera housing. All fastening bolts and screws should be checked and tightened each year. Cables should be examined for damage and degradation. Wiper blades if fitted should be replaced. If housings are removed, check the seals and replace if perished.

26.8   **Security Alarm Indication Systems.** Once an alarm is triggered, various systems may be activated to indicate the presence of the intruder. The following alarm systems are commonly used. Thanks to Dolphin Marine Security (www.marine-security.co.uk.) for their assistance.

    a.   **Strobe Light.** The mounting of a high intensity Xenon strobe light on a high location for maximum visibility is the most common indication method. Many install a blue light, but you simply cannot see it easily, which is why police forces worldwide now use a red/blue/white light combination on vehicles. I usually install an orange xenon strobe light.

    b.   **Audible Alarm.** Install the highest two-tone output siren that is available. Put one outside and one inside. A high decibel output unit inside can be very painful to an intruder, and simply cut short his stay. Several different alarm signals can panic or disorientate the thief.

    c.   **Interlocking Systems.** The interlocking of various systems to the alarm is another popular method:

        (1)   Deck and foredeck spotlights, as well as any lights on targas and fly bridges, can be interlocked to come on with alarm activation.

        (2)   Mobile phone dial-out and pager. These options automatically dial out to designated pagers and cell phones.

        (3)   GPS tracking. This is an autodialing system with a pre-recorded message via the GSM phone and allows PC based tracking. Global coverage uses Inmarsat D+.

        (4)   Camera systems. These can be small discrete CCD low light cameras, or vandal proof pan and tilt color cameras. They can be coupled to a video recorder.

        (5)   Volvo has an electronic immobilizer that shuts off the engine fuel feed for those intent on stealing the boat.

    d.   **Time Delays.** Entry and exit delays give you time to leave after you activate the alarm, or to disable the alarm when you return. I prefer to fit a remote isolator hidden in a locker, and have minimal delay. Legally you may have to ensure that there is a reset function. Generally, laws restrict operation to 10 minutes, and then alarms must cease. A popular method of really ambitious thieves is to set off the alarm and come back when the silence returns, so ensure that it is an auto reset type.

e.   **Back-to-Base Alarms.** This method of alarm monitoring transmits a radio signal back to a 24-hour monitoring station for action. These systems can monitor all vessel alarms, including bilge levels, smoke and fire detection, gas detection and security. You can do this via Internet to your own home computer.

f.   **Precautions.** These additional steps also help deter thieves. Place clear notices at all access points, stating that vessel is protected by alarms. Place an outside alarm in the cockpit. Hide valuables and keep curtains drawn. Put a light and radio on a time switch, with a few variable times, not just the same time every evening.

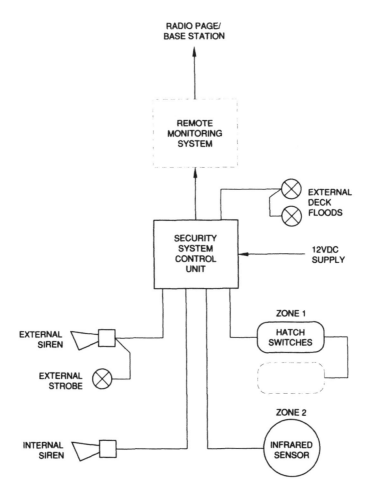

Figure 26-2 Security Systems

Entertainment Systems

27.1   Satellite TV. There are some very sophisticated TV systems available including Applied Satellite Technology (AST) (www.satcomms.com); KVH TracVision and SeaTel. Systems operate on the C-Band (3.7-4.2 GHz) and the Ku-Band (10.7-12.95 GHz), and some are dual frequency. The units use a control unit, and auto-tracking gyro-stabilized antenna dishes housed in a radome. Radomes have sizes ranging from 0.6 to 1.5m. As satellite tracking has to be fast and accurate to remain locked on, units also have pitch and roll sensors, with 3-axis servos and track satellites while compensating for vessel pitch, roll and yaw. These sensors use rate gyro sensors and inclinometers. Companies are now investing heavily in research and development; AST has made significant advances in parabolic reflector efficiency, reduced weights and more precise tracking. They have a 4-axis design compensating for elevation, pitch and roll, azimuth and active skew to maximize signal quality. Some units also have integral GPS receivers that supplement the NMEA gyro data. With the power on, typical satellite acquisition times are around 5 minutes. There are several search modes including auto, manual, search and scan modes. The servo is normally a high torque brushless motor. Installation principles are virtually the same as for Inmarsat antennas. As satellites transmit to limited areas, reception is dependent on being within the footprint. Footprints are generally limited to coastal and landmass areas, and proper selection of the correct tracking frequency is necessary. Power consumption is typically 3–5 amps. There are over 300 TV channels available in Europe and many more in the US and elsewhere, CD quality music and high speed Internet downlinks are available.

   a.   **European Barges.** On many barges in Europe you will see small domestic type satellite dishes. They are set up at the required azimuth and elevation each night. Some people I know have taken a subscription at home and transferred the demodulator and dish to the boat. Some channels and elevations include Telecom 2B and Telekom 2B (5°W); Telecom 2A (8°W), Astra 1A–1D (19.2°E); Eutelsat II F1/Hotbird (13°E); Eutelsat II F3/Hotbird (16°E); Eutelsat II F2/Hotbird (10°E). The dishes are small and easy to mount, and on inland waterways there are no motion problems to overcome. Demodulator set-up usually causes the most problems so read and understand the operations manual.

   b.   **Maintenance and Troubleshooting.** Systems should be inspected on a routine basis, with the system switched off and isolated. Inspect cables for chafing or damage. Radome interiors should be checked for water ingress and corrosion. All nuts and bolts should be checked and tightened. Some units have desiccant cartridges and these should be replaced if saturated. Faults are usually due to incorrect setup, satellite acquisition problems, or wrong satellite selection. Systems also have comprehensive monitoring and menu based systems, and reading the manuals is important.

27.2 **Television.** There are a range of TVs designed for 12- and 24-volt operation. For long-distance passage makers multi-system units with NSTC and PAL reception are available. Television aerials and their performance on vessels are a controversial subject, given the often over-optimistic claims by some manufacturers. They are also expensive. Comparable performance with home aerials should not be expected, and attempting to get a reasonable picture while under way is generally out of the question. The off-watch crew should stick to DVDs and videos. At anchorages, the principal problem is getting a good picture, without the continual ghosting that occurs in varying degrees of severity as you swing around. The ghosting problem largely depends on the path of the transmitted signal, and the frequency characteristics of the transmission.

    a.   **Signal Distortion.** Transmission signals are essentially straight line and do not bend significantly when meeting obstructions. The effect is one of creating shadows and areas of low signal behind the obstruction. Reflection of the signal also alters the direction of propagation causing signals to arrive at the aerial from a direction other than the straight-line path from the transmitter. The receiver ultimately receives two signals that arrive at times different to each other. The effect is the reception of a distorted signal pattern. The dis-

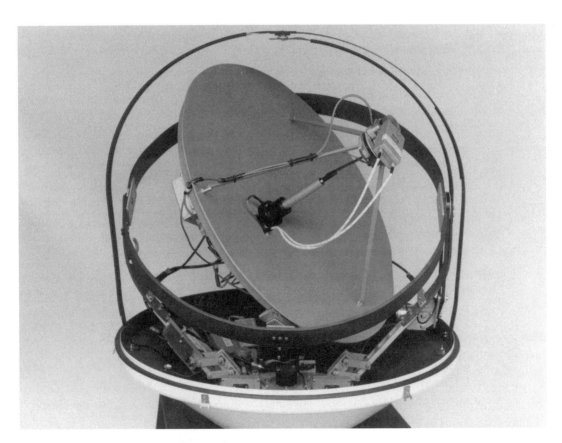

Figure 27-1 AST Satellite TV Systems, *Courtesy of Applied Satellite Technology*

tortion of signal occurs from a number of sources that include hills, other boats, rigging and reflection off the water surface.

b. **Signal Polarization.** Signal transmissions are generally horizontally polarized. When signal is reflected, the polarization is altered, causing distortion.

c. **Transmission Systems.** The variety of TV transmission systems in use is confusing. The main systems are M/NTSC (US, Canada, Guam, most of South America); B.G/PAL (Australia, Netherlands, Spain, Portugal, Italy, Canary Islands.); I/PAL (UK, South Africa); L/SECAM (France).

27.3 **TV Aerials.** There are a number of aerial types:

a. **Directional Aerials.** These aerials can be aligned with the transmitted signal. Intended for domestic use, they may be of use if you live on board and rarely venture out from the marina, but at an anchorage they are fairly useless, as you must continually adjust the aerial.

b. **Omni-directional Aerials.** These aerials are able to receive transmission signals consistently and are not affected by the vessel swinging at anchor. This type of aerial does not discriminate between directly transmitted or reflected signals. Commonly a ring or loop, the aerial is hoisted when required. These aerials do have a problem with reception of reflected signal from any masts and rigging, and perform poorly in marinas where many other vessels are tied up.

c. **Active Aerials.** These units have typically a fiberglass or plastic dome, with an integral omni-directional loop aerial element inside. The signal is amplified to compensate for the smaller aerial and performance depends on a good gain value within the amplifier unit. These aerials are also designed for the reception of UHF signals as well as AM/FM radio transmissions, which eliminates the need for additional aerials.

d. **Installation Factors.** The following factors should be considered when mounting and installing aerials:

(1) **Aerial Height.** Install the aerial as high as possible. I recently installed one of the very low profile Omnimax Gazelle units, which is small, and compact.

(2) **Aerial Cables.** Cables should always be low loss coaxial (RG59), which is normally 75-ohm impedance.

27.4 **Video and DVD Players.** The video has been the mainstay of on-board entertainment, however the DVD is far more practical. DVD discs are recorded in 4 digital audio formats, (Dolby Digital, DTS, MPEG and Linear PCM). Depending on the DVD player, all may be output to the sound system or amplifier. It is not recommended to attempt to play discs not rated for the player, as player damage is possible. Discs for other regions will be indicated on displays and not play or be ejected. Common faults are damaged or scratched discs that cause skipping, failure to play or disc rejection. Vibration can also cause skipping and location should be checked. Failure to play can also be caused by moisture on the laser pickup, which can be rectified by leaving the player on to warm up for an hour. Picture problems are usually caused by incorrect settings, poor cable connections, or the disc has incompatible copy prevention guards on them. Sometimes power off, removal of the plug for 30 seconds and restarting will solve problems, which are often caused by static, lightning, electrical noise or simple improper operation. Remember that any switch off causes a loss in settings. Current demands are relatively small, typically around 1 amp. Combined with an average TV consumption of 3 amps, it will take around 8-amp hours for the average movie. It is a good idea to place a cover or bag over unused players with a bag of silica gel and perhaps a corrosion inhibitor, as players are not marine grade.

27.5   Computers. The range of options with computers is now astounding. For entertainment you can play games, play music on the CD drive and drive some external speakers or simply have the hard disk full of MPEG files. DVDs can be watched which does away with the TV and video requirements. Lastly you can install a TV demodulator and aerial, and watch television wherever you are. These can accept NTSC and PAL transmissions, and allow a compact TV system to be used on board. (See chapter 16.)

27.6   Stereos. Units specifically designed for vehicles are obviously the choice for smaller boats, while larger boats will put on quality shore-type systems. Choose units that are designed for RVs and more rugged duty. A good option is the use of a 5 or 10 CD cartridge pack from Sony, Kenwood, Alpine and Pioneer which give a lot of music without reloading. There are radio/cassette players that are marinized with front covers.

27.7   Satellite Radios. This great new entertainment system from Sirius uses digital satellite radio broadcast system, with 50 channels of music, and 50 news, sports and entertainment channels. Contact them at www.siriusradio.com.

27.8   Speakers. A speaker produces sound when the cone moves back and forth, compressing air in waves that produce the sound. Best sound is produced along a line projecting outwards from cone center. Sound also radiates at around 45° of the main axis in a cone configuration. If not listening in this zone, sound reflects and distorts off other surfaces. The average speaker requires air space of at least one cubic foot. When the cone moves forward a vacuum is created, and as it moves back the air is compressed. Small cavities behind speakers will reduce the cone movement, and you will get a lower bass response, as low frequencies require more air movement. I installed Bose environmental speakers that cope with damp air and still sound great. Also be aware that magnetics on the speaker cones can affect navigation instruments so install them well away from compasses and GPS.

Troubleshooting, Testing and Basic Theory

28.1   **Troubleshooting.** Troubleshooting has a definite philosophy that should be understood and followed if it is to be effective. Troubleshooting is a logical process of evaluating a system, and how it operates. It involves collecting evidence, such as burn marks or heat, unusual sounds, acrid smells, temperature variations etc. This can be supported by using instruments correctly and analyzing the data displayed on them. This information forms the basis for testing theories and assumptions, so that the precise fault can be identified and subsequently rectified. The following factors must be considered in any troubleshooting exercise.

    a.   **Systems Knowledge.** Understand the basic operations of the equipment. It is common to find that faults are in fact only improperly operated equipment. If there is a basic understanding of the system, it is considerably easier to break down the system into functional blocks, which makes the process much easier. A circuit diagram will show all of the components in a system.

    b.   **Systems Configuration.** Understand where all the system components are installed, where connections and cables are and where supply voltages originate.

    c.   **Systems Operation Parameters.** Understand what is normal during operation, and what are the parameters or operating range of the system. All too often, expectations are very different from the realities.

    d.   **Test Equipment.** Understand how to use a basic multimeter. Be able to make the simple tests of voltage and continuity of conductors.

28.2   **Troubleshooting Procedure.** The following approach should be used:

    a.   **System Inputs.** Check that the system has the correct power input. Don't assume anything. For example there may be a voltage input but it may be too low. Check it with a multimeter.

    b.   **System Outputs.** Does the system have an output? Is the required voltage or signal being put out? If there is input and no output, then you have already isolated the main problem.

    c.   **Fault Isolation.** In any troubleshooting exercise, split the system in two. This method is ideal when troubleshooting lighting circuits. It instantly isolates the problem into a specific and smaller area.

    d.   **Fault Complexity.** Most problems usually turn out to be rather simple. Start with the basics, and don't try to apply complex theoretical ideas you do not fully understand. Stand back and think first.

    e.   **Failure Causes.** When a fault has been isolated and repaired, ascertain why the failure has occurred, if possible.

28.3   How To Use a Multimeter. The majority of tests can be carried out using a multimeter. A multimeter, as the name suggests, is able to perform a range of electrical measurements. There are two types of multimeters, analog and digital. An analog meter has a needle to show the readings. The digital meter (DMM) displays the test values numerically on a display. Manual ranging meters require selection of measurement ranges, and auto-ranging automatically types select the best measurement range.

    a.   **Voltage Tests (AC and DC).** The volt is the unit of electrical pressure, and equals the force required to cause a current to flow against a resistance. The basic equation is $E = I \times R$. It is the most useful of all measurements, either to detect that it is present or to precisely measure voltage levels. I perform 95% of all my troubleshooting on complex oil rigs and commercial vessels with this function alone. The voltmeter is connected across the supply or equipment, which is negative probe to negative and positive-to-positive to measure the voltage potential between the two. Reversal of probes will simply show a negative reading. If the DMM is not auto-ranging, set the scale to the one that exceeds the expected or operating voltage of the circuit under test. To analyze results:

        (1)   If the voltage is missing, this indicates that the circuit supply is switched off, or the circuit is possibly broken, such as a connection or a wire (positive or negative), or a faulty switch or circuit breaker.

        (2)   If the voltage is low, this indicates that the supply voltage to circuit from the battery is low, or that additional resistance is in the circuit, such as a faulty connection.

    b.   **Continuity Tests.** The continuity test requires the use of the ohms setting. It is simply to test whether a circuit is closed or open. Many multimeters also incorporate a beeper to indicate a closed condition. Power must be switched off before testing. Set the scale to one of the megohm ranges. Touch the probes together to verify operation, and then place the probes on each wire of the circuit under test. What you are looking for is a simple over-range reading if the circuit is open, and low or no resistance if it is closed.

    c.   **Resistance Tests.** Resistance is resistance to the flow of electrons, and fundamental laws were formulated by George Ohm and called Ohms Law. The ratio of a voltage through a conductor to a current flowing in it is constant, and is equal to the resistance of the conductor. The basic equation is $R = E/I$. If DMM is not auto-ranging, set the range switch to the circuit under test, typically the 20-ohm range is used. Turn off circuit power, and discharge any capacitors. When testing, do not touch probes with fingers as this may alter readings. Prior to testing, touch the probes together to see that the meter reads zero.

    d.   **Current Tests.** Current is the rate of electron flow in a conductor in amperes, and the basic equation is $I = E/R$.

        (1)   **Direct Current (DC).** This is the movement of electrons through a conductor in a single direction only. The ammeter function of a multimeter is rarely used or required, although some use it for measuring leakage currents. The switchboard ammeter normally can be used for all measurements. The ammeter is always connected in series with a circuit, as it is a measurement of current passing through the cable. The circuit should be switched off before inserting the ammeter in circuit. Most DMM have maximum DC measurement ratings of 10 amps only, and it is a little used function.

(2) **Alternating Current (AC).** This is the movement of electrons through a conductor in one direction, followed by a reversed movement in the other. The cycle is referred to as a sinusoidal waveform. In normal practice all references to voltage, current and power values are what is termed Root Mean Squared (RMS) values. This is the maximum value multiplied by a constant, which in AC systems is 0.707. The frequency of AC is measured in cycles per second, and the measurement unit is the Hertz (Hz). In most systems this is nominally 50Hz or 60Hz, although aircraft operate at 400Hz. AC current measurements are made using a clamp-on current meter.

e. **Power.** The watt is the unit of energy or power. The basic equation is $P = E \times I$. In AC systems power factor is included so that $P = E \times I \, Cos$. Power can be tested using a wattmeter, as it is in domestic situations using watt hour meters. Power meters also may be installed on generator panels and display in Kw. In most circumstances it is simply calculated using voltage and current readings.

f. **Capacitors.** When an insulator or electrolyte separates 2 metal plates, a potential difference exists. Excess electrons on the negative plate exert attraction on positive plate when the potential difference is removed this reverses charge and then discharges. Unit of capacity is the farad and microfarad.

g. **Diode.** A diode is a semiconductor one-way valve, consisting of an anode and cathode. It allows electrons to flow one way only and has a high resistance the other way. To test a diode, where a diode test position is not included on the multimeter set, place a probe on each side. It will read low resistance in the forward direction and high resistance in the reverse or blocking direction. This is why they are often called blocking diodes. Diodes are used to form full wave bridge rectifiers that convert AC to DC. To test, each diode must be checked as a separate diode, in the forward and reverse direction.

28.4 **Meter Maintenance.** Look after your meter. Do not drop it or let it get wet. A few basics will ensure reliability and safety:

a. **Probes.** Keep the probes in good condition. On many probes the tips sometimes rotate out, and a probe may came out and short across the terminals under test. Another problem is the solder connections of test leads break away due to twisting and movement.

b. **Cables.** Cables should be kept clean and insulation undamaged. Cables do age and crack. Do not attempt to test higher voltages, in particular AC voltages, if the cables are damaged. People have received severe shocks or been killed due to faulty leads. If a cable is damaged, replace it.

    c.   **Batteries.** Replace the internal battery every 12 months, or at least carry a spare. Many meters will have a low battery warning function.

28.5   **Before Requesting Service Technicians.** I remember an episode when a boat arrived in from a Pacific cruise and the skipper told me that his radar had been out for some months. He could only get the display partially working, but there was no picture. I went to the stern-mounted scanner, and simply flipped on the local power switch. Imagine his reaction, he simply had forgotten to check it. Grown men do cry. Consider the following points before calling for service:

    a.   Did I operate the equipment properly? Read the manual again and go back to basics. Only when you are sure that you have operated the equipment properly and it doesn't work should you call the service technician.

    b.   Are all the plugs in and power on? It is amazing how many people forget to plug in an aerial or to put the power on. If the power is on at the breaker and not at the equipment, double-check that the circuit connection on the back of the switchboard is not disconnected. Check that the equipment fuse has not ruptured. Check the obvious.

    c.   What you were doing immediately prior to the fault? A great number of faults occur immediately after working on unrelated systems. Check to see if you inadvertently disturbed a connection.

    d.   Write down clearly the fault and the situation when the unit failed. If a profile can be built up, it may point to some other factors. Not only will it assist the service person but also it may assist you in solving the problem and avoiding an expensive callout.

    e.   Keep a good technical file on board. If possible, obtain copies of all the technical manuals. No service technician can carry or get every manual. It will save you money if you give him the information, as time will be saved.

    f.   Clean up the area to be worked on. It is quite unfair to expect service people to work on filthy engines and dirty bilges. If you don't mind grime tracked through the boat, then ignore this advice, and if the fellow is good he simply may decline to come back again.

    g.   Have a good tool kit ready. It is impossible to carry on to every boat a complete tool set. Any assistance like this is greatly appreciated. Make sure your flashlights work, and empty or clear any locker through which equipment is accessed.

28.6   **Spare Parts and Tools.** To maintain a reasonable level of self-sufficiency, the following tools and equipment should be carried on board every vessel. The list should be used as your itemized checklist.

Table 28-1 Tools and Spares List

Recommended Tools	Consumables and Spares
Electrical pliers	Self bonding tape (2 rolls)
Long nose pliers	Insulation tape (2 rolls)
Side cutters	Denso tape (2 rolls)
Cable crimpers (Ratchet type)	Heatshrink tubing
Set electrical screwdrivers	Spiral wrapping
Set Phillips head screwdrivers	Nylon cable ties, black (3 sizes)
Soldering iron (Gas)	50m 2.5mm twin tinned cable
Soldering iron (12 volt)	100m 2.5mm single tinned cable
Roll solder	Circuit breaker (15A)
Adjustable wrench	Lamp-bicolor (2)
File, small half round	Lamp-stern/masthead (2)
File, small round	Lamp-anchor (2)
Socket wrench set	Switchboard indicator lamps (2)
Bearing puller set	Butt crimp connectors
Wire brush	Alternator regulator
Junior hacksaw	Alternator
Battery powered drill	Alternator warning light
Ring spanner set (offset)	Start relay (if fitted)
Set Allen keys	Alternator fuses (if fitted)
Digital multimeter	Fuses for electronics equipment
Meter battery	Anchor windlass fuses (2)
Set jumper wires & clips (Tandy)	Brushes-windlass (if fitted)
	Brushes-starter motor (if fitted)
	Brushes-refrigerator motor (if fitted)
	Brushes-alternator
	Coaxial connectors
	Battery terminals (2)
	Bearings for AC motors
	Engine fan belts (2 each)
	Electrical cleaner, CRC, (2 cans)
	Water dispersant, WD40 (2 cans)
	Silicon grease (1 tube)
	Silicon compound (1 tube)
	Petroleum jelly (Vaseline) (1 can)
	Anti-seize lubricant (Copper Slip)
	Distilled water (1 gal)
	Boeshield B-19 (3 cans)

Table 28-2 Basic Three Language Electrical Glossary

English	French	Spanish
Audible alarm	Avertisseur sonore	Bocina electrónica
Alternator	Alternateur	Alternador
Alternator rating	Puissance de l'alternateur	Potencia del alternador
Alarm panel	Tableau des alarmes	Tarjeta instrumentos
Battery	Batterie	Batería (Accumulador)
Bolt	Boulon	Perno, tornillo
Circuit breaker	Disjoncteur, interrupteur	Fusible
Connection	Cablage	Conexión
Circuit diagram	Schéma de cablage electrique	Eschema de conexiónes electricas
Current (electrical)	Courant	Corriente
Drive belt	Courroie de transmission	Correa de ventilador
Disconnect	Déconnecter, isoler	Desconectar
Electrician	Electricien	Electricista
Element	Elément	Resistencia
Fault	Faute	Defecto
Ignition switch	Contact (moteur)	Llave de contacto
Insulation	Isolement	Aislamiento
Current level	Intensité (amps)	Intensidad
Fuse	Fusible	Fusible
Ground (earth)	Mettre à la masse	Conectar con masa
Lights	Feux	Luz
Light bulb	Ampoule électrique	Bombilla, foco
Lightning	Eclair	Relámpago, rayo
Navigation lights	Feux de position	Luz de navegación
Overheat	Surchauffe	Recalentarse
Oil pressure sensor	Sonde de pression d'huile	Sensor presión aceite
Pressure gauge	Manomètre d'huile	Manómetro de aceite
Preheating glowplugs	Bougies de préchauffage	Bujia de precalentamiento
Relay	Relais	Relé
Recharge	Recharge de batterie	Recargar
Short circuit	Court-circuit	Cortocircuito
Starter motor	Démarreur	Motor de arranque
Sensor	Capteur/sonde	Sensor
Switch	Bouton poussoir/interrupteur	Pulsador
Tachometer	Compte-tours	Tacometro
Temperature sensor	Sonde de température	Sensor temperatura
Transmitter	Emetteur	Transmisor
Voltmeter	Voltmètre	Voltimetro
Voltage	Tension de système	Tensión del systema
Voltage drop	Chute de tension	Caida de voltaje
Water pump	Pompe à eau	Bomba de agua
Wire	Cable ou fil (électrique)	Alambre
Engine not starting	Le moteur ne démarre pas	El motor no arranca

BIBLIOGRAPHY

American Boat and Yacht Council (ABYC) Recommendations

Browns Nautical Almanac.

Donat, Hans . *Engine Monitoring on Motor Boats.* VDO Marine, 1985

Graves, Frederick. *Mariners Guide to Single Sideband.* SEA, 1992

International Regulations for Preventing Collisions at Sea, 1972

Lloyd's Rules for Yachts and Small Craft

Mychael, *Electric Circuits and Machines* McGraw Hill, 1972

Nories Nautical Tables. Imray, Laurie, Norie and Wilson, 1991

Warren, Nigel. *Metal Corrosion in Boats.* UK: Adlard Coles and US: Sheridan House, 1980

ACKNOWLEDGMENTS

Many thanks to Grahame MacCleod for the Visio 2000 illustrations, Paul Checkley for the Autocad illustrations; Lt Cdr Ian Bullock; Adrian Gomm (Thales Brasil) as well as colleagues at Global Maritime (www.globalmaritime.com) and Pride International (www.prideinternational.com) and the numerous friends and companies for their assistance, and for allowing me the use of various drawings, service manuals and circuits used as reference material. They are cited with their websites in the manual. Also special thanks to the Cruising Association UK.

INDEX